Fo
Florida

Fodor's Travel Publications, Inc.
New York • Toronto • London • Sydney • Auckland

 Published in the United States by Fodor's Travel Publications, Inc., a subsidiary of Random House, Inc., New York, and simultaneously in Canada by Random House of Canada Limited, Toronto. Distributed by Random House, Inc., New York.

ISBN 0-679-02293-7

Grateful acknowledgement is made to Alfred A. Knopf, Inc. for permission to reprint excerpts from *Tropical Splendor: An Architectural History of Florida* by Hap Hatton. Copyright © 1987 by Hap Hatton. Reprinted by permission of Alfred A. Knopf, Inc.

Fodor's Florida

Editor: Alison Hoffman
Area Editor: Herb Hiller
Editorial Contributors: April Athey, Al Burt, Peter Coan, Andy Collins, Michael Etzkin, Jeff Goldsmith, Ann Hughes, Kathryn Kilgore, Peter Oliver, Marcy Pritchard, G. Stuart Smith, Karen Feldman Smith
Creative Director: Fabrizio La Rocca
Cartographer: David Lindroth
Illustrator: Karl Tanner
Cover Photograph: Edward Slater/Southern Stock Photos

Design: Vignelli Associates

Special Sales

Fodor's Travel Publications are available at special discounts for bulk purchases (100 copies or more) for sales promotions or premiums. Special editions, including personalized covers, excerpts of existing guides, and corporate imprints, can be created in large quantities for special needs. For more information write to Special Marketing, Fodor's Travel Publications, 201 E. 50th St., New York, NY 10022. Inquiries from Canada should be sent to Random House of Canada, Ltd., Marketing Department, 1265 Aerowood Dr., Mississauga, Ontario L4W 1B9. Inquiries from the United Kingdom should be sent to Fodor's Travel Publications, 20 Vauxhall Bridge Rd., London, England SW1V 2SA.

MANUFACTURED IN THE UNITED STATES OF AMERICA
10 9 8 7 6 5 4 3 2 1

Contents

Maps

Foreword

Florida is one of the world's most popular tourist destinations. Visitors from far and near are attracted to the state's sandy beaches, warm and sunny climate, and theme parks such as Walt Disney World. Travelers find Florida rich in historic sites, vast stretches of wildlife preserves, recreational trails, fine restaurants, accommodations to suit every budget, and shopping. Our Florida writers have put together information on the widest possible range of activities, and within that range present you with selections of events and places that will be safe, worthwhile, and of good value. The descriptions we provide are just enough for you to make your own informed choices from among our selections.

We wish to express our gratitude to those who have helped with this guide, including the Florida Division of Tourism, especially Dean Sullivan and Rosetta Stone Land; the Florida Department of Natural Resources, especially Mary Ann Koos; the Greater Fort Lauderdale Convention and Visitors Bureau, in particular Francine Mason and Jennifer Meriam; Mary Louise English at the Greater Miami Convention and Visitors Bureau; the Palm Beach County Convention and Visitors Bureau, especially Jennifer Clark; Warren Zeiller with the South Dade Visitors Information Center; Richard Altman at M. Silver Associates; Stuart Newman and Associates, assuredly Jean Gomez; Geiger & Associates; and Delta Airlines, particularly Dean Breest; and Joan and Peter Jefferson in Stuart, Florida.

While every care has been taken to assure the accuracy of the information in this guide, the passage of time will always bring change, and, consequently, the publisher cannot accept responsibility for errors that may occur.

All prices and opening times quoted here are based on information available to us at press time. Hours and admission fees may change, however, and the prudent traveler will avoid inconvenience by calling ahead.

Fodor's wants to hear about your travel experiences, both pleasant and unpleasant. When a hotel or restaurant fails to live up to its billing, let us know, and we will investigate.

Send your letters to the editors of Fodor's Travel Publications, 201 E. 50th St., New York, NY 10022.

Highlights'93 and Fodor's Choice

Highlights '93

Statewide Trends Severe budget shortages in 1992 jeopardized Florida's nation-leading endangered land acquisition program, and slowed environmental reform in everything from parks maintenance to trail-improvement funding. The action has shifted to the local level and is receiving a lot of attention from volunteer groups.

In 1991 and 1992, as a manatee protection measure, 13 coastal counties in Florida imposed boat speed regulations through much of their inland waters.

Also in 1992 a new smoking law that requires restaurants with a seating capacity of 50 people or more to provide a nonsmoking section for at least 35% of their seats went into effect.

Everglades Survival of **Everglades National Park** is still far from assured, regardless of efforts made in 1991 by governments and the sugar and dairy industries to clean up pollutants from Lake Okeechobee. In 1992, the nonprofit American Rivers declared the Everglades the fourth most endangered river in North America.

Florida Keys Quickening devastation of the reef off the Florida Keys is leading to last-ditch efforts to stave off demise. Everyone in the region awaits the new management plan for the **Florida Keys National Marine Sanctuary** to be issued early in 1993 by the National Oceanographic and Atmospheric Administration. Meanwhile, new construction moratoriums have been mandated by the Monroe County Commission to slow growth.

Fort Lauderdale Inspired by a wedding of culture and leisure, Fort Lauderdale has turned its downtown riverfront into one of Florida's must-see attractions. The 1¼-mile tropically planted linear park along the north shore of the **New River** ties together the newly opened **Museum of Science and Discovery**, the **Broward Center for the Performing Arts**, the **Esplanade** setting for community festivals, historic **Stranahan House**, and the fashionable shops of **Las Olas Boulevard.** Meanwhile, the beachfront glows stylishly with landscaped medians, decorative pedestrian promenades, and superb Mediterranean details on signage and street furniture.

Miami Feeding on its own international publicity, Miami Beach's **Art Deco District** has become Florida's number one people-watching place. The city's contribution to leisure sport has become round-the-clock ogling from the sidewalk cafés along Ocean Drive. The mainland of this exotic metropolis newly sports the **Florida Marlins,** its National League baseball team. Scheduled to start before year's end are extensions of the downtown **Metromover,** the elevated rapid transit system that's as much a sightseeing joy as it is commuter boon. A ride in the cars will offer spectacular views of Biscayne Bay on the northern Omni District extension, and a new high-bridge river crossing into the southern Brickell District.

Northwest Florida **Flagler County** continues to be the fastest growing county in the entire state.

Palm Beach and Palm Beach Counties By the start of 1993, the free motorized shuttle will be transporting passengers through downtown West Palm Beach as part of continuing work on West Palm's new **Inter-Modal Transfer Facility,** scheduled to open in 1994. The system will link local, inter-county, and interstate rail and surface transportation systems. It's part of a downtown revitalization which late in 1992 saw the opening of the $53-million **Kravis Performing Arts Center** in the downtown **Cultural Arts District.** Also already moved in: the **Palm Beach Opera** and **Ballet Florida.** Next on line, opening in 1994, will be the $25-million **Palm Beach Performing Arts Public School.**

The Panhandle This region of Florida is still enjoying its reputation of having some of the best beaches in the country, according to a 1991 study by the University of Maryland's Laboratory for Coastal Research. Among the top-rated beaches are **Grayton Beach, Perdido Key, St. Joseph State Park,** and **Eastern Perdido Key.**

Southwest Florida In 1992 Tampa welcomed **The Lightning,** the new expansion ice-hockey team.

Fodor's Choice

No two people will agree on what makes a perfect vacation, but it's fun and helpful to know what others think. We hope you'll have a chance to experience some of Fodor's Choices yourself while visiting Florida. For detailed information about each entry, refer to the appropriate chapter in this guidebook.

Sights

The Gulf of Mexico at sunset, particularly at Mallory Square in Key West, where sunset watching is an evening ritual

The boardwalk at Royal Palm Hammock in the Everglades

Art Deco District in Miami Beach

Downtown Miami from the elevated Metromovers

Views of Miami Beach and Biscayne Bay from the 18th floor of the Metro-Dade Center

Cruise ships departing from the cruise port at Dodge Island, as seen from Watson Island on MacArthur Causeway

The new Riverwalk cultural facilities and oceanfront aesthetics in Fort Lauderdale

The main span of Sunshine Skyway Bridge, St. Petersburg

The Palm Beach Bicycle Trail along Lake Worth

Route A1A, along the oceanfront through southern Palm Beach County

Gulf of Mexico beaches seen from a fixed-wing glider at Clearwater

White tigers at Busch Gardens, Tampa

Singing Apes of Borneo, Central Florida Zoo, Sanford

IlluminNations in Walt Disney World's Epcot Center, Orlando

The view from the battlements at the Castillo de San Marcos, St. Augustine

San Agustin Antiguo, a restored Spanish colonial village in St. Augustine

Edison's and Ford's homes, with adjoining museum displaying many of their inventions, Fort Myers

The Vizcaya Museum and Gardens in Miami

Hotels

Cheeca Lodge, Islamorada (*Very Expensive*)

Grand Bay Hotel, Coconut Grove (*Very Expensive*)

Little Palm Island, Little Torch Key (*Very Expensive*)

Marquesa Hotel, Key West (*Very Expensive*)

The Breakers, Palm Beach (*Very Expensive*)

Brazilian Court, Palm Beach (*Very Expensive*)

South Seas Plantation, Captiva Island (*Very Expensive*)

Amelia Island Plantation, Amelia Island (*Expensive–Very Expensive*)

Jacksonville Omni Hotel, Jacksonville (*Expensive–Very Expensive*)

Sandestin Beach Resort, Destin (*Expensive–Very Expensive*)

Peabody Orlando, Orlando (*Expensive–Very Expensive*)

Don CeSar Hotel, St. Petersburg Beach (*Expensive*)

Caribbean Beach Resort, Walt Disney World (*Moderate*)

Miami River Inn, Miami (*Moderate*)

Casa Rosa Inn, Kissimmee (*Inexpensive*)

Restaurants

Grand Cafe, Coconut Grove (*Very Expensive*)

Louie's Back Yard, Key West (*Very Expensive*)

Mark's Place, North Miami Beach (*Very Expensive*)

Bern's Steak House, Tampa (*Expensive*)

Cafe Chauveron, Bay Harbor Islands (*Expensive*)

Casa Rolandi, Coral Gables (*Expensive*)

Chalet Suzanne, Orlando (*Expensive*)

Chef Allen, North Miami Beach (*Expensive*)

Topaz Cafe, Flagler Beach (*Moderate*)

Jamie's, Pensacola (*Moderate*)

Flamingo Cafe, Destin (*Inexpensive–Moderate*)

Homestead, Jacksonville (*Inexpensive*)

Romeros, Orlando (*Inexpensive*)

Beaches

Crystal Beach Wayside Park

The Fort Pickens area of Gulf Islands National Seashore

Grayton Beach, near Destin

John U. Lloyd Beach State Recreation Area, Dania

Pier Park, at the southern tip of Miami Beach and Lummus Park

Bill Baggs Cape Florida State Recreation Area, Key Biscayne

Sarasota County beaches

Delnor-Wiggins Pass State Recreation Area, Naples

Events

The Boggy Bayou Mullet Festival in October, Niceville

Light Up Orlando in November, Orlando

The ground shaking underfoot as a rocket soars spaceward from Cape Canaveral

King Orange Jamboree Parade preceding the Orange Bowl football game, Miami

Village Wine Festival, each February, Walt Disney World

Carnaval Miami, including the *Calle Oche* Open House, in early March in the Little Havana district of Miami

Coconut Grove and Winter Park arts festivals

Saturday morning farmers' markets in Coconut Grove and Winter Park

Sports

Walking, jogging, or cycling on the new, largely complete 35-mile Pinellas Trail that runs through the heart of urban Tarpon Springs, Dunedin, Clearwater, and St. Petersburg

Fishing from the Redington Long Pier, or game fishing for the big ones off the Florida Keys

A jai alai game at any of the many frontons throughout the state

The Orange Bowl Classic football game and its two attendant tennis tournaments, Miami

The new Florida Marlins of the National Baseball League

A round of golf at Key Biscayne Golf Course

Golfing at any of the challenging courses around Orlando

After Hours

For local color, a drink at Captain Tony's, the original Sloppy Joe's, Hemingway's favorite bar in Key West

Comedy Corner, Palm Beach

Ragtime Tavern for Dixieland and classic jazz, Atlantic Beach

Tobacco Road bar and restaurant, Miami

Sliders, Fernandina Beach

Florida

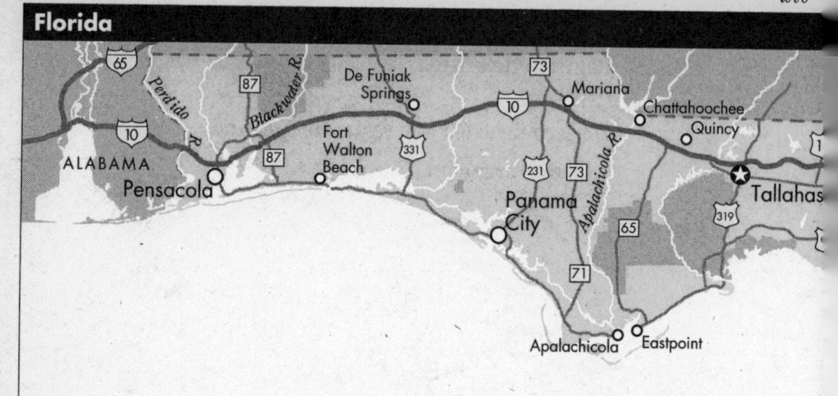

Gulf of Mexico

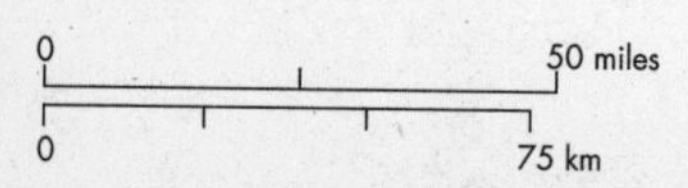

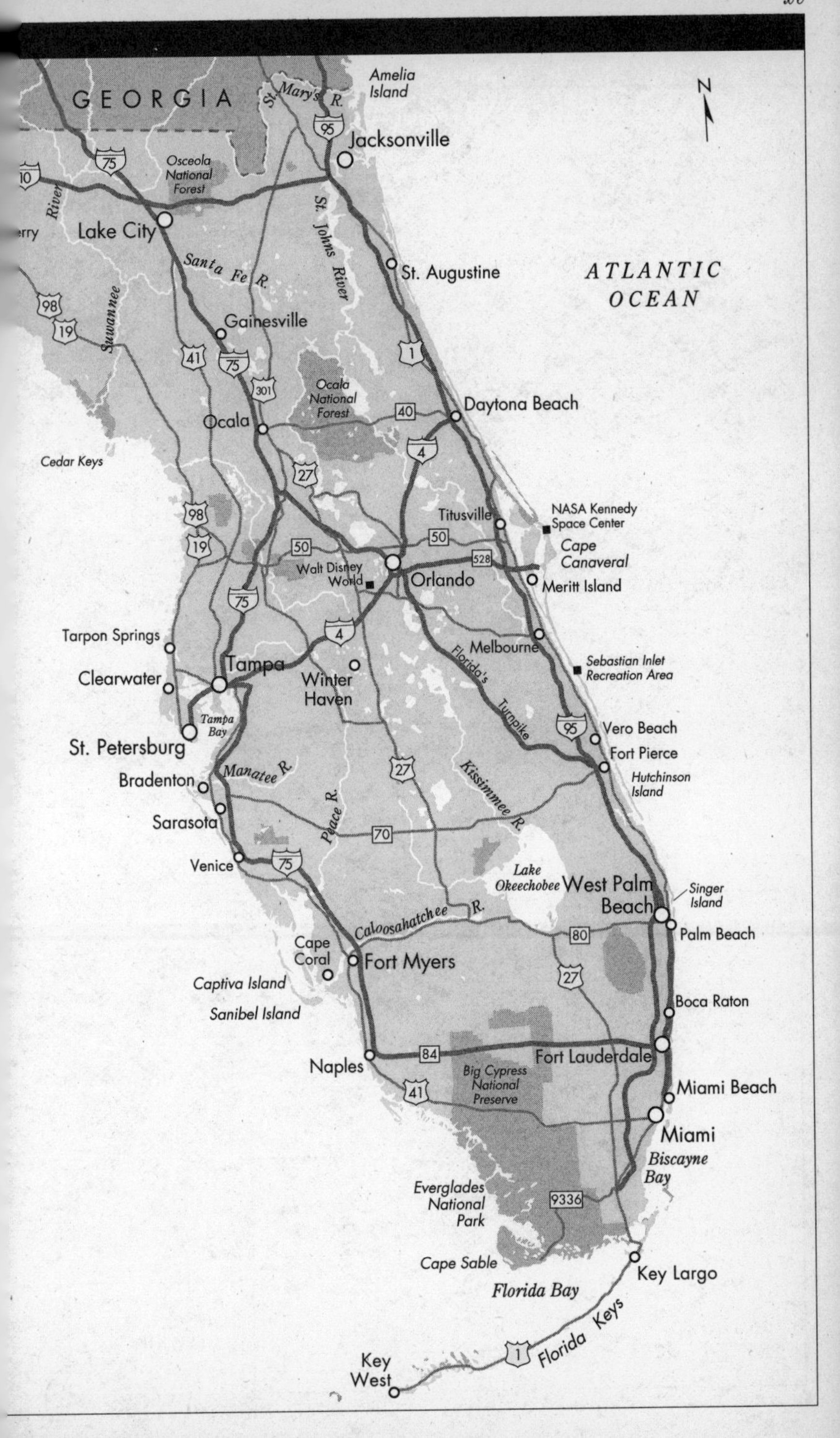
GEORGIA
Amelia Island
St. Mary's R.
95
Jacksonville
75
10
Osceola National Forest
River
Lake City
St. Johns River
Santa Fe R.
St. Augustine
ATLANTIC OCEAN
98
19
Suwannee
Gainesville
41
75
1
301
Ocala National Forest
Ocala
40
Daytona Beach
4
Cedar Keys
27
98
Titusville
NASA Kennedy Space Center
50
19
50
Cape Canaveral
528
Walt Disney World
Orlando
Meritt Island
75
Tarpon Springs
4
Melbourne
Florida's Turnpike
Sebastian Inlet Recreation Area
Tampa
Clearwater
Winter Haven
Tampa Bay
95
Vero Beach
St. Petersburg
Fort Pierce
27
Kissimmee R.
Hutchinson Island
Bradenton
Manatee R.
Sarasota
Peace R.
70
Venice
75
Lake Okeechobee
West Palm Beach
Singer Island
Caloosahatchee R.
Palm Beach
80
Cape Coral
Fort Myers
27
Captiva Island
Sanibel Island
Boca Raton
84
Fort Lauderdale
Naples
Big Cypress National Preserve
41
Miami Beach
Miami
Biscayne Bay
Everglades National Park
9336
Cape Sable
Key Largo
Florida Bay
Florida Keys
1
Key West

The United States

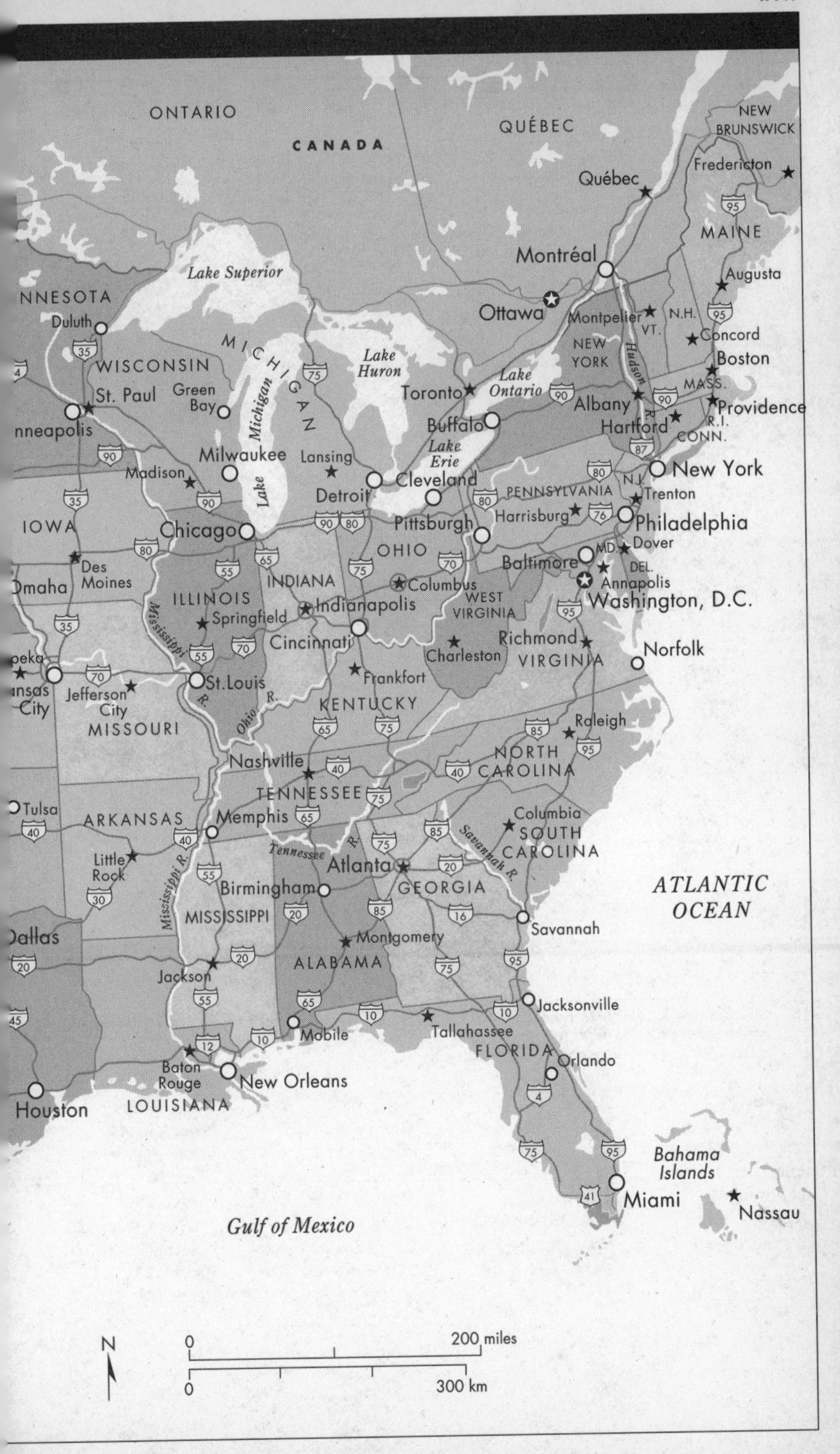
ONTARIO
CANADA
QUÉBEC
NEW BRUNSWICK
Fredericton
Québec
MAINE
Montréal
Augusta
Lake Superior
Ottawa
Montpelier
VT.
N.H.
Concord
NEW YORK
Hudson R.
Boston
MASS.
Providence
R.I.
CONN.
Albany
Hartford
Lake Ontario
Toronto
Buffalo
Lake Huron
MICHIGAN
Lake Michigan
WISCONSIN
Duluth
St. Paul
Green Bay
Milwaukee
Madison
Lansing
Detroit
Lake Erie
Cleveland
Pittsburgh
New York
N.J.
Trenton
PENNSYLVANIA
Harrisburg
Philadelphia
Dover
MD.
DEL.
Baltimore
Annapolis
Washington, D.C.
Chicago
IOWA
Des Moines
Omaha
INDIANA
OHIO
Columbus
WEST VIRGINIA
ILLINOIS
Springfield
Indianapolis
Cincinnati
Charleston
Richmond
VIRGINIA
Norfolk
Mississippi R.
St. Louis
Jefferson City
MISSOURI
Ohio R.
Frankfort
KENTUCKY
Raleigh
NORTH CAROLINA
Nashville
TENNESSEE
Tulsa
ARKANSAS
Memphis
Columbia
SOUTH CAROLINA
Savannah R.
Tennessee R.
Atlanta
GEORGIA
Little Rock
Birmingham
ATLANTIC OCEAN
MISSISSIPPI
Savannah
Dallas
Montgomery
ALABAMA
Jackson
Jacksonville
Mobile
Tallahassee
FLORIDA
Baton Rouge
New Orleans
Orlando
Houston
LOUISIANA
Bahama Islands
Miami
Nassau
Gulf of Mexico
N
0
200 miles
0
300 km

World Time Zones

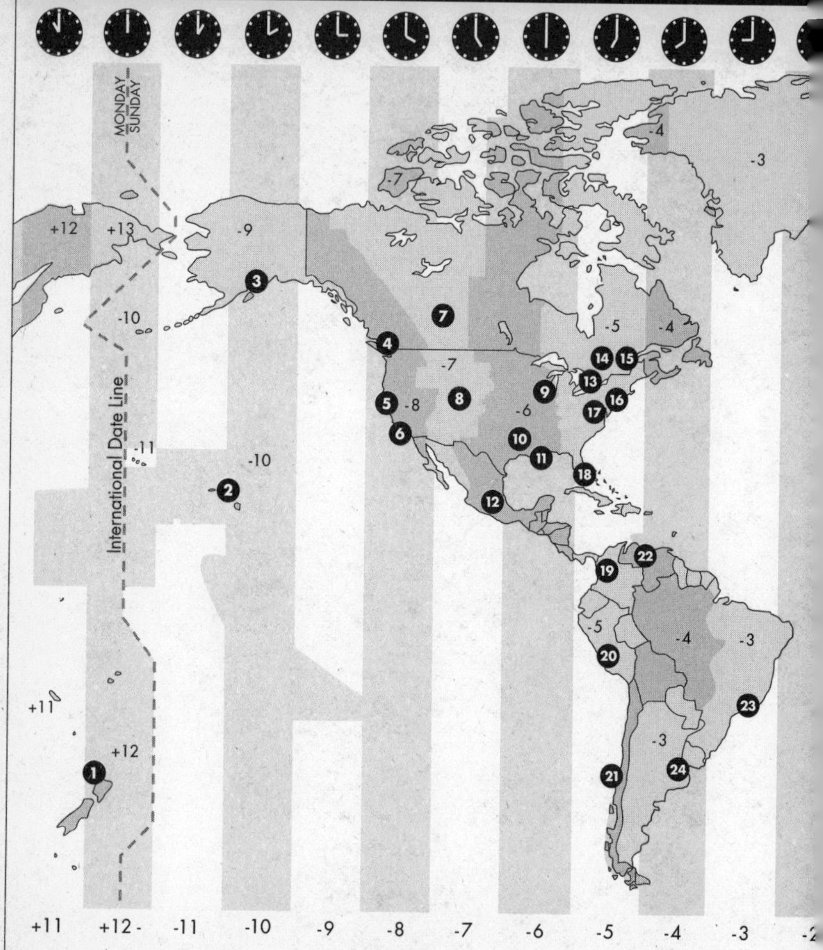

+11 +12 -11 -10 -9 -8 -7 -6 -5 -4 -3

Numbers below vertical bands relate each zone to Greenwich Mean Time (0 hrs.). Local times frequently differ from these general indications, as indicated by light-face numbers on map.

Algiers, **29**
Anchorage, **3**
Athens, **41**
Auckland, **1**
Baghdad, **46**
Bangkok, **50**
Beijing, **54**
Berlin, **34**
Bogotá, **19**
Budapest, **37**
Buenos Aires, **24**
Caracas, **22**
Chicago, **9**
Copenhagen, **33**
Dallas, **10**
Delhi, **48**
Denver, **8**
Djakarta, **53**
Dublin, **26**
Edmonton, **7**
Hong Kong, **56**
Honolulu, **2**
Istanbul, **40**
Jerusalem, **42**
Johannesburg, **44**
Lima, **20**
Lisbon, **28**
London (Greenwich), **27**
Los Angeles, **6**
Madrid, **38**
Manila, **57**

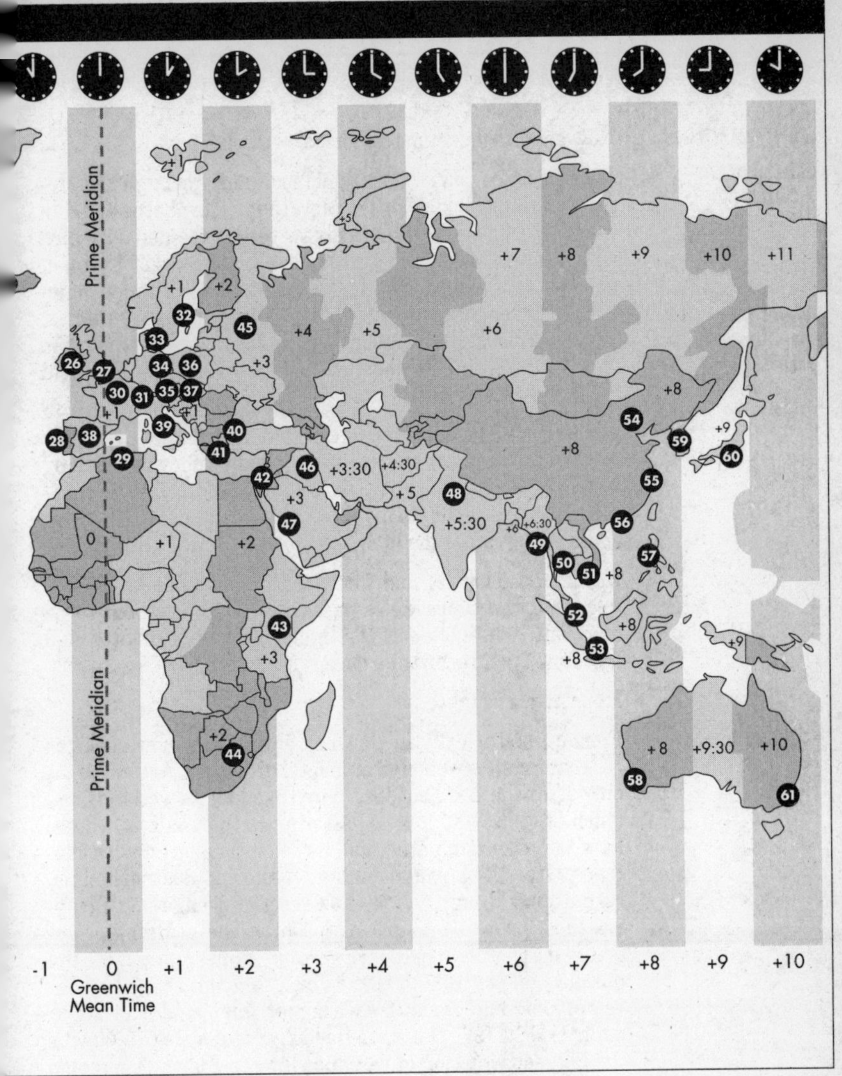

Mecca, **47**
Mexico City, **12**
Miami, **18**
Montréal, **15**
Moscow, **45**
Nairobi, **43**
New Orleans, **11**
New York City, **16**
Ottawa, **14**
Paris, **30**
Perth, **58**
Reykjavík, **25**
Rio de Janeiro, **23**
Rome, **39**
Saigon (Ho Chi Minh City), **51**
San Francisco, **5**
Santiago, **21**
Seoul, **59**
Shanghai, **55**
Singapore, **52**
Stockholm, **32**
Sydney, **61**
Tokyo, **60**
Toronto, **13**
Vancouver, **4**
Vienna, **35**
Warsaw, **36**
Washington, D.C., **17**
Yangon, **49**
Zürich, **31**

Introduction

By Herb Hiller

Editor of the Ecotourism Society Newsletter, *Herb Hiller is also a freelance writer whose pieces often focus on backroads travel and cycling.*

How about a museum to Florida's motels?

Impertinence comes easy while browsing through the Museum of the Florida Keys in Marathon. The photos and dioramas display a world that only yesterday teemed with bird and fish life, deer and gators, scrub flats laced by mangroves, randomly canopied by palm and hardwood hammocks. Over all hung pewter skies of dawn, blue skies, purple skies, storm skies, red skies of sunset. Rimming the shore for 220 miles was the reef, a magical other world spangled beneath the sea.

Outside the museum, along the Overseas Highway, urban hustle shouts down the magic—splendor elbowed aside by motels, gas stations, RV parks, fast-food chains, convenience stores, shell shops, dive shops, dives. A barrage of come-ons assaults the land.

But suppose nature and The Good Life really are compatible; that the times we're passing through turn out to be aberrant, the evidence of blight confined to photos and dioramas, last record of a once reigning folly?

Hope newly brightens.

Florida, historically in thrall to developers, now seeks to redress a century of environmental disasters. Action comes only after the state has lost more than half its wetlands and much of its upland forests, after more than half its waters have been contaminated, and its coasts cankered with concrete. Growth-management laws in the mid-80s marked the turnaround. Tough policies now restrict dredge-and-fill operations, protect mangroves, prohibit the bridging of unbridged islands, preserve beach dunes, finance the purchase of critical lands and riverfront threatened by development, and authorize stringent fines against wanton polluters. In 1991 the state fined Lykes Bros. $670,000 for the biggest violation of wetlands laws in Florida's history; U.S. Sugar $3.7 million for dumping toxic waste. An ambitious Everglades restoration plan, for the first time in Florida—maybe in America—requires agribusiness to pay for cleaning up its pollution. Along the Lake Wales Ridge, the first U.S. refuge for endangered plants, has nearly been authorized by Congress. To the north, the route of the Cross State Barge Canal that began gouging through pristine jungle of the Oklawaha River will instead become a nature trail.

What choice for a state choking on its own growth? Even skeptics of the pro-environment movement can't deny Florida's dilemma. For more than 100 years, Florida's allure has engendered Florida's ruin. What but natural bounty drew the early northerners who ravaged the state's bird populations, tore out its orchids, burned tree snail habitats, massacred gators? What but climate continues to draw hundreds of new residents daily, swelling Florida's population to fourth place in the nation, likely to surpass New York by the turn of the century?

Few people any longer doubt the need for the state to limit its growth. What may have been acceptable policy only brief years ago no longer serves either those already settled here or those who visit. Florida vacationers can freely choose from a still wide array of the state's pleasures. Increasingly, the choices will be guided by environmental restraint.

Juan Ponce de Leon was only the first European to stumble upon the bounty. Long before the Spanish invasion, Native Americans had already discovered the area's restorative springs, the fishing and hunting grounds along both coasts, and along the lakes and rivers. Spain named the land for its conspicuous feature. They called the place *Florida*, land of flowers. But the Spanish never stopped to smell the fragrance: Florida dissappointed them. Gold was what they were after and Florida produced none of that.

None of the Europeans made much of Florida. The land was too wet, and the Indians, tricked and harassed, constantly fought back. Even after acquisition by the United States in 1821 and following statehood in 1845, Florida attracted few permanent settlers (except for the ancient cities of St. Augustine and Pensacola). Three wars were fought during the 23-year period that ended in 1858, before stubborn natives were removed and Americans could safely begin to develop the state. Except for early canal builders who pushed beyond perimeter plantations into marshy mid-state, and except for railroaders who linked Atlantic and Gulf ports to facilitate commerce in cotton and timber, settlement of the state had to await the end of the Civil War.

Florida: what potential, but how meagerly realized. Florida was chiefly a haven for the sick. In winter, ailing northerners made their way to the healing springs along the Suwannee River to bathe and drink the sulphurous waters, but otherwise to lounge bored. North Florida—and north Florida was all anyone knew but for licentious Key West—was becoming the national rest home.

Epidemics of malaria and yellow fever swept the state. Lurid reports described brigands, and worse, snakes and alligators that imperiled homesteads, carried off dogs and children. Florida was hardly a place for a new worldly elite.

In an attempt to recast Florida's reputation, railroaders cleverly enlisted poet Sidney Lanier to counter the scary reports by composing flowery tracts about Florida's charms. Responding to the writer's prose, the curious began arriving, but often to their regret. They soon learned that to complete their journeys to ballyhooed St. Augustine involved 16 hours of bumpy going merely to get from Savannah to Jacksonville; in Jacksonville they had to transfer to sooty steamers that traveled up the St. Johns River to Tocoi, and finally, a narrow-gauge railroad took them bouncing another 15 miles to their destination. No wonder once they arrived they stayed the winter!

One who responded to less purple prose was Staten Islander Ralph Middleton Munroe, who shared Transcendentalist Ralph Waldo Emerson's ideas that man had gotten the civilizing process wrong and should start over again in the wilderness. A designer of shallow draft sailing boats, Munroe eventually settled at Jack's Bight, where he formed the community of Coconut Grove.

Munroe convinced early Grove settlers Charles and Isabella Peacock to open an inn, which in the winter of 1882–83, became the first lodging along Florida's lower east coast. The Peacock Inn quickly attracted Bahamian staff, and so settled the first of Miami's ethnic communities. When the inn was later closed, Munroe himself began putting up winter guests. His Camp Biscayne for years drew an intellectually prominent clientele, attracted by the clean bay waters and hospitality best reflected in the Camp Biscayne motto, "Insofar as possible, the hotel atmosphere is eliminated." Coconut Grove, when annexed years later in 1925, would become the oldest district in the city of Miami, and even today, though burdened by trendy excess, it remains a sanctuary of some vital Florida spirit.

Meanwhile in 1881, Hamilton Disston—a wealthy toolmaker from Philadelphia—offered the state $1 million and his promise to drain Florida's swamps, in return for 4-million Florida acres. The deal defined Florida's modern era. The state, eager to get ahead, would cast its lot with monopolists who, in the rough-and-tumble Protestant ethos of the late 19th century, seemed divinely appointed to exploit the enormous resources of America.

The state next turned to the two Henrys: railroaders Henry Plant and Henry Flagler. Plant heaped sophistications on a barely civilized Gulf Coast; Flagler more opulently tamed the east.

By the time of his first Florida visit in 1878, Flagler—the partner of John D. Rockefeller in Standard Oil—was one of the richest men in America, and notorious. To achieve his goals, Flagler engaged, bribed, and suborned state legislators. Ill luck made the match between Flagler and Florida.

Flagler's sickly wife needed a winter in the sun, and where else but Florida? Predictably, the journey was a horror. Hotels in Jacksonville and St. Augustine were horrendous, accommodating a depressingly sick winter crowd. Still, St.

Augustine appealed to Flagler, if not for what it was then, for what it might become.

In 1882, widowed, he returned, and again two years later (now remarried to his deceased wife's former nurse). Flagler engaged a pair of New York architects to design the grandest hotel Florida had ever seen. He bought up the little rail line that tortuously linked Jacksonville and St. Augustine, and bridged the St. Johns River, thereby eliminating the need for ferries. Flexing his imperial muscle, Flagler was remaking Florida. When in 1888 his $2.5 million Ponce de Leon Hotel opened as centerpiece of a revitalized St. Augustine, Flagler debuted an electrifying social season. No more would Florida represent a gray hospice of the sick, instead it was a festive realm of the cultured and wealthy.

Henry Plant achieved the same for Tampa by creating a second, more southerly hub for the wintering well-to-do. There, in 1891, Plant opened his $3-million hotel, the Tampa Bay. At the peak of their eminence, he and Flagler would claim millions of acres from Florida, and gain tens of thousands more from landowners who induced the two Henrys to lay rails their way. Florida, aboard the gilded chariot of champions, was racing into the 20th century.

Reaching south, Flagler extended his railroad from its terminus at Palatka on the St. Johns back to the coast where he acquired and expanded another hotel, the Ormond Beach. Society followed, as Flagler indulged winter colonists with imaginative forms of recreation. Laborers pedaled wicker rickshaws called Afromobiles; and sportier types amused themselves as they raced their new motorcars on the hard-packed sand. Henry Plant, meanwhile, at another of his west-coast resorts, paved the first asphalt track for the newly popular sport of racing bicycles, and lavished an entire golf course—the first in Florida conceived as a resort amenity—on his immense Belleview Hotel on the bluffs of Clearwater Bay. The promotions bloated in tandem with luxury: Upon opening, the Belleview brochure proclaimed "The caprice of wind and wave seems to have anchored here . . . Nature's wondrous charm lies on this pink-shelled, sun-kissed coast . . . The freshest ring of the true metal of real romance seems to hover between land and sky."

Flagler continued tracking the coast, amassing acreage all the way. At the point where the Gulf Stream swept closest to the Florida shore, Flagler bought an entire island, burned out the inhabitants, and created the opulent new American Riviera he called Palm Beach. His magnificent Royal Poinciana Hotel—opened in 1894—lasted only 40 years. The Breakers—another of his great creations—however, twice rebuilt after fires, remains among Florida's finest accommodations. On the mainland side of Lake Worth, Flagler built West Palm Beach to house the workers and keep them separate from the upper crust across the water.

Land that was not suitable for his guests' strolls or golf games, Flagler assigned for agriculture and homesteading. Flagler made his money by transporting settlers to Florida. Settlers farmed the lands he gained from the state and he shipped their produce north, and he profitted again. But the vast tracts around Lake Okeechobee turned over to cattle ranching and vegetable farming begot the systematic pollution of the huge lake; flooding of the lake led inexorably to demands by ranchers and growers for ditching and diking the Kissimmee–Okeechobee–Everglades and the present crisis in south Florida water management.

After freeze decimated his croplands in 1895, Flagler determined to push farther south. Hence, in 1896, he brought the railroad to Miami (until then an Indian trading post), then, at the turn of the century, seized by his own manifest destiny, Flagler began the overseas extension of his railroad to Key West. He proceeded unmindful of the havoc construction caused to fisheries of Florida Bay, denied responsibility for slavelike treatment of workers, and irresponsibly left his workers unprepared for the 1906 hurricane that was to kill 200 of them. His railroad reached Key West six years later—a larger-than-life achievement that Florida would come to boast as its "natural" way of doing things. Flagler was hailed as one of history's great engineers. He died within the year.

Florida everywhere was being massively altered. Too bad for the nature visitors came for. Citrus planters extended cultivation from along the lower St. Johns south into the lakes district where the lee of surrounding hills protected trees from winter freeze. Citrus came to foul surface and groundwater with pesticides, which eventually led to the death of entire lakes and the demise of once-thriving freshwater fishing resorts. Phosphate mining lowered the water table and reduced to trickles the flows of springs which for years had supported the state's spa resorts.

Regardless of their hegemony, not only Flagler and Plant but all Florida's captains of enterprise have claimed partiality to tourism, even if they preserved only pockets of nature after cloaking the state otherwise in ill-fitting ways. They saw themselves as imperial hosts, without whom Florida would have remained beyond the pale of development: They portrayed themselves sympathetic to what remained of the state's natural beauty so Florida could continue to attract northern dreamers for whom the name Florida remained ever magic.

Flagler and Plant of course became synonymous with their hotels. Among secondary Florida figures, S. Davies Warfield of the Seaboard Air Line Railroad opened his Seminole Country Inn in Indiantown—for a brief improbable time the terminus of his line—first as a hunting and fishing lodge for cronies, later to the public. Citrus barons, planting their way down state, raised a legion of once grand hotels, today moldering relics scraping the skies over Lakeland, Haines City, and Lake Wales. Cane lords of Lake Okeechobee opened the Clewiston Inn in its namesake town, where its antebellum style befits the byzantine politics that still characterize Florida sugar. South of Tallahassee Ed Ball opened the Wakulla Springs Lodge in the heart of a nature preserve that has become a park run by the state. Elsewhere throughout Florida, hundreds—thousands—of moms and pops leapt to the opportunity like Flaglers and Plants before them, erecting hotels, motels, and campgrounds along virtually every mile of roadway.

Almost 100 years after Flagler purlayed his stature with Standard Oil into Florida eminence, Walt Disney, trading on his own enormous reputation, created the ultimate empire, the ultimate realm of tourism. Disney, too, found his abettors in government. Florida granted Disney extraordinary tax breaks and near-sovereign control over rule-making throughout his fiefdom. Typically, a compliant Orlando newspaper remained silent when privy to Disney plans in the early '60s, thus vouchsafing Disney's acquisition of 28,000 acres for $5.5 million.

In Florida's dawning environmental age, however, even The Mouse gets caught at the cookie jar. In 1990 the Environmental Protection Agency levied a fine of $550,000 against Disney for hazardous materials violations. Disney paid another $95,000 the following year to settle claims for maltreating birds of prey naturally drawn to the park's wildlife. Contrary to understandings that helped secure its grant of quasi-governmental status, Disney, in 1990, chose to compete against some Central Florida governments for tax-exempt bond funds, successfully pocketing $57.7 million to upgrade its sewer system at a time when Orange County sought the same state-authorized dollars to build low-income housing.

As Florida has grown disenthralled with its potentates, and as communities spawned by developers have matured, citizens have become more aware of the potential and real problems the state faces—in many cases they've sought to correct environmental depredations that have been committed in the name of what attracted them to Florida in the first place. In addition to green legislation, Floridians supported financing for new cultural institutions and increased parks and trails. They support an acclaimed mix of quality restaurants, several new major league sports teams, and mammoth year-round street festivals, all of which also attract vacationers.

Bahamians, for example, who make up Florida's largest contingent of overseas visitors, fly over early each June to celebrate with mainland kin the annual Bahamian heritage festival called Goombay. In February, Latins come from around the Americas for Carnaval Miami and its hip-swiveling finale, the salsa-spiced Calle Ocho Festival. The annual Miami Book Fair—now the largest book event in America—attracts bibliophiles from around the hemisphere each November. Sportsmen come for special events: the Breeders Cup at Gulfstream Track in Fort Lauderdale each October and the winter polo season at the Palm Beach Polo and Country Club. Who knows how many more may schedule vacations to coincide with games of the new Tampa Bay Lightning in the National Hockey League. Speed Weeks and the biannual summer seasons of the London Philharmonic Orchestra have become major draws for Daytona Beach, while as many as can find a room anywhere within 50 miles pack Key West for the annual Hallowe'en Fantasy Fest.

No city in Florida, however, more decisively ties quality of life to tourism than Fort Lauderdale. The 1¼-mile Riverwalk, downtown, has become a magical setting for shaded promenades and al fresco entertainment. New performing-arts and fine-arts venues are enabling residents and visitors to enjoy year-round cultural entertainment. Along the beachfront—for years infamous for spring break debauchery—2½ miles of shore road attest to the good life by the sea.

Miami, the big bad boy of Florida cities, tar-brushed by "Miami Vice," is remarkably cosmopolitan, more Latin than imaginable, with a firming grip on its history. The mix works best in south Miami Beach where the Art Deco District, once a seedy retirement strip, has spurred preservation throughout the metropolis. The Deco District newly sparkles as Florida's top people attraction, where café society and day-trippers ogle the lollipop-colored deco hotels and the broad monochrome beach across Ocean Drive. In Coconut Grove, the new Cocowalk shops, cinemas, and smart bistros have renewed that sense of life-as-art that dates from Munroe's earliest indulgence of bohemian society. The nightly ritual of ogle-and-be-ogled gridlocks the village on weekends. A one-minute walk from Cocowalk, Coconut Grove of 100 years ago lives at the Barnacle, the old Munroe homestead, open to visitors as a state park.

The rich and famous of Palm Beach County and the Treasure Coast tax themselves to support and patronize arts and recreational facilities unequaled in the state. Palm Beach County alone has 15 theaters and theater companies, 15 music and dance companies or series, 26 museums and galleries, and more than 70 parks. The Loxahatchee River in Martin County is Florida's only river officially designated wild and scenic. The beaches of Martin, St. Lucie, and Indian River counties are broad and rarely crowded. Worth Avenue in Palm Beach attracts shoppers with its grand reputation: Tiffany's was lately added to the roster of internationally known merchants. Downtown West Palm Beach, where the $60 million Kravis Performing Arts Center is scheduled to open by 1993, is reviving as an arts and dining district.

Along the lower west coast, Naples to the far south boasts the best environmental planning in Florida. Even the grandest hotels—the Ritz-Carlton and the Registry Resort—as well as baronial new residential estates lay to the back or to the side of coastal wetlands. Today marshes front the posh new communities, linked only by boardwalks to the beach. Preservationists esteem Olde Naples, environmentalists the Corkscrew Swamp Sanctuary by the Audubon Society, and lovers of the arts the new $19 million Philharmonic Performing Arts Center.

Lee County, farther north, stands out for its nature preserves, shelling beaches, and unbridged barrier islands. The region is not very developed, but where building has occurred along the coast, the style is informal to quirky. Each town retains a distinctive character, including sometimes crowded Sanibel and Captiva Islands, Cabbage Key, clubby Useppa Island, and patrician Boca Grande. Since 1988 the county has collected ⅓ cent of its tourist development tax solely to buy, protect, and improve beaches and parks. The J.N. "Ding" Darling National Wildlife Refuge occupies 5,030 acres of Sanibel—more than 30% of its land area.

Sarasota County delights with the circus and arts legacies John Ringling and heiress Bertha Palmer. Local and visitor kids have been privileged for more than 60 years that the Ringling Bros. and Barnum & Bailey Circus has wintered in Venice. Adults enjoy the John and Mable Ringling Museum of Art; Ca' d' Zan, the Venetianlike palace that was the Ringling home; the Asolo State Theatre, and historic Spanish Point in Osprey. In addition, the county boasts numerous other arts-related attractions.

Urban Tampa Bay offers much more than Busch Gardens and beaches. Tarpon Springs with its heritage of Greek sponge fisheries, and Safety Harbor with its landmark and namesake spa, are two of Florida's cherished communities. Downtown St. Petersburg charms with its well-maintained parklike plazas, the historic Stouffer Vinoy Resort, and the new Dali Museum. Downtown Tampa's art district includes the new Museum of African-American Art, the restored 1926 Tampa Theater, and the Henry B. Plant Museum of Art, to name a few venues.

Florida's environmental turn shows best where tourism has been slow to take hold—mainly where beaches are few or where railroaders never laid track. In late 1991 nine counties along the mid-Gulf Coast north of Tampa Bay banded together as "The Nature Coast," to flaunt their lakes and bubbling springs, hilly inland stretches, and marshes.

Most Florida visitors will be heading too fast to Disney or home again to visit the Big Scrub. Upper mid-state lacks name attractions. So much the better. White board fences through Marion County tidily mark off thoroughbred ranches that rival Kentucky's Blue Grass for breeding racing champions. The old clapboard and brick towns of McIntosh and Micanopy date from early in the 19th century. Paynes Prairie provides habitat for sandhill cranes and bison. Cross Creek, where Marjorie Kinnan Rawlings wrote *The Yearling,* in 1990 gained protection from quick-buck promoters who were about to erect the usual mishmash to cash in on the publicity from the film version of Rawlings' *Cross Creek.* At the Devil's Millhopper you can descend a 221-foot walkway to the bottom of a 120-foot deep sinkhole, and at O'Leno State Park watch the Santa Fe River swirl underground. At Ichetucknee State Park you can tube the mighty "Itch." Nearby you can dive a dozen or more pellucid springs.

Reach to Pensacola through Florida's Panhandle, where in lie many of the state's most beautiful and most surprising parks, including Florida Caverns, Falling Waters, Natural Bridge. Botanical fanciers especially will enjoy Eden State Gardens, Maclay State Gardens, and Torreya State Park—the latter with bluffs that rise 150 feet above the Apalachicola River. The Panhandle has Florida's finest beaches, including Grayton in south Walton County, rated best in mainland America in a landmark 1991 study by the University of Maryland's Laboratory for Coastal Research. Pensacola has three designated historic districts, two listed in the National Register. Seaside in Walton County, with its shell- and picket-lined lanes too narrow for automobiles, is America's most acclaimed revival of early 20th-century planning. In Tallahassee, an 8-mile downtown trail links 50 historic buildings and sites, most open to the public.

Florida's northeast celebrates the state's earliest affair with tourism. North of St. Augustine lies Fernandina Beach, its turn-of-the-century look preserved in a vibrant historic core. Jacksonville is a brawny port city that feels more southern than tropical. Arts thrive, gentility survives. With its muscular skyline and bridges, its working river that's equally a source of recreation, its historic residential neighborhoods—three in the National Register—Jacksonville is America's 17th most populous city and largest in land mass. It's Florida's sleeping giant, on the way south to St. Augustine—America's oldest city—Ormond Beach, and Daytona Beach.

In Orlando, construction is ready to begin on a new $600-million magnetic levitation rail system to whisk visitors between Orlando International Airport and the south end of International Drive. Rides start three years later. Lake

Eola Park, with its mile-round jogging path, in the late '80s was reclaimed from vagrants and remade the healthy heart of the city with a $900,000 amphitheater, swan boats, night-lit fountain, and landscaping that draw Orlandoans downtown the way Disney draws from around America. Leu Botanical Gardens features the largest collection of camellias in eastern North America. Also not to miss: Winter Park with the most beautiful shopping street in Florida, along Park Avenue, as well as the Morse Museum, the nearby Maitland Art Center, and the Cornell Fine Arts Museum and the plush velvet Annie Russell Theatre at lakeside Rollins College. Head east and in an hour you're at Spaceport U.S.A. at Cape Canaveral.

As for the Keys, what's in store?

In 1990, reacting to long-term environmental decline, President Bush signed a law that designated the Keys a national marine sanctuary. The ruling made most of the islands off-limits for federally assisted development projects, and turned responsibility for preparing a management plan by 1993 over to the National Oceanic and Atmospheric Administration. While everybody lobbies the effort, county government—under threat of massive fines by the state—has set a maximum of 255 building permits a year for the next 10 years as a way to insure that the population doesn't grow so large that all can't be evacuated within 30 hours in case of a hurricane alert. For the next five years the county commission says it will issue no more hotel or motel permits, but it remains to be seen if the ban will be enforced and what effect the new sanctuary management plan will have on other construction.

Late in 1991, a University of Georgia report forecast the death of the reefs off the Florida Keys within 10 years. Will that forecast convince people that the resource is too valuable to continue abusing it? Will Floridians finally accept limits to growth elsewhere in the state?

Maybe they should permit just one more building in the Keys. Maybe just a museum to Florida's motels.

1 Essential Information

Before You Go

Tourist Information

Contact the **Florida Division of Tourism** for information on tourist attractions and answers to questions about traveling in the state.

In Florida: 126 Van Buren St., Tallahassee 32399, tel. 904/487–1462 or 1463.

In Canada: Canadian travelers can get assistance from U.S. Travel in Toronto, tel. 416/595–0335.

In the United Kingdom: British travelers can get assistance from the **U.S. Travel and Tourism Administration** (USTTA–Premier House, 77 Oxford St., London W1R 1RB, tel. 071/439–4773).

For additional information, contact the regional tourist bureaus and chambers of commerce in the areas you wish to visit (*see* individual chapters for listings).

Tour Groups

If you prefer to leave the driving to someone else, consider a package tour. Although you will have to march to the beat of a tour guide's drum rather than your own, you are likely to save money on airfare, hotels, and ground transportation. For the more experienced or adventurous traveler, a variety of special-interest and independent packages are available. Listed below is a sampling of available options. Check with your travel agent or the Florida Division of Tourism (904/487–1462) for additional resources.

When considering a tour, be sure to find out exactly what expenses are included (particularly tips, taxes, side trips, additional meals, and entertainment); ratings of all hotels on the itinerary and the facilities they offer; cancellation policies for you and for the tour operator; and, if you are traveling alone, the cost for a single supplement. Most tour operators request that bookings be made through a travel agent; there is no additional charge for doing so.

General-Interest Tours

Globus-Gateway/Cosmos (95–25 Queens Blvd., Rego Park, NY 11374, tel. 718/268–7000 or 800/221–0090) offers a 10-day "Best of Florida" tour. **Domenico Tours** (751 Broadway, Bayonne, NJ 07002, tel. 201/823–8687 or 800/554–TOUR) offers packages to Orlando, Miami Beach, Palm Beach, St. Petersburg, Ft. Lauderdale, and Miami Beach/Bahamas/Walt Disney World. **Gadabout Tours** (700 E. Tahquitz Canyon Way, Palm Springs, CA 92262–6761, tel. 619/325–5556 or 800/952–5068) offers a nine-day tour of Florida, including a cruise to the Bahamas. **Tauck Tours** (11 Wilton Rd., Westport, CT 06881, tel. 203/226–6911 or 800/468–2825) offers tours of the resort areas of southern Florida and the Florida Keys, as well as trips to major attractions in central Florida.

Special-Interest Tours

Adventure

Sobek's International Explorers Society (Box 1089, Angels Camp, CA 95222, tel. 209/736–4524) will take you canoeing through the Florida Everglades or island-hopping by sailboat off the Gulf Coast of Florida in their "Adventure Sail Escape."

Wilderness Southeast (711 Sandtown Rd., Savannah, GA 31410, tel. 912/897–5108) runs rugged trips through the Everglades and places like the Okefenokee Swamp in Georgia. Also available is a four-day trip through central Florida, beginning with canoeing excursions in Ocala National Forest and ending with a snorkeling expedition on the Gulf Coast.

Nature Capt. Vicki Impallomeni (23 Key Haven Terr., Key West 33040, tel. 305/294–9731), a native-born Key Wester and environmental authority, operates day-long and half-day charters in the backcountry of the Florida Keys. She is especially effective with families with young children. Visit the loggerhead turtle on Sanibel Island, off Florida's Gulf Coast, with conservationists in an outing arranged by **Smithsonian Associates Travel Program** (1100 Jefferson Dr., SW, Washington, DC 20560, tel. 202/357–4700). You must pay a $20 fee to become a member of the Smithsonian to take any of the trips offered in the program.

Package Deals for Independent Travelers

American FlyAAway Vacations (tel. 800/321–2121) offers city packages with discounts on hotels and car rentals. The airline offers a "Fly and Drive" package to the entire state as well as a number of three- and four-day trips to Orlando and its environs, including Sea World and Disney World. **Delta Airlines** (tel. 800/872–7786) offers a wide variety of packages in Florida, including trips to Disney World, Daytona, Ft. Lauderdale, Miami, Key West, Tampa, Orlando, Sarasota, Ft. Myers, and Marco Island. **American Express** (300 Pinnacle Way, Norcross, GA 30093, tel. 800/241–1700 or, in GA, 800/421–5785) has similar city packages, with complimentary admission to certain area attractions. Also check with **Continental Airlines** (tel. 800/634–5555), **TWA Getaway Vacations** (tel. 800/GETAWAY), and **United Airlines** (tel. 800/328–6877) for packages.

Tips for British Travelers

Government Tourist Offices The **U.S. Travel and Tourism Administration** (Box 1EN, London W14 1EN, tel. 071/439–7433, fax 071/439–1152) will give you advice on your trip to Florida and can send brochures and an information packet.

Passports and Visas You will need a valid 10-year passport (£15) to enter the United States. You do not need a visa so long as you are visiting either on business or pleasure; are staying for less than 90 days; have a return ticket; are flying with a major airline (in effect, all airlines that fly to the United States); and a completed visa waiver form I–94W (supplied either at the airport of departure or on the plane and to be handed in on arrival). Otherwise you can obtain a U.S. Visitors Visa either through your travel agent or by post from the **United States Embassy** (Visa and Immigration Dept., 5 Upper Grosvenor St., London W1A 2JB, tel. 071/499–3443). The embassy no longer accepts visa applications made by personal callers. No vaccinations are required.

Customs Visitors age 21 or over can take in 200 cigarettes or 50 cigars or 2 kilograms of tobacco; one U.S. liter of alcohol; and duty-free gifts to a value of $100. Do not try to take in meat or meat products, seeds, plants, fruits, etc. Avoid illegal drugs like the plague.

Returning to Britain you may bring home: (1) 200 cigarettes or 100 cigarillos or 50 cigars or 250 grams of tobacco; (2) two liters of table wine with additional allowances for (a) one liter of alcohol over 22% by volume (38.8 proof, most spirits) or (b) two liters of alcohol under 22% by volume (fortified or sparkling wine) or (c) two more liters of table wine and (3) 60 milliliters of perfume and 250 milliliters of toilet water; and (4) other goods up to a value of £32, but not more than 50 liters of beer or 25 mechanical lighters.

Insurance We recommend that you insure yourself to cover health and motoring mishaps through **Europ Assistance** (252 High St., Croydon, Surrey CRO 1NF, tel. 081/680–1234).

It is also wise to take out insurance to cover loss of luggage (though check that this isn't already covered in any existing home-owner's policy). Trip-cancellation insurance is another wise buy. **The Association of British Insurers** (51 Gresham St., London EC2V 7HQ, tel. 071/600–3333) will give comprehensive advice on all aspects of vacation insurance.

Tour Operators Numerous tour operators offer packages to Florida. Here we list just a few; contact your travel agent to find companies best suited to your needs and pocketbook.

Albany Travel (Manchester) Ltd. (Royal London House, 196 Deansgate, Manchester M3 3NF, tel. 061/833–0202) offers a 10-day "Florida Highlights" escorted coach tour that includes Orlando, the Everglades, Key West, and Miami. There are also flight/hotel/car rental packages to several Florida resorts.

British Airways Holidays (Atlantic House, Hazelwick Ave., Three Bridges, Crawley, W. Sussex RH10 1NP, tel. 0293/518022) has a variety of Gold Coast and Gulf Coast packages, multi-center and fly-drive holidays and flight bargains.

Cosmosair (Ground Floor, Dale House, Tiviot Dale, Stockport, Cheshire SK1 1TB, tel. 061/480–5799) offers a 15-day, escorted "Highlights of Florida" coach tour that includes Miami, Orlando, Cape Canaveral, and the Everglades. Self-drive itineraries are also available.

Jetsave Travel Ltd. (Sussex House, London Rd., East Grinstead, W. Sussex RH19 1LD, tel. 0342/312033) offers a variety of Gulf Coast and East Coast holidays in luxury homes, apartments, and hotels.

Airfares If you want to make your own way to Florida and need a reasonably priced ticket, try the small ads in the daily or Sunday newspapers or in magazines such as *Time Out*. You should be able to pick up something at rock-bottom prices. Be prepared to be flexible about your dates of travel and book as early as possible.

Also check out the APEX tickets offered by the major airlines, which are another good option. As we went to press, round-trip tickets to Orlando and Miami ranged from £508 to £559 for low and high season. Be sure to ask if there are any hidden extras, since airport taxes and supplements can increase the price dramatically.

Car Rental There are offices of the major car rental companies in most large towns, and you can either make your arrangements before you leave or when you get to your destination.

Avis (Hayes Gate House, Uxbridge Rd., Hayes, Middlesex UB4 0JN, tel. 081/848–8733) offers seven days' rental of a Chevrolet Cavalier at $105; extra days start at $26 per day.

Hertz (Radnor House, 1272 London Rd., Norbury, London SW16 4XW, tel. 081/679–1799) offers an "Affordable USA" program. Most rental offers include unlimited mileage, but don't forget to budget for the price of gas, local taxes, and collision insurance. Also check out the fly–drive offers from tour operators and airlines; some good bargains are usually available.

When to Go

Florida is a state for all seasons, although most visitors prefer October–April, particularly in southern Florida.

Winter is the height of the tourist season, when southern Florida is crowded with "snowbirds" fleeing the cold weather in the North. Hotels, bars, discos, restaurants, shops, and attractions are all crowded. Hollywood and Broadway celebrities appear in sophisticated supper clubs, and other performing artists hold the stage at ballets, operas, concerts, and theaters.

During the winter season, the Magic Kingdom at Disney World is more magical than ever, especially from mid-December through January 2, with daily parades and other extravaganzas. The crowds are overwhelming then, too. Winter fairs and festivals, art shows, parades, and fiestas take place in other parts of the state as well. In Tarpon Springs, youths dive for a golden cross during the Epiphany Festival on January 6. And in Tampa, the new multiethnic Bamboleo Festival attract enormous crowds in mid-winter.

Summer in Florida, as smart budget-minded visitors have discovered, is often hot and very humid, but the season is made bearable along the coast by ocean breezes. Besides, many hotels lower their prices considerably during summer. In the Panhandle, though, summer is the peak season.

Families who want to explore Disney World (including the Magic Kingdom, Epcot Center, MGM Studios), Sea World, Universal Studios Florida, Busch Gardens, and other outstanding attractions will find crowds in summer—but fewer during the week when children return to school in September.

For the college crowd, spring vacation is still the time to congregate in Florida, especially in Panama City Beach and the Daytona Beach area; Fort Lauderdale, where city officials, in their effort to refashion Fort Lauderdale more as a family resort, no longer indulges young revelers, so is much less popular with college students than it once was.

For senior citizens, September–December is the time for discounts to many attractions and hotels in Orlando and along the Pinellas Suncoast in the Tampa Bay area. The Panhandle is an excellent bargain all winter.

Climate What follows are average daily maximum and minimum temperatures for major cities in Florida.

Key West (The Keys)	**Jan.**	76F	24C	**May**	85F	29C	**Sept.**	90F	32C
		65	18		74	23		77	25
	Feb.	76F	24C	**June**	88F	31C	**Oct.**	83F	28C
		67	19		77	25		76	24
	Mar.	79F	26C	**July**	90F	32C	**Nov.**	79F	26C
		68	20		79	26		70	21
	Apr.	81F	27C	**Aug.**	90F	32C	**Dec.**	76F	24C
		72	22		79	26		67	19

Miami	**Jan.**	74F	23C	**May**	83F	28C	**Sept.**	86F	30C
		63	17		72	22		76	24
	Feb.	76F	24C	**June**	85F	29C	**Oct.**	83F	28C
		63	17		76	24		72	22
	Mar.	77F	25C	**July**	88F	31C	**Nov.**	79F	26C
		65	18		76	24		67	19
	Apr.	79F	26C	**Aug.**	88F	31C	**Dec.**	76F	26C
		68	20		77	25		63	17

Orlando	**Jan.**	70F	21C	**May**	88F	31C	**Sept.**	88F	31C
		49	9		67	19		74	23
	Feb.	72F	22C	**June**	90F	32C	**Oct.**	83F	28C
		54	12		72	22		67	19
	Mar.	76F	24C	**July**	90F	32C	**Nov.**	76F	24C
		56	13		74	23		58	14
	Apr.	81F	27C	**Aug.**	90F	32C	**Dec.**	70F	21C
		63	17		74	23		52	11

Current weather information for over 750 cities around the world may be obtained by calling **WeatherTrak** information service at 900/370–8728 or in TX, 900/575–8728. A taped message will tell you to dial the three-digit access code for the destination you're interested in. The code is either the area code (in the United States) or the first three letters of the foreign city. For a list of all access codes, send a stamped, self-addressed envelope to Cities (9B Terrace Way, Greensboro, NC 27403). For further information, phone 800/247–3282.

Festivals and Seasonal Events

Top seasonal events in Florida include Speed Week's auto racing celebration in Daytona Beach and the Miami Film Festival—both in February; Florida Derby Festival from March through April; Sunfest in Palm Beach in May; and Key West's celebration of Hemingway Days in July. For exact dates and details about the following events, call the listed numbers or inquire from local chambers of commerce.

Early Jan.: Polo Season opens at the Palm Beach Polo and Country Club (13420 South Shore Blvd., West Palm Beach 33414, tel. 407/793–1440).
Jan. 6: Greek Epiphany Day includes religious celebrations, parades, music, dancing, and feasting at the St. Nicholas Greek Orthodox Cathedral (Box 248, Tarpon Springs 34689, tel. 813/937–6109).
Mid-Jan.: Art Deco Weekend spotlights Miami Beach's historic district with an Art Deco street fair, a 1930s-style Moon Over Miami Ball, and live entertainment (1244 Ocean Dr., Miami Beach 33119, tel. 305/672–2014).

Mid-Jan.: Taste of the Grove Food and Music Festival is a popular fund-raiser put on in Coconut Grove's Peacock Park by area restaurants (tel. 305/442–2001).

Mid-Jan.: Martin Luther King, Jr., Festivals are celebrated in Miami and Tampa (7225 S.W. 24th St., Miami 33155; and 1420 N. Tampa St., Tampa 33602, tel. 813/223–8615).

Late Jan.: South Florida Fair and Exposition takes place in West Palm Beach (Box 15915 West Palm Springs 33416–5915, tel. 407/793–0333).

Late Jan.: Bamboleo Festival is the new, big city-sanctioned Tampa event, with parade, flotilla, and other street festivities, that replaces a former Tampa tradition, the Gasparilla and Pirate Fest celebrations (Tampa/Hillsborough Convention & Visitors Assn., 111 Madison St., Ste. 1010, Tampa 33601–0519, tel. 813/223–1111).

Late Jan.: Miami Rivers Blues Festival takes place on the south bank of the river next to Tobacco Road (626 S. Miami Ave., Miami 33130, tel. 305/374–1198).

Late Jan. or early Feb.: Key Biscayne Art Festival is an annual juried show of 175 talented artists at the entrance to Cape Florida State Park (Key Biscayne Rotary Club, Box 490174, Key Biscayne 33149, tel. 305/361–5207).

Feb.: Florida Strawberry Festival in Plant City celebrates its winter harvest for two weeks, with country music stars, rides, exhibits, and strawberry delicacies (tel. 813/752–9194).

Feb.: Olustee Battle Festival in Lake City, the second largest Civil War reenactment in the nation after Gettysburg, features a memorial service, crafts and food festival, 10K run, and parade (Box 1847, Lake City 32056, tel. 904/755–5666).

Early Feb.–late Feb.: Speed Weeks is a three-week celebration of auto racing that culminates in the famous Daytona 500 in Daytona Beach (Daytona International Speedway, Drawer S, Daytona Beach 32015, tel. 904/254–2700).

Feb–Mar.: Winter Equestrian Festival includes more than 1,000 horses and three grand-prix equestrian events at the Palm Beach Polo and Country Club in West Palm Beach (tel. 407/798–7000).

First weekend in Feb.: Sarasota Classic is a major event on the LPGA tour (Classic, Box 2199, Sarasota 33578).

Feb.–Mar.: Scottish Festival and Games features a variety of events in Key Biscayne (tel. 305/757–6730).

Mid-Feb.: Florida State Fair includes carnival rides and 4-H competitions in Tampa (Box 11766, Tampa 33680, tel. 813/621–7821).

Mid-Feb.: Miami Film Festival is 10 days of international, domestic, and local films sponsored by the Film Society of America (444 Brickell Ave., Suite 229, Miami 33131, tel. 305/377–FILM).

Mid-Feb.: Florida Manatee Festival in Crystal River focuses on both the river and the endangered manatee (tel. 904/795–3149).

Mid-Feb.: Florida Citrus Festival and Polk County Fair in Winter Haven showcases the citrus harvest with displays and entertainment (Box 9229, Winter Haven 33883, tel. 813/293–3175).

Mid-Feb.: Islamorada Sportfishing Festival features a weekend of fishing, arts and crafts, races, and prizes (tel. 305/664–2321).

Mid-Feb.: Coconut Grove Art Festival is the state's largest (tel. 305/447–0401).

Last full weekend in Feb.: Labelle Swamp Cabbage Festival is a salute to the state tree, the cabbage palm (tel. 813/675–0125).
First weekend in Mar.: Sanibel Shell Fair is the largest event of the year on Sanibel Island (tel. 813/472–2155 or 813/472–4709).
Early Mar.: Azalea Festival is a beauty pageant, arts and crafts show, and parade held in downtown Palatka and Riverfront Park (tel. 904/328–1503).
Early Mar.: Carnaval Miami is a carnival celebration staged by the Little Havana Tourist Authority (970 S.W. First St., Miami 33130, tel. 305/836–5223).
Early Mar.: Bike Week is a major motorcycle racing event at Daytona International Speedway that always takes place three weeks after the Daytona 500 (tel. 904/255–0981).
Mid-Mar. and early July: Arcadia All-Florida Championship Rodeo is professional rodeo at its best (Rodeo, Box 1266, Arcadia 33821, tel. 813/494–3773).
Mid-Mar.–early May: Springtime Tallahassee is a major cultural, sporting, and culinary event in the capital (tel. 904/224–5012).
Late Mar.: Port Canaveral Seafood Festival requires hearty appetites at Cape Canaveral (tel. 407/459–2200).
Apr.: Arts in April presents a series of visual and performing arts events produced by local independent arts organizations (Elizabeth Kurz, Office of the Mayor, 1 City Commons, 400 S. Orange Ave., Orlando 32801, tel. 407/246–2221).
Early Apr.: Spring Arts Festival attracts more than 300 artists and craftspeople from across the country to Gainesville (tel. 904/372–1976).
Early Apr.: Delray Affair is the biggest event in the area and features arts, crafts, and food.
Early Apr.–late May: Addison Mizner Festival in Boca Raton celebrates the 1920s in Palm Beach County (tel. 800/242–1774).
Palm Sunday: Blessing of the Fleet is held on the bay front in St. Augustine (tel. 904/829–5681).
Mid-Apr.: Cedar Key Sidewalk Arts Festival is celebrated in one of the state's most historic towns (tel. 904/543–5600).
Mid-Apr.: Pompano Seafood Festival includes one of the nation's premier billfish tournaments, plus area restaurants that showcase their offerings (tel. 305/941–2940).
Easter Sunday: Easter Sunrise Service in Orlando is held at Sea World (tel. 407/351–3600).
Late Apr.: River Cities Festival is a three-day event in Miami Springs and Hialeah that focuses attention on the Miami River and the need to keep it clean (tel. 305/887–1515).
Late Apr.–early May: Sun 'n' Fun Festival includes a bathtub regatta, golf tournament, and nighttime parade in Clearwater (tel. 813/462–6531 or 813/461–0011).
Late Apr.–early May: Conch Republic Celebration in Key West honors the founding fathers of the Conch Republic, "the small island nation of Key West" (tel. 305/294–4440).
First weekend in May: Sunfest includes a wide variety of cultural and sporting events in West Palm Beach (tel. 407/659–5980).
Mid-May: Arabian Nights Festival in Opa-locka is a mix of contemporary and fantasy-inspired entertainment (tel. 305/953–2821).
Mid-May: Tropicool Fest for two weeks draws thousands to more than 30 concerts, and arts and sports events all around town (Kris Paradis, 362 U.S. 41 N, Naples 33940, tel. 813/262–6141).
Mid-June: Fiesta of Five Flags in Pensacola celebrates de

Luna's landing with dancing and reenactments of the event (tel. 904/433–6512).

First weekend in June: Miami-Bahamas Goombay Festival in Miami's Coconut Grove, celebrates the city's Bahamian heritage (tel. 305/443–7928).

Early–mid-June: Billy Bowlegs Festival in Fort Walton Beach is a week of entertaining activities in memory of a pirate who ruled the area in the late 1700s (tel. 904/267–1216).

July 4: Firecracker Festival in Melbourne is one of the state's most colorful Independence Day celebrations (tel. 407/724–5400).

Mid-July: Hemingway Days Festival in Key West includes plays, short-story competitions, and a Hemingway look-alike contest (tel. 305/294–4440).

Mid-July: The Greater Jacksonville King Fish Tournament offers a number of cash prizes (tel. 904/241–7127).

Aug.: Boca Festival Days includes many educational, cultural, and recreational activities in Boca Raton (tel. 407/338–7070).

Mid-Aug.: Shark Tournament at Port of the Islands on Marco Island awards prizes for the largest shark in three categories; at Port of the Islands Resort and Marina (Rte. 41, Marco Island 33937, tel. 800/237–4173. Contact: Art Ogden, Port of the Islands Resort and Marina, 2500 Tamiami East, Naples 33961).

Labor Day: Worm Fiddler's Day is the biggest day of the year in Caryville (tel. 904/548–5571).

Early Sept.: Pioneer Florida Day is celebrated at the Pioneer Florida Museum in Dade City (tel. 904/567–0262).

Early Sept.: Anniversary of the Founding of St. Augustine is held on the grounds of the Mission of Nombre de Dios (tel. 904/247–4242).

Mid- to late Sept.: Festival Miami is three weeks of performing and visual arts sponsored by the University of Miami. (University of Miami School of Music, 6200 San Amaro Dr., Coral Gables 33124–1514, tel. 305/284–3941).

Late Sept.: Pensacola Seafood Festival means food and entertainment in Pensacola (tel. 904/433–6512).

Oct.: Jacksonville Jazz Festival is a three-day event featuring jazz superstars, performances, arts and crafts, food, and the Great American Jazz Piano Competition (tel. 904/353–7770).

Oct.: Destin Seafood Festival is a two-day affair where you can sample smoked amberjack, fried mullet, or shark kabobs (tel. 904/837–6241).

Mid-Oct.: Florida State Chili Cookoff Championship at Port of the Islands Resort in the Everglades means all the chili you can eat (25000 Tamiami Trail E., Naples 33961, tel. 800/237–4173).

Late Oct.: Banyan Art Festival attracts craftspeople and artists to Coconut Grove (tel. 305/444–7270).

Late Oct.: Boggy Bayou Mullet Festival is a three-day hoedown in celebration of the "Twin Cities," Valparaiso/Niceville, and the famed scavenger fish, the mullet (tel. 904/678–5077).

Late Oct.: Fantasy Fest in Key West is an unrestrained Halloween costume party, parade, and town fair (tel. 305/296–1817).

Early Nov.: Light Up Orlando is a street celebration of bands, international foods, and the Queen Kumquat Sashay Parade (tel. 407/363–5800).

Early Nov.: Florida Seafood Festival is Apalachicola's celebration of its seafood staple with oyster-shucking-and-consumption contests and parades (tel. 904/653–8051.)

Mid-Dec.: Walt Disney World's Very Merry Christmas Parade in

the Magic Kingdom (Walt Disney World, Box 10000, Lake Buena Vista 32830–1000).
Mid-Dec.: Grand Illumination is a colorful display in St. Augustine (tel. 904/829–5681).
Late Dec.: Coconut Grove King Mango Strut is a parody of the Orange Bowl Parade (tel. 305/858–6253).

What to Pack

Pack light, because porters and luggage trolleys are hard to find. Luggage allowances on domestic flights vary slightly from airline to airline. Most allow three checked pieces and two carryons. In all cases, check-in luggage cannot weigh more than 70 pounds per bag or be larger than 62 inches (length + width + height) and carryons must fit under the seat or in the overhead luggage compartment.

The northern part of the state is much cooler in the winter than is the southern part. Winters are mild in the Orlando area, with daytime temperatures in the 70s and low 80s. But the temperature can dip to the 50s, even in the Keys, so take a sweater or jacket, just in case. Farther north, in the Panhandle area, winters are cool and there's often frost at night.

The Miami area and the Tampa/St. Petersburg area are warm year-round and often extremely humid during the summer months. Be prepared for sudden summer storms, but leave the plastic raincoats at home because they're uncomfortable in the high humidity.

Dress is casual throughout the state, with sundresses, jeans, or walking shorts appropriate during the day. A pair of comfortable walking shoes or sneakers is a must for the major theme parks. A few of the better restaurants request that men wear jackets and ties, but most do not. Be prepared for air-conditioning bordering on freezing, especially in the Miami/Fort Lauderdale areas.

You can swim in most of peninsular Florida year-round. Be sure to take a sun hat and a good sunscreen because the sun can be fierce, even in the winter.

An extra pair of glasses, contact lenses, or prescription sunglasses is always a good idea; it is important to pack any allergy medication you may need.

Cash Machines

Virtually all U.S. banks belong to a network of ATMs (automatic teller machines), which dispense cash 24 hours a day in cities throughout the country. There are some eight major networks in the United States, the largest of which are **Cirrus,** owned by MasterCard, and **Plus,** affiliated with Visa. Some banks belong to more than one network. These cards are not automatically issued; you have to ask for them. Cards issued by American Express, Visa, and MasterCard may also be used in the ATMs, but the fees are usually higher than the fees on bank cards, and there is a daily interest charge on the "loan," even if monthly bills are paid on time. **Express Cash** allows American Express cardholders to withdraw up to $1,000 in a seven-day period (21 days overseas) from their personal checking accounts at ATMs worldwide. Gold-card members can receive up to $2,500 in a seven-day period (21 days overseas). Express Cash is not a cash advance service; only money already in the linked checking account can be withdrawn. Every transaction carries a 2% fee with a minimum charge of $2 and a maximum of $6. Apply for a PIN (Personal Identification number) and link your accounts at least 2–3 weeks before departure.

Each network has a toll-free number you can call to locate machines in a given city. The Cirrus number is 800/424–7787; the Plus number is 800/843–7587; the Express Cash number is 800/CASH–NOW. Check with your bank for fees and for the amount of cash you can withdraw per day.

Traveling with Film

If your camera is new, shoot and develop a few rolls before leaving home. Pack some lens tissue and an extra battery for your built-in light meter. Invest about $10 in a skylight filter and screw it onto the front of your lens; it will protect the lens and also reduce haze.

Film doesn't like hot weather. If you're driving in summer, don't store film in the glove compartment or on the shelf under the rear window. Put it behind the front seat on the floor, on the side opposite the exhaust pipe.

On a plane trip, never pack unprocessed film in check-in luggage; if your bags get X-rayed, say goodbye to your pictures. Always carry undeveloped film with you through security and ask to have it inspected by hand. (It helps to isolate your film in a plastic bag, ready for quick inspection.) Inspectors at American airports are required by law to honor requests for hand inspection.

The newer airport scanning machines used in all U.S. airports are safe for anything from five to 500 scans, depending on the speed of your film. The effects are cumulative; you can put the same roll of film through several scans without worry. After five scans, though, you're asking for trouble.

If your film gets fogged and you want an explanation, send it to the National Association of Photographic Manufacturers (550 Mamaroneck Ave., Harrison, NY 10528). It will try to determine what went wrong. The service is free.

Car Rentals

Florida is a car renter's bazaar, with more discount companies offering more bargains—and more fine print—than anywhere else in the nation. If you're planning to rent a car in Florida, shop around for the best combination rate for car and airfare. Jacksonville, for example, is often somewhat cheaper to fly into than Miami, but Miami's car-rental rates are usually lower than Jacksonville's. In major Florida cities, peak-season rates for a subcompact average around $110 a week, often with unlimited mileage. Some companies advertise peak-season promotional rates as low as $69 a week with unlimited mileage, but only a few cars are available at this rate, and you may have to pay twice as much if you keep the car less than seven days! Some of these companies require you to keep the car in the state and are quick to charge for an extra day when you return a vehicle late.

Avis (tel. 800/331–1212), **Budget** (tel. 800/527–0700), **Dollar** (tel. 800/800–4000), **Hertz** (tel. 800/654–3131), **National** (tel. 800/227–7368), **Sears** (tel. 800/527–0770), and **Thrifty** (tel. 800/367–2277) maintain airport and city locations throughout Florida. So do **Alamo** (tel. 800/327–9633) and **General** (tel. 800/327–7607), which offer some of the state's lowest rates. **Rent-A-Wreck** (tel. 800/535–1391) and **Ugly Duckling** (tel. 800/843–3825) rent used cars throughout the state, usually with more stringent mileage restrictions. Neither operation, however, has locations in Orlando.

Besides the national rental companies, several regional and local firms offer good deals in major Florida cities. These include **Auto Host** (tel. 800/448–4678), **Payless** (tel. 800/237–2804), **Superior** (tel. 800/237–8106), **USA** (tel. 800/872–2277), and **Value** (tel. 800/327–2501). In Fort Lauderdale, local companies include **Aapex Thompson** (tel. 305/566–8663) and **Air and Sea** (tel. 305/764–1008). In Orlando, try **InterAmerican Car Rental** (tel. 407/859–0414) and **Rainbow Rent-A-Car** (tel. 407/240–9791). In Tampa–St. Petersburg call **A-Florida Rent-A-Heap** (tel. 813/581–4805). In Miami, **Superior Rent-A-Car** (tel. 305/649–7012) is a local budget company, as are **Pass** (tel. 305/444–3923) and **InterAmerican Car Rental** (tel. 305/871–3030). Down in Key West, try **Tropical Rent-a-Car** (tel. 305/294–8136).

It's always best to know a few essentials *before* you arrive at the car-rental counter. Find out what the collision damage waiver (CDW), usually an $8–$12 daily surcharge, covers and whether your corporate or personal insurance already covers damage to a rental car (if so, bring a photocopy of the benefits section along). More and more companies are now holding renters responsible for theft and vandalism damages if they don't buy the CDW; in response, some credit card and insurance companies are extending *their* coverage to rental cars. These include **Chase Manhattan Bank Visa Cards** (tel. 800/645–7352), and **Dreyfus Consumer Bank Gold and Silver MasterCards** (tel. 800/847–9700). Find out, too, if you must pay for a full tank of gas whether you use it or not, and make sure you get a reservation number.

Traveling with Children

Publications ***Family Travel Times*** is an 8- to 12-page newsletter published 10 times a year by **Travel with Your Children.** The $35 subscription includes access to back issues and twice-weekly opportunities to call in for specific advice. Send $1 for a sample issue.

Great Vacations with Your Kids: The Complete Guide to Family Vacations in the U.S., second edition, by Dorothy Ann Jordon and Marjorie Adoff Cohen (E. P. Dutton, 375 Hudson St., New York, NY 10014, tel. 212/366–2000) details everything from city vacations to adventure vacations to child-care resources.

Periodicals for parents that are filled with listings of events, resources, and advice are available free at such places as libraries, supermarkets, and museums; ***Florida Parent*** (Box 2321, Boca Raton 33427, tel. 305/776–3305), a monthly, covers Palm Beach, Broward, and Dade counties.

Hotels Florida may have the highest concentration of hotels with organized children's programs in the United States. The following list gives examples of the kinds of services and activities offered by some of the major chains. It is by no means exhaustive. Be sure to ask about children's programs when you make a reservation.

Club Med (40 W. 57th St., New York, NY 10019, tel. 800/CLUB-MED) opened its new Sandpiper resort village in Port St. Lucie, including a "Baby Club" (4–23 months), "Mini Club" (2 years and up), and "Kids Club" (8 years and up). **Guest Quarters Suite Hotels** (Fort Lauderdale and Tampa locations, tel. 800/424-2900) offers the luxury of two-room suites with kitchen facilities and children's menus in the restaurant. It also allows children under 18 to stay free in the same suite with their parents. Two **Sonesta International Hotels** (tel. 800/766-3782) have children's programs: Sonesta Villa Resort Orlando and Sonesta Beach Hotel Key Biscayne. The **Hyatt Regency Grand Cypress** at Orlando (1 Grand Cypress Blvd., Orlando 32819, tel. 407/239-1234 or 800/228-9000) staffs a year-round Camp Gator for kids 5–15, but only Saturday and Sunday, Friday and Saturday evenings, and during holiday periods. There's a Children's Creative Center at the **Delta Orlando Resort** (5715 Major Blvd., Orlando 32819, tel. 407/351-3340). Also look for children's programs at **Marriott's Harbor Beach Resort** (3030 Holiday Dr., Fort Lauderdale 33316, tel. 305/525-4000 or 800/228-9290); Shamu's Playhouse at the **Stouffer Orlando Resort** (6677 Sea Harbor Dr., Orlando 32821, tel. 407/351-5555 or 800/468-3571); **Amelia Island Plantation Resort** (Rte. A1A, Amelia Island 32034, tel. 904/261-6161); **Holiday Inn Main Gate East** at Disney World (5678 Space Coast Hwy., Kissimmee 32741, tel. 407/396-4488 or 800/465-4329); **Holiday Inn Lake Buena Vista** (13351 S.R. 535, Lake Buena Vista 32830, tel. 800/366-6299); **La Concha Holiday Inn** (430 Duval St., Key West 33040, tel. 305/296-2991 or 800/227-6151); and **Marriott's Marco Island Resort** (400 S. Collier Blvd., Marco Island 33937, tel. 813/394-2511 or 800/228-9290); and the **Radisson Suite Beach Resort in Marco Island** (the Marco Munchkins program for ages 3–6, Radisson Rascals, 7–12) (600 S. Collier Blvd., Marco Island 33937, tel. 813/394-4100 or 800/333-3333). Most **Days Inn** hotels (tel. 800/325-2525) charge only a nominal fee for children under 18 and allow kids 12 and under to eat free (many offer efficiency-type apartments, too).

Condo Rentals See ***The Condo Lux Vacationer's Guide to Condominium Rentals in the Southeast*** by Jill Little (Vintage Books/Random House, New York; $9.95).

Home Exchange Exchanging homes is a surprisingly low-cost way to enjoy a vacation in another part of the country. A good choice for home exchange in the United States is the **Vacation Exchange Club, Inc.** (Box 820, Haleiwa, HI 96712, tel. 800/638-3841). The club publishes four directories a year, in January, March, July, and September, and updated, late listings throughout the year. Annual membership, which includes your listing in one book, a newsletter, and copies of all publications (mailed first class) is $50.

Getting There On domestic flights, children under 2 who do not occupy a seat travel free. Various discounts apply to children 2–12. Reserve a seat behind the bulkhead of the plane, which offers more legroom and can usually fit a bassinet (supplied by the airline). At the same time, inquire about children's meals, snacks, or special dietary needs, which are addressed by most airlines. (See "TWYCH's Airline Guide," in the February 1990 and 1992 issues of ***Family Travel Times,*** for a rundown of the services offered by 46 airlines.) Regulations about infant travel on airplanes are in the process of changing. Until they do, however, if you want to be sure your infant is secure, you must bring your own car seat and buy your baby a separate ticket. The booklet *Child Infant Safety Seats Acceptable for Use in Aircraft* is available from the Federal Aviation Administration (APA–200, 800 Independence Ave., SW, Washington, DC 20591, tel. 202/267–3479). If you opt to hold your baby on your lap, do so with the infant outside the seat belt rather than inside it so he or she doesn't get crushed in case of a sudden stop.

Hints for Disabled Travelers

Visitors may request the "Florida Services Directory for the Physically Challenged Traveler" from the Florida Department of Commerce, Division of Tourism (126 W. Van Buren St. Tallahassee 32399-2000, tel. 904/487–1462).

The Information Center for Individuals with Disabilities (Fort Point Place, 1st floor, 27–43 Wormwood St., Boston, MA 02210, tel. 617/727–5540—voice and TDD) offers useful problem-solving assistance, including lists of travel agents that specialize in tours for the disabled.

Moss Rehabilitation Hospital Travel Information Service (1200 W. Tabor Rd., Philadelphia, PA 19141–3099, tel. 215/456–9600; TDD 215/456–9602) provides information on tourist sights, transportation, and accommodations in destinations around the world. There is a small fee.

Mobility International USA (Box 3551, Eugene, OR 97403, tel. 503/343–1284) is a membership organization with a $20 annual fee offering information on accommodations, organized study, and so forth.

The Society for the Advancement of Travel for the Handicapped (SATH, 347 5th Ave., Suite 610, New York, NY 10016, tel. 212/447–7284) offers access information. Annual membership costs $45, or $25 for senior travelers and students. Send $1 and a self-addressed envelope.

The **National Park Service** provides a **Golden Access Passport** free of charge to those who are medically blind or have a permanent disability; the passport covers the entry fee for the holder and anyone accompanying the holder in the same private, noncommercial vehicle and a 50% discount on camping, boat launching, and parking. All charges are covered except lodging. Apply for the passport in person at any national recreation facility that charges an entrance fee; proof of disability is required. For additional information, write to the National Park Service (Box 37127, Washington, DC 20013–7127).

Greyhound/Trailways (tel. 800/752–4841) will carry a disabled person and companion for the price of a single fare.

Amtrak (tel. 800/USA–RAIL; TDD 800/523–6590) requests 72 hours' notice to provide redcap service, special seats, or wheelchair assistance at stations equipped to provide this service. All disabled and elderly passengers are entitled to a 15% discount on the lowest available fare. Reduced-price fares are also available for children. For a free copy of ***Access Amtrak,*** a guide to its services for elderly and disabled travelers, write to Amtrak (National Railroad Corporation Passenger Services, 60 Massachusetts Ave., NE, Washington, DC 20002).

Publications **Twin Peaks Press** (Box 129, Vancover, WA 98666, tel. 206/694–2462; 800/637–2256 for orders only) specializes in books for the disabled. Add $2 postage for the first book; $1 each additional book. ***Travel for the Disabled*** ($9.95) offers a comprehensive list of guidebooks and facilities geared to the disabled. ***Directory of Travel Agencies for the Disabled*** ($12.95) lists more than 350 agencies throughout the world. ***Wheelchair Vagabond*** ($9.95) helps independent travelers plan for extended trips in cars, vans, or campers. Twin Peaks also offers a "Traveling Nurse's Network," which provides registered nurses trained in all medical areas to accompany and assist disabled travelers.

Access America: An Atlas and Guide to the National Parks for Visitors with Disabilities (published by Northern Cartographic, Box 133, Burlington, VT 05402, tel. 802/860–2886) contains detailed information about access for the 37 largest and most visited national parks in the United States. This award-winning book costs $44.95 plus $5 shipping directly from the publisher.

Hints for Older Travelers

The **American Association of Retired Persons** (AARP, 601 E. St., NW, Washington, DC 20049, tel. 202/434–2277) has two programs for independent travelers: (1) the Purchase Privilege Program, which offers discounts on hotels, airfare, car rentals, RV rentals, and sightseeing, and (2) the AARP Motoring Plan, provided by Amoco, which offers emergency aid (road service) and trip-routing information for an annual fee of $33.95 per person or per married couple. The AARP also arranges group tours, cruises, and apartment living all over the world through "AARP Travel Experience from American Express" (400 Pinnacle Way, Suite 450, Norcross, GA 30071, tel. 800/659–5678). AARP members must be 50 or older. Annual dues are $5 per person or per married couple.

If you're planning to use an AARP or other senior-citizen identification card to obtain a reduced hotel rate, mention it at the time you make your reservation, not when you check out. At participating restaurants, show your card to the maître d' before you're seated, because discounts may be limited to certain set menus, days, or hours. When renting a car, be sure to ask about special promotional rates which might offer greater savings than the available discount.

Travel Industry and Disabled Exchange (TIDE, 5435 Donna Ave., Tarzana, CA 91356, tel. 818/368–5648) is an industry-based organization with a $15-per-person annual membership fee. Members receive a quarterly newsletter and a directory of travel agents for the disabled.

National Council of Senior Citizens (1331 F St., NW, Washington, DC 20004, tel. 202/347–8800) is a nonprofit advocacy group with some 5,000 local clubs across the country. Annual membership is $12 per person or couple. Members receive a monthly newspaper with travel information and an ID for reduced rates on hotels and car rentals.

Mature Outlook (6001 N. Clark St., Chicago, IL 60660, tel. 800/336–6330), a subsidiary of Sears Roebuck & Co., is a travel club for people over 50, offering discounts at Holiday Inns and a bimonthly newsletter. Annual membership is $9.95 per person or per married couple. Instant membership is available at Sears stores and participating Holiday Inns.

Golden Age Passport is a free lifetime pass to all parks, monuments, and recreation areas run by the federal government. People 62 and over should pick one up in person at any national park that charges admission. A driver's license or other proof of age is required.

September Days Club (tel. 800/241–5050) is run by the moderately priced Days Inns of America. The $12 annual membership fee for individuals or couples over 50 entitles them to reduced car rental rates and reductions of 15%–50% at 95% of the chain's more than 350 motels. Members also receive *Travel Holiday Magazine Quarterly* for updated information and travel articles.

Elderhostel (75 Federal St., 3rd floor, Boston, MA 02110–1941, tel. 617/426–7788) is an innovative, low-cost educational program for people aged 60 or over (only one member of a traveling couple needs to qualify). Participants live in dorms on 1,600 campuses in the United States and around the world. Mornings are devoted to lectures and seminars, afternoons to sightseeing and field trips. The fee includes room, board, tuition (in the United States and Canada), and round-trip transportation (overseas). Special scholarships are available for those who qualify financially.

Saga International Holidays (120 Boylston St., Boston, MA 02116, tel. 800/343–0273) specializes in group travel for people over age 60. A selection of variously priced tours allows you to choose the package that best meets your needs.

Publications ***The Senior Citizen's Guide to Budget Travel in the United States and Canada*** is available for $5.95 (including shipping) from Pilot Books (103 Cooper St., Babylon, NY 11702, tel. 516/422–2225).

Although Florida probably attracts more elderly people than any other state, the state publishes no booklet addressed directly to senior citizens.

Senior-citizen discounts are common throughout Florida, but there are no set standards. Some discounts, like those for prescriptions at the Eckerd Drug chain, require that you fill out a card and register. The best bet is simply to ask whether there is a senior-citizen discount available on your purchase, meal, or hotel stay.

Further Reading

Suspense novels that are rich in details about Florida include Elmore Leonard's *La Brava*, John D. MacDonald's *The Empty Copper Sea*, Joan Higgins's *A Little Death Music*, and Charles Willeford's *Miami Blues*. Pat Frank's *Alas Babylon* describes a fictional nuclear disaster in Florida.

Marjorie K. Rawlings's classic, *The Yearling*, poignantly portrays life in the brush country, and her *Cross Creek* re-creates the memorable people the author knew in her 13 years of living at Cross Creek. Peter Matthiessen's *Killing Mister Watson* recreates turn-of-the-century lower southwest Florida of the Ten Thousand Islands in a tale about a prosperous killer in an Everglades settlement of hardscrabble pioneers.

Look for *Princess of the Everglades*, a novel about the 1926 hurricane by Charles Mink, and *Snow White and Rose Red* and *Jack and the Beanstalk*, Ed McBain's novels about Matthew Hope, an attorney who practices law in a Florida gulf city. Pat Booth's novel *Palm Beach* describes the glitzy Palm Beach scene. *The Tourist Season* is Carl Hiaasen's immensely funny declaration of war against the state's environment-despoiling hordes. His latest is *Native Tongue*. New—from sexy hot to mystic cool—are Pat Booth's *Miami*, and Sam Harrison's *Birdsong Ascending*. T.D. Allman's *Miami* is the best of a recent flock of titles about the city.

Other recommended novels include *Florida Straits*, by Laurence Shames; Evelyn Mayerson's *No Enemy But Time; To Have and Have Not*, by Ernest Hemingway; *The Day of the Dolphin*, by Robert Merle; and *Their Eyes Were Watching God*, by Zora Neale Hurston.

Among the recommended nonfiction books are *Key West Writers and Their Homes*, Lynn Kaufelt's tour of homes of Hemingway, Wallace Stevens, Tennessee Williams, and others; *The Everglades: River of Grass*, by Marjory S. Douglas; *Florida*, by Gloria Jahoda, published as part of the Bicentennial observance; *Miami Alive*, by Ethel Blum; and *Florida's Sandy Beaches*, University Press of Florida. Mark Derr's *Some Kind of Paradise* is an excellent review of the state's environmental follies; John Rothchild's *Up for Grabs*, equally good, is about Florida's commercial lunacy. Good anthologies include *The Florida Reader: Visions of Paradise* (Maurice O'Sullivan and Jack Lane, eds.); *The Rivers of Florida* (Del and Marty Marth, eds.), and *Subtropical Speculations: An Anthology of Florida Science Fiction* (Richard Mathews and Rick Wilber, eds.).

Arriving and Departing

By Plane

Most major U.S. airlines schedule regular flights into Florida, and some, such as Delta and United Airlines, serve the Florida airports extensively.

Delta and USAir all have regular service into Jacksonville, Daytona Beach, Orlando, Melbourne, West Palm Beach, Fort Lauderdale, Miami, Fort Myers, Tampa, Tallahassee, Gainesville, and Key West. Delta also flies into Sarasota, Naples, Pensacola, and Fort Pierce.

Other major airlines that serve the Florida airports include Continental, American, American Trans Air, Northwest, United, and TWA. Many foreign airlines also fly into some of the major airports in Florida; the smaller, out-of-the-way airports are usually accessible through the commuter flights of major domestic carriers.

Packages that combine airfare and vacation activities at special rates are often available through the airlines. For example, Delta (tel. 800/872–7786) offers travel packages to Disney World in Orlando (*see* Package Deals for Independent Travelers).

When booking reservations, keep in mind the distinction between nonstop flights (no stops and no changes), direct flights (no changes of aircraft, but one or more stops), and connecting flights (one or more changes of planes at one or more stops). Connecting flights are often the least expensive, but they are the most time-consuming, and the biggest nuisance.

Smoking Smoking regulations prohibit smoking on all domestic flights under six hours. This rule applies to both domestic and foreign carriers.

Carry-on Luggage Passengers are usually limited to two carry-on bags. For bags stored under your seat, the maximum dimensions are 9″ × 14″ × 22″. For bags that can be hung in a closet, the maximum dimensions are 4″ × 23″ × 45″. For bags stored in an overhead bin, the maximum dimensions are 10″ × 14″ × 36″. Any item that exceeds the specified dimensions will generally be rejected as a carryon and handled as checked baggage. Keep in mind that an airline can adapt these rules to circumstances; on an especially crowded flight, don't be surprised if you are allowed only one carry-on bag.

In addition to the two carryons, passengers may also bring aboard: a handbag (pocketbook or purse), an overcoat or wrap, an umbrella, a camera, a reasonable amount of reading material, an infant bag, and crutches, a cane, braces, or other prosthetic device upon which the passenger is dependent. Infant/child safety seats can also be brought aboard if parents have purchased a ticket for the child or if there is space in the cabin.

Note that these regulations are for U.S. airlines only. Foreign airlines generally allow one piece of carry-on luggage in tourist class, in addition to handbags and bags filled with duty-free goods. Passengers in first and business class may also be allowed to carry on one garment bag. It is best to check with your airline ahead of time to find out what its exact rules are regarding carry-on luggage.

Checked Luggage Luggage allowances vary slightly from airline to airline. Many carriers allow three checked pieces; some allow only two. It is best to consult with the airline before you go. In all cases, check-in luggage cannot weigh more than 70 pounds per piece or be larger than 62 inches (length + width + height).

Lost Luggage On domestic flights, airlines are responsible for lost or damaged property only up to $1,250 per passenger. If you're carrying valuables, either take them with you on the airplane or purchase additional insurance for lost luggage. Some airlines will issue additional luggage insurance when you check in, but many do not. Insurance for lost, damaged, or stolen luggage is available through travel agents or directly through various insurance companies. Two that issue luggage insurance are **Tele-Trip** (Box 31685, 3201 Farnam St., Omaha, NE 68131–0618, tel. 800/228–9792), a subsidiary of Mutual of Omaha, and **The Travelers Insurance Corporation** (Ticket and Travel Dept., 1 Tower Sq., Hartford, CT 06183–5040, tel. 203/277–0111 or 800/243–3174). Tele-Trip operates sales booths at airports, and it also issues insurance through travel agents. Tele-Trip will insure checked or hand luggage through its travel insurance packages. Rates vary according to the length of the trip. The Travelers will insure checked or hand luggage at $500–$2,000 valuation per person, for a maximum of 180 days. Rates for 1–5 days for $500 valuation are $10; for 180 days, $85.

Other companies with comprehensive policies include **Access America, Inc.,** a subsidiary of Blue Cross–Blue Shield (Box 11188, Richmond, VA 23230, tel. 800/334–7525 or 800/284–8300) and **Near Services** (450 Prairie Ave., Suite 101, Calumet City, IL 60409, tel. 708/868–6700 or 800/654–6700).

Before you go, itemize the contents of each bag in case you need to file an insurance claim. Be certain to put your home address on each piece of luggage, including carry-on bags. If your luggage is stolen and later recovered, the airline will deliver the luggage to your home free of charge.

By Car

Three major interstates lead to Florida from various parts of the country. I–95 begins in Maine, runs south through New England and the Mid-Atlantic states, and enters Florida just north of Jacksonville. It continues south past Daytona Beach, the Space Coast, Vero Beach, Palm Beach, and Fort Lauderdale, eventually ending in Miami.

I–75 begins at the Canadian border in Michigan and runs south through Ohio, Kentucky, Tennessee, and Georgia before entering Florida. The interstate moves through the center of the state before veering west into Tampa. It follows the west coast south to Naples, then crosses the state and ends in Miami.

California and all the most southern states are connected to Florida by I–10. This interstate originates in Los Angeles and moves east through Arizona, New Mexico, Texas, Louisiana, Mississippi, and Alabama before entering Florida at Pensacola on the west coast. I–10 continues straight across the northern part of the state until it terminates in Jacksonville.

Travelers heading from the Midwest or other points west for the lower east coast of Florida will want to use Florida's Turnpike from Wildwood, which crosses the state for 321 miles and goes as far as Florida City. In 1990 and 1991 toll cards were replaced at many locations with coin-drops. Eight service plazas were all attractively rebuilt in 1989 at a cost of $28 million and feature a mix of fast-food restaurants. For current information on tolls and other services, call the Florida Turnpike public information number (tel. 800/447–1781).

Speed Limits In Florida the speed limits are 55 mph on the state highways, 30 mph within city limits and residential areas, and 55–65 mph on the interstates and on Florida's Turnpike. These limits may vary, so be sure to watch road signs for any changes.

By Train

Amtrak (tel. 800/USA-RAIL) provides service to Orlando, Tampa, Miami, Tallahassee, Jacksonville, and several other major cities in Florida.

By Bus

Greyhound/Trailways passes through practically every major city in Florida, including Jacksonville, Daytona, Orlando, West Palm Beach, Fort Lauderdale, Miami, Sarasota, Tampa, Tallahassee, and Key West. For information about bus schedules and fares, contact your local Greyhound Information Center.

Staying in Florida

Tourist Information

The **Florida Division of Tourism** operates **welcome centers** on I–10, I–75, I–95, U.S. 231 (near Graceville), and in the lobby of the new Capitol in Tallahassee (Department of Commerce, 126 Van Buren St., Tallahassee 32399, tel. 904/487–1462).

Shopping

Malls in Florida are full of nationally franchised shops, major department-store chains, and one-of-a-kind shops catering to a mass audience. Small shops in out-of-the-way places, however, often have the best souvenirs and most special gift items.

Indian Artifacts Native American crafts are abundant, particularly in the southern part of the state, where you'll find billowing dresses and shirts, hand-sewn in striking colors and designs. At the Miccosukee Indian Village, 25 miles west of Miami on the Tamiami Trail (U.S. 41), as well as at the Seminole and Miccosukee reservations in the Everglades, you can also find handcrafted dolls and beaded belts.

Seashells The best shelling in Florida is on the beaches of Sanibel Island off Fort Myers. Shell shops, selling mostly kitsch items, abound throughout Florida. The largest such establishment is The Shell Factory near Fort Myers (*see* Shopping in Chapter 10).

Citrus Fruit Fresh citrus is available most of the year, except in summer. Two kinds of citrus grow in Florida: the sweeter and more costly Indian River fruit from a thin ribbon of groves along the east coast, and the less-costly fruit from the interior. After killer freezes in 1984, 1985, and 1989 ruined many groves in the Orlando area, the interior growers began planting in warmer areas south and west of Lake Okeechobee.

Citrus is sold in ¼, ½, ¾, and full bushels. Many shippers offer special gift packages with several varieties of fruit, jellies, and other food items. Some prices include U.S. postage, others may not. Shipping may exceed the cost of the fruit. If you have a choice of citrus packaged in boxes or bags, take the boxes. They are easier to label, are harder to squash, and travel better than the bags.

Malls and Boutiques The Greater Miami area has many look-alike shopping strips and malls with the same retail and discount shops. You'll find finer boutiques in specialty malls such as Cocowalk in Coconut Grove (*see* Exploring Coral Gables/Coconut Grove/South Miami in Chapter 4) and the Bal Harbour Shops (9700 Collins Ave., Bal Harbour 33154, tel. 305/866–0311). For ½ mile, Flagler Street, in the heart of downtown Miami, is the nation's most important import–export center, where bargain items for international travelers include cameras, electronics, and jewelry (*see* Exploring Downtown Miami in Chapter 4). Bayside Marketplace provides entertainment along with boutiques. The Caribbean Marketplace offers good Haitian imports.

Fort Lauderdale's finest shops cluster along six blocks of Las Olas Boulevard (*see* Exploring Fort Lauderdale in Chapter 6) and at the 150-store Galleria At Fort Lauderdale (2414 E. Sunrise Blvd., tel. 305/564–1015).

For the ultimate Florida shopping experience, stroll Palm Beach's Worth Avenue (*see* Shopping in Chapter 7). Here you'll find shops like Brooks Brothers and Tiffany's tucked between galleries selling ancient Chinese art or Oriental rugs, gourmet restaurants, one-of-a-kind jewelry stores, and chocolatiers. On the other hand, if your ultimate shopping experience is a discount mall, a must is the new Sawgrass Mills Mall in western Broward County (*see* Shopping in Chapter 6).

In Tampa, visit Old Hyde Park Village in one of the city's oldest neighborhoods. Some of the most successful countemporary retailers have set up shops (712 S. Oregon Ave., tel. 813/251–3500). Harbour Island features specialty shops plus dining, dancing, and boat tours (610 S. Harbour Island Blvd., tel. 813/228–7807). South of Tampa Bay on Florida's west coast, St. Armand's Circle in Sarasota has many elegant clothing shops and fine restaurants (*see* Shopping in Chapter 10). North of Tampa Bay in Tarpon Springs, you'll enjoy exploring sponge shops and savoring Greek fare along Dodecanese Boulevard.

Winter Park's Park Avenue provides a picturesque mile of shops with distinctly residential character alongside the town's namesake park.

Shops at the World Showcase in Epcot Center at Walt Disney World offer unusual lines of clothing, decorative items, gifts, and fine wines from many parts of the globe.

To shop and dine in a gracious 19th-century setting, visit the commercial heart of old Pensacola in the Palafox Historic District and the adjoining Seville Historic District centered around Seville Square. At the Quayside Thieves Market (712 S. Palafox St., tel. 904/433–9930), antiques shops and a flea market occupy a historic 19th-century warehouse beside the port. Specialty shops in Pensacola's historic district offer art, Christmas decorations, cookware, fine gifts, linens, and out-of-print books (*see* Exploring Pensacola in Chapter 11).

To travel even farther back in time, stroll the four-block pedestrian zone on St. George Street in Old St. Augustine. Shoppers are serenaded by street musicians as they pause to window-wish or peer into dimly lit shops to watch craftspeople at work. Just north, Jacksonville Landing, in its namesake city, provides a festive marketplace on the St. Johns River.

Antiques lovers should explore Micanopy, south of Gainesville off I–75; the Antiques Mall in St. Augustine's Lightner Museum; on U.S. 1 north of Dania Beach Boulevard in Dania; and S.W. 28th Lane and Unity Boulevard in Miami (near the Coconut Grove Metrorail station). Saturday farmers' markets are popular in Coconut Grove, Coral Gables, Orlando, and Winter Park.

Beaches

No point in Florida is more than 60 miles from saltwater. This long, lean peninsula is bordered by a 526-mile Atlantic coast from Fernandina Beach to Key West and a 792-mile coast along the Gulf of Mexico and Florida Bay from Pensacola to Key West. If you were to stretch Florida's convoluted coast in a straight line, it would extend for about 1,800 miles. What's more, if you add in the perimeter of every island surrounded by saltwater, Florida has about 8,500 miles of tidal shoreline—more than any other state except Alaska. Florida's coastline comprises about 1,016 miles of sand beaches.

Visitors unaccustomed to strong subtropical sun run a risk of sunburn and heat prostration on Florida beaches, even in winter. The natives go to the beach early in the day or in the late afternoon. If they must be out in direct sun at midday, they limit their sun exposure and strenuous exercise, drink plenty of liquids, and wear hats. Wherever you plan to swim, ask if the water has a dangerous undertow.

The state owns all beaches below the mean high-tide line, even in front of hotels and private resorts, but gaining access to the public beach can be a problem along much of Florida's coastline. You must pay to enter and/or park at most state, county, and local beachfront parks. Where hotels dominate the beach frontage, public parking may be limited or nonexistent.

Along the Atlantic Coast from the Georgia border south through the Daytona Beach area the beaches are broad and firm. In Daytona Beach you can drive on them. Some beachfront communities in this area charge for the privilege; others provide free beach access for vehicles.

From the Treasure Coast south, erosion has affected the beaches. Major beach rehabilitation projects have been completed in Fort Lauderdale, the Sunny Isles area of north Dade County, Miami Beach, and Key Biscayne.

In the Florida Keys, coral reefs and prevailing currents prevent sand from building up to form beaches. The few Keys beaches are small, narrow, and generally have little or no sandy bottom.

On the Gulf Coast, Captiva Island is losing sand to neighboring Sanibel Island, where a stroll beside the water at sunrise or sunset can be a truly sensual experience. Currents bring all sorts of unusual shells onto Sanibel's beach, and scatter sharks' teeth across Venice and Caspersen beaches in south Sarasota County. Siesta Beach in Sarasota County claims to have Florida's softest white sand. At the north end of Longboat Key in Manatee County, accretion has built a magnificent beach in the vicinity of Beer Can Island. Much of that sand came from Coquina Beach and Bradenton Beach, county parks that remain popular despite their dwindling supply of sand. In Pinellas County, visit Caladesi Island State Park to experience what all the barrier islands used to look like.

In Florida's Panhandle, Gulf Island National Seashore administers 150 miles of beach frontage notable for its sugarlike sand and the impressive dune formations near Fort Walton Beach. Expect the beaches outside Panama City and Pensacola to be crowded on summer weekends.

Participant Sports

The Governor's Council on Physical Fitness and Sports (1330 N.W. 6th St., Gainesville 32601, tel. 904/336–2120) puts on the annual **Sunshine State Games** in July each year in a different part of the state, and promotes the business of sports. Call for information on events.

Bicycling Bicycling is popular throughout Florida. The terrain is flat in the south and gently rolling along the central ridge and in much of the Panhandle. Most cities of any size have bike-rental shops, which are good sources of information on local bike paths.

Florida's Department of Natural Resources (Div. of Recreation and Parks, Mail Station 585, 3900 Commonwealth Blvd., Tallahassee 32399–3000, tel. 904/487–4784) is developing three overnight bicycle tours of different areas of the state. The tours will vary in length between 100 and 450 miles (for 2–6 days of cycling), and will use state parks for rest stops and overnight camping.

Florida's Department of Transportation (DOT) publishes free bicycle trail guides, which you can request from the state bicycle–pedestrian coordinator (605 Suwannee St., Mail Station 19, Tallahassee 32399-0450, tel. 904/487–1200). DOT also sells 7 maps for bicycle trips of 35 to 300 miles. Write to Maps and Publications, 605 Suwannee St., Mail Station 12, Tallahassee 32399–0450, tel. 904/488–9220. Cost: $1 plus 6% sales tax per map.

For information on local biking events and clubs, contact **Florida Bicycle Association** (Box 16652, Tampa 33687–6652, tel. 800/FOR BIKE or 210 Lake Hollingsworth #1707, Lakeland 33803, tel. 813/985–4326). In Greater Miami, contact Dade County's bicycle–pedestrian coordinator (Office of the County Manager, Metro-Dade Government Center, 111 N.W. 1st St., Suite 910, Miami 33128, tel. 305/375–4507). Contact Florida's DOT (*see* above) for names of other bike coordinators around the state.

For specific information about Florida's rails-to-trails network contact the Department of Natural Resources (*see* above).

Canoeing The best time to canoe in Florida is winter, the dry season, when you're less likely to get caught in a torrential downpour or be eaten alive by mosquitoes.

The Everglades has areas suitable for flat-water wilderness canoeing that are comparable to spots in the Boundary Waters region of Minnesota. Other popular canoeing rivers include the Blackwater, Juniper, Loxahatchee, Peace, Oklawaha, Suwannee, St. Marys, and Santa Fe. A free guide issued by the Florida Department of Natural Resources (DNR), ***Florida Recreational Trails System Canoe Trails,*** describes nearly 950 miles of designated canoe trails and support services along 36 Florida creeks, rivers, and springs (Div. of Recreation and Parks, Bureau of Operational Services, MS 535, 3900 Commonwealth Blvd., Tallahassee 32399–3000, tel. 904/488–7896). Contact individual national forests, parks, monuments, reserves, and seashores for information on their canoe trails. Local chambers of commerce have information on canoe trails in county parks.

Two Florida canoe-outfitter organizations publish free lists of canoe outfitters who organize canoe trips, rent canoes and canoeing equipment, and help shuttle canoeists' boats and cars. ***Canoe Outpost System*** is a brochure listing six independent outfitters serving 11 Florida rivers (Rte. 7, Box 301, Arcadia 33821, tel. 813/494–1215). The **Florida Association of Canoe Liveries and Outfitters (FACLO)** publishes a free list of 33 canoe outfitters who organize trips on 28 creeks and rivers (Box 1764, Arcadia 33821).

Fishing In Atlantic and Gulf waters, fishing seasons and other regulations vary by location, and by the number and size of fish of various species that you may catch and retain. For a free copy of the annual ***Florida Fishing Handbook,*** write to the Florida Game and Fresh Water Fish Commission (620 S. Meridian St., Tallahassee 32399–1600, tel. 904/488–1960).

Opportunities for saltwater fishing abound from the Keys all the way up the Atlantic Coast to Georgia and up the Gulf Coast to Alabama. Many seaside communities have fishing piers that charge admission to anglers (and usually a lower rate to watchers). These piers usually have a bait-and-tackle shop. Write the **Florida Sea Grant Extension Program** for a free list of Florida fishing piers (Rm. G-022, McCarty Hall, University of Florida, Gainesville 32611, tel. 904/392–1771).

Inland, there are more than 7,000 freshwater lakes to choose from. The largest—448,000-acre **Lake Okeechobee,** the fourth-largest natural lake in the United States—is home to bass, bluegill, speckled perch, and succulent catfish (which the locals call "sharpies"). In addition to the state's many natural freshwater rivers, South Florida also has an extensive system of flood-control canals. In 1989 scientists found high mercury levels in largemouth bass and warmouth caught in parts of the Everglades in Palm Beach, Broward, and Dade counties, and warned against eating fish from those areas. Warnings have since been extended to parts of northern Florida.

It's easy to find a boat-charter service that will take you out into deep water. Some of the best are found in the Panhandle, where small towns like Destin and Fort Walton Beach have huge fleets. The Keys, too, are dotted with charter services, and Key West has a sportfishing and shrimping fleet as extensive as what you would expect to find in large cities. Depending on your taste, budget, and needs, you can charter anything from an old wooden craft to a luxurious, waterborne palace with state-of-the-art amenities.

Licenses are required for both freshwater and saltwater fishing. The fees for a saltwater fishing license are $30 for nonresidents and $12 for residents. A nonresident seven-day saltwater license is $15. Nonresidents can purchase freshwater fishing licenses good for 10 days ($15) or for one year ($30); residents pay $12 for an annual license. Combined annual freshwater fishing and hunting licenses are also available at $22 for residents.

Golf Except in the heart of the Everglades, you'll never be far from one of Florida's more than 1,050 golf courses. Palm Beach County, the state's leading golf locale with 130 golf courses, also houses the home offices of the National Golf Foundation and the Professional Golfers Association of America. Many of the best golf courses in Florida allow visitors to play without being members or hotel guests. *See* Chapter 3, The Florida Fifty, for details on the state's best courses.

Especially in winter, you should reserve tee-off times in advance. Ask about golf reservations when you make your lodging reservations.

Horseback Riding Trail and endurance riding are popular throughout the state, with seven state parks providing overnight camping with stables, facilities, and 14 parks with trails and campgrounds for horses. Amelia Island offers horseback riding on the beach. Spring and fall meetings for riders are held. In the fall they meet in Altoona in the Ocala National Forest; in the spring, in a different location. For more information, contact **AHOOF** (Affiliated Horse Organization of Florida, Box 448, Laurel 34272, tel. 813/484–6449).

Hunting Hunters in Florida stalk a wide variety of resident game animals and birds, including deer, wild hog, wild turkey, bobwhite quail, ducks, and coots. A plain hunting license costs $11 for Florida residents, $150 for nonresidents, except nonresidents from Alabama who pay $100. Nonresidents can get a 10-day hunting license for $25, except for nonresidents from Georgia, who pay $121.

Each year in June, the **Florida Game and Fresh Water Fish Commission** announces the dates and hours of the fall hunting seasons for public and private wildlife-management areas. Hunting seasons vary across the state. Where hunting is allowed, you need the landowner's written permission—and you must carry that letter with your hunting license in the field. Trespassing with a weapon is a felony. For a free copy of the annual ***Florida Hunting Handbook,*** contact the game commission (620 Meridian St., Tallahassee 32399–1600, tel. 904/488–4676).

Jogging, Running, and Walking All over Florida, you'll find joggers, runners, and walkers on bike paths and city streets—primarily in the early morning and after working hours in the evening. Some Florida hotels have set up their own running trails; others provide guests with information on measured trails in the vicinity. The first time you run in Florida, be prepared to go a shorter distance than normal because of higher heat and humidity.

Two major Florida festivals include important running races. Each year in December the **Capital Bank Orange Bowl 10K,** one of the state's best-known running events, brings world-class runners to Miami. In April, as part of the Florida Keys annual Conch Republic Days, runners congregate near Marathon on one of the world's most spectacular courses for the **Seven Mile Bridge Run.**

Local running clubs all over the state sponsor weekly public events for joggers, runners, and walkers. For a list of local clubs and events throughout the state, call or send a self-addressed stamped envelope to the **Florida Athletics Congress** (1330 N.W. 6th St., Gainesville 32601, tel. 904/378–6805). For information about events in south Florida contact the 1,500-member **Miami Runners Club** (7900 S.W. 40th St., Miami 33155, tel. 305/227–1500).

Scuba Diving and Snorkeling South Florida and the Keys attract most of the divers and snorkelers, but the more than 300 dive shops throughout the state schedule drift-, reef-, and wreck-diving trips for scuba divers all along Florida's Atlantic and Gulf coasts. The low-tech pleasures of snorkeling can be enjoyed all along the Overseas Highway in the Keys and elsewhere where shallow reefs hug the shore.

Inland in north and central Florida divers explore more than 100 grottoes, rivers, sinkholes, and springs. In some locations, you can swim with manatees ("sea cows"), which migrate in from the sea to congregate around warm springs during the cool winter months. Ginnie Springs (Rte. 1, Box 153, High Springs 32643, tel. 904/454–2202 or 800/874–8571), near Branford, is one of Florida's most famous springs. Crystal Lodge Dive Center in the Econo Lodge (525 N.W. 7th Ave., Crystal River 32629, tel. 904/795–6798) is a popular gateway to river-diving in the Crystal River in central Florida.

Contact the **Dive Industry Association** for lists of advertisers who provide services for boaters, divers, and fisherfolk. The Keys packet is $6.95, and the all-inclusive Florida state packet, $14.95 (Teall's Inc., 111 Saguaro La., Marathon 33050, tel. 305/743–3942).

Tennis Many Florida hotels have a resident tennis pro and offer special tennis packages with lessons. Many local park and recreation departments throughout Florida operate modern tennis centers like those at country clubs, and most such centers welcome nonresidents, for a fee. For general information and schedules for amateur tournaments, contact the **Florida Tennis Association** (801 N.E. 167th St., Suite 301, North Miami Beach 33162, tel. 305/652–2866).

Trails Trails for biking, canoeing, sea-kayaking, hiking, horseback riding, and jogging are getting new attention in Florida. Contact the **State Trails Coordinator** in the Bureau of Park Planning, Department of Natural Resources (3900 Commonwealth Blvd., Tallahassee 32399-3000, tel. 904/487–4784). Impetus stems from the **Florida Trail Association** (Box 13708, Gainesville, FL 32604, tel. 800/343–1882 in FL, 904/378–8823 outside FL), which since 1964 has developed more than 1,000 miles of trail through the state, including more than 300 miles of certified Florida National Scenic Trail; and from the Florida Chapter of the **Rails-to-Trails Conservancy** (2545 Blairstone Pines Dr., Tallahassee, FL 32301, tel. 904/942–2379).

Parks and Nature Preserves

Although Florida is the fourth-most-populous state in the nation, there are 9,711,043 acres of public and private recreation facilities set aside in national forests, parks, monuments, reserves, and seashores; state forests and parks; county parks; and nature preserves owned and managed by private conservation groups.

On holidays and weekends, crowds flock to Florida's most popular parks—even to some on islands that are accessible only by boat. Come early or risk being turned away. In winter, northern migratory birds descend on the state. Many resident species breed in the warm summer months, but others (such as the wood stork) time their breeding cycle to the winter dry season. In summer, mosquitoes are voracious and daily afternoon thundershowers add to the state's humidity, but this is when the sea turtles come ashore to lay their eggs and when you're most likely to see frigate birds and other tropical species.

National Parks The federal government maintains no centralized information service for its natural and historic sites in Florida. You must contact each site directly for information on current recreational facilities and hours. To obtain a copy of **Guide and Map of National Parks of U.S.**, which provides park addresses and facilities lists, write to U.S. Government Printing Office,

Washington, DC 20402. GPO No. 024005008527. Cost: $1.25 (no tax or postage).

In 1908 the federal government declared the keys around what is now **Fort Jefferson National Monument** in the Dry Tortugas a wildlife sanctuary to protect the sooty tern. **Everglades National Park** was established in 1947. Other natural and historic sites in Florida under federal management include **Big Cypress National Preserve** and **Biscayne National Park** in the Everglades, **Canaveral National Seashore** in central Florida, **Castillo De San Marcos National Monument** in north Florida, **De Soto National Monument** in Bradenton, the 130-acre **Fort Caroline National Memorial** on the St. Johns River in Jacksonville, **Fort Matanzas National Monument** south of St. Augustine, and **Gulf Islands National Seashore** in north Florida.

The federal government operates three national forests in Florida. The **Apalachicola National Forest** encompasses 557,000 acres of pine and hardwoods in two ranger districts across the northern coastal plain (west Apalachicola District; east Wakulla District). The 336,000-acre **Ocala National Forest** includes the sandhills of the Big Scrub (*see* the essay in Chapter 2). Cypress swamps and numerous sinkhole lakes dot the 157,000-acre **Osceola National Forest.**

National wildlife refuges in Florida include the **Great White Heron National Wildlife Refuge** and **National Key Deer Refuge** (in the Keys), **Loxahatchee National Wildlife Refuge** near Palm Beach, **J. N. "Ding" Darling National Wildlife Refuge** in southwest Florida, and **Merritt Island National Wildlife Refuge.** The federal government also operates the **Key Largo National Marine Sanctuary, Looe Key National Marine Sanctuary,** and the **Florida Keys National Marine Sanctuary,** largest in the national system, established in 1990.

State Parks

The **Florida Department of Natural Resources** is responsible for hundreds of historic buildings, landmarks, nature preserves, and an expanding state park system. When you request a free copy of the ***Florida State Park Guide,*** mention which parts of the state you plan to visit. For information on camping facilities at the state parks, ask for the free ***Florida State Parks, Fees and Facilities*** and ***Florida State Parks Camping Reservation Procedures*** brochures (Marjory Stoneman Douglas Bldg., MS 535, 3900 Commonwealth Blvd., Tallahassee 32399–3000, tel. 904/488–7896).

Private Nature Preserves

In 1905, Audubon Society warden Guy Bradley died while protecting the egrets nesting at Cuthbert Rookery, in what is now Everglades National Park. Private efforts to preserve Florida's fragile ecosystems continue today, as the **National Audubon Society** and the **Nature Conservancy** acquire and manage sensitive natural areas.

Wood storks nest at the National Audubon Society's **Corkscrew Swamp Sanctuary** near Naples. On Big Pine Key, Audubon has leased acreage without charge to the U.S. Fish and Wildlife Service in the **National Key Deer Refuge.** Audubon also controls more than 65 other Florida properties, including islands, prairies, forests, and swamps. Visitation at these sites is limited. For information, contact National Audubon Society, Sanctuary Director (Miles Wildlife Sanctuary, RR 1, Box 294, W. Cornwall Rd., Sharon, CT 06069, tel. 203/364–0048).

Five of the preserves managed by the Nature Conservancy are open to the public: **Apalachicola Bluffs & Ravines** in Liberty County, **Blowing Rocks Preserve** *(see* Exploring Treasure Coast, Chapter 7), the 970-acre **Cummer Sanctuary** in Levy County, the 320-acre **Janet Butterfield Brooks Preserve** near Bristol in Hernando County, the 42-acre **Matanzas Pass Wilderness Preserve** on Estero Island (between Bay and School Streets east of the 3000 block of Estero Boulevard in Fort Myers Beach) and the **Tiger Creek Preserve** at 225 E. Stuart Ave., Lake Wales in Polk County. Additionally, the 150-acre **Spruce Creek Preserve** in Volusia County opened in early 1991.

For access to these tracts, information on self-guided tour information, and a guide to the Conservancy's holdings contact the Florida Chapter of the Nature Conservancy (2699 Lee Rd., Ste. 500, Winter Park 32789, tel. 407/628–5887). Visitors are welcome at the Winter Park office and at offices in Miami, Key West, Lake Wales, Tallahassee, and West Palm Beach. *Rivergate Plaza Bldg., 444 Brickell Ave., Ste. 224, Miami 33131, tel. 305/530–8585; 201 Front St., Bldg. 21, Key West 33040, tel. 305/296–3880; 225 E. Stuart Ave., Lake Wales 33859, tel. 813/678–1551; 625 N. Adams St., Tallahassee 32301, tel. 904/222–0199; Comeau Bldg., 319 Clematis St., Ste. 611, West Palm Beach 33401, tel. 407/833–4226. Open weekdays 9–5.*

Dining

Florida regional cuisine changes as you move across the state, based on who settled the area and who now operates the restaurants. But always you can expect seafood to be a staple on nearly every menu. Look for Minorcan cuisine in St. Augustine, and the traditional Miccosukee and Seminole Indian fried bread, catfish, and frogs' legs at tribe-owned restaurants in the Everglades. South Florida's diverse assortment of Latin American restaurants offers the distinctive national fare of Argentina, Brazil, Colombia, Cuba, El Salvador, Mexico, Nicaragua, and Puerto Rico as well as West Indian delicacies from the Bahamas, Haiti, and Jamaica, and an acclaimed new tropical-Continental-nouvelle fusion that originated in Miami.

The influence of earlier Hispanic settlements remains in Key West and Tampa's Ybor City.

All over Florida, Asian cuisine no longer means just Chinese. Indian, Japanese, Pakistani, Thai, and Vietnamese specialties are now available. Continental cuisine (French, German, Italian, Spanish, and Swiss) is also well represented all over Florida. Many of these restaurants have excellent wine lists. Bern's Steak House in Tampa has the largest wine list in the state—7,000 labels!

Every Florida restaurant claims to make the best Key lime pie. Pastry chefs and restaurant managers take the matter very seriously—they discuss the problems of getting good lime juice and maintaining top quality every day. Traditional Key lime pie is yellow, not green, with an old-fashioned Graham cracker crust and meringue top. The filling should be tart, and chilled but not frozen. Some restaurants serve their Key lime pie with a pastry crust; most substitute whipped cream for the more temperamental meringue. Each pie will be a little different. Try several, and make your own choice.

Ratings Category	Cost*: Major Cities	Cost*: Other Areas
Very Expensive	over $50	over $40
Expensive	$30–$50	$25–$40
Moderate	$15–$30	$10–$25
Inexpensive	under $15	under $10

**per person, excluding drinks, service, and 6% sales tax*

Lodging

Hotels and Motels All the major hotel and motel chains are represented in Florida. Holiday Inn, Marriott, and Quality Inns operate under a variety of brand names offering varying levels of amenities and prices.

Although many hotels in Florida have affiliated with a chain to get business from its central reservation system, some fine hotels and resorts still remain independent. They include the Brazilian Court, The Breakers in Palm Beach, Chalet Suzanne in Lake Wales, the Park Plaza in Winter Park, the Governors Inn in Tallahassee, and Pier House in Key West.

The Florida Hotel & Motel Association (FH&MA) publishes an ***Annual Travel Directory*** which you can obtain without charge from the **Florida Division of Tourism** (Department of Commerce, 126 Van Buren St., Tallahassee 32399, tel. 904/487–1462). You can also order it from the FH&MA if you send a stamped, addressed No. 10 envelope and $1 for handling (117 W. College Ave., Box 1529, Tallahassee 32301–1529, tel. 904/224–2888).

Ratings Category	Cost*: Major Cities	Cost*: Other Areas
Very Expensive	$150 peak season $100 off-peak	$100
Expensive	$120–$150 peak season $80–$100 off-peak	$70–$100
Moderate	$80–$120 peak season $50–$80 off-peak	$40–$70
Inexpensive	under $80 peak season under $50 off-peak	under $40

**All prices are for a standard double room, excluding 6% state sales tax (some counties also have a local sales tax), and nominal (1%–4%) tourist tax.*

Alternative Lodgings Small inns and guest houses are becoming increasingly numerous and popular in Florida. Many offer the convenience of bed-and-breakfast accommodations in a homelike setting; many, in fact, are in private homes, and the owners treat you almost like a member of the family. **Inn Route, Inc.** (525 Simonton St., Key West 33040, tel. 305/294–6712), a statewide association of small, architecturally distinctive historic inns, will send you a free brochure newly published in 1992. You can also order the award-winning ***Guide to the Small and Historic Lodgings of***

Florida, a paperback book updated every two years, the latest one in 1993 (Pineapple Press Inc., Drawer 16008, Sarasota 34239, tel. 813/952–1085. Cost: $14.95 plus 6% sales tax).

Bed-and-breakfast referral and reservation agencies in Florida include: **Bed & Breakfast Co., Tropical Florida** (Box 262, Miami 33243, tel. 305/661–3270), **Bed & Breakfast East Coast** (Box 1373, Marathon 33050, tel. 305/743–4118), **Open House Bed & Breakfast,** (Box 3025, Palm Beach 33480, tel. 407/842–5190), **Southern Comfort Reservation & Referral Service** (8021 S.E. Helen Terr., Hobe Sound 33455, tel. 407/546–6743), and **Suncoast Accommodations of Florida** (8690 Gulf Blvd., St. Petersburg Beach 33706, tel. 813/360–1753).

Camping and RV Facilities

Contact the national parks and forests you plan to visit directly for information on camping facilities (*see* National Parks, above). For information on camping facilities in state parks, contact the Florida Department of Natural Resources (*see* State Parks, above).

The free annual ***Florida Camping Directory*** lists 200 commercial campgrounds in Florida with 50,000 sites. It's available at Florida welcome centers, from the Florida Division of Tourism, and from the **Florida Campground Association** (1638 N. Plaza Dr., Tallahassee 32308–5364, tel. 904/656–8878).

Vacation Ownership Resorts

Vacation ownership resorts sell hotel rooms, condominium apartments, or villas in weekly, monthly, or quarterly increments. The weekly arrangement is most popular; it's often referred to as "interval ownership" or "time sharing." Of more than 2,500 vacation ownership resorts around the world, some 400 are in Florida, with the heaviest concentration in the Disney World/Orlando area. Most vacation ownership resorts are affiliated with one of two major exchange organizations—**Interval International** (6262 Sunset Dr., Penthouse One, S. Miami 33143, tel. 305/666–1861 or 800/828–8200) or **Resort Condominiums International** (3502 Woodview Trace, Indianapolis, IN 46268–3131, tel. 317/876–8899 or 800/338–7777). As an owner, you can join your resort's exchange organization and swap your interval for another someplace else in any year when you want a change of scene. Even if you don't own an interval, you can rent at many vacation ownership resorts where unsold intervals remain and/or owners have placed their intervals in a rental program. For rental information, contact the exchange organizations (Worldex, tel. 800/722–1861; Resort Condominiums International, tel. 800/654–5000), the individual resort, or a local real estate broker in the area where you want to rent.

Credit Cards

Throughout the book credit card abbreviations refer to the following: AE, American Express; D, Discover; DC, Diners Club; MC, MasterCard; and V, Visa.

2 Portraits of Florida

In Search of the Real Florida

By April Athey

A free-lance writer based in Tallahassee, April Athey has been writing about her home state for magazines and newspapers since 1977. Her work has appeared in many publications, including the New York Times, Chicago Tribune, Christian Science Monitor, Frequent Flyer, *and* Gulfshore Life.

It's hard to imagine a Florida without a magic kingdom, a spaceport to the stars, interstate highways, or high-rise beachfront hotels. But such a Florida exists, and today the state's natural and historical treasures are being imitated, refurbished, restored, and recognized for their lasting appeal.

Even the state's leader in family entertainment—Walt Disney World—is imitating and popularizing Old Florida with its new Grand Floridian Beach Resort, featuring gabled roofs and Victorian balustrades that were typical of Florida's turn-of-the-century beach resorts. Disney officials say the resort recalls the days when John D. Rockefeller, Thomas Edison, and even President Theodore Roosevelt led the annual winter pilgrimage to Florida's warm shores.

There are those who recall the day when Walt Disney World's fantasy lands and futuristic hotels opened in 1971, setting a technological standard in entertainment that may still be unrivaled. The owners of natural attractions like Silver Springs, Weeki Wachee, and Homosassa Springs struggled to keep the attention of technology-hungry Americans. The lush jungle-lined rivers, exotic wildlife, and crystal-clear spring waters somehow paled in contrast to the make-believe, never-a-dull-moment amusements for which the Disney corporation had become famous. The convenience of a one-stop, no-surprise vacation apparently made real wilderness cruises, beaches, wildlife, and historical attractions passé.

To see and appreciate the real thing, one had to leave the interstate highways and brave a few side roads. Because not many tourists cared to take the road less traveled, many owners of natural attractions were forced to expand their offerings with man-made amusements. If budgets weren't sweet enough to permit this sort of commercialization, the attractions (usually the lesser-known botanical gardens, great homes, and wildlife reserves) saw lean years.

Fortunately, the cycle is coming full circle. Technology-harassed Americans are now looking for the good old days, and Florida is obliging them.

Today, developers of new resorts are focusing attention on the Florida of the 19th century. New resorts not only imitate Old Florida architecture but also, through their landscaping, recall when the only silhouettes scraping Florida's sky were of stout cabbage palms, mossy oaks, towering cypress, and hardy evergreens.

Maintaining the ecological integrity of the land and its often-endangered inhabitants has become an increasing concern of developers. The Grand Cypress Resort in Orlando was designed to be complemented by a stand of native cypress, and the Registry Resort in Naples nestles at the edge of a 1,000-acre nature preserve, through which a $1-million boardwalk was built to provide access to the beach and protection for the delicate sand dunes.

St. Augustine is the oldest permanent European settlement in the United States—with an extensive historic district to prove it—and was the first Florida resort popularized by Henry Flagler when he brought his Florida East Coast Railroad and friends south for the winter. Key West was the last resort Flagler helped build. His Casa Marina hotel still stands, having been restored and expanded under management by Marriott. The island's "conch houses" also are being restored, and many have been converted into guest houses and restaurants. Flagler also put Palm Beach and its sister, West Palm Beach, on the map. Though his original wooden hotels burned to the ground, his private estate is now the Flagler Museum.

Sharing space with the glinting glass of skyscrapers are the castlelike villas and Old Florida-style homes of former Florida residents. You can tour Ca'd'Zan, the bay-side villa that John Ringling and his wife Mable built, which now is part of the Ringling Museums Complex in Sarasota. Like an oasis in the middle of Miami's asphalt-and-concrete desert, the palatial bay-front estate of John Deering, with its formal gardens and surrounding natural jungles (Vizcaya Museum and Gardens), may be toured daily. Visit Thomas Edison's Winter Home in Fort Myers, and dine out on Cabbage Key, the tiny island accessible by boat (offshore from Captiva)—the retreat of mystery writer Mary Roberts Rinehart. Ormond Beach has reminders of its heyday, when John D. Rockefeller and friends made the riverfront Ormond Hotel a world-renowned wintering spot. Rockefeller eventually built his winter home, The Casements, across the street from the hotel, and both still stand proudly by the shores of the Halifax River, just north of Daytona Beach. The Casements is now an art museum and site of an annual antique-auto show.

Fort Jefferson, the Civil War island fortress on which Samuel Mudd—the physician who treated Lincoln's assassin—was imprisoned, is only a seaplane flight away from tropical Key West. On Key West are the 19th-century fortifications—East and West Martello Towers—one now home to the city's historical museum, and the other the setting of the garden club. Recently excavated and open to the public on Key West is Fort Zachary Taylor. Living-history interpretations are conducted daily at Fort Clinch, a Civil War fortress in Fernandina Beach, and at Fort Foster in Hillsborough State Park, just west of Tampa. Speaking of

Tampa, the next time you order a rum and Coke, remember that the concoction was invented there by Teddy Roosevelt's Rough Riders.

In addition to the monuments of recent history, there are the archaeological reminders of Florida's first residents, the aboriginal Indians who greeted European explorers and expatriates. Several state parks preserve treasured archaeological sites, like Hontoon Island on the St. Johns River, Tomoka River State Park, near Daytona Beach (both sites of Timucuan Indian settlements), and Jonathan Dickinson State Park, near the Palm Beaches (site of a Quaker shipwreck and their subsequent imprisonment by Jaega Indians).

These and later Indians left their place names as a lasting legacy—names like Ichetucknee (now a tubing river north of Gainesville), Pensacola, Apalachicola, Tequesta, Kissimmee, Chassahowitzka (a national wildlife refuge near Homosassa Springs), Okeechobee (a 590-square-mile inland lake), Ocala, and Tallahassee (the state capital).

Victorian homes with gingerbread-trimmed wraparound verandas, shaded by sloping tin roofs, are being restored and operated as bed-and-breakfast inns or chic restaurants. Check out K. C. Crump on the River in Homosassa Springs, near Ocala in central Florida, a posh new restaurant in a restored, turn-of-the-century homestead. In Ocala, the newest B&B is the Seven Sisters Inn, which serves gourmet fare. Florida's B&Bs have increased from an estimated five in 1980 to more than 50 in 1988.

Main Street programs are flourishing throughout the state, revitalizing the business/entertainment districts of towns like Winter Park, Orlando, DeLand, and Quincy (in northwest Florida).

Historic hotels and inns, once threatened by wrecking crews, are living new lives. Check out the Heritage in St. Petersburg, a restored, 60-year-old hotel (the original Florida "cracker" home in the backyard now serves as an atrium-greenhouse bar); or book a weekend at Apalachicola's 100-year-old Gibson Inn.

Waterfront redevelopment projects like Miami's Bayside and Jacksonville Landing (Rouse Marketplace developments) are focusing fresh attention on the inlets and bays that once harbored renegade pirates and adventurous pioneers.

Quiet waterfront hamlets, built during the boom in steamboat travel—Sanford and Crescent City are good examples—are beginning to blossom again with the reemergence of riverboat cruising.

Wildlife and wilderness, once overlooked in favor of make-believe amusements, are once again attracting awed attention. In response, Silver Springs turned back the clock with a complete Victorian redesign.

Oddly enough, it may be easier to find an Old Florida vacation experience now than it was 20 years ago.

Though serving to popularize Old Florida, newcomers and their artful imitations are no substitutes for the real thing. The wilderness, wildlife, and historic homes and resorts are already here to enjoy.

Washed by both the Gulf of Mexico and the Atlantic Ocean, Florida seems to be more water than land. Underground freshwater rivers course through the limestone bedrock of its north and central highlands, often boiling to the surface and flowing overland to the sea. A bird's-eye view reveals a peninsula whose upper reaches are dotted and crisscrossed by hundreds of lakes and streams and whose ragged southern borders are home to a vast, shallow river of grass called the Everglades and a maze of mangrove clumps called the Ten Thousand Islands. From the town of Everglades City, on Florida's southwest tip, sightseeing boats meander through the maze of islands, and just off the Tamiami Trail (U.S. 41), on the north-central boundary of Everglades National Park, you can climb the observation deck at Shark Valley Overlook for a good look at the river of grass.

This view, perhaps more than anything, helps to remind people of what Floridians are trying to recapture.

The Florida Scrub

By Al Burt

A roving writer-columnist for The Miami Herald *for the past 15 years, Al Burt specializes in Florida's history, natural habitat, and future. He has written two books on the state*—Becalmed in the Mullet Latitudes *and* Florida: A Place in the Sun. *In 1974, Burt left Miami's city life to make his base in his beloved Scrub Country, near Melrose in north Florida.*

Understanding Florida requires at least some knowledge of the historic Scrub Country, the oldest, the driest, the harshest, and, in some ways, the most delicate part of the state. In water-loving Florida, the Scrub struggles to remain a desert outlaw.

If you have ever walked a beach and observed how the tides and the wind have rolled the sterile sands into a long, graceful dune on which grow a few scraggly, scratchy plants, you may have gotten some idea about Florida's unique Scrub Country and its peculiar beauty.

The Scrub, which once covered most of Florida with bone-dry sandhills, is the legitimate kin to a desert, and it's full of puzzles. The life forms there are persistent, thrifty, and fragile. Once, you could look across the low profile of its vegetation and see odd "islands" of fertility, little oases of tall trees and green life, while all around was the stunted, prickly, vulnerable Scrub growth. They were like oddly matched siblings of nature, growing up side by side, but, by freakish accident, one had been denied its vitamins.

The name came from an early and natural lack of appreciation. It was scrubby country, not like the scenic Florida of the travel books. Except in those "islands," it lacked the towering slash pines and the comfortable shade of large-crowned live oaks and the open landscapes beneath. The Scrub was a place unto itself, with few easy pleasures, and it was not good for conventional farming.

Loving the Scrub came easiest if you grew up with it, if it came naturally to you. Sometimes it became a fierce, protective thing, like a stubbornly loyal Cracker Mama who adored the scrawniest of her children most because it was the misfit.

Flooding rains leached quickly through Scrub sands and left them dry as ever. Rosemary bushes, prickly pears, saw palmettos, sand pines, sandburs, gnarled dwarf oaks, and other scraggly little trees commonly grew there.

The deep sand made it difficult to walk with shoes on. The sands in summer burned the soles of bare feet with temperatures of 135–140 degrees. Everything in the Scrub seemed to scratch and claw at you, fighting for life.

Rattlesnakes loved it. Exotic little creatures (in addition to raccoons, bobcats, and deer), some of them now rare and endangered, made it home—scrub jays, lizards, skinks, gopher frogs and gopher tortoises, exotic mice, red widow spiders, and such.

For years, big patches of the Scrub Country, especially if they were inland and off the main tracks, lay abandoned. If they attracted anyone, it was likely to be the young, who sometimes found the sandhills great places for exploring or play, sliding down them, burrowing into them, and holding beer parties and buggy chases on the tricky sand.

The Scrub did not rebound easily from such use, but nobody cared. The track of a jeep across virgin scrub vegetation might take unaided nature years to erase. That was minor compared with what else happened in the history of the Scrub.

It began when Florida began. The Scrub probably was the first part of Florida to emerge from the ocean, geologists say. Its dunes or sandhills formed under pressures of wind and tides as the ocean levels rose and fell during the ice ages. Great, irregular ridges took shape, almost like terraces. Time altered them into graceful sandhills.

The original Scrub Country became the Central Highlands of Florida, which stretches from east of Gainesville in the north-central part of the state south for some 200 miles and flatten out into the prairies of Lake Okeechobee. In places, the elevation reaches 300 feet.

For Florida, those great sandhills became Sierra Citrus, center of one of its greatest trademark industries. The well-drained Scrub lands were easily cleared and were perfect for oranges—once the growers added fertilizers and artificial irrigation.

You can ride that ridge today in one of the state's most scenic inland drives and imagine the beginning. U.S. 27, a fine highway, rolls up and down those great sandhills, past a series of lakes, along the fringes of Disney World country, and through miles and miles of green and seasonally fragrant citrus groves. (Even though the freezes of recent winters blighted many of them, the scene remains impressive.)

Like smaller versions of the Central Highlands, lesser dunes trailed away to the ocean. All had similar characteristics, but closer to the coast there were subtle changes, particularly if they were close enough to get the windblown ocean spray.

The dunes and the life on them also differed in their northern stretches, where the climate was temperate and subject to more seasonal changes than in southern Florida. In the south, the influence of the Gulf Stream and the more prominent crosswinds from the gulf and the ocean produced an exotic subtropical climate.

Scrub Country was high ground. Water did not collect there, but in strategic or special places development did, especially along the coast. Around the turn of the century, Henry Flagler built his pioneering railroad partially on a high dune ridge running down the east coast. Then he opened up cities like Palm Beach, Miami, and eventually Key West to tourists and development.

For the most part, the Scrub Country was an ugly duckling among Florida real estate developers. Many wanted to use it as raw material or take advantage of its special location, but few perceived it as anything that was uniquely beautiful or valuable in itself. As a result, 90% or more of this original Florida scene no longer exists.

The sand, some of it as fine as sugar, was mined for construction materials. Great areas were leveled for shopping centers and other development. Subdivisions turned dune ripples into square blocks of cottages. Water was piped in, and developers covered these desert sands with St. Augustine grass.

Except for exploiters, the Scrub Country had few advocates. The most notable of them was the writer, Marjorie Kinnan Rawlings, an easterner. Rawlings's work elevated one area of the Scrub into legend.

In 1928, Rawlings fled the rigors of newspaper life in Rochester, NY, and settled in an old Cracker house by an orange grove in an unlikely little village oasis called Cross Creek. She sought inspiration in isolation and frontier surroundings. The creek (between Ocala and Gainesville) was a lane of water connecting two large lakes in north-central Florida.

Her love of the creek and its people expanded to the areas nearby, which included a significant piece of Scrub Country known locally as the Big Scrub. To enrich her knowledge of it, she lived for a while with a family in the Scrub, hunted there, and befriended the Crackers who chose it as a place to live.

Rawlings's novels, particularly *The Yearling*, which won the Pulitzer Prize and then was made into a popular movie, realistically acknowledged but nevertheless romanticized the Big Scrub. She depicted the impoverished Crackers as primitives who lived by their own code—a code that she clearly thought had a noble base.

Rawlings gave the Big Scrub and Florida's Scrub Country a national identity. Within the past few years, her book of essays on Cross Creek and a short story entitled "Gal Young 'Un" also were made into well-received movies. Those films renewed and enlarged Rawlings's loving images of the Cross Creek area and the Big Scrub. Since then, the importance of the Scrub as a unique plant and animal habitat has been recognized. Scientists and conservationists have dedicated themselves to its study and preservation.

Rawlings's books became especially significant because the largest remaining area of Scrub left in Florida, modified though it may be, is the one she idealized. It lies in the central and western portions of the 380,000-acre Ocala National Forest (a multiple-use forest that permits hunting and camping) and still is called the Big Scrub.

The Big Scrub contains the world's largest stand of sand pines. Many of them occur naturally, but, because in some areas the pines were planted in rows so neat that the natural poetry of the forest is altered, some have criticized it as a sand-pine plantation. In either case, both the pines and the patches of dunes, as close as the road shoulders, are visible from the car during a drive through the forest. The area illustrates how sand pines and other scrub vegetation, over time, tend to close and fill in an area, giving it a canopy above and a soil below slowly being altered by collections of natural forest debris, especially leaves, fallen limbs, and root systems. This cycle can change the natural characteristics of the Scrubs, unless fire (the sand pine is highly flammable) or timbering activities interfere. Even so, the Scrub retains its mysteries. Even the foresters cannot always predict with certainty that the Scrub cycle will begin again after a fire.

Most of Florida's Scrub Country is now scattered in bits and pieces around the state. You have to search and guess and inquire locally. Aside from the Ocala forest, a visitor can see examples of it in the Jonathan Dickinson State Park, 13 miles south of Stuart on U.S. 1.

In that same area, you may see from the highway a typical patch of surviving Scrub—a high roadside dune topped by a windswept sand pine, so stressed that it seems picturesquely oriental. The same sand pine, seen in the Ocala Forest, may grow bushy and erect and look like an ideal Christmas tree.

Finding examples of the Scrub elsewhere becomes a matter of travel and identification, of looking for inland dunes left untouched by development. Where there is a low, sandy hill there could be scrub. You can find areas of it down the east coast, from St. Augustine to West Palm Beach, in northeast Florida near the coast and along Rte. AIA, and there are some that sweep back off the Panhandle beaches in northwest Florida. Little of the scrub, however—except that in public parks—has tourist convenience for study and enjoyment. Even in the state and national forests, the sandy footing, the heat, and the numerous insects discourage all but the most hardy explorers.

At least two large tracts are being maintained for scientific research. The University of Florida owns several thousand acres of Scrub east of Gainesville, and the Archbold Biological Station (established in 1941) has 3,800 acres of distinctive Scrub near Lake Placid on the southern slope of the Central Highlands. These are not open for public roaming, however.

One good thing to remember is that, globally, Florida lies in the zone of the great deserts, including the Sahara, so the Scrub is not out of character. Florida began with those ocean sands that bleached into dunes and sandhills and then into the variety that visitors enjoy today.

Remembering the past explains a lot about the true nature of Florida, no matter how wet it looks right now. The Scrub Country reminds us that the makings of a desert are still there, waiting.

Miami Beach Art Deco

By Hap Hatton

Born and raised in Florida, Hap Hatton now lives in New York City, where he is in charge of still photography for PBS station WNET 13. His previous books include The Tent Book *and* The Virgin Homeowner's Handbook.

By 1910 Miami Beach had failed first as a coconut plantation, then as an avocado farm. Now it was being tried as a residential development. It took 10 years to create the present landmass. Carl Fisher, the Hoosier millionaire who financed much of the dredging and land-clearing, envisioned the area as a playground for the wealthy. Interspersed between his opulent hotels were huge estates on lots running 400 feet in from Biscayne Bay. Meanwhile, the southern portion of the barrier island was developed by the Lummus brothers, who plotted smaller lots for a middle-class resort. Scarcely had the dredging begun than the Lummus brothers in 1912 opened the Ocean Beach Realty Company, the first real estate office on the beach. Steady growth was interrupted by World War I, but then Miami Beach took off—until the collapse of the Florida real estate boom and the ensuing Depression.

By 1936, assisted by an expanding tourist industry, south Florida had emerged from the Depression. Hundreds of small hotels and apartment buildings were constructed on the small Lummus lots at the rate of 100 a year until 1941, making Miami Beach one of the few cities in the United States to have a building boom during the Depression. Ernest Hemingway's brother Leicester, also a writer, explains the phenomenon:

During the Depression, people needed to let go. . . . They became wild on Miami Beach. . . . They didn't watch their nickels. . . . [Architects] were determined not to use any older styles like the Spanish. . . . They wanted something modern, so they smoothed out all the Spanish things. They smoothed everything until you got the feeling that life was smooth. The buildings made you feel all clean and new and excited and happy to be there.

The style that prevailed in South Miami Beach was a zesty, crowd-pleasing Art Deco built by a handful of architects and contractors. Many of the architects were not formally trained but freely adapted national design trends to this tropical setting, creating a uniformity in style and scale rarely found in an urban setting. Called Miami Beach Art Deco (the name Tropical Deco has also been applied to the style), this brand of Art Deco was both relatively inexpensive to construct and offered a slick, dramatic, fashionable appearance, while its strong visual tropical symbols—

"Floridiana"—impressed upon visitors the unique charms of the area.

Florida didn't invent the decorative vegetative and animal motifs that dominated the more ornate Miami Beach Art Deco buildings, but it raised them to new stylistic heights with facade bas-reliefs of cast or dyed stone, etched windows, and decorative metalwork on doors and porches.

Flowers, especially voluptuous gladiolus, alluded to the fecund floral paradise. Nymphs and nudes hedonistically stressed sensuous youth and romance. Fountains as well as sunbursts and symbolic zigzag equivalents of rays conjured up the life-renewing natural properties of the climate. Animals such as peacocks, flamingos, greyhounds, herons, and pelicans were chosen for their romantic associations, arabesque shapes, and exaggerated proportions. Originally, most of the buildings were stark white, with trims of azure blue, ocean turquoise, blazing yellow, palm tree green, erotic pink, or purples and mauves that evoked tropical sunsets, bougainvillea, and feelings both sensuous and exotic.

The sense of place is strong among these Deco buildings, leaving no doubt that this is the tropics, far from the cold, gray, sooty, industrial North.

The variances in Miami Beach Art Deco reflected what was occurring economically and architecturally on the national scene. Among others, four prevalent Deco styles comprise Miami Beach Art Deco.

Art Deco. The earliest buildings adapted the original Art Deco style's sharply angular massing with shallow stepped-back facades. Ornate bas-relief panels often framed large central openings. The French love of luxurious, sensuous textures such as crystal, mother-of-pearl, and unusual woods translated into indigenous Florida oolitic limestone, etched glass, stucco, and terrazzo (a cast agglomerate of marble or granite particles in colored and polished cement).

Depression Moderne. By 1937 the mode had shifted to a deco with the more austere look of the reigning International Style. Art Moderne's vertical stucco bands, flat roof with stepped parapet, and facade symmetry were still there, but with an increased horizontal emphasis that would later become dominant in streamlining. Depression Moderne was also readapted for government buildings such as the Miami Beach Post Office, and called PWA Moderne for the Public Works Administration.

Streamlined Moderne. By 1939, a full-blown aerodynamic Moderne featured curved forms, applied racing stripes that accentuated horizontal emphasis, and "eyebrow" shading of the windows with cantilevered slabs to reduce the angle of penetration of the sun. The continuously wrapped stucco surfaces expressed concepts associated with travel and speed. Here the angularity of the originally imported Art Moderne was entirely replaced by soft flowing masses accented with horizontal lines and rows of windows. This phase combined smooth, sweeping curves with straight lines of the machine age in simple, definite, contrasting shapes. Combinations of Cubism's suggestion of dimensionality, Futurism's romance with speed, and Surrealist fantasy are cited as sources of inspiration. This streamlining restored the fun and humor drained by Depression Moderne.

Mannerism. A final development of Miami Beach streamlining was called Resort Mannerism or Mannerist Moderne (from Mannerism, a late 16th-century reaction against the High Renaissance characterized by a deliberate distortion of the existing artistic and architectural repertoire; it gave way to the Baroque, and today the term is associated with the exaggeration and/or distortion of existing themes). Resort Mannerism included Nautical Moderne, with its exaggerated and literal invocations of ships at sea with porthole windows, decklike balconies, and flagstaffs. This mature Moderne emphasized sinuous curves, stylized directional ornament, and bold projections, marking a conscious search by architects both here and in Europe for a unique form to express contemporary modernity. Never a pure style, it even incorporated highlights from the Spanish Mediterranean, such as sloping tile roofs or colored ceramic tiles. The late 1930s film influence brought soaring "trylons" or space-age needles to roofs and facades. This Flash Gordon touch turned the buildings visually into spaceships with Hollywood stage-set lobbies that were also referred to as Cinema Style and Hollywood Style.

Larger Deco hotels did make their appearance, but, by and large, the area known as Old Miami Beach consists of two- and three-story hostelries small in scale and rich in expression. Deco architecture prevailed here later than anywhere else in the country, until World War II abruptly terminated construction. By 1941, most hotels were occupied by the military in training for the war effort. After the war, the area began to decline as Miami Beach continued its development northward.

In 1979, one square mile of Miami Beach became this country's first 20th-century national historic district. It reflects a trend in architecture that took place between the two world wars, when more than 500 Art Deco structures went up in one small area. It is not only the largest and most cohesive concentration of Art Deco buildings in the world but the first historic district that has registered buildings less than 50 years old. It sits on one of the best pieces of real estate in Florida, perhaps on the entire East Coast.

The fight for preservation of these landmarks has raged for years between developers who want to erect more profitable high-rise condominiums and the local Miami Design

Preservation League, founded by Barbara Baer Capitman. A former art historian and now president of the Art Deco Society of Miami, she held her first organizational meeting in 1976 with six people and spoke of the area's potential as "capital of the Art Deco world." Capitman attracted 100 volunteers to survey and research the locality. Then the battle was launched that resulted in tax and zoning incentives for the owners of Deco buildings who preserve their original structures.

Developers fought back and, to block the legislation, lobbied successfully for an ordinance that required 100% owner approval for historic district designations (51% is standard). This ordinance was later struck down when, to avoid costly litigation, Miami Beach changed its ordinance to 51% approval. Some local businessmen see the preservation issue as one of property rights versus government coercion. A few, however, realize that the Art Deco district will yield them long-term beneficial results: It will create a desirable cultural center and provide a sense of identity vital to establishing Miami Beach as a unique city rather than a second-rate Las Vegas.

Because no corresponding local legislation had been passed to protect the district, its designation on the National Register of Historic Places did not prevent demolition of several landmark Art Deco hotels. The turning point came in July of 1986, when Richard Hoberman, president of the Miami Design Preservation League, orchestrated a campaign to secure designation of two key areas: a quarter-mile district covering Ocean Drive/Collins Avenue (from Fifth to Sixteenth streets) as well as Espanola Way, a six-block street that includes a 1920s Spanish theme village. Hoberman packed the city commission chambers with supporters wearing "Deco-pink" ribbons to witness the decisive 6–1 vote. Local designation means that a design review board must approve all renovation work for appropriateness, all new construction must be compatible with surrounding buildings, and—most important—there will be a six-month moratorium on demolition to allow time for other investors to step in. Now prospective developers need not fear that their preservation efforts will be invalidated by high rises, and successful rehabilitation within these two districts should help in the essential designation of additional areas. Things are looking good: Already one developer has turned a million-dollar profit in 10 months by restoring and reselling one of the district's Art Deco hotels. Seven years after federal recognition, the city fathers have finally understood the economic benefits of preservation.

The preservation movement on Miami Beach has generated admiration for Art Deco, and south Florida developers have invested millions of dollars building imitation Deco residential communities for those who want the look of Deco but wish to live outside the troubled inner-city area.

These new homes have much of the generic look of huge housing developments, despite their attempt to blend International Style and Deco. They feature stepped walls and entrances, porthole windows, geometric shapes, and two-tone pastel colors. Builders toned down the bright Deco colors to Necco wafer hues of quiet pastels when a local homeowners' association complained of the bright aqua, peach, and intense pinks. This "switch rather than fight" approach is an attempt to sidestep the complex problems of gentrification. The buildings themselves mark a rejection of International Style anonymity, a recognition of the value of Art Deco, and a positive trend in Miami's search for its own architectural identity.

Meanwhile, in the Deco District the tax credits to be obtained by rehabilitating these architectural treasures have brought developers into the area, and dozens of hotels and apartment houses are being refurbished. The small hotels average 60 to 120 rooms, many having been converted to "pullmanettes" (rooms with kitchenettes). For the past quarter-century these have been popular with mostly Jewish and Eastern European retirees, and a decade ago more than half of the south Beach population was 65 or older. With retirement communities now proliferating in south Florida, for about a decade Miami Beach has ceased to be a destination point for the elderly, and now the percentage is less than one-quarter.

By its nature, rehabilitation means modernization and deviation from original design schemes, and nowhere is this more apparent than in color restoration. The original white with vivid color accents has been rejected in favor of a palette of Post-Modern cake-icing pastels now associated with the former television series "Miami Vice." Leonard Horowitz, the designer who introduced these colors, rationalized that because the neighborhood had deteriorated and much of the original vegetation had died, there was justification for using a plethora of color. Finally, white is being reintroduced.

The buildings of the Miami Beach Historical District chronicle more than a decade of historic cultural change and served the emotional needs of the public in a time of national crisis. No orthodox academic style has accomplished this. Whatever their historical significance or their eventual evaluation as art, these Miami Art Deco habitations are built to the human scale where the desires of the people are met rather than dictated to by sociological or aesthetic theory. Such a value in buildings has generally been condescended to or given mere lip service by respected architects who consider the tastes of the public beneath contempt. Yet the art of living cannot be measured by formal architectural standards of purity or style, only by the pleasure of the time and place. Miami Beach Art Deco created this quality of life with consummate success.

Today, the buildings still hold magic for visitors and inhabitants. Although the romance is slightly tarnished by peeling facades, and idealistic dreams have succumbed to more jaded views, there is still a sense of desire and expectation in the air. There is a glamour about these buildings that invites thoughts of moonlit walks on sparkling beaches, movie-screen romances, dancing under starry skies. There is a sadness, too, of once-vital dreams lost, either demolished or covered over with gaudy wallpaper and wall-to-wall carpeting. But this special fantasy of Florida still twinkles seductively among the vast pile of urban mediocrity that threatens to engulf the Miami Beach Deco District.

3 The Florida Fifty

Golfing Throughout the State

By Peter Oliver

A New York–based writer, Peter Oliver specializes in sports and travel. He is the author of The Insider's Guide to the Best Skiing in New England.

When it comes to golf, Florida is, far and away, the top dog among U.S. states. If you doubt it, the state can round up a host of statistics as evidence. More than one of every 10 rounds of golf played in the United States is played in Florida. The roughly 3 million golfers who visit Florida annually far exceeds the number of golfers who visit any other state. They bring their wallets with them, too, shelling out more than $1.5 billion directly on golf and $5 billion in related spending. Put in perspective, that combined figure exceeds the gross national product of more than half of the countries of the world.

Most significantly, Florida has more golf courses than any other state. Present count tallies more than 1,000, with about 100 other courses in either the planning stages or under construction. According to a National Golf Foundation estimate, the number of courses in Florida will approach 1,500 by the year 2000.

Many of these grounds, however, are (and will be) private. Still, at last count roughly two-thirds were either public courses, "semiprivate" courses, or private courses allowing limited access to the public (for example, courses extending privileges to guests of nearby hotels). So if you're on your way to Florida with a mind to play golf, you'll have more than 600 courses to choose from.

A big part of the appeal of Florida golf is its year-round availability. Although a few courses might close for a day or two in the fall to reseed greens, and a few in the north might delay morning tee times in winter because of occasional frost, it's still fair to say that you can golf in Florida 365 days a year. That's why a large number of touring professionals—players such as Jack Nicklaus and Greg Norman—have settled here.

What sort of play can golfers visiting Florida expect? It's no state secret that Florida is flat; with a highest elevation of 345 feet, Florida can't claim many naturally rolling courses. And the few that can be found are mostly in the northwest. Don't be deceived, though, into thinking that the natural flatness of the Florida landscape is an assurance of flat fairways or greens. The world's leading golf-course designers, including Tom Fazio, Jack Nicklaus, and Ed Seay have compensated by creating lots of manmade rolls and undulations. No designer, however, has been more notable in this regard than Pete Dye, pioneer of the "stadium" style (courses designed to accommodate large tournament audiences) of golf-course construction.

The two characteristics most common to Florida play are water and sand. "I don't think there's a course in Florida that doesn't have water on at least a few holes, and usually on more than 14," says Alan Smith, director of golf at the Marriott at Sawgrass, one of Florida's top golf resorts. That shouldn't be a surprise in a flat state with a high water table; as Smith points out, "A lot of times, lakes and canals have been created just to move water out of the way to make fairways." Sand is also a natural part of the Florida environment, although many courses import special fine-grain sand to fill traps. Regardless of the sand's origin, it is plentiful; it isn't unusual to come across a hole in Florida with 10 or more traps, and several courses have more than 100 traps each. In some ways, however, Florida sand works to the golfer's advantage. The sandy soil drains well after rain and also provides a surface more forgiving in playing iron shots than denser, clay-rich soil more common elsewhere.

What this adds up to is a premium on accuracy when it comes to approach shots. While Florida fairways are characteristically wide, greens tend to be heavily bunkered or protected by water. A diabolically popular invention of Florida course builders is the island green, completely surrounded by water. The best strategy for tackling this, says Smith, is discretion: "Don't be greedy in your shot selection (for example, shoot for the center of the green and don't cut corners). Otherwise, bring plenty of extra golf balls."

One other element that often comes into play in Florida is wind. This is particularly true at seaside courses, of which there are many in a state with more than 3,000 miles of coastline. But wind can also be a vexing factor inland, where it swirls and becomes unpredictable as it moves through tall pine and palm trees. If all of this sounds unfairly treacherous, golfers can take heart in the fact that deep rough is uncommon as a penalizing element in Florida play; short rough is especially prevalent during the winter.

Finally, keep in mind that for most of the year, Florida greens are seeded with Bermuda grass. Golfers used to putting on bent-grass greens found in other parts of the country might find that the speed (on the slow side) and grain of Bermuda greens takes time to get used to.

The Florida Fifty

In a state with more than 1,000 courses, coming up with only 50 recommended courses is no easy task. In creating a "Florida Fifty," some properties in the state are easily eliminated: those that are private or those with policies for public play that are unusually restrictive. Nine-hole and par-3 (sometimes called "executive") courses also have not been considered. That still leaves hundreds of courses from which to choose.

This list is a sampling of the broad range of what is available in Florida, from inexpensive municipal courses to luxurious resort courses. Compiled after consulting several experts on Florida golf as well as various golf magazines, books, and guides, this index includes those courses repeatedly cited as being among Florida's best. This does not, however, mean these are the only ones worth playing in the state. Also, although just one course has been highlighted at each of the multicourse resorts cited, other courses at these resorts (for example, Doral, Grand Cypress, Palm-Aire, PGA National) may also be among Florida's best. For that reason, the *total* number of holes at any resort is listed, and the number includes the holes of the featured course.

Yardages included are of the featured course and are calculated from the championship, or blue, tees. The championship length represents a course at its most difficult; most golfers won't play any of the courses at anywhere near the listed length, but yardage is a useful indication of a course's length relative to other courses listed. Courses are typically 400–800 yards shorter from the regular men's tees and 1,000–1,500 yards shorter from the regular women's tees. With its large retirement population, Florida also has many facilities with "seniors" tees, usu-

Florida Golf Courses

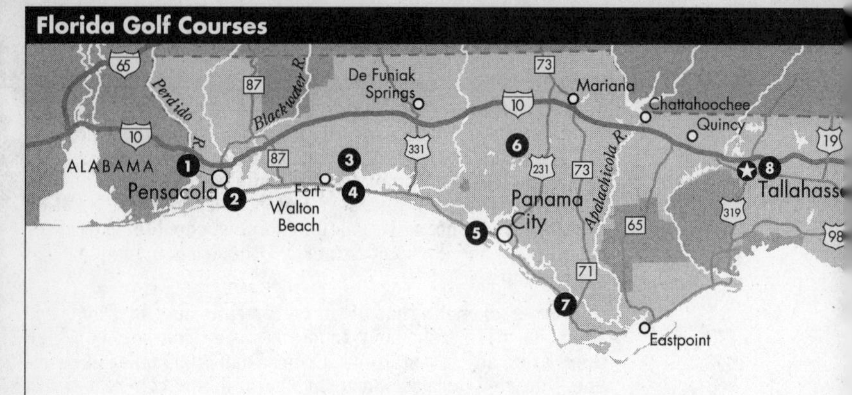

Gulf of Mexico

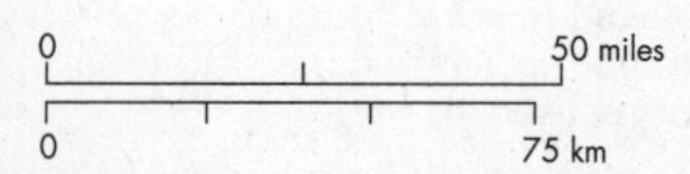

Panhandle

Bay Point Yacht & Country Club, **5**

Bluewater Bay Resort, **3**

Perdido Bay Resort, **1**

St. Joseph's Bay Country Club, **7**

Sandestin Golf Club, **4**

Sunny Hills Country Club, **6**

Tiger Point Country Club, **2**

Northeast Florida

Amelia Island Plantation, **9**

Golden Ocala Golf Club, **16**

Indigo Lakes Resort, **15**

Killearn Inn & Golf Club, **8**

Marriott at Sawgrass, **10**

Ponce de Leon Golf Club, **13**

Ponte Vedra Inn & Club, **11**

Ravines Golf & Country Club, **12**

Sheraton Palm Coast, **14**

Orlando Area

Grand Cypress Golf Club, **19**

Grenelefe Resort, **21**

Mission Inn Golf & Tennis Resort, **17**

Timacuan Golf & Country Club, **18**

Walt Disney World Resort, **20**

Willowbrook Golf Club, **22**

Southwest Florida

Bloomingdale Golfers Club, **26**

Cape Coral Golf & Tennis Resort, **30**

Eastwood Golf Club, **32**

Innisbrook Resort & Golf Club, **25**

Lely Flamingo Island Golf Club, **34**

Lochmoor Country Club, **31**

Longboat Key, **27**

Naples Beach Hotel Golf Club, **35**

Pelican's Nest, **33**

Plantation Golf & Country Club, **29**

Plantation Inn Golf Club, **23**

Saddlebrook Golf Club, **24**

Sun 'n Lakes Golf Club, **28**

Palm Beach

Boca Raton Resort & Club, **43**

Boynton Beach Municipal Golf Course, **42**

Breakers Hotel Golf Club, **39**

Emerald Dunes Golf Club, **40**

Indian River Plantation, **36**

Palm Beach Polo & Country Club, **41**

PGA National Golf Club, **37**

Royal Palm Beach Country Club, **38**

Fort Lauderdale

Bonaventure Resort & Spa, **45**

Colony West Country Club, **46**

The Oaks Golf & Racquet Club, **44**

Miami

Don Shula's Golf Club, **49**

Doral Hotel Golf Club, **48**

Key Biscayne Golf Club, **50**

Turnberry Isle Country Club, **47**

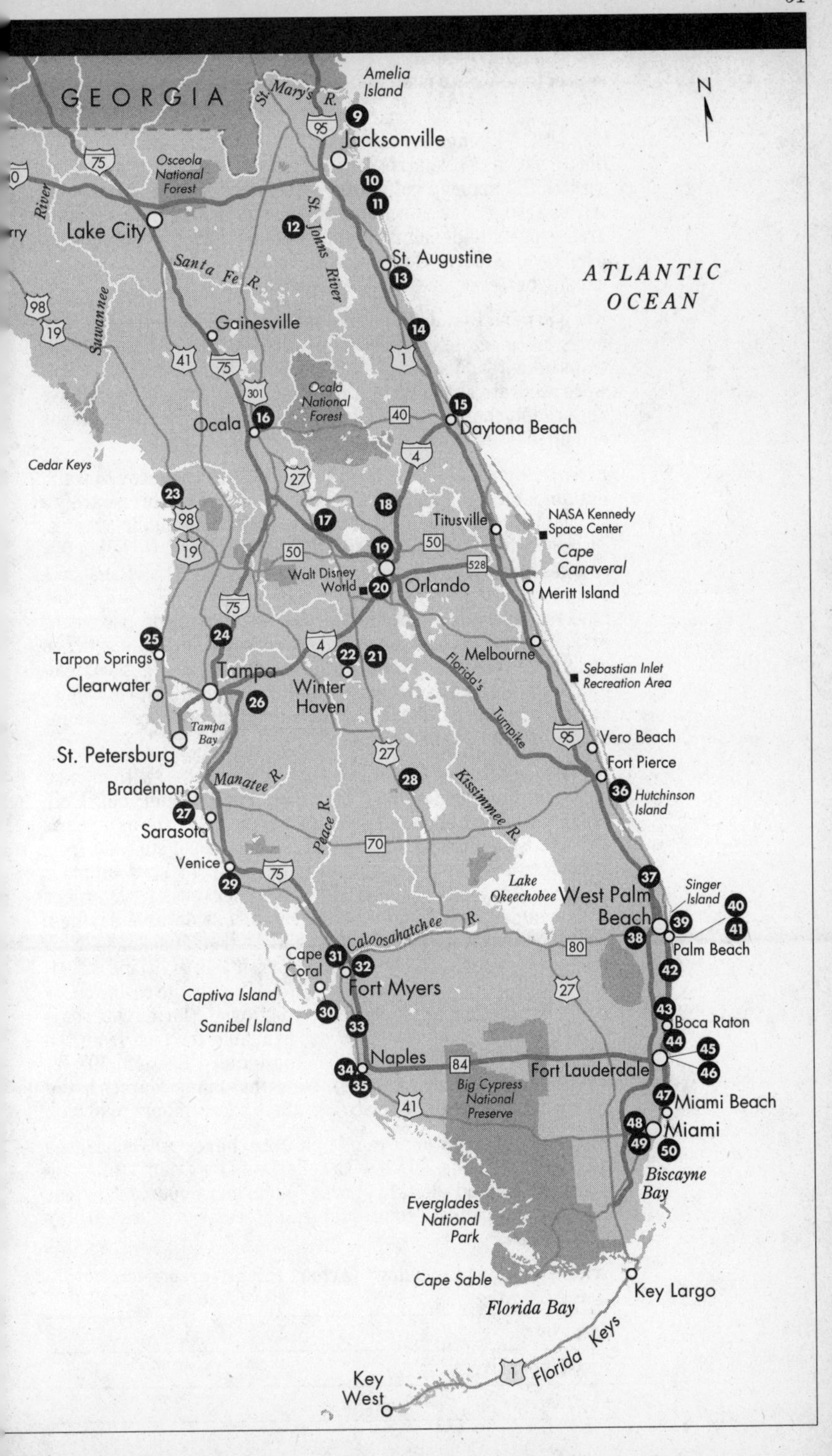
GEORGIA
ATLANTIC OCEAN
Amelia Island
St. Mary's R.
Jacksonville
Osceola National Forest
Lake City
St. Johns River
Santa Fe R.
St. Augustine
Suwannee
Gainesville
Ocala National Forest
Ocala
Daytona Beach
Cedar Keys
Titusville
NASA Kennedy Space Center
Cape Canaveral
Walt Disney World
Orlando
Meritt Island
Melbourne
Tarpon Springs
Tampa
Clearwater
Winter Haven
Florida's Turnpike
Sebastian Inlet Recreation Area
Tampa Bay
St. Petersburg
Vero Beach
Fort Pierce
Manatee R.
Kissimmee R.
Hutchinson Island
Bradenton
Sarasota
Peace R.
Venice
Lake Okeechobee
West Palm Beach
Singer Island
Caloosahatchee R.
Palm Beach
Cape Coral
Fort Myers
Captiva Island
Sanibel Island
Boca Raton
Naples
Fort Lauderdale
Big Cypress National Preserve
Miami Beach
Miami
Biscayne Bay
Everglades National Park
Cape Sable
Key Largo
Florida Bay
Florida Keys
Key West

ally in front of the women's tees and often designated as gold. A few designers—notably Jack Nicklaus—include five or more sets of tee boxes to make courses playable for varying golf abilities.

The USGA ratings are also from the championship tees and indicate a course's relative difficulty; the rating is the average a scratch (0-handicap golfer) should expect to score. Any course with a rating of two or more strokes higher than par is considered especially demanding and generally suitable only for experienced golfers. Courses with ratings below their par are usually better choices for less experienced golfers.

Keep in mind that a golf course tends to be a work-in-progress; holes are often lengthened or shortened, greens are rebuilt, traps added, and so forth. The statistics and descriptions here were accurate at the time of publication, but courses may have undergone changes—even major overhauls—by the time you end up playing them.

Because Florida courses tend to be flat, most are easy to walk, but unfortunately for people who enjoy walking, this is rarely a consideration any more in Florida. Except on public courses, carts are usually required throughout the state, though a few courses allow late-afternoon players to walk. The official reason is that carts help speed up play, which is generally true; however, operators concede that the cart concession also means extra revenue. A note for anyone interested in walking, when and where it is permitted: In Florida, where the "golf community" is a pervasive concept, walking distances *between* holes can be substantial, a real-estate ploy to allow more space for course-side homes and condos.

Greens fees are per person, regular-season rates, with mandatory cart fees (per person) included, where applicable. Note that greens fees, especially at resort courses, can be as much as 50% more during the high season, which runs generally from February to May, or substantially lower in slow summer months. Many resorts also offer golf packages, with greens fees included, which may represent a considerable savings. There are also companies that specialize in golf packages. Notable among these is **Golfpac Inc.** (Box 940490, Maitland 32794, tel. 407/660–8277 or 800/327–0878). An invaluable resource for any golfer seeking a comprehensive listing of Florida courses is *The Official Florida Golf Guide,* available for free from the Florida Division of Tourism (Visitor Inquiry Section, 107 W. Gaines St., Tallahassee 32399). Note that many courses listed in this publication as "private" do allow nonmembers to play.

Most courses (even some municipal ones) have dress codes, the standard requiring shirts with collars and long pants (often no jeans) or Bermuda-length shorts. While many courses are less than militant in dress-code enforcement, come prepared to play by the rules.

Prices quoted in the following chart refer to greens fees:

Catagory	**Cost**
Very Expensive	over $75
Expensive	$50–$75

Moderate	\$20–\$50
Inexpensive	under \$20

Northeast Florida

Amelia Island Plantation. The Tom Fazio–designed Long Point course is unusual for Florida: It features water on only three holes. Cedars, oaks, marshes, and ocean views make scenery a strong point. *Hwy. A1A S. Amelia Island 32034, tel. 904/261–6161 or 800/874–6878. Yardage: 6,750. Par: 72. USGA rating: 72.5. Total number of holes: 45. Greens fees: very expensive. Cart: mandatory. Special policies: must be a resort guest. Course facilities: restaurant, driving range, accommodations.*

Golden Ocala Golf Club. Ron Garl designed this course with several "replica" holes, including one of the famed, par-3 Postage Stamp hole at Royal Troon, Scotland; and also of the 12th and 13th holes at Augusta National, home of the Masters. *7300 U.S. 27 NW, Ocala 32675, tel. 904/622–0172. Yardage: 6,755. Par: 72. USGA rating: 72.2. Total number of holes: 18. Greens fees: moderate. Cart: mandatory. Special policies: tee times available a week in advance for weekdays, 3 days in advance for weekends. Facilities: driving range.*

Indigo Lakes Resort. Headquarters of the Ladies Professional Golf Association, Indigo Lakes is distinguished by its oversize greens, each averaging more than 9,000 square feet. *2620 Volusia Ave., Daytona Beach 32020, tel. 904/258–6333 or 800/874–9918. Yardage: 7,123. Par: 72. USGA rating: 73.5. Total number of holes: 18. Greens fees: expensive–moderate. Cart: mandatory. Special policies: club members and resort guests only before noon; afternoon public tee times up to a day in advance. Facilities: restaurant, driving range, accommodations.*

Killearn Inn & Golf Club. Gently rolling fairways and clusters of large oak trees give this course its distinctive character. The course hosts the Centel Classic, which in 1992 offered the largest prize purse on the Ladies Professional Golf Association tour. *100 Tyron Circle, Tallahassee 32308, tel. 904/893–2186 or 800/476–4101. Yardage: 7,022. Par: 72. USGA rating: 73.9. Total number of holes: 27. Greens fees: moderate. Cart: optional. Special policies: must be an inn guest. Facilities: restaurant, accommodations.*

Marriott at Sawgrass. With 99 holes, this is one of Florida's largest golfing compounds. The Pete Dye–designed TPC Stadium course—famed for its island 17th hole—vexes even top pros who compete in the Tournament Players Championship. *110 TPC Blvd., Ponte Vedra Beach 32082, tel. 904/273–3235. Yardage: 6,857. Par: 72. USGA rating: 74. Total number of holes: 99. Greens fees: very expensive. Cart: mandatory. Special policies: must be a hotel guest or the guest of a club member. Facilities: restaurant, driving range, accommodations.*

Ponce de Leon Golf Club. This is an older style Florida course, originally designed by Donald Ross. Here, marshland tends to be more of a backdrop to play than a hazard, as opposed to newer courses where marshy areas are more likely to have been converted into ponds or lakes that are very much in play. *4000 U.S. 1N, St. Augustine 32085, tel. 904/829–5314. Yardage:*

6,878. Par: 72. USGA rating: 72.9. Total number of holes: 18. Greens fees: moderate. Cart: mandatory. Special policies: tee times may be made one year in advance. Facilities: restaurant, driving range, accommodations.

Ponte Vedra Inn & Club. Designed by Robert Trent Jones, Sr., the Ocean course features an island hole—the 147-yard 9th said to have inspired Pete Dye's design of the 17th at the nearby TPC Stadium course—and plays tough when the wind is up. *200 Ponte Vedra Blvd., Ponte Vedra Beach 32082, tel. 904/285–1111 or 800/234–7842. Yardage: 6,515. Par: 72. USGA rating: 68.9. Total number of holes: 36. Greens fees: moderate. Cart: mandatory. Special policies: private course; must be an inn guest or guest of a member. Facilities: restaurant, driving range, accommodations.*

Ravines Golf & Country Club. Trees, rolling terrain, and deep ravines (hence the name) lend to a type of play atypical of Florida, where longer, flat courses with many water hazards are the norm. *2932 Ravines Rd., Middleburg 32068, tel. 904/282–7888. Yardage: 6,784. Par: 72. USGA rating: 72.7. Total number of holes: 18. Greens fees: moderate. Cart: mandatory. Special policies: weekday reservations available a week in advance; 2 days in advance for weekends. Facilities: restaurant, driving range, accommodations.*

Sheraton Palm Coast. The Matanzas Woods course, one of four 18s open to resort guests, is an Arnold Palmer/Ed Seay design, featuring rolling fairways and large greens. *300 Clubhouse Dr., Palm Coast 32137, tel. 904/445–3000. Yardage: 6,985. Par: 72. USGA rating: 73.3. Total number of holes: 72. Greens fees: moderate. Cart: mandatory. Special policies: none. Facilities: restaurant, driving range, accommodations.*

The Panhandle

Bay Point Yacht & Country Club. The Lagoon Legend course, used for the PGA Tour's qualifying school, is a watery monster, with the beast coming into play on 16 holes. Completed in 1986, the Lagoon Legend has been rated by magazines among the 1980s top new courses in the United States. *100 Delwood Beach Rd., Panama City Beach 32411, tel. 904/234–3307 or 800/874–7105. Yardage: 6,942. Par: 72. USGA rating: 73. Total number of holes: 36. Greens fees: moderate. Cart: mandatory. Special policies: tee times available 2 months in advance; lower greens fees for resort guests. Facilities: restaurant, driving range, accommodations.*

Bluewater Bay Resort. Generally ranked among the top courses in the state's northwest by golf magazines, this Tom Fazio–designed layout features thick woods, with water and marshy areas on several holes. *Box 247, 1950 Bluewater Blvd., Niceville 32578, tel. 904/897–3613 or 800/874–2128. Yardage: 6,808. Par: 72. USGA rating: 72.6. Total number of holes: 27. Greens fees: moderate. Cart: optional after 1 PM; $12–$14 per cart. Special policies: walking permitted after 1 PM. Facilities: restaurant, driving range, accommodations.*

Perdido Bay Resort. This course demands accuracy: On the par-5 11th, for example, water lines both sides of the fairway and the front of the green. *1 Doug Ford Dr., Pensacola 32507, tel. 904/492–1223 or 800/874–5355. Yardage: 7,154. Par: 72.*

USGA rating: 73.8. Total number of holes: 18. Greens fees: moderate. Cart: mandatory. Special policies: open to public; preferred tee times for club members and resort guests. Facilities: restaurant, driving range, accommodations.

St. Joseph's Bay Country Club. Length is not a factor on this public course but water is: it winds around 16 ponds. *Rte. C-30 S, Port St. Joe, 32456, tel. 904/227–1751. Yardage: 6,673. Par: 72. USGA rating: 71.8. Total number of holes: 18. Greens fees: inexpensive. Cart: optional weekdays; $13 per cart. Special policies: carts required on weekends. Facilities: restaurant, driving range.*

Sandestin Golf Club. The Links course requires play around and across canals on most of its holes. After little water on the first three holes, the fourth—a par-5 of 501 yards and ranked as one of Florida's toughest—is flanked by a lagoon and marsh. *Emerald Coast Pwky., Destin 32541, tel. 904/267–8144 or 800/277–0800. Yardage: 6,676. Par: 72. USGA rating: 72.5. Total number of holes: 45. Greens fees: expensive. Cart: mandatory weekends. Special policies: tee time preference and reduced greens fees for resort guests. Facilities: restaurant, driving range, accommodations.*

Sunny Hills Country Club. Typical of Florida, this course has plenty of sand, but atypically, only one hole features a water hazard. *1150 Country Club Blvd., Sunny Hills 32428, tel. 904/773–3619. Yardage: 6,888. Par: 72. USGA rating: 71.6. Total number of holes: 18. Greens fees: inexpensive. Cart: optional after 11 AM; $14 per cart. Special policies: carts required for tee times before 11 AM except Tues. and Thurs.; tee times available up to 2 days in advance. Facilities: restaurant, driving range.*

Tiger Point Country Club. In the design of the East course, Jerry Pate and Ron Garl built many "spectator mounds," a relatively modern design feature that frames greens. *1255 Country Club Dr., Gulf Breeze 32561, tel. 904/932–1333. Yardage: 7,033. Par: 72. USGA rating: 73.9. Total number of holes: 36. Greens fees: moderate. Cart: mandatory. Special policies: tee times available 4 days in advance. Facilities: restaurant, driving range.*

Orlando Area

Grand Cypress Golf Club. The New Course—a Jack Nicklaus re-creation of the famed Old Course in St. Andrews, Scotland—comes complete with hidden "pot" bunkers, deep enough to have stairs for entry and exit, in the fairways. *1 N. Jacaranda, Orlando 32836, tel. 407/239–4700. Yardage: 6,773. Par: 72. USGA rating: 72.1. Total number of holes: 45. Greens fees: very expensive. Cart: optional, with a $10 greens-fee reduction for walkers. Special policies: must be a resort guest; tee times available 2 months in advance. Facilities: restaurant, driving range, accommodations.*

Grenelefe Resort. Length is the key here: The West course, designed by Robert Trent Jones, Sr., plays to 7,325 yards from the championship tees. An absence of water hazards (there are just two ponds) softens the course somewhat. *3200 Rte. 546, Grenelefe 33844, tel. 813/422–7511 or 800/237–9549. Yardage: 7,325. Par: 72. USGA rating: 75. Total number of holes: 54. Greens fees: expensive. Cart: mandatory. Special policies: tee* *times may be booked 90 days in advance. Facilities: restaurant, driving range, accommodations.*

Mission Inn Golf & Tennis Resort. Originally built 60 years ago, this course is a mixed bag, featuring island greens typical of Florida as well as elevated tees and tree-lined fairways more characterisic of courses in the Carolinas and the Northeast. *10400 C.R. 48, Howey-in-the-Hills 34737, tel. 904/324–3885 or 800/874–9053. Yardage: 6,770. Par: 72. USGA rating: 73.5. Total number of holes: 36. Greens fees: expensive. Cart: mandatory. Special policies: open to public; tee times available a week in advance. Facilities: restaurant, accommodations.*

Timacuan Golf & Country Club. This is a two-part course designed by Ron Garl: Part I, the front nine, is open, with lots of sand; Part II, the back nine, is heavily wooded. *550 Timacuan Blvd., Lake Mary 32746, tel. 407/321–0010. Yardage: 7,019. Par: 72. USGA rating: 73.5. Total number of holes: 18. Greens fees: moderate. Cart: mandatory. Special policies: reserved until noon on weekends for members; tee times available 3 days in advance. Facilities: restaurant, driving range.*

Walt Disney World Resort. Where else would you find a sand trap shaped like the head of a well-known mouse? The Magnolia course, played by the pros in the Walt Disney World Oldsmobile Golf Classic, is long but forgiving, with extra-wide fairways. The resort also features a "Wee Links" for preteen golfers. *Magnolia Dr., Box 10000, Lake Buena Vista 32830, tel. 407/824–2270. Yardage: 7,190. Par: 72. USGA rating: 73.9. Total number of holes: 99. Greens fees: expensive. Cart: mandatory. Special policies: tee times 30 days in advance for resort guests; a week in advance for the public. Facilities: restaurant, driving range, accommodations.*

Willowbrook Golf Club. This is a relatively short municipal course, but lack of length is balanced by plenty of water, especially on the par-5 17th hole. *4200 Hwy. 544 N., Winter Haven 33881, tel. 813/299–7889. Yardage: 6,335. Par: 72. USGA rating: 70.5. Total number of holes: 18. Greens fees: inexpensive. Cart: optional; $8 per cart. Special policies: tee times available 6 days in advance. Facilities: driving range, snack bar.*

Southwest Florida

Bloomingdale Golfers Club. Playing here can be like playing in an open-air aviary, because there are, reportedly, more than 60 bird species (including a bald eagle) in residence on the course. For golfers, however, birdies and eagles are hard to come by on this water- and tree-lined course. *1802 Natures Way Blvd., Valrico 33594, tel. 813/685–4105. Yardage: 7;165. Par: 72. USGA rating: 74.5. Total number of holes: 18. Greens fees: expensive. Cart: mandatory. Special policies: club members only from 11:30 AM Fri.–Sun. Facilities: driving range, restaurant.*

Cape Coral Golf & Tennis Resort. This course tests those who think themselves expert in sand play. Although not long and not difficult, the course is guarded by more than 100 bunkers. *4003 Palm Tree Blvd., Cape Coral 33904, tel. 813/542–7879. Yardage of the featured course: 6,649. Par: 72. USGA rating: 71.6. Total number of holes: 18. Greens fees: moderate–inexpensive. Cart: mandatory. Special policies: tee times available*

3 days in advance. Facilities: restaurant, driving range, accommodations.

Eastwood Golf Club. Included on many lists of America's best public courses, Eastwood demands accuracy, with tight fairways, water, and well-bunkered greens. *4600 Bruce Herd La., Fort Myers 33905, tel. 813/275–4848. Yardage: 6,772. Par: 72. USGA rating: 73.3. Total number of holes: 18. Greens fees: inexpensive. Cart: mandatory before 3 PM in season; $15–$20. Special policies: carts mandatory before 3 PM in season. Facilities: driving range.*

Innisbrook Resort & Golf Club. Innisbrook's Copperhead course, generally ranked among Florida's toughest, has several long, dogleg par-4s. *U.S. 19, Tarpon Springs 34685, tel. 813/942–2000. Yardage: 7,062. Par: 72. USGA rating: 74.4. Total number of holes: 63. Greens fees: expensive. Cart: mandatory. Special policies: must be a resort guest or a member of a U.S. or Canadian resort. Facilities: restaurant, driving range, accommodations.*

Lely Flamingo Island Club. This Robert Trent Jones course was completed in 1991 and is the first of a planned three at this resort-in-the-making. Multilevel greens are guarded by a fleet of greedy bunkers, but the wide, rolling fairways generally keep errant drives in play. *8004 Lely Resort Blvd., Naples 33962, tel. 813/793–2223. Yardage: 7,171. Par: 72. USGA rating: 73.9. Total number of holes: 18. Greens fees: very expensive–expensive. Cart: mandatory. Special policies: tee times available 3 days in advance. Facilities: driving range, restaurant.*

Lochmoor Country Club. The course is well-maintained for a heavily played public links and winds around lakes and through tall palms and pine trees. *3911 Orange Grove Blvd., North Fort Myers 33903, tel. 813/995–0501. Yardage: 6,950. Par: 72. USGA rating: 70.6. Total number of holes: 18. Greens fees: moderate. Cart: optional after 2 PM; $10. Special policies: carts mandatory until after 2 PM. Facilities: restaurant, driving range.*

Longboat Key. Water, water everywhere: Amid canals and lagoons, the Islandside course brings water into play on all but one hole, and play can be especially tough when the wind comes off Sarasota Bay or the Gulf of Mexico. *301 Gulf of Mexico Dr., Longboat Key 34228, tel. 813/383–8821. Yardage: 6,890. Par: 72. USGA rating: 74.2. Total number of holes: 45. Greens fees: expensive. Cart: mandatory. Special policies: tee times required 3 days in advance. Facilities: restaurant, driving range, accommodations.*

Naples Beach Hotel Golf Club. Originally built in 1930, this is one of Florida's oldest courses. Although the course is short and flat, the strategic bunkering can make for challenging play. *851 Gulf Shore Blvd. N., Naples 33940, tel. 813/261–2222. Yardage: 6,462. Par: 72. USGA rating: 70.6. Total number of holes: 18. Greens fees: expensive. Cart: mandatory. Special policies: additional greens fees for non-hotel guests. Facilities: restaurant, driving range, accommodations.*

Pelican's Nest. A Tom Fazio design, the course is lined with thick vegetation—cypress, pine, oak, and palm trees—and swampland. Recent renovations to the elegant and enormous clubhouse and meticulous groundskeeping make the Pelican's Nest a haven for guests of Naples's luxury resorts. *4450 Bay Creek Dr. SW, Bonita Springs 33923, tel. 813/947–4600. Yardage: 6,940. Par: 72. USGA rating: 70.8. Total number of holes: 27. Greens fees: very expensive–expensive. Cart: mandatory. Special policies: public course, limited number of caddies in winter. Facilities: restaurant, driving range.*

Plantation Golf & Country Club. Local knowledge can be helpful on the Bobcat course: With water on 16 holes and greens not visible from the tee on 12 holes, shot placement and club selection are critical. *500 Rockley Blvd., Venice 34293, tel. 813/493–2000. Yardage: 6,862. Par: 72. USGA rating: 73.4. Total number of holes: 36. Greens fees: moderate. Cart: mandatory. Special policies: tee times available 2 days in advance, Bobcat course open to members and resort guests only Jan.–Apr. Facilities: restaurant, driving range, accommodations.*

Plantation Inn Golf Club. The Championship course winds through pines and natural lakes. An assortment of tee boxes makes the course playable for golfers of varying ability levels. *9301 W. Fort Island Trail, Crystal River 32629, tel. 904/795–4211 or 800/632–6262. Yardage: 6,654. Par: 72. USGA rating: 71.6. Total number of holes: 27. Greens fees: moderate. Cart: optional off-season; $14 per person. Special policies: tee times available 7 days in advance, 2 days in advance in Feb. and Mar.; walking restricted in peak season. Facilities: restaurant, driving range, accommodations.*

Saddlebrook Golf Club. The Saddlebrook course, designed by Arnold Palmer, is relatively short, but the premium is on accuracy, with lots of water to avoid, and large undulating greens make four-putting a constant concern. *5700 Saddlebrook Way, Wesley Chapel 33543, tel. 813/973–1111 or 800/729–8383. Yardage: 6,603. Par: 70. USGA rating: 71.5. Total number of holes: 36. Greens fees: very expensive. Cart: mandatory. Special policies: open to public, with tee time preference given to resort guests. Facilities: restaurant, driving range, accommodations.*

Sun 'n Lakes Golf Club. The course has a "wilderness" reputation: deer are often spotted on the fairways, and playing from the rough can be like playing from a jungle. *5306 Columbus Circle, Sebring 33872, tel. 813/385–4830. Yardage: 7,024. Par: 72. USGA rating: 74.8. Total number of holes: 18. Greens fees: moderate. Cart: mandatory. Special policies: tee times available a day in advance; Wed. AM ladies only, Thurs. Jan.–Apr., men only after noon. Facilities: restaurant, driving range, accommodations.*

Fort Lauderdale

Bonaventure Resort & Spa. Plenty of trees, water, and bunkers line the East course. The highlight hole is the par-3 third, with the green fronted by a waterfall. *250 Racquet Club Rd., Fort Lauderdale 33326, tel. 305/389–3300 or 800/327–8090. Yardage: 7,011 yards. Par: 72. USGA rating: 71. Total number of holes: 36. Greens fees: moderate. Cart: mandatory. Special policies: tee times available 3 days in advance. Facilities: restaurant, driving range, accommodations.*

Colony West Country Club. There is water on 14 of the Championship course's holes, with the most interesting hole the 12th, a par-4 through a cypress forest. *6800 N.W. 88th Ave., Tamarac 33321, tel. 305/726–8430. Yardage: 6,864. Par: 71. USGA Rating: 73.9. Total number of holes: 36. Greens fees: moderate. Cart: mandatory. Special policies: tee times available 3 days in advance. Facilities: restaurant.*

The Oaks Golf & Racquet Club. The Cypress, the most challenging of five courses, has familiar Florida features: lots of palms and greens well protected by sand and water. *3701 Oaks Clubhouse Dr., Pompano Beach 33069, tel. 305/978–1737 or 800/336–2108. Yardage: 6,910. Par: 72. USGA rating: 73.3. Total number of holes: 36. Greens fees: moderate. Cart: mandatory. Special policies: tee times a day in advance. Facilities: restaurant, driving range, accommodations.*

Miami

Don Schula's Golf Club. Large greens and elevated tees—unusual in south Florida—are features of the championship course. For golfers who can't get enough, there's also a lighted par-3 course at night. *N.W. 154th St., Miami Lakes 33014, tel. 305/821–1150 or 800/247–4852. Yardage: 7,055. Par: 72. USGA rating: 73. Total number of holes: 18. Greens fees: moderate. Cart: mandatory, $15. Special policies: open to public; reservations no more than 2 days in advance. Facilities: restaurant, driving range, accommodations.*

Doral Hotel Golf Club. The 18th hole on the Blue course, nicknamed "the Blue Monster" and venue for the Doral Open, rates among the hardest finishing holes on the PGA Tour. Veteran pro Ray Floyd reportedly called it the toughest par-4 in the world. *4400 N.W. 87th Ave., Miami 33178, tel. 305/592–2000 or 800/327–6334. Yardage: 7,065. Par: 72. USGA rating: 73. Total number of holes: 99. Greens fees: very expensive–expensive. Cart: mandatory. Special policies: open to public but tee time preference for hotel guests; extra greens fees for Blue course. Facilities: restaurant, driving range, accommodations.*

Key Biscayne Golf Club. Regularly rated highly among U.S. public courses, this one—the site of the Royal Caribbean Classic on the PGA Seniors Tour—is surrounded by mangrove swamps and inhabited by many bird species and alligators. *6700 Crandon Blvd., Key Biscayne 33149, tel. 305/361–9129. Yardage: 7,070. Par: 72. USGA rating: 74. Total number of holes: 18. Greens fees: moderate. Cart: optional after 1 PM, $14 per cart. Special policies: walking permitted after 1 PM; tee times available a day in advance. Facilities: restaurant, driving range.*

Turnberry Isle Country Club. The South course, which has hosted the PGA Senior Championship, is a Robert Trent Jones design that mixes old and new: a double green, similar to those at the Old Course at St. Andrews, Scotland, and an island green (on the 18th hole), a common feature of modern design. *199th St. and Biscayne Blvd., North Miami Beach 33180, tel. 305/932–6200 or 800/327–7028. Yardage: 7,200. Par: 72. USGA rating: not available. Total number of holes: 36. Greens fees: expensive. Cart: mandatory. Special policies: open to hotel guests and club members only; tee times 2 days in advance. Facilities: restaurant, driving range, accommodations.*

Palm Beach

Boca Raton Resort & Club. It's not so much the course as the celebrity aura that serves as an attraction here. When you play this one, you follow in the footsteps (or cart tracks) of Frank Sinatra and Gerald Ford, among others. *501 E. Camino Real, Boca Raton 33432, tel. 407/395–3000 or 800/327–0101. Yardage: 6,682. Par: 71. USGA rating: 71.7. Total number of holes: 36. Greens fees: expensive. Cart: mandatory. Special policies: open to resort guests and club members only; tee times up to 4 days in advance. Facilities: restaurant, driving range, accommodations.*

Boynton Beach Municipal Golf Course. The rolling terrain of this relatively short public course is unusual for the generally flat Palm Beach area. *8020 Jog Rd., Boynton Beach 33437, tel. 407/969–2200. Yardage: 6,340. Par: 71. USGA rating: 70.1. Total number of holes: 27. Greens fees: inexpensive. Cart: mandatory. Special policies: none. Facilities: driving range, snack bar.*

Breakers Hotel Golf Club. The Ocean course, designed by Donald Ross and among Florida's oldest, compensates for its shortness with tight fairways and small greens. *1 S. County Rd., Palm Beach 33480, tel. 407/655–6611 or 800/833–3141. Yardage: 6,008. Par: 70. USGA rating: 68. Total number of holes: 36. Greens fees: expensive. Cart: mandatory. Special policies: hotel guests and members only; free shuttle bus to West Course, 11 mi. off-site. Facilities: restaurant, driving range, accommodations.*

Emerald Dunes Golf Club. This Tom Fazio–designed course gets official credit as the 1,000th course to open in Florida and was considered one of the best new courses in the United States in 1990. *2100 Emerald Dunes Dr., West Palm Beach 33411, tel. 407/684–4653. Yardage: 7,006. Par: 72. USGA rating: 73.8. Total number of holes: 18. Greens fees: very expensive–expensive. Cart: mandatory. Special policies: tee times available 3 days in advance. Facilities: restaurant, driving range.*

Indian River Plantation. The course, a par-61, is classically Florida—flat, with lots of palms and bunkers, made tricky by ocean breezes. *555 N.E. Plantation Rd., Hutchinson Island 33494, tel. 407/225–3700 or 800/444–1432. Yardage: 4,042. Par: 61. USGA rating: 57.6. Total number of holes: 18. Greens fees: moderate. Cart: mandatory; price included in greens fees. Special policies: open to resort guests and members only; resort guests can book one tee time up to 2 weeks in advance. Facilities: restaurant, driving range, accommodations.*

Palm Beach Polo & Country Club. The Dunes course—the resort's newest—is a Ron Garl/Jerry Pate design with Scottish touches such as pot bunkers and grass traps. *13198 Forest Hill Blvd., West Palm Beach 33414, tel. 407/798–7000 or 800/327–4204. Yardage: 7,050. Par: 72. USGA rating: 73.4. Total number of holes: 45. Greens fees: expensive. Cart: mandatory. Special policies: open to resort guests and club members only; tee times up to 2 days in advance. Facilities: restaurant, driving range, accommodations.*

PGA National Golf Club. The Champion course, recently redesigned by Jack Nicklaus, demands length and accuracy, with more than 100 traps as well as water on 17 holes. It is the course used for the PGA Seniors Championship. *1000 Ave. of Champions, Palm Beach Gardens 33418, tel. 407/627–1800. Yardage: 7,022. Par: 72. USGA rating: 74.4. Total number of holes: 90. Greens fees: very expensive–expensive. Cart: mandatory. Special policies: must be a resort guest or golf pro; higher greens fees for the Champion course. Facilities: restaurant, driving range, accommodations.*

Royal Palm Beach Country Club. The course is longer than most public courses, but most holes are open, with few water hazards. *900 Royal Palm Beach Blvd., Royal Palm Beach 33411, tel. 407/798–6430. Yardage: 7,067. Par: 72. USGA rating: 72.5. Total number of holes: 18. Greens fees: moderate. Cart: mandatory. Special policies: tee times available 3 days in advance. Facilities: restaurant, driving range.*

4 Miami and Miami Beach

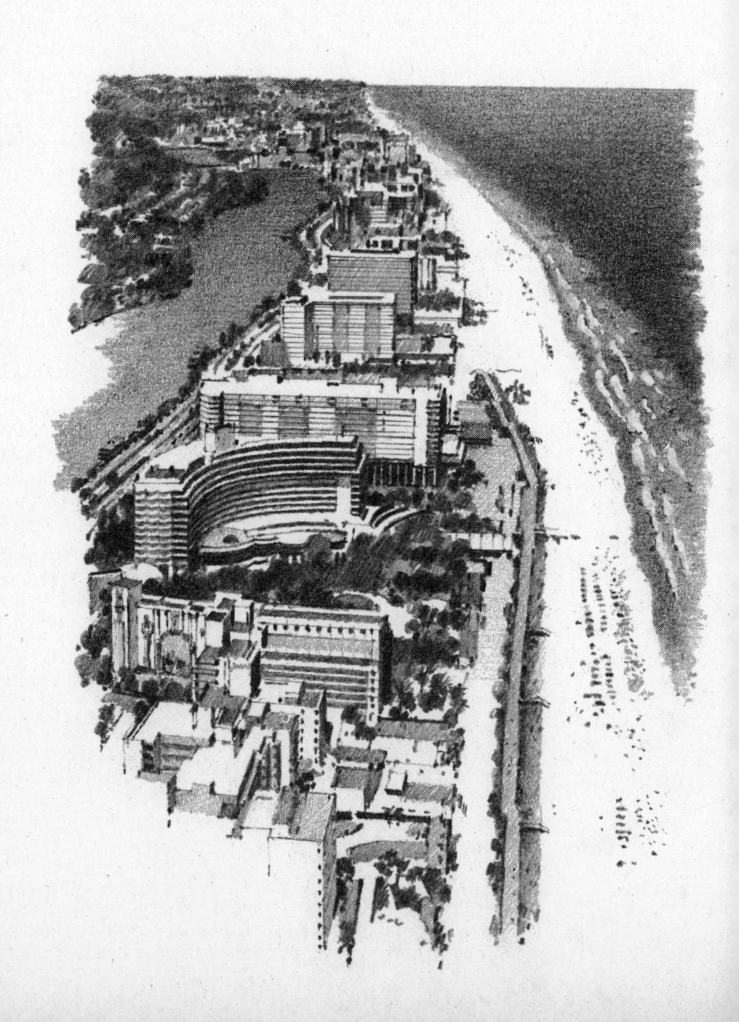

Introduction

What they say about Miami is true. The city *is* different. Miami is different from what it once was and it's different from other cities. Once a sleepy southern resort town, Miami today is a burgeoning giant of international commerce and finance as well as a place to find pleasure and relaxation. Like all big cities, Miami inspires the first-time visitor with hopes and dreams. Also as in other cities, many of these hopes and dreams can be sidetracked by crime and violence.

Miami's natural difference can be detected when you fly into the city. Clinging to a thin ribbon of dry land between the marshy Everglades and the Atlantic Ocean, Miami remains vulnerable to its perennial mosquitoes, periodic flooding, and potential devastation by hurricanes. These perils give life in Miami a flavor of urgency, a compulsion to prosper and party before the dream ends.

Miami may be the wrong place for a city, but it's the right place for a crossroads. Long before Spain's gold-laden treasure ships passed offshore in the Gulf Stream, the Calusa Indians who lived here had begun to trade with their mainland neighbors to the north and their island brethren to the south. Repeating this prehistoric pattern, many U.S. and multinational companies now locate their Latin American headquarters in Greater Miami because no other city can match its airline connections to the Western Hemisphere.

That same ease of access, coupled with a congenial climate, attracts hordes of Latin tourists—especially in Miami's steamy summer months (South America's winter), when domestic visitors from the northern United States are less in evidence. Access and climate also explain why Miami has become what *Newsweek* calls "America's Casablanca." Whenever a Latin American or Caribbean government erupts in revolution and economic chaos, the inevitable refugees flock inexorably to Miami (where they open restaurants).

Even without a revolution, Miami's cosmopolitan character and entrepreneurial spirit attract other immigrants from all over the world. The favorably cheap U.S. dollar has lured European tourists and commercial interests as well, spurring new European air connections. Alitalia, Air France, British Airways, Iberia, KLM, Lufthansa, Sabena, Swissair, and Virgin Atlantic have all newly begun or expanded service into Miami. In 1991, more than 10 million visitors arrived in Miami, a record, especially in the face of the Gulf War and recession.

Today, almost half of Greater Miami's population is Hispanic—the majority from Cuba, with significant populations from Colombia, El Salvador, Nicaragua, Panama, Puerto Rico, and Venezuela. About 150,000 French- and Creole-speaking Haitians also live in Greater Miami, as do Brazilians, Chinese, Germans, Greeks, Iranians, Israelis, Italians, Jamaicans, Lebanese, Malaysians, Russians, Swedes, and more—a veritable Babel of tongues. Most either know or are trying to learn English. You can help them by speaking slowly and distinctly.

Try not to think of Miami as a melting pot. Where ethnic and cultural diversity are the norm, there's less pressure to conform. Miamians practice matter-of-factly the customs they brought here—much to the consternation of other Miamians whose customs differ. The community wrestles constantly with these tensions and sensitivities.

As a big city, Miami has its share of crime, violence, and drug trafficking. And though the city dubiously led the nation in car thefts in 1992, you probably won't find the city's seamy underside unless you go looking for it. Still, just to make sure, and reflecting a new maturity, the Greater Miami Chamber of Commerce in 1991 began issuing a bilingual pamphlet with tips for avoiding crime while vacationing in the city. The hope is that more than ever visitors will find in Miami a multicultural metropolis that works and plays with vigor and that welcomes you to share its celebration of diversity.

Essential Information

Arriving and Departing by Plane

Airport **Miami International Airport (MIA),** 6 miles west of downtown Miami, is Greater Miami's only commercial airport. MIA has the nation's second-largest volume of international passenger and cargo traffic, and in 1991 was 10th busiest passenger airport in the world, ahead of New York's Kennedy International. MIA's busiest hours, when flight delays may occur, are 11 AM–8 PM. MIA contains 118 aircraft gates along seven concourses. Road improvements speed access into the departure area southbound from S.R. 112.

The airport has undertaken a $2 billion expansion program that will require much of the decade to complete; passengers will mainly notice expanded gates for American (concourses D and part of E) and United Airlines (concourse F, where Pan Am used to operate). A new 18-gate arrival/departure concourse A will go into construction by 1993, and will probably be completed in 1995. Improvements will help reduce congestion at concourses C, H, and F, all to be rebuilt; work on F is set for completion by 1993, and on C and H, by 1994. A largely underused convenience for passengers who have to get from one concourse to another in this long, linear terminal is the moving, cushioned Skywalk, one level up from the departure level, with access points at every concourse.

When you fly out of MIA, plan to check in 55 minutes before departure for a domestic flight and 90 minutes before departure for an international flight. Services for international travelers include 24-hour multilingual information and paging phones and foreign currency conversion booths throughout the terminal. An information booth with multilingual staff and 24-hour currency exchange are at Concourse E.

Between the Airport and Center City
By Bus

Metrobus. The county's Metrobus system has one benefit—its modest cost—if you're willing to put up with the inconveniences of infrequent service, scruffy equipment, and the circuitous path that many routes follow. Some routes from the airport are #7 to downtown (operates every 40 minutes from 6 AM to 10 PM; 9–5 on weekends); #37 South to Coral Gables and South Miami (operates every 30 minutes from 6 AM to 10 PM); #37 North to Hialeah (operates every 30 minutes from 5:30 AM to 11:30 PM); "J" to Coral Gables (operates every 30 minutes from 6 AM to 12:30 AM); #42 to Coconut Grove (operates hourly from 5:40 AM to 6:30 PM); and "J" east to Miami Beach (operates every 30 minutes from 4:30 AM to 11:30 PM). *Tel. 305/638–6700. Fare: $1.25 (exact change), transfer 25¢; 60¢ with 10¢ transfer for senior citizens and students.*

By Taxi For trips originating at MIA or the Port of Miami, a $1 toll is added to the meter fare—except for the flat-fare trips described below. You'll pay a $14 flat fare between MIA and the Port of Miami, in either direction.

For taxi service from the airport to destinations in the immediate vicinity, ask a uniformed county taxi dispatcher to call an **ARTS (Airport Region Taxi Service)** cab for you. These special blue cabs will offer you a short-haul flat fare in two zones: an inner-city ride is $5; an outer-city fare is $8. Maps are posted in cab windows on both sides.

SuperShuttle vans transport passengers between MIA and local hotels, the Port of Miami, and even individual residences on a 24-hour basis. The company's service area extends from Palm Beach to Monroe County (including the Lower Keys). Drivers provide narration en route. It's best to make reservations 24 hours before departure, although the firm will try to arrange pickups within Dade County on as little as four hours' notice. *For information and reservations from inside MIA, tel. 305/871–8488. Reservations outside MIA, tel. 305/871–2000 (Dade and Monroe counties) or 305/674–1700 (Broward and Palm Beach counties). Pet transport fee: $5. Lower rate for 2nd passenger in same party for many destinations. Children 3 and under ride free with parents. AE, DC, MC, V.*

By Limousine **Bayshore Limousine** has chauffeur-driven four-door town cars and stretch limousines available through the 24-hour reservation service. It serves Miami, Fort Lauderdale, Palm Beach, and the Keys. *11485 S.W. 87th Ave., Miami, tel. 305/253–9046, 235–3851, or 858–5888. AE, MC, V.*

Arriving and Departing by Car, Train, and Bus

By Car The main highways into Greater Miami from the north are Florida's Turnpike (toll) and I–95. From the northwest, take I–75 or U.S. 27 into town. From the Everglades to the west, use the Tamiami Trail (U.S. 41). From the south, use U.S. 1 and the Homestead Extension of Florida's Turnpike. In 1993 and 1994 the Brickell Avenue (U.S. 1) bridge—a major north–south artery into downtown—will be closed. Drivers will have to use I–95. Construction will begin in late 1993/early 1994 on flyover ramps in the Golden Glades interchange, while by 1994 construction is scheduled for completion on upgrades between N.W. 58th and 95th streets, on new ramps where I–95 and S.R. 836 meet, and on a new off-ramp southbound onto N.W. 8th Street. Widening the six lanes of the MacArthur Causeway and accompanying installation of safety shoulders along this road (bordered on both sides by water) is expected to be completed in the summer of 1993.

Rental Cars Five rental-car firms—**Avis Rent-a-Car** (tel. 800/331–1212), **Dollar Rent-a-Car** (tel. 800/800–4000), **Hertz Rent-a-Car** (tel. 800/654–3131), **National Rent-a-Car** (tel. 800/328–4567), and **Value Rent-a-Car** (tel. 800/327–2501)—have booths near the baggage claim area on MIA's lower level—a convenience when you arrive.

By Train **Amtrak's** two trains between Miami and New York City, the *Silver Meteor* and *Silver Star*, make different stops along the way. Each has a daily Miami arrival and departure.

Amtrak's "All Aboard" fare is the most economical way to travel to Florida, if you have time to meet the length-of-stay requirements. Trains run full all year, except in October and May. For the best fare, contact Amtrak as soon as you decide to take a trip. Ask for Amtrak's 1992 travel planner. *Amtrak Station, 8303 N.W. 37th Ave., Miami 33147. For recorded arrival/departure information, tel. 305/835–1200; package and express service, tel. 305/835–1225. Advance reservations required. Reservations: Amtrak Customer Relations, 400 N. Capitol St., NW, Washington, DC 20001, tel. 800/USA–RAIL in the U.S., 800/4AMTRAK in Canada.*

The 4-year old **Tri-Rail** commuter train system connects Miami with Broward and Palm Beach Monday–Saturday. Call for schedule and details on weekly and monthly passes. *Suite 200, 1 River Plaza, 305 S. Andrews Ave., Fort Lauderdale, FL 33301, tel. 305/728–8445 or 800/TRI–RAIL.*

By Bus **Greyhound/Trailways** buses stop at five bus terminals in Greater Miami. *700 Biscayne Blvd., Miami, tel. 305/379–7403 (fares and schedules only). No reservations.*

Getting Around Miami

Greater Miami resembles Los Angeles in its urban sprawl and traffic congestion. You'll need a car to visit many of the attractions and points of interest listed in this book. Some are accessible via public transportation.

A department of county government, the Metro-Dade Transit Agency, runs the public transportation system. It consists of more than 450 Metrobuses on 74 routes, the 21-mile Metrorail elevated rapid transit system, and the 1.9-mile Metromover in downtown Miami. Free maps, schedules, and a First-Time Rider's Kit are available. *6601 N.W. 72nd Ave., Miami 33166. Maps by Mail, tel. 305/638–6137. For route information, tel. 305/638–6700 daily 6 AM–11 PM. Fare $1.25, transfer 25¢, exact change only.*

By Train Metrorail runs from downtown Miami north to Hialeah and south along U.S. 1 to Dadeland. *Service every 7½ minutes in peak hours, every 15–30 minutes other times. Weekdays 6 AM–midnight, weekends 6:30 AM–6:30 PM. Runs until midnight on weekends for special events such as the Orange Bowl parade. Fare: $1.25.*

Metromover's two loops circle downtown Miami, linking major hotels, office buildings, and shopping areas (*see* Exploring Downtown Miami, below). An extension of Metromover (north to the Omni district and south to Brickell Ave. at Coral Way) began in 1991 and is expected to be completed by 1994. *Service every 90 seconds. Weekdays 6:30 AM–midnight, weekends 8:30 AM–midnight. Later for special events. Fare 25¢.*

By Bus Metrobus stops are marked by blue-and-green signs with a bus logo and route information. The frequency of service varies widely. Obtain specific schedule information in advance for the routes you want to ride. *Tel. 305/638–6700.*

By Taxicab There are some 2,000 taxicabs in Dade County. Fares are $1.10 for the first ⅐ mile, 20¢ for each additional ⅐ mile; waiting time 20¢ for each ⅘ minute. No additional charge for extra passengers, luggage, or road and bridge tolls. Taxi companies with dispatch service are **All American Taxi** (tel. 305/947–3333), **Central Taxicab Service** (tel. 305/534–0694), **Diamond Cab Company** (tel. 305/545–7575), **Dolphin Cab** (tel. 305/948–6666), **Magic City Cab Company** (tel. 305/757–5523), **Metro Taxicab Company** (tel. 305/888–8888), **Miami-Dade Yellow Cab** (tel. 305/633–0503), **Miami Springs Taxi** (tel. 305/888–8541), **Society Cab Company** (tel. 305/757–5523), **Speedy Cab** (tel. 305/861–9999), **Super Yellow Cab Company** (tel. 305/888–7777), **Tropical Taxicab Company** (tel. 305/945–1025), and **Yellow Cab Company** (tel. 305/444–4444). Many now accept credit cards. Inquire when you call.

It is recommended that you be on your guard when traveling by cab in Miami, as some drivers are rude and unhelpful, and have even been known to take advantage of visitors who are unfamiliar with their destinations or the layout of the city. If it's possible, avoid taking a cab; if you must, try to be familiar with your route and destination.

By Car Finding your way around Greater Miami is easy if you know how the numbering system works. Miami is laid out on a grid with four quadrants—northeast, northwest, southeast, and southwest—which meet at Miami Avenue and Flagler Street. Miami Avenue separates east from west and Flagler Street separates north from south. *Avenues* and *courts* run north-south; *streets*, *terraces*, and *ways* run east-west. *Roads* run diagonally, northwest-southeast.

Many named streets also bear numbers. For example, Unity Boulevard is N.W. and S.W. 27th Avenue, LeJeune Road is N.W. and S.W. 42nd Avenue. However, named streets that depart markedly from the grid, such as Biscayne Boulevard and Brickell Avenue, have no corresponding numerical designations. Dade County and most other municipalities follow the Miami numbering system.

In Miami Beach, *avenues* run north-south; *streets*, east-west. Numbers rise along the beach from south to north and from the Atlantic Ocean in the east to Biscayne Bay in the west.

In Coral Gables, all streets bear names. Coral Gables uses the Miami numbering system for north-south addresses but begins counting east-west addresses westward from Douglas Road (S.W. 37th Ave.).

Hialeah has its own grid. Palm Avenue separates east from west; Hialeah Drive separates north from south. *Avenues* run north-south and *streets* east-west. Numbered streets and avenues are designated west, east, or southeast.

Important Addresses and Numbers

Tourist Information The Greater Miami Convention and Visitors Bureau has opened satellite tourist information centers in Miami Beach (Miami Beach Chamber of Commerce, 1920 Meridian Ave., 33139, tel. 305/672–1270), and in Homestead–Florida City (South Dade Visitors Information Center, 1160 U.S. 1, Florida City 33034, tel. 305/245–9180 or 800/852–8675). Additional satellite centers were to open in 1992 at Bayside downtown and in

Miami Beach and at the corner of Lincoln Road and Washington Avenue. Contact the bureau for locations and hours or to request information by mail.

Visitor Services, Greater Miami Convention and Visitors Bureau (701 Brickell Ave., Suite 2700, Miami 33131, tel. 305/539–3063 or 800/283–2707); Surfside Tourist Board (9301 Collins Ave., Surfside 33154, tel. 305/864–0722).

Chambers of Commerce

Greater Miami has a central chamber—the **Greater Miami Chamber of Commerce** (1601 Biscayne Blvd., Miami 33132, tel. 305/350–7700)—as well as more than 20 local chambers of commerce, each promoting its individual community. Most maintain racks of brochures on tourist information in their offices and will send you information about their community.

Coconut Grove Chamber of Commerce (2820 McFarlane Rd., Coconut Grove 33133, tel. 305/444–7270).
Coral Gables Chamber of Commerce (50 Aragon Ave., Coral Gables 33134, tel. 305/446–1657).
Gold Coast Chamber of Commerce (1100 Kane Concourse, Suite 210, Bay Harbor Islands 33154, tel. 305/866–6020). Serves the beach communities of Bal Harbour, Bay Harbor Islands, Golden Beach, North Bay Village, Sunny Isles, and Surfside.
Key Biscayne Chamber of Commerce (Key Biscayne Bank Bldg., 95 W. McIntyre St., Key Biscayne 33149, tel. 305/361–5207).
Miami Beach Chamber of Commerce (1920 Meridian Ave., Miami Beach 33139, tel. 305/672–1270).
North Miami Chamber of Commerce (13100 W. Dixie Hwy., North Miami 33181, tel. 305/891–7811).
Greater South Dade/South Miami Chamber of Commerce (6410 S.W. 80th St., South Miami 33143–4602, tel. 305/661–1621).

Emergencies

Dial 911 for **police** and **ambulance.** You can dial free from pay phones.

Telecommunication lines for the hearing impaired are used by hearing-impaired travelers with telecommunication devices (TDD) to reach TDD-equipped public services:

Fire/Police/Medical/Rescue (tel. 305/595–4749 TDD)
Operator and Directory Assistance (tel. 800/855–1155 TDD)
Deaf Services of Miami (5455 SW 8th St., Room 255, Miami, tel. 305/444–2211 TDD or voice 305/444–2266). Operates 24 hours..

Ambulance

Randle Eastern Ambulance Service Inc. Serves Greater Miami. Meets air ambulances and takes patients to hospitals. Services include advanced life-support systems. *35 S.W. 27th Ave., Miami 33135, tel. 305/642–6400. Open 24 hrs. AE, MC, V.*

Hospitals

The following hospitals have 24-hour emergency rooms:

Miami Beach: *Mt. Sinai Medical Center* (4300 Alton Rd., Miami Beach, tel. 305/674–2200; physician referral, tel. 674–2273). Just off Julia Tuttle Causeway (I–195).

St. Francis Hospital (250 W. 63rd St., Miami Beach, tel. 305/868–2770; physician referral, tel. 305/868–2728). Near Collins Ave. and north end of Alton Rd.

Central: *University of Miami/Jackson Memorial Medical Center.* Includes Jackson Memorial Hospital, a county hospital with Greater Miami's only trauma center. Near Dolphin Expressway. Metrorail stops a block away. *1611 N.W. 12th Ave., Miami, tel. 305/325-7429. Emergency room, tel. 305/585-6901. Interpreter service, tel. 305/549-6316. Patient relations, tel. 305/549-7341. Physician referral, tel. 305/547-5757.*

Mercy Hospital (3663 S. Miami Ave., Coconut Grove, tel. 305/285-2171; physician referral, tel. 305/285-2929). Greater Miami's only hospital with an emergency boat dock.

Miami Children's Hospital (6125 S.W. 31st St., tel. 305/662-8280; physician referral, ext. 2563).

South: *Baptist Hospital of Miami* (8900 N. Kendall Dr., Miami, tel. 305/596-6556; physician referral, tel. 305/596-6557).

24-Hour Pharmacies

Of some 300 pharmacies in Greater Miami, only five are open 24 hours a day. Most pharmacies open at 8 or 9 AM and close between 9 PM and midnight. Many pharmacies offer local delivery service.

Eckerd Drugs. 1825 Miami Gardens Dr. N.E. (185th St.), North Miami Beach, tel. 305/932-5740 and 9031 S.W. 107th Ave., Miami, tel. 305/274-6776.

Walgreens. 500-B W. 49th St. (Palm Springs Mall), Hialeah, tel. 305/557-5468; 12245 Biscayne Blvd., Miami, tel. 305/893-6860; 5731 Bird Rd., Miami, tel. 305/666-0757.

Physician Referral Services

Dade County Medical Association (1501 N.W. N. River Dr., Miami, tel. 305/324-8717). Office open weekdays 9-5 for medical referral.

East Coast District Dental Society (420 S. Dixie Hwy., Suite 2E, Coral Gables, tel. 305/667-3647). Office open weekdays 9 AM-4:30 PM for dental referral. Services include general dentistry, endodontics, periodontics, and oral surgery.

Guided Tours

Orientation Tours

Old Town Trolley of Miami. Ninety-minute narrated tours of Miami and 90-minute tours of Miami Beach leave Bayside Marketplace every half hour between 10 and 4. *Box 12985, Miami 33101, tel. 305/374-8687. Miami and Miami Beach tours: $14 adults, $5 children 3-12. No credit cards.*

Special-Interest Tours

Air Tours

Air Tours of Miami offers 1-hour sightseeing tours of Miami, the Everglades, and nearby waters in a Piper Seneca II six-seater. *1470 N.E. 123rd St., Ste. 602, Miami, tel. 305/893-5874. Tours depart from Opa-locka Airport; inquire for directions. Cost: $75 adults, $50 children, minimum of 3 adults, maximum of 5. Reservations required. Other tours to Key West, Orlando, Southeast Florida, and Caribbean are offered. AE, MC, V.*

Gold Coast Helicopters. This family business offers Bell-47 helicopter rides that last eight minutes or longer. *15101 Biscayne Blvd., N. Miami, tel. 305/940-1009. Cost: $60 for 1 or 2, for 8 min. Longer rides cost more. Reservations advised.*

Boat Tours

Heritage of Miami II. Miami's official tall ship, an 85-foot steel sailing schooner, docks at Bayside Marina. Carries up to 49 passengers for day sailing, sleeps 16; children and cameras welcome. Ice and ice chest on board, soft drinks for sale; bring your own food. Standard Biscayne Bay day trip lasts two hours. Reservations recommended. *3145 Virginia St., Coconut Grove*

33133, tel. 305/442–9697. Cost: $10 adults, $5 children under 12. Sails daily, weather permitting.

Island Queen and ***Good Times Too*** are a pair of 150-passenger double-decker tour boats that dock at Bayside Marketplace (401 Biscayne Blvd.) and offer 90-minute narrated tours of Port of Miami and Millionaires' Row. *Cost: $10 adults, $5 children. Tel. 305/379–5119. Tours daily.*

Nikko Gold Coast Cruises. Two 150-passenger boats based at Haulover Park Marina specialize in water tours to major Greater Miami attractions. *10800 Collins Ave., Miami Beach, tel. 305/945–5461. Tours include Bayside Marketplace ($9.59 adults, $5.33 children under 13); Seaquarium ($27.64/$18.06, including admission); Vizcaya ($18.11/$9.59, including admission); and 2-hr sightseeing trips at 10 AM and 2 PM ($7.95/ $4.19). (Second price is for children under 13.)*

History Tours

Art Deco District Tour. Meet your guide at 10:30 AM Saturday and Sunday, 5 PM Wednesday at the Leslie Hotel (1244 Ocean Dr., Miami Beach), the **Miami Design Preservation League's** welcome center, for a 90-minute tour. Wear comfortable shoes. Also available is the League's *Art Deco District Guide*, a book with six detailed walking or driving tours of the square-mile Art Deco District on Miami Beach. *Bin L, Miami Beach 33119, tel. 305/672–2014. Cost: $6 for tour, $10 for book.*

Prof. Paul George. Explore Miami's history with a professional historian on a 3-hour walking tour of downtown. Paul George is a history professor at Miami-Dade Community College and the past-president of the Florida Historical Society. His tour begins either on the north bank of the Miami River behind the Hyatt Regency Hotel, 400 S.E. 2nd Ave., or at Bayside Marketplace (*see* Exploring Downtown Miami, below). Wear comfortable walking shoes and a hat. Tours are usually held Saturdays, 9 AM–1 PM, and by appointment. George also gives 2½-hour walking tours of Brickell Avenue, Buena Vista, Coconut Grove, Coral Gables, Little Havana, Miami's old City Cemetery, the Miami Beach Art Deco District, historic Morningside, Southside, and Fort Lauderdale and Fort Lauderdale Beach. *1345 S.W. 14th St., Miami, tel. 305/858–6021, $10 adults, $7 children 7–14, under 7 free.*

Rickshaw Tours

Majestic Rickshaw. Look for rickshaws along Main Highway in Coconut Grove's Village Center (75 N.E. 156 St., Biscayne Gardens, tel. 305/256–8833) nightly 8 PM–2 AM in Coconut Grove. Rickshaw holds two adults. $3 per person for 10-minute ride through Coconut Grove, $6 per person for 20-minute lovers' moonlight ride down to Biscayne Bay. No credit cards.

Self-Guided Tours

The Junior League of Miami publishes five excellent self-guiding tours to architectural and historical landmarks in Coconut Grove, Coral Gables, downtown Miami, the northeast, and south Dade. *2325 Salzedo, Coral Gables 33134, tel. 305/ 443–0160. Cost: $3 each.*

Exploring Miami

Exploring Downtown Miami

Numbers in the margin correspond to points of interest on the Downtown Miami map.

Orientation From a distance you see downtown Miami's future—a 21st-century skyline already stroking the clouds with sleek fingers of steel and glass. By day, this icon of commerce and technology sparkles in the strong subtropical sun; at night, it basks in the man-made glow of floodlights.

Staid, suited lawyers and bankers share the sidewalks with Hispanic merchants wearing open-neck, intricately embroidered shirts called *guayaberas*. Fruit merchants sell their wares from pushcarts. European youths with backpacks stroll the streets. Foreign businessmen haggle over prices in import–export shops. You hear Arabic, Chinese, Creole, French, German, Hebrew, Hindi, Japanese, Portuguese, Spanish, Swedish, Yiddish, and even a little English now and then.

With effort, you can find remnants of downtown Miami's past, though still less this year than last, when two venerable hotels, the McAlister and the Columbus, were demolished. Most of the city's "old" downtown buildings date from only the 1920s and 1930s—an incongruity if you're from someplace that counts its past in centuries. Remember that Miami is a young city, incorporated in 1896 with just 3,000 residents. A Junior League book, *Historic Downtown Miami*, locates and describes 27 older structures in and near downtown, including 21 you can see in a two-hour self-guided walking tour of slightly more than a mile.

Touring Downtown Miami Parking downtown is inconvenient and expensive. If you're staying elsewhere in the area, leave your car at an outlying Metrorail station and take the train downtown. Metromover, a separate light-rail mass-transit system, circles the heart of the city on twin elevated loops. No part of the downtown tour is more than 2 blocks from one of Metromover's nine stations. We've organized the tour around those stations, so you can ride Metromover directly to the downtown attractions that interest you most.

❶ ❷ When you get off the Metrorail train at **Government Center Station,** notice the **Dade County Courthouse** (73 W. Flagler St.). It's the building to the east with a pyramid at its peak, where turkey vultures roost in winter. Built in 1928, it was once the tallest building south of Washington, D.C.

❸ As you leave the Metrorail station, you'll enter **Metro-Dade Center,** the county government's 30-story office building. Designed by architect Hugh Stubbins, it opened in 1985.

❹ Across N.W. 1st Street from Metro-Dade Center stands the **Metro-Dade Cultural Center** (101 W. Flagler St.), opened in 1983. The 3.3-acre complex is a Mediterranean expression of architect Philip Johnson's postmodern style. An elevated plaza provides a serene haven from the city's pulsations and a superb setting for festivals and outdoor performances.

The Center for the Fine Arts, an art museum in the tradition of the European *kunsthalle* (exhibition gallery), has no permanent collection but it organizes and borrows temporary exhibitions on many artistic themes. Shows scheduled for early 1993 include "Florida Collects" and "Portrait Drawings from the Portrait Gallery of London." *Tel. 305/375–1700. Admission: $5 adults, $2 children 6–12, under 6 free. Donations Tues. Open Tues.–Sat. 10–5, Thurs. 10–9, Sun. noon–5.*

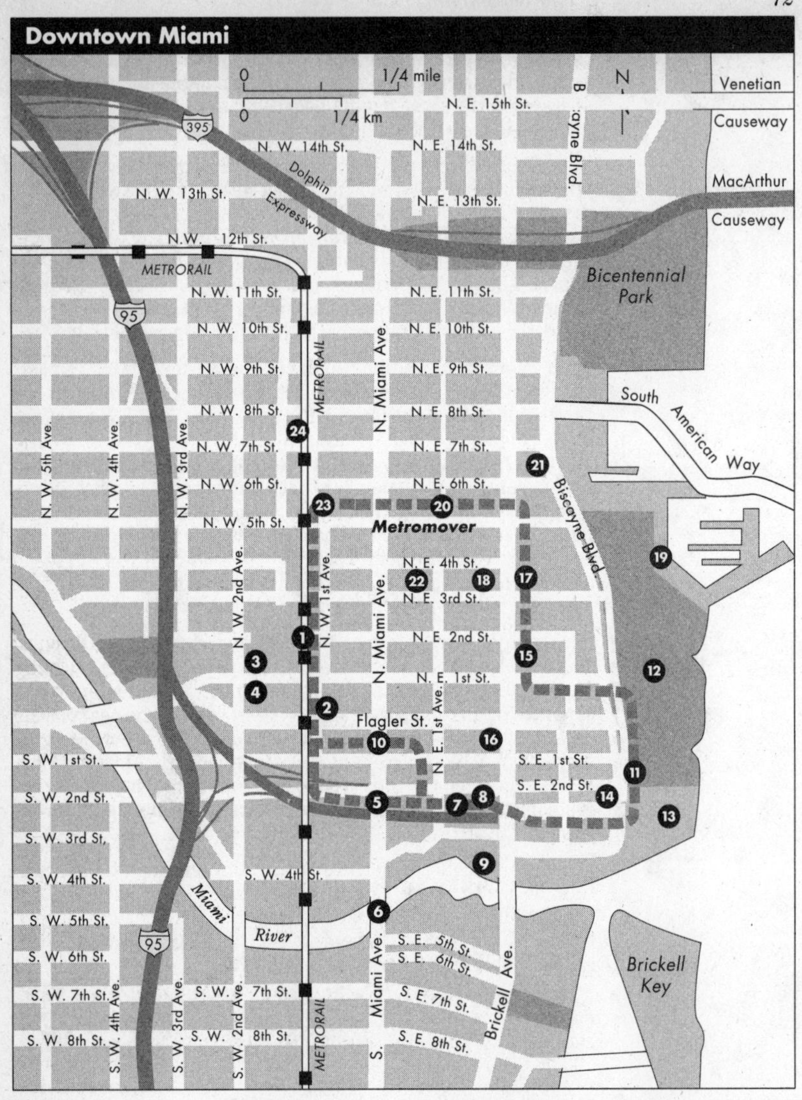

Bayfront Park, **12**
Bayfront Park Station, **11**
Bayside Marketplace, **19**
College Bayside Station, **17**
Dade County Courthouse, **2**
Edcom Station, **20**
First St. Station, **15**
Ft. Dallas Park Station, **5**
Freedom Tower, **21**
Government Center Station, **1**
Gusman Center, **16**
Hotel Inter-Continental Miami, **13**
International Place, **8**
James L. Knight International Center, **9**
Knight Center Station, **7**
Metro-Dade Center, **3**
Metro-Dade Cultural Center, **4**
Miami Arena, **24**
Miami Ave. Bridge, **6**
Miami Ave. Station, **10**
Miami-Dade Community College, **18**
Southeast Financial Center, **14**
State Plaza/Arena Station, **23**
U.S. Courthouse, **22**

The Historical Museum of Southern Florida is a regional museum that interprets the human experience in southern Florida from prehistory to the present. Artifacts on permanent display include Tequesta and Seminole Indian ceramics, clothing, and tools; a 1920 streetcar; and an original edition of Audubon's *Birds of America. Tel. 305/375–1492. Admission: $4 adults, $2 children 6–12, under 6 free. Donations Mon. Open Mon.–Sat. 10–5, Thurs. 10–9, Sun. noon–5.*

The Main Public Library has 3,231,306 holdings as of late 1991 and a computerized card catalog. Inside the entrance, look up at the rotunda mural, where artist Edward Ruscha interpreted a quotation from Shakespeare: "Words without thought never to heaven go." You'll find art exhibits in the auditorium and second-floor lobby. *Tel. 305/375–BOOK. Open Mon.–Sat. 9–6, Thurs. 9–9, Sun. 1–5. Closed Sun. May–mid-Oct.*

At Government Center Station, you can also transfer to Metromover's inner and outer loops through downtown. We've listed the stations and their attractions in sequence along the outer loop.

5 6 The first stop is **Ft. Dallas Park Station.** If you disembark here, you're a block from the **Miami Ave. Bridge,** one of 11 bridges on the river that open to let ships pass. From the bridge approach, watch freighters, tugboats, research vessels, and luxury yachts ply this busy 5-mile waterway.

Time Out Stroll across the bridge to **Tobacco Road** for a drink, snack, or meal. Built in 1912, this friendly neighborhood pub was a speakeasy during Prohibition. *626 S. Miami Ave., tel. 305/374–1198. Open weekdays 11:30 AM–5 AM, weekends 12:30 PM–5 AM. Lunch weekdays 11:30–2:30. Dinner nightly. AE, DC, MC, V.*

7 8 The next Metromover stop, **Knight Center Station,** nestles inside the **International Place** (100 S.E. 1st St.), a wedge-shape 47-story skyscraper designed by I. M. Pei & Partners. The building is brilliantly illuminated at night. Inside the Tower, 9 follow signs to the **James L. Knight International Center** (400 S.E. 2nd Ave., tel. 305/372–0929), a convention and concert hall adjoining the Hyatt Regency Hotel.

At the Knight Center Station, you can transfer to the inner 10 loop and ride one stop to the **Miami Avenue Station,** a block south of **Flagler Street,** downtown Miami's commercial spine. Like most such thoroughfares, Flagler Street lost business in recent years to suburban malls—but unlike most, it found a new lease on life. Today, the ½-mile of Flagler Street from Biscayne Boulevard to the Dade County Courthouse is the most important import-export center in the United States. Its stores and arcades supply much of the world with bargain automotive parts, audio and video equipment, medical equipment and supplies, photographic equipment, clothing, and jewelry.

Time Out Walk about 2½ blocks north of Flagler Street to **The Eating Place,** an open-air Jamaican restaurant as authentic as any in Kingston. The jukebox pours reggae onto Miami Avenue while waitresses pour the native beer, Red Stripe, which goes well with the oxtail stew or curried goat. *240 N. Miami Ave., tel. 305/375–0156. Open daily 8–6:30. No credit cards.*

(11) (12) If you stay on the outer loop, you'll come next to **Bayfront Park Station,** opposite **Claude and Mildred Pepper Bayfront Park,** which extends from Biscayne Boulevard east to the edge of the bay. Japanese sculptor Isamu Noguchi redesigned the park just before his death in 1989; it now includes a memorial to the *Challenger* astronauts, an amphitheater, and a fountain honoring the late Florida congressman Claude Pepper and his wife. (13) Just south of Bayfront Park, the lobby of the **Hotel Inter-Continental Miami** (100 Chopin Plaza) contains *The Spindle,* a huge sculpture by Henry Moore.

West of Bayfront Park Station stands the tallest building in (14) Florida, the 55-story **Southeast Financial Center** (200 S. Biscayne Blvd.), with towering royal palms in its 1-acre Palm Court plaza beneath a steel-and-glass space frame. Just north on the boulevard is where a 2-mile beautification is to begin in fall 1992 of Biscayne Boulevard. The new mosaic tile sidewalks will follow a design of Brazilian landscape architect Roberto Burle Marx.

(15) (16) The next Metromover stop, **First Street Station,** places you a block north of Flagler Street and the landmark **Gusman Center for the Performing Arts,** an ornate former movie palace restored as a concert hall. Gusman Center resembles a Moorish courtyard with twinkling stars in the sky. Performances here include the Miami City Ballet, directed by Edward Villella, and the New World Symphony, a unique, advanced-training orchestra led by Michael Tilson Thomas. Gusman Center: *174 E. Flagler St., Miami 33131. Box office tel. 305/372–0925;* ballet: *905 Lincoln Rd., Miami Beach 33139, tel. 305/532–4880;* symphony: *555 Lincoln Rd., Miami Beach 33139, tel. 305/673–3330.*

(17) (18) The **College/Bayside Station** Metromover stop serves the downtown campus of **Miami-Dade Community College,** where, in building 1, you can browse through two fine galleries: the Centre Gallery on the third floor, and the Frances Wolfson Art Gallery on the fifth floor, which houses traveling exhibitions of contemporary art. *300 N.E. 2nd Ave., tel. 305/237–3278. Admission free. Open weekdays 9–5:30.*

College/Bayside Station is also the most convenient Metro- (19) mover stop for **Bayside Marketplace,** a waterside entertainment and shopping center built by the Rouse Company, between Bayfront Park and the entrance to the Port of Miami. Bayside's 235,000 square feet of retail space include 150 specialty shops, pushcarts in the center's Pier 5 area, outdoor cafés, and an international food court. The center adjoins the 145-slip Miamarina, where you can see luxurious yachts moored; you can also ride in an authentic 36-foot-long Venetian gondola. Pier 5 extends to a fisherman's wharf, where you can buy fresh seafood or sign on for a deep-sea or bay-fishing charter with any of 35 boats. Street performers entertain free throughout the day and evening, and live bands perform on the marina stage daily. *401 Biscayne Blvd., tel. 305/577–3344, for gondola rides 305/529–7178. Open Mon.–Sat. 10–10, Sun. noon–8; extended hours for restaurants and outdoor cafés.*

Just north of Bayside a twin-span bridge with five traffic lanes, completed in 1991, gives new access to the Port of Miami.

As Metromover rounds the curve between College/Bayside (20) (21) Station and **Edcom Station,** look northeast to see **Freedom Tow-**

er (600 Biscayne Blvd.), where the Cuban Refugee Center processed more than 500,000 Cubans who entered the United States to flee Fidel Castro's regime in the 1960s. Built in 1925 for the *Miami Daily News*, this imposing Spanish-baroque structure was inspired by the Giralda, an 800-year-old bell tower in Seville, Spain. After years in derelict condition, Freedom Tower was renovated in 1988 and opened for office use in 1990, though oddly, it has remained untenanted. To see it up close, walk north from Edcom Station to N.E. 6th Street, then 2 blocks east to Biscayne Boulevard.

A 2-block walk south from Edcom Station will bring you to the **U.S. Courthouse,** a handsome keystone building erected in 1931 as Miami's main post office. On the second-floor central courtroom is *Law Guides Florida Progress*, a huge depression-era mural by artist Denman Fink. *300 N.E. 1st Ave. Building open weekdays 8:30–5; during those hours, security guards will open courtroom on request. No cameras or tape recorders allowed in building.*

From **State Plaza/Arena Station,** walk two blocks north on N.W. 1st Avenue to the new **Miami Arena** (721 N.W. 1st Ave., tel. 305/530–4444), home of the Miami Heat, a National Basketball Association team. Other sports and entertainment events take place at the arena, which is also one block east of the Overtown Metrorail Station.

Just across the Miami River from downtown, a canyon of tall buildings lines **Brickell Avenue,** a southward extension of S.E. 2nd Avenue that begins in front of the Hyatt Regency Hotel (400 S.E. 2nd Ave.). For the best views, drive Brickell Avenue from north to south. You'll pass the largest concentration of international banking offices in the United States.

South of S.E. 15th Street several architecturally interesting condominiums rise between Brickell Avenue and Biscayne Bay. Israeli artist Yacov Agam painted the rainbow-hued exterior of **Villa Regina** (1581 Brickell Ave.). Arquitectonica, a nationally prominent architectural firm based in Miami, designed three of these buildings: **The Palace** (1541 Brickell Ave.), **The Imperial** (1627 Brickell Ave.), and **The Atlantis** (2025 Brickell Ave.).

At S.E. 25th Road, turn right, follow signs to **I–95,** and return to downtown Miami on one of the world's most scenic urban highways. Paralleling Brickell Avenue and soaring 75 feet above the Miami River, I–95 offers a superb view of the downtown skyline. At night, International Place is awash with light, and, on the adjoining Metrorail bridge, a neon rainbow glows—Rockne Krebs's 3,600-foot-long light sculpture, *The Miami Line*. Just beyond the river, take the Biscayne Boulevard exit back to S.E. 2nd Avenue in front of the Hyatt Regency Hotel.

Miami Beach

Numbers in the margin correspond to points of interest on the Miami Beach map.

Orientation Most visitors to the Greater Miami area don't realize that Miami and Miami Beach are separate cities. Miami, on the mainland, is south Florida's commercial hub. Miami Beach, on 17 islands offshore in Biscayne Bay, is sometimes considered America's Riviera, luring refugees from winter to its warm sunshine, sandy beaches, and graceful palms.

In 1912, what would become Miami Beach was little more than a sandspit in the bay. Then Carl Graham Fisher, a millionaire promoter who built the Indianapolis Speedway, began to pour much of his fortune into developing the island city.

Ever since, Miami Beach has experienced successive waves of boom and bust—thriving in the early 1920s and the years just after World War II, but also enduring the devastating 1926 hurricane, the Great Depression, travel restrictions during World War II, and an invasion of criminals released from Cuba during the 1980 Mariel boatlift.

Today, a renaissance is under way as Miami Beach revels in the architectural heritage of its mile-square Art Deco District. About 650 significant buildings in the district are listed on the National Register of Historic Places.

The term Art Deco describes the modern architecture that emerged in the 1920s and 1930s. Its forms are eclectic, drawn from nature (including birds, butterflies, and flowers); from ancient Aztec, Mayan, Babylonian, Chaldean, Egyptian, and Hebrew designs; and from the streamlined, aerodynamic shapes of modern transportation and industrial machinery. For detailed information on touring the Art Deco District, contact the Miami Design Preservation League (*see* Guided Tours, above).

Driving Tour of Miami Beach

In our exploration, we direct you from the mainland to Miami Beach and through a cross section of the Art Deco District and the elegant residential neighborhood surrounding the La Gorce Country Club.

From the mainland, cross the **MacArthur Causeway** (Rte. 41) to Miami Beach. To reach the causeway from downtown Miami, turn east off Biscayne Boulevard north of N.E. 11th Street. From I–95, turn east onto I–395. The eastbound Dolphin Expressway (Rte. 836) becomes I–395 east of the I–95 interchange. As you approach the MacArthur Causeway bridge across the Intracoastal Waterway, *The Miami Herald* building looms above Biscayne Bay on your left.

❶ Cross the bridge to **Watson Island,** created by dredging in 1931. To your right is **Chalk's International Airlines** seaplane base (Watson Island, tel. 305/371–8628), the oldest scheduled international air carrier; it was bought in 1991 by Atwood Enterprises. Chalk's added seaplane service to Key West in 1991, and future plans include service to Havana. To your left across the causeway drive is the **Japanese Garden,** which has stone lanterns, a rock garden, and an eight-ton, eight-foot-tall statue of Hotei, Japanese god of prosperity. Industrialist Kiyoshi Ichimura gave the one-acre garden to the City of Miami in 1961 as an expression of friendship.

East of Watson Island, the causeway leaves Miami and enters ❷ Miami Beach. On the left, you'll pass the bridge to **Palm** and ❸ **Hibiscus islands** and then the bridge to **Star Island.** Celebrities who have lived on these islands include Al Capone (93 Palm Ave., Palm Island), author Damon Runyon (271 Hibiscus Island), and actor Don Johnson (8 Star Island).

East of Star Island, the causeway mounts a high bridge. Look ❹ left to see an island with an obelisk, the **Flagler Memorial Mon-**

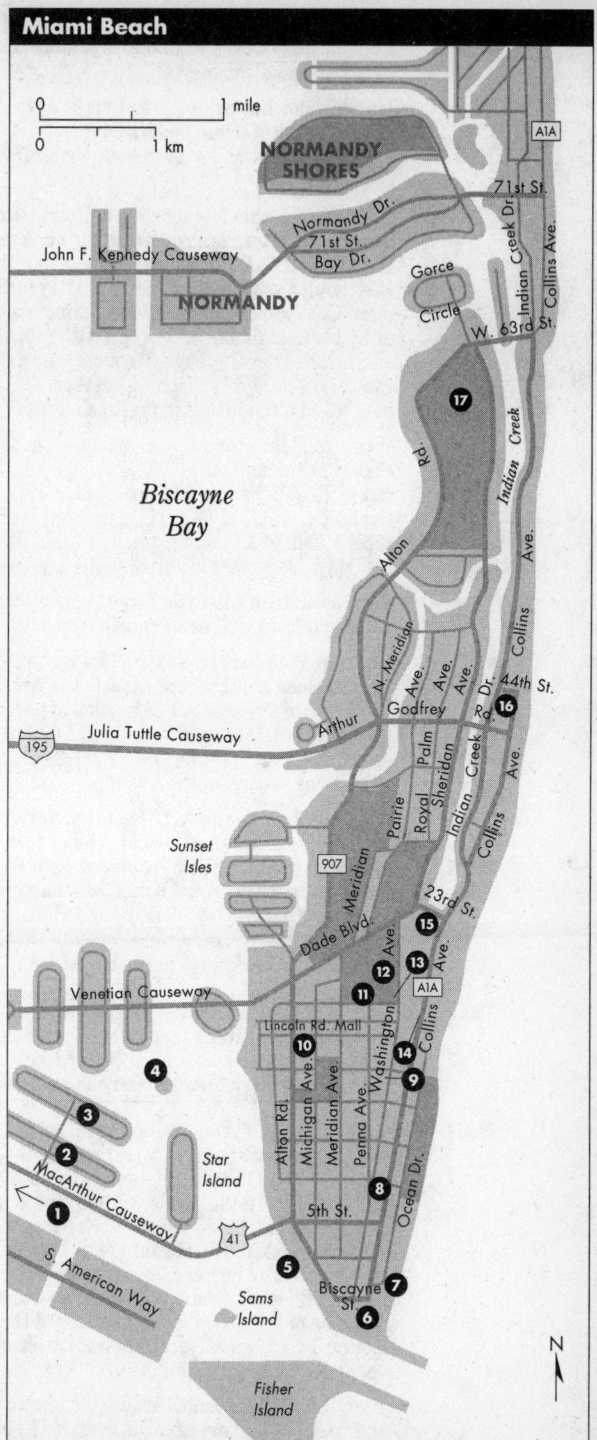
Miami Beach
0
1 mile
0
1 km
NORMANDY SHORES
NORMANDY
A1A
71st St.
Normandy Dr.
71st St.
Bay Dr.
John F. Kennedy Causeway
Gorce
Circle
W. 63rd St.
Indian Creek Dr.
Collins Ave.
Biscayne
Bay
Alton
Rd.
Indian Creek
Ave.
Collins
N. Meridian
Ave.
Ave.
Ave.
Dr.
44th St.
Godfrey
Rd.
Arthur
Julia Tuttle Causeway
195
Palm
Sheridan
Creek
Indian
Royal
Pairie
Ave.
Collins
Sunset
Isles
907
Meridian
23rd St.
Dade Blvd.
Ave.
Ave.
A1A
Venetian Causeway
Lincoln Rd. Mall
Washington
Collins
Alton Rd.
Michigan Ave.
Meridian Ave.
Penna Ave.
Star
Island
MacArthur Causeway
Ocean Dr.
5th St.
41
S. American Way
Sams
Island
Biscayne
St.
Fisher
Island
N

ument. The memorial honors Henry M. Flagler, who built the Florida East Coast Railroad to Miami, opening south Florida to tourism and commerce.

5 Just beyond the bridge, turn right onto Alton Road past the **Miami Beach Marina** (300 Alton Rd., tel. 305/673–6000), where dive boats depart for artificial reefs offshore in the Atlantic Ocean.

6 Continue to the foot of Alton Road, turn left on Biscayne Street, then go right at Washington Avenue to enter **South Pointe Park** (1 Washington Ave.). From the 50-yard Sunshine Pier, which adjoins the mile-long jetty at the mouth of Government Cut, you can fish while watching huge ships pass. No bait or tackle is available in the park. Other facilities include two observation towers, volleyball courts, and a Crawdaddy's Restaurant and Lounge (1 Washington Ave., tel. 305/673–1708) with inside and outside dining for lunch (dinner, inside only).

7 When you leave the park, continue right to the foot of Biscayne Street at Ocean Drive. The sea here offers the best surfing in Miami Beach. **Penrod's Beach Club and South Beach Raw Bar** (1 Ocean Dr., tel. 305/538–1117) is noted for its food, drink, game tables, volleyball courts, and late-night dancing, weekends to 5 AM; May–December, Thursday, Friday, and Saturday.

Turn around on Biscayne Street, going back the way you came, and go right on Collins Avenue.

8 Return to 5th Street, go a block east to Ocean Drive, and turn left. A block north at 6th Street, the **Art Deco District** begins. Take Ocean Drive north past a line of pastel-hued Art Deco hotels on your left and palm-fringed Lummus Park and the beach on your right. Turn left on 15th Street, and left again at the next corner onto Collins Avenue.

Now drive along the Art Deco District's two main commercial streets. Take Collins Avenue south, turn right at 5th Street, and right again at the next corner onto **Washington Avenue,** an interesting mixture of delicatessens, produce markets, and stores selling Jewish, Cuban, and Haitian religious books and artifacts. Most intriguing on the avenue is the eclectic **Botánica La Caridad** (651 Washington Ave., tel. 305/538–7961).

Time Out Turn right on 12th Street to **Muff'n Man** (234 12th St., tel. 305/538–6833). Multiberry, apple, and cinnamon-raisin muffins and brownies and cookies are baked here daily. The interior is filled with Deco District photos and silk pillows.

---

9 Back on Washington Avenue, go past 14th Street to **Espanola Way,** a narrow street of Mediterranean-revival buildings constructed in 1925 and frequented through the years by artists and writers. In the 1930s, Cuban bandleader Desi Arnaz performed in the Village Tavern, now part of the **Clay Hotel & AYH International Youth Hostel** (1438 Washington Ave., tel. 305/534–2988). The hostel caters to young visitors from all over the world who seek secure, inexpensive lodgings within walking distance of the beach. On both sides of the revived street a collection of imaginative clothing, jewelry, and art shops has opened.

Turn left onto Espanola Way, go 3 blocks to Meridian Avenue, and turn right. Three blocks north of Espanola Way is **Lincoln**

Road Mall, a landscaped shopping thoroughfare known during its heyday in the 1950s as "Fifth Avenue of the South." Trams shuttle shoppers along the mall, which is closed to all other vehicular traffic between Washington Avenue and Alton Road.

Park in the municipal lot ½-block north of the mall to stroll ❿ through the **Lincoln Road Arts District,** where 5 blocks of storefronts on Lincoln Road from Pennsylvania Avenue to Lenox Avenue have been transformed into galleries, studios, classrooms, and art-related boutiques and cafés.

The arts district also includes the 500-seat **Colony Theater** (1040 Lincoln Rd., tel. 305/674–1026), a former movie house. Now it's a city-owned performing arts center featuring dance, drama, music, and experimental cinema. At 541–545 Lincoln Road, the **New World Symphony,** a national advanced training orchestra, rehearses and performs in a classical Art Deco theater (tel. 305/673–3331).

From the parking lot, go to the first main street north of Lincoln Road Mall and turn right. You're on 17th Street, named **Hank Meyer Boulevard** for the local publicist who persuaded the late comedian Jackie Gleason to broadcast his TV show from Miami Beach in the 1950s. Two blocks east on your left, ⓫ beside the entrance to **Miami Beach City Hall** (1700 Convention Center Dr., tel. 305/673–7030), stands *Red Sea Road,* a huge red sculpture by Barbara Neijna.

⓬ Also to your left is the **Miami Beach Convention Center** (1901 Convention Center Dr., tel. 305/673–7311), doubled in size in 1988 to 1.1 million square feet of exhibit space.

Behind the Convention Center, at the northwest end of the parking lot near Meridian Avenue, is the **Holocaust Memorial** (1933–45 Meridian Ave., tel. 305/538–1663 or 305/538–1673), a monumental sculpture and graphic record in memory of the 6 million Jewish victims of the Holocaust. A garden conservatory (2000 Convention Center Dr., tel. 305/673–7256) next door is worth a visit but has limited public hours.

Continuing 2 more blocks east, you'll see another large sculp- ⓭ ture, *Mermaid,* by Roy Lichtenstein, in front of **Jackie Gleason Theater of the Performing Arts** (1700 Washington Ave., tel. 305/673–7300), where Gleason's TV show originated. Now the 3,000-seat theater hosts touring Broadway shows and classical music concerts. Near the sculpture, stars appearing in the theater since 1984 have left their footprints and signatures in concrete. This **Walk of the Stars** includes George Abbott, Julie Andrews, Leslie Caron, Carol Channing, and Edward Villella. For information about the Broadway show series, which each year presents five or six major productions (or other performances), contact the box office (505 17th St., tel. 305/673–8300) around the corner.

Return to Ocean Drive, turn right to the Leslie Hotel and the **Art Deco District Welcome Center** (1244 Ocean Dr., tel. 305/672–2014), open weekdays 10–6, Saturdays 10–5.

Go 1 block west to Collins Avenue, turn right (north) toward three of the largest Art Deco hotels, built in the 1940s with streamlined tower forms reflecting the 20th century's transportation revolution: The round dome atop the tower of the 11- ⓮ story **Hotel National** (1677 Collins Ave., tel. 305/532–2311) resembles a balloon. The tower at the 12-story **Delano Hotel** (1685

Collins Ave., tel. 305/538–7881) sports fins suggesting the wings of an airplane or a Buck Rogers spaceship. The 11-story **Ritz Plaza** (1701 Collins Ave., tel. 305/534–3500) rises to a cylindrical tower resembling a submarine periscope.

Turn left on Collins Avenue. At 21st Street, turn left beside the Miami Beach Public Library in Collins Park, go 2 blocks to Park 15 Avenue, and turn right. You're approaching the **Bass Museum of Art,** which houses a diverse collection of European art, including *The Holy Family*, a painting by Peter Paul Rubens; *The Tournament*, a 16th-century Flemish tapestry; and works by Albrecht Dürer and Henri de Toulouse-Lautrec. Park behind the museum and walk around to the entrance past massive tropical baobab trees. *2121 Park Ave., tel. 305/673–7530. Admission: $2 adults, $1 students with ID, children 16 and under free. Some exhibitions may be more expensive. Donations Tues. Open Tues.–Sat. 10–5, Sun. 1–5.*

Return on 21st Street or 22nd Street to Collins Avenue and turn left. As you drive north, a triumphal archway looms ahead, framing a majestic white building set in lush vegetation beside a waterfall and tropical lagoon. This vista is an illusion—a 13,000-square-foot outdoor mural on an exterior wall of 16 the **Fontainebleau Hilton Resort and Spa** (4441 Collins Ave., tel. 305/538–2000). Artist Richard Haas designed the mural to illustrate how the hotel and its rock-grotto swimming pool would look behind the wall. Locals call the 1,206-room hotel "Big Blue." It's the giant of Miami Beach, with 190,000 square feet of meeting and exhibit space.

Go left on 65th Street, turn left again at the next corner onto Indian Creek Drive, and right at 63rd Street, which leads into Alton Road, a winding, landscaped boulevard of gracious 17 homes styled along Art Deco lines. You'll pass the **La Gorce Country Club** (5685 Alton Rd., tel. 305/866–4421), which developer Carl Fisher built and named for his friend Oliver La Gorce, then president of the National Geographic Society.

To return to the mainland on the MacArthur Causeway, stay on Alton Road south to 5th Street, then turn right.

Little Havana

Numbers in the margin correspond to points of interest on the Miami, Coral Gables, and Key Biscayne map.

Orientation More than thirty years ago, the tidal wave of Cubans fleeing the Castro regime flooded an older neighborhood just west of downtown Miami with refugees. This area became known as Little Havana. Today, with a half-million Cubans widely dispersed throughout Greater Miami, Little Havana remains a magnet for Cubans and Anglos alike. They come to experience the flavor of traditional Cuban culture.

That culture, of course, functions in Spanish. Many Little Havana residents and shopkeepers speak almost no English. If you don't speak Spanish, point and smile to communicate.

Touring Little Havana Begin this tour in downtown Miami, westbound on Flagler Street. Cross the Miami River to Little Havana, and park near Flagler Street and Ronald Reagan Avenue (S.W. 12th Ave.) to explore a thriving commercial district.

❶ Continue west on Flagler Street to Teddy Roosevelt Avenue (S.W. 17th Ave.) and pause at **Plaza de la Cubanidad,** on the southwest corner. Redbrick sidewalks surround a fountain and monument with a quotation from José Martí, a leader in Cuba's struggle for independence from Spain: "*Las palmas son novias que esperan.*" (The palm trees are girlfriends who will wait.)

❷ Turn left at Douglas Road (S.W. 37th Ave.), drive south to **Calle Ocho** (S.W. 8th St.), and turn left again. You are now on the main commercial thoroughfare of Little Havana.

Time Out For a total sensory experience, have a snack or meal at **Versailles,** a popular Cuban restaurant. Etched-glass mirrors lining its walls amplify bright lights, and there's the roar of rapid-fire Spanish. Most of the servers don't speak English; you order by pointing to a number on the menu (choice of English or Spanish menus). Specialties include *palomilla,* a flat beefsteak; *ropa vieja* (literally, old clothes), a shredded-beef dish in tomato sauce; and *arroz con pollo,* chicken and yellow rice. *3555 S.W. 8th St., tel. 305/445–7614. AE, DC, MC, V. Open Sun.–Thurs. 8 AM–2 AM, Fri. 8 AM–3:30 AM, Sat. 8 AM–4:30 AM.*

East of Unity Boulevard (S.W. 27th Ave.), Calle Ocho becomes a one-way street eastbound through the heart of Little Havana, where every block deserves exploration. If your time is limited, we suggest the 3-block stretch from S.W. 14th Avenue to S.W. 11th Avenue. Parking is more ample west of Ronald Reagan Avenue (S.W. 12th Ave.).

❸ At Calle Ocho and Memorial Boulevard (S.W. 13th Ave.) stands the **Brigade 2506 Memorial,** commemorating the victims of the unsuccessful 1961 Bay of Pigs invasion of Cuba by an exile force. An eternal flame burns atop a simple stone monument with the inscription: "*Cuba—A Los Martires de La Brigada de Asalto Abril 17 de 1961.*" The monument also bears a shield with the Brigade 2506 emblem, a Cuban flag superimposed on a cross. Walk a block south on Memorial Boulevard from the Brigade 2506 Memorial to see other monuments relevant to Cuban history, including a statue of José Martí.

❹ When you return to your car, drive 5 blocks south on Ronald Reagan Avenue to the **Cuban Museum of Art and Culture.** Created by Cuban exiles to preserve and interpret the cultural heritage of their homeland, the museum has expanded its focus to embrace the entire Hispanic art community. In 1989, some artists who had previously exhibited in Havana were invited to show here. Because of political conditions concerning U.S./Cuba relations, this event has caused controversy for the museum. Albeit controversial, the museum survives and mounts temporary exhibitions and shows works from its small permanent collection. *1300 S.W. 12th Ave., tel. 305/858–8006. Donation requested. Open Wed.–Sun. 1–5.*

To return to downtown Miami, take Ronald Reagan Avenue back north to S.W. 8th Street, turn right, go east to Miami Avenue or Brickell Avenue, turn left, and go north across the Miami River.

Coral Gables/Coconut Grove/South Miami

Orientation This tour directs you through three separate communities, each unique in character. Two of them, Coral Gables and South

Miami, Coral Gables, and Key Biscayne

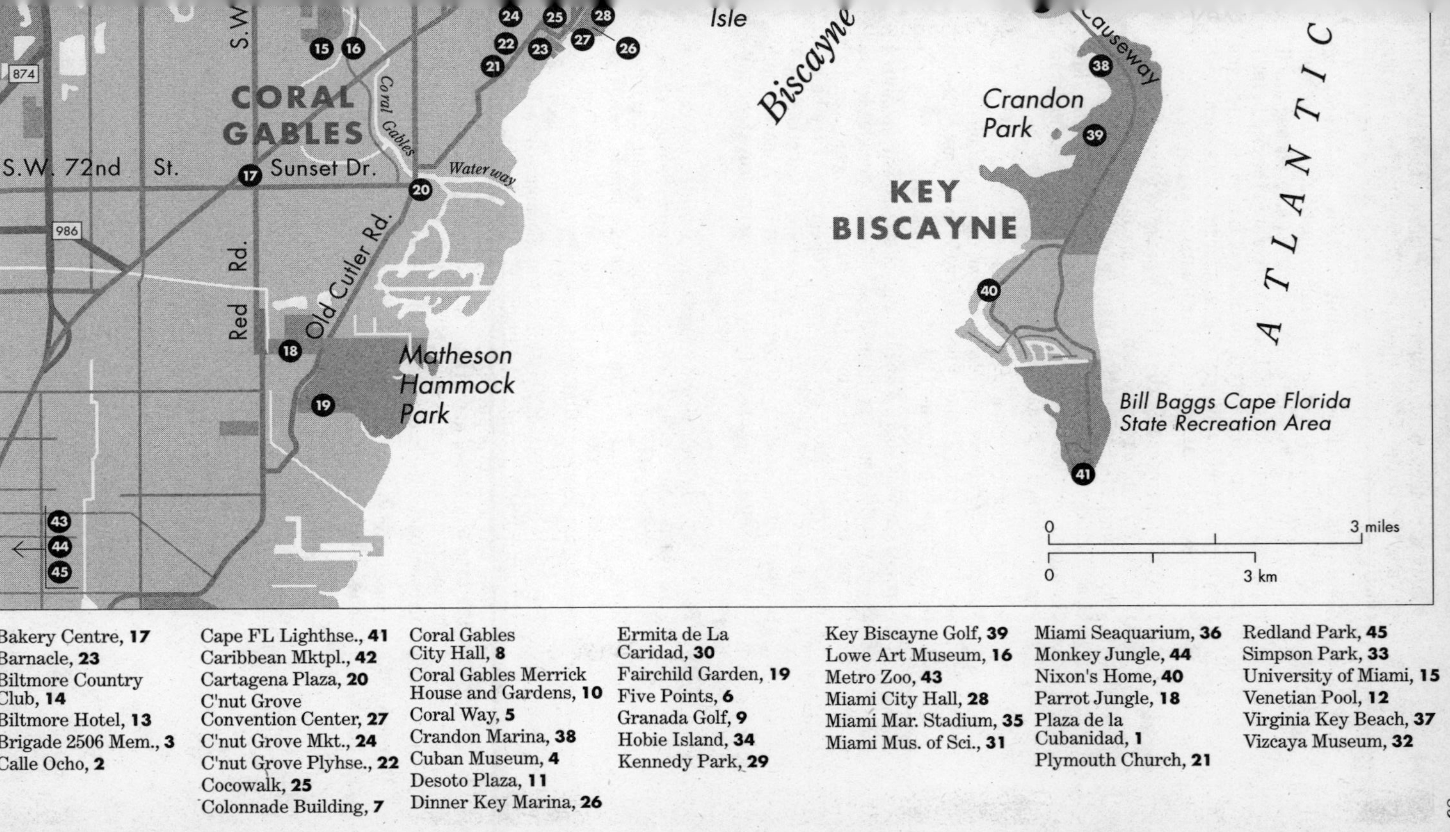

Bakery Centre, **17**
Barnacle, **23**
Biltmore Country Club, **14**
Biltmore Hotel, **13**
Brigade 2506 Mem., **3**
Calle Ocho, **2**
Cape FL Lighthse., **41**
Caribbean Mktpl., **42**
Cartagena Plaza, **20**
C'nut Grove Convention Center, **27**
C'nut Grove Mkt., **24**
C'nut Grove Plyhse., **22**
Cocowalk, **25**
Colonnade Building, **7**
Coral Gables City Hall, **8**
Coral Gables Merrick House and Gardens, **10**
Coral Way, **5**
Crandon Marina, **38**
Cuban Museum, **4**
Desoto Plaza, **11**
Dinner Key Marina, **26**
Ermita de La Caridad, **30**
Fairchild Garden, **19**
Five Points, **6**
Granada Golf, **9**
Hobie Island, **34**
Kennedy Park, **29**
Key Biscayne Golf, **39**
Lowe Art Museum, **16**
Metro Zoo, **43**
Miami City Hall, **28**
Miami Mar. Stadium, **35**
Miami Mus. of Sci., **31**
Miami Seaquarium, **36**
Monkey Jungle, **44**
Nixon's Home, **40**
Parrot Jungle, **18**
Plaza de la Cubanidad, **1**
Plymouth Church, **21**
Redland Park, **45**
Simpson Park, **33**
University of Miami, **15**
Venetian Pool, **12**
Virginia Key Beach, **37**
Vizcaya Museum, **32**

Miami, are independent suburbs. The third, Coconut Grove, was annexed to the City of Miami in 1925 but still retains a distinctive personality.

Coral Gables, a planned community of broad boulevards and Spanish Mediterranean architecture, justifiably calls itself "The City Beautiful." Developer George E. Merrick began selling Coral Gables lots in 1921 and incorporated the city in 1925. He named most of the streets for Spanish explorers, cities, and provinces. Street names are at ground level beside each intersection on whitewashed concrete cornerstones.

The 1926 hurricane and the Great Depression prevented Merrick from fulfilling many aspects of his plan. The city languished until after World War II but then grew rapidly. Today, Coral Gables has a population of about 41,000. In its bustling downtown, more than 100 multinational companies maintain headquarters or regional offices.

A pioneer farming community that grew into a suburb, **South Miami** today retains small-town charm, despite a failed, oversized shopping mall called The Bakery Centre, constructed on the former site of Holsum Bakery.

Coconut Grove is south Florida's oldest settlement, inhabited as early as 1834 and established by 1873, two decades before Miami. Its early settlers included Bahamian blacks, "conchs" from Key West, and New England intellectuals. They built a community that attracted artists, writers, and scientists to establish winter homes. By the end of World War I, more people listed in *Who's Who* gave addresses in Coconut Grove than anyplace else.

To this day, Coconut Grove reflects the pioneers' eclectic origins. Posh estates mingle with rustic cottages, modest frame homes, and starkly modern dwellings—often on the same block. To keep Coconut Grove a village in a jungle, residents lavish affection on exotic plantings while battling to protect remaining native vegetation.

The historic center of the Village of Coconut Grove went through a hippie period in the 1960s, laid-back funkiness in the 1970s, and a teenybopper invasion in the early 1980s. Today, the tone is upscale, and urban, with a mix of galleries, boutiques, restaurants, and bars and sidewalk cafés. On the weekends it's particularly trendy and congested.

Driving Tour

This tour begins in downtown Miami. Go south on S.E. 2nd Avenue, which becomes Brickell Avenue and crosses the Miami River. Half a mile south of the river, turn right onto **Coral Way,** (5) which at this point is S.W. 13th Street. Within ½ mile, Coral Way doglegs left under I–95 and becomes S.W. 3rd Avenue. It continues another mile to a complex intersection, **Five Points,** (6) and doglegs right to become S.W. 22nd Avenue.

Along the S.W. 3rd Avenue and S.W. 22nd Avenue segments of Coral Way, banyan trees planted in the median strip in 1929 arch over the roadway. The banyans end at the Miami/Coral Gables boundary, where **Miracle Mile** begins. This 4-block stretch of Coral Way, from Douglas Road (37th Ave.) to Le Jeune Road (42nd Ave.) in the heart of downtown Coral Gables, is really ½-mile long. To stroll the full mile, walk up one side and down the other. Miracle Mile's 160 shops range from chain restaurants and shoe stores to posh boutiques and beauty salons. The stores are numbered from 1 to 399. As you go west, numbers and quality both increase. Request a complete directory from the Miracle Mile Association (220 Miracle Mile, Suite 218, Coral Gables 33134, tel. 305/445-0591).

7 **The Colonnade Building** (133-169 Miracle Mile, Coral Gables) on Miracle Mile once housed George Merrick's sales office. Its rotunda bears an ornamental frieze and a Spanish-tile roof 75 feet above street level. The Colonnade Building has been restored and connected to the new 13-story Colonnade Hotel and an office building that echoes the rotunda's roofline.

The ornate Spanish Renaissance structure facing Miracle Mile 8 just west of Le Jeune Road is **Coral Gables City Hall,** opened in 1928. It has a three-tier tower topped with a clock and a 500-pound bell. Inside the domed ceiling, a mural by artist Denman Fink depicting the four seasons can be seen from the second floor. *405 Biltmore Way, Coral Gables, tel. 305/446-6800. Open weekdays 7:30-5.*

Proceed west to the corner of Segovia Avenue, turn right, then 9 left onto Coral Way. You'll pass the **Granada Golf Course** (2001 Granada Blvd., Coral Gables, tel. 305/460-5367), one of two public courses in the midst of the largest historic district of Coral Gables.

One block west of the golf course, turn right on Toledo Street to 10 park behind **Coral Gables Merrick House and Gardens,** George Merrick's boyhood home. The city acquired the dwelling in 1976 and restored it to its 1920s appearance. It contains Merrick family furnishings and artifacts. *907 Coral Way, Coral Gables, tel. 305/460-5361. Admission: $2 adults, $1 children. Open Sun. and Wed. 1-4.*

Return to Coral Way, turn right, then left at the first stoplight. Now you're southbound on Granada Boulevard, approaching 11 **DeSoto Plaza and Fountain,** a classical column on a pedestal with water flowing from the mouths of four sculpted faces. The closed eyes of the face looking west symbolize the day's end. Denman Fink designed the fountain in the early 1920s.

Follow the traffic circle almost completely around the fountain to northeast-bound DeSoto Boulevard. On your right in the 12 next block is **Venetian Pool,** a unique municipal swimming pool transformed from a rock quarry. *2701 DeSoto Blvd., Coral Gables, tel. 305/460-5356. Admission (nonresident): $4 adults, $3.50 teens, $1.60 children under 12. Free parking across DeSoto Blvd. Summer hours: weekdays 11-7:30, weekends 10-4:30; winter hours: Tues.-Fri. 11-4:30, weekends 10-4:30.*

From the pool, go around the block with right turns onto Almeria Avenue, Toledo Street, and Sevilla Avenue. You'll return to the DeSoto Fountain and take DeSoto Boulevard southeast to 13 emerge in front of **The Biltmore Hotel** (1200 Anastasia Ave., Coral Gables, tel. 305/445-1926). Like the Freedom Tower in downtown Miami, the Biltmore's 26-story tower is a replica of the Giralda Tower in Seville, Spain. Unfortunately, after extensive renovations the hotel closed and plans for its future are still unclear. However, open to the public is the Biltmore Golf Course, known for its scenic and competitive layout, and for having the largest hotel pool in the United States, with a capacity of 1.25 million gallons. In 1992 a $1.4-million renovation restored the course to its original Donald Ross design.

Just west of The Biltmore Hotel stands a separate building, ⑭ **The Biltmore Country Club,** which the city restored in the late 1970s. It's a richly ornamented Beaux Arts–style structure with a superb colonnade and courtyard. On its ground floor are facilities for golfers. In the former club lounge, meeting rooms include one lofty space paneled with veneer from 60 species of trees. In 1989 the structure was reincorporated into The Biltmore Hotel, of which it was an original part.

From the hotel, turn right on Anastasia Avenue, go east to Granada Boulevard, and turn right. Continue south on Granada Boulevard over a bridge across the **Coral Gables Waterway,** which connects the grounds of The Biltmore Hotel with Biscayne Bay. In the hotel's heyday, Venetian gondolas plied the waterway, bringing guests to a bayside beach.

At Ponce de León Boulevard, turn right. On your left is Metrorail's Stonehenge-like concrete structure, and on your ⑮ right, the **University of Miami**'s 260-acre main campus. With about 13,000 full-time, part-time, and noncredit students, UM is the largest private research university in the Southeast.

Turn right at the first stoplight to enter the campus and park in ⑯ the lot on your right designated for visitors to UM's **Lowe Art Museum.** The Lowe's permanent collection of 8,000 works includes Renaissance and Baroque art, American paintings, Latin American art, and Navajo and Pueblo Indian textiles and baskets. The museum also hosts traveling exhibitions. *1301 Stanford Dr., Coral Gables, tel. 305/284–3535 for recorded information, 305/284–3536 for museum office. Admission: $4 adults, $3 senior citizens, $2 students, children under 6 free. Open Sun. 12–5, Tues.–Sat. 10–5.*

Now exit the UM campus on Stanford Drive, pass under Metrorail, and cross Dixie Highway. Just beyond the Burger King on your right, bear right onto Maynada Street. Turn right at the next stoplight onto **Sunset Drive.** Fine old homes and mature trees line this officially designated "historic and scenic road" that leads to and through downtown South Miami.

On the northwest corner of Sunset Drive and Red Road (57th Ave.), note the pink building with a mural in which an alligator seems ready to devour a horrified man. This trompe l'oeil fantasy, *South Florida Cascade,* by illusionary artist Richard Haas, ⑰ highlights the main entrance to **The Bakery Centre** (5701 Sunset Dr., South Miami, tel. 305/662–4155).

On the third level of The Bakery Centre, the **Miami Youth Museum** features cultural arts exhibits, hands-on displays, and activities to enhance a child's creativity and inspire interest in artistic careers. At press time there is talk that the museum may move to another location. Call ahead. *5701 Sunset Dr., S. Miami, tel. 305/661–ARTS. Admission: $3 adults, senior citizens and children under 1 free. Open weekdays 10–5, weekends 11–5; closed holidays.*

Go south on Red Road and turn right just before Killian Drive ⑱ (S.W. 112th St.) into the grounds of **Parrot Jungle,** where more than 1,100 exotic birds are on display. Many of the parrots, macaws, and cockatoos fly free, but they'll come to you for seeds, which you can purchase from old-fashioned gumball machines. Attend a trained-bird show, watch baby birds in training, and pose for photos with colorful macaws perched on your arms.

The "jungle" is a natural hammock surrounding a sinkhole. Stroll among orchids and other flowering plants nestled among ferns, bald-cypress trees, and massive live oaks. Other highlights include a primate show, small-wildlife shows, a children's playground, and a petting zoo. Also see the cactus garden and Flamingo Lake, with a breeding population of 75 Caribbean flamingos. Opened in 1936, Parrot Jungle is one of Greater Miami's oldest and most popular commercial tourist attractions. *11000 S.W. 57th Ave., Miami, tel. 305/666–7834. Admission: $10.50 adults, $6 children 3–12. Open daily 9:30–6. Café opens 8 AM.*

From Parrot Jungle, take Red Road ⅓ mile south and turn left at Old Cutler Road, which curves north along the uplands of south Florida's coastal ridge. Visit 83-acre **Fairchild Tropical Garden,** the largest tropical botanical garden in the continental United States. *10901 Old Cutler Rd., Coral Gables, tel. 305/667–1651. Admission: $5 adults, children under 13 free with parents. Hourly tram rides, $1 adults; 50¢ children under 13. Open daily except Christmas 9:30–4:30.*

North of the garden, Old Cutler Road traverses Dade County's oldest and most scenic park, **Matheson Hammock Park.** The Civilian Conservation Corps developed the 100-acre tract of upland and mangrove swamp in the 1930s on land donated by a local pioneer, Commodore J. W. Matheson. The park's most popular feature is a bathing beach, where the tide flushes a saltwater "atoll" pool through four gates. *9610 Old Cutler Rd., Coral Gables, tel. 305/666–6979. Parking fee for beach and marina $3 per car, $5 per car with trailer. Limited upland parking free. Park open 6 AM–sundown. Pool lifeguards on duty winter 8:30 AM–6 PM, summer 7:30 AM–7 PM.*

Continue north on Old Cutler Road to **Cartagena Plaza,** cross the Le Jeune Road bridge over the waterway, and turn right at the first stoplight onto Ingraham Highway. Four blocks later, you're back in the City of Miami, at the south end of Coconut Grove. Follow Ingraham Highway to Douglas Road and turn right at the next stoplight onto Main Highway. You're following old pioneer trails that today remain narrow roads shaded by a canopy of towering trees.

One block past the stoplight at Royal Palm Avenue, turn left onto Devon Road in front of **Plymouth Congregational Church.** Opened in 1917, this handsome coral-rock structure resembles a Mexican mission church. The front door, of hand-carved walnut and oak with original wrought-iron fittings, came from an early-17th-century monastery in the Pyrenees. *3400 Devon Rd., Coconut Grove, tel. 305/444–6521. Ask at the office to go inside the church, weekdays 9–4:30. Service Sun. 10 AM.*

When you leave the church, go around the block opposite the church. Turn left from Devon Road onto Hibiscus Street, left again onto Royal Palm Avenue, and left at the stoplight onto Main Highway.

You're now headed for the historic **Village of Coconut Grove,** a trendy commercial district with redbrick sidewalks and more than 300 restaurants, stores, and art galleries.

Parking can be a problem in the village—especially on weekend evenings, when police direct traffic and prohibit turns at some intersections to prevent gridlock. Be prepared to walk several blocks from the periphery into the heart of the Grove.

22 As you enter the village center, note the apricot-hued Spanish rococo **Coconut Grove Playhouse** to your left. Built in 1926 as a movie theater, it became a legitimate theater in 1956 and is now owned by the State of Florida. The playhouse presents Broadway-bound plays and musical revues and experimental productions in its 1,100-seat main theater and 100-seat cabaret-style Encore Room. *3500 Main Hwy., Coconut Grove, tel. 305/442-4000, box office; tel. 305/442-2662, administrative office. Parking lot: $2 daytime; $4 evenings.*

23 Benches and a shelter opposite the playhouse mark the entrance to **The Barnacle,** a pioneer residence that is now a state historic site. Commodore Ralph Munroe built The Barnacle in 1891. Its broad, sloping roof and deeply recessed verandas channel sea breezes into the house. A central stairwell and rooftop vent allow hot air to escape. Many furnishings are original. While living at the Barnacle, Munroe built shoal-draft sailboats. One such craft, the ketch *Micco,* is on display. *3485 Main Hwy., Coconut Grove, tel. 305/448-9445. Admission: $2. Reservations required for groups of 8 or more; others meet ranger on porch of Barnacle house. Open Thurs.–Mon. 9–4; tours 10, 11:30, 1, and 2:30; closed Tues. and Wed.*

Time Out Turn left at the next street, Commodore Plaza, and pause. Cafés at both corners overflow the brick sidewalks. Try the **Green Streets Cafe** on the south side; this French gourmet café features—among other fare—16 kinds of muffins and a superb Greek-style salad bulging with brine-soaked olives and feta cheese. *3110 Commodore Plaza, Coconut Grove, tel. 305/444-0244. Inside and outdoor service and carryouts available. MC, V. Open 6:30–3.*

---

24 If your timing is right, visit the **Coconut Grove Farmers Market,** a laid-back, Brigadoon-like happening that appears as if by magic each Saturday on a vacant lot. To get there from Commodore Plaza, go north to Grand Avenue, cross McDonald Avenue (S.W. 32nd Ave.), and go a block west to Margaret Street. Vendors set up outdoor stands to offer home-grown tropical fruits and vegetables (including organic produce); honey, seafoods, macrobiotic foods; and ethnic fare from the Caribbean, the Middle East, and Southeast Asia. Nonfood items for sale include plants, handicrafts, candles, jewelry, and homemade clothing. A masseur plies his trade, musicians play, and the Hare Krishnas come to chant. People-watching is half the fun. *Open Sat. 8–3.*

25 Now return to the village center. On your left is **Cocowalk,** a multilevel open mall of Mediterranean-style brick courtyards and terraces overflowing with people. Opened early in 1991, Cocowalk has revitalized Coconut Grove's nightlife. The mix of shops, restaurants, and theaters has renewed the Grove by creating a new circuit for promenading between these attractions and the historic heart of the Grove along Commodore Plaza. The area now teems with Manhattan-like crowds, especially on weekend evenings. Across Virginia Street is **Mayfair,** an artistic but aloof mall originally built for the extravagant, free-spending South Americans who no longer come.

Leaving the village center, take McFarlane Road east from its intersection with Grand Avenue and Main Highway. Peacock Park, site of the first hotel in southeast Florida, is on your right. Ahead, seabirds soar and sailboats ride at anchor in 26 **Dinner Key Marina** (3400 Pan American Dr., Coconut Grove, tel. 305/579–6980), named for a small island where early settlers held picnics. With 580 moorings at eight piers, all renovated in 1990, it's Greater Miami's largest marina.

McFarlane Road turns left onto South Bayshore Drive. Turn right at the first stoplight onto Unity Boulevard (S.W. 27th Ave.), and go east into a parking lot that serves the marina and 27 the 105,000-square-foot **Coconut Grove Convention Center** (2700 S. Bayshore Dr., Coconut Grove, tel. 305/579–3310), where antique, boat, and home-furnishings shows are held.

28 At the northeast corner of the lot is **Miami City Hall,** which was built in 1934 as the terminal for the Pan American Airways seaplane base at Dinner Key. The building retains its nautical-style art deco trim. *3500 Pan American Dr., Coconut Grove, tel. 305/250–5400. Open weekdays 8–5.*

From City Hall, drive west on Pan American Drive toward South Bayshore Drive, with its pyramidlike Grand Bay Hotel. Turn right on South Bayshore Drive, and go north past 29 **Kennedy Park.** Leave your car in the park's lot north of Kirk Street and walk toward the water. From a footbridge over the mouth of a small tidal creek, you'll enjoy an unobstructed view across Biscayne Bay to Key Biscayne. Film crews use the park often to make commercials and Italian westerns.

From South Bayshore Drive, turn right, and go north past the entrance to Mercy Hospital, where South Bayshore Drive becomes South Miami Avenue. At the next stoplight beyond the hospital, turn right on a private road that goes past St. 30 Kieran's Church to **Ermita de La Caridad**—Our Lady of Charity Shrine—a conical building 90 feet high and 80 feet wide overlooking the bay so worshipers face toward Cuba. A mural above the shrine's altar depicts Cuba's history. *3609 S. Miami Ave., Coconut Grove, tel. 305/854–2405. Open daily 9–9.*

Return to South Miami Avenue, turn right, go about 3/10 of a 31 mile, and turn left to the **Miami Museum of Science and Space Transit Planetarium,** where in 1991 the museum added 3,200 square feet of new exhibition spaces, new classrooms, 90 more parking spaces, and a new Mediterranean facade. This is a participatory museum, chock-full of sound, gravity, and electricity displays for children and adults alike to manipulate and marvel at. A wildlife center houses native Florida snakes, turtles and tortoises, birds of prey, and large wading birds. *3280 S. Miami Ave., Miami, tel. 305/854–4247; 24-hour Cosmic Hotline for planetarium show times and prices, 305/854–2222. Admission to museum: $6 adults, $4 children 3–12; to planetarium shows $5 adults, $2.50 children and senior citizens; to laser light shows $6 adults, $2.50 children and senior citizens. Open daily 10–6.*

32 Across South Miami Avenue is the entrance to **Vizcaya Museum and Gardens,** an estate with an Italian Renaissance–style villa built in 1912–16 as the winter residence of Chicago industrialist James Deering. The house and gardens overlook Biscayne Bay on a 30-acre tract that includes a native hammock and more than 10 acres of formal gardens and fountains. You

can leave your car in the Museum of Science lot and walk across the street or drive across and park in Vizcaya's own lot.

The house contains a total of 70 rooms, with 34 rooms of antique furniture, paintings, sculpture, and other decorative arts, open to the public. These objects date from the 15th through the 19th centuries, representing the Renaissance, Baroque, Rococo, and Neoclassic styles. *3251 S. Miami Ave., Miami, tel. 305/579–2813. Admission: $8 adults, $4 children 6–12. Guided 45-min tours available, group tours by appointment. House open 9:30–4:30; ticket booth open until 4:30, garden until 5:30. Closed Christmas.*

As you leave Vizcaya, turn north (left from the Museum of Science lot, right from the Vizcaya lot) onto South Miami Avenue. (33) Continue to 17th Road and turn left to **Simpson Park.** Enjoy a fragment of the dense tropical jungle—large gumbo-limbo trees, marlberry, banyans, and black calabash—that once covered the entire five miles from downtown Miami to Coconut Grove. You'll get a rare glimpse of how things were before the high-rises towered. Avoid the park during summer when mosquitoes whine as incessantly today as they did 100 years ago. You may follow South Miami Avenue the rest of the way downtown or go back two stoplights and turn left to the entrance to the Rickenbacker Causeway and Key Biscayne.

Virginia Key and Key Biscayne

Government Cut and the Port of Miami separate the dense urban fabric of Miami Beach from Greater Miami's playground islands, Virginia Key, and Key Biscayne. Parks occupy much of both keys, providing congenial upland with facilities for basking on the beach, golf, tennis, softball, and picnicking—plus uninviting but ecologically valuable stretches of dense mangrove swamp. Also on the keys are several marinas, an assortment of water-oriented tourist attractions, and the no longer laid-back village where Richard Nixon set up his presidential vacation compound. In 1991, residents of Key Biscayne voted to incorporate their island as Dade County's 28th municipality.

Driving Tour

To reach Virginia Key and Key Biscayne, take the **Rickenbacker Causeway** across Biscayne Bay from the mainland at Brickell Avenue and S.W. 26th Road, about 2 miles south of downtown Miami. A fitness pathway for biking and jogging parallels the causeway. In 1990 a new bike lane was added in each direction of the causeway from the new high bridge to the village of Key Biscayne. An older and somewhat uprooted path still meanders as a scenic alternative through pine forests and marsh, and here and there through parking lots. *Toll: $1 per car, bicycles and pedestrians free.*

About 200 feet east of the tollgate (just across the first low (34) bridge), you can rent windsurfing equipment on **Hobie Island.** *Sailboards Miami, Box 16, Key Biscayne 33149, tel. 305/361–SAIL. Cost: $17 per hour for 10 hours, $9.50 for each hour thereafter; $39 for a 2-hour windsurfing lesson. Open daily 9:30–dusk.*

The **Old Rickenbacker Causeway Bridge,** built in 1947, is now a fishing pier. The west stub begins about a mile from the tollgate. Park near its entrance and walk past fishermen tending their lines to the gap where the center draw span across the Intracoastal Waterway was removed. There you can watch boat traffic pass through the channel, pelicans and other seabirds soar and dive, and porpoises cavort in the bay.

The new high-level **William M. Powell Bridge** rises 75 feet above the water to eliminate the need for a draw span. The panoramic view from the top encompasses the bay, keys, port, and downtown skyscrapers, with Miami Beach and the Atlantic Ocean in the distance. The speed limit is 45 mph, and you can't stop on the bridge, so park in the fishing pier lot and walk up.

35 Next along the causeway stands the 6,536-seat **Miami Marine Stadium** (3601 Rickenbacker Causeway, Miami, tel. 305/361–6732), where summer pop concerts take place and name entertainers occasionally perform. You can join the audience on land in the stadium or on a boat anchored just offshore. Fourth of July concertgoers enjoy a spectacular fireworks display that is visible for miles up and down the bay.

36 Down the causeway from Marine Stadium at the **Miami Seaquarium,** Lolita, a killer whale, cavorts in a huge tank. She performs two or three times a day, as do sea lions and dolphins in separate shows. Exhibits include a shark pool, 235,000-gallon tropical reef aquarium, and manatees. *4400 Rickenbacker Causeway, Miami, tel. 305/361–5705; Admission: $16.95 adults, $13.95 senior citizens, $11.95 children 3–12. Open daily 9:30–6.*

37 Opposite the causeway from the Seaquarium, a road leads north to **Virginia Key Beach,** a City of Miami park, with a 2-mile stretch of oceanfront, shelters, barbecue grills, ball fields, nature trails, and a fishing area. Ask for directions at the entrance gate. *Cost: $2 per car.*

In 1992, a 400-acre portion on the west side of this mangrove-edged island was dedicated as the **Virginia Key Critical Wildlife Area.** Birds to be seen here include reddish egrets, black-bellied plovers, black skimmers, and roseate spoonbills—but only May through July. Undisturbed the other nine months, the area will be more amenable to migratory shorebirds.

38 From Virginia Key, the causeway crosses **Bear Cut** to the north end of Key Biscayne, where it becomes Crandon Boulevard. The **Crandon Park Marina,** behind Sundays on the Bay restaurant, sells bait and tackle. *4000 Crandon Blvd., Key Biscayne, tel. 305/361–1161. Open 7–5 weekdays, 7–6 weekends.*

Beyond the marina, Crandon Boulevard bisects 1,211-acre **Crandon Park.** Turnouts on your left lead to four parking lots, adjacent picnic areas, ball fields, and 3.3 miles of beach. *Parking: $2 per car. Open daily 8 AM–sunset.*

39 On your right are entrances to the **Key Biscayne Golf Course** and the **International Tennis Center,** where in 1992 a $16.5-million, 7,500-seat tennis stadium was being constructed in preparation for the March 1993 Lipton International Players Championships.

40 From the traffic circle at the south end of Crandon Park, Crandon Boulevard continues for two miles through the developed portion of Key Biscayne. You'll come back that way, but first detour to the site of **President Nixon's home** (485 W. Matheson Dr.). Turn right at the first stoplight onto Harbor

Drive, go about a mile, and turn right at Matheson Drive. A later owner enlarged and totally changed Nixon's home.

Emerging from West Matheson Drive, turn right onto Harbor Drive and go about a mile south to Mashta Drive; follow Mashta Drive east past Harbor Drive to Crandon Boulevard, and turn right.

You are approaching the entrance to **Bill Baggs Cape Florida State Recreation Area,** named for a crusading newspaper editor whose efforts prompted the state to create this 406-acre park. The park includes 1¼ miles of beach and a seawall along Biscayne Bay where anglers catch bonefish, grouper, jack, snapper, and snook. There is a nature trail with native plants now rare on Key Biscayne.

Also in the park is the oldest structure in south Florida, the (41) **Cape Florida Lighthouse,** erected in 1825 to help ships avoid the shallows and reefs offshore. In 1836 a band of Seminole Indians attacked the lighthouse and killed the keeper's helper. You can no longer climb the 122 steps to the top of the 95-foot-tall lighthouse because the structure awaits about $1 million in repairs—a sum that Dade Heritage Trust, the local preservation society, is endeavoring to raise. *1200 S. Crandon Blvd., Key Biscayne, tel. 305/361–5811. Admission to park: $3.25 per vehicle; to lighthouse and keeper's residence: $1 per person, under age 6 free. Park open all year 8–sunset. Lighthouse tours daily except Tues. at 1, 2:30, and 3:30.*

When you leave Cape Florida, follow Crandon Boulevard back to Crandon Park through Key Biscayne's commercial center, a mixture of posh shops and stores catering to the needs of the neighborhood. On your way back to the mainland, pause as you approach the Powell Bridge to admire the downtown Miami skyline. At night, the brightly lit International Place looks from this angle like a clipper ship running under full sail before the breeze.

Little Haiti

Of the more than 150,000 Haitians who have settled in Greater Miami, some 60,000 live in Little Haiti, a 200-block area on Miami's northeast side. More than 400 small Haitian businesses operate in Little Haiti.

For many Haitians, English is a third language. French is Haiti's official language, but much day-to-day conversation takes place in Creole, a French-based patois. Smiling and pointing will bridge any language barrier you may encounter.

This tour takes you through the Miami Design District on the margin of Little Haiti, then along two main thoroughfares that form the spine of the Haitian community. The tour begins in downtown Miami. Take Biscayne Boulevard north to N.E. 36th Street, turn left, go about 4⁄10 of a mile west to North Miami Avenue. Turn right, and go north through the **Miami Design District,** where about 225 wholesale stores, showrooms, and galleries feature interior furnishings and decorative arts.

Little Haiti begins immediately north of the Design District in an area with some of Miami's oldest dwellings, dating from the dawn of the 20th century through the 1920s land-boom era.

Drive the side streets to see elegant Mediterranean-style homes, and bungalows with distinctive coral-rock trim.

Return to North Miami Avenue and go north. A half-block east on 54th Street is the tiny storefront office of the **Haitian Refugee Center** (119 N.E. 54th St., tel. 305/757–8538), a focal point of activity in the Haitian community.

Continue north on North Miami Avenue past the former Cuban consulate, a pretentious Caribbean-Colonial mansion that is now the clinic of Haitian physician Lucien Albert (5811 N. Miami Ave., tel. 305/758–2700).

North of 85th Street, cross the Little River Canal into **El Portal,** a tiny suburban village of modest homes where more than a quarter of the property is now Haitian-owned. Turn right on N.E. 87th Street and right again on N.E. 2nd Avenue. You are now southbound on Little Haiti's main commercial street.

Time Out Stop for Haitian breads and cakes made with coconut and other tropical ingredients at **Baptiste Bakery.** *7488 N.E. 2nd Ave., tel. 305/756–1119. Open 7–7, sometimes later.*

Along N.E. 2nd Avenue between 79th Street and 45th Street, rows of storefronts in faded pastels reflect a first effort by area merchants to dress up their neighborhood and attract outsiders.

More successful—aesthetically, if not yet commercially—is (42) the **Caribbean Marketplace,** which the Haitian Task Force (an economic development organization) opened in 1990. Its 10 or so merchants sell handmade baskets, Caribbean art and craft items, books, videos, and ice cream. *Tel. 305/758–8708, 5927 N.E. 2nd Ave., Miami.*

This concludes the Little Haiti tour. To return to downtown Miami, take N.E. 2nd Avenue south to N.E. 35th Street, turn left, go east one block to Biscayne Boulevard, and turn right to go south.

South Dade

This tour directs you to major attractions in the suburbs southwest of Dade County's urban core. A Junior League book, *Historic South Dade,* locates and describes 40 historic structures and attractions in a South Dade County driving tour. You can contact the Junior League *(2325 Salzedo Dr., Coral Gables, tel. 305/443–0160)* for additional information.

From downtown Miami, take the Dolphin Expressway (Rte. 836) west to the Palmetto Expressway (Rte. 826) southbound. Bear left south of Bird Road (S.W. 40th St.) onto the Don Shula Expressway (Rte. 874). Exit westbound onto Killian Drive (S.W. 104th St.) and go west to Lindgren Road (S.W. 137th Ave.). Turn left and go south to S.W. 128th Street, the entrance to the Tamiami Airport and **Weeks Air Museum,** where aircraft on display include a World War I–vintage Sopwith Camel (of Snoopy fame), and a B–17 Flying Fortress bomber and P–51 Mustang from World War II. *14710 S.W. 128th St., tel. 305/233–5197. Admission: $5 adults, $4 seniors, $3 children 12 and under. Open daily 10–5.*

43 Continue south on Lindgren Road to Coral Reef Drive (S.W. 152nd St.). Turn left and go east to **Metro Zoo** and the **Gold Coast Railroad Museum.**

Metro Zoo covers 290 acres and is cageless; animals roam free on islands surrounded by moats. In "Wings of Asia," a 1.5-acre aviary, hundreds of exotic birds from southeast Asia fly through a rain forest beneath a protective net enclosure. The zoo has 3 miles of walkways, a monorail with four stations, and an open-air amphitheater for concerts. Paws, a petting zoo for children, opened in 1989 and features three shows daily. *12400 Coral Reef Dr. (S.W. 152nd St.), tel. 305/251–0400 for recorded information; 305/251–0401 for other information. Admission: $8.79 adults, $4.53 children 3–12. Admission for Florida residents with proof of citizenship (Mon.–Sat. 9:30–11 AM) $5.33 adults, $2.66 children. Admission includes monorail tickets. AE, MC, V. No credit cards at snack bar. Gates open daily 9:30–4. Park closes at 5:30.*

The railroad museum's collection includes a 1949 Silver Crescent dome car; and the *Ferdinand Magellan*, the only Pullman car ever constructed specifically for U.S. presidents, used by Roosevelt, Truman, Eisenhower, and Reagan. *12450 Coral Reef Dr. (S.W. 152nd St.), tel. 305/253–0063. Train rides weekends, holidays. Admission: weekdays $3 adults, $2 children; weekends $5/$3. Includes 20-min train ride. Open weekdays 10–3, weekends 10–5.*

Return to Coral Reef Drive, turn right (east) to the Homestead Extension of Florida's Turnpike, take the turnpike south, exit at Hainlin Mill Drive (S.W. 216th St.), and turn right. Cross South Dixie Highway (U.S. 1), go 3 miles west, and turn right 44 into **Monkey Jungle,** home to more than 400 monkeys representing 35 species—including orangutans from Borneo and Sumatra, golden lion tamarins from Brazil, and brown lemurs from Madagascar. Performing monkey shows begin at 10 AM and run continuously at 45-minute intervals. The walkways of this 30-acre attraction are caged; the monkeys roam free. *14805 Hainlin Mill Dr. (S.W. 216 St.), tel. 305/235–1611. Admission: $9.85 adults, $8.85 senior citizens, $5.35 children 4–12. AE, D, MC, V. Open daily 9:30–5.*

Continue west on Hainlin Mill Drive to Krome Avenue (S.W. 177th Ave.). Cross Krome to Redland Road (S.W. 187th Ave.). Turn left to Coconut Palm Drive (S.W. 248th St.). You are at 45 the **Redland Fruit & Spice Park,** a Dade County treasure since 1944, when it was established as a 20-acre showcase of tropical fruits and vegetables. More than 500 varieties of exotic fruits, herbs, spices, and nuts from throughout the world grow here, including poisonous plants. There are 50 varieties of bananas, 40 varieties of grapes, and 100 varieties of citrus. A gourmet and fruit shop offers many varieties of tropical fruit products, jellies, seeds, aromatic teas, and reference books. *24801 S.W. 187th Ave. (Redland Rd.), tel. 305/247–5727. Admission: $1 adults, 50¢ children; fee for guided weekend tours (1 and 3 PM): park admission plus $1.50 adults, $1 children. MC, V. Open daily 10–5.*

Drive east on Coconut Palm Drive (S.W. 248th St.) to Newton Road (S.W. 157th Ave.). Turn right and go south to **Orchid Jungle,** where you can stroll under live-oak trees to see orchids, ferns, bromeliads, and anthuriums, and peer through the windows of an orchid-cloning laboratory. *26715 S.W. 157th Ave., Homestead, tel. 305/247-4824 or 800/344-2457. Admission: $5 adults, $4 senior citizens and children 13-17, $1.50 children 6-12. Open daily 8:30-5:30.*

Continue south on Newton Road to South Dixie Highway (U.S. 1), and turn left. Almost immediately, you'll find **Coral Castle of Florida** on your right. It was built by Edward Leedskalnin, a Latvian immigrant, between 1920 and 1940. The 3-acre castle has a 9-ton gate a child can open, an accurate working sundial, and a telescope of coral rock aimed at the North Star. *28655 South Dixie Hwy., Homestead, tel. 305/248-6344. Admission: $7.75 adults, $4.50 children 6-12. MC, V. Open daily 9-9.*

To return to downtown Miami after leaving Coral Castle, take South Dixie Highway to Biscayne Drive (S.W. 288th St.) and go east to the turnpike. Take the turnpike back to the Don Shula Expressway (Rte. 874), which leads to the Palmetto Expressway (Rte. 826), which leads in turn to the Dolphin Expressway (Rte. 836).

Miami for Free

Concerts **PACE** (Performing Arts for Community and Education, tel. 305/681-1470; 305/237-1718 for recorded information on upcoming events) supports free concerts in parks and cultural and religious institutions throughout the Greater Miami area.

University of Miami School of Music (1314 Miller Dr., tel. 305/284-6477) offers many free concerts at the Coral Gables campus.

Museums Some museums are free all the time. Others have donation days, when you may pay as much or as little as you wish.

Parks There are 28 national, state, and county parks in metro Miami with a variety of beaches, picnic shelters, barbecue grills, playgrounds, trails, athletic fields, and other facilities. Most are open free to the public. For a list and for information about hours of use, contact the **Greater Miami Convention & Visitors Bureau** (*see* Important Numbers and Addresses, above).

What to See and Do with Children

Greater Miami is a family-oriented vacation destination. Most of the major hotels can provide access to baby-sitting for young children.

American Police Hall of Fame and Museum. Here you can view more than 10,000 law enforcement-related items, including weapons, a jail cell, and an electric chair, as well as a 400-ton marble memorial listing the names of more than 3,000 police officers killed in the line of duty since 1960. *3801 Biscayne Blvd., tel. 305/891-1700. Open daily 10-5:30. Admission: $3 adults, $1.50 senior citizens and children 6-12.*

Ancient Spanish Monastery. This is the oldest building in the western hemisphere, dating from 1141 in Segovia, Spain. Newspaper magnate William Randolph Hearst had it removed in pieces and stored it in California for 25 years. In 1954 Miami developers rebuilt it at its present site. *16711 W. Dixie Hwy., N. Miami Beach, tel. 305/945-1461. Open Mon.-Sat. 10-5,*

Sun. noon–5. Admission: $4 adults, $2.50 senior citizens, $1.50 students (12–18), $1 children (7–12).

Ice Castle Skating Arena. This state-of-the-art ice skating arena includes a complete blade shop, skate rentals, snack bar, and video arcade. *255 N.E. 2nd Dr., Homestead, tel. 305/255–4144 (recording) or 305/245–2020. Reservations advised. Admission: $3.50–$7.50, depending on activity and time of day; skate rental $1.*

Shopping

Except in the heart of the Everglades, visitors to the Greater Miami area are never more than 15 minutes away from a major shopping area. Downtown Miami long ago ceased to be the community's central shopping hub. Today Dade County has more than a dozen major malls, an international free zone, and hundreds of miles of commercial streets lined with storefronts and small neighborhood shopping centers. Many of these local shopping areas have an ethnic flavor, catering primarily to one of Greater Miami's immigrant cultures.

In the Latin neighborhoods, children's stores sell *vestidos de fiesta* (party dresses) made of organza and lace. Men's stores sell the *guayabera*, a pleated, embroidered shirt that replaces the tie and jacket in much of the tropics. Traditional bridal shops display formal dresses that Latin families buy or rent for a daughter's *quince*, a lavish 15th-birthday celebration.

No standard store hours exist in Greater Miami. Phone ahead. When you shop, expect to pay Florida's 6% sales tax unless you have the store ship your goods out of Florida.

Shopping Districts

Fashion District

Greater Miami is the fashion marketplace for the southeastern United States, the Caribbean, and Latin America. Many of the 500 garment manufacturers in Miami and Hialeah sell their clothing locally, in more than 30 factory outlets and discount fashion stores in the Miami Fashion District, east of I-95 along 5th Avenue from 29th Street to 25th Street. Most stores in the district are open Monday–Saturday 9–5, and accept credit cards.

Miami Free Zone

The Miami Free Zone (MFZ) is an international wholesale trade center where the U.S. Customs Service supervises the exhibition and sales space. You can buy goods duty-free for export or pay duty on goods released for domestic use. More than 140 companies sell products from 75 countries, including aviation equipment, chemicals, clothing, computers, cosmetics, electronics, liquor, and perfumes. The 51-acre MFZ is five minutes west of Miami International Airport off the Dolphin Expressway (Rte. 836), and about 20 minutes from the Port of Miami. *Miami Free Zone, 2305 N.W. 107th Ave., tel. 305/591–4300. Open weekdays 9–5.*

Cauley Square

A tearoom and craft, antiques, and clothing shops now occupy this complex of clapboard, coral-rock, and stucco buildings erected 1907–20 for railroad workers who built and maintained the line to Key West. Three festivals are held each year—the first Saturday in March, the last Saturday in July, and first Saturday in November—when 10 acres of booths are set up for the sale of crafts. Turn right off U.S. 1 at S.W. 224th Street.

22400 Old Dixie Hwy., Goulds, tel. 305/258–3543. Open Mon.–Sat. 10–4:30, Sun. from Thanksgiving to Christmas Eve 12–5.

Books Greater Miami's best English-language bookstore, **Books & Books, Inc.,** specializes in books on the arts, architecture, Floridiana, and contemporary and classical literature. Collectors enjoy browsing through the rare-book room upstairs, which doubles as a photography gallery. Frequent poetry readings and book signings. *296 Aragon Ave., Coral Gables, tel. 305/442–4408, and 933 Lincoln Rd. (Sterling Bldg.), Miami Beach, tel. 305/532–3222. AE, MC, V. Coral Gables store open weekdays 10–8, Sat. 10–7, Sun. noon–5. Miami Beach store open Mon.–Thurs. 10–9, Fri. and Sat. 10–midnight, Sun. noon–5.*

Children's Books and Toys The friendly staff at **A Likely Story** will help you choose books and educational toys that are appropriate to your child's interests and stage of development. *5740 Sunset Dr., South Miami, tel. 305/667–3730. MC, V. Open Mon.–Sat. 10–6.*

A good choice north in the city is **A Kid's Book Shoppe.** *1849 N.E. Miami Gardens Dr., No. Miami Beach, tel 305/937–2665.*

Beaches

Miami Beach From Haulover Cut to Government Cut, a broad sandy beach extends for 10 continuous miles. Amazingly, it's a man-made beach—a marvel of modern engineering to repair the ravages of nature.

Along this stretch, erosion had all but eliminated the beach by the mid-1970s. Waves threatened to undermine the seawalls of hotels and apartment towers. From 1977 to 1981, the U.S. Army Corps of Engineers spent $51.5 million to pump tons of sand from offshore, restoring the beach to a 300-foot width. Between 21st and 46th streets, Miami Beach built boardwalks and protective walk-overs atop a sand dune landscaped with sea oats, sea grape, and other native plants whose roots keep the sand from blowing away.

The new beach lures residents and visitors alike to swim and stroll. More than 7 million people visit the 7.1 miles of beaches within the Miami Beach city limits annually. The other 2.9 miles are in Surfside and Bal Harbour. Here's a guide to where kindred spirits gather:

The best windsurfing on Miami Beach occurs at First Street, just north of the Government Cut jetty, and at 21st Street. You can also windsurf at Lummus Park at 10th Street and in the vicinity of 3rd, 14th, and 21st streets. Lifeguards discourage windsurfing from 79th Street to 87th Street. The best area is south of town at Hobie Island/Virginia Key.

City of Miami Beach beaches are open daily with lifeguards, winter 8–5, summer 9–sunset. Bal Harbour and Surfside have no lifeguards; beaches open daily 24 hours. Beaches free in all three communities; metered parking nearby.

County Park Beaches Metropolitan Dade County operates beaches at several of its major parks. Each county park operates on its own schedule that varies from day to day and season to season. Phone the park you want to visit for current hours and information on special events.

Crandon Park. Atlantic Ocean beach, popular with young Hispanics and with family groups of all ethnic backgrounds. *4000 Crandon Park Blvd., Key Biscayne, tel. 305/361–5421. Admission: $3 per car. Open daily 8:30–5.*

Haulover Beach Park. Atlantic Ocean beach. A good place to avoid crowds. Lightly used compared to other public beaches, except on weekends and in the peak tourist season, when it attracts a diverse crowd. *10800 Collins Ave., Miami, tel. 305/947–3525. Admission: $3 per car. Open daily 8–sunset.*

Cape Florida

Bill Baggs Cape Florida State Recreation Area (*see* Exploring Virginia Key and Key Biscayne, above).

Participant Sports

Miami's subtropical climate is ideal for active people, a place where refugees from the frozen north can enjoy warm-weather outdoor sports, such as boating, swimming, and golf, all year long. During Miami's hot, humid summers, people avoid the sun's strongest rays by playing early or late in the day. We've listed below some of the most popular individual and group sports activities.

Bicycling

Dade County has about 100 miles of off-road bicycling trails. In 1992 the county issued a color-coded map outlining Dade's 4,000 miles of roads suitable for bike travel. The map is available for $3.50 from area bike shops or from the Dade County Bicycle Coordinator, Metropolitan Planning Organization (111 N.W. 1st St., Ste. 910, Miami 33128, tel. 305/375–4507). Also, for information on dozens of monthly group rides contact the **Everglades Bicycle Club** (Box 430282, S. Miami 33243–0282, tel. 305/598–3998).

Among the best shops for renting bicycles is **Dade Cycle** (3216 Grand Ave., Coconut Grove, tel. 305/444–5997).

Golf

From the famed "Blue Monster" at the Doral Resort & Country Club to the scenic Key Biscayne Golf Course overlooking Biscayne Bay, Greater Miami has more than 30 private and public courses. For information, contact the appropriate Parks and Recreation Department: Metro-Dade County (tel. 305/579–2968), City of Miami (tel. 305/575–5256), and City of Miami Beach (tel. 305/673–7730).

Spa

The **Doral Saturnia International Spa Resort** opened in 1987 on the grounds of the Doral Resort and Country Club. Formal Italian gardens contain the spa pool and a special waterfall under which guests can enjoy natural hydromassage from the gentle pounding of falling water. The spa's 100-foot-high atrium accommodates a 5,000-pound bronze staircase railing created in 1920 by French architect Alexandre Gustave Eiffel and fabricated by artist Edgar Brandt for Paris's Bon Marché department store. The spa combines mud baths and other European pampering techniques with state-of-the-art American fitness and exercise programs. A one-day sampler is available. *8755 N.W. 36th St., Miami 33178, tel. 305/593–6030. 48 suites. Facilities: 4 exercise studios (2 with spring-loaded floors), 2 outdoor heated pools, indoor heated pool, David fitness equipment, beauty salon, 2 restaurants. AE, DC, MC, V.*

Water Sports

Marinas

Listed below are the major marinas in Greater Miami. The dock masters at these marinas can provide information on other marine services you may need. Also ask the dock masters for *Teall's Tides and Guides, Miami-Dade County,* and other local nautical publications.

The U.S. Customs Service requires boats of less than five tons that enter the country along Florida's Atlantic Coast south of Sebastian Inlet to report to designated marinas and call U.S. Customs on a direct phone line. The phones, located outside marina buildings, are accessible 24 hours a day. U.S. Customs phones in Greater Miami are at Haulover Marina and Watson Island Marina (both listed below).

Dinner Key Marina. Operated by City of Miami. Facilities include dockage with space for transients and a boat ramp. *3400 Pan American Dr., Coconut Grove, tel. 305/579–6980. Open daily 7 AM–11 PM.*

Haulover Park Marina. Operated by county lessee. Facilities include a bait-and-tackle shop, marine gas station, and boat launch. *15000 Collins Ave., Miami Beach, tel. 305/945–3934. Open weekdays 7 AM–5 PM, weekends 7 AM–6 PM.*

Miami Beach Marina. Facilities include dockage, boat ramp, fueling station, bait and tackle, and bathrooms with showers. This is one of five locations for renting Club Nautico power boats (Pier E, 300 Alton Rd., Miami Beach, tel. 305/673–2502). *300 Alton Rd., Miami Beach, tel. 305/673–6000. Open daily 8–6; 24-hr guard with communications capability.*

Watson Island Marina. City of Miami marina. Facilities include bait and tackle, boat ramp, and fuel. When the marina is busy, it stays open until all boaters are helped. *1050 MacArthur Causeway, Miami, tel. 305/371–2378. Open Mon.–Thurs. 7:30 AM–8 PM, Fri. 7:30–10, Sat. and Sun. 6:30–10, and often open later.*

Sailing Dinner Key and the Coconut Grove waterfront remain the center of sailing in Greater Miami, although sailboat moorings and rentals are located along other parts of the bay and up the Miami River. For instruction and rentals, Easy Sailing offers a fleet ranging from 19 to 127 feet for rent by the hour or for the day. Services include sailboat lessons, scuba diving lessons and certification, and on-board catering. *Dinner Key Marina, 3400 Pan American Dr., tel. 305/858–4001 or 800/780–4001. Reservation and advance deposit required. Open daily 9–sunset.*

Windsurfing **Beach Sports International.** You can rent windsurfers and hobie cats, and arrange parasailing at this shop just north of the Art Deco District. *2401 Collins Ave., Miami Beach 33140, tel. 305/538–0752. AE, MC, V. Open daily 8:30–6.*

Sailboards Miami (tel. 305/361–SAIL).

Diving Summer diving conditions in greater Miami have been compared to those in the Caribbean. Winter diving can be adversely affected when cold fronts come through. Dive-boat schedules vary with the season and with local weather conditions.

Fowey, Triumph, Long, and Emerald Reefs all are shallow 10- to 15-foot dives that are good for snorkelers and beginning divers. These reefs are on the edge of the continental shelf, a quarter of a mile from depths greater than 100 feet. You can also paddle around the tangled prop roots of the mangrove trees that line Florida's coastline, peering at the fish, crabs, and other on-shore creatures that hide there.

Dive Boats and Instruction. Look for instructors who are affiliated with PADI (Professional Association of Dive Instructors) or NAUI (National Association of Underwater Instructors).

Divers Paradise Corp (4000 Crandon Blvd., Key Biscayne, tel. 305/361–DIVE). Complete dive shop and diving charter service, including equipment rental and scuba instruction. PADI affiliation. *AE, DC, MC, V. Open weekdays 10–6, weekends 7:30–6.*

Omega Diving International. Private instruction throughout Greater Miami. Equipment consultation and specialty courses, including instructor training and underwater photography. PADI affiliation. *13885 S.W. 70th Ave., Miami, tel. 305/238–3039 or 800/255–1966. Open daily 8–6.*

Bubbles Dive Center. This all-purpose dive shop is located right at the Miami Beach marina. PADI affiliation. *2671 S.W. 27th Ave., Miami, 33133, tel. 305/856–0565. AE, MC, V. Open Mon.–Sat. 10 AM–6 PM. Closed Sun.*

Tennis

Greater Miami has more than 60 private and public tennis centers, of which 11 are open to the public. All public tennis courts charge nonresidents an hourly fee.

Coral Gables

Biltmore Tennis Center. Ten well-maintained hard courts. Site of annual Orange Bowl Junior International Tennis Tournament for children 14 and under in December. *1150 Anastasia Ave., tel. 305/460–5360. Nonresident day rate $4.30, night rate $5 per person per hour. Open weekdays 8 AM–10 PM, weekends 8–8.*

Miami Beach

Flamingo Tennis Center. Has 19 well-maintained clay courts. Site of the Rolex–Orange Bowl Junior International Tennis Tournament for teenagers 12–18. *1000 12th St., tel. 305/673–7761. Cost: day $2.13, night $2.65 per person per hour. Open weekdays 8 AM–9 PM, weekends 8–7.*

Metropolitan Dade County

International Tennis Center. Has 17 Laykold Cushion Plus hard courts, six lighted. Reservations necessary for night play. Closed to public play for about two weeks before and after the annual Lipton International Players Championship in March. *7300 Crandon Blvd., Key Biscayne, tel. 305/361–8633. Open daily 8 AM–10 PM. Cost: days $2, nights $3 per person per hour. Rental rackets $5 per hour.*

Spectator Sports

Greater Miami offers a broad variety of spectator sports events, including such popular pastimes as football and baseball, and more specialized events, such as boat racing and rugby. Major stadium and arena diagrams appear in the Community Interest Pages of the telephone directory. However, the community lacks a central clearinghouse for sports information and ticket sales.

Generally you can find daily listings of local sports events on the last page of the sports section in *The Miami Herald.* The weekend section on Friday carries detailed schedules and coverage of spectator sports.

Orange Bowl Festival. The activities of the annual Orange Bowl and Junior Orange Festival take place early November–late February. Best-known for its **King Orange Jamboree Parade**

and the **Federal Express/Orange Bowl Football Classic,** the festival also includes two tennis tournaments: the **Rolex–Orange Bowl International Tennis Championships** for top amateur national and international tennis players 18 and under, and an international tournament for players 14 and under.

Auto Racing

Hialeah Speedway. The Greater Miami area's only independent raceway holds stock-car races on a ⅓-mile asphalt speedway in a 5,000-seat stadium. Five divisions of stock cars run weekly. The Marion Edwards, Jr., Memorial Race for late-model stock cars is in November. Located on U.S. 27, ¼ mile east of Palmetto Expressway (Rte. 826). *3300 W. Okeechobee Rd., Hialeah, tel. 305/821–6644. Admission: $10 adults, under 12 free. Open every Sat. late Jan.–early Dec. Gates open 6 PM, racing 7:30–11.*

Grand Prix of Miami. Currently held in February or April each year for the Camel GT Championship on a 1.9-mile, E-shape track in downtown Miami, south of MacArthur Causeway and east of Biscayne Boulevard. Drivers race three hours; the one completing the most laps wins. Sanctioned by International Motor Sports Association (IMSA). At press time the site of the 1993 Grand Prix was in question. *Miami Motor Sports, Inc., 7254 S.W. 48th St., Miami 33155, tel. 305/662–5660. Tickets available from Miami Motor Sports, Inc., tel. 305/665–RACE or Ticketmaster (see* Important Addresses and Numbers, above).

Baseball

Florida Marlins. The Marlins—members of the Eastern Division of the National League—will play all home games at the beautiful Joe Robbie Stadium where the Miami Dolphins established major league sports in Florida in 1966. For transportation information, *see* Football, below.

Basketball

Miami Heat. Fifth 41 home-game season November–April for Miami's National Basketball Association team. *Tickets: Miami Arena, Miami 33136–4102, tel. 305/577–HEAT or Ticketmaster (see* Important Addresses and Numbers, above).

Dog Racing

The Biscayne Kennel Club and the Flagler Dog Track in Greater Miami divide the annual racing calendar. Check with the individual tracks for dates.

Biscayne Kennel Club. Greyhounds chase a mechanical rabbit around illuminated fountains in the track's infield. Near I–95 at N.W. 115th Street. *320 N.W. 115th St., Miami Shores, tel. 305/754–3484. Admission: table seats $1, grandstand $1, clubhouse $2, sports room $3. Parking 50¢–$2. Season: late Apr. into July and Oct.–Dec.*

Flagler Dog Track. Inner-city track in the middle of Little Havana, five minutes east of Miami International Airport off Dolphin Expressway (Rte. 836) and Douglas Road (corner of N.W. 37th Ave. and 7th St.). *401 N.W. 38th Ct., Miami, tel. 305/649–3000. General admission $1, clubhouse $3, parking 50¢–$2. Open Apr.–July and Sept.–Oct. Dates may fluctuate; call ahead for exact times.*

Football

Miami Dolphins. President Tim Robbie took over for his dad in late 1989 after the curmudgeonly Joe Robbie passed away. Miami has the elder Robbie to thank for a state-of-the-art football arena—Joe Robbie Stadium—that the late president named for himself.

JRS, as the stadium is called, has 73,000 seats and a grass playing-field surface with built-in drainage under the sod to carry off rainwater. It's on a 160-acre site, 16 miles northwest of downtown Miami, one mile south of the Dade-Broward county line, accessible from I–95 and Florida's Turnpike. On game days, the Metro-Dade Transit Authority runs buses to the stadium. Bus information, tel. 305/638–6700.

Dolphins tickets: *Miami Dolphins, Joe Robbie Stadium, 2269 N.W. 199th St., Miami 33056, tel. 305/620–2578. Open weekdays 10–6, Sat. during season. Also available through Ticketmaster* (see *Important Addresses and Numbers, above*).

Horse Racing

Calder Race Course. Opened in 1971, Calder is Florida's largest glass-enclosed, air-conditioned sports facility. This means that Calder actually has two racing seasons, one in fall or winter, another in spring or summer. Contact the track for this year's dates. In May, Calder holds the Tropical Park Derby for three-year-olds, the last major race in Florida before the Kentucky Derby. On the Dade-Broward county line near I–95 and the Hallandale Beach Boulevard exit, ¾ mile from Joe Robbie Stadium. *21001 N.W. 27th Ave., Miami, tel. 305/625–1311. General admission $2, clubhouse $4, programs 75¢, parking $1–$3. Gates open 10:30 AM, post time 12:30 PM, races end about 5:30.*

Hialeah Park. A superb setting for thoroughbred racing, Hialeah's 228 acres of meticulously landscaped grounds surround paddocks and a clubhouse built in a classic French-Mediterranean style. Since it opened in 1925, Hialeah Park has survived hurricanes and now seems likely to survive even changing demographics as the racetrack crowd has steadily moved north and east, away from Hialeah. This grand old park has a dismal 1989 season, and no racing took place the next two seasons. However, the track saw racing again in 1991–92, and dates for the 1992–93 season are likely to be between November and January. Even if you're not a race fan, during racing season you can take advantage of the early gate opening Saturday and Sunday mornings and breakfast at Hialeah Park. You can watch the horses work out, explore Hialeah's gardens, munch on breakfast fare of tolerable palatability, and admire the park's breeding flock of 600 Cuban flamingos. Hialeah Park opens daily for free tours 9–5. Metrorail's Hialeah Station is on the grounds of Hialeah Park. *2200 E. 4th Ave., Hialeah, tel. 305/885–8000. Gates open during race season at 10:30, post time 12:30 or 1. Races end 5:30. Other times of year, park open Mon.–Sat. 10–5. Admission $2 grandstand, $4 clubhouse. Parking $1–$3.*

Jai Alai

Miami Jai-Alai Fronton. This game, invented in the Basque region of northern Spain, is the world's fastest. Jai-alai balls, called *pelotas*, have been clocked at speeds exceeding 170 mph. The game is played in a 176-foot-long court called a *fronton*. Players climb the walls to catch the ball in a *cesta*—a woven basket—with an attached glove. You bet on a team to win or on the order in which teams will finish. Built in 1926, Miami Jai-Alai is the oldest fronton in America. Each evening, it presents 13 games—14 on Friday and Saturday—some singles, some doubles. Located a mile east of Miami International Airport. *3500 N.W. 37th Ave., Miami, tel. 305/633–6400. Admission: $1, clubhouse $5. Dinner available. AE, D, DC, MC, V. Open nightly early Nov.–late Apr. and May–late Sept., 7:10–mid-*

night; closed Sun. year-round and Tues. and Wed. Mar.–Apr. Matinees Mon., Wed., and Sat. noon–5.

Soccer **Miami Freedom.** Miami's entry in the newly consolidated American Professional Soccer League typically plays a seven-game exhibition season followed by an eight-game home season at the Orange Bowl (1400 N.W. 4th St.). Day games start at 2 PM. *1801 Coral Way, Miami, tel. 305/446–3136. Tickets: $5 adults, $3 children 14 and under and senior citizens (admission subject to change).*

Tennis **Lipton International Players Championship (LIPC).** This 10-day spring tournament at the 64-acre International Tennis Center of Key Biscayne is one of the largest in the world in terms of attendance. The two main professional tennis organizations—Association of Tennis Professionals and Women's International Tennis Association—helped create this tournament and own part of it. *7300 Crandon Blvd., Key Biscayne, tel. for tickets 305/361–5252 or Ticketmaster (see* Important Addresses and Numbers, above).

Dining

By Rosalie Leposky

Updated by Herb Hiller

You can eat your way around the world in Greater Miami, enjoying just about any kind of cuisine imaginable, and in every price category. The rich mix of nationalities here encourages individual restaurateurs and chefs to retain their culinary roots. Thus, Miami offers not just Latin fare but dishes distinctive to Spain, Cuba, Nicaragua, and other Hispanic countries; not just Oriental fare but specialties of China, India, Thailand, Vietnam, and other Asian cultures. And don't neglect American fare just because it's not "foreign." In recent years the city has gained eminence for the distinctive cuisine introduced by chefs who have migrated north from the tropics, and here combine fresh, natural foods—especially seafoods—with classically inspired dedication. Dining is definitely one of the signs of Miami's coming of age.

Highly recommended restaurants are indicated by a star ★.

Category	Cost*
Very Expensive	over $55
Expensive	$35–$55
Moderate	$15–$35
Inexpensive	under $15

**per person, excluding drinks, service, and 6% sales tax*

American
Downtown Miami
★

The Pavillon Grill. The mahogany, jade marble, and leather appointments of the restaurant's salon and dining room exude the conservative bias of an English private club. A harpist plays, and the attentive staff serves regional American fare, including items that are low in calories, cholesterol, and sodium for diners who are on restricted diets. Specialties include tournedos of Pacific salmon in a light cream-herb sauce and duck in two acts: duck breast with caramelized apples, and grilled leg on greens. For dessert, the restaurant features a gratin of berries perfumed with Cointreau in an almond cream sauce. The menu changes often, but there's always an extensive wine list. *100*

Miami Gdns. Dr.
Palmetto Expwy.
Okeechobee Rd.
Florida's Turnpike (W. Dade Expwy.)
Palmetto Expwy.
N.W. 57th Ave.
Red Rd.
W. 49th St.
E. 49th St.
8th Ave.
N.W. 135th St.
N.W. 27th Ave.
N.W. 103rd St.
N.W. 95th St.
E. 25th St.
N.W. 79th St.
N.W. 72nd Ave.
N.W. 58th St.
Hialeah Dr.
N.W. 62nd St.
N.W. 54th St.
N.W. 36th St.
N.W. 87th Ave.
Diary Rd.
Robert Frost Expwy.
N.W. 36th St.
N.W. 20th St.
Dolphin Expwy.
N.W. 7th St.
W. Flagler St.
W. Flagler St.
S.W. 8th St.
Tamiami Trail
S.W. 8th St.
MIAMI
Gratigny Rd.
NORTH MIAMI
N.W. 7th Ave.
N.E. 135th St.
N.E. 6th Ave.
NORTH MIAMI BEACH
N. Miami Beach Blvd.
Miami Gdns. Dr.
Biscayne Blvd.
Broad Causeway
N.E. 103rd St.
N.E. 95th St.
N. Miami Ave.
N.W. 2nd Ave.
Biscayne Blvd.
JFK Causeway
Julia Tuttle Causeway
Venetian Causeway
MacArthur Causeway
Bay
Collins Ave.
MIAMI BEACH
OCEAN
N

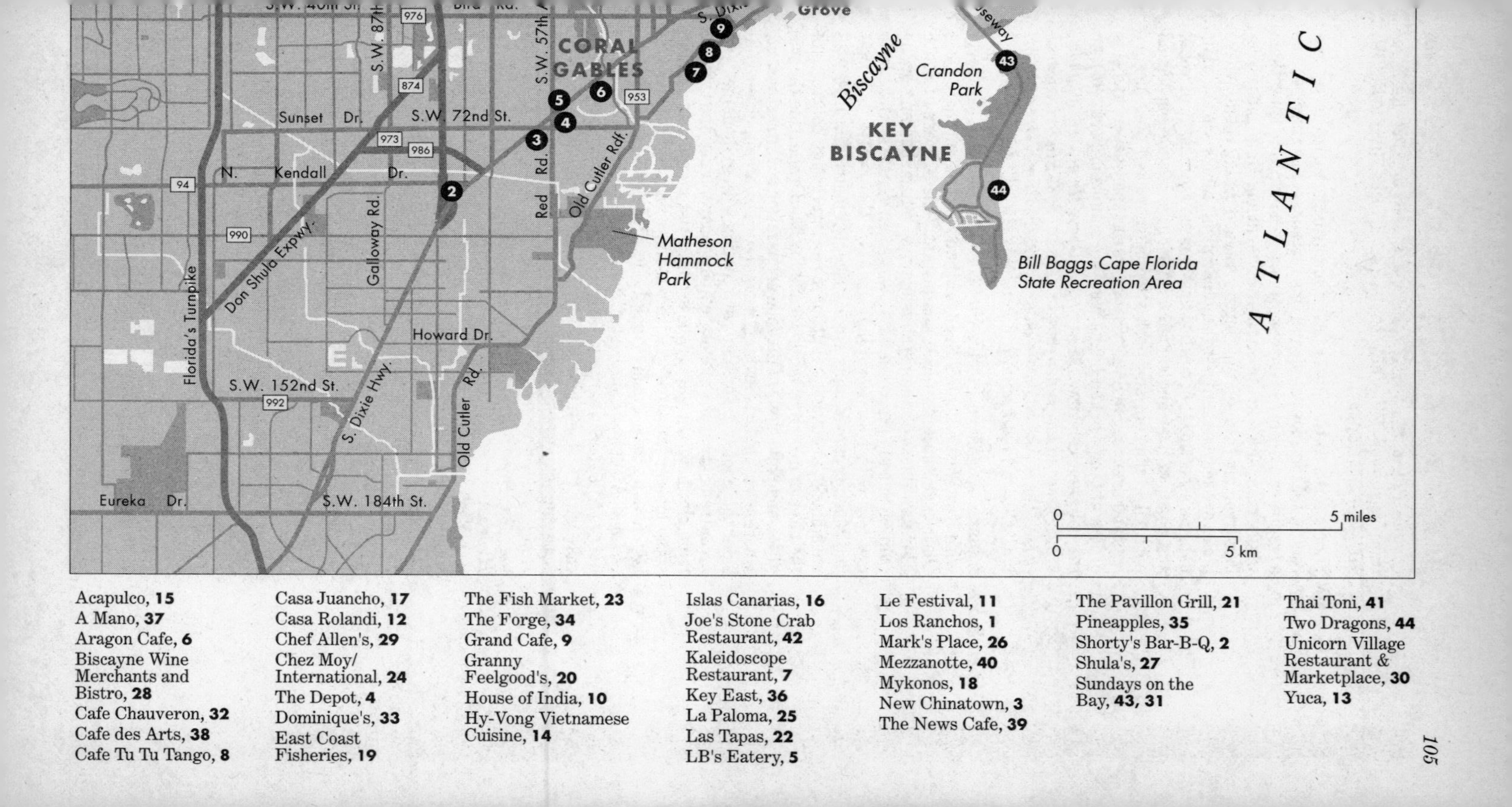
CORAL GABLES
KEY BISCAYNE
Biscayne
ATLANTIC
Crandon Park
Matheson Hammock Park
Bill Baggs Cape Florida State Recreation Area
Grove
S.W. 87th
S.W. 57th
S.W. 72nd St.
Sunset Dr.
N. Kendall Dr.
Red Rd.
Old Cutler Rd.
Galloway Rd.
Don Shula Expwy.
Florida's Turnpike
Howard Dr.
S.W. 152nd St.
S. Dixie Hwy.
Old Cutler Rd.
Eureka Dr.
S.W. 184th St.
976
874
973
986
953
94
990
992
0
5 miles
0
5 km
Acapulco, 15
A Mano, 37
Aragon Cafe, 6
Biscayne Wine Merchants and Bistro, 28
Cafe Chauveron, 32
Cafe des Arts, 38
Cafe Tu Tu Tango, 8
Casa Juancho, 17
Casa Rolandi, 12
Chef Allen's, 29
Chez Moy/ International, 24
The Depot, 4
Dominique's, 33
East Coast Fisheries, 19
The Fish Market, 23
The Forge, 34
Grand Cafe, 9
Granny Feelgood's, 20
House of India, 10
Hy-Vong Vietnamese Cuisine, 14
Islas Canarias, 16
Joe's Stone Crab Restaurant, 42
Kaleidoscope Restaurant, 7
Key East, 36
La Paloma, 25
Las Tapas, 22
LB's Eatery, 5
Le Festival, 11
Los Ranchos, 1
Mark's Place, 26
Mezzanotte, 40
Mykonos, 18
New Chinatown, 3
The News Cafe, 39
The Pavillon Grill, 21
Pineapples, 35
Shorty's Bar-B-Q, 2
Shula's, 27
Sundays on the Bay, 43, 31
Thai Toni, 41
Two Dragons, 44
Unicorn Village Restaurant & Marketplace, 30
Yuca, 13

Chopin Plaza, tel. 305/577–1000, ext. 4494 or 4462. Reservations recommended. Jacket required. Closed Sun. AE, DC, MC, V. Very Expensive.

Kendall (S.W. Suburb)

Shorty's Bar-B-Q. Shorty Allen opened his barbecue restaurant in 1951 in a log cabin, and this restaurant has since become a tradition. Parents bring their teenage children to show them where mom and dad ate on their honeymoon. Huge fans circulate fresh air through the single screened dining room, where meals are served family-style at long picnic tables. On the walls hang an assortment of cowboy hats, horns, saddles, an ox yoke, and heads of boar and caribou. Specialties include barbecued pork ribs, chicken, and pork steak slow-cooked over hickory logs and drenched in Shorty's own warm, spicy sauce, and side orders of tangy baked beans with big chunks of pork, corn on the cob, and coleslaw. *9200 South Dixie Hwy., tel. 305/665–5732. A second location opened in 1989 at 5989 South University Dr., Davie, tel. 305/680–9900. No reservations. Dress: informal. Closed Thanksgiving, Christmas. MC, V. Inexpensive.*

Miami Beach

A Mano. Acclaimed Florida chef Norman Van Aken (formerly with Key West's Louie's Backyard) opened this intimate Deco District restaurant in 1991 and instantly made it one of South Florida's finest dining establishments. When speaking of the tropical cuisine prepared here, Van Aken says it's "Old World methods with New World ingredients." Terra-cotta floor tiles and black-trimmed aqua chairs accent a mottled orange wall with black panels, contributing to the interesting contrasts of the interior design. *A mano* means "by hand, reflecting the tradition and philosophy of the food preparation at the restaurant, where everything is lovingly prepared. For an appetizer consider the triple-decker blue corn tortilla with grilled duck and accoutrements such as smoky chipotle mayonnaise and tropical fruit chutney. On any given evening the menu may include spiny lobster tail stir-fry with wasabi, soba noodles, and ginger–lemon grass–tamari vinaigrette, among other inspired offerings. A separate dessert menu boasts such delectables as berry trifle, pecan caramel tart, and "fallen" chocolate-cognac cake with passion fruit chantilly. There's an extensive wine list with some expensive choices. *1140 Ocean Dr. (in the Betsy Ross Hotel), Miami Beach, tel. 305/531–6266. Reservations recommended. Dress: casual but neat. Closed Mon. AE, DC, MC, V. Expensive.*

Key East. This is a favorite hangout for the art, theater, and bookish crowd who get their kicks from the natural foods and naturally good-natured ways of a fast-moving staff. Because of its location near a number of theaters the waiters are experts at filling orders before curtain time. Dine outside where you can watch Rollerbladers brake for the bluesy sounds or other musical offerings. Big salads and fresh homemade pastas go well with the crusty sourdough rolls that keep coming. There's nothing deep-fried, and no salt is used in preparation. Try a crispy baked fruit dessert. *647 Lincoln Rd. Mall, tel. 305/672–3606. Closed Sun., Thanksgiving, Christmas, New Year's Day. No reservations. Casual but neat. AE, MC, V. Moderate.*

The News Cafe. Owners Mark Soyka, who trained on the cosmopolitan beach scene in Tel Aviv, and Jeffrey Dispenzieri from New York, are right on the money here with quick, friendly waiters and waitresses who don't hurry the guests who have come to shmooze or the intellects who are deep in a Tolstoi novel picked out of the book rack. A raw bar has been added in back with 15 stools, but most visitors prefer seating outside to feel the salt breeze and look at the beach. This is the hippest joint on Ocean Drive. Offering a little of this, and a little of that—bagels, pâtés, chocolate fondue—The News Cafe attracts people who come here for a snack, light meal, or aperitif, and invariably, to indulge in the people parade. *800 Ocean Dr., tel. 305/538–6397. No reservations. Dress: casual. AE, DC, MC, V. Open 24 hours. Inexpensive.*

North Miami Beach

★ **Chef Allen's.** Thirty more seats have been added, thus reducing the waiting time for this top-of-the-line restaurant. Also new is the bar and full-liquor service. In this Art Deco world of glass block, neon trim, and fresh flowers, your gaze nonetheless remains riveted on the kitchen. Chef Allen Susser designed it with a picture window, 25 feet wide, so you can watch him create new American masterpieces almost too pretty to eat. Specialties include mesquite-grilled rare tuna with glazed onions and cranberry chutney, and lamb medallions with pinenuts and wilted spinach garnished with goat cheese. Among the dessert choices are white-chocolate macadamia nut torte, chocolate pizza, and a sugar junkie's delight—scoops of chocolate, raspberry, caramel, and pistachio ice cream floating in caramel sauce. Fine wines by the glass from a wine bar. *19088 N.E. 29th Ave., tel. 305/935–2900. Reservations accepted. Dress: informal. AE, MC, V. Expensive.*

★ **Mark's Place.** Since 1986, owner/chef Mark Militello has cooked regional Florida fare in a special oak-burning oven imported from Genoa. The menu changes nightly, based on the availability of fresh ingredients, but typical selections include appetizers of rock shrimp hash with cayenne mustard sauce and red pepper aioli, grilled shrimp with curried infused oil, and ginger and tropical fruit paella; for salad, try calamari with spinach, mint, sweet mango, and red bell pepper (many of the vegetables are organically grown by staffers). Entrees may include porcini-crusted cobia with fricassee of lobster, mango, and colorful pepper; grilled swordfish with rosemary, pinenuts, and vegetable couscous; and duck with chayote, plantains, green apple, and red onion confit. For dessert, the chocolate espresso torte with a hazelnut crust and a warm apple tart with homemade vanilla and caramel sauce receive high ratings. *2286 N.E. 123rd St., North Miami 33181, tel. 305/893–6888. Reservations advised. Dress: neat but casual. AE, DC, MC, V. Closed Thanksgiving, Christmas. No lunch weekends. Expensive.*

South Miami

The Depot. Aptly named, this restaurant is situated across the highway from where trains to Key West once ran and near the site of the old Larkins depot (in what was once the town of South Miami). Lit with oil font chandeliers and wall lamps and as long as a Pullman car, The Depot is decorated with mahogany paneling and stained-glass transoms. Glass-topped tables are placed over dimly lit model railroad layouts that operate on 90-second timers. As pleasing as the ambience is the menu, which, in addition to featuring some of the finest beef in town, also includes snapper *fruits de mer* (sauteed fillet of snapper topped with scallops and shrimp in a white wine garlic butter suace); black pepper fettucini tossed with smoked salmon and bell peppers in a light cream sauce, and grilled sea scallops and shiitake mushrooms with tropical fruit coulis. *5830 S. Dixie Hwy., tel. 305/665–6261. Reservations advised. Dress: neat but casual. AE, DC, MC, V. Moderate.*

West Dade **Shula's.** Surrounded by memorabilia of coach Don Shula's perfect 1972 season with the Miami Dolphins, you can drink or dine in this shrine for the NFL-obsessed. The certified black angus beef is almost an afterthought to the icons that include quarterback Earl Morall's rocking chair, assistant coach Howard Schnellenberger's pipe, and the autographed playbook from President Nixon to coach Shula. The Sports Ticker fills in for any gaps in conversation, ditto—in season—the weekly stat sheets of all NFL games. The ladies room mirrors the Orange Bowl locker room from where the magic took place, with pictures of the beefy perfect-season squad. Otherwise it's steaks, prime rib, and fish (including dolphinfish) in a woody, fireplace-cheered and cedar-shingled setting—not to mention its location on the grounds of Miami Lakes. *15400 N.W. 77th Ave., tel. 305/821–1150. Reservations advised. Dress: neat but casual. AE, DC, MC, V. Expensive–Moderate.*

Chinese
Key Biscayne **Two Dragons.** Run like a small family restaurant, the ingredients served in this Chinese restaurant are all fresh and entrees are prepared to order. Specialties include a Cantonese seafood nest (shrimp, scallops, and crabmeat with Chinese vegetables in a nest of crisp noodles), an orange beef Mandarin, and Szechuan eggplant with a spicy garlic-mustard sauce guaranteed to clear the sinuses. Dine in an intimate pagodalike booth behind hanging curtains of wooden beads or at an open table overlooking an outdoor Oriental garden. A Japanese steak house—the "second dragon"—serves Teppanyaki-style cuisine at six cooking tables in a separate room. *Sonesta Beach Hotel, 350 Ocean Dr., tel. 305/361–2021. Reservations advised. Dress: neat but casual. AE, D, DC, MC, V. Dinner only. Closed 2 weeks in Sept. Moderate.*

South Miami **New Chinatown.** This spacious 200-seat restaurant offers bright and busy family dining. The big menu features Cantonese, Mandarin, Szechuan, and sizzling Teppan regional choices, as well as chow mein, chop suey, and moo goo gai pan. Vegetarians can find steamed Chinese vegetables among five special entrées or order any of the more than 60 dishes without meat. Entrées include hot and spicy *mo-po-to-fu* (bean curd sautéed with fresh scallions) with or without ground pork; orange chicken; and lotus prawns in a garlic and Hoisin sauce. New Chinatown will reduce but not eliminate the MSG in dishes, insisting the taste suffers. *5958 S. Dixie Hwy., tel. 305/662–5649 or 662–5650. No reservations. Dress: casual. AE, MC, V. Closed Thanksgiving. Moderate.*

Continental
Coconut Grove
★ **Grand Cafe.** Understated elegance at all hours is the hallmark—a bilevel room with pink tablecloths and floral bouquets, sunbathed by day, dim and intimate after dark. Japanese-born, French-trained executive chef Katsuo Sugiura creates "international" cuisine (the menu theme changes every six weeks—look for special Brazilian, Caribbean, Cajun, and Oriental specialties), combining ingredients from all over the world in pleasing presentations that intrigue the palate. Specialties include black linguini (colored with squid ink); fresh smoked salmon; a superbly rich she-crab soup with roe, sherry, and cayenne pepper; "boned" Maine lobster presented in the shape of a lobster, with artichokes and a cream sauce of vermouth and saffron. Dessert specialties include a white-chocolate and pistachio mousse with blackberry sauce and Beaujolais essence. *2669 S. Bayshore Dr., tel. 305/858–9600.*

Reservations advised. Jacket preferred. AE, DC, MC, V. Very Expensive.

Kaleidoscope Restaurant. The tropical ambience here extends to a choice of indoor or outdoor seating—all in air-conditioned comfort, because fans blow cold air around a glass-roofed terrace overlooking a landscaped courtyard. Specialties include pastas and seafood. *3112 Commodore Plaza, tel. 305/446–5010. Reservations advised. Dress: casual. AE, DC, MC, V. Moderate.*

Coral Gables

Aragon Cafe. If George Merrick, the founder of Coral Gables, entered the bar of Aragon Cafe, he would see on display some of his mother's hand-painted china and silver. In this restaurant designed to look old and classy, subdued lighting emanates from gaslight-style chandeliers and etched-glass wall lights. The menu emphasizes fresh Florida seafoods, and reflects Merrick's desire to re-create the best of the Mediterranean in a Florida setting. Specialties include seafood minestrone made with shrimp, scallops, clams, new potatoes, carrots, and kidney and green beans; grilled goat cheese in banana leaves; grilled Florida dolphinfish with native starfruit sauce; and tuna steak au poivre in a mushroom-based sauce of peppercorns and cream. Dessert offerings include a white-chocolate terrine with pistachio sauce. *180 Aragon Ave. in the Colonnade Hotel, Coral Gables 33134, tel. 305/448–9966. Reservations advised. Jacket required. Free valet parking. AE, DC, MC, V. No lunch Sat. Closed Sun. Expensive.*

Miami Beach

The Forge. Miraculously reopened in late 1991 after a devastating fire, The Forge has in fact gained something: improved intimacy. Seats have been reduced by 300 to 175 through the loss of several rooms, which may reopen in time. Otherwise, this landmark (often compared to a museum) still stands behind a facade of 19th-century Parisian mansions, where an authentic forge once stood. Dinner is served in intimate dining salons, each with its own historical artifacts, including a 250-year-old chandelier that hung in James Madison's White House. A fully stocked wine cellar contains an inventory of 380,000 bottles—including more than 500 dating from 1822 (and costing as much as $35,000) and recorked in 1989 by experts from Domaines Barons de Rothschild. Specialties include veal chop with mushrooms and grapes and pear-scented breast of chicken beaujolais. Desserts are extravagant; try the famous blacksmith pie. *432 Arthur Godfrey Rd., tel. 305/538–8533. Reservations advised. Dress: casual but neat. AE, DC, MC, V. Dinner only. Expensive.*

North Miami

La Paloma. This fine Swiss Continental restaurant offers a total sensory experience: fine food, impeccable service, and the ambience of an art museum. In sideboards and cases throughout, owners Werner and Maria Staub display ornate European antiques that they have spent decades collecting. The treasures include Baccarat crystal, Limoges china, Meissen porcelains, and Sevres clocks. The staff speaks Spanish, French, German, Portuguese, or Arabic. Specialties include fresh local fish and seafood; Norwegian salmon Caroline (poached, served on a bed of spinach with hollandaise sauce); Wiener schnitzel; lamb chops à la *diable* (coated with bread crumbs, mustard, garlic, and herbs), veal chop with morrel sauce, chateaubriand; and for dessert, passion-fruit sorbet and kiwi soufflé with raspberry sauce. *10999 Biscayne Blvd., tel. 305/891–0505. Reser-*

vations advised. Jacket preferred. AE, MC, V. No lunch. Closed Mon., July, and part of Aug. Expensive.

Biscayne Wine Merchants and Bistro. In this 35-seat retail beer and wine store with a deli counter, strangers often become friends while sharing tables and sampling the merchandise. Owners Jan Sitko and Esther Flores stock about 300 wines (sold by the glass or bottle) and 92 brands of beer. The menu changes daily but always includes bean and cream soups. Typical fare may include chicken Crustaces (a chicken breast stuffed with leeks, dill, and crab with a light dill sauce) and daily fresh fish specials such as dolphin, shark, snapper, swordtail, wahoo, and salmon. Sitko and Flores like to create new dishes with fresh herbs, spices, fruits, and vegetables. One favorite is a tangy-sweet sauce with jalapeño and citrus. *12953 Biscayne Blvd., North Miami, tel. 305/899–1997. No reservations. Dress: informal. AE, MC, V. No lunch Sat., Sun. Closed Thanksgiving, Christmas, New Year's Day, sometimes other holidays. Moderate.*

Cuban
Coral Gables
★

Yuca. This high-style Cuban eatery is chicly designed with track lighting, blond woods, tiles, and art prints. The cuisine is presented colorfully also, by chef Douglas Rodriguez, who takes good advantage of the tropical foods available in Miami. Entrées include meat-filled empanadas with a pickled garlic rémoulade arranged with watercress and lime. Also featured are homemade gnocchi of malanga and sweet potato served with picadillo; and grilled loin pork chops with roasted cumin seed and carmelized onion butter served with moros and avocado. Owner Efrain Veiga relocated to expanded quarters in 1991. *177 Giralda Ave., tel. 305/444–4448. Dress: neat but casual. No lunch weekends. Reservations required. AE, DC, MC, V. Closed Thanksgiving, Christmas, New Year's Day. Expensive.*

Little Havana

Islas Canarias. A gathering place for Cuban poets, pop music stars, and media personalities. Wall murals depict a Canary Islands street scene and an indigenous dragon tree (*Dracaena draco*). The menu includes such Canary Islands dishes as baked lamb, ham hocks with boiled potatoes, and *tortilla Española* (a Spanish omelet with onions and chorizo, a spicy sausage), as well as Cuban standards, including palomilla steak, and fried kingfish. Don't miss the three superb varieties of homemade chips—potato, malanga, and plantain. Islas Canarias has another location in Westchester at Coral Way and S.W. 137th Ave. *285 N.W. Unity Blvd. (N.W. 27th Ave.), tel. 305/649–0440. No reservations. Dress: informal. No credit cards. Open Christmas Eve and New Year's Eve to 6 PM. Inexpensive.*

Family Style
Coral Gables

LB's Eatery. Town and gown meet at this sprout-laden haven a ½-block from the University of Miami's baseball stadium. Kitschy food-related posters plaster the walls of this relaxed restaurant with low prices. Since there are no waiters, you order at the counter and pick up your food when called. Vegetarians thrive on LB's salads and daily meatless entrées, such as lasagna and moussaka. Famous for Saturday night lobster. (If you plan to come after 8, call ahead to reserve a lobster.) Other specialties include barbecued baby-back ribs, lime chicken, croissant sandwiches, and carrot cake. *5813 Ponce de León Blvd., tel. 305/661–7091. No reservations. Dress: informal. MC, V. Closed Sun., all major holidays. Inexpensive.*

French
Coral Gables

Le Festival. The modest canopied entrance to this classical French restaurant understates the elegance within. Decor includes etched-glass filigree mirrors and light pink walls. Appetizers of salmon mousse, baked oysters with garlic butter, and lobster in champagne sauce en croute lead the way for special entrées such as rack of lamb (for two), and medallions of veal with two sauces—a pungent, creamy lime sauce and a dark port-wine sauce with mushrooms. Dinners come with real french-fried potatoes. Don't pass up dessert here; the mousses and soufflés are positively decadent. *2120 Salzedo St., tel. 305/442–8545. Reservations required for dinner and for lunch parties of 5 or more. Dress: neat but casual. AE, DC, MC, V. No lunch weekends. Closed Sat. noon, all day Sun., and Sept.–Oct. Expensive.*

Miami Beach
★ **Dominique's.** Woodwork and mirrors from a Vanderbilt home and other demolished New York mansions create an intimate setting for a unique nouvelle cuisine dining experience. Specialties include exotic appetizers, such as buffalo sausage, sautéed alligator tail, and rattlesnake-meat salad; rack of lamb (which accounts for 35% of the restaurant's total sales) and fresh seafood; and an extensive wine list. The restaurant also serves brunch on Sunday. *Alexander Hotel, 5225 Collins Ave., tel. 305/865–6500 or 800/327–6121. Reservations advised. Jacket recommended. AE, DC, MC, V. Very Expensive.*

★ **Cafe Chauveron.** After a lapse of service, this café again reigns as doyen of traditional French cuisine in Miami. The international clientele is personally looked after by an attentive, multilingual staff. Stellar Chef Jean-Claude Plihon offers Escoffier cookery with a nouvelle presentation in a setting that overlooks Indian Creek. Consider as appetizer the crab cake with chives, cayenne, saffron, and a touch of garlic in lobster sauce. A *feuillete* of lobster is elegant in its pastry shell. The broiled pheasant with truffle and goose liver pâté is flambéed with cognac and served with fried potato slivers filled with inoke and chanterelle mushrooms. The bouillabaise is suffused with saffron in an herbed fish stock and includes mussels, scallops, lobster, clams, and shrimp. For dessert, indulge in a Grand Marnier soufflé served with raspberry, chocolate, and custard sauce. *9561 E. Bay Harbor Dr., tel. 305/866–8779. Jacket required. Reservations advised. Closed June–Sept. AE, DC, MC, V. Expensive.*

Cafe des Arts. Enjoy French-provincial cuisine in an Art Deco setting amid tropical plants, antiques, and an art gallery that changes every six to eight weeks. Indoor and outdoor seating. Specialties include smoked-salmon pasta with artichokes, mushrooms, and brie sauce; braised duck in grape sauce; and seafood salad. *918 Ocean Dr., tel. 305/534–6267. Reservations advised. Dress: casual. AE, MC, V. No lunch. Moderate.*

Greek
Southwest Miami
Mykonos. A family restaurant serving typical Greek fare since 1974 in a Spartan setting—a single 74-seat room adorned with Greek travel posters. Specialties include gyro; moussaka; marinated lamb and chicken; calamari (squid) and octopus sautéed in wine and onions; and sumptuous Greek salads thick with feta cheese and briny olives. *1201 Coral Way, tel. 305/856–3140. Reservations accepted for dinner. Dress: informal. AE, MC, V. Open Sun. at 5 PM. Closed July 4, Thanksgiving, Christmas Eve, New Year's Eve, New Year's Day. Inexpensive.*

Haitian
Little Haiti
Chez Moy International. Seating is outside on a shaded patio or in a pleasant room with oak tables and high-backed chairs. Specialties include *grillot* (pork boiled, then fried with spices);

fried or boiled fish; stewed goat; and conch with garlic and hot pepper. Try a tropical fruit drink such as sweet sop (also called *anon* or *cachiman*) or sour sop (also called *guanabana* or *corrosol*) blended with milk and sugar, and sweet potato pie for dessert. *1 N.W. 54th St., tel. 305/756–7540. Reservations accepted. Dress: casual. No smoking. No credit cards. Inexpensive.*

Indian
Coral Gables

House of India. The haunting strains of sitar music lull diners at this popular spot in Coral Gables. Vegetarian and nonvegetarian specialties include hot coconut soup with cardamom, milk, rose water, and sugar; curried goat; and authentic chicken tandoori, cooked in a clay oven. The weekday luncheon buffet is a good bargain. Another location is in Fort Lauderdale at 3060 N. Andrews Avenue (tel. 305/566–5666). *22 Merrick Way, tel. 305/444–2348. Weekend reservations accepted. Dress: casual. AE, MC, V. Closed Labor Day, Thanksgiving, Christmas. Moderate.*

Italian
Coral Gables
★

Casa Rolandi. Italian art and two working brick ovens add a warm feeling here. Among the tasty entrées you'll find *agnolotti Fiorentina* (spinach pasta stuffed with ricotta cheese and topped with tomato sauce and sage); *fusilli al pesto* with pine nuts, parsley, basil and olive oil, parmesan cheese, and a touch of cream; and *tortelloni de fonduta al sugo d'arrosto di vitello e tartufi* (homemade cheese tortelloni served with a veal juice demiglaze and pared white truffles). The snapper *livornesa*—a special—comes with compote of green and yellow squash, radicchio, and parslied potato arranged artfully on a plate shaped like a scallop shell. All meals come with a pita-style house bread baked with virgin olive oil. For dessert, the *tiramisù* is a winner. *1930 Ponce de León Blvd., tel. 305/444–2187. Reservations required. Dress: neat but casual. AE, DC, MC, V. No lunch Fri.–Sun. Closed Thanksgiving, Christmas, New Year's Day. Expensive.*

Miami Beach

Mezzanotte. Chic, but not intimate, this restaurant is noted for fine food at moderate prices. Among the entrées is *zuppe nettuno*, with fish, octopus, squid, and crab served with angel hair pasta. The *spiedano Romano* includes sautéed porcini mushrooms under melted fontina cheese in a white wine sauce, and capers with mustard and garlic served over bread. Mezzanotte is known for its pastas, especially the *capellini primavera*, and for its veal dishes, including *piccata* (lemon butter sauce and roasted peppers), *lombata* (lightly breaded with radicchio, endive, tomatoes, and onions), and six scaloppines. Desserts are decadent. *1200 Washington Ave., tel. 305/673–4343. Reservations accepted for parties of 5 or more. Dress: neat but casual. AE, DC, MC, V. No lunch. Moderate.*

Latin
Coconut Grove

Cafe Tu Tu Tango. Brilliant artists such as local William DeLaVega set up their easels in the rococo-modern arcades of this eclectic, imaginative café-lounge on the second story of the highly popular Cocowalk. All the while, throngs of people frequent this place to savor the frittatas, *cosas frías*, and empanadas. Hot recorded jazz sets the mood and you can sit indoors or out; the latter offers some of the best people-watching in the entire South. Between the oak floors and the paddle-fans on the ceiling, guests at the more than 250 seats graze on chips, dips, breads, and spreads. House specials include crusted tempura-like "fritangas" of ham and crabmeat, and *boniato relleno* (white sweet tubers stuffed with picadillo). A few wines are available, but nothing that costs too much. Don't miss out on this place. *3015 Grand Ave. (Cocowalk), tel. 305/529–2222. Open Mon.–Wed. and Sun. 11:30 AM–midnight, Thurs. 11:30 AM–1 AM, Fri. and Sat. 11:30 AM–2 AM. No reservations. Dress: casual but neat. AE, DC, MC, V. Closed Christmas. Moderate.*

Mexican
Little Havana

Acapulco. Authentic Mexican cuisine is served in an intimate 70-seat room with adobe walls, wooden beams, tabletops of Mexican tiles, and sombreros and serapes on the walls. As soon as you sit down, a waiter descends on you with a free, ample supply of *totopos,* homemade corn chips served hot and crunchy, salt free, with a fiery *pico de gallo* sauce. Specialties include a rich, chunky guacamole; *carnitas asadas* (marinated pork chunks in lemon and butter sauce); *mole poblano* (chicken in chocolate sauce); shrimp and rice in a cherry wine sauce; and combination platters of tacos, burritos, and enchiladas. *727 N.W. Unity Blvd. (N.W. 27th Ave.), tel. 305/642–6961. Weekend reservations recommended. Dress: informal. AE, DC, MC, V. Moderate.*

Natural
Downtown Miami

Granny Feelgood's. "Granny" is a shrewd gentleman named Irving Field, who caters to health-conscious lawyers, office workers, and cruise-ship crews at five locations. Since 1989 Jack Osman has owned the original Granny's, and with Field plans to franchise locations outside Miami. Specialties include chicken salad with raisins, apples, and cinnamon; spinach fettucini with pinenuts; grilled tofu; apple crumb cake; and carrot cake. *190 S.E. 1st Ave., tel. 305/358–6233. No reservations. Dress: casual. No smoking. AE, MC, V. Closed Sun. Inexpensive.*

Miami Beach

Pineapples. Art Deco pink pervades this health-food store and restaurant. Specialties include Chinese egg rolls; lasagna filled with tofu and mushrooms; spinach fettucini with feta cheese, fresh garlic, walnuts, and cream sauce; and salads with a full-flavored Italian-style dressing. *530 Arthur Godfrey Rd., tel. 305/532–9731. No reservations. Dress: casual. No smoking. AE, MC, V. Closed Rosh Hashanah, Yom Kippur. Moderate.*

North Miami Beach
★

Unicorn Village Restaurant & Marketplace. Ten years after opening a 1960s-style health food store and restaurant, Terry Dalton relocated his top-notch natural foods restaurant to the Shoppes at the Waterways in 1990. Now with 300 seats (up from the original 80), the restaurant caters to vegetarian and nonvegetarian diners. In an outdoor setting of free-form ponds and fountains by a bayfront dock, or in a plant-filled, natural-woods interior under three-story-high wood-beamed ceilings sun-bright with skylights, guests enjoy spinach lasagna, a Tuscan vegetable sauté with Italian seasonings, grilled honey-mustard chicken, wok-barbecued shrimp, spicy seafood cakes; fresh fish, poultry, and Coleman natural beef; and the Unicorn's spring roll of uncooked veggies wrapped in a thin rice paper with cellophane noodles. The 16,000-square-foot food market is the largest natural foods source in Florida and features desserts all baked on premises. *3565 N.E. 207th St., tel. 305/933–8829. No reservations. Dress: casual. No smoking. MC, V. Moderate.*

Nicaraguan
Little Managua

Los Ranchos. Julio Somoza, owner of this busy establishment and nephew of Nicaragua's late president, Anastasio Somoza, fled to south Florida in 1979. Somoza sustains a tradition begun 30 years ago in Managua, when the original Los Ranchos instilled in Nicaraguan palates a love of Argentine-style beef—lean, grass-fed tenderloin with *chimichurri*, a green sauce of chopped parsley, garlic, oil, vinegar, and other spices. Nicaragua's own sauces are a tomato-based marinara and the fiery *cebollitas encurtidas*, with slices of jalapeño pepper and onion pickled in vinegar. Specialties include *chorizo* (sausage); *cuajada con maduro* (skim cheese with fried bananas); and shrimp sautéed in butter and topped with a creamy jalapeño sauce. *125 S.W. 107th Ave., tel. 305/221–9367. Also at Bayside Marketplace, tel. 305/375–8188. Reservations advised, especially on weekends. Dress: casual. Nightly entertainment. AE, DC, MC, V. Closed Good Friday, Christmas Eve, New Year's Day. Moderate.*

Seafood
Downtown Miami

The Fish Market. Tucked away in a corner of the Omni International Hotel's lobby, this fine restaurant boasts a kitchen staff fluent in seafood's complexities. The menu changes with availability of fresh fish, fruits, and vegetables, but typical menu items may include sautéed dolphin in a basil-perfumed olive oil; fillet of pompano; pan-baked red snapper; and Florida lobster tail. Daily seafood specials might include bluefish, dolphin, lemon sole, marlin, pompano, redfish, sea bass, sea trout, tuna, and a whole, peppery yellowtail. The chocolate pecan tart and pistachio chocolate terrine with orange cream sauce are just two of the featured desserts. *Biscayne Blvd. at 16th St., 33132, tel. 305/374–0000. Jacket recommended. Reservations advised. Free valet parking. AE, DC, MC, V. No lunch Sat.; closed Sun. Expensive.*

East Coast Fisheries. This family-owned restaurant and retail fish market on the Miami River features fresh Florida seafood from its own 38-boat fleet in the Keys. From tables along the second-floor balcony railing, watch the cooks prepare your dinner in the open kitchen below. Specialties include a complimentary fish-pâté appetizer, blackened pompano with owner David Swartz's personal herb-and-spice recipe, lightly breaded fried grouper, and a homemade Key lime pie so rich it tastes like ice cream. *360 W. Flagler St., tel. 305/373–5515. Dress: casual. Beer and wine only. AE, MC, V. Moderate.*

Key Biscayne

Sundays on the Bay. Two locations overlook the water: the Crandon Park Marina at Key Biscayne and Salty's, as it's now called, on the Intracoastal Waterway at Haulover. Both have inside dining and outdoor decks, bars, live bands playing island music and top-40 hits nightly, and an energetic young serving staff. Specialties from an extensive seafood menu include conch fritters, conch chowder (tomato-based, served with sherry and Tabasco sauce), and baked grouper topped with crabmeat and shrimp scampi. *Key Biscayne: 5420 Crandon Blvd., tel. 305/361–6777; Haulover Beach Park: 10880 Collins Ave., tel. 305/945–5115. Reservations advised for Sun. brunch. Dress: casual. AE, D, DC, MC, V. Moderate.*

Miami Beach

Joe's Stone Crab Restaurant. A south Florida tradition since 1913, Joe's is a family restaurant in its fourth generation. You go to wait, people watch, and finally settle down to an ample à la carte menu. About a ton of stone crab claws are served daily, with drawn butter, lemon wedges, and a piquant mustard sauce (recipe available). Popular side orders include a vinegary coleslaw, salad with a brisk vinaigrette house dressing, creamed garlic spinach, french-fried onion rings and eggplant, and hash brown potatoes. Save room for dessert—a slice of

Key-lime pie with graham cracker crust and real whipped cream or apple pie with a crumb-pecan topping. *227 Biscayne St., tel. 305/673–0365; 800/780–CRAB (for carry out orders or overnight shipping). No reservations. Dress: casual, but no T-shirts or tank tops. To minimize wait, come for lunch at 11:30, for dinner at 5 or after 9. AE, DC, MC, V. Closed May 15–Oct. 15. Moderate.*

Spanish
Downtown Miami

Las Tapas. Overhung with dried meats and enormous show breads, this popular spot offers a lot of imaginative creations. *Tapas*—"little dishes"—come in appetizer-size portions to give you a variety of tastes during a single meal. Specialties include *la tostada* (smoked salmon on melba toast, topped with a dollop of sour cream, across which are laid baby eels, black caviar, capers, and chopped onion) and *pincho de pollo a la plancha* (grilled chicken brochette marinated in brandy and onions). Also available are soups, salads, sandwiches, and standard-size dinners. *Bayside Marketplace, 401 Biscayne Blvd., tel. 305/372–2737. Reservations for large parties only. Dress: casual. AE, DC, MC, V. Moderate.*

Little Havana
★

Casa Juancho. A meeting place for the movers and shakers of Miami's Cuban community, Casa Juancho serves a cross section of Spanish regional cuisines. The interior recalls old Castile: brown brick, rough-hewn dark timbers, and walls adorned with colorful Talavera platters. Strolling Spanish balladeers will serenade you. Specialties include *cochinillo Segoviano* (roast suckling pig), and *parrillada de mariscos* (fish, shrimps, squid, and scallops grilled in a light garlic sauce) from the Pontevedra region of northwest Spain. For dessert, the *crema Catalana* has a delectable crust of burnt caramel atop a rich pastry custard. The wine list includes fine labels from Spain's Rioja region. *2436 S.W. 8th St., tel. 305/642–2452. Reservations advised; not accepted after 8 PM Fri. and Sat. Dress: casual but neat. AE, DC, MC, V. Closed Christmas Eve. Expensive.*

Thai
Miami Beach

Thai Toni. Thai silks, bronze Buddhas, ceiling drapes, and two raised platforms for guests who want to dine seated on cushions highlight this fine eatery. The mellow, Thai Singha beer sets you up for the spicy grilled squid appetizer or the vegetarian or pork *pad Thai* (rice noodles tossed with shrimp, egg, bean sprouts, and peanuts). Traditional entrées include a hot-and-spicy deep-fried whole snapper garnished with basil leaves and mixed vegetables. Try the homemade lemonade. *890 Washington Ave., tel. 305/538–THAI. Dress: neat but casual. AE, MC, V. Dinner only. Moderate.*

Vietnamese
Little Havana
★

Hy-Vong Vietnamese Cuisine. Under new ownership since 1989, the magic continues to pour forth from the tiny kitchen of this 36-seat restaurant as it has since 1980. Now the word is out, so come before 7 PM to avoid a wait. Specialties include spring rolls, a Vietnamese version of an egg roll, with ground pork, cellophane noodles, and black mushrooms wrapped in homemade rice paper; a whole fish panfried with *nuoc man* (a garlic-lime fish sauce); and thinly sliced pork, barbecued with sesame seeds and fish sauce, served with bean sprouts, rice noodles, and slivers of carrots, almonds, and peanuts. *3458 S.W. 8th St., tel. 305/446–3674. Reservations accepted for 5 or more. Dress: casual. No smoking. No credit cards. Closed lunch and Mon., American and Vietnamese/Chinese New Years, and 2 weeks in Aug. Moderate.*

Lodging

Few urban areas can match Greater Miami's diversity of hotel accommodations. The area has hundreds of hotels and motels with lodgings in all price categories, from $8 for a night in a dormitory-style hostel bed to $2,000 for a night in the luxurious presidential suite atop a posh downtown hotel.

As recently as the 1960s, many hotels in Greater Miami opened only in the winter to accommodate Yankee "snowbirds." Now all stay open all year. In summer, they cater to European and Latin American vacationers who find Miami quite congenial despite the heat, humidity, and intense thunderstorms almost every afternoon.

Although some hotels (especially on the mainland) have adopted year-round rates, many still adjust their rates to reflect the ebb and flow of seasonal demand. The peak occurs in winter, with only a slight dip in summer when families with schoolchildren take vacations. You'll find the best values between Easter and Memorial Day (a delightful time in Miami but a difficult time for many people to travel), and in September and October (the height of hurricane season).

The list that follows is a representative selection of the best hotels and motels, organized geographically.

The rate categories in the list are based on the all-year or peak-season price; off-peak rates may be a category or two lower.

Highly recommended places are indicated by a star ★.

Category	Cost*
Very Expensive	over $120
Expensive	$90–$120
Moderate	$50–$90
Inexpensive	under $50

**All prices are for a standard double room, excluding 6% state sales tax and nominal tourist tax.*

Coconut Grove

★ **Grand Bay Hotel.** This modern high rise overlooking Biscayne Bay features rooms with traditional furnishings and original art. The building's stairstep facade, like a Mayan pyramid, gives each room facing the bay a private terrace, but the best views come from rooms at the northeast corner that look out on downtown Miami. Only slightly more special than most rooms is 814, Luciano Pavarotti's two-level suite with a baby-grand piano, circular staircase, and canopied king-size bed. You can rent it when he's not there. Most remarkable, however, is the meticulous attention the staff pays to guests' desires. *2669 S. Bayshore Dr., Coconut Grove 33133, tel. 305/858–9600. 181 rooms with bath, including 49 suites, 20 nonsmoker rooms. Facilities: outdoor pool, hot tub, health club, saunas, masseur, afternoon tea in lobby, gourmet restaurant, lounge, poolside bar. AE, DC, MC, V. Very Expensive.*

Grove Isle. This luxurious mid-rise urban resort sits on a 26-acre island and adjoins the equally posh condominium apartment towers and private club. Developer Martin Margulies displays selections from his extensive private art collection on the premises (*see* Exploring Coconut Grove, above). The over-sized rooms have patios, bay views, ceiling fans, and tropical decor with area rugs and Spanish tiles; rooms with the most light and best bay view are 201–205. *4 Grove Isle Dr., Coconut Grove 33133, tel. 305/858–8300. 49 rooms with bath, including 9 suites. Facilities: outdoor freshwater pool and whirlpool; 12 tennis courts; 85-slip marina; running track around the island; in-room refreshment bar and coffee maker; free cable TV; restaurant with indoor and outdoor seating. AE, DC, MC, V. Very Expensive.*

Mayfair House. This European-style luxury hotel sits within an exclusive open-air shopping mall (*see* Exploring Coconut Grove, above). Public areas have Tiffany windows, polished mahogany, marble walls and floors, and imported ceramics and crystal. Also impressive is the glassed-in elevator that whisks you to the corridor on your floor; a balcony overlooks the mall's central fountains and walkways. In all suites, outdoor terraces face the street, screened from view by vegetation and wood latticework. Each has a Japanese hot tub on the balcony or a Roman tub in the suites. Otherwise, each suite is unique in size and furnishings. Sunset (Room 505) is one of 48 suites with antique pianos. Some aspects of the building's design are quirky; you can get lost looking for the ballroom or restaurant, and, in many rooms, you must stand in the bathtub to turn on the water. The worst suite for sleeping is Featherfern (Room 356), from which you can hear the band one floor below in the club. *3000 Florida Ave., Coconut Grove 33133, tel. 305/441–0000 or 800/433–4555. 181 suites, including 22 nonsmoker suites. Facilities: rooftop recreation area with sauna in a barrel, small outdoor freshwater swimming pool; snack bar. AE, DC, MC, V. Very Expensive.*

Doubletree Hotel at Coconut Grove. This high rise with a bay view was built in 1970 and renovated in 1988. Large rooms—most with balconies—have comfortable chairs, armoires, original artwork, and either a mauve or turquoise color scheme. Best rooms are on upper floors with bay views. Homemade chocolate-chip cookies are offered to arriving guests. *2649 S. Bayshore Dr., Coconut Grove 33133, tel. 305/858–2500 or 800/528–0444. 190 rooms with bath, including 32 nonsmoker rooms, and 3 rooms for handicapped guests. Facilities: outdoor freshwater pool, 2 tennis courts, restaurant, bar. Casablanca, a private club, is on the top floor. AE, DC, MC, V. Expensive.*

Coral Gables

The Biltmore Hotel. A historic high rise built in 1926, the Biltmore was restored and renovated in 1986 and reopened as a luxury hotel. Upper-floor rooms facing north and east toward the airport, downtown Miami, and Biscayne Bay have the most spectacular views. The hotel has been in foreclosure but is expected to reopen in 1993. *1200 Anastasia Ave., Coral Gables 33134, tel. 305/445–1926 or 800/445–2586. 275 rooms with bath, including 45 suites. Facilities: 18-hole championship golf course, 10 lighted tennis courts, health spa with sauna, pool, restaurant, coffee shop, lounge. AE, DC, MC, V. Very Expensive.*

★ **The Colonnade Hotel.** The twin 13-story towers of this $65-million hotel, office, and shopping complex dominate the heart of Coral Gables. Architectural details echo the adjoining two-story Corinthian-style rotunda on Miracle Mile from which 1920s developer George Merrick sold lots in his fledgling city.

Miami Area Lodging

N
Miami Gdns. Dr.
Palmetto Expwy.
Red Rd.
27th Ave.
7th Ave.
N.E. 6th Ave.
N. Miami Beach Blvd.
NORTH MIAMI BEACH
Biscayne Blvd.
N.E. 135th St.
N.W. 135th St.
NORTH MIAMI
Broad Causeway
Gratigny Rd.
N.W.
8th Ave.
Okeechobee Rd.
W. 49th St.
E. 49th St.
N.W. 103rd St.
N.E. 103rd St.
N.W. 95th St.
N.E. 95th St.
Collins Ave.
W. 4th Ave.
E. 25th St.
N.W. 79th St.
JFK Causeway
N.W. 72nd Ave.
N. Miami Ave.
N.W. 2nd Ave.
N.W. 58th St.
N.W. 62nd St.
Hialeah Dr.
N.W. 54th St.
MIAMI BEACH
OCEAN
N.W. 36th St.
Robert Frost Expwy.
Julia Tuttle Causeway
W. 87th Ave.
Diary Rd.
Miami Riv
75
95
441
1
27
9
860
826
817
856
909
915
932
944
A1A
14
15
16
17
18
19
20

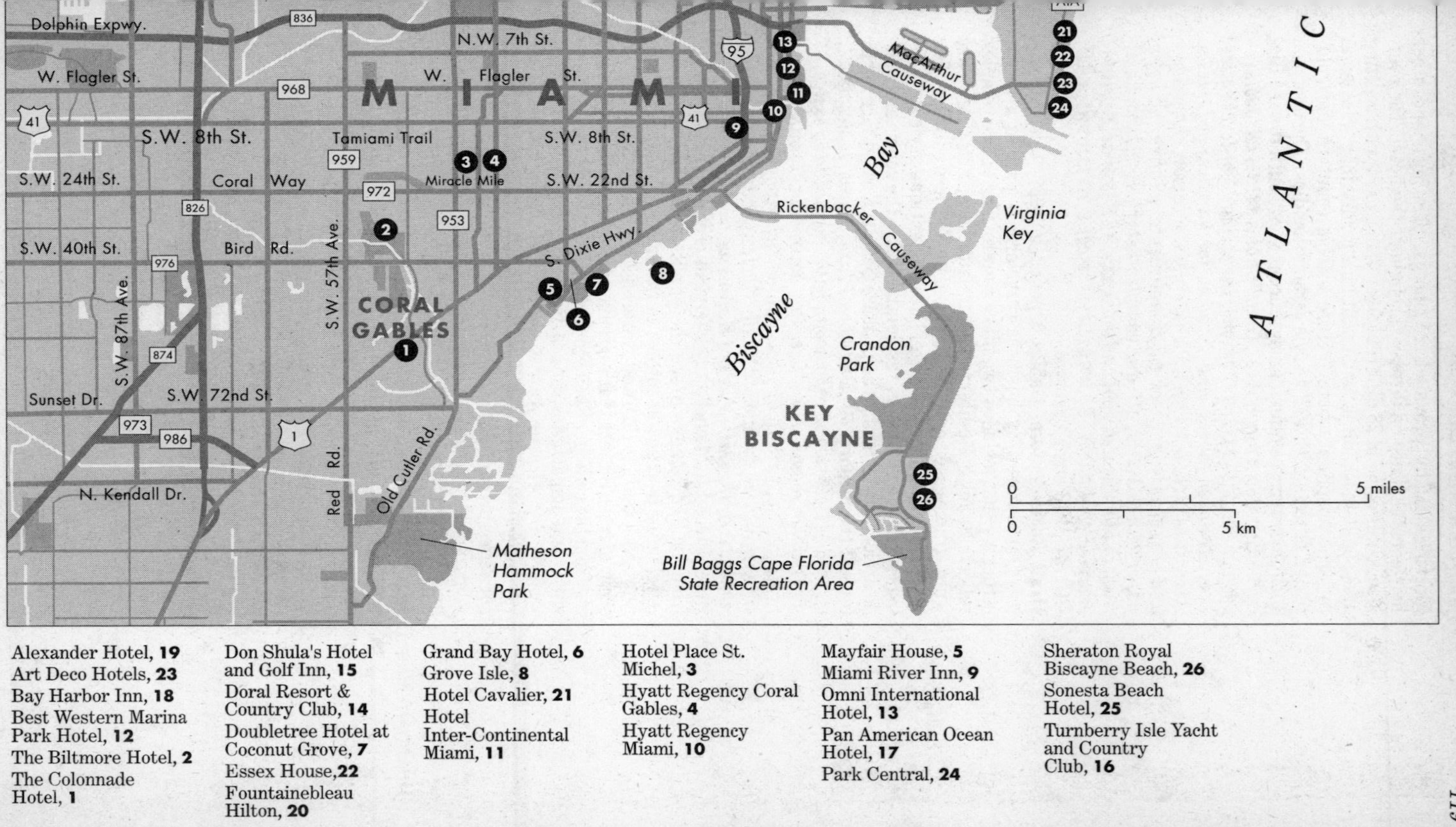

Alexander Hotel, **19**
Art Deco Hotels, **23**
Bay Harbor Inn, **18**
Best Western Marina Park Hotel, **12**
The Biltmore Hotel, **2**
The Colonnade Hotel, **1**
Don Shula's Hotel and Golf Inn, **15**
Doral Resort & Country Club, **14**
Doubletree Hotel at Coconut Grove, **7**
Essex House, **22**
Fountainebleau Hilton, **20**
Grand Bay Hotel, **6**
Grove Isle, **8**
Hotel Cavalier, **21**
Hotel Inter-Continental Miami, **11**
Hotel Place St. Michel, **3**
Hyatt Regency Coral Gables, **4**
Hyatt Regency Miami, **10**
Mayfair House, **5**
Miami River Inn, **9**
Omni International Hotel, **13**
Pan American Ocean Hotel, **17**
Park Central, **24**
Sheraton Royal Biscayne Beach, **26**
Sonesta Beach Hotel, **25**
Turnberry Isle Yacht and Country Club, **16**

Merrick's family provided old photos, paintings, and other heirlooms that are on display throughout the hotel. The oversize rooms come in 26 different floor plans, each with a sitting area, built-in armoires, and traditional furnishings of mahogany. The hospitality bars feature marble counters and gold-plated faucets with 1920s-style ceramic handles. The pool on a 10th-floor terrace offers a magnificent view south toward Biscayne Bay. *180 Aragon Ave., Coral Gables 33134, tel. 305/441-2600 or 800/533-1337. 157 rooms, including 17 bi-level suites, 18 nonsmoker rooms, and 4 rooms for handicapped guests. Amenities include terry-cloth bathrobes, minibar, champagne and orange juice at check-in, complimentary coffee and newspaper with wake-up call, and complimentary shoeshine. Facilities: outdoor heated pool and Jacuzzi with 2 saunas, Nautilus exercise equipment, 24-hr room service, 2 restaurants. AE, DC, MC, V. Very Expensive.*

★ **Hyatt Regency Coral Gables.** Opened in 1987, this highrise hotel, patronized by business travelers, is part of a megastructure that includes two office towers. The entire complex reflects Spanish Mediterranean architecture, with tile roofs, white-frame casement windows, and pink-stucco exterior. The hotel's interior decor of pastel hues and antique-style furnishings gives a comfortable, residential feel to the rooms and public areas. Rooms facing the pool are best; the worst face north toward the airport. *50 Alhambra Plaza, Coral Gables 33134, tel. 305/441-1234. 242 rooms with bath, including 50 suites, 45 nonsmoker rooms. Facilities: two ballrooms, 1 with restaurant, lounge, fifth-floor pool, outdoor whirlpool, health club with Nautilus equipment, Life Cycles, sauna, and steam rooms. AE, DC, MC, V. Very Expensive.*

★ **Hotel Place St. Michel.** Art Nouveau chandeliers suspended from vaulted ceilings grace the public areas of this intimate jewel in the heart of downtown Coral Gables. The historic low-rise hotel, built in 1926 and restored 1981–86 is filled with the scent of fresh flowers that's circulated by the paddle fans hanging from the ceilings. Each room has its own dimension, personality, and imported antiques from England, Scotland, and France. *162 Alcazar Ave., Coral Gables 33134, tel. 305/444-1666 or 800/247-8526. 28 rooms with bath, including 3 suites. Facilities: welcome basket of fruit and cheese in every room, morning newspaper, Continental breakfast, restaurant, lounge, French snack shop. AE, DC, MC, V. Expensive.*

Downtown Miami

★ **Hotel Inter-Continental Miami.** Stand on the fifth-floor recreation plaza and gaze up at this 34-story granite monolith that appears to be arching over you. The grain in the lobby's marble floor matches that in *The Spindle*, a massive centerpiece sculpture by Henry Moore. With all that marble, the lobby could easily look like a mausoleum—and did before the addition of palm trees, colorful umbrellas, and oversize wicker chairs and tables. Atop a five-story atrium, a skylight lets the afternoon sun pour in. The triangular hotel tower offers bay, port, and city views that improve with height. *100 Chopin Plaza, Miami 33131, tel. 305/577-1000 or 800/327-3005. 644 rooms with bath, including 34 suites, 48 nonsmoker rooms; corner rooms have extra-wide doors for handicapped guests. Facilities: outdoor heated freshwater pool beside the bay, ¼-mile jogging track with rubber surface, in-room minibar, restaurants, lounge. AE, DC, MC, V. Very Expensive.*

Hyatt Regency Miami. This centrally located, 24-story convention hotel adjoins the James L. Knight International Center (*see* Exploring Downtown Miami, above). Nestled beside the Brickell Avenue Bridge on the north bank of the Miami River, the Hyatt offers views of tugboats, freighters, and pleasure craft from its lower lobby. The best rooms are on the upper floors, facing east toward Biscayne Bay. A $7-million room renovation began in 1991. *400 S.E. 2nd Ave., Miami 33131, tel. 305/358-1234 or 800/233-1234. 615 rooms with bath, 25 suites, 43 nonsmoker rooms, 17 rooms for handicapped guests. Facilities: outdoor freshwater pool, $10 admission to nearby Downtown Athletic Club, in-room safe, in-house pay-TV movies, 2 restaurants, lounge. AE, DC, MC, V. Very Expensive.*

Omni International Hotel. A 20-story hotel built in 1977, the Omni stands atop a 10.5-acre shopping and entertainment complex that includes J. C. Penney, a number of specialty shops, the Children's Workshop child-care center, and a hand-made Italian wood carousel. The lowest hotel floor is five stories up; rooms on upper floors have spectacular views of downtown Miami and Biscayne Bay. Many rooms feature a blue-and-tan color scheme and mahogany furniture. *1601 Biscayne Blvd., Miami 33132, tel. 305/374-0000 or 800/THE-OMNI. 535 rooms, including 50 suites, 25 nonsmoker rooms, and 2 rooms for handicapped guests. Facilities: outdoor heated pool on a terrace 5 stories above street, lobby bar, terrace café, restaurant (The Fish Market), access to nearby health club and spa. AE, DC, MC, V. Very Expensive.*

Best Western Marina Park Hotel. Centrally located, this mid-rise hotel, owned by a French chain, has an inviting tiled lobby filled with wicker furnishings. Pastel-color rooms, also with rattan amenities, provide soft mattresses and trilingual TV. The best views are from east rooms that overlook Bayside and the Port of Miami. *340 Biscayne Blvd., Miami 33132, tel. 305/371-4400 or 800/327-6565. 200 rooms with bath, including 25 suites. Facilities: pool, restaurant, bar. AE, D, DC, MC, V. Expensive-Moderate.*

★ **Miami River Inn.** Preservationist Sallye Jude has restored this landmark property (the oldest continuously operating inn south of St. Augustine) as an oasis of country hospitality at the edge of downtown. It is a 10-minute walk across the 1st Street Bridge to the heart of the city, and a few hundred feet from José Martí Park (one of the city's prettiest). The inn—dating to 1904—consists of five clapboard buildings that are the only concentration of houses remaining from that period. The inn offers 40 antiques-filled rooms with breakfast area, small meeting space, outdoor pool and patio, and an oval lawn. As part of the same property—officially designated the Riverside Historic District—four modified-Deco mid-century masonry buildings house long-term renters. The best rooms are second- and third-story river-views with stunning vistas of the city. Avoid the tiny rooms in building "D" that overlook the stark condo to the west. *118 S.W. S. River Dr., Miami 33130, tel. 305/325-0045. 40 rooms (39 with bath, some with tub only). Facilities: freshwater outdoor pool and heated Jacuzzi, use of refrigerator, AC, heat, phones, small meeting room. Rate includes Continental breakfast. Moderate.*

Key Biscayne

Sheraton Royal Biscayne Beach Resort and Racquet Club. Art Deco pinks, wicker furniture, and chattering macaws and cockatoos in the lobby set the tone for this three-story beachfront resort set amid the waving fronds of coconut palms. Built in

1952 and restored in 1985, this laid-back hotel maintains a casual demeanor. All rooms have garden and bay views; most have terraces. *555 Ocean Dr., Key Biscayne 33149, tel. 305/361–5775. 192 rooms with bath, including 4 oceanfront suites, 17 junior suites with kitchenette, 15 nonsmoker rooms. Facilities: ¼-mi of ocean beach, 2 outdoor freshwater heated pools, children's wading pool, 10 tennis courts (4 lighted), sailboats, windsurfers, Hobie Cats, aquabikes, snorkeling kits, rental bicycles, pay-TV movies, unisex beauty salon, restaurant, lounge. AE, DC, MC, V. Very Expensive.*

★ **Sonesta Beach Hotel & Tennis Club.** Among the features of this eight-story beachfront resort are the displays of museum-quality modern art pieces by prominent painters and sculptors. Don't miss Andy Warhol's three drawings of rock star Mick Jagger in the hotel's disco bar, Desires. The best rooms, on the eighth floor, face the ocean. All guest rooms were completely renewed in 1991 and 1992. *350 Ocean Dr., Key Biscayne 33149, tel. 305/361–2021 or 800/SONESTA. 290 rooms with bath, including 12 suites and 11 villas (3-, 4-, and 5-bedroom homes with full kitchens and screened-in pools). Facilities: 750-ft ocean beach, outdoor freshwater heated Olympic-size pool and whirlpool, water sports including sailboarding, 10 tennis courts (3 lighted); health center with Jacuzzi, steam rooms, aerobic dance floor, weight room, massage room, and tanning room; gift shops; restaurants, snack bar, deli, lounge with live entertainment. AE, DC, MC, V. Very Expensive.*

Miami Beach

Fontainebleau Hilton Resort and Spa. The Miami area's foremost convention hotel boasts an opulent lobby with massive chandeliers, a sweeping staircase, and new meeting rooms in Art Deco hues. There are always some rooms in the hotel that are under renovation; most recently completed in mid-1992, as part of a $10 million program, are 375 rooms in the north tower building, which have been redone in a tropical theme and have new bathroom fixtures. Decor is varied; you can request a '50s look or one that's contemporary. Upper-floor rooms in the Chateau Building have the best views. *4441 Collins Ave., Miami Beach 33140, tel. 305/538–2000. 1,206 rooms with bath, including 60 suites, 120 nonsmoker and handicapped rooms. Facilities: ocean beach with 30 cabanas, 2 outdoor pools (one fresh, one salt), marina, windsurfing, parasailing, Hobie Cats, volleyball, 3 whirlpool baths, 7 lighted tennis courts, health club with exercise classes, saunas, free children's activities, 12 restaurants and lounges, Tropigala nightclub. AE, DC, MC, V. Very Expensive.*

★ **Pan American Ocean Hotel, A Radisson Resort.** This beach hotel—built in 1954—sits back from Collins Avenue behind a refreshing garden of coconut palms and seasonal flowers. In 1992 all guest rooms received a facelift. The best view is from rooms 330, 332, and 333 on the third floor of the north wing, which overlooks the ocean. Direct north- and south-facing rooms have only a sliver view of ocean or bay. *17875 Collins Ave., Miami Beach 33160, tel. 305/932–1100 or 800/327–5678. 146 rooms, including 4 suites and handicapped rooms. Facilities: 400 ft of ocean beach, outdoor heated pool, 4 hard-surface tennis courts, tennis pro and pro shop, 2 shuffleboard courts, 9-hole putting green, exercise room, volleyball, beauty salon, coffee shop, pool gazebo bar, terrace lounge and oceanfront restaurant, ping-pong room, video game room, card room, free shuttle service to Bal Harbour and Aventura shopping malls, coin* *laundry, minibar in all rooms. AE, D, DC, MC, V. Very Expensive.*

Park Central. Across the street from the glorious beach, this seven-story mauve, turquoise, and white deco hotel—with wraparound corner windows—makes all the right moves to stay in front of the deco revival. Most of the high-fashioned models visiting town come to this property, which dates back to 1937. Black-and-white photos of old beach scenes, hurricanes, and familiar faces attest to the hotel's longevity. Stylishly, rooms are decorated with Philippine mahogony furnishings—originals that have been restored. An Italian theme prevails, with the Barocco Beach restaurant and espresso served in the lobby. *640 Ocean Dr., 33139, tel. 305/538–1611, fax 305/534–7520. 80 rooms with bath. Facilities: restaurant, bar, espresso bar. AE, DC, MC, V. Very Expensive–Expensive.*

★ **Alexander Hotel.** A spa and diet center was added in 1990 to this 16-story hotel that offers ocean and bay views from every suite, all of which have antique furnishings or reproductions and original art. Suites facing south have the best views. A computer keeps track of the mattresses, so you can request the degree of firmness you prefer. *5225 Collins Ave., Miami Beach 33140, tel. 305/865–6500. 212 suites, each with 2 baths, 2 phones, kitchen, minibar, free cable movies, daily newspaper. Facilities: ocean beach, 2 outdoor heated freshwater pools, 4 poolside Jacuzzis, cabanas, Sunfishes and catamarans for rent, Dominique's gourmet restaurant, and coffee shop. AE, DC, MC, V. Expensive.*

Bay Harbor Inn. Here you'll find down-home hospitality in the most affluent zip code in the county. Retired Washington lawyer Sandy Lankler and his wife Celeste operate this 35-room lodging in two sections—two moods. The buildings are modern, but townside furnishings are antiques. Townside is the oldest building in Bay Harbor Islands, vaguely Georgian in style but dating from 1940. Behind triple sets of French doors under fan windows, the lobby is full of oak desks, handmills, grandfather clocks, historical maps, and potted plants. Rooms are antiques-filled and no two are alike. Along Indian Creek the inn incorporates the former Albert Pick Hotella, a shipshape tropical-style set of rooms on two floors off loggias surrounded by palms with all rooms facing the water. Mid-century modern here, and chintz. The popular The Palms restaurant is located both townside and creekside. *9660 East Bay Harbor Dr., Bay Harbor Islands 33154, tel. 305/868–4141. 36 rooms with bath, including 12 suites and penthouse. Facilities: outdoor freshwater pool, 2 restaurants, lounge. Complimentary Continental breakfast and champagne tea. AE, DC, MC, V. Expensive.*

Essex House. From the beginning, this has been one of the premiere lodgings of the Art Deco era. It was all here to start: designed by architect Henry Hohauser, Everglades mural by Earl LaPan. Here are the ziggurat arches, the hieroglyph-style ironwork, etched glass panels of flamingos under the palms, five-foot rose medallion Chinese urns. Hallways have recessed showcases with original deco sculptures. The original 66 rooms from 1938 are now 41, plus two petite suites, six grand. Amenities include complete turndown service with clothes hung and shoes polished, designer linens and towels, all feather-and-down pillows and sofa rolls, and individually controlled air conditioning and central heat plus ceiling fans. The rooms are soundproofed from within (otherwise unheard of in beach properties of the thirties), and rooms to the east have extra thick windows to reduce the band noise from a nearby hotel. Smallest rooms are yellow-themed and face north. Best are the two-room oceanview suites: 305 and 308, and 205 and 208. Continental breakfast is free. *1001 Collins Ave., Miami Beach 33139, tel. 305/534–2700, 800/55–ESSEX. 64 rooms and suites with bath. Facilities: breakfast room. AE, MC, V. Expensive.*

Hotel Cavalier. Rooms in this three-story beachfront hotel have period maple furnishings, new baths, and air conditioning. The Cavalier is popular with the film and fashion industry; many guests are artists, models, photographers, and writers. The best rooms face the ocean; the worst are on the ground floor, rear south, where the garbage truck goes by in the morning. *1320 Ocean Dr., Miami Beach 33139, tel. 305/534–2135 or 800/338–9076. 44 rooms with bath, including 2 suites. Amenities include Evian water and flowers in all rooms, Continental breakfast in lobby of adjacent Cardozo Hotel. AE, D, DC, MC, V. Expensive.*

Art Deco Hotels. Four hotels, which kicked off revival of the Deco District a decade ago, as well as the **Hotel Cavalier,** were bought at auction in 1992 by local developers who have excellent reputations in South Beach revival. These include the **Hotel Cardozo,** which dates from 1939, the **Hotel Leslie** from 1937, the **Hotel Carlyle** from 1941, and the **Victor Hotel** from the same period (the last two recently closed). All are attractively decorated in Art Deco pinks, whites, and grays. Many contain original walnut furniture, restored and refinished. Rooms are comfortable but small; inspect your room before registering to assure that it meets your needs; all have air conditioning, but most of the time you won't need it—especially if you're in one that faces the water, where a sea breeze usually blows. *1244 Ocean Dr., Miami Beach 33139, tel. 305/534–2135 or 800/338–9076. 220 rooms with bath, including suites. Facilities: restaurants, bar with live entertainment in the Carlyle. AE, DC, MC, V. Expensive–Moderate.*

North Dade
★
Turnberry Isle Yacht and Country Club. In 1991, a two-year, $80-million redevelopment project was completed, adding a 271-room, three-wing Mediterranean-style resort and club, new restaurants, and the *Ms. Turnberry* (a custom-built yacht) to this upscale condominium community on a 300-acre bayfront site. Guests can also choose from the European-style Marina Hotel, the Yacht Club, or the Mizner-style Country Club Hotel beside the golf course—340 rooms in all. Interiors of the oversize rooms feature light woods and earth-tone colors, a nautical-blue motif at the hotel, large curving terraces, Jacuzzis, honor bar, and in-room safes. *1999 W. Country Club Dr., Aventura 33180, tel. 305/932–6200, 800/327–7028, 340 rooms with bath, including 40 suites. Facilities: Ocean Club with 250 feet of private beach frontage, diving gear, Windsurfers and Hobie Cats for rent, and complimentary shuttle service to the hotel; 4 outdoor freshwater pools; 24 tennis courts (18 lighted); 2 Robert Trent Jones–designed 18-hole golf courses; helipad; marina with moorings for 117 boats up to 150 ft; full-service spa with physician, nutritionist, saunas, steam rooms, whirlpools, facials, herbal wraps, Nautilus exercise equipment, indoor racquetball courts, and outdoor jogging course; 5 private restaurants, lounge, nightly entertainment. AE, DC, MC, V. Very Expensive.*

West Dade
Don Shula's Hotel and Golf Inn. This low-rise suburban resort is part of a planned town developed by Florida Senator Bob

Graham's family about 14 miles northwest of downtown Miami. The golf resort opened in 1962 and added two wings in 1978. Its decor is English-traditional throughout, rich in leather and wood. All rooms have balconies. The inn opened in 1983 with a typically Florida-tropic look—light pastel hues and furniture of wicker and light wood. In both locations, the best rooms are near the lobby for convenient access; the worst are near the elevators. *Main St., Miami Lakes 33014, tel. 305/821–1150. 301 rooms with bath, including 32 suites. Facilities: 2 outdoor freshwater heated pools; 9 lighted tennis courts; golf (18-hole par-72 championship course, lighted 18-hole par-54 executive course, golf school); saunas, steam rooms, and whirlpools; 8 indoor racquetball courts; Shula's Athletic Club with Nautilus fitness center; full-size gym for volleyball and basketball; aerobics classes; restaurants and lounges; shopping discount at Main St. shops. AE, DC, MC, V. Very Expensive.*

★ **Doral Resort & Country Club.** Millions of airline passengers annually peer down upon this 2,400-acre jewel of an inland golf and tennis resort while fastening their seat belts. It's 4 miles west of Miami International Airport and consists of eight separate three- and four-story lodges nestled beside the golf links. The resort follows a tropical theme, with light pastels, wicker, and teak furniture. All guest rooms have minibars; most have private balconies or terraces with views of the golf courses or tennis courts. This is the site of the Doral Ryder Open Tournament, played on the Doral "Blue Monster" golf course. *4400 N.W. 87th Ave., Miami 33178, tel. 305/592–2000. 650 rooms with bath, including 58 suites. Facilities: five 18-hole golf courses, and a 9-hole, par-3 executive course; pro shop and boutique; 15 tennis courts (4 lighted), Olympic-size heated outdoor freshwater pool; 3-mi jogging and bike path; bicycle rentals; lake fishing; restaurants and lounges; transportation to beach. AE, DC, MC, V. Very Expensive.*

The Arts

Performing arts aficionados in Greater Miami will tell you they survive quite nicely despite the area's historic inability to support a professional symphony orchestra. In recent years, this community has begun to write a new chapter in its performing arts history.

The New World Symphony, a unique advanced-training orchestra, marks its sixth season in 1993. The Miami City Ballet has risen rapidly to international prominence in its seven-year existence. The opera company ranks with the nation's best, and a venerable chamber music series brings renowned ensembles to perform here. Several churches and synagogues also run classical music series with international performers.

In theater, Miami offers English-speaking audiences an assortment of professional, collegiate, and amateur productions of musicals, comedy, and drama. Spanish theater also is active. High hopes and funding have lately buoyed prospects that the nonprofit regional repertory theater **Miami's Skyline** (tel. 305/358–7529) may present productions by 1993. Call for information.

In the cinema world, the Miami Film Festival attracts more than 45,000 people annually to screenings of new films from all over the world—including some made here.

Arts Information. Strongest on reviews, also with comprehensive listings, is Greater Miami's English-language daily newspaper, *The Miami Herald*, which publishes information on the performing arts in its Weekend Section on Friday and the Lively Arts Section on Sunday. Phone ahead to confirm details before you go.

If you read Spanish, check *El Nuevo Herald* (a Spanish version of *The Miami Herald*) or *Diario Las Américas* (the area's largest independent Spanish-language paper) for information on the Spanish theater and a smattering of general performing arts news.

Another good source of information on the performing arts is the calendar in *Miami Today*, a free weekly newspaper available each Thursday in downtown Miami, Coconut Grove, and Coral Gables. The best, most complete source is the *New Times*, a free weekly distributed throughout Dade County each Wednesday.

The free *Greater Miami Calendar of Events* is published twice a year by the Dade County Cultural Affairs Council (111 N.W. 1st St., Ste. 625, Miami, tel. 305/375–4634).

Guide to the Arts/South Florida is a pocket-size monthly publication covering all the cultural arts in Greater Miami, Broward, and Palm Beach. *Kage Publications, 2340 N.E. 171st St., North Miami Beach, tel. 305/956–7801. Annual subscription $15; individual copy $2. No credit cards.*

Real Talk/WTMI (93.1 FM) provides concert information on its Cultural Arts Line (tel. 305/358–8000, ext. 9398).

Ticketmaster. You can use this service to order tickets for performing arts and sports events by telephone. A service fee is added to the price of the ticket. *Tel. 305/358–5885 (Dade), 305/523–3309 (Broward), or 407/839–3900 (Palm Beach). AE, MC, V.*

Art In addition to museums described in the self-guided tours, other museums of interest include:

Black Heritage Museum: In 1991 the dispersed collections of the museum found a permanent home on the first level of the Miracle Center, a vertical shopping mall. Rotating exhibits add to permanent collections that include carvings from Africa, artifacts of Black Americana, and vestiges and arts of local history. *Miracle Center, 3301 Coral Way, Miami, tel. 305/446–7304. Admission free. Open weekdays 11–4, weekends 1–4.*
North Miami Center of Contemporary Art: Rotating exhibits feature contemporary paintings, photographs, and Florida artworks. Avant-garde films are also screened. *12340 N.E. 8th Ave., N. Miami, tel. 305/893–6211. Admission free. Open weekdays 10–4, Sat. 1–4.*
South Florida Art Center: The center houses the workrooms of emerging and established visual artists of the Lincoln Road Arts District. The artists open their studios and showrooms to the public. The center and studios hold an open house the third Friday of each month from 7–10 PM. *924 Lincoln Rd., Miami Beach, tel. 305/674–8278. Admission free. Open Mon.–Fri. 12–7, Sat. 12–5, closed Sun.*
Bacardi Art Gallery: This unusual, tiled Bacardi Imports building exhibits works by local and international artists in its not-for-profit art gallery. Tours are available in English and Span-

ish if requested in advance. *2100 Biscayne Blvd., tel. 305/573–8511. Admission free. Open weekdays 9–5.*

Bakehouse Art Complex: Built as the Flowers Bakery in the 1920s, this two-story masonry building was revived in 1987 as a gallery and studios for area artists. The best time to visit is for the monthly Second Sunday, when, from 1 to 5 PM, artists meet with visitors. New to the complex are the **Miami Jewelry Institute** and **Threshold Gallery of Art,** showing ceramics, basketry, fiber, and glass. *561 N.W. 32nd St., tel. 305/576–2828. Admission free. Open Tues.–Fri. 10–4.*

Ballet

Miami City Ballet. Florida's first major fully professional resident ballet company. Edward Villella, the artistic director, was principal dancer of the New York City Ballet under George Balanchine. Now the Miami City Ballet re-creates the Balanchine repertoire and introduces new works of its own. Miami City Ballet performances are at the Dade County Auditorium; the Broward Center for the Performing Arts; Bailey Concert Hall, also in Broward County; at the Raymond F. Kravis Center for the Performing Arts; and at the Naples Philharmonic Center for the Arts. Demonstrations of works in progress are at the 800-seat Lincoln Theater in Miami Beach. Villella narrates the children's and works-in-progress programs. *905 Lincoln Rd., Miami Beach 33139, tel. 305/532–7713. Ticketmaster (see* Important Addresses and Numbers, above*). Season: Sept.–Mar. AE, MC, V.*

Cinema

The Alliance Film/Video Project. Cutting-edge cinema from around the world is featured, with special midnight shows. *927 Lincoln Rd. Mall, suite 119, Sterling Building, Miami Beach 33139, tel. 305/531–8504.*

The Miami Film Festival. During 10 days in February, new films from all over the world are screened in the Gusman Center for the Performing Arts. Tickets and schedule: *444 Brickell Ave., Ste. 229, Miami 33131, tel. 305/377–3456. AE, MC, V. Ticketmaster (see* Important Addresses and Numbers, above).

Concerts

Concert Association of Florida. A not-for-profit organization, directed by Judith Drucker, this is the South's largest presenter of classical artists. Ticket and program information: *555 Hank Meyer Blvd. (17th St.), Miami Beach 33139, tel. 305/532–3491. AE, MC, V.*

Friends of Chamber Music (44 W. Flagler St., Miami 33130, tel. 305/372–2975) presents an annual series of chamber concerts by internationally known guest ensembles, such as the Beaux Arts Trio, I Musici, and the Juilliard String Quartet.

Drama

Check *Guide to the Arts/South Florida* for a complete English-language theater schedule. Traveling companies come and go; amateur groups form, perform, and disband. Listed below are the more enduring groups of Greater Miami's drama scene.

Acme Acting Company. Thought provoking, on-the-edge theater by new playwrights is presented during winter and summer seasons at the Colony Theater (1040 Lincoln Rd. Mall, Miami Beach, tel. 305/674–1026). *174 E. Flagler St., Miami, tel. 305/372–1718.*

Actor's Playhouse. This six-year-old professional equity company, based in Kendall, performs adults' and children's productions year-round. *8851 S.W. 107th Ave., Miami 33176, tel. 305/595–0010.*

Area Stage. This company emphasizes new works. *645 Lincoln Rd., Miami Beach, tel. 305/673–8002.*

Coconut Grove Playhouse. Arnold Mittelman, artistic director, stages Broadway-bound plays and musical reviews and experimental productions. *3500 Main Hwy., Coconut Grove 33133, tel. 305/442–4000. AE, D, MC, V.*

Minorca Playhouse. The playhouse is the long-established home of several theater companies, including the Florida Shakespeare Theatre and the Hispanic Theatre Festival. *323 Minorca Ave., Coral Gables, tel. 305/446–1116.*

New Theatre. Productions here showcase contemporary and classical plays. *65 Almeria St., Coral Gables 33134, tel. 305/443–5909.*

Ring Theater. The University of Miami's Department of Theatre Arts presents eight complete plays a year, two each season, in this 311-seat hall. *University of Miami, 1380 Miller Dr., Coral Gables 33124, tel. 305/284–3355. AE, MC, V.*

Opera

Greater Miami Opera. Miami's resident opera company presents two complete casts for four or five operas in the Dade County Auditorium. The International Series brings such luminaries as Placido Domingo and Luciano Pavarotti; the National Series features rising young singers in the principal roles, with the same sets and chorus, but with more modest ticket prices. All operas are sung in their original language, with titles in English projected onto a screen above the stage. *1200 Coral Way, Miami 33145, tel. 305/854–7890. AE, D, MC, V. Ticketmaster (*see *Important Addresses and Numbers, above). Box office open weekdays 9–4.*

Symphony

New World Symphony. Although Greater Miami still has no resident symphony orchestra, the New World Symphony, conducted by Michael Tilson Thomas, helps to fill the void. Musicians aged 22–30 who have finished their academic studies perform here before moving on. *541 Lincoln Rd., Miami Beach 33139, box office tel. 305/673–3331, main office 305/673–3330. AE, MC, V. Ticketmaster (*see *Important Addresses and Numbers, above). Season: Oct.–Apr.*

Theaters

Dade County Auditorium (2901 W. Flagler St., Miami 33135, tel. 305/545–3395) satisfies patrons with 2,498 comfortable seats, good sight lines, and acceptable acoustics.

Jackie Gleason Theater of the Performing Arts (TOPA, 1700 Washington Ave., Miami Beach 33139, tel. 305/673–7700 for information; 305/673–8300 for ticket sales for the Broadway Series). In 1990 TOPA completed a $23-million, three-year series of improvements that have finally provided adequate acoustics and good visibility for all 2,750 seats.

Gusman Center for the Performing Arts (174 E. Flagler St., Miami 33131, tel. 305/372–0925). Located in downtown Miami, the center has 1,739 seats made for sardines—and the best acoustics in town. An ornate former movie palace, the hall resembles a Moorish courtyard. Lights twinkle, starlike, from the ceiling.

Gusman Concert Hall (1314 Miller Dr., Coral Gables 33124, tel. 305/284–2438). This 600-seat hall on the University of Miami's Coral Gables campus has good acoustics, and plenty of room. Parking is a problem when school is in session.

Jan McArt's International Room (Marco Polo Hotel, 19201 Collins Ave., Miami Beach 33180, tel. 305/932–7880) is the new Miami-area venue for musicals, which are performed year-round in the 270-seat hotel theater.

Spanish Theater Spanish theater prospers, although many companies have short lives. About 20 Spanish companies perform light comedy, puppetry, vaudeville, and political satire. To locate them, read the Spanish newspapers. When you phone, be prepared for a conversation in Spanish. Most of the box-office personnel don't speak English.

Teatro Avante. Three to six productions are staged annually at El Carrosel (235 Alcazar Ave., tel. 305/445–8877). A Hispanic theater festival is held each May. *Box 453005, Miami 33245–3005, tel. 305/858–4155.*

Prometeo. This theater has produced three to four bilingual Spanish-English plays a year for 19 years. *Miami-Dade Community College, New World Center Campus, 300 N.E. 2nd Ave., Miami, tel. 305/237–3263. Admission free. Call for invitation.*

Teatro de Bellas Artes. A 255-seat theater on Calle Ocho, Little Havana's main commercial street, Teatro de Bellas Artes presents eight Spanish plays and musicals a year. *2173 S.W. 8th St., Miami, tel. 305/325–0515. No credit cards. Dramas Fri.–Sat. 9 PM and Sun. 3 PM. Musical comedy Sat. midnight and Sun. 9 PM. Recitals Sun. 6 PM.*

Nightlife

Greater Miami has no concentration of night spots like Bourbon Street in New Orleans or Rush Street in Chicago, but nightlife thrives throughout the Miami area in scattered locations, including Miami Beach, Little Haiti, Little Havana, Coconut Grove, the fringes of downtown Miami, and south-suburban Kendall. Individual clubs offer jazz, reggae, salsa, various forms of rock-and-roll, and top-40 sounds on different nights of the week. Some clubs refuse entrance to anyone under 21; others set the age limit at 25.

For current information, see the Weekend Section in the Friday edition of *The Miami Herald;* the calendar in *Miami Today,* a free weekly newspaper available each Thursday in downtown Miami, Coconut Grove, and Coral Gables; and *New Times,* a free weekly distributed throughout Dade County each Wednesday.

Love 94 (WLVE, 93.9 FM) sponsors an entertainment line with information on touring groups of all kinds, except classical (tel. 305/654–9436). Blues Hot Line lists local blues clubs and bars (tel. 305/666–6656). Jazz Hot Line lists local jazz programs (tel. 305/382–3938).

On Miami Beach, where the sounds of jazz and reggae spill into the streets, fashion models and photographers frequent the lobby bars of small Art Deco hotels.

Throughout the Greater Miami area, bars and cocktail lounges in larger hotels operate discos nightly, with live entertainment on weekends. Many hotels extend their bars into open-air courtyards, where patrons dine and dance under the stars throughout the year.

Bars **Cactus Cantina.** An unpretentious local hangout, this presents live music every night but Thursday—comedy night. The food and beer selections are tops. *630 6th St., Miami Beach, tel. 305/*

532–5095. Open weekdays, 5–5, weekends 5–7. Cover on weekends.

Churchill's Hideaway. This enclave of Anglicism in Little Haiti is popular with cruise-line employees and international sports fans. Its satellite dish picks up BBC news programs, and a Sharp Six System VHS plays foreign-format tapes of international soccer and rugby games. Not for the unadventurous. Live music Tuesday and Thursday through Saturday. *5501 N.E. 2nd Ave., Miami, tel. 305/757–1807. No credit cards. Open Mon.–Thurs. 11 AM–1 AM, Fri. 11 AM–3 AM, Sat. 9:30 AM–3 AM, Sun. noon–2 AM, but sometimes it opens earlier and closes later. Call ahead.*

Hungry Sailor. This small English-style pub is decorated with nautical charts, marine flags, and flotsam and jetsam. It's Coconut Grove's answer to *the pub* with six English/Irish ales and beers on tap plus 18 varieties of bottled brews. The "Sailor" serves, in addition to English-American food, traditional Caribbean clam chowder and other island tidbits. Reggae and calypso nightly. *3064½ Grand Ave., Coconut Grove, tel. 305/444–9359. AE, DC, MC, V. Open 11:30 AM–2:30 AM.*

Mac's Club Deuce. This South Miami Beach gem shows off top international models who pop in to have a drink, shoot some pool. All you get late at night are minipizzas, but the pizzazz lasts, akin to that of the bar scene in *Star Wars,* they'll tell you. One of the best. *222 14th St., Miami Beach, tel. 305/673–9537. No credit cards. Open daily 8 AM–5 AM.*

Stuart's Bar-Lounge. *Esquire* called Stuart's (built 1926) one of the best new bars of 1987. Six years later locals still favor it. It is decorated with beveled mirrors, mahogany paneling, French posters, pictures of old Coral Gables, and art nouveau lighting. *162 Alcazar Ave., Coral Gables, tel. 305/444–1666. Open Mon.–Sat. 5 PM–12:30 AM. AE, DC, MC, V. Closed Sun.*

Taurus Steak House. The bar, built in 1922 of native cypress, nightly draws an over-30 singles crowd that drifts outside to a patio. A band plays on weekends. *3540 Main Hwy., Coconut Grove, tel. 305/448–0633. AE, DC, MC, V. Open weekdays 11:30 AM–midnight, Fri.–Sun. 11:30 AM–3. Dinner nightly.*

Tobacco Road. This bar, opened in 1912, holds Miami's oldest liquor license. Upstairs, in space occupied by a speakeasy during Prohibition, local and national blues bands perform Friday and Saturday and in scheduled weeknight concerts. Excellent bar food. *626 S. Miami Ave., Miami, tel. 305/374–1198. AE, DC, MC, V. Open weekdays 11:30 AM–5 AM, weekends 1 PM–5 AM. Lunch served weekdays. Dinner served Sun.–Thurs.*

Tropics International Restaurant. Music from right-on jazz to rhythm-and-blues, and no cover charge, make Tropics worth popping into. This Memphis-style bar was created by Victor Farinas, one of Miami's top nouveau designers. And if the heat's up, bring your suit and take a dip in the pool where there's live music Thursday through Saturday nights. International menu. *960 Ocean Dr., Miami Beach, tel. 305/531–5335. AE, D, DC, MC, V. Open Mon.–Thurs. 11 AM–2 AM, Fri. 11 AM–4 AM, Sat. 8:30 AM–4 AM, Sun. 8:30 AM–2 AM.*

Comedy Clubs

Coconut Grove. Three comedy clubs make the scene in this popular part of town: **Coconuts Comedy Club** at the Peacock Cafe (2977 McFarlane Rd., tel. 305/446–2582) and at the Howard Johnson Motor Lodge (Golden Glades Interchange, 16500 N.W. 2nd Ave., tel. 305/940–7371); the **Improv** (3015 Grand Ave., tel. 305/441–8200) in the new Cocowalk indoor/out mall;

and the long-standing and outrageous **Mental Floss** (3138 Commodore Plaza, tel. 305/448–1011).

Uncle Funny's Comedy Club. This 1990s version of vaudeville comedy thrives with humor that's adult, but not obscene. Two acts per show; new performers each week. *Mark Twain's Riverboat Playhouse, 13700 N. Kendall Dr., Miami, tel. 305/388–1992. MC, V. $6 cover Fri., $7 Sat., both nights have 2-drink-minimum policy. Shows weekends 9:30 and 11:30.*

Disco/Jazz/ Rock Clubs

Baja Beach Club. Waiters and waitresses dress in beach attire as they cater to the 6,000 or so people who go through here on the weekends. You'll find three bars under one roof and a very popular balcony where customers hang out to watch the goings-on in the heart of Coconut Grove, below. There's live entertainment, lots of sports events, dancing, and good food. *3015 Grand Ave., Cocowalk in Coconut Grove, tel. 305/445–0278. AE, MC, V. All rooms open until 5 AM. Sports Bar opens 11 AM; Baja Beach Club 5 PM; Music Room 8 or 9 PM.*

Copacabana Supper Club. In 1992, a gala new South American revue with up to 40 cast members was introduced Friday through Sunday nights, complete with chorus line, song and dance, and individual performers. During the week expect theme nights. Complete restaurant service. *3600 S.W. 8th St., Miami, tel. 305/443–7020. AE, MC, V. Open Wed.–Sun. 5:30 PM–4 AM. Reservations advised.*

Stringfellows. Opened in May 1989, Peter Stringfellow's Coconut Grove club has been attracting guests from international artistic, business, and social circles, many of whom are already familiar with Stringfellow's other clubs in London and New York. Guests enter through green glass doors decorated with an etched-glass butterfly crest and ascend to the club's second-floor restaurant and nightclub. The restaurant, decorated with art-deco furnishings, pink tablecloths, and fresh orchids, features well-prepared international cuisine. The nightclub, which opens at 11:30, features rock music pumped through a state-of-the-art sound system and a sophisticated light system capable of producing hundreds of variations. *3390 Mary St., Miami 33133, tel. 305/446–7555. Reservations advised. Club cover charge: $10 Tues.–Thurs., $15 Sat. AE, DC, MC, V. Closed Sun., Mon., Christmas. À la carte menu served 8 PM–2:30 AM, late-night supper from 2:30–4 AM. Club open 11 PM–5 AM.*

Stefano's of Key Biscayne. Live band performs nightly, 7–11 PM. Then this northern Italian restaurant becomes a disco, complete with wood dance floor. *24 Crandon Blvd., Key Biscayne, tel. 305/361–7007. AE, DC, MC, V. Open 5 PM–5 AM nightly.*

Nightclubs

Three trendy new clubs that have opened in South Beach include the **Paragon** (1235 Washington Ave., Miami Beach 33139, tel. 305/534–1235; $10 cover, open Thurs.–Sat.) that draws a gay crowd, **Van Dome** (1532 Washington Ave., Miami Beach 33139, tel. 305/534–4288; cover $10 Saturday, variable Fri.), in a former synagogue, and **The Whiskey** (1250 Ocean Dr., Miami Beach 33139, tel. 305/531–0713; cover $5 Fri. and Sat. only, open nightly), a spinoff of Manhattan's pop Paramount Plaza Hotel bar.

Mako's Bay Club. This new Top-40 club on the north side of town, close by Bay Vista Campus of Florida International University, has been a quick hit among the younger set since its late 1991 opening. *17290 Biscayne Blvd., No. Miami Beach,* *tel. 305/944–7805. Cover: $3 to $5. AE, DC, MC, V. Open nightly 9 PM–6 AM, from 6 PM Sat.*

Les Violins Supper Club. This standby has been owned for 26 years by the Cachaidora-Currais family, who ran a club and restaurant in Havana. Live dance band. Wood dance floor. Dinner. *1751 Biscayne Blvd., Miami, tel. 305/371–8668. Open 7 PM. Closes Tues.–Thurs. and Sun. 1 AM, Fri. 2 AM, Sat. 3 AM. Reservations advised. AE, D, DC, MC, V. Closed Mon.*

Club Tropigala at La Ronde in the Fontainebleau Hilton Hotel. A seven-level round room decorated with orchids, banana leaves, and philodendrons to resemble a tropical jungle, this club is operated by owners of Les Violins. Two bands play Latin music for dancing on the wood floor. One live costumed show Wednesday, Thursday, and Friday; two Wednesday, Thursday, Sunday, some Friday, and Saturday. Dinner. Long wait for valet parking. *4441 Collins Ave., Miami Beach, tel. 305/672–7469. Reservations advised. AE, DC, MC, V. Open Wed.–Sun. 7 PM, or later.*

Performance Art Club

Miami Arts Asylum. Arty Bohemianism flourishes here in painting, sculpture, performance, music. Attire and attitudes make it eclectic and electric. *1445 Washington Ave., Miami Beach, tel. 305/532–0922. Call for nights, hours, admission.*

5 The Everglades

Introduction

By George and Rosalie Leposky

Updated by Herb Hiller

Greater Miami is the only metropolitan area in the United States with two national parks in its backyard: Everglades and Biscayne. The long-term survival of both parks is threatened by environmental problems.

Everglades National Park, created in 1947, was meant to preserve the slow-flowing "river of grass" that was under stress from channelizing and from weirs installed for flood control. But the water has been steadily more polluted by pesticide runoff from dairy, sugar cane, and vegetable growers and, in turn, the disrupted flow has caused further subtle but steady changes in Everglades wildlife habitat and the quickening demise of Florida Bay. Visitors to the park over the years note diminished numbers of birds; the black bear has been eliminated and the Florida panther reduced to near extinction. In 1992 the nonprofit group American Rivers declared the Everglades the fourth most endangered river in North America.

Biscayne National Park, established as a national monument in 1968, and 12 years later expanded and upgraded to park status, is mostly underwater. The park includes the northernmost sections of Florida's tropical reef, which is under assault from the polluted and massive freshwater outflow of the canals that drain the Everglades, as well as from direct damage to corals by boat anchors and from commercial shipping that runs off course and onto the reefs.

At some levels, the state and federal governments have joined environmentalists who are trying to stem the damage. Local populations that once resisted any interference with their agricultural policies grudgingly cooperate. Meanwhile, new motels, shopping centers, and restaurants have opened; old ones are sprucing up in Homestead and Florida City, gateways to the parks. City officials have created a historic district downtown that promotes restoration of Homestead's commercial heart. It's all an effort to house, feed, and amuse many of the million visitors who will explore the Everglades in 1992—and the 100,000 hardy souls who will discover Biscayne.

If you intend to spend just one day at Everglades National Park, take the 38-mile main park road from the Main Visitor Center to Flamingo to see a cross section of the park's ecosystems: hardwood hammock (tree islands), freshwater prairie, pineland, freshwater slough, cypress, coastal prairie, mangrove, and marine/estuarine.

The Gulf Coast and Key Largo ranger stations and the Flamingo Visitor Center offer access to the mangroves and marine habitats—Gulf Coast in the Ten Thousand Islands region along the Gulf of Mexico near Everglades City; Flamingo and Key Largo in Florida Bay. You can take tour boat rides from Everglades City and Flamingo through this ecosystem (*see* Guided Tours, below) and hire a fishing guide to show you where the big ones bite (*see* Participant Sports and Outdoor Activities, below).

Biscayne National Park encompasses almost 274 square miles, of which 96% are under water. Biscayne includes 18 miles of inhospitable mangrove shoreline on the mainland and 45 mangrove-fringed barrier islands seven miles to the east across Biscayne Bay. The bay is a lobster sanctuary and a nursery for fish, sponges, and crabs. Manatees and sea turtles also frequent its warm, shallow waters.

The islands (called keys) are fossilized coral reefs that emerged from the sea when glaciers trapped much of the world's water supply during the Ice Age. Today a tropical hardwood forest grows in the crevices of these rocky keys.

East of the keys, coral reefs 3 miles seaward attract divers and snorkelers (*see* Participant Sports and Outdoor Activities, below). Biscayne is the only national park in the continental United States with living coral reefs and is the nation's largest marine park.

The park boundary encompasses the continental shelf to a depth of 60 feet. East of that boundary, the shelf falls rapidly away to a depth of 400 feet at the edge of the Gulf Stream.

Essential Information

Getting Around

By Plane
Commercial Flights

Miami International Airport (MIA) is the closest commercial airport to Everglades National Park and Biscayne National Park. It's 34 miles from Homestead and 83 miles from the Flamingo resort in Everglades National Park.

By Car

From the north, the main highways to Homestead-Florida City are U.S. 1, the Homestead Extension of the Florida Turnpike, and Krome Avenue (Rte. 997/old U.S. 27).

From Miami to Biscayne National Park, take the turnpike extension to the Tallahassee Road (S.W. 137th Ave.) exit, turn left, and go south. Turn left at North Canal Drive (S.W. 328th St.), go east, and follow signs to park headquarters at Convoy Point. The park is about 30 miles from downtown Miami.

From Homestead to Biscayne National Park, take U.S. 1 or Krome Avenue (Rte. 997) to Lucy Street (S.E. 8th St.). Turn east. Lucy Street becomes North Canal Drive (S.W. 328th St.). Follow signs about 8 miles to the park headquarters.

From Homestead to Everglades National Park's Main Visitor Center and Flamingo, take U.S. 1 or Krome Avenue (Rte. 997/ Old U.S. 27) south to Florida City. Turn right (west) onto Rte. 9336. Follow signs to the park entrance. The Main Visitor Center is 11 miles from Homestead; Flamingo is 49 miles from Homestead.

To reach the western gateway to Everglades National Park, take U.S. 41 (the Tamiami Trail) west from Miami. It's 40 miles to the Shark Valley Information Center and 83 miles to the Gulf Coast Ranger Station at Everglades City.

To reach the south end of Everglades National Park in the Florida Keys, take U.S. 1 south from Homestead. It's 27 miles to the Key Largo Ranger Station (between MM 98 and 99 on the Overseas Hwy.).

Rental Cars

American Eagle Rent-A-Car, (28400 S. Dixie Hwy., Homestead, 33033, tel. 305/245–0300; 305/247–0873), **Enterprise Rent-a-Car** (30428 S. Fed. Hwy., Homestead 33030, tel. 305/ 246–2056). Rental cars also available at MIA.

By Van

Super Shuttle. 11-passenger air-conditioned vans operate between MIA and Homestead. Service on demand from MIA; go to Super Shuttle booth outside most luggage areas on lower level. 24-hour advance reservation requested returning to MIA. *Tel. 305/871–2000. 24-hr daily service. $26–$35 per person depending on zip code in Homestead, $5 each additional person traveling together. 10% discount for round-trips anyplace in Dade County. AE, DC, MC, V.*

The Airporter. Five shuttle bus services a day run between the Holiday Inn, Homestead (with a stop at the Holiday Inn, Cutler Ridge), and the airport. Service from Homestead is between 8 AM and 6:20 PM; from the airport between 9:15 AM and 7:30 PM. Trips take approximately one hour. The airport station is in the bus loop in front of Concourse E. *One-way fares $15. Reservations required. Tel. 305/247–8874, 305/247–8877.*

By Bus

Metrobus. Route 1A runs from Homestead to MIA only during peak weekday hours: 6:30–9 AM and 4–6:30 PM.

Greyhound/Trailways operates three trips daily north to near Miami International Airport, but the trip is not direct. The Greyhound/Trailways depot (4111 N.W. 27th St.) is about a $5 cab ride from the airport. Coming from the airport to connect with one of Greyhound's three daily buses south to Homestead, you can take an ARTS (Airport Region Taxi Service) car for about $5 (including the normal $1 surcharge on cab service from MIA),stopping at the Homestead Bus Station (5 N.E. 3rd Rd., tel. 305/247–2040).

By Taxi

Homestead Yellow Cab Company. Service in Homestead-Florida City area. Full service to and from Flamingo and the tour boats in Biscayne National Park. Service from Homestead to MIA. *416 N.E. 1st Rd., Homestead, tel. 305/247–7777. No credit cards.*

By Boat

U.S. Customs. The nearest U.S. Customs phones to the two national parks are at **Watson Island Marina** (1050 MacArthur Causeway, Miami, tel. 305/371–2378), about 25 nautical miles to Biscayne National Park headquarters, 50 nautical miles to Flamingo; and **Tavernier Creek Marina** (MM 90.5, U.S. 1, Tavernier, tel. 305/252–0194 from Miami, 305/852–5854 from the Keys), about 48 nautical miles to Biscayne National Park headquarters, 25 nautical miles to Flamingo.

Scenic Drives

Main road to Flamingo in Everglades National Park. It's 38 road miles from the Main Visitor Center to Flamingo, across six distinct ecosystems (with access from the road to two others). Highlights of the trip include a dwarf cypress forest, the ecotone (transition zone) between saw grass and mangrove forest, and a wealth of wading birds at Mrazek and Coot Bay ponds. Boardwalks and trails along the main road and several short spurs allow you to see the Everglades without getting your feet wet. Well-written interpretive signs en route will help you understand this diverse wilderness.

Tamiami Trail. U.S. 41 from Miami to the Gulf Coast crosses the Everglades and the Big Cypress National Preserve. Highlights of the trip include sweeping views across the saw grass to the Shark River Slough, a visit to the Miccosukee Indian Reservation, and the Big Cypress National Preserve's variegated pattern of wet prairies, ponds, marshes, sloughs, and strands.

It's 83 miles to the Gulf Coast Ranger Station at Everglades City.

Guided Tours

Tours of Everglades National Park and Biscayne National Park typically focus on native wildlife, plants, and park history. Concessionaires operate the Everglades tram tours and the boat cruises in both parks. In addition, the National Park Service organizes a variety of free programs at Everglades National Park. Ask a ranger for the daily schedule.

Orientation Tours

Since 1980 **All Florida Adventure Tours** has operated from one-day to two-week tours that emphasize nature, history, and ecology. Custom tours also arranged upon request. *8263–B S.W. 107th Ave., Miami 33173–3729, tel. 305/270–0219. MC, V.*

Special-Interest Tours

Agricultural Tour

Agricultural Guided Tour. Seasonal 2½-hour narrated bus tour leaves from the State Farmers Market in Florida City and visits among 2,400 nurseries and 90,000 acres of groves and farmed land that produces such unusual fruit crops as mamey sapote, mangos, papayas, plantains, and popular tropical root crops that include calabaza, malanga, and yucca. *300 N. Krome Ave., Florida City 33034, tel. 305/248–6798. Cost: $10 adults, $8 youths 12–17, children under 12 free. No credit cards. Tours Dec. 1–Apr. 1, weekdays 9 and 1:30.*

Air Tours

Air Tours of South Florida. Three 50-minute narrated tours cover either the Everglades, Florida Keys, or Miami and Miami Beach; an 80-minute Grand Circle Tour covers all. *Homestead General Aviation Airport, 28720 S.W. 217th Ave., Homestead 33030, tel. 305/248–1100 or 800/628–3610. Cost: $59 per person for 50-min tour, $110 for 80-min, minimum 2 people. Reservations recommended. AE, MC, V. Open daily 9 AM–4 PM.*

Airboat Rides

Buffalo Tiger's Florida Everglades Airboat Ride. The former chairman of the Miccosukee tribe will take you on a 35-minute airboat ride through the Everglades, with a stop at an old Indian camp. Opportunities to watch birds, turtles, and alligators. *Tour location: 12 mi west of Krome Ave., 20 mi west of the Miami city limits (Rte. 997), tel. 305/559–5250. Cost: $8 adults, $5 children under 10. No credit cards. Open daily 10–5 winter, 10–6 summer. Closed Fri. Sept. and Oct.*

Coopertown Airboat Ride. This 30-minute airboat ride through the Everglades saw grass takes you to two hammocks (subtropical hardwood forests) and alligator holes. Bird-watching opportunities. *Tamiami Trail, 5 mi west of Krome Ave., 15 mi west of Miami city limits, tel. 305/226–6048. Cost: $7 per person for 3 or more; minimum $18 for the boat. No credit cards. Open daily 8 AM–dusk.*

Everglades Alligator Farm. A 4-mile, 30-minute tour of the River of Grass leaves at least every half hour and includes free tour of an alligator farm. Big improvements have been made at this site since 1991, with new fencing, new landscaping, and a new gift shop. *40351 S.W. 192nd Ave., tel. 305/AIRBOAT. Cost: $9 adults, $8 senior citizens, $4.50 children 4–12, under 4 free. AE, D, MC, V. Open daily 9–5.*

Boat Tours

Biscayne National Park Tour Boats. You'll ride to Biscayne National Park's living coral reefs 10 miles offshore on a 53-foot glass-bottom boat. A separate tour to Elliott Key visitor center, on a barrier island 7 miles offshore across Biscayne Bay, is conducted only in winter, based on demand, when mosquitoes are less active. *East end of North Canal Dr. (S.W. 328th St.), Homestead, tel. 305/247–2400. Glass-bottom boat cost: $16.50 adults, $8.50 children, $24.50 snorkelers. Elliott Key tour Sun. only at 10 AM, if demand warrants, prices same as for glass-bottom-boat tour. Reservations required. MC, V. Office open daily 8:30–6. Phone for daily schedule.*

Back Country Tour. A two-hour cruise from Flamingo Lodge Marina & Outpost Resort aboard a 40-passenger pontoon boat covers 12–15 miles through tropical estuaries fringed with impenetrable mangrove forests. You may see manatees, dolphins, sharks, alligators, and many species of bird life, including bald eagles. *Flamingo Marina, Flamingo, tel. 305/253–2241 or 813/695–3101; fax 813/695–3921. Cruises daily. Tours Nov.–Apr. Phone for schedule. Reservations accepted. Cost: $10.50 adults, $5 children 6–12, under 6 free. AE, DC, MC, V.*

Everglades National Park Boat Tours. Sammy Hamilton operates three separate 14-mile tours through the Ten Thousand Islands region along the Gulf of Mexico on the western margin of the park. *Everglades National Park's Gulf Coast Ranger Station on Rte. 29, about 3 mi south of U.S. 41 (Tamiami Trail), tel. 813/695–2591 or in FL 800/445–7724. Phone for schedule. Cost: $10 adults, $5 children 6–12, under 6 free. MC, V. Office open daily 8:30–5.*

Florida Bay Cruise. A 90-minute tour of Florida Bay from Flamingo Lodge Marina & Outpost Resort aboard *Bald Eagle*, a 90-passenger pontoon boat. The tour offers a close look at bird life on rookery islands in the bay and on sandbars during low tide. In winter, you're likely to see white pelicans; in summer, magnificent frigatebirds. Also offers backcountry and sunset tours. *Flamingo Marina, Flamingo, tel. 305/253–2241 or 813/695–3101. Phone for schedule. Reservations accepted. Cost: $7.75 adults, $3.75 children 6–12. AE, DC, MC, V. Cruises daily.*

Florida Boat Tours. Back-country tours outside Everglades National Park in Everglades City area. Runs three 24-passenger airboats for 30-minute rides, 48-passenger pontoon boat and airboat for one-hour cruise, which includes visit to Indian Village; departure is from Everglades City. Boats are Coast Guard approved. *Tel. 813/695–4400 or in FL 800/282–9194. Phone for schedule. Cost: $12 adults, $6 children 4–12. MC, V.*

Tram Tours

Wilderness Tram Tour. Snake Bight is an indentation in the Florida Bay shoreline near Flamingo. You can go there aboard a 48-passenger screened tram on this two-hour tour through a mangrove forest and a coastal prairie to a 100-yard boardwalk over the mud flats at the edge of the bight. It's a good birding spot. Tram operates subject to mosquito, weather, and trail conditions. Driver has insect repellent on board. *Departs from Flamingo Lodge gift shop 10:30 AM, 1:30 and 3:30, tel. 305/253–2241 or 813/695–3101. Reservations accepted. Cost: $7 adults, $3.50 children 6–12. AE, DC, MC, V.*

Shark Valley Tram Tours. The trams take a new 15-mile loop road, which is elevated, has 200 culverts, and is considerably less flood prone when the summer rains come. Propane- and gas-powered trams travel into the interior, stopping at a 50-foot observation tower on the site of an oil well drilled in the 1940s. From atop the tower, you'll view the Everglades' vast "river of grass" sweeping south toward the Gulf of Mexico. The trams are covered but have open sides, so carry rain gear. (Plastic raincoats are sold for $1.) *Shark Valley entrance to Everglades National Park, 40 mi west of Miami off U.S. 41 (Tamiami Trail), tel. 305/221–8455. Cost: $7 adults, $3.50 12 and under, $6.25 senior citizens. No credit cards. Open daily all year 9–4. Reservations recommended Dec.–Mar.*

Personal Guides

Swampland Airboat Tours. Collier County native and licensed guide Donald McDowell will take up to six people on day or night tours of the Big Cypress National Preserve. Pick-ups arranged at any of six landings. *Box 619, Everglades City 33929, tel. 813/695–2740. Cost: 1–2 persons $60/hr., $10 each additional person up to 6. Reservations required.*

Flamingo Lodge Marina & Outpost Resort. Captains of charter fishing boats are available to give individual tours out of Flamingo. Make reservations several weeks in advance through the marina store. *TW Services Inc., Everglades National Park, Box 428, Flamingo 33030, tel. 305/253–2241 or 813/695–3101. Cost: $265 a day (for up to 3 persons), $165 a half day. Additional persons $20 each. AE, DC, MC, V. Available year-round.*

Historical Attraction

Florida Pioneer Museum. This down-home collection of articles from daily life evokes the homestead period on the last frontier of mainland America. Housed in three yellow structures from the early 20th century—the relocated Homestead East Coast Railway Station, railway agent's house, and a caboose—the collections recall a time when Henry Flagler's railroad vaulted the Florida Keys on its epic extension to Key West, and when Homestead and Florida City were briefly the take-charge supply outposts. The agent's house was moved to the museum grounds in 1964, the station in 1976. *826 N. Krome Ave., Florida City 33034, tel. 305/246–9531. Donation: $3 adults, $1 children. Open daily 1–5. Closed major holidays.*

Important Addresses and Numbers

Tourist Information

South Dade Visitors Information Center. *160 U.S. 1, Florida City 33034, tel. 305/245–9180 or 800/388–9669. Open daily 8–6.*

Greater Homestead-Florida City Chamber of Commerce. (43 N. Krome Ave., Homestead 33030, tel. 305/247–2332).

Emergencies

Homestead, Florida City, and unincorporated Dade County use the same emergency number, 911. You can dial free from pay phones.

In the national parks, the rangers perform police, fire, and medical-emergency functions. Look for the rangers at park visitor centers and information stations, or phone the park switchboards: Biscayne (tel. 305/247–2044); Everglades (tel. 305/247–6211).

Hospitals

South Miami Hospital of Homestead. 24-hour emergency room. *160 N.W. 13th St., Homestead, tel. 305/248–3232. Physician referral service, tel. 305/248–DOCS.*

Marine Phone Numbers

Biscayne National Park (tel. 305/247–2044). Rangers staff Elliott Key Visitor Center and Adams Key Information Center around the clock and can call the mainland on ship-to-shore radio. Park headquarters on Convoy Point open daily 8:30–6 winter, 9–5 summer. Park open 8–sunset year-round.

Florida Marine Patrol. Law-enforcement arm of the Florida Department of Natural Resources. Boating emergencies: 24-hour tel. 305/325–3346. Natural resource violations, including marine fishery laws, mangrove cuttings, manatee reports, filling of wetlands. *Tel. 305/325–3346.*

National Weather Service. National Hurricane Center office in Coral Gables supplies local forecasts. *Open weekdays 7:30–5, tel. 305/665–0429. For 24-hr weather recording, tel. 305/661–5065.*

U.S. Coast Guard

Miami Beach Coast Guard Base (tel. 305/535–4314 or 305/535–4315, VHF-FM Channel 16). Local marine emergencies, search-and-rescue, and reporting of navigation hazards.

Exploring the Everglades

Biscayne National Park

Numbers in the margin correspond to points of interest on the Everglades and Biscayne National Parks map.

Because 96% of Biscayne National Park's acreage is under water, you must take a boat ride to visit most of it and snorkel or scuba dive to appreciate it fully. If you don't have your own boat, a concessionaire will take you to the coral reefs 10 miles offshore. These dome-shape patch reefs—some the size of a student's desk, others as broad as a large parking lot—rely on the delicate balance of temperature, depth, light, and water quality that the park was created to maintain.

A diverse population of colorful fish flits through the reefs: angelfish, gobies, grunts, parrot fish, pork fish, wrasses, and many more.

From December through April, when the mosquito population is relatively quiescent, you can comfortably explore several of the mangrove-fringed barrier islands 7 miles offshore. Tropical hardwood forests cloak the upper reaches of these fossilized coral reefs.

The list below describes the facilities at each of Biscayne National Park's visitor service areas, and also at the Metro-Dade County parks within the national park's boundaries.

1. **Adams Key Information Station.** Boat dock, picnic area, rest rooms, short nature trail. Ranger station has ship-to-shore radio contact with mainland. Day use only.

2. **Boca Chita Key.** Mark C. Honeywell, former president of Minneapolis's Honeywell Co., bought this island in 1937 and built the ornamental lighthouse, rainwater catchment cisterns, a wall, and other buildings of coral rock. There is a boat dock, picnic area, and rest rooms. Lighthouse open on occasion; ask rangers.

3. **Convoy Point Information Station.** Park headquarters. New $8 million administration and visitor center with exhibits, docks, and boardwalk is scheduled to open by 1993. Currently small visitor center and outdoor kiosk with bulletin boards. Launch-

The Everglades and Biscayne National Parks

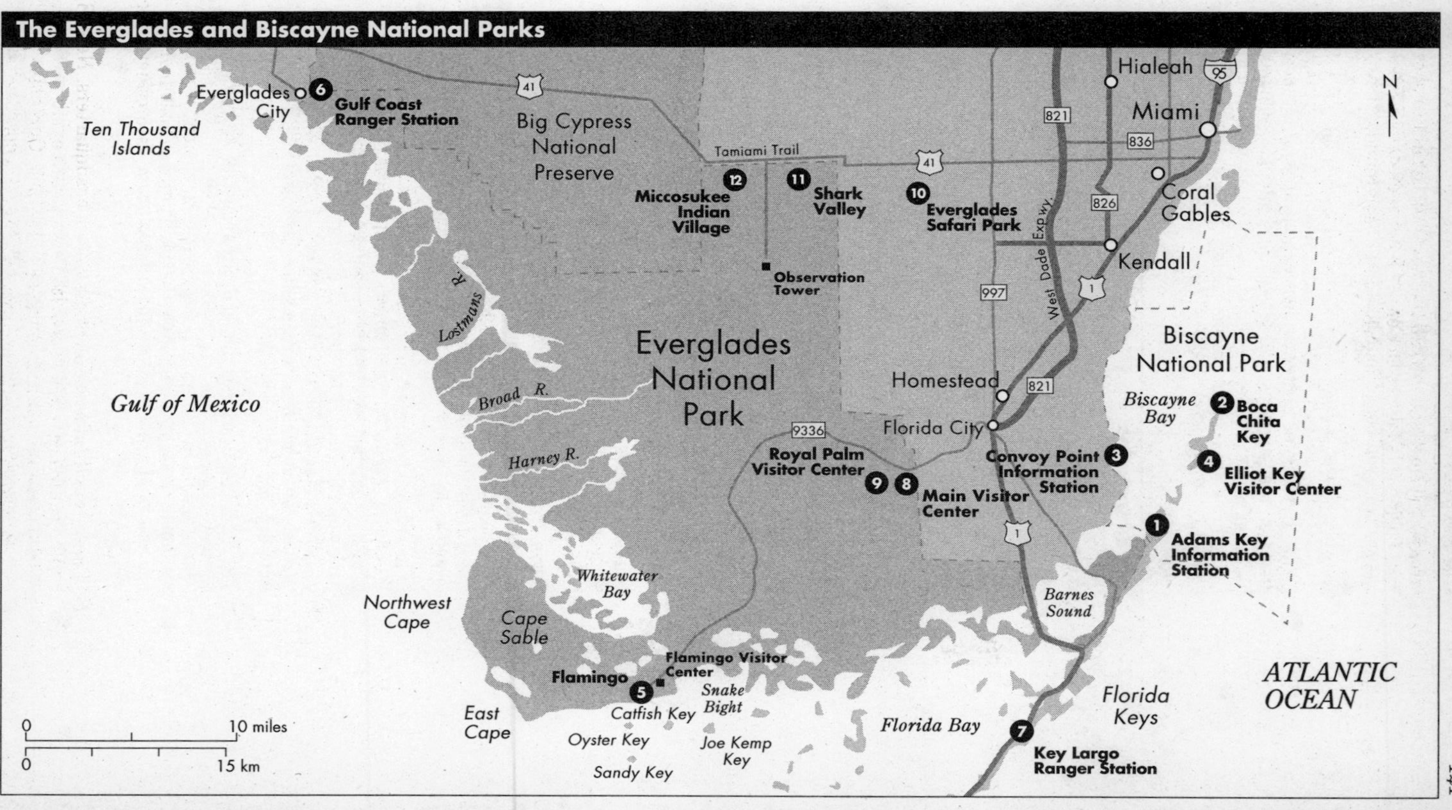

ing ramp for canoes and sailboards. Boardwalk over shallow water near shore to jetty and path along jetty. Picnic area. Dock where you board tour boats to reefs and Elliott Key. *At east end of North Canal Dr. (S.W. 328th St.), Homestead, tel. 305/247–PARK. Admission free. Open year-round.*

4 **Elliott Key Visitor Center.** Indoor exhibit area on second floor displays coral, sponges, and sea-turtle shells on a "touching table" that children especially enjoy. A screened enclosure under the exhibit area houses picnic tables, bulletin boards, and a slide show. *Tel. 305/247–PARK. Open most weekends and holidays 10–4.*

The Everglades

Winter is the best time to visit Everglades National Park. Temperatures and mosquito activity are moderate. Low water levels concentrate the resident wildlife around sloughs that retain water all year. Migratory birds swell the avian population. Winter is also the busiest time in the park. Make reservations and expect crowds at Flamingo, the main visitor center, and Royal Palm—the most popular visitor service areas.

In spring the weather turns increasingly hot and dry. After Easter, fewer visitors come, and tours and facilities are less crowded. Migratory birds depart, and you must look harder to see wildlife. Be especially careful with campfires and matches; this is when the wildfire-prone saw-grass prairies and pinelands are most vulnerable.

Summer brings intense sun and billowing clouds that unleash torrents of rain on the Everglades. Thunderstorms roll in almost every afternoon, bringing the park 90% of its annual 60-inch rainfall from June through October. Water levels rise. Wildlife disperses. Mosquitoes hatch, swarm, and descend on you in voracious clouds. It's a good time to stay away, although some brave souls do come to explore. Europeans constitute 80% of the summer visitors.

Summer in south Florida lingers until mid-October, when the first cold front sweeps through. The rains cease, water levels start to fall, and the ground begins to dry out. Wildlife moves toward the sloughs. Flocks of migratory birds and tourists swoop in, as the cycle of seasons builds once more to the winter peak activity.

Whenever you come, we urge you to experience the real Everglades by getting your feet wet—but most people who visit the park won't do that. Boat tours at Everglades City and Flamingo, a tram ride at Shark Valley, and boardwalks at several locations along the main park road allow you to see the Everglades with dry feet.

The list below describes the facilities at each of the park's visitor service areas.

5 **Flamingo.** Museum, lodge, restaurant, lounge, gift shop, marina, and campground. *Mailing address: Box 279, Homestead 33030, tel. 305/247–6211 (Park Service), tel. 305/253–2241 (Everglades Lodge). Visitor center open daily 8–5.*

6 **Gulf Coast Ranger Station.** Visitor center, where back-country campers pick up required free permits; exhibits; gift shop. *Follow Everglades National Park signs from Tamiami Trail*

(U.S. 41) south on Rte. 29, tel. 813/695–3311. Admission free. Open daily in winter 7–4:30, reduced hours in summer.

7 **Key Largo Ranger Station.** No exhibits, no docks, chiefly for canoers. *98710 Overseas Hwy., Key Largo, tel. 305/852–5119. Not always staffed; phone ahead. Admission free.*

8 **Main Visitor Center.** Exhibits, film, bookstore, park headquarters. *11 mi west of Homestead on Rte. 9336, tel. 305/242–7700. Visitor center open 8–5. Admission: $5 per car (good for 7 days); $2 per person on foot, bicycle, or motorcycle; U.S. senior citizens over 62 free. Park open 24 hrs.*

9 **Royal Palm Visitor Center.** Anhinga Trail boardwalk, Gumbo Limbo Trail through hammock, museum, bookstore, vending machines. *Tel. 305/242–7700. Open 8–4:30, with ½ hour off for lunch.*

10 **Everglades Safari Park.** This commercial attraction includes an airboat ride, jungle trail, observation platform, alligator wrestling, wildlife museum, gift shop, and restaurant. *9 mi west of Krome Ave., 17 mi west of Miami city limits, on Tamiami Trail (U.S. 41), tel. 305/226–6923 or 305/223–3804. Admission: $10 adults, $5 children under 12. No credit cards. Open daily 8:30–5.*

11 **Shark Valley.** Tram tour, ¼-mile boardwalk, hiking trails, rotating exhibits, bookstore. *Box 42, Ochopee 33943, tel. 305/221–8776. Open daily 8:30–5. Admission: $3 per car, $1 per person on foot, bicycle, or motorcycle (good for 7 days); U.S. senior citizens over 62 free. 2-hr. tram tours: $7 adult, $3.50 12 and under. Departures every hour between 9 and 4 in winter, less frequently in summer. Reservations recommended Dec.–Mar. No credit cards. Show Shark Valley admission receipt at Main Visitor Center and pay only the difference there.*

12 **Miccosukee Indian Village.** Near the Shark Valley entrance to Everglades National Park, the Miccosukee tribe operates an Indian village as a tourist attraction. You can watch Indian families cooking and making clothes, dolls, beadwork, and baskets. You'll also see an alligator-wrestling demonstration. The village has a boardwalk and a museum. *On Tamiami Trail (U.S. 41) 25 mi west of Miami. Mailing address: Box 440021, Miami 33144, tel. 305/223–8380. Admission: $5 adults, $3.50 children. Airboat rides: $7 for 30-min trip to another Indian camp on an island in the heart of the Everglades. Open daily 9–5.*

Shopping

Biscayne National Park

Biscayne National Park Tour Boats. T-shirts, snorkeling and diving gear, snacks, and information on Biscayne National Park are available at park headquarters north of the canal. A dive shop van with air compressor is parked south of the canal at Homestead Bayfront Park. *Tel. 305/247–2400. MC, V. Open daily. Office open 8–6.*

Everglades National Park

Flamingo Lodge Marina & Outpost Resort (*see* Participant Sports, below). The gift shop sells mosquito repellent, Everglades guides, popular novels, T-shirts, souvenirs, and artwork. *Tel. 305/253–2241 or 813/695–3101. AE, DC, MC, V. Open Nov.–Mar. 9–8, though hours are extended during high season.*

Florida City **Robert Is Here.** A remarkable fruit stand. Robert grows and sells (in season) any tropical fruit that will grow. Near Everglades National Park. *19200 Palm Dr. (S.W. 344th St.), tel. 305/246–1592. No credit cards. Open daily 8–7.*

Homestead Homestead's main shopping streets are Homestead Boulevard (U.S. 1), Krome Avenue (Rte. 997), where the heart of old Homestead has been historically themed with brick sidewalks, now attracting many antique stores, and Campbell Drive (S.W. 312th St., N.E. 8th St.). Shopping centers with major department stores are 10–20 miles north of Homestead along South Dixie Highway (U.S. 1).

Participant Sports and Outdoor Activities

Most of the sports and recreational opportunities in Everglades National Park and Biscayne National Park are related in some way to water or nature study, or both. Even on land, be prepared to get your feet wet on the region's marshy hiking trails. In summer, save your outdoor activities for early or late in the day to avoid the sun's strongest rays and use a sunscreen. Carry mosquito repellent at any time of year.

Water Sports

Boating

Carry aboard the proper *NOAA Nautical Charts* before you cast off to explore the waters of the parks. The charts cost $15.95 each and are sold at many marine stores in south Florida, at the Convoy Point Visitor Center in Biscayne National Park, and in Flamingo Marina.

Waterway Guide (southern regional edition) is an annual publication, which many boaters use as a guide to these waters. Bookstores all over south Florida sell it, or you can order it directly from the publisher. *Communications Channels, Book Department, 6255 Barfield Rd., Atlanta, GA 30328, tel. 800/233–3359. Cost: $32.95 plus $3 shipping and handling.*

Canoeing

The subtropical wilderness of southern Florida is a mecca for flat-water paddlers. In winter, you'll find the best canoeing that the two parks can offer. Temperatures are moderate, rainfall is minimal, and the mosquitoes are tolerable.

Before you paddle into the back country and camp overnight, get a required free permit from the rangers in the park where you plan to canoe (at Convoy Point, Elliott Key, and Adams Key for Biscayne; at Everglades City or Flamingo for Everglades. The Biscayne permit isn't valid for Everglades, and vice versa).

You don't need a permit for day trips, but tell someone where you're going and when you expect to return. Getting lost out here is easy, and spending the night without proper gear can be unpleasant, if not dangerous.

At Biscayne, you can explore five creeks through the mangrove wilderness within 1½ miles of park headquarters at Convoy Point.

Everglades has six well-marked canoe trails in the Flamingo area, including the southern end of the 100-mile Wilderness Waterway from Flamingo to Everglades City. North American Canoe Tours in Everglades City runs a three-hour shuttle service to haul people, cars, and canoes 151 road-miles between Everglades City and Flamingo.

The vendors listed below all rent aluminum canoes. Most have 17-foot Grummans. Bring your own cushions.

Biscayne National Park Tour Boats. At Convoy Point in Biscayne National Park. *Tel. 305/247–2400. Cost: $5 per hr., $17.50 for 4 hrs, $22.50 per day. No launch fee. MC, V. Office open daily 8:30–6.*

Everglades National Park Boat Tours. Gulf Coast Ranger Station in Everglades City. *Tel. 813/695–2591, in FL 800/445–7724. Cost: $15 per half day, $20 per day; Flamingo–Everglades City shuttle costs $100 round-trip with two canoes. MC, V. Open daily 8:30–4:30.*

North America Canoe Tours at Glades Haven. This outfitter rents canoes and runs guided Everglades trips approved by the National Park Service. *800 S.E. Copeland Ave., Box 5038, Everglades City 33929, tel. 813/695–4666. Canoes $20 the first day, $18 per day thereafter. Outfitter in 1990 opened a bed-and-breakfast in Everglades City called The Ivey House. Inquire for rates. No children under age 8 on guided tours. No pets in park campsites. Reservations required. MC, V. Open daily 7 AM–9 PM; guided trips Nov. 1–Mar. 31.*

Marinas Listed below are the major marinas serving the two parks. The dock masters at these marinas can provide information on other marine services you may need.

Black Point Marina. Facilities at this 155-acre Metro-Dade County Park with a hurricane-safe harbor basin, 5 miles north of Homestead Bayfront Park, include storage racks for 300 boats, 178 wet slips, 10 ramps, fuel, a bait-and-tackle shop, canoe-launching ramp, power-boat rentals, police station, and outside grill serving lunch and dinner, with bar. Shrimp fleet docks at the park. At east end of Coconut Palm Drive (S.W. 248th St.). From Florida's Turnpike, exit at S.W. 112th Avenue, go 2 blocks north, and turn east on Coconut Palm Drive. *24775 S.W. 87th Ave., Naranja, tel. 305/258–4092. AE, MC, V (restaurant only). Office open daily 8:30–5; park open 6 AM–sundown; restaurant open Thurs.–Sun. 11 AM–midnight. AE, MC, V.*

Marine Management. At Black Point Marina. Rents 15- to 20-foot open fishermen boats and bow riders. *Tel. 305/258–3500. MC, V. Open winter, weekdays 8–5, weekends 7–5; summer, weekdays until 6, weekends 7:30. Opening and closing times may vary. Closed Christmas.*

Pirate's Spa Marina. Just west of Black Point Park entrance. Shrimp boats dock along canal. Facilities include boat hoist, wet and dry storage, fuel, bait and tackle, and boat rental. *8701 Coconut Palm Dr. (S.W. 248th St.), Naranja, tel. 305/257–5100. No credit cards. Open weekdays 7 AM–sundown, weekends open 6 AM.*

Flamingo Lodge Marina & Outpost Resort. Fifty-slip marina rents 40 canoes, 10 power skiffs, 5 houseboats, and several private boats available for charter. There are two ramps, one for Florida Bay, the other for Whitewater Bay and the back country. The hoist across the plug dam separating Florida Bay from the Buttonwood Canal can take boats up to 26 feet long. A small marina store sells food, camping supplies, bait and tackle, and automobile and boat fuel. *Tel. 305/253–2241 from Miami, 813/*

695–3101 from Gulf Coast. AE, DC, MC, V. Open winter 6 AM–7 PM, summer 7–6.

Homestead Bayfront Park Bait and Tackle. Facilities include dock and wet slips, fuel, bait and tackle, ice, boat hoist, and ramp. The marina is near Homestead Bayfront Park's tidal swimming area and concessions. *North Canal Dr., Homestead, tel. 305/245–2273. AE, MC, V. Open weekdays 7–5, weekends 7–6; in the summer daily until 7.*

Diving

Dive Boats and Instruction

Biscayne National Park Tour Boats. This is the official concessionaire for Biscayne National Park. The center provides equipment for dive trips and sells equipment. Snorkeling and scuba trips include about 2 hours on the reefs. *Reef Rover IV and V*, aluminum dive boats, each carries up to 49 passengers. The resort course and private instruction lead to full certification. *Office and dive boat at Convoy Point. Mailing address: Box 1270, Homestead 33030, tel. 305/247–2400. Cost: $24.50 snorkeling, $34.50 scuba. Reservations required. Children welcome. AE, MC, V. Open daily 8–6. Snorkeling and scuba trips daily 1:30–5 PM; group charters any day.*

Dive Zone. This is the last dive store north of the Keys, and it rents, sells, and repairs diving equipment. Staff teaches all sport-diving classes, including resort course, deep diver, and underwater photography. The center does not have a boat; instead they use dive boats at Homestead Bayfront Park and at other places in the Keys. NAUI and PADI affiliation. *35414 S. Dixie Hwy., Florida City 33034, tel. 305/248–4050. AE, D, DC, MC, V.Open weekdays 10–8, Fri. 10–10; Sat. and Sun. 7–5. Open 24 hours during annual 4-day sport divers' lobster season (in July or Aug.).*

Fishing

The rangers in the two parks enforce all state fishing laws and a few of their own. Ask at each park's visitor centers for that park's specific regulations.

Swimming

Homestead Bayfront Park. This saltwater atoll pool, adjacent to Biscayne Bay, which is flushed by tidal action, is popular with local family groups and teenagers. Highlights include a newly installed tot lot playground, ramps for disabled people including a ramp that leads into the swimming area, and four new barbecues in the picnic pavilion. *N. Canal Dr., Homestead, tel. 305/247–1543. Admission: $3 per car, $5 admission on boat ramp, hoist available for $10. Open daily, 7 AM to sundown.*

Elliott Key. Boaters like to anchor off Elliott Key's 30-foot-wide sandy beach, the only beach in Biscayne National Park. It's about a mile north of the harbor on the west (bay) side of the key.

Bicycling and Hiking

Biscayne National Park. Elliott Key's resident rangers lead informal nature walks on a 1½-mile nature trail. You can also walk the length of the 7-mile key along a rough path that developers bulldozed before the park was created.

Everglades National Park. Shark Valley's concessionaire has rental bicycles. You may ride or hike along the Loop Road, a 15-mile round-trip. Yield right of way to trams. *Shark Valley Tram Tours, Box 1729, Tamiami Station, Miami 33144, tel. 305/221–8455. Cost: $2 per hr. No reservations. No credit cards. Rentals daily 8:30–3, return bicycles by 4.*

Ask the rangers for *Foot and Canoe Trails of the Flamingo Area*, a leaflet that also lists bike trails. Inquire about water levels and insect conditions before you go. Get a free back-country permit if you plan to camp overnight.

Dining

Although the two parks are wilderness areas, there are restaurants within a short drive of all park entrances: between Miami and Shark Valley along the Tamiami Trail (U.S. 41), in the Homestead-Florida City area, in Everglades City, and in the Keys along the Overseas Highway (U.S. 1). The only food service in either park is at Flamingo in the Everglades.

The list below is a selection of independent restaurants on the Tamiami Trail, in the Homestead–Florida City area, and at Flamingo. Many of these establishments will pack picnic fare that you can take to the parks. (You can also find fast-food establishments with carryout service on the Tamiami Trail and in Homestead-Florida City.)

Highly recommended restaurants are indicated by a star ★.

Category	Cost*
Very Expensive	over $60
Expensive	$40–$60
Moderate	$20–$40
Inexpensive	under $20

**per person, excluding drinks, service, and 6% sales tax.*

Flamingo
American

Flamingo Restaurant. The view from this three-tier dining room on the second floor of the Flamingo Visitor Center will knock your socks off. Picture windows overlook Florida Bay, giving you a bird's-eye view (almost) of soaring eagles, gulls, pelicans, terns, and vultures. Try to dine at low tide when flocks of birds gather on a sandbar just offshore. Specialties include a flavorful, mildly spiced conch chowder; teriyaki chicken breast; and pork loin roasted Cuban-style with garlic and lime. The tastiest choices, however, are the seafood. If marlin is on the dinner menu, order it fried so that the moisture and flavor of the dark, chewy meat are retained. Picnic baskets available. They will cook the fish you catch if you clean it at the marina. *At Flamingo Visitor Center in Everglades National Park, Flamingo, tel. 305/253–2241 from Miami, 813/695–3101 from Gulf Coast. Reservations advised at dinner. Dress: casual. AE, DC, MC, V. Closed early May–mid-Oct. (The snack bar and Buttonwood Lounge at the marina store stay open all year to serve pizza, sandwiches, and salads.) Moderate.*

Florida City
Italian
★

Richard Accursio's Capri Restaurant and **King Richard's Room.** One of the oldest family-run restaurants in Dade County—since 1958—this is where locals dine out—business groups at lunch, the Rotary Club each Wednesday at noon, and families at night. Specialties include pizza with light, crunchy crusts and ample toppings; mild, meaty conch chowder; mussels in garlic-cream or marinara sauce; Caesar salad with lots of cheese and anchovies; antipasto with a homemade, vinegary Italian dressing; pasta shells stuffed with rigatoni cheese in tomato sauce; yellowtail snapper Française; and Key lime pie with plenty of real Key lime juice. *935 N. Krome Ave., Florida City, tel. 305/*

247–1544. Reservations advised. Dress: casual. AE, D, MC, V. Closed Sun. except Mother's Day. Closed Christmas. Moderate–Inexpensive.

Homestead
American

Potlikker's. This southern country-style restaurant takes its name from the broth—*pot liquor*—left over from the boiling of greens. Live plants dangle from the sides of open rafters in the lofty pinelined dining room. Specialties include a lemon-pepper chicken breast with lemon sauce, fresh-carved roast turkey with homemade dressing, and at least 11 different vegetables to serve with lunch and dinner entrées. For dessert, try Key lime pie—four inches tall and frozen; it tastes great if you dawdle over dessert while it thaws. *591 Washington Ave., tel. 305/248–0835. No reservations. Dress: casual. AE, MC, V. Closed Christmas Day. Inexpensive.*

Tiffany's. This country French cottage with shops and restaurant under a big banyan tree looks like a converted pioneer house with its high-pitched roof and lattice. That's because fourth-generation Miamian Rebecca DeLuria, who built it in 1984 with her husband, Robert, wanted a place that reminded her of the Miami she remembered. Teaberry-colored tables, moiré satin-like floral placemats, marble-effect floor tiles, fresh flowers on each table, and lots of country items lend to the tea-room style found here. Featured entrées include hot crabmeat au gratin, asparagus supreme (rolled in ham with hollandaise sauce), quiche of the day, and fettucini Alfredo. Homemade desserts are to die for: old-fashioned (very tall) carrot cake, strawberry whipped cream cake, and a harvest pie with double crust that layers apples, cranberries, walnuts, raisins, and a caramel topping. Stop in on Sunday for brunch, or any morning Monday–Saturday for breakfast. *22 N.E. 15th St., tel. 305/246–0022. Reservations accepted. Dress: neat but casual. AE, MC, V. No dinner. Closed Memorial Day, Labor Day, Christmas, New Year's Day. Inexpensive.*

Mexican

El Toro Taco. The Hernandez family came to the United States from San Luis Potosí, Mexico, to pick crops. They opened this Homestead-area institution in 1971. They make salt-free tortillas and nacho chips with corn from Texas that they cook and grind themselves. The cilantro-dominated salsa is mild for American tastes; if you like more fire on your tongue, ask for a side dish of minced jalapeño peppers to mix in. Specialties include chile rellenos (green peppers stuffed with meaty chunks of ground beef and topped with three kinds of cheese), and chicken *fajitas* (chunks of chicken marinated in Worcestershire sauce and spices, grilled in butter with onions and peppers, and served with tortillas and salsa). Bring your own beer and wine; the staff will keep it cold for you and supply lemon for your Corona beer. *1 S. Krome Ave., tel. 305/245–5576. No reservations. Dress: casual. No credit cards. Inexpensive.*

Seafood

Mutineer Restaurant. Former Sheraton Hotels builder Allan Bennett built this roadside restaurant with its indoor-outdoor fish and duck pond solid and stylish as a big-city hotel at a time (1980) when Homestead was barely on the map. Bilevel dining rooms (doubled in size in 1990) are up-scale with sea-scene dividers in etched glass, striped velvet chairs, original pirate art, stained glass, and a few portholes, but there's no excess. The Wharf Lounge behind its solid oak doors on ballbearing brass hinges is equally imaginative with magnified aquarium and nautical antiques such as a crow's nest with real stuffed crow, gold parrot, and treasure chest. The big menu features 18 seafood entrées plus another half dozen daily seafood specials, as well as game, ribs, and steaks. Favorites include quail & tail (quail stuffed with blended wild rice and a broiled Florida lobster tail), and snapper Oscar (topped with crabmeat and asparagus). Bathrooms are tiled and mirrored as beautifully as in hotel suites. Enjoy live music Thursday–Saturday evenings. *11 S.E. 1st Ave., tel. 305/245–3377. Reservations accepted. Dress: neat but casual. AE, D, DC, MC, V. Moderate.*

Tamiami Trail
American

The Pit Bar-B-Q. This place will overwork your salivary glands with its intense aroma of barbecue and blackjack oak smoke. You order at the counter, then come when called to pick up your food. Specialties include barbecued chicken and ribs with a tangy sauce, french fries, coleslaw, and a fried biscuit, and catfish, frogs' legs, and shrimp breaded and deep-fried in vegetable oil. *16400 S.W. 8th St., Miami, tel. 305/226–2272. Dress: casual. No reservations. Closed Christmas Day. MC, V. Inexpensive.*

American Indian

Miccosukee Restaurant. Murals with Indian themes depict women cooking and men engaged in a powwow. Specialties include catfish and frogs' legs breaded and deep-fried in peanut oil, Indian fry bread (a flour-and-water dough deep-fried in peanut oil), pumpkin bread, Indian burger (ground beef browned, rolled in fry bread dough, and deep-fried), and Indian taco (fry bread with chili, lettuce, tomato, and shredded cheddar cheese on top). *On Tamiami Trail, near the Shark Valley entrance to Everglades National Park, tel. 305/223–8380, ext. 332. No reservations. Dress: casual. AE, DC, MC, V. Inexpensive.*

Floridian

Coopertown Restaurant. A rustic 30-seat restaurant full of Floridiana, including alligator skulls, stuffed alligator heads, alligator accessories (belts, key chains, and the like). Specialties include alligator and frogs' legs, breaded and deep-fried in vegetable oil, available for breakfast, lunch, or dinner. *22700 S.W. 8th St., Miami, tel. 305/226–6048. Reservations accepted. Dress: casual. No credit cards. Inexpensive.*

Lodging

Many visitors to the two parks stay in the big-city portion of Greater Miami and spend a day visiting one or both of the parks. For serious outdoors people, such a schedule consumes too much time in traffic and leaves too little time for nature-study and recreation.

At Shark Valley, due west of Miami, you have no choice. Only the Miccosukee Indians live there; there is no motel.

Southwest of Miami, Homestead has become a bedroom community for both parks. You'll find well-kept older properties and shiny new ones, chain motels, and independents. Prices tend to be somewhat lower than in the Miami area.

Hotel and motel accommodations are available on the Gulf Coast at Everglades City and Naples.

The list below is a representative selection of hotels and motels in the Homestead area. Also included are the only lodgings inside either park. The rate categories in the list are based on the all-year or peak-season price; off-peak rates may be a category or two lower.

Category	Cost*
Very Expensive	over $120
Expensive	$90–$120
Moderate	$50–$90
Inexpensive	under $50

**per room, double occupancy, excluding 6% state sales tax and modest resort tax*

Flamingo Lodge Marina & Outpost Resort. This rustic low-rise wilderness resort, the only lodging inside Everglades National Park, is a strip of tentative civilization 300 yards wide and 1½ miles long. Accommodations are basic but attractive and well kept. An amiable staff with a sense of humor helps you become accustomed to alligators bellowing in the sewage-treatment pond down the road, raccoons roaming the pool enclosure at night, and the flock of ibis grazing on the lawn. The rooms have wood-paneled walls, contemporary furniture, floral bedspreads, and art prints of flamingos and egrets on the walls. Most bathrooms are near the door, so you won't track mud all over the room. Television reception has been improved with addition of a satellite dish, but you don't come here to watch TV. All motel rooms face Florida Bay but don't necessarily overlook it. The cottages are in a wooded area on the margin of a coastal prairie. Ask about reserving tours, skiffs, and canoes when you make reservations. Also inquire about the *M/V Bald Eagle*, the new 100-passenger tour boat for day and sunset cruises. *Box 428, Flamingo 33090, tel. 305/253–2241 from Miami, 813/695–3101 from Gulf Coast. 125 units with bath, including 101 motel rooms, one 2-bath suite for up to 8 people, 24 kitchenette cottages (2 for handicapped guests). Facilities: screened outdoor freshwater pool, restaurant, lounge, marina, marina store with snack bar, gift shop, coin laundry. AE, DC, MC, V. Lodge, marina, and marina store open all year; restaurant, lounge, and gift shop closed May 1–Oct. 31. Moderate.*

Holiday Inn. This low-rise motel is situated on a commercial strip. The best rooms look out on the landscaped pool and adjoining Banana Bar. Rooms have contemporary walnut furnishings and firm, bouncy mattresses. A guest laundry and fitness room were added in 1992. *990 N. Homestead Blvd., Homestead 33030, tel. 305/247–7020 or 800/HOLIDAY. 150 rooms with bath. Facilities: outdoor freshwater pool, restaurant and lounge with nightly entertainment, poolside bar, cable TV, massage shower heads. AE, D, DC, MC, V. Moderate.*

Knights Inn. Opened in 1987, this low-rise lodging is set on a commercial strip next door to a McDonald's. Beds are a foot longer than normal, and the mattresses are firm. The inn is decorated in English half-timber style, inside and out. *401 U.S. 1, Florida City 33034, tel. 305/245–2800. 108 rooms, 11 fully equipped kitchenettes, 27 for handicapped guests. Facilities: outdoor freshwater pool, free HBO and TV movies, free ice, free local phone calls, coffee bar in lobby, security at night. AE, D, DC, MC, V. Moderate.*

Hampton Inn. This two-story, 102-unit motel just off the highway has good clean rooms and some public-friendly policies.

There's a free Continental breakfast daily, free local calls, and the TV gets the Disney Channel at no extra charge. All rooms have at least two upholstered chairs, twin reading lamps, and a desk and chair. Units are color-coordinated and carpeted. Baths have tub-showers. *124 E. Palm Dr., Florida City 33034, tel. 800/426-7866, 305/247-8833. Facilities: outdoor pool. AE, D, DC, MC, V. Moderate–Inexpensive.*

Camping

Biscayne National Park

You can camp on designated keys 7 miles offshore at primitive sites or in the backcountry. Carry all your food, water, and supplies onto the keys, and carry all trash off when you leave. Bring plenty of insect repellent. *Free. No reservations. No ferry or marina services. For backcountry camping, obtain a required free permit from rangers at Adams Key, Convoy Point, or Elliott Key.*

Everglades National Park

All campgrounds are primitive, with no water or electricity. Come early to get a good site, especially in winter. Bring plenty of insect repellent. *Admission: $8 per site in winter, free in summer, except for walk-in sites at Flamingo, which are $4. Stay limited to 14 days Nov. 1–Apr. 30. Check-out time 10 AM. Register at campground. Open all year.*

Long Pine Key. 108 campsites, drinking water, sewage dump station.

Flamingo. 235 drive-in sites, 60 walk-in sites, drinking water, cold-water showers, and sewage dump station.

Backcountry. 48 designated sites (2 accessible by land, others only by canoe), 14 with chickees (raised wood platforms with thatch roofs). All have chemical toilets, including the 29 ground sites. Four chickee sites and nine of the ground sites are within an easy day's canoeing of Flamingo; five of the ground sites are within an easy day's canoeing of Everglades City. Call ahead for information on handicap accessibility and updates. Carry all your food, water, and supplies in; carry out all trash. Get free permit from rangers at Everglades City or Flamingo. Permits issued for a specific site. Capacity and length of stay limited. Call for daily updates, but sites available first come, first served. *Flamingo Ranger Stn., Backcountry Reservations Office, Box 279, Homestead 33034, tel. 305/242-7700, 813/695-3101, ext. 182.*

6 Fort Lauderdale

Introduction

Updated by Herb Hiller

If you think of Fort Lauderdale only as a spring-break mecca for collegians seeking sun, suds, and surf, your knowledge is both fragmentary and out of date. The 1960 film *Where the Boys Are* attracted hordes of young people to the city's beaches. And because Fort Lauderdale became a popular place for students on spring break, upscale visitors shunned the city at that time and, unfortunately, year-round as well. City officials intentionally discouraged college revelers after a record number of 350,000 appeared in 1985; by 1991 that number dropped to fewer than 15,000 (most have relocated to Daytona Beach and Panama City), while for the second straight year metropolitan visitorship neared a record five million.

Fort Lauderdale today emphasizes year-round family tourism focused on a wide assortment of sports and recreational activities, an extensive cultural calendar, artistic and historic attractions, and fine shopping and dining opportunities.

Sandwiched between Miami to the south and Palm Beach to the north along southeast Florida's Gold Coast, Fort Lauderdale is the county seat of Broward County. The county encompasses 1,197 square miles—17 square miles less than the state of Rhode Island. Broward County has 23 miles of Atlantic Ocean beach frontage, and it extends 50 miles inland to the west. A coastal ridge rising in places to 25 feet above sea level separates the coastal lowlands from the interior lowlands of the Everglades.

Broward County is named for Napoleon Bonaparte Broward, Florida's governor from 1905 to 1909. His drainage schemes around the turn of the century opened much of the marshy Everglades region for farming, ranching, and settlement. In fact, the first successful efforts at large-scale Everglades drainage took place within Broward County's boundaries.

Fort Lauderdale's first known white settler, Charles Lewis, established a plantation along the New River in 1793. The city is named for a fort that Major William Lauderdale built at the river's mouth in 1838 during the Seminole Indian wars.

The area was still a remote frontier when Frank Stranahan arrived in 1892 to operate an overnight camp on the river. Stranahan began trading with the Indians in 1901 and built a store, which later became his residence. It's now a museum.

Fort Lauderdale incorporated in 1911 with just 175 residents, but it grew rapidly during the Florida boom of the 1920s. Today the city's population of 150,000 remains relatively stable, while suburban areas bulge with growth. Broward County's population is expected to reach 1.4 million in 1995—more than double its 1970 population of 620,000. Most of the recent gains reflect changes in inland Broward's 28 municipalities. Once a home for retirees, Broward County now attracts younger working-age families as well.

New homes, offices, and shopping centers have filled in the gaps between older communities along the coastal ridge. Now they're marching west along I–75, I–595, and the Sawgrass Expressway. There the mammoth new Sawgrass Mills Mall (*see* Shopping, below) is a magnet for further development of the east Everglades. Meanwhile, downtown Fort Lauderdale is building skyscrapers and civic centers downtown to cement its position as the county's financial, commercial, and cultural hub. Chief facilities include the Broward County Main Library; the Broward Center for the Performing Arts, which opened in 1991; the Museum of Art; and the 2-mile Riverwalk (*see* Exploring Fort Lauderdale, below), where construction is complete on the north side of the New River. Distinguished from riverfront development in other Florida cities, the renewal project emphasizes historical, educational, and scenic attractions.

Broward County is developing a concentration of clean high-technology industries, including computer manufacturing, data processing, and electronics. Port Everglades, a major deep-water seaport, handles refined petroleum products and general cargo. A cruise terminal at Port Everglades caters to luxury liners, leaving the mass-market cruise business to the Port of Miami. A new $49-million, tri-level convention center opened in 1991 at Port Everglades, where next to come is a 33-acre, $250-million retail complex with a new hotel, shopping and dining mall, and cruise terminal all tied together with climate-controlled skywalks. A special-events hotline (tel. 305/765–4466), provides information about seasonal events. Information for senior citizens regarding special discounts at area lodgings, restaurants, and attractions is also provided; ask for the "Senior Super Saver" directory.

To accommodate the traffic that comes with all this growth, the Florida Department of Transportation in 1991 completed a major expansion of Broward County's road system (*see* Getting Around By Car, below). Even if you're stuck in traffic, you can still enjoy Broward County's near-ideal weather. The average temperature is about 75 degrees (winter average 66 degrees, summer average 84 degrees). Rainfall averages 65 inches a year, with 60% of the total occurring in afternoon thunderstorms June–October. The warm, relatively dry winters help to give the county about 3,000 hours of sunshine a year.

Essential Information

Arriving and Departing by Plane

Airport **Fort Lauderdale–Hollywood International Airport (FLHIA),** (tel. 305/357–6100), 4 miles south of downtown Fort Lauderdale, is Broward County's major airline terminal. To get there off I–95, take the I–595 east exit to U.S. 1 and follow the signs to the airport entrance. From the south (Miami), exit on Griffin Road to U.S. 1 and follow the signs to the airport. In 1991 the airport completed the lengthening of its runways to 9,000 feet to accommodate jumbo jets. As a result, international charter service has expanded dramatically from the United Kingdom, Scandinavia, and Germany. Among North American carriers, Continental, Delta, USAir, United, Northwest Airlines, Braniff International, TWA, Air Canada, and American Airlines have all augmented their Fort Lauderdale schedules.

Between the Airport and Center City **Broward Transit**'s bus route No. 1 operates between the airport and its main terminal at N.W. 1st Street and 1st Avenue in the center of Fort Lauderdale. Service north from the airport begins daily at 5:40 AM; the last bus from the downtown terminal to the airport leaves at 9:30 PM. The fare is 85¢. Limousine service is available from **Airport Express** (tel. 305/527–8690) to all parts of Broward County. Fares range from $6 to $13 or more per person, depending on distance. Fares to most Fort Lauderdale beach hotels are in the $6–$8 range. Pickup points are at each of the new terminals.

Arriving and Departing by Car, Train, and Bus

By Car The access highways to Broward County from the north or south are Florida's Turnpike, I–95, U.S. 1, and U.S. 441; for a more scenic—and slower—drive, Rte. A1A, which generally parallels the beach area. The I–75 (Alligator Alley) connects Broward County with the west coast of Florida and recently has been expanded and upgraded to a four-lane interstate highway. The primary access road to Broward County from the west is I–595, paralleled by Rte. 84.

By Train **Amtrak** provides daily service to Broward County, with stops at Hollywood, Fort Lauderdale, and Deerfield Beach. *Fort Lauderdale station, 200 S.W. 21st Terr., tel. 305/463–8251; reservations, tel. 800/872–7245.*

Tri-Rail, which connects Broward, Dade, and Palm Beach counties, has six stations in Broward. All stations are west of I–95. Service operates daily except Sunday. Morning service begins northbound and southbound before 6:00; last trains leave from Miami and West Palm Beach around 7:30 PM. *Tel. 305/728–8445 or 800/TRI–RAIL (in Dade, Broward, and Palm Beach counties).*

By Bus **Greyhound/Trailways** (513 N.E. 3rd St., Ft. Lauderdale, tel. 305/764–6551).

Getting Around

By Car North-south I–95 now ties to east-west I–595, which carries high-speed traffic from westernmost Broward County to Fort Lauderdale–Hollywood International Airport in about 20 minutes. Except during rush hour, Broward County has become easy to get around.

Major bottlenecks in Broward are expected through mid-1994 on the 2-mile stretch of I–95 between S.R. 84 and Sunrise Boulevard, the last section of I–95 in the county to be scheduled for widening.

Car Rentals Rental car stations located directly in FLHIA include **Avis** (tel. 305/359–3255), **Budget** (tel. 305/359–4700), **Dollar** (tel. 305/359–7800), **Hertz** (tel. 305/359–5281), and **National** (tel. 305/359–8303).

By Bus **Broward County Mass Transit** serves the entire county. The fare is 85¢ (senior citizens, handicapped persons, and students 40¢) plus 10¢ for a transfer, with some bus routes starting as early as 5 AM; some continuing to 9 PM. Call for route information (tel. 305/357–8400). There are also special seven-day tourist passes for $8 that are good for unlimited use on all county buses. These are available at some hotels and at Broward County libraries.

By Taxi It's difficult to hail a taxi on the street; sometimes you can pick one up at a major hotel. Otherwise, phone ahead. Fares are not cheap; meters run at the rate of $2.20 for the first mile and

$1.50 for each additional mile, waiting time 25¢/minute. The major company serving the area is **Yellow Cab** (tel. 305/565–5400).

By Water Taxi **Water Taxi** (tel. 305/565–5507) provides service along the Intracoastal Waterway between Port Everglades and Commercial Boulevard 10 AM–1 AM. In 1992 new service began between Atlantic Boulevard and Hillsboro Boulevard in Pompano Beach. Taxis operate between noon and midnight. The boats stop at more than 30 restaurants, hotels, shops, and nightclubs; the fare is $4.50 one way, $9 round-trip, all-day pass $12 (no credit cards, reservations accepted).

Important Addresses and Numbers

Tourist Information The main office of the **Greater Fort Lauderdale Convention & Visitors Bureau** (tel. 305/765–4466) is at 200 E. Las Olas Boulevard, Suite 1500. The office is open weekdays 8:30–5. The Greater Fort Lauderdale Chamber of Commerce (tel. 305/462–6000, 800/22–SUNNY for brochures) is at 512 N.E. 3rd Ave., 33301. Other communities in Broward County also have individual chambers of commerce, including Dania (Box 838, Dania 33004, tel. 305/927–3377), Hollywood (4000 Hollywood Blvd., Ste. 265–South, Hollywood 33021, tel. 305/985–4000), Deerfield Beach (1601 E. Hillsboro Blvd., Deerfield Beach 33441, tel. 305/427–1050), and Pompano Beach (2200 E. Atlantic Blvd., Pompano Beach 33062, tel. 305/941–2940).

Emergencies Dial 911 for **police** and **ambulance** in an emergency.

Poison Control (tel. 800/282–3171).

Hospitals. The following hospitals have a 24-hour emergency room: **Holy Cross Hospital** (4725 N. Federal Hwy., Fort Lauderdale, tel. 305/771–8000; physician referral, tel. 305/776–3223), **Imperial Point Hospital** (6401 N. Federal Hwy., Fort Lauderdale, tel. 305/355–4888; physician referral, tel. 305/776–8500), and **Broward General Medical Center** (1600 S. Andrews Ave., Fort Lauderdale, tel. 305/355–4400; physician referral, tel. 305/355–4888).

24-Hour Pharmacies. Eckerd Drug (1385 S.E. 17th St., Fort Lauderdale, tel. 305/525–8173; and 154 University Dr., Pembroke Pines, tel. 305/432–5510). **Walgreens** (2855 Stirling Rd., Fort Lauderdale, tel. 305/981–1104; 5001 N. Dixie Hwy., Oakland Park, tel. 305/772–4206; and 289 S. Federal Hwy., Deerfield Beach, tel. 305/481–2993).

Special Services **Telecommunications for the Hearing-Impaired.** United Hearing and Deaf Services operates weekdays 8:30 to 5 (4850 W. Oakland Park Blvd., Suite 207, Lauderdale Lakes, tel. 305/731–7208). A telephone relay service operates 24 hours a day, seven days a week (tel. 305/731–7200).

Access for Handicapped Persons. Throughout Broward County, beaches, hotels, cruise ships, cultural centers, and rental cars are equipped with facilities for disabled people. The newest installation is a cedar wheelchair ramp on Fort Lauderdale Beach that leads to the water's edge. Expanded parking offers direct access to the beach. Other wheelchair-accessible facilities include Fisherman's Wharf, Ocean World, Jungle Queen cruise ship, Discovery Center, and Fort Lauderdale Historical Society. For details, contact the Greater Fort Lauderdale Convention & Visitors Bureau (Dept. MS, 200 E. Las Olas, Ste. 1500, Fort Lauderdale 33301, tel. 305/765–4466).

Guided Tours

The ***Jungle Queen*** operates a 155-passenger single-deck boat, and a 578-passenger double-decker designed to resemble an old-time steamboat. Both travel day and night up the New River through the heart of Fort Lauderdale. Three-hour day cruises depart 10 and 2 (adults $6.95, children 2–12 $4.95); four-hour dinner cruises at 7 ($20.95). The same company sends boats to Miami's Bayside Marketplace. All cruises leave from the Bahia Mar dock on Rte. A1A. *Tel. 305/462–5596 (Broward County), 305/947–6597 (Dade County). No credit cards.*

Las Olas Horse and Carriage operates Tuesday through Sunday evening between 7 and midnight. The New River Tour lasts 20 minutes and goes through the Riverwalk area ($8 per person); the Colee-Hammock Tour is 30 minutes and takes in old Fort Lauderdale ($12 per person). A new Royal Palm Tour through residential neighborhoods, Colee-Hammock, and Las Olas Boulevard takes 1¼ hours ($90 for up to 6 persons). Transportation between Las Olas Boulevard and the Broward County Center for the Performing Arts is available either one-way or round-trip ($45 or $80, for up to 6). *610 E. Las Olas Blvd., tel. 305/763–7393. Reservations advised.*

River/Walking Tours are co-sponsored by the Fort Lauderdale Historical Society. A two-hour tour of the New River and a portion of the Intracoastal Waterway runs Saturday mornings from 10 to noon. The boat leaves from the Chart House Restaurant dock (301 S.W. 3rd Ave.) and the tour costs $13.50. Walking tour schedules vary by season but generally last 2–3 hours with a limit of 20 persons. *219 S.W. 2nd Ave., Fort Lauderdale 33301, tel. 305/463–4431. Reservations required. MC, V.*

South Florida Trolley Tours (tel. 305/522–7701; 305/528–6340 driver's night beeper) offers fully narrated 90-minute tours on *Lolly the Trolley* daily from 9 to 5. The trolley stops at all major hotels from Rte. A1A and Sunrise Boulevard to 17th St. and Eisenhower Boulevard. Pick-ups are generally along Las Olas Boulevard, but with reservations the trolley can also pick up passengers elsewhere nearby. Passengers can board and reboard the trolley all day for $10 per person and thus can sightsee, dine, and shop at their own pace (children 7–12 $5, under 6 free). *MC, V.*

Exploring Fort Lauderdale

Numbers in the margin correspond to points of interest on the Fort Lauderdale Area map.

Central Fort Lauderdale is diverse, picturesque, and surprisingly compact. Within a few blocks you'll find modern high-rise office buildings; a historic district with museums, restaurants, and antiques shops; a scenic riverfront drive; upscale shopping; and the only vehicular tunnel in Florida—all within 2 miles of the beach.

This tour begins on the beach at Las Olas Boulevard and Rte. A1A. Go north on Rte. A1A along **the beach,** with hotels, restaurants, and shops on your left, the ocean on your right.

Through much of this stretch, the beach road (Rte. A1A) and beachfront are being improved with planters, palms, and a beachfront wall of ornamental entrances, whorled and scrolled in European styling. Throughout the beach area, distinctive signage, street furniture, and a central wave theme will unify the area and become the symbol of the beachfront revitalization. The entire project will stretch 2½ miles and cost approximately $26 million. More than ever, the boulevard will be worth promenading. As part of improvements, a new road is being constructed west of present Hwy. A1A which will accommodate southbound traffic. Turn left off A1A at Sunrise Boulevard, then right into **Hugh Taylor Birch State Recreation Area.** Amid the 180-acre park's tropical greenery, you can stroll along a nature trail, visit the Birch House Museum, picnic, play volleyball, pitch horseshoes, ride a rental bike or paddleboats, and canoe. *3109 E. Sunrise Blvd., tel. 305/564–4521; concessions tel. 305/564–4572. Admission: $3.25 per car. Open 8–sundown. Ranger-guided nature walks Fri. 10:30.*

❷ You can visit the **Bonnet House** anytime but winter. To do so, when leaving the park, cross Sunrise Boulevard south. This lyrical house built by artist Frederic Bartlett is on land he was given by his first father-in-law, Hugh Taylor Birch. The house and its subtropical 35-acre estate has since been donated to the Florida Trust for Historic Preservation. From May through November the house is open to visitors with its original works of art, including whimsically carved animals, a swan pond, and, most of all, its tranquility. *900 N. Birch Rd., tel. 305/563–5393. Reservations required. Admission $7.50 adults, $5 senior citizens, students, and military personnel; children under 6 free.*

Leaving Bonnet House, return to A1A, go south to Las Olas Boulevard, turn right, and cross the Intracoastal Waterway. ❸ You're now westbound through **The Isles,** Fort Lauderdale's most expensive and prestigious neighborhood, where the homes line a series of canals with large yachts beside the seawalls. When you reach the mainland, Las Olas becomes an upscale shopping street with Spanish-Colonial buildings housing high-fashion boutiques, jewelry shops, and art galleries. The heart of the **Las Olas Shopping District** is from S.E. 11th Avenue to S.E. 6th Avenue.

❹ Turn left on S.E. 6th Avenue, and visit **Stranahan House,** home of pioneer businessman Frank Stranahan, and oldest standing structure in Fort Lauderdale. He arrived in 1892 and began trading with the Seminole Indians. In 1901 he built a store, and later made it his home. Now it's a museum with many of the Stranahans' furnishings on display. Friday evening socials are held September through May from 5:30 to 8 and are a good way to meet local people. For $5 the social includes three drink tickets, food, and house tours. *1 Stranahan Pl. (335 S.E. 6th Ave.), tel. 305/524–4736. Admission: $3, $2 children under 12. Open Wed., Fri., Sat. 10–3:30.*

Return to Las Olas Boulevard, turn right on Andrews Avenue, ❺ and park in one of the municipal garages. Visit the **Museum of Art,** which features a major collection of works from the CoBrA (Copenhagen, Brussels, and Amsterdam) movement, plus American Indian, pre-Columbian, West African, and Oceanic ethnographic art. Edward Larabee Barnes designed the museum building, which opened in 1986. In late 1991, the museum opened its exhibit of the $50 million collection of 224 works by

Fort Lauderdale Area

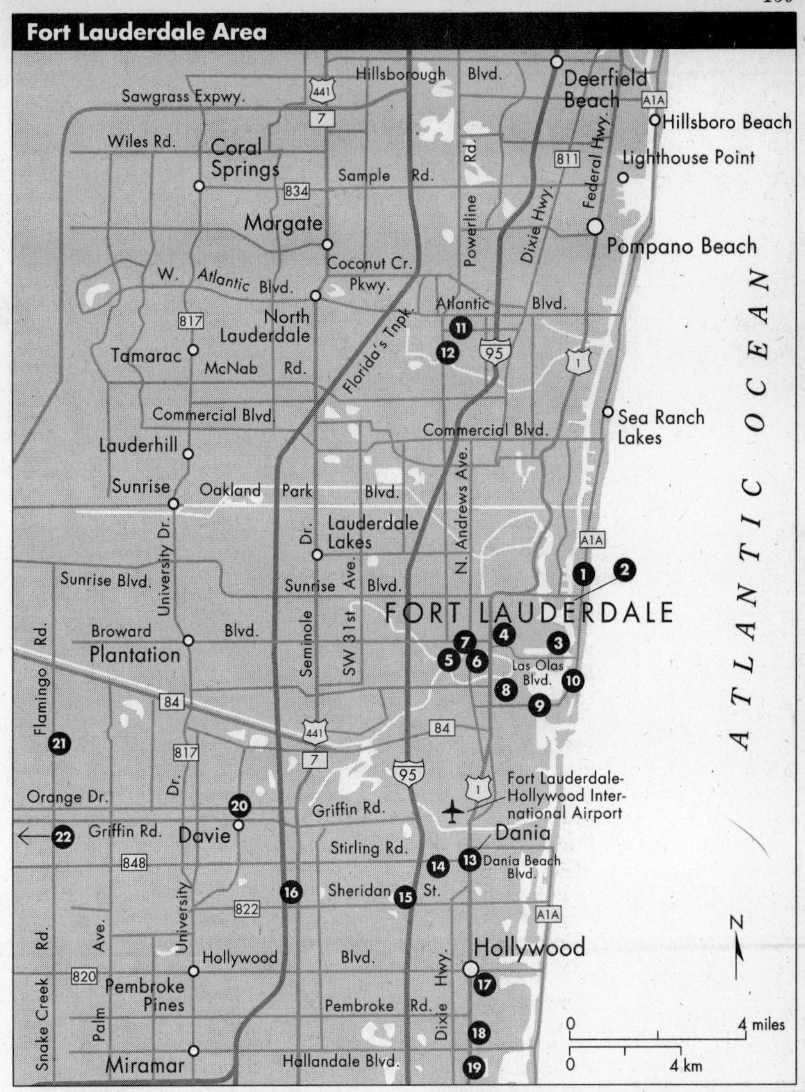

Art and Cultural Center of Hollywood, **17**
Atlantis the Water Kingdom, **14**
Bonnet House, **2**
Brooks Memorial Causeway, **9**
Broward County Main Library, **6**
Dania Jai-Alai Palace, **13**
Davie Arena for Rodeo, **20**
Everglades Holiday Park and Campground, **22**
Flamingo Gardens, **21**
Gulfstream Park Race Track, **19**
Hollywood Greyhound Track, **18**
Hugh Taylor Birch State Recreation Area, **1**
International Swimming Hall of Fame Museum and Pool, **10**
The Isles, **3**
Museum of Art, **5**
Ocean World, **8**
Pompano Harness Track, **11**
Quiet Waters Park, **12**
Riverwalk, **7**
Seminole Native Village, **16**
Stranahan House, **4**
Topeekeegee Yugnee Park, **15**

celebrated Ashcan School artist William Glackens and other early-20th-century American painters. Portions of this largest donation of art on record in Florida were expected to be on view in 1992. *1 E. Las Olas Blvd., tel. 305/525–5500. Admission: $3.25 adults, $2.75 seniors, $1.25 students, free under 12. Free 1-hr highlight tours Tues. 1 and 6:30 PM, Thurs. and Fri. at 1, Sat., Sun. 2 PM. Open Tues. 11–9, Wed.–Sat. 10–5, Sun. noon–5. Parking nearby in municipal garage.*

6 Walk 1 block north to the **Broward County Main Library.** Designed by Marcel Breuer, the library is distinguished by its display of many works from Broward's Art in Public Places program, including a painting by Yaacov Agam, wood construction by Marc Beauregard, an outdoor aluminum-and-steel sculpture by Dale Eldred that responds to the sun and artificial night lights, and ceramic tile by Ivan Chermayeff. Productions from theater to poetry readings are presented in a 300-seat auditorium. *100 S. Andrews Ave., tel. 305/357–7444; 305/357–7457 for self-guided Art in Public Places walking tour brochure. Admission free. Open. Mon.–Thurs. 10–9, Fri.–Sat. 9–5, Sun. 1–5. Closed holidays.*

Go north to Broward Boulevard, turn left between 5th and 6th avenues into the Arts and Science District parking garage. You 7 can now walk to the palm-lined **Riverwalk.** As part of a planned multi-million-dollar revitalization of downtown Fort Lauderdale, the 2-mile, $4.65 million Riverwalk consists of 28.8 open and developed acres that connect the following: the **Arts and Science District,** with the new $52 million Broward Center for the Performing Arts (which opened in 1991); the **Historic District/Entertainment Center** that houses many museums and restaurants, and the historic Stranahan House and Riverside Hotel. **The Broward Center for the Performing Arts** (tel. 305/462–0222) includes the 2,700-seat Au-Rene Theater for major productions, and the 595-seat Amaturo Theater for more intimate performances. More than 550 programs a year are planned. The Arts and Science District features an indoor-outdoor **Esplanade** (opened in 1990), and an education and performance park for children with exhibits that offer informative lessons on south Florida's climate and environment.

Just north of the esplanade is the **Discovery Center,** which includes a science museum in the **New River Inn,** Fort Lauderdale's first hotel, and a pioneer residence museum in the restored **King-Cromartie House.** The museum is a child-oriented place with hands-on exhibits that explore optical illusions and bend rays of light, an insect zoo, a glass-front beehive, a loom, a computer center, and a small planetarium. The center will be replaced by a new $29 million, 300,000-square-foot **Museum of Discovery and Science** by 1993, and will include a 300-seat IMAX theater. *231 S.W. 2nd Ave., tel. 305/462–4115. Admission: $5, $4 children and seniors, children under 3 free. Open Tues.–Fri. and Sun. noon–5; Sat. and school holidays in winter 10–5. Museum closed Mon. in summer.*

East of the Esplanade along the Riverwalk is the **Fort Lauderdale Historical Society Museum,** which surveys the city's history from the Seminole Indian era to World War II. A model in the lobby depicts old Fort Lauderdale. The building also houses a research library and a bookstore. *219 S.W. 2nd Ave., tel. 305/463–4431. Admission $2 adults, $1 children 6–12, children under 6 free. Open Tues.–Sat. 10–4, Sun. 1–4.*

Return to your car; go to Broward Boulevard, turn right and go east to Federal Highway (U.S. 1). Turn right and go south through the **Henry E. Kinney Tunnel,** named for a founder of Fort Lauderdale; Florida's only tunnel dips beneath Las Olas Boulevard and the New River.

8 Continue south on Federal Highway to S.E. 17th Street, then turn left. About a mile east is the entrance to **Ocean World,** an intimate marine park. Six shows daily feature trained dolphins and sea lions. Display tanks hold sharks, sea turtles, alligators, and river otters. You can feed and pet a dolphin here. *1701 S.E. 17th St., tel. 305/525-6611. Admission: $9.95 adults, $7.95 children 4–12, under 4 free. Boat tour admission: $6 adults, $5 children 4–12, under 4 free. Tours at 12:30, 2:50, and 5:05 last about an hour. Open 10–6, last show starts 4:15.*

Across 17th Street is the new **Greater Fort Lauderdale/Broward County Convention Center,** home of boat shows, antique shows, and mammoth meetings.

9 Go east on S.E. 17th Street across the **Brooks Memorial Causeway** over the Intracoastal Waterway, and bear left onto Seabreeze Boulevard (Rte. A1A). You'll pass through a neighborhood of older homes set in lush vegetation before emerging at the south end of Fort Lauderdale's beachfront strip. On your left at **Bahia Mar Resort & Yachting Center,** novelist John McDonald's fictional hero, Travis McGee, is honored with a plaque at the marina where he docked his houseboat. *801 Seabreeze Blvd., tel. 305/764-2233 or 800/327-8154.*

10 Three blocks north, visit the **International Swimming Hall of Fame Museum and Pool,** where in 1991 a new 10-lane, 50-meter pool with locker rooms and weight rooms was completed. Also included is an expanded exhibition building that features photos, medals, and other souvenirs from major swimming events around the world. *1 Hall of Fame Dr., museum tel. 305/462-6536, pool tel. 305/523-0994. Museum admission: $3 adults, $2 children 6–21, senior citizens, and military personnel, $5 family. Pool admission: $3 nonresident adults, $2 nonresident students, $1 resident students, senior citizens, military personnel. Open Mon.–Sat. 10–5, Sun. 11–4.*

This concludes the central Fort Lauderdale tour. To return to the starting point, continue north on Seabreeze Boulevard to Las Olas Boulevard.

Broward

Time Out To start a brief exploration of the North Broward, take I–95 North to Cypress Creek Road. Turn west 2 miles to 21st Avenue, then right on 21st to the first light (McNab Road), right again onto 20th Avenue, and right to the end of the street. On your left in a warehouse district is **Acme Smoked Fish** where, in a scene reminiscent of New York's East Side in its sights and smells, you're among deli mavens relishing the smoked salmon, whitefish, and herrings. Acme also sells deli meats and crackers so you can nosh while soaking up the atmosphere. *6704 N.W. 20th Ave., tel. 305/974-8100. No credit cards. Open Tues.–Sat. 9–4.*

Return to I–95 and go north to the Atlantic Boulevard exit and go west to Power Line Road, which will lead you to the popular

⓫ **Pompano Harness Track** (1800 S.W. 3rd St., Pompano Beach), Florida's only harness track. Early in 1992 the 327-acre facility was put up for sale after six years of unprofitable operations. For now, however, it's business as usual. The Top 'O The Park restaurant overlooks the finish line. Post time: 7:30; call for dates, tel. 305/972–2000.

⓬ A unique water skiing cableway is at **Quiet Waters Park,** just north of the racetrack, on Power Line Road. **Ski Rixen** (tel. 305/429–0215) offers waterskiing lessons for beginners, plus skis and life vests. A cable pulls the skiers. If you're skilled enough, you can try all sorts of variations to the two-hand, two-ski way of skimming across the water. *Tel. 305/360–1315. Admission: weekdays free, weekends and holidays $1 driver, 75¢ per passenger; children under 5 free. Open daily 8–sunset.*

Return to Atlantic Boulevard and turn east to Hwy. A1A. Turn north along scenic route A1A passing Lighthouse Point, the brightest light in the southeast; Hillsboro Beach, with its million-dollar homes along the ocean and the Intracoastal Waterway; and Deerfield Beach, with its popular public facilities.

Southern Broward

In southern Broward County, an exploration can include Native American crafts and lifestyles, high-stakes pari-mutuel wagering, and a unique natural park, all within the same driving loop.

⓭ Start with the **Dania Jai-Alai Palace** (301 E. Dania Beach Blvd., Dania, tel. 305/428–7766), offering one of the fastest games on the planet from early November–April (winter season) and May–November (summer season).

⓮ Follow Dania Beach Boulevard west to U.S. 1, turn left, go south to Stirling Road, turn right, and go west to **Atlantis The Water Kingdom,** one of the world's largest water-theme parks. It has 2 million gallons of water in 45 pools and water slides up to seven stories high, plus children's entertainment. Highlights include a wave pool and an activity pool with trolleys, slides, and rope ladders, and a new attraction known as The Awesome Twosome, a pair of completely enclosed slides that take two at a time. Riders on Thunderball, the steepest water slide, reach speeds near 40 mph. The park sets minimum and maximum height requirements for participants in some activities. *2700 Stirling Rd., Hollywood, tel. 305/926–1000. Admission: $13.95 adults, $6.95 senior citizens over 55, $10.95 children 3–11. Summer hours 10 AM to between 5 and 10 PM; phone for hours at other times of year.*

⓯ Travel on I–95 south to the Sheridan Street exit, then west to **Topeekeegee Yugnee Park.** Rentals include sailboats, sailboards, paddleboats, and canoes. *3300 N. Park Rd., tel. 305/985–1980. Admission weekends and holidays: $1 car and driver, 75¢ each passenger, children under 6 free. Open daily sunrise–sunset.*

⓰ Drive from Sheridan Street west to U.S. 441/Rte. 7, turn right, and go north through the **Seminole Native Village,** a reservation of the never-conquered Seminole Indian tribe. The Indians sell native arts and crafts and run a high-stakes bingo parlor (4150 N. Rte. 7, tel. 305/961–5140, for recorded information or 305/961–3220, for general information). Four bingo games dai ly; call recording for information. Continue north to **Anhinga Indian Museum and Art Gallery,** where Joe Dan and Virginia Osceola display a collection of artifacts from the Seminoles and other American Indian tribes. They also sell contemporary Indian art and craft objects. *5791 S. Rte. 7, tel. 305/581-8411. Open daily 9-5. MC, V.*

17 Newly opened in 1992 was the **Art and Cultural Center of Hollywood,** set in a 1924 Mediterranean-style one-time residence. The community hopes that the Sunday concerts and daily art exhibits will help to revitalize the downtown area. Additional galleries and a museum store are planned for the future. *1650 Harrison St., Hollywood, tel. 305/921-3274. Admission: $2 Wed.-Sat., $3 Sun. concerts, donations accepted Tues. Open Tues.-Sat. 10-4, Sun. 1-4.*

18 From U.S. 441/Rte. 7 south to Pembroke Road go east to Federal Highway to the **Hollywood Greyhound Track** (831 N. Federal Highway, Hallandale, tel. 305/454-9400). Open day after Christmas until late April.

19 Take Federal Highway south to **Gulfstream Park Race Track** (901 S. Federal Hwy., tel. 305/454-7000), home of the Florida Derby, one of the southeast's foremost horse racing events, and the Breeders Cup. Race dates always during winter.

Inland

Between the coastal cities and the watery wilderness of the Everglades, urban sprawl is rapidly devouring Broward County's citrus groves and cow pastures. If you go inland, you can still find vestiges of the county's agricultural past.

20 The **Davie Arena for Rodeo** at Orange Drive and Davie Road holds rodeos throughout the year. *6591 S.W. 45th St. (Orange Dr.), Davie 33314, tel. 305/797-1145. Admission for jackpot events: $4 adults, $2 children; five-star rodeo, $8 adults, $5 children.*

Now, take Davie Road south past Orange Drive, cross the South New River Canal, and turn right on Griffin Road. Go half a mile west to **Spykes Grove & Tropical Gardens,** where the entire family can hop aboard a tractor-pulled tram for a 15-minute tour of working citrus groves, which have been in operation since 1944. A bear born in captivity, gators, prairie dogs, roosters, and peacocks also are on exhibit. *7250 Griffin Rd., tel. 305/583-0426. Admission free. Tours hourly 11-4. Open daily Oct.-June, 9-5:30.*

21 Head 7 miles west on Griffin Road and turn right onto Flamingo Road to **Flamingo Gardens.** Flamingo Island offers gators, crocodiles, river otters, birds of prey, a plant house, and Everglades Museum in the pioneer Wray Home. A new, 23,000-square-foot walk-through aviary was added in 1991. Admission includes a 1½-hour guided tram ride through a citrus grove and wetlands area. *3750 Flamingo Rd., tel. 305/473-2955. Admission: $6 adults, $2.50 children 4-12. Senior citizens and AAA members 20% discount. Open daily 9-5.*

22 Return to Griffin Road and go almost 8½ miles west until the road ends at the edge of the Everglades. There you'll find **Everglades Holiday Park and Campground,** which offers a 60-minute narrated airboat tour and an alligator-wrestling show

featuring Seminole Indians. The park has a 100-space campground that accommodates recreational vehicles and tents. *21940 Griffin Rd., Ft. Lauderdale 33332, tel. 305/434–8111 (Broward County), 305/621–2009 (Miami). Tour: $12 adults, $6 children, under 3 free. MC, V.*

What to See and Do with Children

Butterfly World. This attraction in Tradewinds Park South is a screened-in aviary in a tropical rain forest on 2.8 acres of land, where thousands of caterpillars pupate and emerge as butterflies. Up to 150 species flit through the shrubbery. Many are so tame they will land on you. Best time to go is in the afternoon; school groups fill the place in the mornings. *3600 W. Sample Rd., Coconut Creek, tel. 305/977–4400. Admission: $7.95 adults, $5 children 3–12, $6.95 senior citizens. AE, MC, V. Open Mon.–Sat. 9–5, Sun. 1–5.*

Discovery Center (*see* Exploring Fort Lauderdale, above).

Ocean World (*see* Exploring Fort Lauderdale, above).

Atlantis The Water Kingdom (*see* Exploring Southern Broward, above).

Shopping

Shopping Districts

Major Malls

Broward Mall, the county's largest upscale shopping center, features such stores as Burdines, J.C. Penney, and Sears. *8000 W. Broward Blvd., Plantation, tel. 305/473–8100. Open Mon.–Sat. 10–9, Sun. noon–5:30.*

Fashion Mall features Macy's and Lord and Taylor among 150 shops, boutiques, and restaurants in a three-level, 669,000-square-foot landscaped, glass-enclosed facility. *University Blvd., Plantation, tel. 305/370–1884. Open Mon.–Sat. 10–9:30, Sun. noon–6.*

Galleria Mall on Sunrise Boulevard, just west of the Intracoastal Waterway, occupies more than one million square feet and includes Neiman-Marcus, Lord & Taylor, Saks Fifth Avenue, and Brooks Brothers. *Tel. 305/564–5015. Open 10–9 Mon.–Sat., noon–5:30 Sun.*

Pompano Fashion Square in Pompano Beach has 110 shops with three department stores and food stalls. *2255 N. Federal Hwy., tel. 305/943–4683. Open Mon.–Sat. 10–9, Sun. noon–5:30.*

Sawgrass Mills Mall is a candy-colored Disney-style discount mall—said to be the largest in America—that opened in late 1990 with more than two million square feet of stores, restaurants, and entertainment activities. The mall sprawls at the intersection of Flamingo Road and Sunrise Boulevard in west Broward *Open Mon.–Sat. 10–9:30, Sun. 11–6.*

Antiques

More than 75 dealers line U.S. 1 (Federal Hwy.) in Dania, a half mile south of the Fort Lauderdale International Airport and a half mile north of Hollywood. Open 10–5 every day but Sunday. Exit Griffin Road East off I–95.

Beaches

The Fort Lauderdale area boasts an average temperature of about 75 degrees and 23 miles of oceanfront beach. Parking is readily available, often at parking meters. At the southern end of Broward County, **John U. Lloyd Beach State Recreation Area** (6503 N. Ocean Dr., Dania) offers a beach for swimmers and sunners, but also 251 acres of mangroves, picnic facilities, fishing, and canoeing. *Open 8 AM–sunset. Park tel. 305/923–2833. Admission: $3.25 per car. Call the park number for information about the concession, scheduled to reopen in 1992.*

Throughout Broward County, each municipality along the Atlantic has its own public beach area. Hollywood also has a 2.5-mile Broadwalk, edged with shops and eateries. Pompano Beach and Lauderdale-by-the-Sea have piers you can fish off of in addition to the beaches. The most crowded portion of beach in this area is along the **Fort Lauderdale "Strip,"** which runs from Las Olas Boulevard north to Sunrise Boulevard.

In past years, there have been serious oil spills and dumpings by freighters and tankers at sea, and the gunk has washed ashore in globules and become mixed with the beach sand. The problem has been somewhat eased, but some hotels still include a tar-removal packet with the toilet amenities. If you're concerned, ask at the desk of your hotel or motel.

Participant Sports

Biking Cycling is popular in Broward County, though statistically this is one of the most dangerous places to ride in Florida. Popular routes are along A1A, especially early in the morning before traffic builds, and many shops along the beach rent bikes. Other popular riding areas are the more rural parts of the county—the **Parkland** area of northwestern Broward and the vast **Weston** community in the southwest. Weston has already installed some 10 miles of the 21 total miles of bike lanes planned for the community. Along the I–595 corridor the Rte. 84 bike path provides 6 miles for off-street cycling from University Drive to Markham Park. However, between Rte. 7 and the Florida Turnpike, Rte. 84 merges with I–595 and is closed to cyclists. Traveling from the east, cyclists along this stretch must use Davie Boulevard; from the west, Peters Road. Both are north of the corridor. South of the corridor, cyclists must use Griffin Road. A new 330-meter velodrome—first in Florida—is scheduled to open by late September 1992 at Brian Piccolo Park in Cooper City, at Sheridan Street and N.W. 101st Avenue. The track will be open to the public most of the time. Visiting cyclists in Broward County can request a new route map scheduled for publication in 1993. For details, contact the **County Bicycle Coordinator** (tel. 305/357–6661).

Diving Good diving can be enjoyed within 20 minutes of the shore along Broward County's 25-mile coast. Among the most popular of the county's 80 dive sites is the 2-mile-wide, 23-mile-long Fort Lauderdale Reef.

Broward County features Florida's most successful artificial reef-building program, which began in 1984 with the sinking of a 435-foot freighter donated by an Oklahoma marine electronics manufacturer. Since then more than a dozen houseboats, ships, and oil platforms have been sunk to provide habitat for fish and other marine life, as well as to help stabilize beaches. The most famous sunken ship is the 200-foot German freighter *Mercedes,* which was blown ashore in a violent Thanksgiving storm onto Palm Beach socialite Mollie Wilmot's pool terrace in 1984; the ship was purposefully sunk. Today it lies a mile off Fort Lauderdale beach. For more information, contact the Greater Fort Lauderdale Convention & Visitors Bureau (*see* Important Addresses and Numbers, above).

Dive Boats and Instruction All **Force E** stores rent scuba and snorkeling equipment. Instruction is available at all skill levels. Dive boat charters are available. *2700 E. Atlantic Blvd., Pompano Beach, tel. 305/943-3483. Open in winter Mon.-Sat. 8-7, Sun. 8-5; in summer weekdays 8-8:30, Sat. 8-7, Sun. 8-5. 2104 W. Oakland Park Blvd., Oakland Park, tel. 305/735-6227. Open winter weekdays 10-8:30, Sat. 8-7, Sun. 8-4; summer weekdays 8 AM-9 PM, Sat. 8-7, Sun. 8-4. AE, D, MC, V.*

Lauderdale Diver offers packages with the Marriott Hotel & Marina and Fort Lauderdale Oceanside Inn, which include transportation to Tugboat Annie's in Dania, from where its 42-foot fully equipped diveboat departs. Dive trips last approximately three to four hours; nonpackage reef trips are also open to divers for $35, to snorkelers for $25, including snorkel equipment; scuba gear is extra. PADI affiliated. *1334 S.E. 17th St. Causeway, Fort Lauderdale, tel. 305/467-2822 or 800/654-2073. AE, D, DC, MC, V. Open in winter weekdays 10-6, Sat. 8-6, Sun. 8-1; in summer weekdays 9-7, Sat. 8-7, Sun. 8-1.*

Pro Dive, the area's oldest diving operation, offers packages with Bahia Mar Resort & Yachting Center, from where its 60-foot fully equipped boat departs. Nonpackage snorkelers can go out for $25 on the 4-hour dive trip, or for $20 on the 2-hour snorkeling trip, which includes snorkel equipment but not scuba gear. *Bahia Mar Resort & Yachting Center, Rte. A1A, Fort Lauderdale, tel. 305/761-3413 or 800/772-DIVE outside FL. AE, MC, V.*

Fishing Deep-sea and freshwater fishing are year-round pursuits in Broward. Fishing piers draw anglers for pompano, amberjack, bluefish, snapper, blue runners, snook, mackerel, and Florida lobsters. Pompano Beach's **Fisherman's Wharf** extends 1,080 feet into the Atlantic. The cost is $1.95 for adults, 95¢ for children under 10; rod-and-reel rental is $4.75. **Anglin's Fishing Pier** in Lauderdale-by-the-Sea reaches 875 feet and can be fished off 24 hours a day. Fishing is $2.50 for adults and $1.75 for children up to 12, tackle rental $5.

Charters Two primary centers for charter boats are Fort Lauderdale's **Bahia Mar Yachting Center,** and the **Fish City Marina** on Highway A1A and Hillsboro Inlet in Pompano Beach. Half-day charters usually run from $200 to $250 for up to six persons; full days between $400 and $475. Skipper and crew plus bait and tackle are included. Split-parties can be arranged at a cost of about $50 per person. Among marinas catering to freshwater fishing are **Sawgrass Recreation** and **Everglades Holiday Park,** where fisherpeople can rent a 14-foot, flat-bottomed John boat carrying up to four persons for about $30-$32.50 for five hours. Tackle rents for $5-$8; bait is extra. For details contact Greater Fort Lauderdale Convention & Visitors Bureau (*see* Important Addresses and Numbers, above).

Golf More than 50 courses, public and private, green the landscape in metro Fort Lauderdale, including some of the most famous championship links—such as the Eagle Trace, Weston Hills (site of the PGA Honda Classic) and the Bonaventure Country Club.

Spas If you watch "Lifestyles of the Rich and Famous" on TV, you'll recognize the names of Greater Fort Lauderdale's two world-famous spas, the Bonaventure Resort & Spa and Palm-Aire Spa Resort. At each resort, women comprise 75%–80% of the spa clientele. Both resorts offer single-day spa privileges to nonguests. Price and availability of services vary with seasonal demand; resort guests have priority. At each resort, day users may receive a body massage, exercise class, facials, herbal wrap, spa-cuisine lunch, and other spa facilities and services. Bring your own sneakers and socks. The spa provides everything else you'll need. Each spa will help you design a personal exercise-and-diet program tied to your lifestyle at home. If you already have an exercise program, bring it with you. If you have a medical problem, bring a letter from your doctor.

Bonaventure Resort and Spa (250 Racquet Club Rd., Fort Lauderdale, tel. 305/389–3300 or 800/327–8090), which underwent a $1-million face-lift in 1992 offers complimentary caffeine-free herbal teas in the morning, fresh fruit in the afternoon. Staff nutritionist follows American Heart Association and American Cancer Society guidelines, and can accommodate macrobiotic and vegetarian diets. Full-service beauty salon open to the public.

Palm-Aire Spa Resort (2601 Palm-Aire Drive N., Pompano Beach, tel. 305/972–3300 or 800/272–5624) is a 192-room, 750-acre health, fitness and stress-reduction spa offering exercise activities, personal treatments, and calorie-controlled meals. It's 15 minutes from downtown Fort Lauderdale.

Spectator Sports

For tickets to sporting events, call Ticketmaster (tel. 305/523–3309).

Baseball The New York Yankees hold spring training in 7,000-seat Fort Lauderdale Stadium (5301 N.W. 12th Ave., Fort Lauderdale, tel. 305/776–1921). The Fort Lauderdale Yankees compete between April and August in the Florida State League, as do the Pompano Beach Miracles at Pompano Municipal Stadium (1799 N.E. 8th St., tel. 305/783–2111).

Rugby The Fort Lauderdale Knights play rough and ready on the green at Holiday Park. *Off Federal Hwy., 2 blocks south of Sunrise Blvd., Fort Lauderdale, tel. 305/561–5263 for a recorded message. Admission free. Games Sept.–Apr., Sat. 2 PM.*

Dining

The list below is a representative selection of independent restaurants in Fort Lauderdale and Broward County, organized by type of cuisine. Unless otherwise noted, they serve lunch and dinner.

Highly recommended restaurants are indicated by a star ★.

Category	Cost*
Very Expensive	over $55
Expensive	$35–$55
Moderate	$15–$35
Inexpensive	under $15

**per person, excluding drinks, service, and 6% sales tax*

American **Burt & Jack's.** This restaurant, situated at the far end and most scenic lookout of Port Everglades, has been around in some capacity since the late 1970s. Finally, after three restaurants failed here, in 1984, Burt Reynolds and Jack Jackson hit it right and, despite scarce signage, diners find their way through the port-management maze. Behind the heavy mission doors and bougainvillea guests are rewarded with Maine lobster, steaks, and chops. The two-story gallery of hacienda-like dining rooms surrounded by glass have stunning views of the Intracoastal Waterway and John U. Lloyd State Park. Come to this very romantic spot Saturday or Sunday early evening for cocktails (served from 4:30, dinner from 5) and watch the cruise ships steam out. *Berth 23, Port Everglades, Fort Lauderdale, tel. 305/522–2878. Reservations advised. Jacket required. Dinner only. AE, DC, MC, V. Closed Christmas. Expensive.*

★ **Cafe Max.** As you enter Cafe Max, you're greeted by the aroma of fragrant spices issuing from the open theater kitchen. The decor includes art deco–style black wood chairs, original creations, and cut flowers. Booth seating is best; the tables are quite close together. Owner-chef Oliver Saucy combines the best of new American cuisine with traditional *escoffier* cooking. Specialties include Anaheim chili peppers stuffed with Monterey Jack cheese; mushroom duxelles served with goat cheese sauce; duck and smoked mozzarella ravioli with sun-dried tomatoes and basil butter; soft-shell crab with fresh tomato-jicama relish; and grilled veal chops. Daily chocolate dessert specials include hazelnut chocolate cappuccino torte and white-chocolate mousse pie with fresh raspberries. Other desserts include fresh fruit sorbets and homemade ice cream served with sauce *anglaise* and fresh raspberries. *2601 E. Atlantic Blvd., Pompano Beach, tel. 305/782–0606. Reservations advised. Dress: neat but casual. Dinner only. AE, D, DC, MC, V. Closed July 4, Super Bowl Sun. Expensive.*

Bimini Boatyard. With sky-high sloped roof, loads of windows, and paddlefans, this is a rarity among architecturally distinctive restaurants: inexpensive menu, ambience, and a quality bar. Try the Sam Adams with a loaf of Bimini bread or buffalo chicken wings. Heartier fare? Go for the *fettuccine al salmone affumicato* (smoked salmon, capers, whole-grain mustard, white wine, cream, and leeks). The extensive menu includes salads, burgers, and dishes from the cookbooks of the Bahamas, Jamaica, and Indonesia (grilled chicken breast with peanut sauce). The restaurant is on the 15th Street canal, and there is seating outside where the yachts tie up, or in. On weekends Bimini hosts progressive jazz bands. *1555 S.E. 17th St., tel. 305/525–7400. Reservations accepted for groups. Dress: casual. Limited menu after 11. AE, MC, V. Closed Christmas. Moderate.*

Ernie's Bar-B-Q & Lounge. Soup you can chew, thick barbecue between slabs of Bahama bread, and a wacky wall collection of

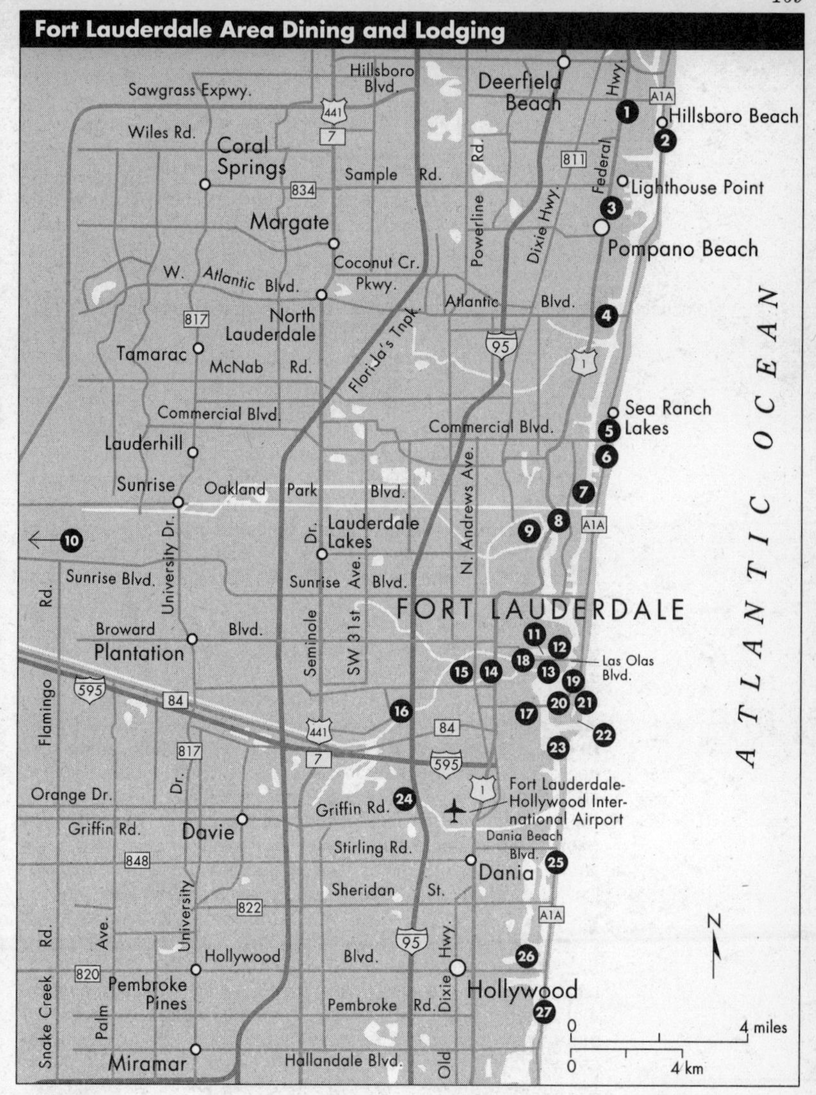

Lodging
Bahia Cabana Beach Resort, **19**
Banyan Marina Apartments, **11**
Carriage House Resort Motel, **2**
Di Vito By the Sea, **26**
Driftwood On the Ocean, **27**
Lago Mar Resort Hotel & Club, **22**
Marriott's Harbor Beach Resort, **21**
Pier 66 Resort and Marina, **20**
Pier Pointe Resort, **6**
Riverside Hotel, **13**
Tropic Seas Resort Motel, **5**

Dining
Bimini Boatyard, **17**
Burt & Jack's, **23**
Cafe Max, **4**
Cap's Place, **3**
Casa Vecchia, **12**
Don Arturo, **24**
Down Under, **7**
Ernie's Bar-B-Q & Lounge, **14**
Grainary Cafe, **1**
Il Tartuffo, **8**
Martha's, **25**
Old Florida Seafood House, **9**
Rennaissance Resturant, **10**
Rustic Inn Crabhouse, **16**
Santa Lucia, **18**
Shirttail Charlie's, **15**

memorabilia from a previous owner make Ernie's a must. Since 1976, Jeff Kirtman (from Brooklyn) has run this two-story eatery, which has an open-deck patio upstairs overlooking six-lane Federal Highway. The downstairs murals tout zany slogans and are adorned with former owner Ernie Siebert's dodo birds. Current owner Kirtman has supplied plenty of new reasons for visiting, including his conch-rich thick chowder, the hot open BBQ pork and beef sandwiches, and the combo ribs and chicken dinner with corn on the cob and baked beans. *1843 S. Federal Hwy., Fort Lauderdale, tel. 305/523-8636. No reservations. Dress: casual. MC, V. Inexpensive.*

Continental

Down Under. When Al Kocab and Leonce Picot opened Down Under in 1968, the Australian government sent them a boomerang as a gift. The name actually describes the restaurant's location, below a bridge approach at the edge of the Intracoastal Waterway. The two-story structure was built to look old, with walls of antique brick deliberately laid off-plumb. Dishes include a classic cobb salad, Florida seafoods—snapper, crab, lobster—duck, and beef Wellington, all in traditional presentations. Other specialties include fresh Belon oysters and littleneck clams from Maine; Florida blue crab cakes; Brutus salad (Down Under's version of Caesar salad); fresh Idaho trout lightly sautéed and topped with Florida blue crab and hollandaise sauce. Desserts include Key lime pie with meringue, crème brûlée, and pecan squares. *3000 E. Oakland Park Blvd., tel. 305/563-4123. Reservations advised. Dress: neat but casual. AE, MC, V. Expensive.*

Martha's. Situated on the Intracoastal across from a 417-acre mangrove preserve, just downstream of the Dania Boulevard Bridge, the restaurant evokes sheer elegance. The downstairs decor includes tables adorned with orchid buds, fanned napery, etched glass dividers, brass, and rosewood, and the outdoor patio is surrounded by a wildly floral mural. Piano music accompanies happy hour, and at night, a band and dancing set a supper-club mood. The upstairs dining area (reached by elevator) is casual, with a tropical setting of painted orchids, stained glass, and wave-shaped outdoor furniture. The same menu downstairs and up features outstanding seafood preparations: flaky dolphin in a court-bouillon; shrimp dipped in a piña colada batter, rolled in coconut, panfried with orange mustard sauce; and snapper prepared 17 ways. An assortment of rolls and banana bread come with entrées. For dessert, try fresh sorbet and vanilla and chocolate ice cream topped with meringue and hot fudge brandy sauce. *6024 N. Ocean Dr., Hollywood, tel. 305/923-5444. Reservations advised. Dress: neat but casual downstairs; casual upstairs. AE, DC, MC, V. Expensive.*

Cuban

Don Arturo. Waiters in tuxedos belie the friendly style of this family-run, romantically lit restaurant popular with the courthouse crowd. Avoid the party room that's near a noisy service area. If you're new to Cuban food, try the tri-steak sampler (chicken filet, palomilla steak, and pork filet), or one of the dinners for two, such as the *zarzuela de mariscos* (assorted seafood and fish smothered in tangy Spanish red sauce). Wash it down with the homemade sangria. English is spoken in this restaurant located four stoplights west of I-95, just north of Davie Boulevard. *1998 S.W. 27th Ave., tel. 305/584-7966 (also at 6522 W. Atlantic Blvd., Margate, tel. 305/968-1608). Reservations accepted. Dress: neat but casual. Dinner only Sun.*

AE, D, DC, MC, V. Closed July 4, Thanksgiving, Christmas, New Year's Day. Moderate.

Italian ★ **Casa Vecchia.** This old house (*casa vecchia*) stands beside the Intracoastal Waterway, surrounded by a formal garden where you can watch boats cruise past. The garden also grows herbs that flavor the restaurant's fare. Casa Vecchia was built in the late 1930s, and diners are encouraged to roam through the building to admire antique furnishings and original statuary and paintings. Spanish tiles decorate Casa Vecchia's walls and many tabletops. The menu changes every three months, but lately it's been leaning toward lighter fare, with specialties such as cannelloni Casa Vecchia (escarole leaves rolled with veal, spinach, and Parmesan cheese), *capellini d'Angelo* (angel hair pasta with sweet peas, prosciutto, and tomato cream sauce), broiled swordfish with charmoula vinaigrette, and an ossobucco. Desserts include full-flavored sorbets of fresh seasonal fruit prepared on the premises and *zabaglione freddo alla frutta* (cold sabayon with Grand Marnier and fresh fruit). *209 N. Birch Rd., tel. 305/463–7575. Reservations advised. Jacket preferred. AE, MC, V. Dinner only. Expensive.*

Santa Lucia. "You gotta taste the ocean," says owner/chef Angelo Ciampa, 43 years in restaurants, who now draws packed houses to his little 12-table storefront restaurant next to the fashionable Riverside Hotel on Las Olas Boulevard. The place smells like it ought to at home: pungent with a lot of subtle wafts. Try the *tuna carpaccio* (fresh tuna with capers, olive oil, parmesan cheese, and fresh Italian parsley) or the *rigatoni à la Russa* (tomato, garlic, hot pepper, parmesan, and basil with a splash of vodka). The *zuccotto* (a homemade sponge cake), is made with whipped cream, liqueurs, roasted pinenuts, almonds, and walnuts. Ask for the Moretti beer, a full-bodied Italian gift to the world. Or choose from three dozen Italian wines. *602 E. Las Olas Blvd., tel. 305/525–9530. Reservations advised. Dress: neat but casual. AE, MC, V. No lunch. Closed Sun. and Mon. in summer; closed Aug. Expensive.*

Il Tartufo. Only 16 tables are set here in a hint of a Ligurian garden with a cherub fountain. Specials include fresh truffles in November and December, but exquisite preparations can be found year-round in this family-run restaurant. Try an antipasto of portobello mushrooms with white wine, garlic, olive oil, herbs, and lemon; or a jumbo shrimp on radicchio flavored with balsamic vinegar, garlic, olive oil, and cilantro. Exceptional pastas include: cannelloni stuffed with parmesan and ricotta cheeses and spinach in a béchamel-tomato sauce; a home-made *pappardelle* pasta (wide noodles) with pesto sauce; and ravioli stuffed with veal in a white Genovese sauce. *2980 N. Federal Hwy., Fort Lauderdale, tel. 305/564–0607. Reservations advised. Dress: casual but neat. AE, MC, V. Dinner only. Closed Mon. Moderate.*

Natural ★ **Grainary Cafe.** Tucked away in the little Palm Plaza on the west side of Federal Highway, this is the premiere natural food restaurant in the county. Recently it expanded from 50 to 90 seats in a café setting, offering gourmet vegetarian food priced for family pocketbooks. Lunch specials include kasha veggie stew, tofu potato casserole with vegetable, and sweet potato ratatouille. In the evening entrées come with brown rice; unlimited bread basket (including macrobiotic brown rice bread, pita, and outstanding sourdough rolls) with miso-tahini spread and soy margarine; as well as soup or salad. House-filleted fresh fish is served in a lemon-ginger sauce, broiled, Cajun-blackened, or in a West Indian sauté that's served hot and spicy or mild and plain. You can get a rice burger with marinara or tahini or a bean and veggie burrito in a corn tortilla with salsa. *847 S. Federal Hwy., Deerfield Beach, tel. 305/360–0824. Reservations accepted. Dress: casual. AE, D, MC, V. BYOB. No lunch Sun. Closed Christmas. Inexpensive.*

Seafood ★ **Cap's Place.** This restaurant, located on an island previously inhabited by a rum runner, boasts having served such celebrities as Winston Churchill, Franklin D. Roosevelt, and John F. Kennedy. "Cap" was Captain Theodore Knight, born in 1871, who floated a derelict barge with partner-in-crime Al Hasis to the area in the 1920s. Today, the rustic restaurant, built atop the site, is run by descendants of Hasis who make freshness and excellence a priority. Baked wahoo steaks are lightly glazed and meaty; the long-cut french fries arouse gluttony; hot and flaky rolls are baked fresh several times a night, and tangy lime pie is the finishing touch. *Cap's Dock, 2765 N.E. 28th Ct., Lighthouse Point, tel. 305/941–0418. Follow the double-line road leading east on N.E. 24th St. off Federal Hwy. 2 blocks north to Pompano Fashion. No reservations. Dress: casual. AE, MC, V. Dinner only. Closed Sun. June–Nov. Expensive–Moderate.*

Old Florida Seafood House. Owner Bob Wickline has run this traditional seafood restaurant since 1978 with a West Virginian's eye toward giving value for money so he keeps his trade: plain on atmosphere, friendly on price. Nothing's frozen, nothing portion-controlled. He'll bring out a whole swordfish to show that it's fresh or take you to the cutting room with him. Best recommendation: Local waiters, waitresses, bartenders, and fellow restaurateurs all patronize the place that's not gourmet, just good. Try the veal Gustav (sautéed veal topped with a lobster tail), and a snapper New Orleans (sautéed with mushrooms and artichokes, laced with a light brown sauce). There's usually a 30-minute wait weekends. *1414 N.E. 26th St., Wilton Manors, tel. 305/566–1044. Also at 4535 Pine Island Rd., Sunrise, tel. 305/572–0444. Dress: neat but casual. AE, MC, V. No Sat. lunch. Closed Thanksgiving. Moderate.*

Rustic Inn Crabhouse. Wayne McDonald started with a cozy one-room roadhouse saloon in 1955 when this was a remote service road just west of the little airport. Now, the plain, rustic place situated around the New River Waterway seats 700. Since its opening, the owners have sold about as many garlic crabs as the other McDonald has sold burgers. Steamed crabs, seasoned with garlic and herbs, spices, and oil, are served with mallets on tables covered with newspapers; peel-and-eat shrimp is served either Key West–style with garlic and butter, or spiced and steamed with Old Bay seasoning. The big menu includes other seafood items as well. Pies and cheesecakes are on offer for dessert. *4331 Ravenswood Rd., Fort Lauderdale, tel. 305/584–1637. No reservations. Dress: casual. AE, D, DC, MC, V. Closed Thanksgiving, Christmas. Moderate.*

Shirttail Charlie's. You can watch the world go by from the outdoor deck or upstairs dining room of Shirttail Charlie's. Boats glide up and down the New River. Sunday–Thursday diners may take a free 30–40 minute after-dinner cruise on the 26-foot, 28-passenger *Shirttail Charlie's Express*, which chugs upriver past an alleged Al Capone speakeasy. Charlie's itself is built to look old, with 1920s tile floor that leans toward the water. Florida-style seafood offerings include an alligator-tail appetizer served with *tortuga* sauce (a béarnaise with turtle broth and sherry); conch served four ways; crab balls; swordfish bites; blackened tuna with Dijon mustard sauce; crunchy coconut shrimp with a not-too-sweet piña colada sauce; and a superbly tart Key lime pie with graham cracker-crust. *400 S.W. 3rd Ave., tel. 305/463–3474. Reservations advised upstairs. Dress: casual but neat. AE, D, MC, V. Moderate.*

Seafood **Renaissance Restaurant.** This gourmet restaurant, in the Bonaventure Resort and Spa, five-star-rated by the Confrérie de la Chaine des Rôtisseurs, features mesquite-grilled seafood and California cuisine with Florida adaptations. You dine in a rain forest setting, with views of a waterfall surrounded by palm and ficus trees, ferns and blooming flowers, and a pond with variegated foot-long carp. Specialties include chilled cream of avocado and cucumber soup; hot cream of poblano pepper soup with chunks of brie; a spinach-and-bean sprout salad with pickled eggs and rosemary vinaigrette dressing; whole wheat fettuccine sautéed with chunks of Maine lobster, scallops, and chives in a lobster sauce; mako shark in a lime-parsley-butter sauce. *250 Racquet Club Rd., tel. 305/389–3300 or 800/327–8090. Reservations required. Jacket preferred. AE, DC, MC, V. Dinner only. Expensive.*

Lodging

In Fort Lauderdale, Pompano Beach, and the Hollywood-Hallandale area, dozens of hotels line the Atlantic Ocean beaches. You can find accommodations ranging from economy motels to opulent luxury hotels with posh, pricey suites. An innovative Superior Small Lodging program, set up by the Greater Fort Lauderdale Convention and Visitors Bureau and administered by the hospitality department of Broward County's Nova University has led to substantial upgrading of many smaller properties. Some are described below. Inland, the major chain hotels along I–95 north and south of the airport cater primarily to business travelers and overnight visitors en route to somewhere else.

Wherever you plan to stay in Broward County, reservations are a good idea throughout the year. Tourists from the northern United States and Canada fill up the hotels from Thanksgiving through Easter. In summer, southerners and Europeans create a second season that's almost as busy. The list below is a representative selection of hotels and motels, organized by price and alphabetically. The rate categories in the list are based on the all-year or peak-season price; off-peak rates may be a category or two lower.

Highly recommended hotels are indicated by a star ★.

Category	**Cost***
Very Expensive	over $120
Expensive	$90–$120

Moderate	$50–$90
Inexpensive	under $50

**All prices are for a standard double room, excluding 6% state sales tax and nominal tourist tax.*

Lago Mar Resort Hotel & Club. The Banks family has owned this sprawling resort since the early 1950s. Under Walter Banks it draws lots of customers back again because of the easygoing management style that leaves guests feeling they're in a much smaller place. After a half-dozen expansions in different architectural styles, the eclectic look helps make guests feel they're in their own compound. Everyone shares the broad beach in this Harbor Beach section of the city, which is cut off from the rowdiness that sometimes affects the beachfront farther north. If you like a larger room, ask for a newer wing, although you'll pay less for the older. *1700 S. Ocean Lane, 33316, tel. 305/523–6511 or 800/255–5246. On the ocean just south of 17th St. causeway. 180 rooms with bath, including 135 suites. Facilities: 2 outdoor heated pools, 4 tennis courts, 2 volleyball courts, 4 shuffleboard courts, miniature golf, putting green, room service. AE, DC, MC, V. Very Expensive.*

Marriott's Harbor Beach Resort. Fort Lauderdale's only AAA-rated five-diamond hotel is a 14-story tower on 16 acres of oceanfront and has a free-form pool with a cascading waterfall. Built in 1984, its guest rooms were renovated in 1989. Room furnishings are light wood with mauve, pink, blue, and green hues; each room has a balcony facing either the ocean or the Intracoastal Waterway. *3030 Holiday Dr., 33316, tel. 305/525–4000 or 800/228–9290. 624 rooms with bath, including 36 suites, 108 nonsmoker rooms, 7 rooms for handicapped guests. Facilities: 1,100 ft of beach frontage, cabanas, windsurfing, Hobie cats, 65-foot catamaran, parasailing, outdoor heated freshwater pool and whirlpool, 5 tennis courts, fitness center, men's and women's saunas, masseuse, 3 boutiques, 5 restaurants, 3 lounges, in-room minibars, HBO, TV movies, complimentary 1-hr. weekly adult bike tours. AE, DC, MC, V. Very Expensive.*

★ **Pier 66 Resort and Marina.** Phillips Petroleum built Fort Lauderdale's landmark high-rise resort, best known for its revolving rooftop Pier Top Lounge. Its tower and lanai lodgings are "tops" from the ground up. The 17-story tower dominates a 22-acre spread that includes a 142-slip marina. A complete spa was added in 1989 and all rooms were renovated in 1989/90. *2301 S.E. 17th St., 33316, tel. 305/525–6666, 800/432–1956 (FL) 800/327–3796 (rest of US). 388 rooms with bath, including 8 suites. Facilities: 7 restaurants and lounges, water taxi to beach, outdoor freshwater pool, heated Jacuzzi, full-service marina with 142 wet slips for boats up to 200 ft long, scuba diving, snorkling, parasailing, small boat rentals, waterskiing, fishing and sailing yacht charters, 2 clay tennis courts, indoor health club with saunas and exercise equipment, massage therapy. AE, DC, MC, V. Very Expensive.*

Bahia Cabana Beach Resort. *Boating Magazine* ranks this resort's waterfront bar and restaurant among the 10 best. Rooms are spread out in five contiguous buildings furnished in tropical-casual style. Best of the 116 rooms and suites are #129—a two-bedroom suite with private terrace overlooking the tanning garden and pool, and #245—a one-bedroom suite with private deck that overlooks the yacht basin and skyline. Rooms in the 500 Building are more motel-like and overlook the parking lot, but rates here are lowest. The bar-restaurant is far enough from guest rooms so that the nightly entertainment does not disturb anyone. *3001 Harbor Dr., Fort Lauderdale 33316, tel. 305/524-1555, 800/BEACHES (U.S.), 800-3BEACH4 (Canada), or 800/922-3008 (FL). 116 rooms and suites with bath. Facilities: 3 heated freshwater pools, Jacuzzi, saunas, marina shuffleboard court, general store, restaurant, cafe, pool bar, patio bar. AE, D, DC, MC, V. Expensive.*

Pier Pointe Resort. Built in the 1950s, this oceanfront resort in Lauderdale-by-the-Sea, a block off the main street (Highway A1A), a block from the fishing pier, and backed by the beach, reminds one of the Gold Coast 40 years ago. The newly aqua-colored canopied entry opens onto two- and three-story buildings (most units with kitchens) set among brick pathways on cabbage palm lawns. The attractive wood pool deck is set off by sea grapes and rope-strung bollards. Rooms are plain, comfortable, and have balconies. All linens and drapes were redone in 1991. *4324 E. Mar Dr., Lauderdale-by-the-Sea 33308, tel. 305/776-5121 or 800/331-6384. 106 suites, efficiencies, and apartments with bath. Facilities: beach, 3 heated freshwater pools, gardens, barbecues. AE, DC, MC, V. Expensive.*

★ **Riverside Hotel.** This six-story hotel, on Fort Lauderdale's most fashionable shopping thoroughfare, was built in 1936, and has been steadily upgraded since 1987. In 1991 and 1992 80 rooms received new soft goods; the rest of the units are scheduled for 1992–1993. In-room coffee makers are a new feature, too. The tropical murals are the work of Bob Jenny, who painted a New Orleans–style mural across 725 square feet of the hotel's Las Olas facade, and whose pieces also appear at the President's Camp David retreat. An attentive staff includes many with the hotel for two decades or more. Each room is unique, with antique oak furnishings, framed French prints on the walls, in-room refrigerators, and European-style baths. Best rooms face south, overlooking the New River; worst rooms, where you can hear the elevator, are the 36 series. *620 E. Las Olas Blvd., 33301, tel. 305/467-0671, 800/325-3280. 117 rooms with bath, including 5 suites, 15 nonsmoker rooms. Facilities: heated freshwater pool beside the New River, 540 ft of dock with mooring space available by advance reservation, volleyball court, 2 restaurants, poolside bar. AE, DC, MC. Expensive.*

Tropic Seas Resort Motel. It's only a block off A1A, but it might as well be a mile. A million-dollar location directly on the beach, the motel is 2 blocks from municipal tennis courts. Built in the 1950s, units are plain but clean and comfortable, with tropical rattan furniture and ceiling fans. Managers Linda and Joe Surace maintain the largely repeat family-oriented clientele. Added features include a weekly wiener roast and rum swizzle party—both are good opportunities to mingle with other guests. *4616 El Mar Dr., Lauderdale-by-the-Sea 33308, tel. 305/772-2555. 16 rooms, efficiencies, apartments with bath. Facilities: beach, heated freshwater pool, shuffleboard, barbecue. AE, D, DC, MC, V. Expensive.*

★ **Banyan Marina Apartments.** Outstanding waterfront apartments on a residential island just off Las Olas Boulevard feature imaginative landscaping that includes a walkway through the upper branches of a banyan tree, dockage for eight yachts, and exemplary housekeeping. Luxurious units with leather sofas, springy carpets, real potted plants, sheer curtains and full drapes, and jalousies for sweeping the breeze in make these apartments as comfortable as any first-class hotel—but for half the price. Also included is a full kitchen, dining area, water view, and beautiful gardens. This is Florida the way you want it to be. *111 Isle of Venice, tel. 305/524–4430, fax 305/764–4870. Canalside just east of downtown on the way to the beach. 10 hotel rooms, efficiencies, and 1- and 2-bedroom apartments. Facilities: swimming pool, waterfront deck. MC, V. Expensive–Moderate.*

★ **Carriage House Resort Motel.** Very clean and tidy, this very good 30-unit beachfront motel sits 1 block from the ocean. Run by a French-American couple, the two-story, all white, black-shuttered colonial-style motel is actually two buildings connected by a second-story sun deck. Steady improvements have been made to the facility, including the addition of new furniture and Bahama beds that feel and look like sofas. Kitchenettes are equipped with quality utensils. Rooms are self-contained and quiet. *250. S. Ocean Blvd., Deerfield Beach 33441, tel. 305/427–7670. 30 rooms, efficiencies, apartments with bath. Facilities: heated pool, shuffleboard. AE, MC, V. Moderate.*

Driftwood on the Ocean. This attractive motel, built in 1959, occupies three buildings, and its lawn faces the beach at the secluded south end of Surf Road. Most units have a kitchen, and all are tropical in feel and have balconies. *2101 S. Surf Rd., Hollywood 33019, tel. 305/923–9528. 49 rooms, efficiencies, apartments with bath; 39 with kitchen. Facilities: beach, heated pool, shuffleboard, bicycles, laundry, barbecue. AE, MC, V. Moderate.*

The Arts and Nightlife

For the most complete weekly listing of events, read the "Showtime!" entertainment insert and events calendar in the Friday *Fort Lauderdale News/Sun Sentinel.*

Tickets are sold at individual box offices and through Ticketmaster (tel. 305/523–3309 in Broward County), a computerized statewide sales system.

The Arts

Theater

Broward Center for the Performing Arts (201 S.W. 5th Ave., Fort Lauderdale, tel. 305/522–5334) is the waterfront centerpiece of Fort Lauderdale's new outdoor complex. More than 500 cultural and recreational-themed events a year are scheduled at the performing arts center, including Broadway musicals, plays, dance, symphony and opera, rock, film, lectures, comedy, and children's theater. *See* Exploring Fort Lauderdale, above, for details.

Parker Playhouse (808 N.E. 8th St., Holiday Park, Fort Lauderdale, tel. 305/764–0700) features Broadway plays, musicals, drama, and local productions.

Sunrise Musical Theatre (5555 N.W. 95th Ave., Sunrise, tel. 305/741–7300) stages Broadway musicals, a few dramatic plays with name stars, and concerts by well-known singers throughout the year. The theater is 14 miles west of Fort Lauderdale Beach via Commercial Boulevard.

Vinnette Carroll Theatre (503 S.E. 6th St., Fort Lauderdale, tel. 305/462–2424), a multiethnic theater company, housed in a renovated church, is known for such Broadway hits as "Your

Arms Too Short to Box with God," and "Don't Bother Me I Can't Cope."

Concerts

Bailey Concert Hall is a popular place for classical music concerts, dance, drama, and other performing arts activities, especially October–April. *Central Campus of Broward Community College, 3501 S.W. Davie Rd., tel. 305/475–6884 for reservations.*

The Florida Philharmonic Orchestra, south Florida's only fully professional orchestra, is Broward-based but performs in six locations in Broward, Dade, and Palm Beach counties. It offers a variety of series and individual-performance tickets; write for schedule. *1430 N. Federal Hwy., 33304, tel. 305/561–2997; (Dade County), 305/945–5180 (Boca Raton) 407/392–5443; (Palm Beach) 407/659–0331; 800/226–1812 (Ticketmaster statewide). Office open weekdays 9–5. AE, MC, V.*

The Fort Lauderdale Opera Guild presents the current production of the Greater Miami Opera and of the Palm Beach Opera, as well as productions of the Guild itself, in the Broward Center for the Performing Arts. For tickets, contact the Guild office. *333 S.W. 2nd St., 33312, tel. 305/728–9700. Office open weekdays 9–5. AE, MC, V.*

Nightlife

Bars and Nightclubs

Cheers. Lots of parties (Capricorns' night, full-moon night, Roseanne Barr sing-alike night) and a "happy birthday club" when celebrants enjoy bottomless mugs, entice those seeking fun to this woody night spot with two bars and dance floor. Monday is New Orleans jazz; other days mainly rhythm and blues. *941 E. Cypress Creek Rd., tel. 305/771–6337. Bands nightly 10:30–3:30, plus Sun. open mike jam session 7–midnight. Grazing menu served 11:30 AM–4 AM. Cover charge Fri. $3. AE, D, MC, V.*

Confetti. Since the mid-1980s, this has been the high energy "in" spot for 35–50 year olds. A DJ spins top 40 tunes for dancers as they are doused with confetti, and helium balloons bob around the 10 bars. Bartenders blow flames and do tricks, waitresses serve blue vodka-based drinks from racks of vials. The Saturday night motto is "come and party with 6,000 of your closest friends." At 11 PM when the upstairs opens you can walk through the game room to the **Reunion Room** with lots of black light and paintings by Art Institute students. The music is alternative and progressive, but if the disco scene isn't your thing, you can tune in one of the four screens that show wildlife videos. *2660 E. Commercial Blvd., tel. 305/776–4081. $5 cover. Open Wed.–Fri. 8–2, Sat. 8–3. Closed Mon.–Tues. Reunion Room features local and national acts 1st set only Fri. 11:30 PM–12:30 AM. Fri. no cover in Confetti 8–10.*

Crocco's is the action place for singles. Free drinks for women Wed. nights from 8 to 11. *3339 N. Federal Hwy., Oakland Park, tel. 305/566–2406.*

Musician Exchange. This 200-seat club, heading into its 17th year, features an eclectic mix of blues, jazz, and rock-and-roll, with reggae on Sundays. Performers include local bands as well as leading musicians like Donovan, John Lee Hooker, Laura Nyro, Carmen McCrae, and Stan Getz. *729 W. Sunrise Blvd., tel. 305/764–1912. Admission price varies with show. National big-name acts Fri. and Sat. Call for schedule and reservations.*

Shirttail Charlie's Downstairs Bar. A scenic place to have a beer or snack and watch boat traffic on the New River through downtown Fort Lauderdale. Entertainment Wed., Thurs. 5–9,

Fri. 5:30–9:30, Sat. 6–10, Sun. 2–6. Informal. *400 S.W. 3rd Ave., tel. 305/463–3474. Open Mon.–Sat. 11:30–10, Sun. 11:30–9.*

Squeeze. Hard-core new-wavers to yuppie types all fit in here. Fluorescent paints create monstrous wildflower effects, and pterodactyls look very 3-D. A juice bar is offered for designated drivers. The younger crowd goes for the black-and-white Alley with its two bars, dance floor, and the giant green chicken-wire sculpture. The special effects are by Michael Hardwick who hit his stride with sculptures at the late Club Nu in Miami Beach. *2 S. New River Dr., tel. 305/522–2068. Tues.–Sat. 8 PM till early morning. $5 cover; Tues. free. Special parties nightly.*

Sushi Blues. A very small restaurant with great Japanese food also plays good music in the evenings. *1836 Young Circle, Hollywood, tel. 305/929–9560.*

Yesterday's. This upscale disco attracts middle-agers but it's no sleeper. Instead it's more like Saturday Night Fever, with pulsing bass, light show, and confetti. There are four bars, a huge wine cellar, and gourmet menu in the opulent Plum Room (private screens by your banquette on request). Tables and booths overlook the Intracoastal. Special late-night gourmet pizzas are offered. *East Oakland Park Blvd. at the Intracoastal, tel. 305/561–4400. Nightly from 8–2 AM, Sat. to 3. Plum Room 7–11, Fri.–Sat. to midnight. Wed. "ladies night," with complimentary drinks 8–10, $1 drinks for unescorted women after 10 PM.*

Comedy Clubs

The Comic Strip. Stand-up comedians from New York work among framed old newspaper funnies—Katzenjammer Kids, Superman, Prince Valiant, L'il Orphan Annie, Hubert, etc.—and there's a full restaurant menu (two-drink minimum—alcoholic and nonalcoholic beverages). *1432 N. Federal Hwy., tel. 305/565–8887. Showtime Sun.–Fri. 9:30, Sat. 8:30 and 11. Subject to change on holidays. AE, MC, V.*

Country/Western

Do-Da's Country Music Emporium. The Frontier Room seats 800 at buckboard tables and has a 2,100-square-foot sunken wood dance floor, popular for square dancing; the smaller pecky-board Tennessee Room seats 100. Glass-and-brick arches enclose the Tex-Mex dining area, Steak House. Do-Da's presents an international buffet during happy hour, weekdays 5–7:30. Otherwise it's ribs, gator, wings, along with the Tex-Mex menu. *700 S. U.S. 441, Plantation, tel. 305/792–6200. Mon.–Tues. 5–2, Wed.–Fri. 5–4, Sat. 6–4. Closed Sun. Live music nightly 9–2. AE, MC, V.*

7 Palm Beach and Palm Beach County

Introduction

Updated by Herb Hiller

Wealth has its privileges. That's the continuing reality of Palm Beach. Those privileges include the finest homes, cars, food, wine, furniture, jewelry, art, clothing, and toys that money can buy—and the right to stare back at the tourists who visit this elegant barrier-island enclave 70 miles north of Miami.

Henry Morrison Flagler created Palm Beach in 1894. Earlier he helped John D. Rockefeller establish the Standard Oil Company, then retired and put his money into Florida railroads and real estate. He bought a small railroad between Jacksonville and St. Augustine and extended it southward. Eventually it was called the Florida East Coast Railroad. Along the rail line he built hotels to generate traffic, including a huge wooden structure, the 2,000-room Royal Poinciana, beside a tidal bay called Lake Worth.

Flagler created an international high-society resort at Palm Beach, attracting the affluent for the Season, New Year's Day to Washington's Birthday. Then they departed for Europe, extolling Palm Beach's virtues and collecting great art to ship back to the mansions they were building on the island.

A workman told Flagler that people liked to picnic along the beach "down by the breakers," so he built a second hotel there in 1896. It burned, was rebuilt, and burned again. The third structure to bear the name The Breakers rose in 1926 and stands today as the grande dame of Palm Beach hostelries.

Socialites and celebrities still flock to The Breakers for charity galas. They browse in the stores along Worth Avenue, regarded as one of the world's classiest shopping districts. They swim on secluded beaches that are nominally public but lack convenient parking and access points. They pedal the world's most beautiful bicycle path beside Lake Worth. And what they do, *you* can do—if you can afford it.

Despite its prominence and affluence, the Town of Palm Beach occupies far less than 1% of the land area of Palm Beach County, which is 521 square miles larger than the state of Delaware and is a remarkably diverse political jurisdiction.

West Palm Beach, on the mainland across Lake Worth from Palm Beach, is the city Flagler built to house Palm Beach's servants; today it's the county seat and commercial center of Palm Beach County, with a population of about 80,000. Both the downtown and uptown areas are undergoing immense revitalization. Among the biggest and most immediate changes are the completion of the 2,200-seat Raymond K. Kravis Center for the Performing Arts (scheduled to open in November 1992) and the $2 million restoration of the historic Seaboard Railroad Station which reopened the year before. Other new and welcome additions to the downtown scene are the Palm Beach Opera, which arrived in 1991, and, at its heels, the Florida Ballet, in 1992.

Making it simpler for residents and visitors to get to and around downtown will be the so-called Inter-Modal, a networking transportation facility that should be operating by 1994. The system will link together all sorts of transport including Amtrak, Greyhound/Trailways, TriRail (a commuter line), CoTran (a county bus system), and taxis. Beginning in 1993 will be a free shuttle service—the first stage of the project's development—which will link up with the downtown commercial district, a 15-block area where some 10,000 square feet of retail space was added in 1992. Already half a dozen new restaurants and trendy bars are in full swing along the 5 blocks of Clematis Street alone.

Lantana, to the south of West Palm Beach, has a large Finnish population. Delray Beach began as an artists' retreat and a small settlement of Japanese farmers, including George Morikami, who donated the land for the beautiful Morikami Museum of Japanese Culture (4000 Morikami Park Rd., Delray Beach 33446, tel. 407/495–0233), to the county park system. The museum is open Tuesday–Sunday 10–5; closed Easter, Thanksgiving, Christmas, New Year's Day. Boca Raton, an upscale community developed by pioneer architect Addison Mizner as a showcase for his Spanish Revival style, retains much of its 1920s ambience through strict zoning. The newest apparition of the Mizner style is the $75 million Mizner Park, a de rigueur–pink civic cultural center and shopping mall with outdoor amenities that opened in 1991.

To the north, Palm Beach Gardens is a golf center, home of the Professional Golfer's Association. Jupiter boasts the Jupiter Theater and a dune-fringed beach that remains largely free of intrusive development.

Many visitors to Palm Beach County don't realize that the borders extend 50 miles inland to encompass the southeastern quadrant of 448,000-acre Lake Okeechobee, the fourth-largest natural lake in the United States. Its bass and perch attract fisherfolk; catfish devotees prize the hearty flavor of succulent Okeechobee "sharpies."

Marinas at Pahokee and Belle Glade provide lake access. In Lake Harbor, about as far west as you can go in Palm Beach County, the state is restoring a lock built early in the 20th century on the Miami Canal.

Palm Beach County is also the main gateway to the Treasure Coast, consisting of Martin, St. Lucie, and Indian River counties along the Atlantic Coast to the north.

Essential Information

Arriving and Departing by Plane

Airport **Palm Beach International Airport (PBIA)** (Congress Ave. and Belvedere Rd., West Palm Beach, tel. 407/471–7400) is equipped with a 25-gate terminal to handle five million passengers a year, and will add up to 24 more gates by 1995.

Between the Airport and City Center Route No. 10 of **Tri-Rail Commuter Bus Service** joins PBIA and Tri-Rail's Palm Beach Airport station during weekday rush hours only. For schedule, call 800/TRI–RAIL. For connections with CoTran (Palm Beach County Transportation Authority) routes, call 407/686–4560 or 407/686–4555 in Palm Beach, 407/272–6350 in Boca Raton–Delray Beach. Route 4–S operates from PBIA to downtown West Palm Beach every two hours on the half hour starting at 7:30 AM until 5:30 PM. Fare is 90¢. Rental car companies that operate directly within PBIA include **Alamo** (tel. 407/684–6806), **Avis** (tel. 407/233–6400), **Budget** (tel. 407/

683–2401), **Dollar** (tel. 407/686–3300), **Hertz** (tel. 407/684–4300), and **National** (tel. 407/233–7350).

Palm Beach Transportation (tel. 407/689–4222) provides taxi and limousine service from PBIA. Reserve at least a day in advance for a limousine. Lowest fares are $1.50 per mile, with the meter starting at $1.25. Depending on your destination, a flat rate may save money. Inquire about minimum fares required for use of credit cards. *MC, V.*

Arriving and Departing by Train and Car

By Train **Amtrak** (201 S. Tamarind Ave., West Palm Beach, tel. 800/872–7245 or 407/832–6169) connects West Palm Beach with cities along Florida's east coast and the northeast daily.

Tri-Rail has six stations in Palm Beach County. For details, call 800/TRI–RAIL or 305/728–8445.

By Car Most visitors explore Palm Beach County by car. I–95 runs north-south, to link West Palm Beach with Miami and Fort Lauderdale to the south. To get to central Palm Beach, exit at Belvedere Road or Okeechobee Boulevard. Southern Boulevard (U.S. 98) runs east-west. From West Palm Beach, take I-95 south to Delray Beach and Boca Raton, north to Palm Beach Gardens and Jupiter.

Getting Around

By Bus CoTran buses require exact change (90¢, 45¢ for seniors and handicapped persons, plus 25¢ for a transfer). Service is provided from 5 AM to 8:30 PM, with individual route variations. For details, call 407/686–4560 or 407/686–4555 (Palm Beach), 407/272–6350 (Boca Raton-Delray Beach).

By Taxi **Palm Beach Transportation** (tel. 407/689–4222). Cab meters start at $1.25. Each mile within West Palm Beach city limits is $1.25; if the trip at any point leaves the city limits, $1.50. Some cabs may charge more. Waiting time is 25¢ per 75 seconds.

Important Addresses and Numbers

Tourist Information **Palm Beach County Convention & Visitors Bureau** (1555 Palm Beach Lakes Blvd., Suite 204, West Palm Beach 33401, tel. 407/471–3995) is open weekdays 8:30–5.

Chamber of Commerce of the Palm Beaches (401 N. Flagler Dr., West Palm Beach 33401, tel. 407/833–3711) is open weekdays 8:30–5.

Palm Beach Chamber of Commerce (45 Cocoanut Row, Palm Beach 33480, tel. 407/655–3282) is open weekdays 9–5.

Deaf Service Center of Palm Beach County (5730 Corporate Way, Suite 230, West Palm Beach 33407, TDD tel. 407/478–3904; toll-free from south Palm Beach County tel. 407/392–6444, voice tel. 407/478–3903) is open weekdays 8–4:30; closed Thanksgiving, Christmas, December 26, and New Year's Day. Relay operates until 9 PM, Saturday 9–noon.

Emergencies Dial 911 for **police** and **ambulance** in an emergency.

Hospitals Three hospitals in West Palm Beach with 24-hour emergency rooms are **Good Samaritan Hospital** (Flagler Dr. and Palm Beach Lakes Blvd., tel. 407/655–5511; doctor-referral, tel. 407/650–6240); **Palm Beach Regional Hospital** (2028 10th Ave., tel. 407/967–7800; doctor-referral, tel. 800/237–6644); and **St. Mary's Hospital** (901 45th St., tel. 407/844–6300; doctor-referral, tel. 407/881–2929).

24-Hour Pharmacies **Eckerd Drugs** (3343 S. Congress Ave., Palm Springs, southwest of West Palm Beach, tel. 407/965–3367; and 7016 Bera Casa Way, Boca Raton, tel. 407/391–8770). **Walgreen Drugs** (1688 Congress Ave., Palm Springs, tel. 407/968–8211; and 7561 N. Federal Hwy., Boca Raton, tel. 407/241–9802).

Guided Tours

Boat Tours **Star of Palm Beach** (900 E. Blue Heron Blvd., Riviera Beach, tel. 407/842–0882) offers sightseeing as well as dinner-dance tours that cruise the Intracoastal Waterway past millionaire row. Two vessels, which depart from Phil Foster Park, include the 250-passenger *Star of Palm Beach*, a replica of a Mississippi paddlewheeler; and a steamboat. *MC, V. Tours operate daily year-round.*

Since 1988, the *Manatee Queen* (1000 U.S. Hwy. 1, Jupiter, tel. 407/744–2191) a 40-foot, 49-passenger Caribbean catamaran, has offered afternoon, sunset, and evening wine-and-cheese cruises on the Intracoastal Waterway between November and May. Cruises include tours up the Loxahatchee River into cypress swamps of the Jonathan Dickinson State Park and depart from Charlie's Crab at Jupiter Harbor.

Wildlife Tour **Tropical Wildlife Tours** (1001 S. Federal Hwy., Lake Worth, tel. 407/582–5947) offers year-round guided tours of Palm Beach and the Everglades that include hotel pick-up and return in a luxurious van. Prices range from $29 to $69. *MC, V.*

Exploring Palm Beach and Palm Beach County

Numbers in the margin correspond to points of interest on the Palm Beach and Palm Beach County map.

Palm Beach is an island community 12 miles long and no more than a ¼-mile across at its widest point. Three bridges connect Palm Beach to West Palm Beach and the rest of the world. This tour takes you through both communities.

Begin at Royal Palm Way and County Road in the center of Palm Beach. Go north on County Road past the Episcopal ❶ church, **Bethesda-by-the-Sea,** built in 1927 by the first Protestant congregation in southeast Florida. Inspiring stained-glass windows and a lofty, vaulted sanctuary grace its Spanish-Gothic design. A stone bridge with an ornamental tile border spans the pond; bubbling fountains feed it. *141 South County Rd., Palm Beach, tel. 407/655–4554. Gardens open 8–5. Services Sun. 8, 9, and 11 AM in winter, 8 and 10 June–Aug.; phone for weekday schedule.*

❷ Continue north on County Road past **The Breakers** (1 S. County Rd., Palm Beach), an ornate Italian renaissance hotel (*see*

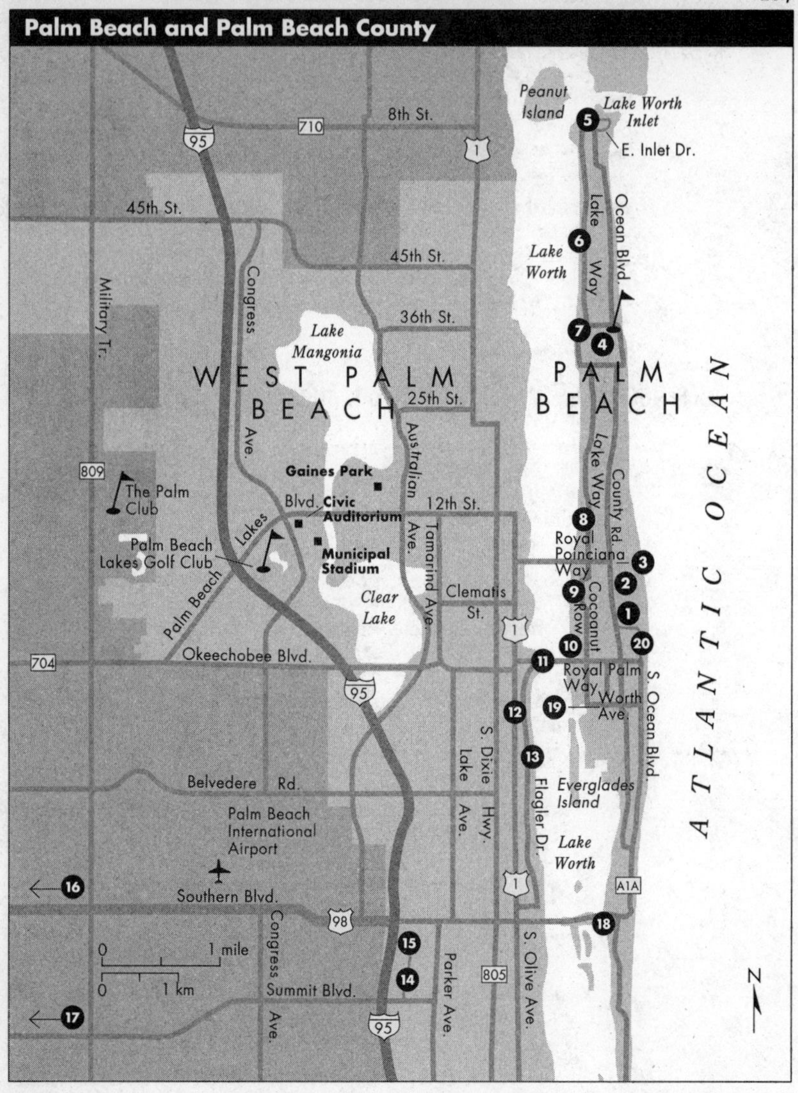

Ann Norton Sculpture Gardens, **13**
Bethesda-by-the-Sea, **1**
The Breakers, **2**
Canyon of Palm Beach, **7**
Dreher Park Zoo, **14**
E. Inlet Drive, **5**
Lion Country Safari, **16**
Mar-A-Lago, **18**
Norton Gallery of Art, **12**
Palm Beach Bicycle Trail, **6**
Palm Beach Biltmore Hotel, **8**
Palm Beach Country Club, **4**
Palm Beach Post Office, **3**
Pine Jog Environmental Sciences Center, **17**
Public Beach, **20**
Royal Palm Bridge, **11**
Society of the Four Arts, **10**
South Florida Science Museum, **15**
Whitehall, **9**
Worth Ave., **19**

Lodging, below) built in 1926 by railroad magnate Henry M. Flagler's widow to replace an earlier hotel, which has burned, twice. Explore the elegant public spaces—especially on a Sunday morning, when you can enjoy the largest champagne brunch in Florida at The Beach Club.

3 Continue north on County Road to Royal Poinciana Way. Go inside the **Palm Beach Post Office** to see the murals depicting Seminole Indians in the Everglades and royal and coconut palms. *95 N. County Rd., Palm Beach, tel. 407/832–0633 or 407/832–1867. Open weekdays 8:30–5.*

4 Continue 3.9 miles north on County Road to the north end of the island, past the very-private **Palm Beach Country Club** and a neighborhood of expansive (and expensive) estates. From the coastal road you can catch glimpses of Singer Island, with its Oz-like scenery.

5 You must turn around at **E. Inlet Drive,** the northern tip of the island, where a dock offers a view of Lake Worth Inlet, the U.S. Coast Guard Reservation on Peanut Island, and the Port of Palm Beach across Lake Worth on the mainland. Observe the no-parking signs; Palm Beach police will issue tickets.

6 Turn south and make the first right onto Indian Road, then the first left onto Lake Way. You'll return to the center of town through an area of newer mansions, past the posh, private Sailfish Club. Lake Way parallels the **Palm Beach Bicycle Trail** along the shoreline of Lake Worth, a palm-fringed path through the backyards of some of the world's priciest homes. Watch on your right for metal posts topped with a swatch of white paint, marking narrow public-access walkways between houses from the street to the bike path.

7 Lake Way runs into Country Club Road, which takes you through the **Canyon of Palm Beach,** a road cut about 25 feet deep through a ridge of sandstone and oolite limestone.

8 As you emerge from the canyon, turn right onto Lake Way and continue south. Lake Way becomes Bradley Place. You'll pass the **Palm Beach Biltmore Hotel,** now a condominium. Another flamboyant landmark of the Florida boom, it cost $7 million to build and opened in 1927 with 543 rooms.

9 As you cross Royal Poinciana Way, Bradley Place becomes Cocoanut Row. Stop at **Whitehall,** the palatial 73-room mansion that Henry M. Flagler built in 1901 for his third wife, Mary Lily Kenan. After the couple died, the mansion was turned into a hotel. In 1960, Flagler's granddaughter, Jean Flagler Matthews, bought the building. She turned it into a museum, with many of the original furnishings on display. The art collection includes a Gainsborough portrait of a girl with a pink sash, displayed in the music room near a 1,200-pipe organ. Exhibits also depict the history of the Florida East Coast Railroad. Flagler's personal railroad car, "The Rambler," is parked behind the building. A tour by well-informed guides takes about an hour; afterwards, you may browse on your own. *Cocoanut Row at Whitehall Way, Palm Beach, tel. 407/655–2833. Admission: $5 adults, $2 children 6–12. Open Tues.–Sat. 10–5, Sun. noon–5. Closed Mon.*

10 Continue south on Cocoanut Row to Royal Palm Way. Turn right and then right again onto the grounds of the **Society of the Four Arts.** This 56-year-old cultural and educational institution

is privately endowed and incorporates an exhibition hall for art, concerts, films, and lectures; a library open without charge; 13 distinct gardens, and the Philip Hulitar Sculpture Garden. *Four Arts Plaza, tel. 407/655–7226. Admission: $20 concerts, $15 lectures, $2.50 Friday films, $1 young people's programs; exhibitions: suggested donation $3; Sun. art films and gallery talks, free. Concert and lecture tickets for nonmembers may be purchased one week in advance. Tickets for Fri. films available at time of showing. Exhibitions and programs, Dec.–mid-Apr., Mon.–Sat. 10–5, Sun. 2–5. Library open Nov.–Apr., Mon.–Sat. 10–5; May–Oct., weekdays 10–5. Gardens open Nov.–Apr., Mon.–Sat. 10–5; Jan.–Apr. 15, Sun. 2:30–5; May–Oct., weekdays 10–5.*

Continue west on Royal Palm Way across the Royal Park Bridge into West Palm Beach. On the mainland side, turn left onto Flagler Drive, which runs along the west shore of Lake Worth. A half-mile south of the **Royal Palm Bridge,** (11) turn right onto Actaeon Street, which is the north edge of a sloping mall leading up to the **Norton Gallery of Art.** (12)

Founded in 1941 by steel magnate Ralph H. Norton, the Norton Gallery boasts an extensive permanent collection of 19th- and 20th-century American and European paintings with emphasis on 19th-century French Impressionists, Chinese bronze and jade sculptures, a sublime outdoor patio with sculptures on display in a tropical garden, and a library housing more than 3,000 art books and periodicals. The Norton also secures many of the best traveling exhibits to reach south Florida. *1451 S. Olive Ave., West Palm Beach, tel. 407/832–5194. Admission free; $5 donation requested. Open Tues.–Sat. 10–5, Sun. 1–5.*

Return to Flagler Drive, go a ½-mile south to Barcelona Road, and turn right again. You're at the entrance to the **Ann Norton Sculpture Gardens,** (13) a monument to the late American sculptor Ann Weaver Norton, second wife of Norton Gallery founder Ralph H. Norton. In three distinct areas of the 3-acre grounds, the art park displays seven granite figures and six brick megaliths. Plantings were designed by Norton, an environmentalist, to attract native birdlife. Native plants include 150 different kinds of palms. Other sculptures in bronze, marble, and wood are on display in Norton's studio. *253 Barcelona Rd., West Palm Beach, tel. 407/832–5328. Admission: $2 adults, children under 12 free. Open Tues.–Sat. noon–4 or by appointment.*

Return again to Flagler Drive and continue south to Southern Boulevard (U.S. 98). Turn right and go west almost a mile, turn left onto Parker Avenue, and go south about a mile. Turn right onto Summit Boulevard, and right again at the next stoplight into the parking lot at the **Dreher Park Zoo.** (14) The 29-acre zoo has more than 400 animals representing more than 100 different species, including an endangered Florida panther. Of special interest are the reptile collection and the petting zoo. *1301 Summit Blvd., West Palm Beach, tel. 407/547–WILD (recording) or 407/533–0887. Admission: $5 adults, $4.50 senior citizens over 60, $3.50 children 3–12. Open daily 9–5.*

(15) About a ¼-mile from the zoo is the **South Florida Science Museum.** Here you'll find hands-on exhibits, aquarium displays with touch-tank demonstrations, planetarium shows, and a chance to observe the heavens Friday nights through the most power-

ful telescope in south Florida (weather permitting). *4801 Dreher Trail N, West Palm Beach, tel. 407/832–1988. Admission: $5 adults, $4.50 senior citizens over 62, $3 students 13–21, $1.50 children 4–12; laser show $2 extra. Planetarium admission: $1.75 extra. Open daily 10–5, Fri. 10–10.*

Leaving the science museum, retrace your path on Summit Boulevard and Parker Avenue to Southern Boulevard (Rte. 80), turn left, and go about 16 miles west to **Lion Country Safari,** where you drive (with car windows closed) on 8 miles of paved roads through a 500-acre cageless zoo where 1,000 wild animals roam free. Lions, elephants, white rhinoceroses, giraffes, zebras, antelopes, chimpanzees, and ostriches are among the species in residence. Try to go early in the day, before the park gets crowded. If you have a convertible or a new car on which you don't want animals to climb, the park will rent you a zebra-stripe, air-conditioned sedan. An adjacent KOA campground offers campers a park discount. *Box 16066, West Palm Beach 33416, tel. 407/793–1084. Admission: $11.95 adults, $9.95 children 3–16, $8.55 senior citizens over 65, under 3 free; car rental $5 per hour. Open daily 9:30–5:30.*

Returning to town on Southern Boulevard, turn right onto Jog Road, left onto Summit Boulevard to the **Pine Jog Environmental Sciences Center.** After 30 years as a limited-admission nature center, in 1991 Pine Jog was opened by Florida Atlantic University to the public. The 150-acre site is mostly undisturbed Florida pine flatwoods. There's a self-guided ½-mile trail, and formal landscaping around the five one-story buildings features an array of native plants. Dioramas and displays show native ecosystems, and environmental education programs are offered. *6301 Summit Blvd., West Palm Beach, tel. 407/686–6600. Admission free. Open weekdays 9–5, weekends 1–4. Closed major holidays.*

Return to Southern Boulevard, turn right, look for the Italianate towers of **Mar-A-Lago** (1100 S. Ocean Blvd.) silhouetted against the sky as you cross the bridge to Palm Beach. Mar-A-Lago, the former estate of breakfast-food heiress Marjorie Meriweather Post, has lately been owned by real estate magnate Donald Trump, who is trying to subdivide it.

Turn north on Ocean Boulevard, one of Florida's most scenic drives. The road follows the dune top, with the beach falling away to surging surf on your right, and some of Palm Beach's most opulent mansions on your left. You will pass the east end of **Worth Avenue** (*see* Shopping, below), regarded by many as the world's classiest shopping street.

As you approach Worth Avenue, the **public beach** begins. Parking meters along Ocean Drive between Worth Avenue and Royal Palm Way signify the only stretch of beach in Palm Beach with convenient public access.

This concludes the tour. To return to its starting point, turn left on Royal Palm Way and go 1 block west to County Road.

What to See and Do with Children

Burt Reynolds Ranch and Mini Petting Farm. Farm and exotic animals can be petted on this 160-acre working horse ranch and feed store complex owned by the famous actor. *16133 Jupiter Farms Rd., Jupiter (2 mi west of I–95 off exit 59-B), tel. 407/*

747–5390. Open daily 10–4:30. Closed major holidays. Admission free.

Children's Museum of Boca Raton at Singing Pines. This learning center for children features hands-on exhibits, workshops, and special programs. *498 Crawford Blvd., Boca Raton, tel. 407/368–6875. Admission: $1. Open Tues.–Sat. noon–4.*

Children's Science Explorium. This museum features 40 hands-on exhibits as well as ongoing special events. On Saturdays there's a science cinema and Wizard's Workshop that features crafts for young children. *Royal Palm Plaza, Suite 15, 131 Mizner Blvd., Boca Raton, tel. 407/395–8401. Admission: $3.50 adults, $3 senior citizens and children over 3. Open Mon.–Sat. 10–5, Sun. noon–5.*

Gumbo Limbo Nature Center. At this unusual nature center, you can stroll a 1,628-foot boardwalk through a dense tropical forest and climb a 50-foot tower to overlook the tree canopy. The forest is a coastal hammock, with tropical species growing north of the tropics. One tree species you're sure to see—the gumbo-limbo, with its red peeling bark—is often called "the tourist tree." A guide to dune plants was published in 1991 in the same format and at the same price as the *Coastal Park Plant Guide* ($4) for Gumbo Limbo, James Rutherford, Red Reef, and Spanish River parks. The guide details the parks' flora, with photos and brief text keyed to numbered posts along the trails. In the nature center building, a diorama depicts the nest of a loggerhead sea turtle along the nearby beach. The center's staff leads guided turtle walks to the beach to see nesting mothers come ashore and lay their eggs. *1801 N. Ocean Blvd., Boca Raton, tel. 407/338–1473. Admission: $3. Ticket must be purchased in advance for the night tour. Open Mon.–Sat. 9–4. Admission free. Turtle walks late May–late July Mon.–Thurs. 9 PM–midnight.*

Off the Beaten Track

Arthur R. Marshall Loxahatchee National Wildlife Refuge

Loxahatchee Refuge is 221 square miles of saw grass marshes, wet prairies, sloughs, and tree islands. You go there to stroll the nature trails, see alligators and birds (including the rare snail kite). You can also fish for bass and panfish, ride an airboat, or paddle your own canoe through this watery wilderness. Loxahatchee refuge was renamed in memory of Art Marshall, a Florida environmental scientist instrumental in Everglades preservation efforts. *Open ½ hr before sunrise–½ hr after sunset. Refuge entrance fee: $3 per car, $1 per pedestrian.*

The refuge has three access points, but only the headquarters has its own facilities and services:

Headquarters

The ranger at the visitor center will show a seven-minute slide presentation on request. Walk both nature trails—a boardwalk through a dense cypress swamp, and a marsh nature trail to a 20-foot-tall observation tower overlooking a pond. A 7-mile canoe trail starts at the boat-launching ramp here. *Entrance off U.S. 441 between Boynton Blvd. (Rte. 804) and Atlantic Ave. (Rte. 806), west of Boynton Beach. Mailing address: Rte. 1, Box 278, Boynton Beach 33437–9741, tel. 407/732–3684 or 407/734–8303.*

Hillsboro Recreation Area At press time the contract for the concession was in the process of changing hands, but it is expected that the new concessionaire will probably provide the same services as the former. The last concessionaire offered airboat rides, boat rentals, guide services, and a store with snacks, fishing tackle, and bait. The airboat ride lasts ½ hour, in a 20-passenger craft with a Cadillac engine; the driver took passengers into the middle of the Everglades, then shut off the engine and explained the unique ecosystem. The following information applies to the former concessionaire, and services, prices, and hours may change. *Entrance off U.S. 441 on Lox Rd. (Rte. 827), 12 mi south of Headquarters and west of Boca Raton.*

20-Mile Bend Recreation Area Boat ramp and fishing area at north end of refuge. *Entrance off U.S. 98/441, due west of West Palm Beach.*

Shopping

Worth Avenue One of the world's strongholds for quality shopping, Worth Avenue runs a ¼ mile east–west across Palm Beach, from the beach to Lake Worth.

The street has more than 250 shops: The 300 block, with a maze of Italianate villas designed by Addison Mizner, retains a quaint charm; the 100 and 200 blocks are more overtly commercial. Most merchants open at 9:30 or 10 AM, and close at 5:30 or 6 PM.

Parking on and around Worth Avenue is quite limited. On-street parking has a strictly enforced one- or two-hour limit. An alternative is Apollo Valet Parking at Hibiscus and Peruvian avenues, a block off Worth Avenue. Merchants will stamp your parking ticket if you buy something (or if you look like a prospective customer); each stamp is good for an hour of free parking.

Apollo's parking deal is just one reason to look presentable when you tour Worth Avenue. Come dressed to feel comfortable, blend in, and indulge your fantasies.

The Worth Avenue Association has strict rules to keep the street chic; no renovations are allowed from December to May, and special sales are limited to 21 consecutive days anytime between April and October.

Many "name" stores associated with fine shopping have a presence on Worth Avenue, including Brooks Brothers, Cartier, F.A.O. Schwarz, Gucci, Hermès, Pierre Deux, Saks Fifth Avenue, Tiffany's, and Van Cleef & Arpels. No other street in the world has such a concentration of these upscale firms—and they tend to send their best merchandise to Worth Avenue to appeal to the discerning tastes of their Palm Beach clientele.

Also appealing to shoppers are the 6 blocks of South County Road, north of Worth Avenue.

Beaches

The widest beaches in Palm Beach County are in the Jupiter area, on Singer Island, and in Boca Raton; many of the beaches in Palm Beach County have begun to erode. Surfing isn't a major draw for this portion of the Atlantic although locals do come out for strong winds and high tides at Palm Beach and Highland

Beach. Clarity of the water, especially in Palm Beach—where the northernmost tropical reef extension runs closest to the shore—affords excellent snorkeling and diving opportunities.

Participant Sports

Biking Bicycle with caution while on city and county roads, especially when there's a lot of traffic. A safe ride, because there are no cross-streets, is the **10-mile path** that borders Lake Worth in Palm Beach, from the Flagler Bridge to the Lake Worth Inlet. For on-the-road rides, group rides, and schedules of longer rides and general cycling savvy, contact the **West Palm Beach Bicycle Club** (Tracy Chambers, Public Affairs Director, tel. 407/659–7644 day, 407/832–9945 evening). Other contacts: **Palm Beach County Bicycle Coordinator** (Wendell Phillips, tel. 407/684–4170); **Boca Raton Bicycle Club** (Jay Lentz, tel. 407/784–7000 day, 407/998–9150 evenings). Rentals, as well as mopeds and rollerblades, are available at **Palm Beach Bicycle Trail Shop,** *223 Sunrise Ave., Palm Beach, tel. 407/659–4583. Open daily 9–5:30. Closed Christmas. AE, MC, V.*

Diving You can drift-dive or anchor-dive along Palm Beach County's 47-mile Atlantic Coast. Drift divers take advantage of the Gulf Stream's strong currents and proximity to shore—sometimes less than a mile. A group of divers joined by nylon line may drift across coral reefs with the current; one member of the group carries a large, orange float that the charter-boat captain can follow. Drift diving works best from Boynton Beach north. South of Boynton Beach, where the Gulf Stream is farther from shore, diving from an anchored boat is more popular. Among the more intriguing artificial reefs in the area is a 1967 Rolls-Royce Silver Shadow in 80 feet of water off Palm Beach.

Dive Boats and Instruction The following **Force E** stores rent scuba and snorkeling equipment and have PADI affiliation and instruction available at all skill levels; dive-boat charters are also available. All shops are closed Thanksgiving, Christmas, and New Year's Day and accept AE, D, MC, V.

1399 N. Military Trail, West Palm Beach, tel. 407/471–2676. Open weekdays 9–8:30, Sat. 8–7, Sun. 8–4.

155 E. Blue Heron Blvd., Riviera Beach, tel. 407/845–2333. Open weekdays year-round. 8–6:30, Sat. 6:30–6:30, Sun. 6:30–4:30.

11911 U.S. 1, Suite 111, N. Palm Beach, tel. 407/624–7136. Open year-round weekdays 10–7, Sat. 8–6, Sun. 8–4.

877 E. Palmetto Park Rd., Boca Raton, tel. 407/368–0555. Open winter, Mon.–Sat. 8–7, Sun. 8–5; summer, weekdays 8 AM–9 PM, weekends same as in winter.

7166 Beracasa Way, Boca Raton, tel. 407/395–4407. Open weekdays 10–9:30 (summer 9–8:30), Sat. 8–7, Sun. 8–4.

Fishing Palm Beach County is fisherfolks' heaven, from deep-sea strikes of fighting sailfish and wahoo to the bass, speckled perch, and bluegill of Lake Okeechobee. In between there are numerous fishing piers, bridges, and waterways where pompano, sheepshead, snapper, and grouper are likely catches. Representative of the fleets and marinas are:

Deep-Sea Fishing **B-Love Fleet.** *314 E. Ocean Ave., Lantana, tel. 407/588-7612. Mornings at 8; afternoons at 1; evenings at 7. $19 per person includes rod, reel, bait.*

Lake Fishing **Slim's Fish Camp.** *Drawer 250, Belle Glade 33430, tel. 407/996-3844. Guided tour 1 or 2 people $185 per day. Boat rental $35 per day. License required: non-Florida resident 7-day permit $16.50, 1-year permit $31.50; Florida resident 1-year permit $13.50.*

J-Mark Fish Camp. *Box 2225, Belle Glade 33430, tel. 407/996-5357. Guided tour 1 or 2 people $200 per day. Boat rental $35 per day (sunrise–sunset). License required.*

Gliding **Glider Rides of America** offers two-passenger rides manned by experienced pilots. Flights last approximately 15–30 minutes. *2633 Lantana Rd., Suite 4, Lantana, tel. 407/965-9101. Open Jan.–Apr., Thurs.–Mon. Reservation required. From 3,000 feet, $39.95 per person; from 4,000, $59.95; from 5,000, $79.95. AE, D, MC, V.*

Golf There are 145 public, private, and semiprivate golf courses in the Palm Beach County area. A **Golf-A-Round** program lets guests at any of 92 hotels in the county golf at one of 10 courses each day, without greens fees, between April and December. For details and for a complete list of courses, contact the Palm Beach County Convention & Visitors Bureau (*see* Important Addresses and Numbers, above).

Spas **Hippocrates Health Institute** was founded in Boston in 1963 by Ann Wigmore and moved to its present 10-acre site in 1987. Guests receive complete examinations by traditional and alternative health-care professionals. Personalized programs include juice fasts and the eating of raw foods. *1443 Palmdale Ct., West Palm Beach, tel. 407/471-8876 or 407/471-8868. AE, MC, V.*

The Spa at PGA National Resort. Styled after a Mediterranean fishing village, the new 17,800-square-foot spa building features six outdoor therapy pools. The facility encompasses 22 rooms for private treatments, including Swedish and shiatsu massage, hydrotherapy and mud treatments, men's and women's Jacuzzis and saunas, and a selection of salon treatments. Also available in a 26,000-square-foot Health & Racquet Center are five racquetball courts, complete Nautilus center, aerobics and dance studios, men's and women's locker rooms, and a fitness-oriented Health Bar. *400 Ave. of the Champions, Palm Beach Gardens 33418-3698; tel. 800/633-9150; 407/627-2000. AE, DC, MC, V.*

Spectator Sports

The *Palm Beach Post's* weekly "TGIF" section on Friday carries information on sports activities. For tickets to Sporting events call **Ticketmaster** (tel. 407/839-3900).

Auto Racing Drag racing, stock car racing, and other two-axle racing takes place at the **Moroso Motorsports Park** (17047 Beeline Hwy., Palm Beach Gardens, tel. 407/622-1400; for information: Box 31907, Palm Beach Gardens 33410, tel. 407/622-1400).

Baseball The **Atlanta Braves** and the **Montreal Expos** both conduct spring training in West Palm Beach's Municipal Stadium, which is also home to the Palm Beach Expos, a Class-A team in the Florida State League. *1610 Palm Beach Lakes Blvd., Box 3087, West Palm Beach 33402, stadium tel. 407/683-6012. Expos tickets: Box 3566, West Palm Beach 33402, tel. 407/689-9121, AE, MC, V. Braves tickets: Box 2619, West Palm Beach 33402, tel. 407/683-6100. No credit cards.*

Greyhound Racing **Palm Beach Kennel Club** opened in 1932 and has 3,000 free seats. Dine in the Paddock Dining Room or watch and eat on the Terrace. Call for schedule. *1111 N. Congress Ave., Palm Beach 33409, tel. 407/683-2222. Admission: 50¢ general admission, $2 dining rooms. Matinees free. Free parking. Wed., Thurs., Sat. 12:30 and 7:30; Tues. and Fri. 7:30; Sun. 1.*

Jai Alai **Palm Beach Jai Alai.** This jai-alai fronton is the site of two world records: for the largest payoff ever, $988,325; and for the fastest ball ever thrown, 188 mph. *1415 45th St., West Palm Beach, ¼ mi east of I-95 off exit 54, tel. 407/844-2444 or 407/427-0009 (toll-free south to Pompano Beach). Admission: 50¢ to $3.50. Senior citizens free Wed., Fri., Sat. matinees. Tues., "ladies' night," women are admitted free. Children 39½" or taller ½-price. Free parking. Sala Del Toro Restaurant. Game time is 7 PM. Schedule changes seasonally. No cameras. Open Sept. to July.*

Equestrian Sports and Polo Palm Beach county is the home of three major polo organizations. Seventy miles north in Vero Beach, the **Windsor Polo and Beach Club** held its first polo match in February 1989. Although only the affluent can support a four-member polo team, admission is free for some games and priced reasonably for others. If you like horses and want to rub elbows with the rich and famous, dress like the locals in tweeds or a good golf shirt and khakis and spend an afternoon watching some of the world's best professional polo players.

Polo teams play under a handicap system in which the U.S. Polo Association ranks each player's skills; a team's total handicap reflects its members' individual handicaps. The best players have a 10-goal handicap. The average polo game lasts about 90 minutes. Each game consists of six periods or chukkers of 7½ minutes each.

Gulf Stream Polo Club, the oldest club in Palm Beach, began in the 1920s and plays medium-goal polo (for teams with handicaps of 8–16 goals). It has six polo fields. *4550 Polo Rd., Lake Worth 33467, tel. 407/965-2057. Play Dec.–April. Games Fri. 3 PM and Sun. 1 PM. Admission free.*

Royal Palm Polo, founded in 1959 by Oklahoma oilman John T. Oxley, has seven polo fields with two stadiums and Oxley's Restaurant. The complex is home to the $100,000 International Gold Cup Tournament. *6300 Old Clint Moore Rd., Boca Raton 33496, tel. 407/994-1876. General admission $5, box seats $15, $3 children and students. High-goal winter season Jan.–Apr. Low-goal summer season June–Oct. Games Sun. 1 and 3 PM.*

Palm Beach Polo and Country Club (*see* Lodging, below). Started in 1979, this is the site each April of the $100,000 Regina World Cup competition. *Stadium address: 13198 Forest Hill, West Palm Beach, 33414, tel. 407/798-7605. General admission $6, reserve $10, lower level $14, upper level $17. AE, MC, V. Games Sun. 3 PM.*

Rugby **Boca Raton Rugby Club** practices on Tuesday and Thursday nights. Home games are played Saturday 2 PM at Boca Raton's

Lake Wyman Park. *For information, contact Allerton "Bing" Towne, president, Florida Rugby Football Clubs, 1580 S.W. 6th Ave., Boca Raton 33486, tel. 407/998–9700 weekdays or 407/395–4259 weekends and nights.*

Dining

The list below is a representative selection of independent restaurants in Palm Beach County, organized geographically, and by type of cuisine within each region of the county. Unless otherwise noted, they serve lunch and dinner.

Highly recommended restaurants are indicated by a star ★.

Category	Cost*
Very Expensive	over $55
Expensive	$35–$55
Moderate	$15–$35
Inexpensive	under $15

**per person, excluding drinks, service, and 6% sales tax*

Boca Raton
Continental

Gazebo Cafe. The locals who patronize this popular restaurant know where it is, even though there is no sign and it's difficult to find: Look for the Barnett Bank Pantry Pride Plaza, a block north of Spanish River Boulevard. Once you find the place, await your table in the open kitchen where chef Paul Sellas (co-owner with his mother Kathleen) and his staff perform a gastronomic ballet. The high noise level of the main dining room has been reduced with an acoustical ceiling but you may still be happier in the smaller back dining room. Specialties include lump crabmeat with an excellent glaze of Mornay sauce on a marinated artichoke bottom; spinach salad with heart of palm, egg white, bacon, croutons, mushrooms, fruit garnish, and a dressing of olive oil and Dijon mustard; Paul Sellas's "classic" bouillabaisse with Maine lobster, shrimp, scallops, clams, and mussels topped with julienne vegetables in a robust broth flavored with garlic, saffron, and tomatoes; and raspberries with a Grand Marnier–Sabayon sauce. The staff can accommodate travelers in seven languages. *4199 N. Federal Hwy., Boca Raton, tel. 407/395–6033. Reservations advised. Jacket preferred. AE, D, DC, MC, V. Closed Sun. except New Year's Eve through Mother's Day. Expensive.*

French
★

La Vieille Maison. This elegant French restaurant occupies a two-story dwelling that dates from the 1920s (hence the name, meaning "old house"). The structure, believed to be an Addison Mizner creation, has been renovated repeatedly, but still retains details which typify the architect's style. Among the unique features of this restaurant is the use of space. Closets and cubbyholes have been transformed into intimate private dining rooms. You may order from a fixed-price or an à la carte menu throughout the year; in summer, a separate fixed-price menu available Sunday through Thursday offers a sampling of the other two at a more modest price. Specialties include *pompano aux pecans* (pompano filets sautéed in butter strewn with pecans under a creamy chardonnay sauce) and *le saumon fumé aux endives* (smoked salmon, onions, and Belgian endive with light vinaigrette). Dessert specialties include *crêpe soufflé au citron* and a chocolate tart. *770 E. Palmetto Park Rd., tel. 407/391–6701 in Boca Raton, 407/737–5677 in Delray Beach and Palm Beach, 305/421–7370 in Ft. Lauderdale. Reservations suggested. Jacket preferred. AE, D, MC, V. Closed Memorial Day, Labor Day, July 4th. Expensive.*

Soul Food

Tom's Place. "This place is a blessing from God," says the sign over the fireplace, to which, when you're finally in and seated (this place draws long lines) you'll add, "Amen!" That's in between mouthfuls of sauce-slathered ribs and chicken cooked in a peppery mustard sauce over hickory and oak. Tom Wright purely brings it on—pork chop sandwich to sweet potato pie. You'll want to leave with a bottle or two of Tom's BBQ sauce: $2.25/pint. You'll return, though, just as Mr. T, Sugar Ray Leonard, Joe Frazier, and a rush of NFL pro players do. You can bet the place is family run. *7251 N. Federal Hwy., tel. 407/997–0920. No reservations. Dress: neat but casual. No credit cards. Open Mon. at 4 PM. Closed all holidays, including Mother's and Father's Day, and for a month around Sept. Inexpensive.*

Jupiter
American

Log Cabin Restaurant. "Too much!" exclaim first-timers, responding to the decor and whopping portions. Everybody takes home a doggie bag, except for the all-you-can-eat meals when the policy is suspended. This rustic roadhouse (very easy to drive past)—with a new porch dining area—has old bikes, sleds, clocks, and quilts hanging from the rafters. For $3.25 you get eggs, French toast, home fries or grits, biscuits and gravy, and coffee. All-you-can-eat specials are featured nightly. *631 N. A1A, tel. 407/746–6877. No reservations. Dress: casual. AE, D, DC, MC, V. Closed Christmas. Inexpensive–Moderate.*

Lighthouse Restaurant. Another family eatery thrives on the Gold Coast and has been for more than 60 years. You'll see the same familiar faces at the counter drinking coffee at 6 AM and midnight. House specialties include roast turkey with giblet gravy, leg of lamb with mint jelly, fresh ham with applesauce, Yankee pot roast, deep-fried Okeechobee catfish, prime rib. "They love my meat loaf and biscuits," manager Renée Jordan says. "But I keep 'em in suspense. They never know when I'm gonna have it." You can get breakfast 24 hours a day, Sunday dinner at noon. *1510 U.S. 1, tel. 407/746–4811. No reservations. Dress: casual. MC, V. Closed Christmas Eve and 1 Sun. night a month (call ahead). Inexpensive.*

Lake Worth
American
★

John G's. About the only time the line lets up here is when the restaurant closes. Otherwise, there's little to complain about: certainly not the service, the price, or the noise. The menu is as big as the crowd: eggs every which way, including a UN of ethnic omelets; big fruit platters; sandwich board superstars; grilled burgers and seafood. The Greek shrimp (seven at recent count) come on fresh linguine topped by feta. Decor is not the thing: a big, open room with tables and counter seats under nautical bric-a-brac. *On the beach, Lake Worth Casino, tel. 407/585–9860. No reservations. Dress: casual. No credit cards. No dinner. Closed Christmas, New Year's Day. Inexpensive.*

Lantana
Seafood

Old House. Line ahead of you? Wait a minute, they'll hammer on a few more seats. Partners Wayne Cordero and Captain Bob Hoddinott are ever expanding this unpretentious seafood house on the Intracoastal Waterway. The premises—the Lyman House—is the oldest house in town, dating to 1889. Out back, a patchwork of shed-like spaces has a seating capacity that now totals 225. Baltimore steamed crab is a specialty, though most of the seafood's from Florida. All dinners come with unlimited salad, fresh baked bread, fries, and parsley potatoes or rice. *300 E. Ocean Ave., tel. 407/533-5220. No reservations. Dress: casual. AE, MC, V. Moderate.*

Palm Beach
American

Chuck & Harold's. Boxer Larry Holmes and thespians Brooke Shields and Burt Reynolds are among the celebrities who frequent this combination power-lunch bar, celebrity sidewalk cafe, and nocturnal big-band/jazz garden restaurant. A blue-and-yellow tent on pulleys rolls back in good weather to expose the garden to the elements. Local businesspeople wheel and deal at lunch in the bar area while quaffing Bass ale on tap. Locals who want to be part of the scenery frequent the front-porch area, next to pots of red and white begonias mounted along the sidewalk rail. Specialties include a mildly spiced conch chowder with a rich flavor and a liberal supply of conch; an onion-crunchy gazpacho with croutons, a cucumber spear, and a dollop of sour cream; a *frittata* (an omelet of bacon, spinach, pepperohcini, potatoes, smoked mozzarella, and fresh tomato salsa); and a tangy Key lime pie with a graham cracker crust and a squeezeable lime slice for even more tartness. *207 Royal Poinciana Way, tel. 407/659-1440. Reservations advised. Dress: neat but casual. AE, DC, MC, V. Moderate.*

Dempsey's. A New York–style Irish pub under the palms: green baize, plaid café curtains, brass rods, burgundy banquettes, *Ring Magazine* covers, open beams, paddlefans, sculpted horse heads, mounted hat racks, horse prints, and antique coach lanterns. George Dempsey was a Florida horse rancher until he entered the restaurant business 13 years ago. This place is packed, noisy, and as electric as Black Friday at the stock exchange when major sports events are on the big TV. Along with much socializing, people put away plates of chicken hash Dempsey (with a dash of Scotch), shad roe, prime rib, and hot apple pie. You go for the scene. Dempsey's is knock-out champ at making it. *50 Cocoanut Row, tel. 407/835-0400. Reservations advised for 6 or more. Dress: neat but casual. AE, MC, V. Closed Thanksgiving, Christmas. Moderate.*

Continental

The Breakers. The main hotel dining area at The Breakers consists of the elegant Florentine Dining Room, decorated with fine 15th-century Flemish tapestries; the adjoining Celebrity Aisle where the maître d' seats his most honored guests; and the Circle Dining Room, with a huge circular skylight framing a bronze-and-crystal Venetian chandelier. Specialties include rack of lamb Dijonnaise; salmon *en croûte* with spinach, herbs and sauce Véronique (a grape sauce); *vacherin glacé* (praline-flavored ice cream encased in fresh whipped cream and frozen in a baked meringue base); and Key lime pie. The Breakers also serves less formally at its Beach Club, where locals flock for the most sumptuous Sunday champagne brunch in Florida, and at the Fairway Cafe in the golf-course clubhouse. *1 S. County Rd., tel. 407/655-6611 or 800/833-3141. Reservations required. Jacket and tie required winter. AE, DC, MC, V. Expensive.*

Ta-boo. Real estate investor Franklyn P. deMarco, Jr. has teamed up with Maryland restaurateur Nancy Sharigan to successfully re-create the legendary Worth Avenue bistro that debuted in 1941. Decorated in gorgeous pinks, greens, and florals, the space is divided into discrete salons: one resembles a courtyard; another, an elegant living room with a fireplace; a third, a gazebo under a skylight. The Tiki Tiki bar is frequented by regulars. The round-the-clock menu includes chicken and arugula from the grill, prime ribs and steaks, gourmet pizzas, and main course salads (a tangy warm steak salad, for instance, comes with grilled strips of marinated filet mignon tossed with greens, mushrooms, tomato, and red onion). *221 Worth Ave., tel. 407/835–3500. Reservations advised. Jacket preferred. AE, MC, V. Closed Christmas. Moderate.*

Deli **TooJay's.** Jewish deli food with California accents best describes this restaurant's menu, with daily specials that may include matzoh ball soup, corned beef on homemade, hand-sliced rye, killer cake with five chocolates, and homemade whipped cream. Naturally, Hebrew National kosher salami layered with onions, muenster cheese, cole slaw, and Russian dressing on rye or pumpernickel is a house favorite. There's also dill-chicken; seafood with crabmeat, shrimp, and sour cream; and for the vegetarians, hummus, tabouleh, and a wheatberry salad. On the high holy days look for carrot *tzimmes* (a sweet compote), beef brisket with gravy, potato pancakes, and roast chicken. Wise-cracking waitresses set the fast pace of this bright restaurant with a high, open packing-crate board ceiling, and windows overlooking the gardens. In addition to this location, Palm Beach County has seven other TooJay's restaurants. *313 Royal Poinciana Plaza, tel. 407/659–7232. No reservations. Dress: casual. AE, MC, V. Beer and wine only. Closed Yom Kippur, Thanksgiving, Christmas. Inexpensive.*

French ★ **Jo's.** This is an intimate, candlelit bistro with flowers on pink cloths, greenery against lattice backdrops, and, after nine years, a well-rehearsed menu. The three-soup sampler is tried and true: buttery lobster bisque, potage St. Germain (green pea soup), and beef consommé. Osso buco, always on the chalkboard, is served with rice and vegetables. Chef Richard Kline, Jo's son, faithfully prepares a moist (but never rare) half roast duckling (boned) with orange demiglaze. For dessert try the fresh apple *tarte tatin* or fresh raspberries Josephine. Jo's is tucked off County Road behind the Church Mouse Thrift Shop. *200 Chilian Ave., tel. 407/659–6776. Reservations advised. Jacket preferred. Dinner only. MC, V. Closed Aug. and Christmas. Expensive.*

Italian **Bice Ristorante.** "Bice" is short for Beatrice, mother of Robert Ruggeri, who founded the Milanese original in 1926. Now in Palm Beach other locations include Paris, New York, Chicago, Washington, Atlanta, and Beverly Hills. Brilliant flower arrangements and Italian stylings—brass, greens, and a dark beige and yellow color scheme—are matched by exquisite aromas of *antipasti* and *pratti del giorni* laced with basil, chive, mint, and oregano. Divine home-baked *focaccia*—a Tuscany-style bread topped with red onion rings—accompanies house favorites such as *robespierre alla moda della bice* (sliced steak topped with arugala salad); *costoletta di vitello impanata alla milanese* (breaded veal cutlet with a tomato shallot salad); and *trancio di spada alla mediterranea* (grilled swordfish with black olives, capers and plum tomatoes). Leave room for *frutta, dolci*, and *gelati*—not an Italian law firm! *313½ Worth Ave., tel. 407/835–1600. Reservations advised. Dress: neat but casual. AE, DC, MC, V. Closed Christmas, New Year's Day. Expensive.*

Seafood **Charley's Crab.** Audubon bird prints, fresh flowers, and French posters accent the walls of this restaurant that sits across the street from the beach. During the season, the dinner line forms early. The raw bar, dropped for the delectable dessert bar a year ago, is back, making meals sumptuous start to finish—even by Palm Beach standards. Dressier than most seafood houses, Charley's offers rooms toward the back of this 315-seater that are particularly fancy and most appropriate for special occassions. Menus change daily. Specialties include 8–10 daily fresh fish specials. *456 S. Ocean Blvd., tel. 407/659–1500. Reservations advised. Dress: casual. AE, D, DC, MC, V. Moderate–Expensive.*

Palm Beach Gardens
Continental
★

The Explorers. You sit in red leather hobnail chairs at tables lit with small brass and glass lanterns. Above you hovers a ceiling mural of stars and the Milky Way; about the room are memorabilia of famous explorers: Daniel Boone, John Glenn, Sir Edmund Hillary, Tenzing Norkay. The à la carte menu includes a variety of international and American regional preparations, including specialties such as a fresh sushi appetizer with soy, wasabi, and pickled ginger; a crab-topped 9-oz. snapper filet; loin of deer with lingonberry conserve; and almond snow eggs, an egg-shaped meringue poached in almond cream, plated between three-fruit coulis (boysenberry, mango, and tamarillo) and garnished with a nest of butter caramel. The Explorers Wine Club meets fortnightly for wine and food tastings and is open to the public for a one-time $5 membership. Contact the club for a schedule of events. *400 Ave. of the Champions, tel. 407/627–2000. Reservations advised. Jacket required. Dinner only. AE, MC, V. Closed Sun.–Mon. May–Sept. Expensive.*

Lodging

The list below is a representative selection of hotels and motels in Palm Beach County. The rate categories in the list are based on the all-year or peak-season price; off-peak rates may be a category or two lower.

Highly recommended hotels are indicated by a star ★.

Category	Cost*
Very Expensive	over $120
Expensive	$90–$120
Moderate	$50–$90
Inexpensive	under $50

**All prices are for a standard double room, excluding 6% state sales tax and nominal tourist tax.*

Very Expensive
★

Boca Raton Resort & Club. Architect and socialite Addison Mizner designed and built the original; the tower was added in 1961, the ultramodern Boca Beach Club, in 1981. In 1991 an eight-year, $55 million renovation was completed that includes, among other revitalizations, the upgrade of 300 accommodations in the tower, soundproofing, a new fitness center, the redesigned Cloister lobby and adjacent golf course, and a new 180-seat restaurant, Nick's Fishmarket, at the Beach Club. In 1992 the 27-story-high Top of the Tower Italian Restaurant opened. Room rates during the winter season are based on the modified American plan (including breakfast and dinner). The rooms in the older buildings tend to be smaller and cozily traditional; those in the newer buildings are light, airy and contemporary in color schemes and furnishings. *501 E. Camino Real, Boca Raton 33431–0825, tel. 407/395–3000 or 800/327–0101. 963 rooms: 100 in the original 1926 Cloister Inn, 333 in the 1931 addition, 242 in the 27-story Tower Building, 214 in the Boca Beach Club, plus the Golf Villas. Facilities: 1½ mi of beach, 4 outdoor freshwater pools, two 18-hole golf courses, 22 tennis courts (2 lighted), health spa, 23-slip marina, fishing and sailing charters, 7 restaurants, 3 lounges, in-room safes. AE, DC, MC, V.*

★ **Brazilian Court.** The color palette at the Brazilian Court captures the magic of the bright Florida sun indoors and out. After a year of management turmoil, the BC, with its 128 courtyard rooms and suites, is again the pick of Palm Beach without snoot. Spread out over half a block, the yellow-stucco facade with gardens and a red tile roof helps you imagine what the place must have been like 67 years ago, at BC's birth. Rooms are brilliantly floral—yellows, blues, greens, with theatrical bed canopies, big white-lattice patterns on carpets, and sunshiny paned windows. Shelf space is small in the bathrooms, but closets will remind you that people once came with trunks enough for the entire season. French doors, bay windows, rattan loggias, cherub fountains, chintz garden umbrellas beneath royal palms are just some of the elements that compose the lyrical style. *301 Australian Ave., Palm Beach 33480, tel. 407/655–7740 or 800/552–0335, 800/228–6852 in Canada. 128 guest rooms and 6 suites. Facilities: swimming pool, 2 restaurants, bar. AE, D, DC, MC, V.*

★ **The Breakers.** This historic seven-story oceanfront resort hotel, built in 1926, enlarged in 1969, and sprawling over 140 acres of splendor in the heart of some of the most expensive real estate in the world, is currently undergoing a five-year, $50-million renovation. In an overall brightening and lightening, more than 400 of its 526 guest rooms have been made over, and its North Loggia has been enlivened with new yellow drapes, yellow sofa cushions, and great pots of yellow mums. At this palatial Italian Renaissance structure, cupids wrestle alligators in the Florentine fountain in front of the main entrance. Inside the lofty lobby, your eyes lift to majestic ceiling vaults and frescoes. The hotel's proud tradition of blending formality with a tropical resort ambiance remains. After 7 PM, men and boys must wear jackets and ties in the public areas. (Ties are optional in summer.) The new room decor follows two color schemes: cool greens and soft pinks in an orchid-patterned English cotton chintz fabric; and shades of blue, with a floral and ribbon chintz. Both designs include white plantation shutters and wall coverings, Chinese porcelain table lamps, and original 1920s furniture restored to its period appearance. The original building has 15 different room sizes and shapes. If you prefer more space, ask to be placed in the newer addition. *1 S. County Rd., Palm Beach 33480, tel. 407/655–6611 or 800/833–3141. 526 rooms with bath, including 42 suites. Facilities: ½ mi of beachfront, outdoor heated freshwater pool, 20 tennis courts, 2 golf courses, health club with Keiser and Nautilus equipment, men's and women's saunas, lawn bowling, croquet, shuffleboard, shopping arcade with upscale boutiques, 4 restaurants, lounge. AE, DC, MC, V.*

★ **The Chesterfield Hotel Deluxe.** You'll be met at the airport in the house Rolls-Royce, whereupon you'll be conveyed to the finest European hotel in Florida. A little pretense, a lot of style, and a super abundance of service marks this 58-room property located a block from Worth Avenue. The Chesterfield may be a Mizner copy, but it's an original achievement in *luxe*. Dating from 1926 when it opened as the Royal Palm, this accommodation has gone through changes, but none have been more enhancing than this current rendition, which used rich chintz, mahogany, leather, and brass. The lobby boasts chintz and plaid with flowered dust ruffles and frou-frou drapes; the Game Room has baize tables so red they could only be a dare; the Library has an aura of brandy in the air after the hunt, with the important newspapers racked and waiting; the Key West–styled pool patio has pink keystone. The dining room is luxuriously adorned in pink and green. No two of the English-country-style bedrooms are alike, but expect lots of wood and brass, with beds recessed into stagey nooks. Details on the upholstery, quilts, ruffles, and drapes keep rooms unique. Baths are travertine with full amenities. *363 Cocoanut Row, Palm Beach 33480, tel. 407/659–5800. 58 rooms and suites with bath. Facilities: heated freshwater pool, restaurant, lounge. AE, D, DC, MC, V.*

The Colony. Still a block from Worth Avenue, The Colony has been a Palm Beach legend since its completion in 1947. But big change in 1990 transformed the lobby into a Park Avenue salon of plush white silks, chandeliers, scenic oils, and a baby grand piano. All of the 119 rooms and suites have also metamorphosed from tropical pastels to cool neutrals. New features include a tiki bar and outdoor grill for casual outdoor dining. Low-rise maisonettes built in the mid-1950s, and apartments from the 1960s, are across the street, as well as seven new villas added in a recently acquired neighborhood house. *155 Hammon Ave., Palm Beach 33480, tel. 407/655–5430, fax 407/832–7318. 106 rooms, including 36 suites and apartments and 7 villas. Facilities: outdoor heated freshwater pool, restaurant serves 3 meals daily, dancing nightly with live band, beauty parlor. AE, D, DC, MC, V.*

The Ocean Grand. This new property at the south end of Palm Beach is cooly elegant, but warm in detail and generous in amenity. Marble, art, fanlight windows through which the sun pours, swagged drapes, chintz, and palms create an ambience of Grecian serenity. In the Restaurant and the Ocean Bistro you'll be serenaded with piano, harp, and guitar music that accompanies the skilled cuisine. In the Living Room cocktails are served daily. Although the hotel's name suggests grandeur, it's more like a small jewel, with only four stories and a long beach. All rooms are spacious—equivalent to some suites in other hotels—and are furnished in finery typical of Palm Beach. Muted natural tones prevail in guest rooms, with teal, mauve, and salmon accents. Each room has a loveseat, upholstered chairs, desk, TV, armoire, and large closet. *2800 S. Ocean Blvd., Palm Beach 33480, tel. 407/582–2800, fax 407/547–1557. 212 rooms, including suites. Facilities: 2 restaurants, lounge, beachfront, heated outdoor freshwater pool, 3 tennis courts, health club, saunas, shops. AE, MC, V.*

PGA National Resort & Spa. The $10 million spa that opened in 1992 is to rave about, as are the limitless sports facilities and The Explorers restaurant (*see* Dining, below). This sprawling resort is the focus of the 2,340-acre PGA National community of 39 neighborhoods and 4,250 residences and is home to the Professional Golfers Association of America and the United States Croquet Association. Its championship golf courses and croquet courts are adorned with 25,000 flowering plants and situated amidst a 240-acre nature preserve. *400 Ave. of the Champions, Palm Beach Gardens 33418 tel. 407/627–2000 or 800/633–9150. 335 rooms and 92 suites, with bath. 36 nonsmoker rooms, 14 rooms for handicapped guests, 80 2-bedroom, 2-bath cottages with fully equipped kitchen. Facilities: 5 golf courses, 19 tennis courts (12 lighted), 5 croquet courts, 5 indoor racquetball courts, outdoor freshwater pool, sand beach on 26-acre lake, sailboats and aquacycles for rent, spa, sauna, whirlpool, aerobic dance studio, 7 restaurants, 2 lounges, inroom minibars and safes. AE, DC, MC, V.*

Palm Beach Polo and Country Club. Individual villas and condominiums are available in this exclusive 2,200-acre resort where Britain's Prince Charles comes to play polo. A polo school is conducted during the sport's season (February–April), and there's a seven-week equestrian festival. Arrange to rent a dwelling closest to the sports activity that interests you: polo, tennis, or golf. Each residence is uniquely designed and furnished by its owner according to standards of quality set by the resort. *13198 Forest Hill Blvd., West Palm Beach 33414, tel. 407/798–7000 or 800/327–4204. 140 privately owned studios, one- and two-bedroom villas, and condominiums available for rental when the owners are away. Facilities: 10 outdoor freshwater pools, 24 grass, clay, and hard-surface tennis courts (20 lighted), two 18-hole golf courses and one 9-hole course, men's and women's saunas, 10 polo fields, and 9 polo barns, equestrian club and trails through a nature preserve, 7 stable barns, 2 lighted croquet lawns, squash and racquetball courts, sculling equipment and instruction, 5 dining rooms. AE, DC, MC, V.*

★ **The Seagate Hotel & Beach Club.** One of the best garden hotels in Palm Beach County if you're looking for value, comfort, style, and personal attention. You can dress up and dine in a smart little mahogany- and lattice-trimmed beachfront salon or have the same Continental fare in casual attire in the equally stylish bar. Lodgings are on the west side of the two-lane road, and it still feels like the country here. The deluxe one-bedroom suite looks sharp in chintz and rattan, with plenty of upholstered pieces. Kitchens in the least expensive studio suites are compact but complete behind foldaway doors. The standard one-bedroom suite has its own touches: make-up lights, double doors between bedroom and living room, and access to bathroom from both. The beachfront facility is actually a private club in which overnight guests can gain membership. Winter rates are high, but after May 1st until mid-November they drop substantially. *400 S. Ocean Blvd., Delray Beach 33483, tel. 407/276–2421, 800/233–3581 (U.S. & Canada). 70 1- and 2-bedroom suites, including 2 penthouses. Facilities: beach, freshwater pool, heated saltwater pool, Jacuzzi, beach cabanas ($10/day), restaurant, lounge. AE, DC, MC, V.*

Expensive–Moderate

Sea Lord Hotel. If you don't need glamor or brand names, and you're not the bed-and-breakfast type, this is for you. Choose from a room that overlooks Lake Worth, the pool, or the ocean while you vacation in this personally run garden-style hideaway. The reasonably priced 20-seat cafe, which attracts repeat clientele, adds to the at-home, comfy feeling you'll get from this place. Rooms are plain but not cheap, and come with carpet, at least one comfortable chair, small or large fridge, and tropical print fabrics. Most were refurbished in 1991. *2315 S. Ocean Blvd., Palm Beach 33480, tel. 407/582–1461. 40 units, including 15 efficiencies and suites all with bath. Facilities: beach, freshwater pool, restaurant. No credit cards.*

Bed-and-Breakfast Rated *Expensive–Moderate* here, the bed-and-breakfast has become a popular alternative to pricey Palm Beach County accommodations. The stand-out is seven-room **Hibiscus House** (501 30th St., West Palm Beach 33407, tel. 407/863–5633). For the entire county, contact **Open House Bed & Breakfast,** *Box 3025, Palm Beach 33480, tel. 407/842–5190.*

The Arts and Nightlife

The *Palm Beach Post,* in its "TGIF" entertainment insert on Friday lists all events for the weekend, including concerts. Admission to some cultural events is free or by donation. Call **Ticketmaster** (407/839–3900) for tickets for performing arts events.

Nightclub **Wildflower Waterway Cafe.** Nightly DJs spin the top of the pops for a mostly young crowd that adores this luxuriantly tropical Boca bistro by the bridge over the Intracoastal Waterway. *551 E. Palmetto Park Rd., Boca Raton, tel. 407/391–0000. Open to 2 AM. Dress: casual but neat. Reservations not accepted except for groups. AE, MC, V.*

Performing Arts Center **Raymond F. Kravis Center for the Performing Arts.** This new $53 million 2,200-seat showcase, scheduled to open by early 1993, will feature high-quality seating, acoustics, and architecture in downtown West Palm Beach. The performance schedule will include about 300 events a year. *701 Okeechobee Blvd., West Palm Beach, tel. 407/833–8300.*

Theater **Caldwell Theatre Company.** In addition to hosting the annual multimedia Mizner Festival each April–May, this professional Equity regional theater, part of the Florida State Theater system, presents four shows in winter. *7783 N. Federal Hwy., Boca Raton 33429, tel. 407/241–7432 (Boca Raton), 407/832–2989 (Palm Beach), 305/462–5433 (Broward County).*

Royal Palm Dinner Theater. The Equity cast performs five or six contemporary musicals each year. *303 S.E. Mizner Blvd., Royal Palm Plaza, Boca Raton 33432, tel. 407/392–3755 or 800/841–6765 in Florida. AE, MC, V. Tues.–Sat. 8 PM, Sun. 6 PM, Wed. and Sat. matinees 2 PM.*

Royal Poinciana Playhouse. The Equity cast performs six productions each year between December and April. *70 Royal Poinciana Plaza, Palm Beach 33480, tel. 407/659–3310.*

Excursion to Treasure Coast

Numbers in the margin correspond to points of interest on the Treasure Coast map.

This excursion north from **Palm Beach** through the Treasure Coast counties of Martin, St. Lucie, and Indian River traverses an area that was remote and sparsely populated as recently as the late-1970s. Resort and leisure-oriented residential development has swollen its population. If you plan to stay overnight or dine at a good restaurant, reservations are a must.

The interior of all three counties is largely devoted to citrus production, and also cattle ranching in rangelands of pine-and-palmetto scrub. St. Lucie and Indian River counties also contain the upper reaches of the vast St. Johns Marsh, headwaters of the largest northward-flowing river in the United States. If you take Florida's Turnpike from Palm Beach north to the Orlando–Disney World area, you will dip into the edge of St. Johns Marsh about 8 miles north of the Fort Pierce exit. Along the coast, the broad expanse of the Indian River (actually a tidal lagoon) separates the barrier islands from the mainland. It's a sheltered route for boaters on the Intracoastal Waterway, a nursery for the young of many saltwater game fish species, and a natural radiator keeping frost away from the tender orange and grapefruit trees that grow near its banks.

Completion of I–95's missing link from Palm Beach Gardens to Fort Pierce in 1987 eliminated the Treasure Coast's last vestiges of relative seclusion. Hotels, restaurants, and shopping malls crowd the corridor from I–95 to the beach throughout the 70-mile stretch from Palm Beach north to Vero Beach. The Treasure Coast has become another link in the chain of municipalities that some Floridians call "the city of U.S. 1."

Of special interest in this area are the sea turtles that come ashore at night from April to August to lay their eggs on the beaches. Conservation groups, chambers of commerce, and resorts organize turtle-watches, which you may join.

Exploring Treasure Coast

❶ This tour takes you north from **Palm Beach** along the coast as far as Sebastian Inlet, but you can break away at any intermediate point and return to Palm Beach on I–95.

❷ From downtown **West Palm Beach,** take U.S. 1 about 5 miles north to Blue Heron Boulevard (Rte. A1A) in Riviera Beach, turn right, and cross the **Jerry Thomas Bridge** onto Singer Island. Sightseeing boats depart from **Phil Foster Park** on the island side of the bridge.

Continue on Rte. A1A as it turns north onto Ocean Boulevard, past hotels and high-rise condominiums to **Ocean Reef Park** (3860 N. Ocean Dr., Riviera Beach, tel. 407/966–6655), a snorkeling spot where the reefs are close to shore in shallow water. You may see angelfish, sergeant-majors, rays, robin fish, and occasionally a Florida lobster (actually a species of saltwater crayfish). Wear canvas sneakers and cloth gloves.

Go north on Rte. A1A to **John D. MacArthur State Park** (10900 Rte. A1A, North Palm Beach, tel. 407/624–6952), which offers more good snorkeling along almost 2 miles of beach, and interpretive walks to the mangrove estuary in the upper reaches of Lake Worth. In 1990 a 4,000-square-foot nature center with a 15-minute video on the natural habitat and two large aquariums was installed. Turtle nesting site walks take place nights during late June and early July.

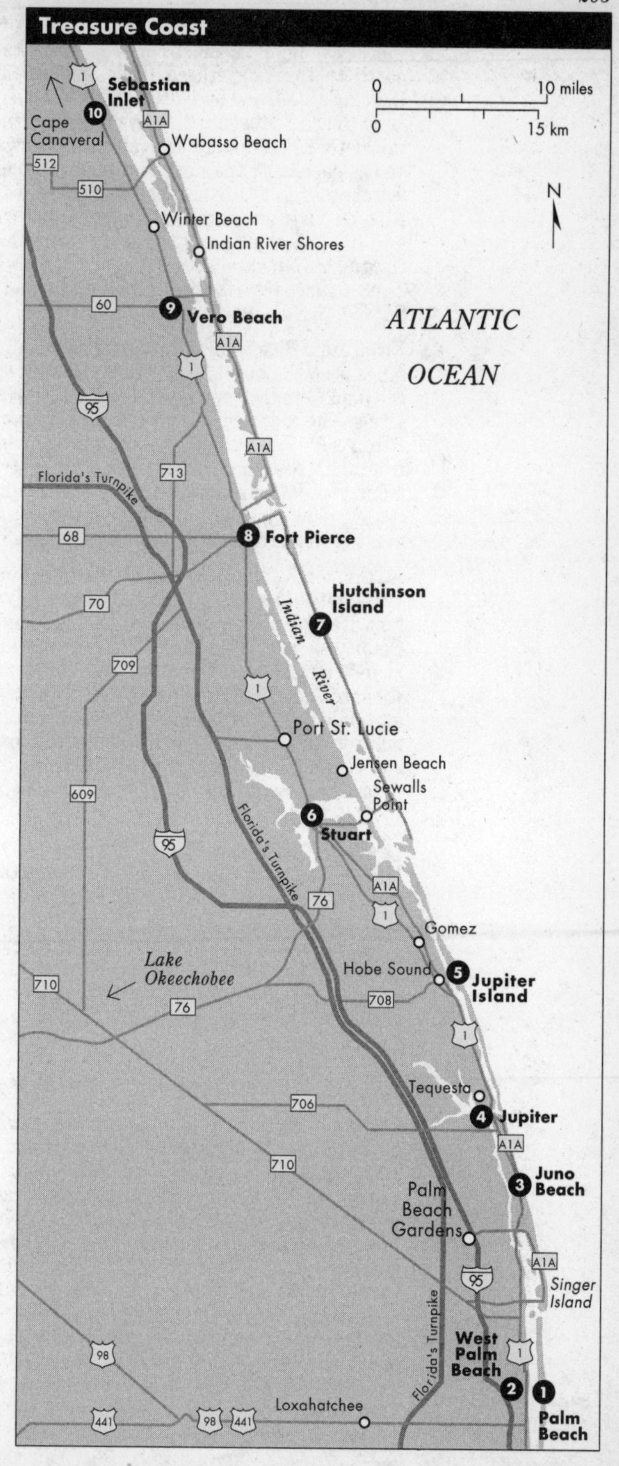
Treasure Coast
Sebastian Inlet
Cape Canaveral
Wabasso Beach
0 10 miles
0 15 km
N
Winter Beach
Indian River Shores
Vero Beach
ATLANTIC OCEAN
Florida's Turnpike
Fort Pierce
Hutchinson Island
Indian River
Port St. Lucie
Jensen Beach
Sewalls Point
Stuart
Gomez
Hobe Sound
Jupiter Island
Lake Okeechobee
Tequesta
Jupiter
Juno Beach
Palm Beach Gardens
Singer Island
West Palm Beach
Palm Beach
Loxahatchee

North of MacArthur State Park, Rte. A1A rejoins U.S. 1, then
3 veers east again 1½ miles north at **Juno Beach.** Take Rte. A1A north to the **Loggerhead Park Marine Life Center of Juno Beach,** established by Eleanor N. Fletcher, "the turtle lady of Juno Beach." Museum displays interpret the sea turtles' natural history; hatchlings are raised in saltwater tanks, tagged and released into the surf. The museum conducts guided turtle watches June 1–July 15, at the height of the nesting season. Also on view are displays of coastal natural history, sharks, whales, and shells, and there are saltwater aquariums. *1111 Ocean Dr., but enter at 1200 U.S. 1, on the west side of the park, Juno Beach, tel. 407/627–8280. Admission free. Open Tues.–Sat. 10–3, Sun. 12–3.*

4 From Juno Beach north to **Jupiter,** Rte. A1A runs for almost 4 miles atop the beachfront dunes. West of the road, about half the land is undeveloped, with endangered native plant communities. The road veers away from the dunes at **Carlin Park** (400 Rte. A1A, Jupiter, tel. 407/964–4420), which provides beach frontage, covered picnic pavilions, hiking trails, a baseball diamond, tot-lot, six tennis courts, and fishing sites. The Park Galley, serving snacks and burgers, is usually open daily sunrise to sunset (closed Christmas Eve and Christmas Day).

At the northwest corner of Indiantown Road and Rte. A1A is **The Jupiter Theater** (formerly the Burt Reynolds Jupiter Theater). Reynolds grew up in Jupiter; his father was a Palm Beach County sheriff. More than 150 Broadway and Hollywood stars have performed here since the theater opened in 1979. In 1989 Richard Akins acquired it and quickly established a reputation for quality productions. In addition to mainstage attractions, a murder mystery series with audience participation has been added, and on some Saturday mornings there is a children's theater presentation. *1001 E. Indiantown Rd., Jupiter, tel. 407/747–5566.*

Leave the theater grounds on Indiantown Road, go west to U.S. 1, and turn right. About a mile north on Jupiter Island, turn right into Burt Reynolds Park to visit the **Loxahatchee Historical Society Museum.** Permanent exhibits completed in 1990 emphasize Seminole Indians, the steamboat era, pioneer life on the Loxahatchee River, shipwrecks, railroads and modern-day development. A pioneer dwelling at the mouth of the river, the Dubois Home, is open Sunday 1–3:30; ask for directions at the museum. *805 N. U.S. 1, Box 1506, Jupiter, tel. 407/747–6639. $3 adults, $2 senior citizens, $1 children 6–18. Open Tues.–Fri. 10–3, weekends 1–4. Closed Mon.*

Continue north on U.S. 1 across the Loxahatchee River and
5 pick up Rte. 707 north from the lighthouse onto **Jupiter Island.** Just north of the Martin County line, stop at the Nature Conservancy's 73-acre **Blowing Rocks Preserve,** where a new information kiosk opened late in 1991. Within the preserve you find plant communities native to beachfront dune, strand (the landward side of the dunes), marsh, and hammock (tropical hardwood forest). Sea grape, cabbage palms, saw palmetto, and sea oats help to anchor the dunes. The floral beauty of Indian blanket, dune sunflower, and goldenrod carpets the ground. A 2.5-acre native-plant nursery opened in 1992, and within the grounds live pelicans, seagulls, ospreys, redbellied and pileated woodpeckers, and a profusion of warblers in spring and fall. A trail takes you over the dune to the beach. Best time to

go is early morning, before the crowds. The parking lot holds just 18 cars, with room for three cars to wait; Jupiter Island police will ticket cars parked along the road shoulder. *Box 3795, Tequesta, tel. 407/575–2297. No food, drinks, ice chests, pets, or spearfishing allowed. No rest rooms. Donation. Open 6–5.*

Continue north through the town of Jupiter Island, a posh community where President Bush's mother and many other notables dwell in estates screened from the road by dense vegetation. Some of the best surfing in Florida is found off Hobe Sound Beach Park, open to the public. At the north end of Jupiter Island, **Hobe Sound National Wildlife Refuge** has a 3½-mile beach where turtles nest and shells wash ashore in abundance. However, high tides and strong winds late in 1991 severely eroded the beach back to the dune. Only at low tide is there beach to walk on (admission: $3 per vehicle). On the mainland at refuge headquarters, visit the **Elizabeth W. Kirby Interpretive Center.** Take Rte. 707 and County Road 708 through the town of Hobe Sound to U.S. 1, then turn left and go about 2 miles south. The center is on the left (east) side of the highway. An adjacent ½-mile trail winds through a forest of sand pine and scrub oak—one of Florida's most unusual and endangered plant communities. *13640 S.E. Federal Hwy., Hobe Sound 33455, refuge tel. 407/546–2067. Trail open sunrise to sunset. Nature center open weekdays 9–11 and 1–3, group tours by appointment.*

From the interpretive center, go south 2½ miles to the entrance to **Jonathan Dickinson State Park.** Follow signs to Hobe Mountain, an ancient dune topped with a tower where you'll have a panoramic view across the park's 10,284 acres of varied terrain. It encompasses sand pine, slash pine, and palmetto flatwoods, mangrove river swamp, and the winding upper northwest fork of the Loxahatchee River, which is part of the federal government's wild and scenic rivers program and populated by manatees in winter and alligators all year. *14800 S.E. Federal Hwy., Hobe Sound, tel. 407/546–2771. Admission: $3.25 per car up to 8 persons, $1 per additional person. Facilities: bicycle and hiking trails, campground, snack bar. Contact State Vending Corp., 16450 S.E. Federal Hwy., Hobe Sound 33455, tel. 407/746–1466 for information and reservations on cabins, rental canoes. 2-hr narrated river cruise: $9 adults, $4 children under 12. Open daily 8–sundown.*

❻ Return to U.S. 1 and proceed north. Quality-of-life values are most apparent in **Stuart**—the county seat—where downtown revival is making this one-time fishing village of fewer than 15,000 residents a magnet for people who want to live and work in a small-town atmosphere. Strict architectural and zoning standards guide civic renewal projects in the older section of Stuart. Recent completions include a 200-seat amphitheater at the foot of St. Lucie Street as centerpiece to the first mile of a 2-mile riverwalk scheduled for completion sometime in 1993. Meanwhile, the old courthouse has been opened for cultural exhibits, and a newly built gazebo features free music performances at noon about once a month. The Lyric Theater has been revived for performing and community events.

❼ Continue north on Rte. A1A to **Hutchinson Island.** At Indian River Plantation, turn right onto MacArthur Boulevard 1.4 miles to the **House of Refuge Museum,** built in 1875 and now restored to its original appearance. It's one of 10 such structures that were erected by the U.S. Life Saving Service (an ancestor of the Coast Guard) to aid stranded sailors along Florida's then-remote Atlantic Coast. The keeper here patrolled the beach looking for shipwreck victims whose vessels foundered on Gilbert's Bar, an offshore reef. Exhibits include antique life-saving equipment, maps, ships' logs, artifacts from nearby wrecks, boatmaking tools, and six tanks of local fish from the ocean and the Indian River. The 35-foot watch-tower in the front yard was used during World War II by submarine spotters. *301 S.E. MacArthur Blvd., Stuart, tel. 407/225–1875. Admission: $1 adults, 50¢ children 6–13, under 6 free. Open Tues.–Sun. 1–4. Closed Mon. and holidays.*

Just south of the House of Refuge Museum, at the southern tip of Hutchinson Island, is **Bathtub Beach,** a public facility ideal for visitors with children because the waters are shallow for about 300 feet offshore and usually calm. At low tides bathers can walk to the reef. Facilities include rest rooms and showers.

Return to Rte. A1A and go ³⁄₁₀ mile north to the expanding **Coastal Science Center** (890 N.E. Ocean Blvd., Stuart 34996, tel. 407/225–0505) of the Florida Oceanographic Society. Its nearly 40-acre site combines a coastal hardwood hammock and mangrove forest. So far, resources include temporary displays about coastal ecology, a library program, and an interpretive nature trail. A visitor center is expected to be completed by early 1993.

Continue up Rte. A1A as far as the Jensen Beach Bridge. Cut back to the mainland and turn right on Indian River Drive, Rte. 707. This scenic road full of curves and dips follows the route of (8) early-20th-century pineapple plantations. In **Fort Pierce,** turn right over the South Beach Causeway Bridge. On the east side, take the first road left onto the grounds of the **St. Lucie County Historical Museum,** where a memorial garden was added in 1991. Enter through a replica of the old **Fort Pierce FEC Railroad Station.** Among exhibits and early-20th-century memorabilia are photos and murals of Indian River Drive, along which you've just driven. A model of downtown Fort Pierce (ca. 1914) is under construction, but may be viewed before its completion, which is set for 1993–1994. Other displays include vintage farm tools, a newly restored 1919 fire engine, replica of a general store, and the restored 1905 Gardner House. *414 Seaway Dr., Fort Pierce, tel. 407/468–1795. Admission: $2 adults, $1 children 6–11, under 6 free. Open Tues.–Sat. 10–4, Sun. noon–4.*

From here, backtrack to the mainland, head north (right), and then turn east across North Beach Causeway. About a mile east, as you approach the ocean, Rte. A1A turns left. Go right instead to visit **Fort Pierce Inlet State Recreation Area,** where a sand bottom creates the Treasure Coast's safest surfing conditions and a nature trail winds through a coastal hammock.

North on Rte. A1A at Pepper Park is the **UDT-Seal Museum,** beside the beach where more than 3,000 Navy frogmen trained during World War II. The museum traces the exploits of Navy divers from the 1944 Normandy invasion through Korea, Vietnam, and astronaut landings at sea. *3300 N. A1A, Ft. Pierce, tel. 407/595–1570. Admission: $1 adults, 50¢ children 6–11, under 6 free. Open Tues.–Sat., 10–4, Sun. noon–4.*

Within a mile north of Pepper Beach, turn left to the parking lot for the 958-acre **Jack Island wildlife refuge,** accessible only by footbridge. The 1.4-mile Marsh Rabbit Trail across the island traverses a mangrove swamp to a 30-foot observation tower overlooking the Indian River. You'll see ospreys, brown pelicans, great blue herons, ibis, and other water birds. Trails cover 4.3 miles altogether.

9 Return to Rte. A1A and go north to **Vero Beach**, an affluent city of about 30,000; retirees comprise half the winter population. In the exclusive Riomar Bay section, north of the 17th Street Bridge, "canopy roads" shaded by massive live oaks cross the barrier island between Rte. A1A and Ocean Drive. **Painted Bunting Lane,** a typical canopy road, is lined with elegant homes—many dating from the 1920s.

The city provides beach-access parks (open daily 7 AM–10 PM, admission free) with boardwalks and steps bridging the foredune. From shore, snorkelers and divers can swim out to explore reefs 100–300 feet off the beach. Summer offers the best diving conditions. At low tide you can see the boiler and other remains of an iron-screw steamer, *Breconshire*, which foundered in 1894 on a reef just south of Beachland Boulevard.

Along Ocean Drive near Beachland Boulevard, a specialty shopping area includes art galleries, antique stores, and upscale clothing stores. Also in this area is **The Driftwood Inn Resort** (3150 Ocean Dr., Vero Beach, tel. 407/231–0550), a unique beachfront hotel (a time-share) and restaurant built in the 1930s by Waldo Sexton, an eccentric plow salesman from Indiana. He used driftwood and other scavenged lumber as well as art treasures salvaged from Palm Beach mansions torn down during the Depression.

Well endowed cultural life in Vero Beach centers around the twin arts facilities in Riverside Park. In the 633-seat **Riverside Theatre** (3250 Riverside Park Dr., Vero Beach, 32963, tel. 407/231–6990), the resident Equity troupe performs six shows a season and hosts road shows and visiting performers. The new $700,000 **Agnes Wahlstrom Youth Playhouse** opened in 1991 and is the home of the Riverside Childrens Theatre. **The Center for the Arts** (3001 Riverside Park Dr., tel. 407/231–0707), opened in 1986, operates the largest museum art school in Florida and houses a collection of 20th-century American art and contemporary Florida sculpture, and presents films, concerts, humanities lectures, seminars, and a year-round program of local and visiting exhibitions.

Continue north on Rte. A1A past the John's Island development. Turn left onto Old Winter Beach Road: The pavement turns to hard-packed dirt as the road curves north, indicating the old **Jungle Trail.** Portions of the trail along the Indian River are still undeveloped, with palms and moss-covered oaks abounding, and provide a glimpse of yesteryear Florida. Continue across paved Wabasso Beach Road (Rte. 510). Although the end of the trail is unmarked, the route is completed at Hwy. A1A, less than a half mile south of **McLarty Museum and Visitor's Center** (13180 N. Hwy. A1A, tel. 407/589–2147, Sebastian; open daily 10–5). Displays here are dedicated to the 1715 hurricane that sank a fleet of Spanish treasure ships. Turn left and
10 proceed 7 miles to **Sebastian Inlet.** The high bridge offers spectacular views as it connects the two sides of the 576-acre **State Recreation Area.** A vast stacking of fisherfolk clambers on jetties, walls, and piers. Sebastian offers the best inlet fishing in

Florida: catch depending on season includes bluefish, flounder, jack, redfish, sea trout, snapper, snook, or Spanish mackerel. Swimming and driftwood collecting are also popular. A concession on the north side of the inlet is open daily from 8–6 in summer and 8–8 in winter, selling fast food, apparel, and souvenirs. The bait shop is open 7–6 year-round. A party boat is available for offshore fishing. Two smaller concessions that serve hot dogs, burgers, and daily specials are also nearby: **Hobo 1** (on the north side) opens when the main concession closes and does not close as long as fisherfolk are around; **Hobo Too** (on the south side), is open from around 11 AM until dark.

Return via Rte. A1A to the Wabasso Beach Road, turn right, and continue via Rtes. 510 and 512 to I–95, turning south to complete the tour.

Spectator Sports

Baseball The **Los Angeles Dodgers** train each March in the 6,500-seat Holman Stadium at Dodgertown 4101 26th St., near the Municipal Airport. *Box 2887, Vero Beach 32961, tel. 407/569–4900.*

The **New York Mets** hold spring training in the 7,300-seat St. Lucie County Sport Complex, home stadium for the Florida League's St. Lucie Mets. A new exit—Exit 63C, St. Lucie West Blvd., off I–95—was opened in 1989. Take it east to Peacock Boulevard, where the stadium is located. *525 N.W. Peacock Blvd., Port St. Lucie 34986, tel. 407/871–2115.*

Polo **Windsor.** Geoffrey and Jorie Kent's polo club featured England's Prince Charles in a special charity game, the Prince of Wales Cup, when it opened in February of 1989. The season usually runs from mid-January to early April. Charity events benefit the international Friends of Conservation, of which Prince Charles is a patron. *3125 Windsor Blvd., Vero Beach 32963, tel. 407/388–5050 or 800/233–POLO.*

Dining

The list below is a representative selection of restaurants on the Treasure Coast, organized geographically, and by type of cuisine within each community. Unless otherwise noted, they serve lunch and dinner.

Highly recommended restaurants are indicated by a star ★.

Category	Cost*
Very Expensive	over $55
Expensive	$35–$55
Moderate	$15–$35
Inexpensive	under $15

**average cost of a 3-course dinner, per person, excluding drinks, service, and 6% sales tax*

The following credit card abbreviations are used: AE, American Express; D, Discover; DC, Diners Club; MC, MasterCard; and V, Visa.

Fort Pierce
Seafood

Mangrove Mattie's. Since its opening five years ago, this upscale rustic spot on Fort Pierce Inlet has provided dazzling views and imaginative decor with food to match. Try the shrimp brochette Key Largo, sizzled with garlic and butter; or on Thursday evenings, build your own roast beef sandwich for $1; and Friday evenings you can get ¼-lb. shrimp for $1. *1640 Seaway Dr., tel. 407/466–1044. Reservations advised. Dress: neat but casual. MC, V. Closed Christmas. Moderate.*

Theo Thudpucker's Raw Bar. Businesspeople dressed for work mingle here with people who come in off the beach wearing shorts. On squally days everyone piles in off the jetty. Specialties include oyster stew, smoked fish spread, conch salad and fritters, fresh catfish, and alligator tail. *2025 Seaway Dr. (South Jetty), tel. 407/465–1078. No reservations. Dress: informal. No credit cards. Closed Christmas, Thanksgiving. Inexpensive.*

Jensen Beach
Continental

11 Maple Street. This 13-table cracker-quaint restaurant sits 2 blocks off the railroad tracks and offers gourmet specialties made from scratch, including a walnut bread with melted fontina cheese appetizer; and shrimp pasta with sun-dried tomatoes, vermouth, and herbs fresh from the garden. While you wait for dinner, prepared to order, you can indulge with beer and wine on the tropical porch or in the flower garden. *3224 Maple Ave., tel. 407/334–7714. Reservations required. Dress: neat but casual. MC, V. Closed Mon.; Mon.–Wed. June–Aug.; no weekend lunches. Moderate.*

Seafood
★

Conchy Joe's. This classic Florida stilt-house full of antique fish mounts, gator hides, and snakeskins dates from the late 1920s, though Conchy Joe's, like a hermit crab sidling into a new shell, only sidled up in '83 from West Palm Beach for the relaxed atmosphere of Jensen Beach. It still feels utterly island where, under a huge Seminole-built *chickee* with a palm through the roof, you get the freshest Florida seafoods from a menu that changes daily—though some things never change: grouper marsala, the house specialty; broiled sea scallops; fried cracked conch. Try the rum drinks with names like Goombay Smash, Bahama Mama, and Jamaica Wind, while you listen to steel band calypsos Thursday through Sunday nights. *3945 N. Indian River Dr., tel. 407/334–1131. No reservations. Dress: casual. AE, MC, V. Closed Thanksgiving, Christmas Eve, Christmas, New Year's Day, Superbowl Sun. Moderate.*

Rio
Continental

The Country Place. Superb dinners are served at this little English country-style restaurant rich in lace, burgundy, and paisley. A pleasant stop on the winding road between Stuart and Jensen Beach, the Country Place exudes coziness. Family culinary tradition stems from Bournemouth brothers Barry (chef) and John (maître d') whose father was a chef on the original *Queen Elizabeth.* Nightly specials may include jumbo scallops in black bean sauce; raspberry duck; or a seafood Wellington: salmon, scallops, shrimp, and crabmeat beautifully layered in a puff pastry on bed of spinach, with plenty fresh basil from Lucky, the Thai waitress and gardener. Save room for the homemade whisky pie, the crème brûlée, or strawberries Grand Marnier. *1205 N.E. Dixie Hwy. (S.R. 707), tel. 407/334–4563. Reservations advised. Dress: casual but neat. Beer and wine only. Dinner only. AE, MC, V. Closed Sun. and Mon. June–Dec; New Year's Day, Super Bowl Sun., Thanksgiving, Christmas. Moderate.*

Stuart
American

The Emporium. Indian River Plantation's coffee shop is an old-fashioned soda fountain and grill that also serves hearty breakfasts. Specialties include eggs Benedict, omelets, and fresh-baked pastries. *555 N.E. Ocean Blvd., Hutchinson Island, tel. 407/225-3700. No reservations. Dress: informal. AE, DC, MC, V. Inexpensive.*

The Porch. This casual indoor/outdoor restaurant overlooks the tennis courts at Indian River Plantation. Specialties include hearty clam chowder, a daily quiche, fried calamari, and two daily selections of fresh fish. *555 N.E. Ocean Blvd., Hutchinson Island, tel. 407/225-3700. No reservations. Dress: informal. AE, DC, MC, V. Inexpensive.*

Continental

★ **The Inlet.** This intimate 60-seat restaurant in the heart of Indian River Plantation features fine dining on gold-rimmed plates in a setting of ethereal pinks and earth tones. Specialties include oysters Rockefeller, creamy lobster bisque with cognac, steak Diane, and fresh snapper. *555 N.E. Ocean Blvd., Hutchinson Island, tel. 407/225-3700. Reservations required. Jacket required. AE, DC, MC, V. No lunch. Closed Sun. and Mon. Expensive.*

★ **Scalawags.** Part of Indian River Plantation's new hotel complex, Scalawags can seat you on a terrace overlooking the marina, in a dining room decorated with original paintings of Florida birds, or in a private 20-seat wine room. Specialties include Caribbean conch soup, sea scallops with fresh dill sauce, seafood ravioli, and rack of lamb. The Sunday champagne brunch is superb. *555 N.E. Ocean Blvd., Hutchinson Island, tel. 407/225-3700. Reservations suggested. Dress: casual but neat. AE, DC, MC, V. Dinner only. Expensive.*

The Ashley. Opened in 1990 this art- and plant-filled 84-seater is on the site of an early Stuart bank that was robbed three times by the Ashley gang. The bank impression has been revived with an old cashier's cage, original tile floor, open-beam ceiling, and brick columns. Breakfast is offered Saturdays and Sundays; lunch and dinner are served daily. The menu appeals with the freshest foods, and features lots of salads, fresh fish, and pastas. *61 S.W. Osceola St., tel. 407/221-9476. Dress: casual but neat. AE, MC, V. Closed major holidays. Moderate.*

Seafood

★ **Mahony's Oyster Bar.** Mike Mahony ensures the personal scale by limiting what he buys to what he can carry on his bike. Well, the beer's trucked in—real stuff like Guinness and Harp, and Molson on draft. Choose from 12 tables and booths, or sit at the 14-stool bar, where Mike's got 13 hot sauces lined up to go with the oysters, clams, and shrimp stew. A chalkboard lists items such as sardines and greens on toast, with green onions, red pepper ring, and parsley and a basic pub salad. Decor consists of wind socks, oars, fish traps and nets, charts, and a couple worshipful paintings of Mike and his bar, and another of Chief Osceola. *201 St. Lucie Ave., tel. 407/286-9757. No reservations. Dress: casual. Beer and wine only. No credit cards. Closed Sun. and dinner Mon.-Wed., major holidays (except St. Patrick's Day), and Aug.-Sept. Inexpensive.*

Vero Beach
American

The Patio. What immediately catches your eye is the tile bar from Spain, the Druze-tribe wood panels from Lebanon, and rafter ceilings and lighting fixtures from the Dodge, Mizner, Rockefeller, and Stotesbury estates. Young professionals to retirees pack the place evenings by 5 when hot hors d'oeuvres—ample as a meal—are served in the happy hour bar. Open 365 days a year, The Patio features big weekly events such as the Friday and Saturday night video sing-alongs and the Sunday all-you-can-eat champagne brunch at $11.95 (60-plus items with endless bubbly and mimosas). Otherwise it's all-American fare, with steaks, prime ribs, chicken, and seafood. *1103 Miracle Mile, Vero Beach, tel. 407/567-7215. Dress: casual but neat. AE, MC, V. Moderate.*

Continental ★ **The Black Pearl.** This intimate restaurant (19 tables) with pink and green art deco furnishings offers entrées that combine fresh local ingredients with the best of the Continental tradition. Specialties include chilled leek-and-watercress soup, local fish in parchment paper, feta cheese and spinach fritters, mesquite-grilled swordfish, and pan-fried veal with crab meat with hollandaise and asparagus. *1409 Rte. A1A, tel. 407/234-4426. Reservations advised. AE, MC, V. Dinner only. Closed major holidays and Super Bowl Sun. Moderate.*

Seafood **Ocean Grill.** Opened by Waldo Sexton as a hamburger shack in 1938, the Ocean Grill has since been refurbished and outfitted with antiques—Tiffany lamps, wrought-iron chandeliers, and Beanie Backus paintings of pirates and Seminole Indians. The menu has also changed with the times and now includes black bean soup, crisp onion rings, jumbo lump crabmeat salad, at least three kinds of fish every day, prime rib, and a tart Key lime pie. *Sexton Plaza (Beachland Blvd. east of Ocean Dr.), tel. 407/231-5409. Reservations accepted for parties of 5 or more. AE, MC, V. Closed weekend lunch, Thanksgiving, Super Bowl Sun., 2 weeks following Labor Day. Moderate.*

Lodging

The list below is a representative selection of hotels and guest houses on the Treasure Coast. The rate categories in the list are based on the all-year or peak-season price; off-peak rates may be a category or two lower.

Highly recommended lodgings are indicated by a star ★.

Category	Cost*
Very Expensive	over $120
Expensive	$90–$120
Moderate	$50–$90
Inexpensive	under $50

**All prices are for a standard double room, excluding 6% state sales tax and nominal tourist tax.*

Stuart ★ **Indian River Plantation.** Situated on a 192-acre tract of land on Hutchinson Island, this resort includes a three-story luxury hotel that is an architectural gem in the Victorian Beach Revival style, with tin roofs, shaded verandas, pink stucco, and much latticework. Seventy new oceanfront rooms and suites with microwave and range-top kitchens opened in 1992. *555 N.E. Ocean Blvd., Hutchinson Island, 34996, tel. 407/225-3700 or 800/444-3389. 200 hotel rooms with bath, including 10 rooms for handicapped guests; 54 1- and 2-bedroom oceanfront condominium apartments with full kitchens. Facilities: 3 pools, outdoor spa, 13 tennis courts (7 lighted), golf course, 77-*

slip marina, power boat and jet-ski rentals, beach club with tiki bar and grill, 5 restaurants. AE, DC, MC, V. Very Expensive.

Guest House **The Homeplace.** The house was built in 1913 by pioneer Sam Matthews who contracted much of the early town construction for railroad developer Henry Flagler. To preserve the structure, present-day developer Jim Smith moved it from Frazier Creek to Creekside Common. The new riverwalk will wrap around the property. Smith's wife Jean Bell has restored the house to its early look, from hardwood floors to fluffy pillows. Fern-filled dining and sun rooms, full of chintz-covered cushioned wicker, overlook a pool and patio. Three guest rooms are Captain's Quarters, Opal's Room, and Prissy's Place. *501 Akron Ave., 34994, tel. 407/220–9148. 3 rooms with bath. Facilities: pool, spa. MC, V. Expensive–Moderate.*

Vero Beach **Guest Quarters Suite Hotel.** Built in 1986, this five-story rose-color stucco hotel on Ocean Drive provides easy access to Vero Beach's specialty shops and boutiques. First-floor rooms have patios opening onto the pool. *3500 Ocean Dr., 32963, tel. 407/231–5666 or 800/742–5388. 55 1- and 2-bedroom suites with bath. Facilities: pool, outdoor pool bar/restaurant, TV, movie rentals. All suites with balconies and ocean views, in-room refrigerators stocked with candy bars, snacks, sodas; coffeemakers; VCRs. AE, D, DC, MC, V. Very Expensive.*

8 The Florida Keys

Introduction

By George and Rosalie Leposky

Updated by Herb Hiller

The Florida Keys are a wilderness of flowering jungles and shimmering seas, a jade pendant of mangrove-fringed islands dangling toward the tropics. The Florida Keys are also a 110-mile traffic jam lined with garish billboards, hamburger stands, shopping centers, motels, and trailer courts. Unfortunately, you can't have one without the other. A river of tourist dollars gushes southward along the only highway—U.S. 1—to Key West. Many residents of Monroe County live by diverting some of that river's green flow to their own pockets, in ways that have in spots blighted the Keys' fragile beauty—at least on the 34 islands linked to the mainland by the 42 bridges of the Overseas Highway. In effect, the Keys' natural resources have paid the price. However, new protective national and state legislation has begun to challenge local landowners, and soon visitors may be asked to share in the cost. In 1990 President Bush approved a new 200-mile-long Florida Keys National Marine Sanctuary (the largest in the nation), for which the National Oceanic and Atmospheric Administration intends to develop a management strategy for the Keys by 1993. The Monroe County Commission in 1991 went on record favoring a five-year moratorium on almost all new development beginning the end of 1992. The State of Florida seems more likely than ever to cooperate.

For now, however, take pleasure as you drive down U.S. 1 through the islands. The silvery blue and green Atlantic, with its great living reef, is on your left, and Florida Bay, the Gulf of Mexico and the back country are on your right. At points the ocean and the gulf are 10 miles apart; on the narrowest landfill islands, they are separated only by the road.

The Overseas Highway varies from a frustrating traffic-clogged trap to a mystical pathway skimming across the sea. There are more islands than you will be able to remember. Follow the little green mile markers by the side of U.S. 1, and even if you lose track of the names of the islands, you won't get lost.

There are many things to do along the way, but first you have to remind yourself to get off the highway, which—lined with junk—still has the seductive power of keeping you to itself. Once you leave this road, you can rent a boat and find a secluded anchorage at which to fish, swim, and marvel at the sun, sea, and sky. To the south in the Atlantic, you can dive to spectacular coral reefs or pursue dolphin, blue marlin, and other deep-water game fish. Along the Florida Bay coastline you can seek out the bonefish, snapper, snook, and tarpon that lurk in the grass flats and in the shallow, winding channels of the back country.

Along the reefs and among the islands are more than 600 kinds of fish. Diminutive deer and pale raccoons, related to but distinct from their mainland cousins, inhabit the Lower Keys. And throughout the islands you'll find such exotic West Indian plants as Jamaica dogwood, pigeon plum, poisonwood, satinwood, and silver and thatch palms, as well as tropical birds like the great white heron, mangrove cuckoo, roseate spoonbill, and white-crowned pigeon.

Another Keys attraction is the weather: in the winter it's typically 10 degrees warmer in the Keys than on the mainland; in the summer it's usually 10 degrees cooler. The Keys also get substantially less rain, around 30 inches annually compared to 55–60 inches in Miami and the Everglades. Most of the rain falls in brief, vigorous thunderstorms on summer afternoons. In winter, continental cold fronts occasionally stall over the Keys, dragging temperatures down to the 40s.

The Keys were only sparsely populated until the early 20th century. In 1905, however, railroad magnate Henry Flagler began building the overseas extension of his east coast Florida railroad south from Homestead to Key West. His goal was to establish a rail link to the steamships that sailed between Key West and Havana, just 90 miles away across the Straits of Florida. The railroad arrived at Key West in 1912 and remained a lifeline of commerce until the Labor Day hurricane of 1935 washed out much of its roadbed. For three years thereafter, the only way in and out of Key West was by boat. The Overseas Highway, built over the railroad's old roadbeds and bridges, was completed in 1938.

Although on the surface the Keys seem homogenous to most mainlanders, they are actually quite varied in terms of population and ambience. Most of the residents of the Upper Keys, which extend from Key Largo to Long Key Channel, moved to Florida from the Northeast and Midwest; many are retirees. Most of the work force is employed by the tourism and service industries. Key Largo, the largest of the keys and the one closest to the mainland, is becoming a bedroom community for Homestead, South Dade, and even the southern reaches of Miami. In the Middle Keys, from Long Key Channel through Marathon to Seven Mile Bridge, fishing and related services dominate the economy. Most residents are the children and grandchildren of migrants from other southern states. The Lower Keys from Seven Mile Bridge down to Key West have a diverse population: native "Conchs" (white Key Westers, many of whom trace their ancestry to the Bahamas), freshwater Conchs (longtime residents who migrated from somewhere else years ago), gays (who now make up at least 20% of Key West's citizenry), Bahamians, Hispanics (primarily Cubans), recent refugees from the urban sprawl of Miami and Fort Lauderdale, transient Navy and Air Force personnel, students waiting tables, and a miscellaneous assortment of vagabonds, drifters, and dropouts in search of refuge at the end of the road.

Essential Information

Arriving and Departing

By Plane Shuttle and connecting flights go to **Key West International Airport** (S. Roosevelt Blvd., tel. 305/296–5439) from the Miami and Orlando International airports. From Miami, you can fly direct to Key West on American Eagle and USAir. From Fort Lauderdale-Hollywood you can fly direct on Delta ComAir. From Orlando you must change planes in Miami unless you fly with Delta ComAir, which has limited nonstop service to Key West as well as connecting service through Fort Lauderdale–Hollywood.

Chalk's (1000 MacArthur Cswy., tel. 305/371–8628 or 800/424–2557), the venerable seaplane service operating out of Miami, flies 17-passenger seaplanes five days a week to Key West: two flights Friday and Sunday (9:15 AM and 2:40 PM), and one flight Monday, Wednesday, and Saturday at 1:05. Depending on how far in advance you buy your ticket, round-trip fare ranges between $124 and $256. Flights land and take off from Key West International Airport while Chalk's continues to look for a suitable marine ramp.

Carriers that provide direct service between Miami and **Marathon Airport** (MM 52, BS, 9000 Overseas Hwy., tel. 305/743–2155) include Airways International (tel. 305/743–0500), and American Eagle (tel. 800/433–7300). **Air Sunshine** (tel. 305/434–8900 in Fort Lauderdale; 800/432–1744 elsewhere in FL) provides direct service between Fort Lauderdale and Marathon.

Between Miami and the Keys

The Airporter. Scheduled van and bus service is available from the lower level of MIA's Concourse E to major hotels in Key Largo ($25 per person) and Islamorada ($28 per person). *88890 Overseas Hwy., Tavernier 33070, MM 88.8, tel. 305/852–3413, 305/852–3306 (Tavernier), 305/247–8874 (Miami). Reservations required.*

Island Taxi. Meets arriving flights at MIA. Reservations are required 24 hours in advance for arrivals, one hour for departures. Accompanied children under 12 ride free. *Tel. 305/664–8181 (Upper Keys), 305/743–0077 (Middle Keys), 305/745–2200 (Lower Keys). Fare from airport to destination for 1 or 2 persons: $80 Key Largo, $100 Islamorada, $175 Marathon, $200 Key West; each additional person $5, except to Key West $10. Inquire for arrangements north of Miami and for van rates.*

By Car

If you want to avoid Miami traffic on the way to the Keys, take the Homestead Extension of Florida's Turnpike; although it's a toll road that carries a lot of commuter traffic, it's still the fastest way to go. From MIA, take LeJeune Road (SW 42nd Ave.) south, turn west on the Dolphin Expressway (Rte. 836) to the turnpike, then go south to the turnpike's southern end. If you prefer traffic to tolls, take LeJeune Road south to U.S. 1 and turn right.

Just south of Florida City, the turnpike joins U.S. 1 and the Overseas Highway begins. Once you cross the Jewfish Creek bridge at the north end of Key Largo, you're officially in the Keys.

From Florida City, you can also reach Key Largo on Card South Road. Go 13 miles south to the Card Sound Bridge (toll: $1), which offers a spectacular view of blue water and mangrove-fringed bays (and of Florida Power & Light Company's hulking Turkey Point nuclear power plant in the distance to your left). At low tide, flocks of herons, ibis, and other birds frequent the mud flats on the margin of the sound. Beyond the bridge, on north Key Largo, the road traverses a mangrove swamp with ponds and inlets harboring the exceedingly rare Florida crocodile. At the only stop sign, turn right onto Route 905, which cuts through some of the Keys' few remaining large tracts of tropical hardwood jungle. You'll rejoin U.S. 1 in north Key Largo 31 miles from Florida City.

Car Rentals

All six of the rental-car firms with booths inside Miami International Airport also have outlets in Key West, which means you can drive into the Keys and fly out. Don't fly into Key West and drive out; the rental firms have substantial drop charges to leave a Key West car in Miami. Some rental car locations other than the airport include **Hertz** (3840 N. Roosevelt Blvd., tel. 305/294–1039 or 800/654–3131); **Keys Jeep Eagle** (1111 Eaton St., tel. 305/294–2883); **National** (2826 N. Roosevelt Blvd., tel. 305/296–7760 or 800/CAR–RENT); and **Tropical Rent A-Car** (1300 Duval St., tel. 305/294–8136). Avis and Hertz also serve Marathon Airport.

Enterprise Rent-A-Car has offices at MIA, several Keys locations, and participating hotels in the Keys where you can pick up and drop off cars when the offices are closed. You can rent a car from Enterprise at MIA and return it there, or leave it in the Keys for a drop charge. *Tel. 305/876–9749 or 800/325–8007 (Miami); 305/451–3998 (Key Largo); tel. 305/292–0220 (Key West). AE, D, DC, MC, V. Open weekdays 8–6, Sat. 9–noon.*

By Bus **Greyhound/Trailways.** Buses traveling between Miami and Key West make 8 scheduled stops, but you can flag down a bus anywhere along the route. *Tel. 305/374–7222 (Miami) for schedule; 24-hr Miami Greyhound Station, Miami Airport, 4111 N.W. 27th St., tel. 305/871–1810; Downtown Miami, 700 Biscayne Blvd., tel. 305/379–7403; Tavernier, tel. 305/852–4666; Big Pine Key, tel. 305/872–4022; Key West, 615½ Duval St., tel. 305/296–9072. No reservations.*

By Boat Boaters can travel to Key West either along the Intracoastal Waterway through Florida Bay, or along the Atlantic Coast. The Keys are full of marinas that welcome transient visitors, but they don't have enough slips for everyone who wants to visit the area. Make reservations in advance, and ask about channel and dockage depth—many Key marinas are quite shallow.

Florida Marine Patrol (MM 49, OS, 2835 Overseas Hwy., Marathon, tel. 305/289–2320).

Coast Guard Group Key West provides 24-hour monitoring of VHF-FM Channel 16. Safety and weather information is broadcast at 7 AM and 5 PM Eastern Standard time on VHF-FM Channel 16 and 22A. *Key West 33040, tel. 305/292–8727. 3 stations in the Keys: Islamorada, tel. 305/664–4404; Marathon, tel. 305/743–6778; Key West, tel. 305/292–8856.*

Getting Around

The only address many people have is a mile marker (MM) number. The markers themselves are small green rectangular signs along the side of the Overseas Highway (U.S. 1). They begin with MM 126 a mile south of Florida City and end with MM 0 on the corner of Fleming and Whitehead streets in Key West. Keys residents also use the abbreviation BS for the Bay Side of U.S. 1, and OS for the Atlantic Ocean Side of the highway.

Florida Visitor Centers and the Florida Department of Commerce distribute *Florida's Official Transportation Map* free. Write to Florida Department of Commerce (Collins Bldg., Tallahassee 32304).

The best road map for the Florida Keys is published by the Homestead/Florida City Chamber of Commerce. You can obtain a copy at the Tropical Everglades Visitor Center in Florida

City, or by mail. *160 U.S. Hwy. 1, Florida City 33034, tel. 305/245–9180. Open daily 8–6. Map costs $2.*

Throughout the Keys, the local chambers of commerce, marinas, and dive shops will offer you the local **Teall's Guide**—a land and nautical map—for $1, which goes to build mooring buoys to protect living coral reefs from boat anchors. The separate guides that used to cover Miami to Key Largo, John Pennekamp Coral Reef State Park and Key Largo National Marine Sanctuary, the Middle Keys, and Marathon-Key West are now in a 12″×18″ complete Florida packet that costs $14.95, postage included. The packet for only the Florida Keys and the Everglades is $5.95. Order from Teall's Florida Guides (111 Saguaro Ln., Marathon 33050, tel. 305/743–3942).

By Car The 18-mile stretch of U.S. 1 from Florida City to Key Largo is a hazardous two-lane road with heavy traffic (especially on weekends) and only two passing zones. Try to drive it in daylight, and be patient day or night. The Overseas Highway is four lanes wide in Key Largo, Marathon, and Stock Island (just north of Key West), but narrow and crowded elsewhere. Expect delays behind large tractor-trailer trucks, cars towing boats, and rubbernecking tourists. Allow at least five hours from Florida City to Key West on a good day. After midnight, you can make the trip in three hours—but then you miss the scenery.

In Key West's Old Town, parking is scarce and costly ($1.50 per hour at Mallory Square, however the first 10 minutes are free). Use a taxicab, bicycle, moped, or your feet to get around. Elsewhere in the Keys, however, having a car is crucial. Gas prices are higher in the Keys than on the mainland. Fill your tank in Miami and top it off in Florida City.

By Bus The **City of Key West Port and Transit Authority** operates two bus lines: Mallory Square (counterclockwise around the island) and Old Town (clockwise around the island). A free Shopping Center Shuttle (Key Plaza to Searstown), which runs Tuesday and Thursday afternoon only, has been resumed. *Tel. 305/292–8165. Exact fare: 75¢, senior citizens and students with ID, children under 5 and handicapped riders 35¢; monthly pass, $20, senior citizens and students $12.*

By Taxi **Island Taxi** offers 24-hour service from Key Largo to Boca Chica Key. Accompanied children ride free. There is service to downtown Key West but no pick-up there. *Tel. 305/664–8181 (Upper Keys), 305/743–0077 (Middle Keys), 305/745–2200 (Lower Keys). Fare: $4 for first 2 mi, then $1.50 per mi.*

Maxi-Taxi Sun Cab System (tel. 305/294–2222 or 305/296–7777) provides 24-hour service in Key West.

By Limousine **Carriage Trade Limousine Service** (tel. 305/296–0000) provides airport van service: $5 per person; cab service: $6 per person. Local metered service, $1.40 first ⅕-mi, 35¢ each additional ⅕-mi. Inquire for group and zone rates.

Important Addresses and Numbers

Tourist Information **Florida Keys & Key West Visitors Bureau** (Box 1147, Key West 33041, tel. 800/FLA-KEYS). Ask for their free accommodations guide.

Local chambers of commerce in Key Largo, Islamorada, Marathon, the Lower Keys, and Key West have visitor centers with information on accommodations, recreation, restaurants, and special events:

Key Largo Chamber of Commerce (MM 106, BS, 105950 Overseas Hwy., Key Largo 33037, tel. 305/451–1414 or 800/822–1088).
Islamorada Chamber of Commerce (MM 82.5, BS, Box 915, Islamorada 33036, tel. 305/664–4503 or 800/FAB–KEYS).
Greater Marathon Chamber of Commerce (MM 48.7, BS, 3330 Overseas Hwy., Marathon 33050, tel. 305/743–5417 or 800/842–9580).
Lower Keys Chamber of Commerce (MM 31, OS, Box 511, Big Pine Key 33043, tel. 305/872–2411 or 800/872–3722).
Greater Key West Chamber of Commerce (402 Wall St., Key West 33040, tel. 305/294–2587 or 800/648–6269).

Emergencies Dial 911 for **ambulance** and **police.**

Hospitals The following hospitals have 24-hour emergency rooms: **Mariners Hospital** (MM 88.5, BS, 50 High Point Rd., Tavernier, Plantation Key 33070; physician-referral service, tel. 305/852–9222), **Fishermen's Hospital** (MM 48.7, OS, 3301 Overseas Hwy., Marathon, tel. 305/743–5533), and **Florida Keys Memorial Hospital** (MM5, BS, 5900 Junior College Rd., Stock Island, tel. 305/294–5531).

Late-Night Pharmacies The Keys have no 24-hour pharmacies. Hospital pharmacists will help with emergencies after regular retail business hours.

Guided Tours

Orientation Tours **The Conch Tour Train.** This 90-minute narrated tour of Key West travels 14 miles through Old Town and around the island. The driver pauses frequently to discuss points of historical interest and to chat with friends. *Boarding Locations: Mallory Sq. Depot every half hour, Roosevelt Blvd. Depot just north of the Quality Inn every hour on the half hour; tel. 305/294–5161. Fare: $11 adults, $5 children. No credit cards. Runs daily 9–4:30.*

Old Town Trolley. Key West has 11 trackless trolley-style buses that run every 30 minutes. The trolleys are smaller than the Conch Tour Train and go places the train won't fit. The narrated trolley tour lasts 90 minutes, passes more than 100 points of interest, and makes 14 stops all around the island. You may disembark at any stop and reboard a later trolley. *1910 N. Roosevelt Blvd., Key West 33040, tel. 305/296–6688. Admission: $12 adults, $5 children. D, MC, V. Runs 9 AM–4:30 PM.*

Special-Interest Tours
Air Tours **Island Aeroplane Tours.** Tours in this open cockpit biplane operate out of Key West International Airport, and up to two people can fly for a quick overview of Key West ($50 for two), to up to 50 minutes for a long look at the offshore reefs ($200 for two, other tours priced in between). Flights operate between 9 AM and sunset. *3469 S. Roosevelt Blvd. (Key West International Airport), tel. 305/294–TOUR. Reservations advised. AE, MC, V.*

Key West Seaplane Service. Enjoy either half-day or full-day trips to the Dry Tortugas in single-engine seaplanes, with flights operating every day, weather permitting. All tours depart Stock Island (last island before Key West). Half-day tours run 8 AM and 12 noon, with two hours on the island; full-day tours leave 8 AM, with six hours on the island. Camping trips from overnight for up to two weeks (you supply all your own gear, including water) also available. Capacity is five passengers per plane. *5603 Junior College Rd., Key West 33040, tel. 305/294–6978. Half-day tours $139 per person, full-day $239; camping trips $259. Reservations required. AE, MC, V.*

Canoe Tours **Canoeing Nature Tours.** Stan Becker leads a full-day 5-mile canoe and hiking trip in the Key Deer National Wildlife Refuge. The trip includes three hours in canoes and four hours exploring Watson Hammock on Big Pine Key. *MM 28, BS, Box 62, Big Pine Key 33043, tel. 305/872–2620. Reservations required. Children welcome; no pets. Box lunch provided. Fee: $65 per person. 9 AM–4 PM.*

Kayak Tours **Mosquito Coast Island Outfitters & Kayak Guides.** Half-day guided sea kayak tours explore the lush backcountry marsh just east of Key West. Two-person kayaks allow a parent to accompany a child. Only bad weather cancels daily year-round departures. *1107 Duval St., Key West. tel. 305/294–7178. Reservations required. Mineral water, granola bars, cap, and snorkel gear provided. Cost: $45 per person. AE, MC, V. 8:45 AM departure, 3 PM return.*

Sunset and Harbor Boat Tours Residents and tourists alike flock to west-facing restaurants, hotel docks, and bars to watch the glowing orb sink into the sea. Hundreds of people gather on Key West's Mallory Square Dock, where street performers and food vendors vie with the sunset for your attention. Throughout the keys, many motor yacht and sailboat captains take paying passengers on sunset cruises. Contact local chambers of commerce and hotels for information.

M/V *Miss Key West* offers a one-hour narrated cruise that explores Key West's harbor up to a half-mile from shore. The 45-passenger, 45-foot motor yacht passes Trumbo Point Navy Base, home of all six of the Navy's hydrofoil guided-missile destroyers. The sundown cruise includes live music. Call for departure times and for additional snorkel trips (all equipment and lessons provided). *Zero Duval St. (booth in front of Ocean Key House), tel. 305/296–8865, in FL 800/238–9815. Admission: harbor and sunset cruise $8 adults, children under 12 free. AE, MC, V. Open 8 AM–11 PM.*

Walking Tours **Pelican Path** is a free walking guide to Key West published by the **Old Island Restoration Foundation.** The tour discusses the history and architecture of 43 structures along 25 blocks of 12 Old town streets. Pick up a copy at the Key West Chamber of Commerce.

Solares Hill's Walking and Biking Guide to Old Key West, by local historian Sharon Wells, contains at least six walking tours of the city and a short tour of the Key West cemetery. Free copies are available from Key West Chamber of Commerce, many hotels and stores.

Water Wildlife Tours, run by native-born Capt. Vicki Impallomeni, an authority on the ecology of Florida Bay and activist for its preservation, features half-day and full-day charters in her 22-ft. Aquasport open fisherman, *The Imp II*. Families especially like exploring with Capt. Vicki because of her ability to teach youngsters. *23 Key Haven Terr., Key West 33040, tel.*

305/294–9731. Tours depart Paradise Marina on Stock Island typically 8:30 and 12:30 for half-day ($250), as early as 7 for full-day ($350), for up to 5 passengers. Reservations necessary, at least a month ahead in winter. AE, MC, V.

Exploring the Florida Keys

Numbers in the margin correspond to points of interest on the Florida Keys map.

The Upper Keys

This tour begins on Key Largo, the northeasternmost of the Florida Keys accessible by road. The tour assumes that you have come south from Florida City on **Card Sound Road** (Rte. 5). If you take the Overseas Highway (U.S. 1) south from Florida City, you can begin the tour with Key Largo Underseas Park. Attractions are listed by island or by mile marker (MM) number.

Cross the **Card Sound Bridge** onto **North Key Largo,** where Card Sound Road forms the eastern boundary of **Crocodile Lakes National Wildlife Refuge.** In the refuge dwell some 300 to 500 crocodiles, the largest single concentration of these shy, elusive reptiles in North America. There's no visitor center here—just 6,800 acres of mangrove swamp and adjoining upland jungle. For your best chance to see a crocodile, park on the shoulder of Card Sound Road and scan the ponds along the road with binoculars. In winter, crocodiles often haul out and sun themselves on the banks farthest from the road. Don't leave the road shoulder; you could disturb tern nests on the nearby spoil banks or aggravate the rattlesnakes.

Take Card Sound Road to Route 905, turn right, and drive for 10 miles through **Key Largo Hammock,** the largest remaining stand of the vast West Indian tropical hardwood forest that once covered most of the upland areas in the Florida Keys. The state and federal governments are busy acquiring as much of the hammock as they can to protect it from further development, and they hope to establish visitor centers and nature trails. For now, it's best to admire this wilderness from the road. According to law-enforcement officials, this may be the most dangerous place in the United States, a haven for modern-day pirates and witches. The "pirates" are drug smugglers who land their cargo along the ocean shore or drop it into the forest from low-flying planes. The "witches" are practitioners of voodoo, *santeria,* and other occult rituals. What's more, this jungle is full of poisonous plants. The most dangerous, the manchineel or "devil tree," has a toxin so potent that rainwater falling on its leaves and then onto a person's skin can cause sores that resist healing. Florida's first tourist, explorer Juan Ponce de León, died in 1521 from a superficial wound inflicted by an Indian arrowhead dipped in manchineel sap.

Continue on U.S. 1 to Transylvania Avenue (MM 103.2) and ❶ turn left to visit the **Key Largo Undersea Park.** The family attractions include an underwater museum that you have to snorkel or dive to, underwater music, and an air-conditioned grotto theater with a 13-minute multimedia slide show devoted to the history of man and sea. *Key Largo Undersea Park, 51 Shoreland Dr., Box 3330, Key Largo, tel. 305/451–2353. Aquarium*

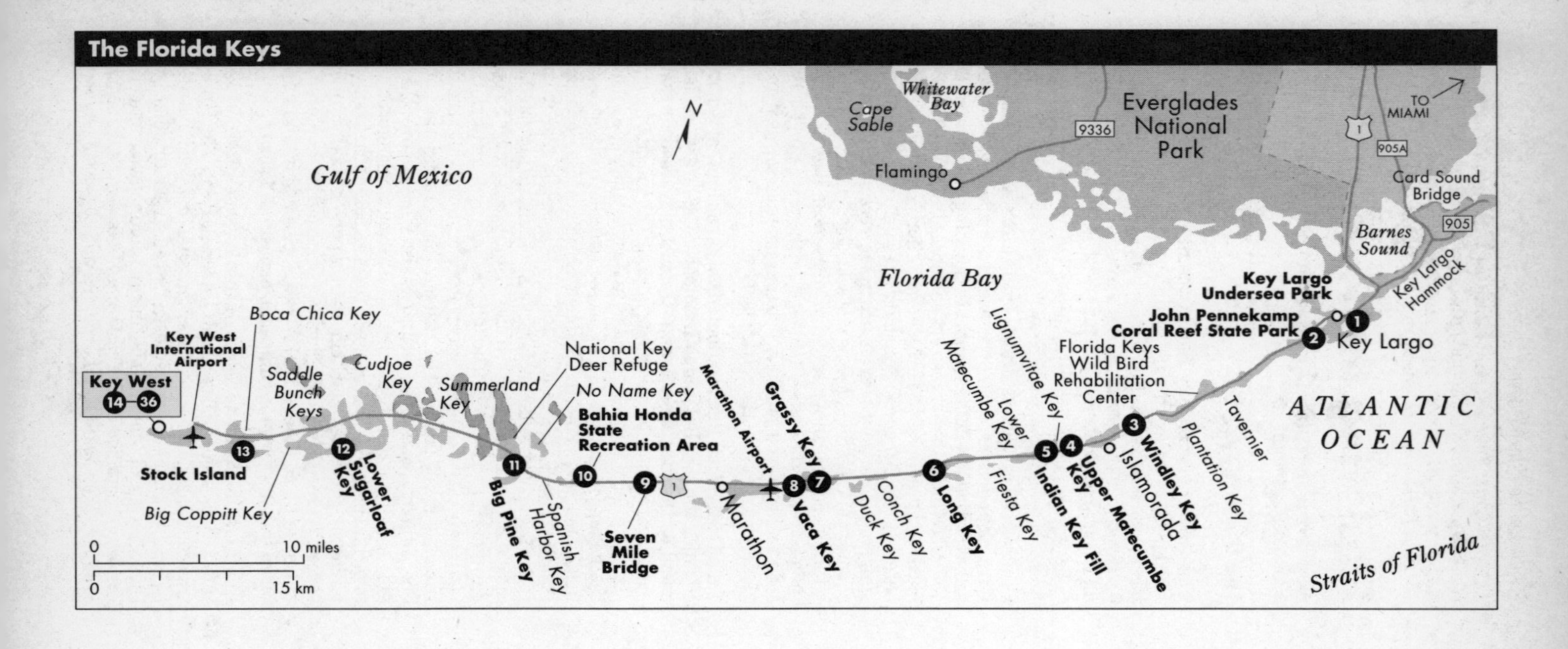
The Florida Keys
Everglades National Park
TO MIAMI
Card Sound Bridge
905A
905
1
9336
Cape Sable
Whitewater Bay
Flamingo
Gulf of Mexico
N
Florida Bay
Barnes Sound
Key Largo Hammock
Key Largo Undersea Park
John Pennekamp Coral Reef State Park
Key Largo
ATLANTIC OCEAN
Straits of Florida
Tavernier
Plantation Key
Florida Keys Wild Bird Rehabilitation Center
Windley Key
Islamorada
Upper Matecumbe Key
Indian Key Fill
Lignumvitae Key
Lower Matecumbe Key
Fiesta Key
Long Key
Conch Key
Duck Key
Grassy Key
Vaca Key
Marathon Airport
Marathon
Seven Mile Bridge
Bahia Honda State Recreation Area
No Name Key
National Key Deer Refuge
Spanish Harbor Key
Big Pine Key
Summerland Key
Cudjoe Key
Lower Sugarloaf Key
Saddle Bunch Keys
Boca Chica Key
Big Coppitt Key
Key West International Airport
Stock Island
Key West
14–36
0 10 miles
0 15 km

theater admission free; scuba fee, including tanks and gear: $20–$30; snorkel fee, including gear: $10, $35 for family of 4. Open daily 9–5.

❷ Return to U.S. 1, turn left, and left again into **John Pennekamp Coral Reef State Park.** The primary attraction here is diving on the offshore coral reefs (*see* Participant Sports, below), but even a landlubber can appreciate the superb interpretive aquarium in the park's visitor center. A concessionaire rents canoes and sailboats and offers boat trips to the reef. The park also includes a nature trail through a mangrove forest, a swimming beach, picnic shelters, a snack bar, a gift shop, and a campground. *MM 102.5, OS, Key Largo, tel. 305/451–1202. Admission: $3.25 per vehicle for up to 8 persons plus $1 each additional, and 50¢ per person county surcharge. Open daily 8 AM–sunset.*

Return to U.S. 1 and turn left. At MM 100, turn left again into the parking lot of the Holiday Inn Key Largo Resort. In the adjoining Key Largo Harbor Marina you'll find the ***African Queen,*** the steam-powered workboat on which Katharine Hepburn and Humphrey Bogart rode in their movie of the same name. Also displayed at the resort is the *Thayer IV*, a 22-foot mahogany Chris Craft built in 1951 and used by Ms. Hepburn and Henry Fonda in Fonda's last film, *On Golden Pond.*

Continuing south on U.S. 1 you'll cross **Plantation Key** (MM 93–87), named for the plantings of limes, pineapples, and tomatoes cultivated here at the turn of the century. In 1991, woodcarver and teacher Laura Quinn moved her **Florida Keys Wild Bird Rehabilitation Center** here. Nowhere else in the Keys can you see birdlife so close up. Many are kept for life because of injuries that can't be healed. Others are brought for rehabilitation and then set free. At any time there's likely to be lots of pelicans, cormorants, terns, and herons of various types. *93600 Overseas Hwy., MM 93.6 BS, Tavernier 33070, tel. 305/852–4486. Admission free, donations accepted. Open daily sunrise–sunset.*

❸ Next comes **Windley Key,** notable for **Theater of the Sea,** where nine dolphins, two sea lions, and an extensive collection of tropical fish swim in the pits of a 1907 railroad quarry. Allow at least two hours to attend the dolphin and sea lion shows and visit all the exhibits, which include an injured birds of prey exhibit, a "bottomless" boat ride, touch tank, shark-feeding pool, and a 300-gallon "living reef" aquarium with invertebrates and small reef fishes. At the entrance is a feeding station for abandoned cats. *MM 84.5, OS, Box 407, Islamorada, tel. 305/664–2431. Admission: $11.75 adults, $6 children 3–12. Swim with dolphins (30-min orientation and 30 min in the water): $65. Reservations required with 50% deposit, minimum age 13, mask and swim fins recommended, life vests optional. Video or still photos $65 (inquire at concession). AE, MC, V. Open daily 9:30 AM–4 PM.*

Watch for the **Hurricane Memorial** (MM 82) beside the highway. It marks the mass grave of 423 victims of the 1935 Labor Day hurricane. Many of those who perished were veterans who had been working on the Overseas Highway; they died when a tidal surge overturned a train sent to evacuate them. The art deco-style monument depicts wind-driven waves and palms bowing before the storm's fury.

4 At the lower tip of **Upper Matecumbe Key,** stop at the **International Fishing Museum** in Bud n' Mary's Marina. The museum contains a collection of antique fishing tackle and a video library with information on fishing activities, fishery conservation, and the natural history of various species of local fishes. The videos don't circulate, but you can watch them in the museum. The museum staff can also help you find a charter captain for deep-sea or back-country fishing. *MM 79.5, OS. For information, contact Bob Epstein, 124 Gardenia St., Tavernier 33070, tel. 305/664–2767 (office), 305/852–8813 (home). Open Mon.–Sat. 9–5, Sun. 9–noon. Admission free.*

5 The dock on **Indian Key Fill** at MM 78, BS, is the closest point on the Overseas Highway to three unusual state parks accessible only by water. The newest of these parks, dedicated in 1989, is **San Pedro Underwater Archaeological Preserve** (*see* Participant Sports, below). State-operated boat tours aboard the M. V. *Monroe* will take you to the other two, **Indian Key State Historic Site** (OS) and **Lignumvitae Key State Botanical Site** (BS). Indian Key was a county seat town and shipwrecker's station until an Indian attack wiped out the settlement in 1840. Dr. Henry Perrine, a noted botanist, was killed in the raid. Today you'll see his plants overgrowing the town's ruins. A virgin hardwood forest still cloaks Lignumvitae Key (where the dock was repaired early in 1991), punctuated only by the home and gardens that chemical magnate William Matheson built as a private retreat in 1919. *MM 78. For information and tour boat reservations, contact Long Key State Recreation Area, Box 776, Long Key, tel. 305/664–4815. Indian Key open daily 8 AM–sunset; Lignumvitae Key open Thurs.–Mon. with 1-hr guided tour (admission: $1 adults, children under 6 free) at 10:30 AM, 1 and 2:30 PM for visitors from private boats. State tour boat admission: $7 adults, $3 children under 12, for 3-hr tours Thurs.–Mon. to Indian Key, 8:30 AM, to Lignumvitae Key, 1:30 PM.*

6 Return to U.S. 1 and turn right. Continue down to **Long Key** (MM 69), where you'll pass a tract of undisturbed forest on the right (BS) just below MM 67. Watch for a historical marker partially obscured by foliage. Pull off the road here and explore **Layton Trail,** named after Del Layton, who incorporated the city of Layton in 1963 and served as its mayor until his death in 1987. The marker relates the history of the Long Key Viaduct, the first major bridge on the rail line, and the Long Key Fishing Club that Henry Flagler established nearby in 1906. Zane Grey, the noted western novelist, was president of the club. It consisted of a lodge, guest cottages, and storehouses—all obliterated by the 1935 hurricane. The clearly marked trail leads through the tropical hardwood forest to a rocky Florida Bay shoreline overlooking shallow grass flats offshore.

Less than a mile below Layton Trail, turn left into **Long Key State Recreation Area,** then left again to the parking area for the **Golden Orb Trail.** This trail leads onto a boardwalk through a mangrove swamp alongside a lagoon where many herons and other water birds congregate in winter. The park also has a campground, a picnic area, a canoe trail through a tidal lagoon, and a not-very-sandy beach fronting on a broad expanse of shallow grass flats. Instead of a pail and shovel, bring a mask and snorkel here to observe the marine life in this rich nursery area. *Box 776, Long Key, MM 67.5 OS, tel. 305/664–4815. Admission: $3.25 per car for up to 8 persons, $1 per additional* *person, plus 50¢ per person county surcharge. Bike rental $10 deposit and $2.14 per hour (includes tax). Open daily 8 AM–sunset.*

The Middle Keys

Below Long Key, the Overseas Highway crosses Long Key Channel on a new highway bridge beside the railroad's **Long Key Viaduct.** The second-longest bridge on the rail line, this 2-mile-long structure has 222 reinforced-concrete arches. It ends at **Conch Key** (MM 63), a tiny fishing and retirement community. Below Conch Key, the causeway on your left at MM 61 leads to **Duck Key,** an upscale residential community and the **Hawk's Cay Resort** (*see* Lodging, below).

7 Next comes **Grassy Key** (MM 59). Watch on the right for the **Dolphin Research Center** and the 35-foot-long concrete sculpture of the dolphin Theresa and her offspring Nat outside the former home of Milton Santini, creator of the original *Flipper* movie. The 14 dolphins here today are free to leave and return to the fenced area that protects them from boaters and predators. *MM 59, BS, Box Dolphin, Marathon Shores, tel. 305/289-0002. Admission: $7.50 adults, $5 donation children 4–12. Walking tours at 10 AM, 12:30, 2 and 3:30 PM. Swim with dolphins (20 min., part of 2½-hr instruction/education program) $65. Children 5–12 swim with an accompanying, paying adult (also $65). Reserve for dolphin swim on the first day of the month for the following month. Visitor center open Wed.–Sun. 9 AM–4 PM, closed Christmas, New Year's Day, Thanksgiving.*

Continuing down U.S. 1, you'll pass the road to **Key Colony Beach** (MM 54, OS), an incorporated city developed in the 1950s as a retirement community. It has a golf course and boating facilities. Soon after, you'll cross a bridge onto **Vaca Key** and enter **Marathon** (MM 53–47), the commercial hub of the Middle Keys.

8

On your right (BS) at 55th Street is **Crane Point Hammock,** a 63-acre tract that includes the last known undisturbed thatch-palm hammock. The Florida Keys Land Trust, a private, non-profit conservation group, paid $1.2 million to acquire the property in 1988. Early in 1990, behind a stunning bronze-and-copper door crafted by Roy Butler of Plantation, Florida, the Trust opened **The Museum of Natural History of the Florida Keys** as the first phase of educational facilities planned for the hammock. A children's museum opened early in 1991. The tract also includes an exotic plant arboretum, several archaeological sites, and the remnants of a Bahamian village with the oldest surviving example of Conch-style architecture outside Key West. Special weekly Hammock tours are offered as part of your admission from November to Easter; bring good walking shoes and bug repellent. *MM 50, BS, 5550 Overseas Hwy., Box 536, Marathon 33050, tel. 305/743-9100. Admission: $4.50 adults, $2.50 senior citizens, $1 children 12–17 and students. Open Mon.–Sat. 9–5, Sun. noon–5.*

9 As you approach the new **Seven Mile Bridge,** turn right at MM 47 to the entrance to the **Old Seven Mile Bridge.** An engineering marvel in its day, the bridge rested on 546 concrete piers spanning the broad expanse of water that separates the Middle and Lower Keys. Monroe County maintains a 2-mile stretch of the old bridge to provide access to **Pigeon Key** (MM 45), where the

county's public schools and community college run marine-science classes in a railroad work camp built around 1908. In 1990 Pigeon Key was placed on the National Register of Historic Places, a status the Old Seven Mile Bridge already enjoyed. *For information, contact James Lewis, Chairman, Pigeon Key Advisory Authority, 2945 Overseas Hwy., Marathon 33050, tel. 305/743-6040.*

Return to U.S. 1 and proceed across the new **Seven Mile Bridge** (actually only 6.79 miles long!). Built between 1980 and 1982 at a cost of $45 million, the new Seven Mile Bridge is the world's longest segmental bridge, with 39 expansion joints separating its cement sections. Each April runners gather in Marathon for the annual Seven Mile Bridge Run.

The Lower Keys

10 At **Bahia Honda State Recreation Area** (MM 36.5) on Bahia Honda Key, you'll find a sandy beach most of the time. Lateral drift builds up the beach in summer; winter storms whisk away much of the sand. The park's Silver Palm Trail leads you through a dense tropical forest where you can see rare West Indian plants, including the Geiger tree, sea lavendar, Key spider lily, bay cedar, thatch and silver palms, and several species found nowhere else in the Florida Keys: the West Indies yellow satinwood, Catesbaea, Jamaica morning glory, and wild dilly. The park also includes a campground, cabins, gift shop, snack bar, marina, and dive shop offering snorkel trips to offshore reefs. *MM 36.5, OS, Rte. 1, Box 782, Big Pine Key, tel. 305/872-2353. Admission: $3.25 per vehicle for up to 8 passengers plus $1 per additional person and 50¢ per person county surcharge. Open daily 8 AM-sunset.*

Cross the Bahia Honda Bridge and continue past Spanish Harbor Key and Spanish Harbor Channel onto **Big Pine Key** (MM 32-30), where prominent signs warn drivers to be on the lookout for Key deer. Every year cars kill 50 to 60 of the delicate creatures. A subspecies of the Virginia white-tailed deer, Key deer once ranged throughout the Lower and Middle Keys, but hunting and habitat destruction reduced the population to fewer than 50 in 1947. Under protection in the **National Key Deer Refuge** since 1954, the deer herd grew to about 750 by the early 1970s. The government owns only about a third of Big Pine Key, however, and as the human population on the remaining land grew during the 1980s, the deer herd declined again until today only 250 to 300 remain. Plans for a new road that may have threatened the remaining deer were canceled in 1991.

To visit the refuge, turn right at the stoplight, then bear left at the fork onto Key Deer Boulevard (Rte. 940). Pass Road Prison No. 426 and a fire tower on the way to Watson Boulevard, then turn left and go about a mile to the **Refuge Headquarters** to see interpretive displays and obtain brochures.

The best place to see Key deer is on **No Name Key,** a sparsely populated island just east of Big Pine Key. To get there, take Watson Boulevard east to Wilder Road, and turn left. You'll go 2 miles from Key Deer Boulevard to the middle of the Bogie Channel Bridge, which links Big Pine and No Name Keys, and 1½ miles from there across No Name Key. If you get out of your car at the end of the road to walk around, close all doors and windows to keep raccoons from wandering in. Deer may turn up along this road at any time of day—especially in early morning and late afternoon. Admire their beauty, but don't try to feed them—it's against the law. To resume your journey, take Wilder Road back to Key Deer Boulevard at the fork just before the stoplight on U.S. 1. Turn right at the stoplight, and continue on down the Keys across **Big Torch, Middle Torch,** and **Little Torch Keys** (named for the torchwood tree, which settlers used for kindling because it burns easily even when green). Next comes **Ramrod Key** (MM 27.5), a base for divers in **Looe Key National Marine Sanctuary** 5 miles offshore (*see* Participant Sports, below).

Time Out Find top dining at **Mangrove Mama's,** a lattice-fronted conch house, remnant from a time when trains outnumbered cars in the Keys *ca.* 1919. Fresh fish, seafoods, some decent beers, and rave-worthy Key lime pie are served. Concrete floors, Keys art on the walls, Tennessee oak bar, and lights twinkling at night in the banana trees are just a few details that contribute to the ambience here. It gets awfully romantic for just down home. *MM 20, BS, tel. 305/745–3030. Reservations accepted. Casual. MC, V. Moderate.*

(12) On **Lower Sugarloaf Key,** you'll find the Sugar Loaf Lodge (MM 17, BS), an attractive motel known for its performing dolphin named Sugar, who lives in a lagoon behind the restaurant (*see* Lodging, below). Follow the paved road northwest from the motel for a ½ mile past an airstrip, and keep going on an unpaved spur. There, in bleak, gravel-strewn surroundings, you'll find a reconstruction of R. C. Perky's **bat tower.** Perky, an early real estate promoter, built the tower in 1929 to attract mosquito-eating bats, but no bats ever roosted in it.

(13) Continue on through the Saddlebunch Keys and Big Coppitt Key to **Boca Chica Key** (MM 10), site of the Key West Naval Air Station. You may hear the roar of jet fighter planes in this vicinity. At last you reach **Stock Island** (MM 5), the gateway to Key West. Pass the 18-hole **Key West Resort Golf Course,** then turn right onto Junior College Road and pause at the **Key West Botanical Garden,** where the Key West Garden Club has labeled an extensive assortment of native and exotic tropical trees.

Key West

Numbers in the margin correspond to points of interest on the Key West map.

In April 1982, the U.S. Border Patrol threw a roadblock across the Overseas Highway just south of Florida City to catch drug runners and illegal aliens. Traffic backed up for miles as Border Patrol agents searched vehicles and demanded that the occupants prove U.S. citizenship. City officials in Key West, outraged at being treated like foreigners by the federal government, staged a mock secession and formed their own "nation," the so-called Conch Republic. They hoisted a flag and distributed mock border passes, visas, and Conch currency. The embarrassed Border Patrol dismantled its roadblock, and now an annual festival recalls the secessionists' victorious exploits.

The episode exemplifies Key West's odd station in life. Situated 150 miles from Miami and just 90 miles from Havana, this tropical island city has always maintained its strong sense of detachment, even after it was connected to the rest of the United States—by the railroad in 1912 and by the Overseas Highway in 1938. The U.S. government acquired **Key West** from Spain in 1819 along with the rest of Florida. The Spanish had named the island Cayo Hueso (Bone Key) in honor of Indian skeletons they found on its shores. In 1822, Uncle Sam sent Commodore David S. Porter to the Keys to chase pirates away.

For three decades, the primary industry in Key West was "wrecking"—rescuing people and salvaging cargo from ships that foundered on the nearby reefs. According to some reports, when business was slow, the wreckers hung out lights to lure ships aground. Their business declined after 1852, when the federal government began building lighthouses along the reefs.

In 1845 the Army started to construct Fort Taylor, which held Key West for the Union during the Civil War. After the war, an influx of Cuban dissidents unhappy with Spain's rule brought the cigar industry to Key West. Fishing, shrimping, and sponge-gathering became important industries, and a pineapple-canning factory opened. Major military installations were established during the Spanish-American War and World War I. Through much of the 19th century and into the second decade of the 20th, Key West was Florida's wealthiest city in per-capita terms.

In the 1920s the local economy began to unravel. Modern ships no longer needed to stop in Key West for provisions, the cigar industry moved to Tampa, Hawaii dominated the pineapple industry, and the sponges succumbed to a blight. Then the Depression hit, and even the military moved out. By 1934 half the population was on relief. The city defaulted on its bond payments, and the Federal Emergency Relief Administration took over the city and county governments.

Federal officials began promoting Key West as a tourist destination. They attracted 40,000 visitors during the 1934–35 winter season. Then the 1935 Labor Day hurricane struck the Middle Keys, sparing Key West but wiping out the railroad and the tourist trade. For three years, until the Overseas Highway opened, the only way in and out of town was by boat.

Ever since, Key West's fortunes have waxed and waned with the vagaries of world affairs. An important naval center during World War II and the Korean conflict, the island remains a strategic listening post on the doorstep of Fidel Castro's Cuba. Although the Navy shut down its submarine base at Truman Annex and sold the property to a real-estate developer, the nearby Boca Chica Naval Air Station and other military installations remain active.

As the military scaled back, city officials looked to tourism again to take up the slack. Even before it tried, Key West had much to sell—superb frost-free weather with an average temperature of 79°F, quaint 19th-century architecture, and a laid-back lifestyle. Promoters have fostered fine restaurants, galleries and shops, and new museums to interpret the city's intriguing past. There's also a growing calendar of artistic and cultural events and a lengthening list of annual festivals—including the Conch Republic celebration in April, Hemingway Days in July, and a Halloween Fantasy Fest rivaling the New Orleans Mardi Gras.

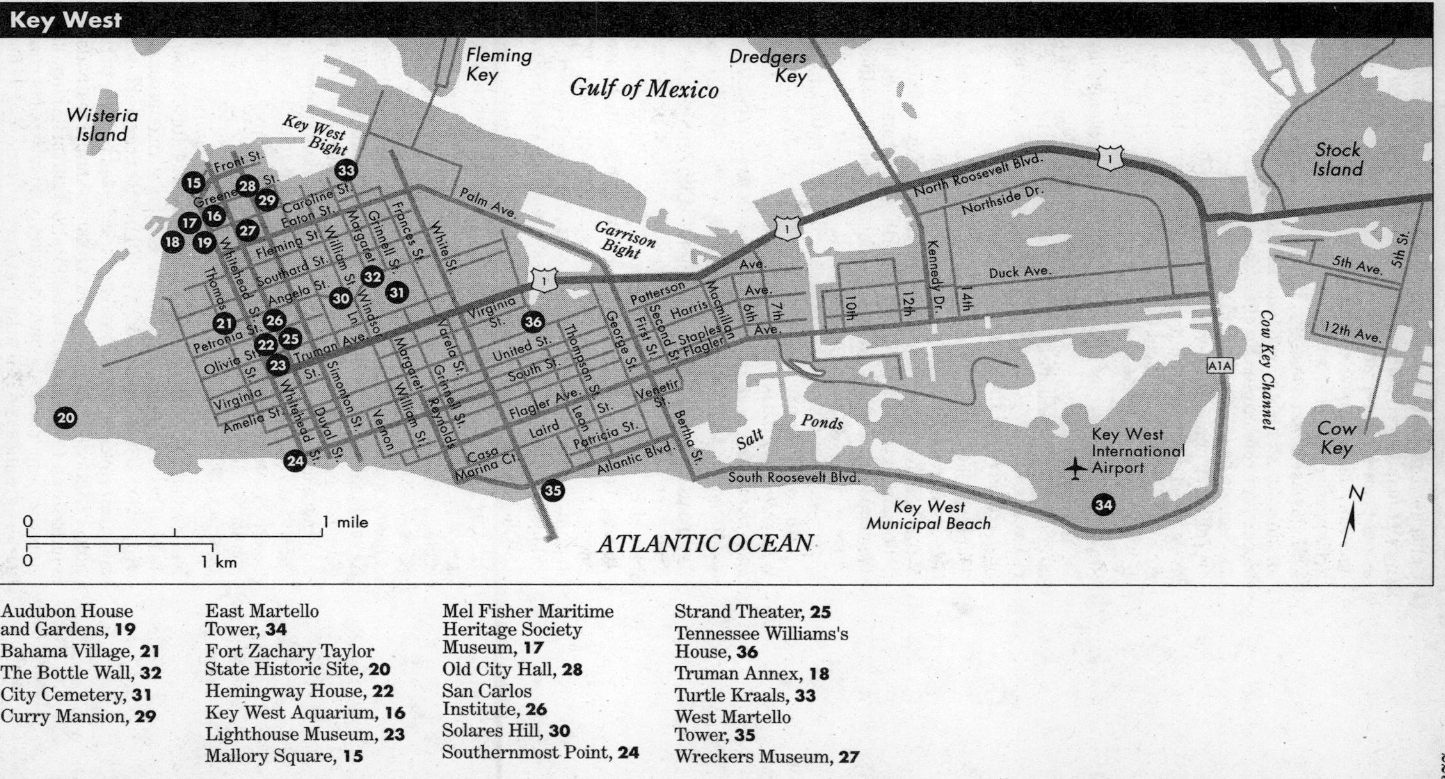

Audubon House and Gardens, **19**
Bahama Village, **21**
The Bottle Wall, **32**
City Cemetery, **31**
Curry Mansion, **29**
East Martello Tower, **34**
Fort Zachary Taylor State Historic Site, **20**
Hemingway House, **22**
Key West Aquarium, **16**
Lighthouse Museum, **23**
Mallory Square, **15**
Mel Fisher Maritime Heritage Society Museum, **17**
Old City Hall, **28**
San Carlos Institute, **26**
Solares Hill, **30**
Southernmost Point, **24**
Strand Theater, **25**
Tennessee Williams's House, **36**
Truman Annex, **18**
Turtle Kraals, **33**
West Martello Tower, **35**
Wreckers Museum, **27**

Gentrification is in the breeze. New city rules say no to retail T-shirt displays on sidewalks, and to amplified sound spilling out of open-air bars. Sundown revelry at Mallory Square has been uneasily reconciled with use of the Mallory Docks by a growing fleet of cruise ships calling at Key West. The rule since 1991 has been that the ships, if staying overnight, have to go offshore for an hour or so at sunset and leave the spectacle unblocked for celebrants. No question—reform is in the air. But the bans on bad taste and loud noise should be seen as part of an overall environmental regard, although it seems the changes more often occur to benefit commercial tourism than the environment. While the wheel turns, begin this tour at Front and Duval streets, near the Pier House hotel and Ocean Key House.

15 Start by going west on Front Street to **Mallory Square,** named for Stephen Mallory, secretary of the Confederate Navy, who later owned the Mallory Steamship Line. On the nearby **Mallory Dock,** a nightly sunset celebration draws street performers, food vendors, and thousands of onlookers.

16 Facing Mallory Square is the **Key West Aquarium,** which features hundreds of brightly colored tropical fish and other fascinating sea creatures from the waters around Key West. A touch tank enables visitors to handle starfish, sea cucumbers, horseshoe and hermit crabs, even horse and queen conchs—living totems of the Conch Republic. Built in 1934 by the Works Progress Administration as the world's first open-air aquarium, the building has been enclosed for all-weather viewing. *1 Whitehead St., tel. 305/296–2051. Guided tours 11 AM, 1, 3, 4:30; shark feeding on every tour. Admission: $5.50 adults, $2.75 children 8–15. Open daily, 10–6 (10–7 in winter).*

Return to Front Street and turn right to **Clinton Place,** where a Civil War memorial to Union soldiers stands in a triangle formed by the intersection of Front, Greene, and Whitehead streets. On your right is the **U.S. Post Office and Customs House,** a Romanesque Revival structure designed by prominent local architect William Kerr and completed in 1891. Tour guides claim that federal bureaucrats required the roof to have a steep pitch so it wouldn't collect snow.

17 On your left is the **Mel Fisher Maritime Heritage Society Museum,** which displays gold and silver bars, coins, jewelry, and other artifacts recovered in 1985 from the Spanish treasure ships *Nuestra Señora de Atocha* and *Santa Margarita*. The two galleons foundered in a hurricane in 1622 near the Marquesas Keys, 40 miles west of Key West. In the museum you can lift a gold bar weighing 6.3 Troy pounds and see a 77.76-carat natural emerald crystal worth almost $250,000. *200 Greene St., tel. 305/294–2633. Museum admission: $5 adults; $4 military, Conch Train and trolley passengers with ticket stub, and AAA members; $1.50 children 6–12. Open daily 10–5; last video showing 4:30.*

18 Mel Fisher's museum occupies a former navy storehouse that he bought from Pritam Singh, the developer of **Truman Annex** (Key West 33040, tel. 305/296–5601). After a $17.25 million fast-start investment followed by a quick stall because of recession, Pritam Singh, the Key West hippie-turned-millionaire, is successfully transforming the 103-acre Truman Annex into a suburban community of pastel, picket, and lattice charm. The parade grounds and barracks that during World War II housed

some 18,000 military and civilian employees now house singles and retirees in affordable condominiums, and families in grassy-yard homes surrounded by colorful bougainvillea and allamanda vines. The whole community is set behind high black wrought iron gates and architecturally designed in the Victorian style that knits Old Town together. Also on the grounds is the **Harry S. Truman Little White House Museum.** Pedestrians and cyclists are welcome on the complex daily between 8 AM and sunset. They'll find a dream community that, though less than full blown, considering the abominations that other developers have dumped on Key West in recent years, is a model of urban good taste. *Museum tel. 305/294–9911. Admission: $6 adults, $3 children 12 and under. Open daily 9–5.*

From Mel Fisher's museum, cross Whitehead Street to visit
19 the **Audubon House and Gardens.** A museum in this three-story dwelling built in the mid-1840s commemorates ornithologist John James Audubon's 1832 visit to Key West. On display are several rooms of period antiques and a large collection of Audubon engravings. There is a self-guided walking tour of the tropical gardens, keyed to an eight-page brochure, and an exquisite collection of porcelains of American birds and foliage by Dorothy Doughty is one in a series of rotating exhibits. In 1989 a children's room was opened, furnished in 18th- and 19th-century antiques. *205 Whitehead St., tel. 305/294–2116. Admission: $5 adults, $1 children 6–12. Open daily 9:30–5.*

Continue up Whitehead Street past **Pigeonhouse Patio Restaurant & Bar** (301 Whitehead St., tel. 305/296–9600). This building was the first headquarters of Pan American World Airways, the first U.S. airline to operate scheduled international air service. The inaugural flight took off from Key West International Airport on October 28, 1927: Passengers paid $9.95 for the 90-mile, 80-minute flight from Key West to Havana aboard *The General Machado*, a Fokker F–7 trimotor.

Turn right onto Southard Street and follow the signs to the
20 **Fort Zachary Taylor State Historic Site.** Built between 1845 and 1866, the fort served as a base for the Union blockade of Confederate shipping during the Civil War. More than 1,500 Confederate vessels captured while trying to run the blockade were brought to Key West's harbor and detained under the fort's guns. What you will see at Fort Taylor today is a fort within a fort. In 1989 a moat was dug to suggest how the fort originally looked when it was surrounded by water. Snorkeling is excellent here because of an artificial reef, except when the wind blows south-southwest and muddies the water. Look for a new concession stand on the beach this winter. *Box 289, tel. 305/292–6713. Free 90-min tour daily at 2 PM. Admission: $3.25 per car for up to 8 passengers, $1 per additional passenger, plus 50¢ county surcharge per person. Park open daily 8–sunset, fort open 8–5.*

Time Out Pause for a libation at the open-air **Green Parrot Bar.** Built in 1890, the bar is said to be Key West's oldest, a sometimes-rowdy saloon where locals outnumber the tourists, especially on weekends when bands play. *601 Whitehead St. (corner of Southard St.), tel. 305/294–6133. No credit cards. Open daily noon–4 AM.*

Return to Thomas Street, turn right 2 blocks to the corner of Petronia Street, and you're at **Blue Heaven,** (729 Thomas St., tel. 305/296–8666), an old blue-on-blue clapboard, peach-and-yellow-trimmed Greek Revival Bahamian house, in the heart of 21 **Bahama Village,** where Bahamians settled Key West a century and a half ago. Blue Heaven is an up-by-the-bootstraps little conch- and Caribbean-food restaurant popular for its take-out. Not too long ago it was a bordello where Ernest Hemingway refereed boxing matches and where Captain Tony in his premayoral days took in the cockfights. There's still a rooster graveyard out back, as well as a water tower hauled here from Little Torch Key in the 1920s.

Time Out Up to your ears in margaritas? Stop by **Casablanca at Bogarts** for an ice-cold pint of Guinness or any of the other imported beers that are on tap. This lively Irish-owned and -run pub is attached to a restaurant (that serves both Irish and Caribbean cuisine) and a guest house. *900 Duval St. (corner of Olivia St.), tel. 305/296–0637. MC, V. Open daily noon–4 AM.*

Return to Whitehead Street east on Petronia Street, turn right 22 1 block to the **Hemingway House,** now a museum dedicated to the novelist's life and work. Built in 1851, this two-story Spanish Colonial dwelling was the first house in Key West to have running water and a fireplace. Hemingway bought the house in 1931 and wrote about 70% of his life's work here, including *A Farewell to Arms* and *For Whom the Bell Tolls*. Three months after Hemingway died in 1961, local jeweler Bernice Dickson bought the house and its contents from Hemingway's estate and two years later opened it as a museum. Of special interest are the huge bed with a headboard made from a 17th-century Spanish monastery gate, a ceramic cat by Pablo Picasso (a gift to Hemingway from the artist), the handblown Venetian glass chandelier in the dining room, and the swimming pool. The museum staff gives guided tours rich with anecdotes about Hemingway and his family and feeds the 42 feline habitants (for the 42 bridges in the Keys), descendants of Hemingway's own 50 cats. Kitten adoptions are possible (for a fee), but there's a five-year waiting list. Tours begin every 10 minutes and take 25–30 minutes; then you're free to explore on your own. *907 Whitehead St., tel. 305/294–1575. Admission: $6 adults, $1.50 children 6–12. Open daily 9–5.*

Down the block and across the street from Hemingway House 23 (behind spic-and-span white picket fence) is the **Lighthouse Museum,** a 92-foot lighthouse built in 1847 and an adjacent 1887 clapboard house where the keeper lived. Both underwent extensive restoration in 1989, and the museum was largely rearranged a year later. You can climb 98 steps to the top of the lighthouse for a spectacular view of the island town, as well as of the first order (biggest) Fresnel lens, installed at a cost of $1 million in the 1860s. On display in the keeper's quarters are vintage photographs, ship models, nautical charts, and lighthouse artifacts from all along the Key reefs. *938 Whitehead St., tel. 305/294–0012. Admission: $3 adults, $1 children 6–12. Open daily 9:30–5.*

Continue to the foot of Whitehead Street, where a huge con-24 crete marker proclaims this spot to be the **Southernmost Point** in the United States. Most tourists snapping pictures of each other in front of the marker are oblivious to Key West's real southernmost point, on a nearby navy base off limits to civilians but visible through the fence to your right. Bahamian vendors of shells and straw hats line the sidewalk and blow a conch horn at passing Conch Tour Trains and Old Town Trolleys.

Turn left on South Street. To your right are two dwellings that both claim to be the **Southernmost House**—the Spanish-style home built in the 1940s at 400 South Street by Thelma Strabel, author of *Reap the Wild Wind*, a novel about the wreckers who salvaged ships aground on the reef in Key West's early days, and the adjoining cream-brick Queen Anne mansion at 1400 Duval Street. Neither is open to the public. Take the next right onto Duval Street, which ends at the Atlantic Ocean and the **Southernmost Beach.** *Admission free. Open daily 7 AM–11 PM.*

Now go north on Duval Street towards downtown Key West. Pause at the **Cuban Club** (1108 Duval St., tel. 305/296–8997). The original building—a social club for the Cuban community—burned in 1983 and has been replaced by shops and luxury condominiums; some of the original facade was retained. Continuing on Duval Street, you'll pass several art galleries from the 1100 block through the 800 block.

Pause to admire the colorful marquee and ornamental facade of (25) the **Strand Theater,** built in 1918 by Cuban craftsmen. After a period as a movie theater, it now offers a variety of live entertainment under the auspices of Clubland at the Strand. *527 Duval St., tel. 305/293–0116.*

(26) Continue on to the **San Carlos Institute,** a Cuban-American heritage center, which houses a museum and research library focusing on the history of Key West and of 19th- and 20th-century Cuban exiles. The San Carlos Institute was founded in 1871 by Cuban immigrants who wanted to preserve their language, customs, and heritage while organizing the struggle for Cuba's independence from Spain. Cuban patriot Jose Martí delivered many famous speeches in Key West from the balcony of the auditorium. Opera star Enrico Caruso sang in the 400-seat hall of the Opera House, which reportedly has the best acoustics of any concert hall in the South. The current building was completed in 1924, replacing the original built in 1871 that burned in the Key West fire of 1886, in which two-thirds of the city was destroyed. A second building succumbed to the hurricane of 1919. After Cuba and the United States broke off diplomatic relations in 1961, the building deteriorated. It was saved from demolition when Miami attorney Rafael A. Peñalver, Jr., secured a $3 million state grant for its restoration. The building reopened January 3, 1992, exactly 100 years after Martí founded the Cuban Revolutionary Party here. Activities include film presentations on the history of Key West and of the Cuban community in the United States, as well as nightly performing arts presentations. *516 Duval St., tel. 305/294–3887. Guided tour, concluding with 30-min film. Admission: $2 adults, $1.50 children. Open daily 9–5.*

(27) Continue north on Duval Street to the **Wreckers Museum,** which is alleged to be the oldest house in Key West. It was built in 1829 as the home of Francis Watlington, a sea captain and wrecker. He was also a Florida state senator, but resigned to serve in the Confederate Navy during the Civil War. Six of the home's eight rooms are now a museum furnished with 18th- and 19th-century antiques. In an upstairs bedroom is an eight-

room miniature dollhouse of Conch architectural design, outfitted with tiny Victorian furniture. *322 Duval St., tel. 305/294–9502. Open daily 10–4; closed Christmas. Admission: $2 adults, 50¢ children 3–12.*

Take Duval Street to Front Street, turn right, go two blocks to Simonton Street, turn right again and go 1 block to Greene Street to see the **Old City Hall,** returned to use after a $1 million restoration. In 1990 the City Commission began meeting here again for the first time since the early 1960s. There is a permanent exhibition of old Key West photographs, including an 1845 Daguerreotype, the oldest known photographic image of Key West. Designed by William Kerr, the architect also responsible for the Customs House, the Old City Hall opened in 1891. It has a rectangular tower with four clock faces and a fire bell. The ground floor, used as a city market for many years, now houses the **Historic Key West Shipwreck Museum.** Among the displays are relics from the *Isaac Allerton,* built at Portsmouth, New Hampshire, in 1838 and sunk off Key West in 1856. The second floor houses the city commission's meeting room and offices of the city government and the Historic Florida Keys Preservation Board (tel. 305/292–6718). *510 Greene St., tel. 305/292–9740. Open daily 10–5. Museum admission: $4 adults, $2 students and children 10–16.*

Time Out Stop next door to the **Cuban Coffee Queen Cafe** (512 Greene St., tel. 305/296–2711), run by a mother/daughter team from Central Chaparra, in Cuba's Oriente Province. Locals love the hot bollos, conch fritters, pigs feet, ham and eggs, sangría, and Cuban coffee.

Return to Simonton Street, go 1 block south to Caroline Street, and turn right to the **Curry Mansion** (*see* Lodging, below). Built in 1899 for Milton Curry, the son of Florida's first millionaire, this 22-room Victorian mansion is an adaptation of a Parisian town house. It has the only widow's walk open to the public in Key West. The owners have restored and redecorated most of the house. Take an unhurried self-guided tour with a comprehensive brochure, which includes floor plans, full of detailed information about the history and contents of the house. *511 Caroline St., tel. 305/294–5349. Admission: $5 adults, $1 children under 12. Open daily 10–5.*

Return to Simonton Street, go south to Angela Street, and turn left. Before you rises **Solares Hill,** the steepest natural grade in Key West. Its summit, the island's loftiest elevation, is 18 feet above sea level.

Now cross Elizabeth Street and bear right onto Windsor Lane to the **City Cemetery.** Turn left onto Passover Lane to the entrance at Margaret Street. Clustered near a flagpole resembling a ship's mast are the graves of 22 sailors killed in the sinking of the battleship U.S.S. *Maine. Guided tours weekends by appointment; call Susan Olsen, tel. 305/296–3913. Admission free. Tour donation: $5. Open sunrise–sunset.*

At the corner of Margaret and Angela streets, pause at **The Bottle Wall.** Hundreds of bottles from vintage champagne to ketchup have been mortared into a homespun work of art that's equally practical. Carolyn Gorton Fuller says she's done it so the dazzle keeps vehicles from missing the curve and crashing into her house. The first wall built 17 years ago went down in a firetruck crash. Note one of the doorsteps of Ms. Fuller's Conch house: the headstone for a grave—in place, she says, when she bought the house.

33 Go up Margaret Street to the harbor docks and visit the **Turtle Kraals,** where the Florida Marine Conservancy runs a hospital for sea creatures. Biologist Linda Bohl maintains a touch tank with horseshoe crabs, sea anemones, sea urchins, and other benign beasts you can fondle—but keep your fingers away from Hawkeye and Gonzo, a churlish pair of 150-pound, 32-year-old hawksbill turtles. A fish pond on the premises gives you a good look at live denizens of local waters, including barracuda, bluefish, lemon and nurse sharks, and yellowtail snapper. *231 Margaret St., tel. 305/294–2640. Admission free; donation accepted. Open 11 AM–1 AM Mon.–Sat., Sun. noon–1 AM.*

Return to Margaret Street and go a block south to Eaton Street, turn left and continue east past White Street, where Eaton Street doglegs to the right into Palm Avenue. You'll cross a causeway and bridge to the corner of **Garrison Bight Yacht Basin,** where many charter-fishing boats dock.

Turn left onto North Roosevelt Boulevard (U.S. 1) and go east. Past the turnoff to Stock Island at the east end of Key West, North Roosevelt Boulevard becomes South Roosevelt Boulevard and turns west. On your left is a small community of houseboats. On your right, just past the entrance to Key West 34 International Airport, stands **East Martello Tower,** one of two Civil War forts of similar design overlooking the Atlantic Ocean. Housed in a portion of this tower are military uniforms and relics of the battleship U.S.S. *Maine,* which was blown up in Havana Harbor in 1898. Also, the **Key West Art and Historical Society** operates a museum in East Martello's vaulted casemates. The collection includes Stanley Papio's "junk art" sculptures, Cuban primitive artist Mario Sanchez's chiseled and painted wood carvings of historic Key West street scenes, memorabilia from movies shot on location in the Keys, and a display of books by many of the 55 famous writers (including seven Pulitzer Prize winners) who live in Key West. Historical exhibits have been developed to present a chronological history of the Florida Keys and are on display. A circular 48-step staircase in the central tower leads to a platform overlooking the airport and surrounding waters. *3501 S. Roosevelt Blvd., tel. 305/296–6206 or 305/296–3913. Admission: $3 adults, $1 children. Open daily 9:30–5.*

Continue west on South Roosevelt Boulevard past Smathers Beach on your left. To your right are the **salt ponds,** where early residents evaporated seawater to collect salt. This area, a vestige of the old Key West, and for years a wildlife sanctuary, in 1991 was saved from intensive development when conservation-minded groups joined forces to acquire the remaining acreage. Today, instead of more condominiums, there's Little Hamaca Park, with a boardwalk leading into the natural area. Where South Roosevelt Boulevard ends at Bertha Street, turn right, then make the first left onto Atlantic Avenue. Near White Street are **Higgs Memorial Beach** (a Monroe County 35 park) and **West Martello Tower,** a fort built in 1861 and used as a lookout post during the Spanish-American War. Within its walls the Key West Garden Club maintains an art gallery and tropical garden. *Tel. 305/294–3210. Donations accepted. Open Wed.–Sun. 10–11:30 AM and 1–3:30 PM.*

Take White Street 9 blocks north to Duncan Street, turn right, (36) and go 3 blocks to **Tennessee Williams's House** (1431 Duncan St., at the corner of Duncan and Leon Sts.), a modest Bahamian-style cottage where the playwright lived from 1949 until his death in 1983.

Shopping

Throughout the Keys many shopping centers cater to the basic needs of locals and visitors alike. In season, supermarkets and roadside stands sell tropical fruits. Look for Key limes (April to January), guavas (August to October), lychee nuts (June), and sapodillas (February to March).

Key West In Key West's Old Town, you'll find specialty shops with international reputations:

Fast Buck Freddie's. Imaginative items you'd never dream of are sold here, including battery-operated alligators that eat Muenster cheese, banana leaf–shaped furniture, fish-shaped flatwear, and every flamingo item anyone's ever come up with. The 100 feet of Duval Street windows change every three weeks and always pick up on holiday themes (witches on broomsticks hang from the ceiling for Fantasy Fest, red carpet is rolled out for Christmas and tree lights are in tropical fish shapes). This is not only a unique place to shop, but it's also a great spot to retreat to when you've had enough sun. *500 Duval St., tel. 305/294–2007. AE, D, MC, V. Open daily 10–6. Closed Thanksgiving, Christmas, Easter.*

Greenpeace. This store, opened in 1983, is operated by Greenpeace, an international conservation organization known for its efforts to prevent the killing of whales and seals. Conservation-oriented educational materials, gift items, and T-shirts are sold here. *719 Duval St., tel. 305/296–4442. AE, MC, V. Open Mon.–Sat. 10–10, Sun. 10–6.*

Key West Aloe. A company founded in a garage in 1971, Key West Aloe today produces some 300 perfume, sunscreen, and skin-care products for men and women. When you visit the factory store, you can watch the staff measure and blend ingredients, then fill and seal the containers. *Main store: 524 Front St., tel. 305/294–5592, 800/445–2563 (US). Open daily 9–8. Factory store: Greene and Simonton Sts. AE, D, DC, MC, V. Open 9–5, production weekdays 9–5. Free self-guided tour.*

Key West Hand Print Fabrics. In the 1960s, Lilly Pulitzer's designs made Key West Hand Print Fabrics famous. Shoppers can watch workers making handprinted fabric on five 50-yard-long tables in the Curry Warehouse, a brick building erected in 1878 to store tobacco. *201 Simonton St., tel. 305/294–9535. AE, MC, V. Open daily 10–6.*

Tikal Trading Co. Since 1975, owners George and Barbara Webb have designed, produced, and sold double-stitched women's clothing of hand-woven Guatemalan cotton. *129 Duval St., tel. 305/296–4463. AE, MC, V. Open daily 10–10.*

Just east of Key West Seaport is Key West Bight. Popular storefronts there include the following:

Old Town Fish Market (513 Green St., tel. 305/294–8046) is one place to go for good daily catches.

Waterfront Baits & Tackle. (201 William St., tel. 305/292–1961). This store sells bait and fishing gear.
Waterfront Fish Market, Inc. (201 William St., tel. 305/294–8046). Fresh seafood is the draw here.
Waterfront Market. (201 William St., tel. 305/294–8418 or 305/296–0778). Health and gourmet foods, deli items, fresh produce, and salads are featured.

Ever since John James Audubon came to Key West in 1832, artists have flocked to the Florida Keys. Today's flourishing art community provides a rich array of merchandise for galleries throughout the Keys.

The Rain Barrel on Islamorada represents 450 local and national artists and has eight resident artists in a 3-acre crafts village attended by free-running cats. The third weekend of March each year the largest arts show of the Keys takes place here, when some 20,000 visitors view the work of 100 artists. *MM 86.7, BS, 86700 Overseas Hwy., Islamorada, tel. 305/852–3084. AE, MC, V. Open daily 9–5; closed Thanksgiving and Christmas.*
Lane Gallery specializes in Key West artists. *1000 Duval St., Key West, tel. 305/294–0067. AE, MC, V. Open daily 11–6; closed Sept.*
Gingerbread Square Gallery, the oldest gallery in Key West, owned by former two-time Key West Mayor Richard Heyman, mainly represents Keys artists who have attained national prominence. *1200 Duval St., Key West, tel. 305/296–8900. AE, MC, V. Open winter, daily 11–6; summer, Thurs.–Mon.*
Haitian Art Co. sells the works of 200-plus Haitian artists. *600 Frances St., Key West, tel. 305/296–8932. AE, D, DC, MC, V. Open daily 10–6.*

Participant Sports

Biking

A bike path parallels the Overseas Highway from Key Largo through Tavernier and onto Plantation Key, from MM 106 (at the Route 905 junction) to MM 86 (near the Monroe County Sheriff's Substation). The **Marathon** area is popular with bikers. Some of the best areas include the paths along Aviation Boulevard on the bay side of Marathon Airport; the new four-lane section of the Overseas Highway through Marathon; Sadowski Causeway to Key Colony Beach; Sombrero Beach Road from the Overseas Highway to the Marathon public beach; the roads on Boot Key (across a bridge from Vaca Key on 20th Street, OS); and a 2-mile section of the old Seven Mile Bridge that remains open to Pigeon Key, where locals like to ride to watch the sunset.

Key West is a cycling town, but many tourists aren't accustomed to driving with so many bikes around, so ride carefully. Some hotels rent bikes to their guests; others will refer you to a nearby bike shop and reserve a bike for you.

Key Largo Bikes stocks adult, children's, and tandem bikes, all single-speed with coaster brakes, and multispeed mountain bikes. *MM 99.4, 99275 Overseas Hwy., Key Largo, tel. 305/451–1910. MC, V. Open Tues.–Sat. 9:30–6.*
KCB Bike Shop rents single-speed adult and children's bikes. *MM 53 (11518 Overseas Hwy.), Marathon, tel. 305/289–1670. MC, V. Open weekdays 8:30–5, Sat. 8:30–2. Closed Sun.*

Keys Moped & Scooter rents beach cruisers with large baskets as well as mopeds and scooters. *523 Truman Ave., Key West, tel. 305/294–0399. AE, D, DC, MC, V. Open daily 9–6. Closed Thanksgiving, Christmas, New Year's Day.*

Camping The State of Florida operates recreational-vehicle and tent campgrounds in **John Pennekamp Coral Reef State Park,** MM 102.5 (Box 487, Key Largo 33037, tel. 305/451–1202); **Long Key State Recreation Area,** MM 67.5 (Box 776, Long Key 33001, tel. 305/664–4815); and **Bahia Honda State Recreation Area,** MM 36.5 (Rte. 1, Box 782, Big Pine Key 33043, tel. 305/872–2353). Bahia Honda also has rental cabins. Best bet to reserve one is to call 8 AM 60 calendar days before your planned visit.

The **Florida Campground Association** (1638 N. Plaza Dr., Tallahassee 32308, tel. 904/656–8878) publishes a free annual directory of over 200 member campgrounds in 11 regions. The Keys are in Region L, which lists 12 commercial campgrounds from Key Largo to Key West. The guide is available at Florida Welcome Centers or by mail.

Diving Although there are reefs and wrecks all along the east coast of Florida, the state's most extensive diving grounds are in the Keys. Divers come for the quantity and quality of living coral reefs within 6 or 7 miles of shore, the kaleidoscopic beauty of 650 species of tropical fish, and the adventure of probing wrecked ships that foundered in these seemingly tranquil seas during almost four centuries of exploration and commerce. A popular dive destination is the 9-foot **Christ of the Deep** statue, a gift to the Underwater Society of America from an Italian dive equipment manufacturer. The statue is about 6 miles east-northeast of Key Largo's South Cut in about 25 feet of water. It's a smaller copy of the 50-foot Christ of the Abysses off Genoa, Italy.

Much of the Keys' expanse of coral reefs is protected in federal, state, and county parks and sanctuaries. From Key Biscayne south almost to Key Largo, **Biscayne National Park** (*see* Chapter 5) encompasses most of Biscayne Bay, its barrier islands, and the patch reefs eastward to a depth of 60 feet. Biscayne National Park's southern boundary is the northern boundary of John Pennekamp Coral Reef State Park and Key Largo National Marine Sanctuary.

John Pennekamp Coral Reef State Park encompasses 78 square miles of coral reefs, sea grass beds, and mangrove swamps on the Atlantic Ocean side of Key Largo. The park is 21 miles long and extends to the seaward limit of state jurisdiction 3 miles offshore. Its reefs contain 40 of the 52 species of coral in the Atlantic Reef System. *MM 102.5, OS, tel. 305/451–1201. Park admission: $3.25 per car for up to 8 persons, plus $1 per additional person, and 50¢ per person county surcharge. Park open daily 8 AM–sunset. Coral Reef Park Co., a concessionaire, offers glass-bottom boat, scuba, sailing, and snorkeling tours: Box 1560, Key Largo 33037, tel. 305/451–1621. AE, MC, V. Concession open daily 8–5:30.*

The **Key Largo National Marine Sanctuary** (Box 1083, Key Largo 33037, tel. 305/451–1644) protects 103 square miles of coral reefs from the eastern boundary of John Pennekamp Coral Reef State Park, 3 miles off Key Largo, to a depth of 300 feet some 8 miles offshore. Managed by the National Oceanic and Atmospheric Administration (NOAA), the sanctuary includes Elbow,

French, and Molasses reefs; the 1852 Carysfort Lighthouse and its surrounding reefs; Christ of the Deep; Grecian Rocks, Key Largo Rocks, and the torpedoed WW II freighter *Benwood*.

San Pedro Underwater Archaeological Preserve. The state recently established this underwater park in 18 feet of water about a mile off the western tip of Indian Key. The *San Pedro* was part of a Spanish treasure fleet wrecked by a hurricane in 1733. You can get there on the *Coral Sea*, a 40-passenger glass-bottom dive and snorkel boat, from the dive shop at Bud 'n' Mary's Fishing Marina. *MM 79.5 OS, Box 1126, Islamorada, tel. 305/664–2211. 3-hr trips at 9 AM and 1:30 PM. Call for reservations. Cost: $15 adults, $7.50 children under 12. AE, D, MC, V.*

Marathon Marine Sanctuary. Monroe County recently established its first underwater park off the Middle Keys in Hawk Channel opposite MM 50, OS. It runs from Washerwoman Shoal on the west to navigation marker 48 on the east. The 2-square-mile park contains a dozen patch reefs ranging from the size of a house to about an acre. *Greater Marathon Chamber of Commerce, MM 49, BS, 330 Overseas Hwy., Marathon, tel. 305/743–5417 or 800/842–9580.*

National Key Deer Refuge (Box 510, Big Pine Key 33043, tel. 305/872–2239) and **Great White Heron National Wildlife Refuge.** Reefs where the Keys' northern margin drops off into the Gulf of Mexico attract fewer divers than the better-known Atlantic Ocean reefs. A favorite Gulf spot for local divers is the Content Keys, 5 miles off Big Pine Key (MM 30).

Looe Key National Marine Sanctuary (Rte. 1, Box 782, Big Pine Key 33043, tel. 305/872–4039). Many divers say Looe Key Reef, 5 miles off Ramrod Key (MM 27.5), is the most beautiful and diverse coral community in the entire region. It has large stands of elkhorn coral on its eastern margin, large purple sea fans, and ample populations of sponges and sea urchins. On its seaward side, it has an almost-vertical dropoff to a depth of 50–90 feet. The reef is named for H.M.S. *Looe*, a British warship wrecked there in 1744.

From shore or from a boat, snorkelers can easily explore grass flats, mangrove roots, and rocks in shallow water almost anywhere in the Keys. You may see occasional small clusters of coral and fish, mollusks, and other sea creatures. Ask dive shops for snorkeling information and directions. Diving and snorkeling are prohibited around bridges and near certain keys.

Dive shops all over the state organize Keys dives and offer diving instruction. South Florida residents fill dive boats on weekends, so plan to dive Monday through Thursday, when the boats and reefs are less crowded.

Jules Undersea Lodge, the world's first underwater hotel, takes reservations 30 days in advance from divers who want to stay in its two-room lodge in 30 feet of water. A resort course for new divers is offered. PADI and NAUI affiliations. *MM 103.2, OS, Box 3330, Key Largo 33037, tel. 305/451–2353. AE, D, MC, V.*

Dive Shops All of the dive shops listed below organize dives, fill air tanks, and sell or rent all necessary diving equipment. All have NAUI and/or PADI affiliation.

Quiescence Diving Service, Inc. Six people per boat. *MM 103.5, BS, 103680 Overseas Hwy., Key Largo, tel. 305/451–2440. AE, MC, V. Open daily 8–6. Closed Thanksgiving, Christmas.*
Capt. Corky's Diver's World of Key Largo. A reef and wreck diving package is available. Reservations accepted for wreck diving of the *Benwood*, Coast Guard cutters *Bibb* and *Duane*, and French and Molasses reefs. *MM 99.5, OS, Box 1663, Key Largo 33037, tel. 305/451–3200, outside FL 800/445–8231. MC, V. Open daily 8–5. Closed Thanksgiving, Christmas.*
Florida Keys Dive Center organizes dives from John Pennekamp Coral Reef State Park to Alligator Light. This center has two Coast Guard–approved dive boats and offers training from introductory scuba through instructor course. *MM 90.5, OS, 90500 Overseas Hwy., Box 391, Tavernier, tel. 305/852–4599 or 800/433–8946. AE, MC, V. Open daily 8–5.*
Treasure Divers, Inc., tucked just across Snake Creek Bridge on Windley Key, is a full-service dive shop with instructors, that arranges dives to reefs, Spanish galleons, and other wrecks. *MM 85.5, BS, 85500 Overseas Hwy., Islamorada, tel. 305/664–5111 or 800/356–9887. AE, MC, V. Open daily 8–5.*
Hall's Dive Center and Career Institute offers trips to Looe Key, Sombrero Reef, Delta Shoal, Content Key, and Coffins Patch. *MM 48.5, BS, 1994 Overseas Hwy., Marathon, tel. 305/743–5929 or 800/331–4255. AE, D, MC, V. Open daily 9–6.*
Looe Key Dive Center. This is the dive shop closest to Looe Key National Marine Sanctuary, a 5-star PADI facility in the lower Keys. In connection with its resort, the center offers overnight dive packages. *MM 27.5, OS, Box 509, Ramrod Key, tel. 305/872–2215 or 800/942–5397. MC, V. Open daily 7:30–6.*
Captain's Corner. Seven full-time instructors provide dive classes in English, French, German, Italian, and Japanese. All captains are licensed dive masters. Reservations are accepted for regular reef and wreck diving, spear and lobster fishing, and archaeological and treasure hunting. The shop also runs fishing charters and a 60-foot dive boat—*Sea Eagle*—which departs daily. *Store at 513 Greene St., Key West, tel. 305/296–8918. Open 9–5. Booth at Zero Duval St., Key West, tel. 305/296–8865. Dive boat departs 9:30 and 1:30. Cost: $20 snorkeling, children half price; $30 scuba. AE, MC, V. Booth open daily 8 AM–11 PM.*

Fishing and Boating

Fishing is popular throughout the Keys. You have a choice of deep-sea fishing on the ocean or the gulf or flat-water fishing in the mangrove-fringed shallows of the backcountry. Each of the areas protected by the state or federal government has its own set of rigorously enforced regulations. Check with your hotel or a local chamber of commerce office to find out what the rules are in the area where you're staying. The same sources can refer you to a reliable charter-boat or party-boat captain who will take you where the right kind of fish are biting.

Glass-bottom boats, which depart daily (weather permitting) from docks throughout the Keys, are popular with visitors who want to admire the reefs without getting wet. If you're prone to seasickness, don't try to look through the glass bottom in rough seas.

Motor yachts, sailboats, Hobie Cats, Windsurfers, canoes, and other water-sports equipment are all available for rent by the day or on a long-term basis. Some hotels have their own rental services; others will refer you to a separate vendor.

Treasure Harbor Marine on Plantation Key rents bare sailboats, from a 19-foot Cape Dory to 65-foot custom-built ketch; and powerboats, from a 32-foot Bayliner to a 42-foot Grand Banks. Captains and provisions available. In 1990 Treasure Harbor combined with Florida-Bahamas Sailing Charters and now offers American Sailing Association courses. Inquire for times and charges. No pets are allowed. *MM 86.5, OS, 200 Treasure Harbor Dr., Islamorada, tel. 305/852–2458 or 800/ FLA–BOATS, fax 305/852–5743. Reservations and advance deposit required; $100 per day captain fee. AE, MC, V. Open 9–6.*

Golf Two of the five golf courses in the Keys are open to the public:

Key Colony Beach Par 3. Nine-hole course near Marathon. *MM 53.5, 8th St., Key Colony Beach, tel. 305/289–1533. Fees: $8 for 9 holes. Open 7:30 AM–7 PM.*
Key West Resort Golf Course. Eighteen-hole course on the bay side of Stock Island. *6450 E. Junior College Rd., Key West, tel. 305/294–5232. Fees: $37.45 18 holes with cart; $27.82 9 holes with cart.*

Beaches

Keys shorelines are either mangrove-fringed marshes or rock outcrops that fall away to mucky grass flats. Most pleasure beaches in the Keys are manmade, with sand imported from the U.S. mainland or the Bahamas. There are public beaches in **John Pennekamp Coral Reef State Park** (MM 102.5), **Long Key State Recreation Area** (MM 67.5), **Sombrero Beach** in Marathon (MM 50), **Bahia Honda State Recreation Area** (MM 36.5), and at many roadside turnouts along the Overseas Highway. Many hotels and motels also have their own small shallow-water beach areas.

When you swim in the Keys, wear an old pair of tennis shoes to protect your feet from rocks, sea-urchin spines, and other potential hazards.

Key West **Smathers Beach.** This beach features almost 2 miles of sand beside South Roosevelt Boulevard. Trucks along the road will rent you rafts, Windsurfers, and other beach "toys."
Higgs Memorial Beach. Near the end of White Street, this is a popular sunbathing spot. A nearby grove of Australian pines provides shade and the **West Martello Tower** provides shelter should a storm suddenly sweep in.
Dog Beach. At Vernon and Waddell streets, this is the only beach in Key West where dogs are allowed.
Southernmost Beach. On the Atlantic Ocean at the foot of Duval Street, this spot is popular with tourists at nearby motels. It has limited parking and a nearby buffet-type restaurant.
Fort Zachary Taylor State Historic Site. The beach here, several hundred yards of shoreline near the western end of Key West, adjoins a picnic area with barbecue grills in a stand of Australian pines. The restoration project begun in 1989 has leveled the beach after much sand erosion. Snorkeling is good except when winds blow from the south-southwest. This beach is relatively uncrowded and attracts more locals than tourists.
Simonton Street Beach. At the north end of Simonton Street, facing the Gulf of Mexico, this is a great place to watch boat traffic in the harbor, but parking here is difficult.
Two hotels in Key West have notable beaches:

Pier House (1 Duval St.) A beach club for locals and patrons of certain nearby guest houses is available here.

Several hotels allow varying degrees of undress on their beaches. Pier House permits female guests on its beach to go topless, and topless bathing is acceptable at the **Atlantic Shores Motel** (510 South St.). Contrary to popular belief, the rangers at Fort Taylor beach do *not* allow nude bathing.

Dining

By Rosalie Leposky

Don't be misled by the expression *Key-easy*. Denizens of the Florida Keys may be relaxed and wear tropical-casual clothes, but these folks take food seriously. A number of young, talented chefs have settled here in the last few years to enjoy the climate and contribute to the Keys' growing image as a fine-dining center. Best-known among them is Doug Shook, who made his reputation at Louie's Backyard, along with lately departed (for Miami Beach's Art Deco District) Norman Van Aken, whose book, *Feast of the Sunlight* (Random House, 1988) describes the delights of Key West's "fusion cuisine," a blend of Florida citrus, seafood, and tropical fruits with Southwestern chilis, herbs, and spices.

The restaurant menus, the rum-based fruit beverages, and even the music reflect the Keys' tropical climate and their proximity to Cuba and other Caribbean islands. The better American and Cuban restaurants serve imaginative and tantalizing dishes that incorporate tropical fruits and vegetables, including avocado, carambola (star fruit), mango, and papaya.

Freshly caught local fish have been on every Keys menu in the past, but that is starting to change. The Keys' growing population has degraded the environment, disrupting fisheries and pricing fishermen out of the local housing market. Because many venerable commercial fish houses have abandoned the business in the past decade, there's a good chance the fish you order in a Keys restaurant may have been caught somewhere else. Since 1985, the U.S. government has protected the queen conch as an endangered species, so any conch you order in the Keys has come fresh-frozen from the Bahamas, Belize, or the Caribbean. Florida lobster and stone crab should be local and fresh from August through March.

Purists will find few examples of authentic Key lime pie: a yellow lime custard in a Graham-cracker crust with a meringue top. Many restaurants now serve a version made with white-pastry crust and whipped cream, which is easy to prepare and hold for sale. For the real thing, try **Papa Joe's** (MM 79.7 BS, Islamorada on Upper Matecumbe Key) or **Mangrove Mama's** (MM 20 BS, Sugarloaf Key).

The list below is a representative selection of independent restaurants in the Keys, organized by mile marker (MM) number in descending order, as you would encounter them when driving down from the mainland. Small restaurants may not follow the hours listed here. Sometimes they close for a day or a week, or cancel lunch for a month or two, just by posting a note on the door.

Highly recommended restaurants are indicated by a star ★.

Category	Cost*
Very Expensive	over $55
Expensive	$35–$55
Moderate	$15–$35
Inexpensive	under $15

**per person, excluding drinks, service, 6% state sales tax, and local tourist tax*

Florida City

Alabama Jack's. In 1953 Alabama Jack Stratham opened his restaurant on two barges at the end of Card Sound Road, 13 miles south of Homestead in an old fishing community between Card and Barnes sounds. The spot, something of a no-man's-land, belongs to the Keys in spirit thanks to the Card Sound toll bridge, which joined the mainland to upper Key Largo in 1969. Regular customers include Keys fixtures such as balladeer Jimmy Buffett, Sunday cyclists, local retirees, boaters who tie up at the restaurant's dock, and anyone else fond of dancing to country-western music and clapping for cloggers. You can also admire the tropical birds cavorting in the nearby mangroves and the occasional crocodile swimming up the canal. Though Jack's been gone since the early 1980s, owner Phyllis Sague has kept the favorites, including peppery homemade crab cakes; crispy-chewy conch fritters; crunchy breaded shrimp; homemade tartar sauce; and a tangy cocktail sauce with horseradish. Ask about availability of a 6-passenger dive boat. *58000 Card Sound Rd., tel. 305/248–8741. No reservations. Dress: casual. No credit cards. Open 8:30–7. Live band Sat.–Sun. 2–7. Moderate.*

Key Largo

Crack'd Conch. Behind the white clapboard lattice exterior and the green and violet trim, foreign money and patrons' business cards festoon the main dining room, where vertical bamboo stakes support the bar. There's also a screened outdoor porch. Specialties include conch (cracked and in chowder, fritters, and salad), fried alligator, smoked chicken, and 89 kinds of beer. *MM 105, OS, Rte. 1, 105045 Overseas Hwy., tel. 305/451–0732. No reservations. Dress: casual. AE. Open Thurs.–Tues. noon–10. Closed Wed.; Tues. from Easter through Memorial Day, and Sept. through Christmas. Moderate.*

Harriette's Retreat. Typical of one of those roadside places where the Coca-Cola sign appears larger than the restaurant's, and where tidying is always in order—although recently Harriette's has seen some refurbishments—this place hangs thick with down-home personality. Owner Harriette Mattson makes it her business to know many of her guests by name, and even takes the trouble to remember what they eat. Wise-cracking waitresses, perfectly styled for this joint, will tell you that the three-egg omelet is usually a six-egg omelet because Harriette has a heavy hand. Light on prices, though, this 48-seater that Harriette calls "a hash house, not a gourmet house" is famous for its breakfasts: featuring steak and eggs with hash browns or grits and toast and jelly for $5.95; or old-fashioned hot cakes with whipped butter and syrup and sausage or bacon for $3.25. Count on a strictly homey, tacky atmosphere with crafts and photos on consignment. *MM 95.7, 95710 Overseas Hwy., BS, Key Largo, tel. 305/852–8689. No reservations. Dress: casual. Open 6–2. No credit cards. Closed Thanksgiving, Christmas. Inexpensive.*

★ **Mrs. Mac's Kitchen.** Hundreds of beer cans, beer bottles, and expired auto license plates from all over the world decorate the walls of this wood-paneled, open-air restaurant. At lunchtime, the counter and booths fill up early with locals. Regular nightly specials are worth the stop: meatloaf on Monday, Mexican on Tuesday, Italian on Wednesday, and seafood Thursday through Saturday. The chili is always good, and the imported beer of the month is $1.50 a bottle or can. Open 7 AM–9:30 PM. *MM 99.4, Rte. 1, tel. 305/451–3722. No reservations. Dress: casual. No credit cards. Closed Sun. and major holidays. Inexpensive.*

Islamorada **Green Turtle Inn.** Photographs of locals and famous visitors dating from 1947 line the walls and stuffed turtle dolls dangle from the ceiling over the bar. Henry Rosenthal, the restaurant's third owner, retains the original menu cover and some of the original dishes. Specialties include a turtle chowder; conch fritters, nicely browned outside, light and fluffy inside; conch salad with vinegar, lime juice, pimiento, and pepper; alligator steak (tail meat) sautéed in an egg batter; and Key lime pie. Whole pies are available for carryout. *MM 81.5, OS, tel. 305/664–9031. No reservations. Dress: casual. AE, D, DC, MC, V. Closed Mon. and Thanksgiving Day. Moderate.*

★ **Marker 88.** The best seats in chef/owner Andre Mueller's main dining room catch the last glimmers of sunset. Hostesses recite a lengthy list of daily specials and offer you a wine list with more than 200 entries. You can get a good steak or veal chop here, but 75% of the food served is seafood. Specialties include a robust conch chowder; banana blueberry bisque; salad Trevisana, made with radicchio, leaf lettuce, Belgium endive, watercress, and sweet-and-sour dill dressing (President Bush's favorite); sautéed conch or alligator steak meunière; grouper Rangoon, served with chunks of papaya, banana, and pineapple in a cinnamon and currant jelly sauce; and Key lime pie. *MM 88 Overseas Hwy., BS, Plantation Key, tel. 305/852–9315. Reservations advised. Dress: casual. AE, DC, MC, V. Dinner only. Closed Mon. Moderate.*

Papa Joe's Landmark Restaurant. Never mind the heavily chlorinated water and the pasty white bread when you can savor succulent dolphin and fresh green beans and carrots al dente. Here, they will still clean and cook your own catch: $8.95 up to 1 pound per person fried, broiled, sautéed; $10.95 any other style, which includes meunière, blackened, coconut-dipped, Cajun, amandine, or Oscar (sautéed, topped with béarnaise sauce, crabmeat, and asparagus). Joe's—which first opened under another name in 1937—reopened in 1991 after an 18-month remodeling project which includes an upper-level, over-the-water tiki bar with 25 seats. "Early American dump," is how owner Frank Curtis describes the look: captain's chairs, mounted fish, hanging baskets, fish buoys, and driftwood strung year-round with Christmas lights. The decor never gets ahead of the food, which is first rate. An early bird menu from 4 to 6 PM is priced $7.95–$8.95. For dessert dive into the Grand Marnier cheesecake, the mud pie, or the rum chocolate cake. *MM 79.7 Overseas Hwy., BS, tel. 305/664–8756. No reservations. Dress: casual. AE, MC, V. Open daily 11–10. Closed Thanksgiving, Christmas. Moderate.*

Whale Harbor Inn. This coral rock building has oyster shells cemented onto the walls, an old Florida Keys bottle collection, and a water mark at the 7-foot mark as a reminder of Hurricane

Donna's fury in 1960. Several restaurant employees rode out the storm in the building's lighthouse tower. The main attraction is a 50-foot-long all-you-can-eat buffet, which includes a stir-fry area for wok cookery and a plentiful supply of shrimp, mussels, crayfish, and snow crab legs. In 1991 seating was expanded from 300 to 400 places in the main Grotto Dining Room, a second buffet set up, and a second lounge opened. The adjoining Dockside Restaurant and Lounge are open for breakfast. The raw bar and grill are open to midnight. *MM 83.5, OS, Upper Matecumbe Key, tel. 305/664-4959. No reservations. Dress: casual. AE, DC, MC, V. Moderate.*

Marathon

Kelsey's. The walls in this restaurant at the Faro Blanco Marine Resort are hung with boat paddles inscribed by the regulars and celebrities such as Joe Namath and Ted Turner. All entrées here are served with fresh-made yeast rolls brushed with drawn butter and Florida orange honey. You can bring your own cleaned and filleted catch for the chef to prepare. Dessert offerings change nightly and may include Mrs. Kelsey's original macadamia pie (even though she's sold out and gone to the old Riverview Hotel in New Smyrna Beach) and Key lime cheesecake. *MM 48, BS, 1996 Overseas Hwy., tel. 305/743-9018. Reservations necessary. Dress: casual. Dinner only. AE, MC, V. Closed Mon. Moderate.*

Ship's Pub and Galley. The collection of historic photos on the restaurant walls depict the railroad era in the Keys, the development of Duck Key, and many of the notables who have visited here. Dinners include soup and a 40-item salad bar with all the steamed shrimp you can eat. Specialties include homemade garlic bread, Swiss onion soup, certified New York Angus beef, at least two fish specials, Florida stone crab claws (in season), and mile-high shoofly mud pie, a 6-inch-high coffee ice-cream pie with a whipped cream topping. The adjoining lounge has live entertainment and a dance floor. *MM 61, OS, tel. 305/743-7000, ext. 3627. Reservations accepted. Dress: casual. Early bird specials. AE, DC, MC, V. Moderate.*

Herbie's Bar. A local favorite for lunch and dinner since the 1940s, Herbie's has three small rooms with two bars. Indoor diners sit at wood picnic tables or the bar; those in the screened outdoor room use concrete tables. Specialties include spicy conch chowder with chunks of tomato and crisp conch fritters with homemade horseradish sauce. Nightly specials. *MM 50.5, BS, 6350 Overseas Hwy., tel. 305/743-6373. No reservations. Dress: casual. No credit cards. Closed Sun. and Easter–Nov. Inexpensive.*

★ **Mile 7 Grill.** This open-air diner built in 1954 at the Marathon end of Seven Mile Bridge has walls festooned with beer cans, mounted fish, sponges, and signs describing individual menu items. Specialties include conch chowder, fresh fish sandwich of the day, and a foot-long chili dog on a toasted sesame roll. Even if you're not a dessert eater, don't pass up the peanut butter pie, served near frozen, in a chocolate-flavored shell. Made with cream cheese, it's a cross between pudding and ice cream. *MM 47.5, BS, 1240 Overseas Hwy., tel. 305/743-4481. No credit cards. Open daily for lunch and dinner. Closed Wed.–Thurs., Christmas Eve–first Fri. after New Year's, and when they want to in Aug.–Sept. Inexpensive.*

Key West
American

★ **Louie's Backyard.** Abstract art and old Key West paintings adorn the interior of this Key West institution, while outside you dine under the mahoe tree and feel the cool breeze coming off the sea. The ambience, however, takes second place to chef Doug Shook's culinary expertise. The loosely Spanish-Caribbean menu changes twice yearly, but might include such house specials as pan-cooked quail stuffed with lobster and wild mushrooms in Madeira sauce or grilled sirloin steak with a rum-tamarind-chili glaze and roasted vegetables. Top off the meal with Louie's lime tart or an irresistible chocolate brownie brulée. *700 Waddell Ave., tel. 305/294–1061. Reservations advised. Dress: casual. AE, DC, MC, V. Very Expensive.*

★ **Pier House Restaurant.** Steamships from Havana once docked at this pier jutting out into the Gulf of Mexico. Now it's an elegant place to dine, indoors or out, and to watch boats gliding by in the harbor. At night the restaurant shines lights into the water, attracting schools of brightly colored parrot fish. The menu emphasizes tropical fruits, spices, and fish and includes grilled sea scallops with black bean cake and *pico de gallo* (tomato, shallots, cilantro, chopped chayote); lobster ravioli in a creamy pesto sauce and salmon caviar; and a seafood catch prepared with tomatillo vinaigrette and saffron aioli. Ordered specially, a poached yellowtail is served with broccoli flowerets and red peppers triangulated on alternate rounds of yellow and green squash. Even simple food becomes art. *1 Duval St., tel. 305/296–4600, ext. 555. Reservations advised. Dress: neat but casual. AE, DC, MC, V. Very Expensive.*

Cafe Marquesa. Only 15 tables and banquettes, the secret of the cafe's success is its openness in all respects. It is open to innovative cuisine, it has a friendly staff, an open kitchen through a *trompe l'oeil* pantry mural—nothing's snooty about this place. Owners of the hotel now attract locals and visitors alike with affordable meals that include arugula salad with sun-dried tomatoes, fresh mushrooms, corn kernels, and bacon; a delicate, generously served blue corn pasta layered with spinach, mushrooms, red bell peppers, ricotta and parmesan cheeses, with a vegetarian béchamel on a bed of zucchini coulis; grilled shrimp with *piripiri* sauce (a salsa of tomatoes, chilis, garlic, cilantro, and shallots). Limitless helpings of the excellent sesame flatbread with black pepper accompany all meals. For dessert try the fruit tart with kiwi, strawberries, and crème fraîche. *600 Fleming St., tel. 305/292–1244. Reservations accepted. Dress: neat but casual. AE, MC, V. Closed lunch and Tues. in summer. Moderate.*

Pepe's Cafe and Steak House. Judges, police officers, carpenters, and fisherpeople rub elbows every morning in their habitual breakfast seats, at three tables and four pine booths under a huge paddlefan. Outdoors are more tables and an open-air bar under a canvas tarp. Pepe's was established downtown in 1909 and moved to the current site in 1962. The specials change nightly: barbecued chicken, pork tenderloin, ribs, potato salad, red or black beans, and corn bread on Sunday; meatloaf on Monday; seafood Tuesday and Wednesday; a full traditional Thanksgiving dinner every Thursday; filet mignon on Friday; and prime rib on Saturday. *806 Caroline St., tel. 305/294–7192. No reservations. Dress: casual. D, MC, V. Moderate.*

Cuban

El Siboney. This family-style restaurant serves traditional Cuban food. Specials include chicken and rice every Friday, oxtail stew with rice and beans on Saturday. Always available are roast pork with *morros* (black beans and white rice) and cassava, paella, and *palomilla* steak. *900 Catherine St., tel. 305/296–4184. No reservations. Dress: casual. No credit cards. Closed*

Thanksgiving, Christmas, New Year's Day, 2 wks in June. Inexpensive.

Delicatessen

Market Bistro. The Pier House's deli and fine-dining snack shop, which recently added an espresso bar, sells the hotel's classic Key lime pie by the slice, as well as a chocolate decadence: a triple chocolate flourless torte with raspberry sauce and rose petals. A cooler holds tropical fruit juices, beer, and mineral water. Other specialties include sandwiches, salads, gourmet cheeses, pâtés, and homemade pastries. *1 Duval St. in the Pier House, tel. 305/296-4600. No reservations. Dress: casual. AE, DC, MC, V. Moderate.*

French

Cafe des Artistes. This intimate 75-seat restaurant occupies part of a hotel building constructed in 1935 by C. E. Alfeld, Al Capone's bookkeeper. Haitian paintings and Keys scenes by local artists decorate the walls. Dining is in two indoor rooms or on a roof-top open deck beneath a big sapodilla tree. Executive chef Andrew Berman presents a French interpretation of tropical cuisine, using fresh local seafood and produce and light, flour-free sauces. Specialties include the restaurant's award-winning lobster with Cognac, served with shrimp in a mango-saffron beurre blanc, the half roast duckling with raspberry sauce, and the *minute de snapper:* paper-thin slices of snapper flash-broiled and served with a tomato and basil sauce. *1007 Simonton St., tel. 305/294-7100. Reservations advised. Dress: neat but casual. AE, MC, V. No lunch. Expensive–Moderate.*

Italian

Antonia's. Since 1979 co-chefs Antonia Berto and Phillip Smith have turned out fluent northern Italian renditions of Keys' seafood with homemade pastas in this 1861 building, formerly the site of the Blue Boar Bar and the hippie coffeehouse Crazy Ophelia's. Behind the stained-glass "615" transom and bay windows is dining at its finest, including such dishes as homemade mozzarella appetizers, whole oven-roasted yellowtail snapper, and the generous dolphin fillet with subtle caper sauce. All pastas and breads are home baked. Many Italian wines are offered by the glass, but consider having a Peroni beer before dinner at the striped canvas–canopied bar overlooked by the bust of Caesar. Room for dessert? Try the tiramisù, cannoli, or Amaretto pie in coconut cream sauce. The ice creams and sorbets are made in house. *615 Duval St., tel. 305/294-6565. Reservations advised. Dress: neat but casual. MC, V. No lunch; Closed 1 month in summer. Moderate.*

Seafood
★

The Buttery. The Buttery's waiters have come to be known as "buttercups," a nickname they share with the house's special drink, a blended frozen concoction of vodka, Kahlúa, Amaretto, coconut milk, and cream. Each of the restaurant's six rooms has its own character. The back room with the bar has wood paneling, skylights, and lots of greenery; a small private dining room in front has green-painted woodwork, a crystal chandelier, and floral wallpaper. Another is eclectically tropical with bamboo chairs, dark louvered shutters, cut-tin lamps, and ceiling fans under the tall eave. All tables have hurricane lamps and fresh flowers. In its 14th year, The Buttery experiments with specials that find their way onto the seasonally changing menu. Lately rave-worthy were the scallops *Tova* (wrapped in salmon atop a spinach hollandaise sauce); steak "Ricardo" (fillets of tenderloin sautéed with mushrooms in Madeira wine sauce); and chilled Senegalese cream of celery soup made with curry, heavy cream, and mango chutney. *1208*

Simonton St., tel. 305/294–0717. Reservations advised. Dress: neat but casual. AE, D, DC, MC, V. Closed 2–3 wks in Sept. No lunch. Moderate.

Half Shell Raw Bar. "Eat It Raw" is the motto, and even off-season the oyster bar keeps shucking. You eat at shellacked picnic tables and benches in a shed, with ship models, life buoys, mounted dolphin, and old license plates hanging overhead. Classic signs offer homage to Keys' passions. Reads one: "Fishing is not a matter of life and death. It's more important than that." Once a fish market, the Half Shell looks out onto the deep-sea fishing fleet. Eat indoors or out. Specials, chalked on the blackboard, may include broiled dolphin sandwich or linguine seafood marinara. The same owners operate The Turtle Kraals Restaurant & Bar on the other side of Land's End Village. *Land's End Marina, tel. 305/294–7496. No reservations. Dress: casual. No credit cards. Moderate–Inexpensive.*

Dockside Bar and Raw Bar. When the crowds get too thick on the Mallory Dock at sunset, you can come up here, have a piña colada and a snack, and watch the action from afar. This establishment, on a 200-foot dock behind Ocean Key House, has a limited but flavorful menu: freshly smoked fish, crunchy conch salad, crispy conch fritters, steamed lobster (in season), potato salad, and shrimp. Live island music is featured nightly. *Ocean Key House, Zero Duval St., tel. 305/296–7701. No reservations. Dress: casual. AE, D, DC, MC, V. Inexpensive.*

Lodging

Some hotels in the Keys are historic structures with a charming patina of age; others are just plain old. Salty winds and soil play havoc with anything manmade in the Keys. Constant maintenance is a must, and some hotels and motels don't get it. Inspect your accommodations before checking in. The best rooms in the Keys have a clear bay or ocean view and a deep setback from the Overseas Highway.

The city of Key West offers the greatest variety of lodgings, from large resorts to bed-and-breakfast rooms in private homes. Altogether there are about 4,000 units (including about 1,500 rooms in close to 60 guest houses) as well as approximately 1,800 condominium apartments that are available for daily or weekly rental through their homeowners associations.

Accommodations in the Keys are more expensive than elsewhere in south Florida. In part this is due to the Keys' popularity and ability to command top dollar, but primarily it's because everything used to build and operate a hotel costs more in the Keys. All materials and supplies must be trucked in, and electric and water rates are among the steepest in the nation.

The Florida Keys and Key West Visitors Bureau provides a free accommodations guide (*see* Important Addresses and Numbers, above). The list below is a representative selection of hotels, motels, resorts, and guest houses. In the Upper, Middle, and Lower Keys outside Key West, we've listed hotels, motels, and resorts by mile marker (MM) number in descending order, as you would encounter them when driving down from the mainland.

Highly recommended hotels are indicated by a star ★.

Category	Cost*
Very Expensive	over $175
Expensive	$110–$175
Moderate	$75–$110
Inexpensive	under $75

**All prices are for a standard double room, excluding 7% state sales tax and local tourist tax.*

Key Largo

Holiday Inn Key Largo Resort & Marina. James W. Hendricks, the Kentucky attorney who restored the *African Queen*, completed renovations and new landscaping at this resort at the Key Largo Harbor Marina in 1989. The hotel was built in 1971, and a new wing was added in 1981. Decor includes blond wood furniture and a pink-and-green color scheme. *MM 100, OS, 99701 Overseas Hwy., 33037, tel. 305/451–2121, 800/HOLIDAY, or 800/THE KEYS. 132 rooms with bath, including nonsmoker rooms and rooms for handicapped guests. Facilities: 2 pools (1 with waterfall), Jacuzzi, marina with 35 transient spaces, gift shop, dive and glass-bottom tour boats, boat rentals. AE, MC, V. Expensive.*

Marina Del Mar Resort and Marina. This resort beside the Key Largo Harbor Canal caters to sailors and divers. All rooms contain original watercolors by Keys artist Mary Boggs and the best rooms are suites 502, 503 and 504, each of which has a full kitchen and plenty of room for large families or dive groups. The fourth-floor observation deck offers spectacular sunrise and sunset views. Advance reservations are suggested for boat slips. *MM 100, OS, Box 1050, 33037, tel. 305/451–4107, 800/451–3483 or 305/451–4107. 76 rooms with bath, including 8 nonsmoker suites, 16 studios with full kitchens, 16 nonsmoker rooms, and 3 rooms for handicapped guests. Facilities: in-room refrigerators, 40-slip full-service marina, showers and washing machines for marina guests, pool, 2 lighted tennis courts, weight room, washers and dryers on all floors, picnic tables, free Continental breakfast in lobby, restaurant and bar with live nightly entertainment, dive packages, diving and snorkeling charters, fishing charters. No pets. AE, DC, MC, V. Expensive.*

Sheraton Key Largo Resort. This is first of the large, amenity-filled, enclave resorts on the way south. Service can be impersonal, as happens at chain resorts, but day by day, one staff person or another wins you over (typically the chambermaids). The look of this four-story hotel, with hanging gardens, fits well in its surroundings. The three-story atrium with its windowpane and coral-rock walls, Mexican tile floor, and rattan furniture strikes the mood. Least desirable rooms are the 230, 330, and 430 series that overlook the parking lot, but all are spacious and comfortable. Mulched nature trails and boardwalks lead through hammocks to mangrove overlooks by the shore. (Bring bug spray for your walk.) Both Cafe Key Largo, for three meals a day, and Christina's, the gourmet dinner-only room, guarantee grand views three stories above the bay. *MM 97, BS, 97000 Overseas Hwy., 33037, tel. 305/852–5553, 800/325–3535 (US), 800/268–9393 (eastern Canada), or 800/268–9330 (western Canada). 200 rooms with bath, including 10 suites. Facilities: 2 heated pools, 2 lighted tennis courts, 2,000-foot labeled nature trail, sailboat and Windsurfer rental, fish-*

ing and dive charters, 21-slip dock for hotel guests, minibars, 2 restaurants, 3 lounges, beauty shop. AE, DC, MC, V. Expensive.

Largo Lodge. No two rooms are the same in this vintage 1950s resort. A dense palm alley sets the mood. Tropical gardens with more palms, sea grapes, and orchids surround the guest cottages. Late in the day, wild ducks, pelicans, herons, and other birds come looking for a handout from long-time owner Harriet "Hat" Stokes. *MM 101.5, BS, 101740 Overseas Hwy., 33037, tel. 305/451–0424 or 800/IN-THE-SUN. 6 apartments with kitchen, 1 efficiency. Facilities: 200 feet of bay frontage, public phone, boat ramp and 3 slips. Call for restrictions. AE, MC, V. Moderate.*

Sunset Cove Motel. Statues of lions, tigers, and dinosaurs seem to be attracting waterbirds that fly in each morning and afternoon, while an orphaned manatee swims by for a daily visit. The 10 guest units all have kitchens and original hand-painted murals. Special discounts are offered to senior citizens and members of conservation groups. *MM 99.5, BS, Box 99, 33037, tel. 305/451–0705. 10 units with bath and a dormitory group house with kitchen for up to 15 people. Facilities: free watersports equipment (canoes, glass-bottom and regular paddleboat, sailboats, trimaran, and Windsurfers), 115-foot fishing pier, boat ramp. MC, V. Moderate.*

Bay Harbor Lodge. Owner Laszlo Simoga speaks German, Hungarian, and Russian and caters to an international clientele. Situated on two heavily landscaped acres, this resort with a rustic wood lodge and several concrete-block structures had all its kitchens and bathrooms retiled in 1990. All cottages got individual barbecues in 1990, and several tiki huts were put up in 1991. Unit 14, a large efficiency apartment with a deck, has a wood ceiling, original oil paintings, and a dining table made from the hatch cover of a World War II Liberty Ship. *MM 97.5, BS, 97702 Overseas Hwy., 33037, tel. 305/852–5695. 16 rooms with bath. Facilities: Jacuzzi, saltwater shower, Olympic weightlifting equipment, individual outdoor barbecues, paddleboat, rowboats, canoes, 2 docks, cable TV, boat-trailer parking. No pets. D, MC, V. Moderate–Inexpensive.*

Islamorada

★ **Cheeca Lodge.** Winner in 1990 of the hotel industry's top environmental award, and host of an annual fund-raising dinner that benefits The Cousteau Society, this 27-acre low-rise resort on Upper Matecumbe Key satisfies both the leisure needs and environmental ethic of affluent travelers. Guests benefit from an underwater snorkel trail that explains marine ecology; Camp Cheeca employs marine science counselors to make learning about the fragile Keys environment fun for children aged 6–12. Biodegradable products are used, most everything is recycled, and the quiet setting is vouchsafed for guests by the resort's ban on motorized watersports that also reduces oily discharges into the water. Preserved at Cheeca is the beachfront pioneer burial ground of the Matecumbe United Methodist Church, and tranquil fish-filled lagoons and gardens surround. Guest rooms and suites feature periwinkle blue/strawberry, and green/hot orange color schemes; all have British Colonial-style furniture of tightly woven wicker, cane, and bamboo. Touches include intriguing hand-painted mirror frames, faintly surreal art prints and romantic waterscapes, and natural shell soapdishes. Ocean Suite 102 has a cathedral ceiling and a screened porch; fourth-floor rooms in the main lodge open onto a terrace with either ocean or bay views. The dining room features a carpet in light blue and ivory that resembles the beautiful, rippled pattern of sand that waves create. *MM 82, Upper Matecumbe Key, Box 527, 33036, tel. 305/664–4651 (Islamorada), or 305/245–3755 (Miami), or 800/327–2888 (US and FL). 203 rooms, including 64 suites, 60 nonsmoker rooms, and 5 rooms for handicapped guests. Facilities: in-room minibar, free golf-cart shuttle service around the resort, 9-hole par-3 executive golf course designed by Jack Nicklaus, 6 lighted tennis courts, 2 heated pools and one saltwater tidal pool, 525-foot fishing pier, 2 restaurants, lounge. Sun. brunch served in the Atlantic's Edge Dining Room. Beach Hut rents Hobie Cats, rafts, snorkeling and fishing gear, parasailing trips, and non-motorized boats. All-year children's program. AE, D, DC, MC, V. Very Expensive.*

Long Key

Lime Tree Bay Resort. Vic Bubnow and Phil DeMontmollin (retired from *The Miami Herald*), new owners since 1990, plan changes at this steadily improving 2.5-acre resort built in 1972. Each room is decorated differently. A palm tree grows through the floor of "The Treehouse," a two-bedroom unit with kitchen that is popular with larger families. You can swim and snorkel in the shallow grass flats just offshore. *MM 68.5, BS, Box 839, Layton, 33001, tel. 305/664–4740. 29 rooms with bath. Facilities: outdoor pool and Jacuzzi, tennis court, power and sailboat rentals, dive boats and charter boats, restaurant. No pets. AE, D, MC, V. Moderate–Inexpensive.*

Marathon

★ **Hawk's Cay Resort.** Morris Lapidus, architect of the Fontainebleau Hilton hotel in Miami Beach, designed this rambling West Indies-style resort, which opened in 1959 as the Indies Inn and Marina. Over the years it has entertained a steady stream of politicians (including Harry Truman, Dwight Eisenhower, and Lyndon Johnson) and film stars who come to relax and be pampered by a friendly, low-key staff. Hawk's Cay retains the comfortable ambience it has always had, even after an $8-million renovation of rooms, public areas, meeting space, and landscaping designed by architect Bill Cox and completed in 1989. The new decor features wickerwork rattan, a sea-green-and-salmon color scheme, and original contemporary artwork in guest rooms and public areas. Most rooms face the water. Twenty-two two-bedroom marina villas are available to hotel guests. *MM 61, OS, 33050, tel. 305/743–7000, 800/432–2242 (FL), 800/327–7775 (US). 177 rooms with bath, including 16 suites, 15 rooms for handicapped guests. Facilities: heated pool, 2 whirlpool spas, 1-mi fitness trail, 8 tennis courts, Tim Farwell's Tennis School, use of Sombrero Golf Course in Marathon, 70-slip full-service marina, PADI-certified and handicap diving certified dive boats, Club Nautico boat rentals, fishing and sailing charter boats, 4 restaurants, complimentary full-breakfast buffet, nightclub, 3 boutique and specialty shops, billiard room, video game room. $18-per-child daily summer and holidays program. AE, D, DC, MC, V. Very Expensive.*

Rainbow Bend Fishing Resort. First you notice the shocking-pink exterior, then the well-kept appearance of this 2.7-acre resort built in the late 1950s as a lumberyard and CIA base. Each guest room is uniquely decorated. A restaurant offering complimentary breakfast overlooks an ample manmade beach and barbecue area, good bonefish flats just a few yards offshore, and a dock with boats available free to guests, except for minimum $5 fuel charge. *MM 58, OS, Grassy Key, Route 1, Box 159, 33050, tel. 305/289–1505. 23 rooms with bath, including 19 suites, and efficiencies. Facilities: heated pool and Jacuzzi, small fishing pier, 4 hrs free use of 15-foot Boston Whaler, free use of sailboats and canoe, complete bait and tackle shop, restaurant. Free full breakfast. AE, MC, V. Expensive.*

Little Torch Key ★

Little Palm Island. The lobby is located off the Overseas Highway on Little Torch Key, but the resort itself is a 3-mile boat ride away on a palm-fringed island at the western end of the Newfound Harbor Keys. There you'll find 14 thatch-roof villas, each with two suites. An additional suite is located in the Great House, a cypress fishing lodge built in 1928. Each suite has a Mexican-tile bath and dressing area, Jacuzzi, beds draped with mosquito netting, and Mexican and Guatemalan wicker and rattan furniture, and a second, outdoor shower. Built on stilts 9 feet above mean high tide, all villas are 20 feet from the water. A 53-ft. motor yacht contains another suite called **The Sweet One.** The island is in the middle of Coupon Bight State Aquatic Preserve and is the closest point of land to the Looe Key National Marine Sanctuary. *MM 28.5, Overseas Highway, Route 4, Box 1036, 33042, tel. 305/872–2524 or 800/343–8567. 30 suites, 1 for handicapped guests. Facilities: air conditioners, wet bars and stocked refrigerators, room safes, heated lagoon-style pool, sauna, tiki bar, gift shop, exercise room, restaurant, 12-slip marina for hotel and restaurant guests, and for visiting yachters. Free on-the-hour launch service 7 AM–11 PM. Pickup from Marathon Airport and Key West International Airport, $80 per couple round-trip. Guided tours and excursions. Restaurant reservations: 305/872–2551. Very Expensive.*

Ramrod Key

Looe Key Reef Resort and Dive Center. The rooms in this two-story motel, which attracts divers because of its scuba facilities, were refurnished in 1987. In the tiny lobby, the front desk doubles as a package liquor store. Rooms are spartan but comfortable, with firm mattresses and ocean-blue bedspreads and carpets. The least desirable rooms are the three singles without a canal view. Guests can make an appointment for free pick-up from the private airstrip on Summerland Key. *MM 27.5, US 1, OS, Box 509, 33042, tel. 305/872–2215 or 800/942–5397 (outside 305 area, and continental U.S.). 23 rooms with bath, 1 for handicapped guests. Facilities: air conditioners, cable TV, outdoor pool, PADI-rated 5-star dive shop, 400 feet of boat dockage, 3 Coast Guard–certified dive boats, restaurant, pool-side tiki bar and raw bar. Dive and snorkel package rates available; discounts for groups. MC, V. Moderate–Inexpensive.*

Lower Sugarloaf Key

Sugar Loaf Lodge. This well-landscaped older motel overlooking mangrove islands and Upper Sugarloaf Sound has one building with soft beds and an eclectic assortment of furniture and another with high ceilings, wall murals, and balconies on the second floor. A friendly dolphin named Sugar inhabits a lagoon just outside the restaurant; diners can watch her perform through a picture window. *MM 17, BS, Box 148, 33044, tel. 305/745–3211. 55 rooms with bath. Facilities: pool, tennis court, 18-hole miniature golf course, restaurant, lounge, free dolphin performances at 9 AM, 1 PM, and 5 PM. AE, D, DC, MC, V. Moderate–Inexpensive.*

Key West
House and Condominium Rentals

Key West Reservation Service makes hotel reservations and helps visitors locate rental properties (hotels, motels, bed-and-breakfasts, oceanfront condominiums, luxury vacation homes). *628 Fleming St., Drawer 1689, 33040, tel. 305/294-7713, 800/356-3567 (FL), 800/327-4831 (US); fax 305/296-6291. AE, MC, V.*

Property Management of Key West, Inc., offers lease and rental service for condominiums, town houses, and private homes, including renovated Conch homes. *1213 Truman Ave., 33040, tel. 305/296-7744. AE, MC, V.*

Hotels and Motels

The Banyan Resort. A time-share resort across the street from the Truman Annex, the Banyan Resort includes five Victorian houses, a former cigar factory listed on the National Registry of Historic Places, and three modern buildings in the Victorian style. The award-winning gardens are a tropical cornucopia of avocado, Barbados cherry, eggfruit, papaya, Persian lime, and sapodilla. The rooms have a gray, maroon, and mauve color scheme and rattan and wicker furniture. *323 Whitehead St., 33040, tel. 305/296-7786 or 800/225-0639. 38 suites with bath. Facilities: 2 pools (1 heated), Jacuzzi, bar. Call for restrictions. AE, D, MC, V. Very Expensive.*

Hyatt Key West. A first for Hyatt, this "baby grand" resort consists of three four-story buildings surrounding a tropical piazza. The lobby features a Mexican terra-cotta tile floor and cherry wood fixtures; the room decor employs mint, lilac, peach, and teal blue hues with light-wood dressers and wicker chairs. *601 Front St., 33040, tel. 305/296-9900, 800/233-1234, 800/228-9005 (HI, AK), or 800/233-1234. 120 rooms with bath, including 4 suites, 16 nonsmoker rooms, and 6 rooms for handicapped guests. Facilities: pool, Jacuzzi, hot tub, fitness room, massage studio, small private manmade beach, bicycle and motor scooter rental, 6-slip marina, 60-ft rental ketch. AE, DC, MC, V. Very Expensive.*

★ **The Marquesa Hotel.** Key West architect Thomas Pope supervised the restoration of this four-story 1884 home and added onto it in a compatible style. The lobby resembles a Victorian parlor, with antique furniture, Audubon prints, fresh flowers, wonderful photos of early Key West, including one of Harry Truman driving by in an open convertible, and a bowl of apples for nibbles. Rooms have Queen Anne and eclectic antique and reproduction furnishings and dotted Swiss curtains. There are marble vanities in some baths, marble floors in others. Continental breakfast is served poolside ($6 extra). *600 Fleming St., 33040, tel. 305/292-1919 or 800/869-4631. 15 rooms with bath. Facilities: heated pool, room service, 24-hr staff, in-room safe, free off-street parking. AE, MC, V. Very Expensive.*

Marriott's Casa Marina Resort. Henry Morrison Flagler's heirs built La Casa Marina in 1921 at the end of the Florida East Coast Railroad line. The entire 13-acre resort revolves around an outdoor patio and lawn facing the ocean. The lobby, with beamed ceiling, polished Dade County pine floor, and wicker furniture and rooms decorated in mauve and green pastels and Key West scenes exude elegance. Among the best rooms are the two-bedroom loft suites with balconies facing the ocean, and the lanai rooms on the ground floor of the main building with French doors opening directly onto the lawn. In 1990 the grand ballroom was opulently restored, and Flagler's (formerly Henry's), the showplace dining room, was made less formal to keep pace with its lighter cuisine that emphasizes pasta and seafood. *1500 Reynolds St., 33040, tel. 305/296–3535, 800/235–4837 (FL), 800/228–9290 (US). 314 rooms with bath, including 63 suites, 16 nonsmoker rooms, 4 rooms for handicapped guests. Facilities: heated pool, whirlpool, 600-ft fishing pier, health club, massage studio and sauna, 3 tennis courts, 2 gift shops, activity center for children, game room, restaurant, poolside bar. Key West Water Sports, a concessionaire, offers deep-sea charter boats, light-tackle fishing, party-boat fishing, Hobie Cats, Sunfish, jet skis, scuba and snorkel trips, bicycle and moped rentals. AE, DC, MC, V. Very Expensive.*

La Concha Holiday Inn. This seven-story Art Deco hotel in the heart of downtown Key West is the city's tallest building and dates to 1926. The lobby's polished floor of pink, mauve, and green marble and a conversation pit with comfortable chairs are among the details beloved by la Concha's guests. Large rooms are furnished with 1920s-era antiques, lace curtains, and big closets. The restorers kept the old building's original louvered room doors, light globes, and floral trim on the archways. You can enjoy the sunset from "The Top," a restaurant and lounge that overlooks the entire island and features Coconuts Comedy Club at the Top on Tuesday and Sunday nights. From Wednesday through Saturday enjoy cocktails at the Palm Court Piano Bar. *430 Duval St., 33040, tel. 305/296–2991, 800/745–2191, 800/HOLIDAY (US). 160 rooms with bath, including 2 suites, 18 nonsmoker rooms, and 8 rooms for handicapped guests. Facilities: pool and sun deck, whirlpool, fitness room, restaurant, 3 bars, bicycle and motor scooter rentals. AE, D, DC, MC, V. Very Expensive–Expensive.*

★ **Pier House.** This is the catbird seat for touring Key West—just off the intersection of Duval and Front streets and within an easy walk of Mallory Square and downtown. Yet inside the hotel grounds you feel the tranquility of a remote tropical island. New since 1990 is the Caribbean Spa: 22 rooms and suites with hardwood floors and two-poster plantation beds. Eleven of the baths convert to steam rooms; the others have whirlpool tubs. In the new rooms (615 and 619 are 1-bedroom suites) you'll be spoiled by the VCRs and a library of movies and CD players with compact discs. You can also avail yourself of a loofa rub, massages, aromatherapy, or facial in the new fitness center. Weathered-gray buildings flank a courtyard filled with tall coconut palms and hibiscus blossoms. Locals gather around the thatch-roof tiki bar at the Beach Club. The complex's eclectic architecture includes an original Conch house. *1 Duval St., 33040, tel. 305/296–4600, 800/327–8340 (US). 142 rooms with bath, including 13 suites in 5 separate low-rise buildings. Facilities: heated pool, 5 bars, 5 restaurants. AE, MC, V. Very Expensive–Expensive.*

Best Western Key Ambassador Inn. If you want to stay in a hotel near the airport, this is the place to visit. Even though the 100 rooms are typical motel style—functional and unluxurious—and the Ambassador was built in 1952, the surroundings are well cared for and the property offers lots of resort features. Each room has a balcony and most offer ocean and pool views. The mood at the pool bar is upbeat and often swings to a reggae sound. A mangrove-lined stream runs through some of the seven acres and connects the salt ponds in the back with the ocean in front across the road. *375 S. Roosevelt Blvd., Key West 33040, tel. 305/296–3500 or 800/432–4315; fax 305/296–9961. 100 rooms. Facilities: outdoor heated pool, outdoor fitness* *course, snack bar and bar, shuffleboard. AE, D, DC, MC, V. Moderate.*

Guest Houses

★ **The Curry Mansion Inn.** Careful dedication to detail by Key West architect Thomas Pope and owners Al and Edith Amsterdam have produced a near-perfect match between the Victorian Curry Mansion (1899) and its modern bed-and-breakfast addition. Each room has a different color scheme using tropical pastels; all rooms have carpeted floors, wicker headboards and furnishings, and quilts from the Cotton Gin Store at MM 94.5 in Tavernier. Rooms 1 and 8, honeymoon suites, feature canopy beds and balconies. Guests are welcome to a complimentary Continental breakfast and happy hour with an open bar and live piano music. *511 Caroline St., 33040, tel. 305/294–5349. 15 rooms with bath, 2 rooms for handicapped guests. Facilities: pool, fridge, wet bars, wheelchair lift. Guests have privileges at Pier House Beach Club. AE, DC, MC, V. Very Expensive–Expensive.*

Island City House. This guest house is actually three separate buildings: the vintage-1880s Island City House and Arch House (a former carriage house) and a 1970s reconstruction of an old cigar factory that once stood on the site. Arch House features a dramatic high carriage entry from the street to the lush courtyard beneath its second story. Floors throughout are pine, and each of the 24 suites is furnished with antiques. Guests share a private tropical garden and are given free Continental breakfasts. *411 William St., 33040, tel. 305/294–5702, 800/621–9405, or 800/634–8230. 24 parlor suites with bath and kitchen. Facilities: pool, Jacuzzi, bike rental. MC, V. Very Expensive–Expensive.*

★ **The Watson House.** Small in number of rooms but big in amenities, this guest house provides utmost privacy with Duval Street convenience: It's a block from the bustle but light years from the hassle. Ed Czaplicki with partner Joe Beres has restored the house to its 1860s Bahamian look that guests find caressingly soothing. The three units are the deco Cabana Suite by the two-tier pool gardens, the William Suite on the second floor of the house with its new wainscoting and wallpapers, and the connecting or private Susan Room, also with new wallpapers. French doors and gingerbread trim dress up the pristine yellow-and-white exterior. *525 Simonton St., 30040, tel. 305/294–6712 or 800/621–9405. 2 suites with bath and full kitchen, one room with bath. Facilities: heated pool, whirlpool, off-street parking. AE, MC, V. Very Expensive–Expensive.*

Artist House. Dressed in French Empire and Victorian style, with lavender shutters on white clapboard, latticework, wrought-iron spear fencing, and a grand tin-shingled turret, this guest home is a real show stopper. All rooms are antique filled and have Dade County pine floors. Among the rooms you'll find a mix-and-match of brocade sofas, Japanese screens, pull-latch doors, clawfoot tubs, four-poster beds, and elaborate moldings. The little garden out back has a Jacuzzi with a stone lion's head, surrounded by a brick deck, and there's a pond. Rates include full breakfast in winter, Continental breakfast in summer. *534 Eaton St., Key West 30040, tel. 305/296–3977 or 800/582–7882; fax 305/296–3210. 5 rooms and suites. Facilities: Jacuzzi, garden. AE, D, DC, MC, V. Very Expensive–Moderate.*

The Arts and Nightlife

The Arts The Keys are more than warm weather and luminous scenery—a vigorous and sophisticated artistic community flourishes here. Key West alone currently claims among its residents 55 full-time writers and 500 painters and craftsmen. Arts organizations in the Keys sponsor many special events, some lasting only a weekend, others spanning an entire season.

The monthly ***Island Navigator,*** Monroe County's only countywide general-interest newspaper, is free at banks, campgrounds, and convenience stores, and other high-traffic businesses. Its monthly community calendar lists cultural and sports events.

Three free publications covering Key West arts, music, and literature are available at hotels and other high-traffic areas:

The weekly ***Island Life,*** the most current and complete, is published by JBM Publications. *517 Duval St., Suite 200, Key West 33040, tel. 305/294-1616. Subscription by mail: $30/year.* ***Solares Hill,*** a monthly community newspaper, is published by Key West Publications, Inc. (1217 White St., Key West 33040, tel. 305/294-3602). In the Upper and Middle Keys, the weekly ***Free Press*** is available at hotels, motels, and retail outlets. *Box 469, Islamorada 33036, tel. 305/664-2266. Subscription by mail: $3/month.*

Theater **Red Barn Theater.** This professional, 94-seat theater in its 13th year performs dramas, comedies, and musicals, including plays by new playwrights. *319 Duval St. (rear), Key West, tel. 305/296-9911. MC, V. Closed some Mons.*

Waterfront Playhouse. This mid-1850s wrecker's warehouse was converted into an 185-seat non-Equity community theater that specializes in comedy and drama. *Mallory Sq., Key West, tel. 305/294-5015. No credit cards. Open Nov.-May.*

Tennessee Williams Fine Arts Center. A 490-seat theater built in 1980 on Stock Island, BS, the center presents chamber music, dance, jazz concerts, plays (dramatic and musical) with national and international stars, and other performing-arts events. *Florida Keys Community College, 5901 W. Junior College Rd., Key West, tel. 305/296-9081, ext. 326. MC, V. Open Nov.-Apr.*

Nightlife
Key Largo **Coconuts Restaurant and Bar.** The soft island music during dinner changes to top 40 after 10 PM. *MM 100, OS, in the Marina Del Mar Resort and Marina, tel. 305/451-4107. AE, DC, MC, V. Open weekdays 11 AM-2 AM, weekends 11-4 AM.*

Key West **Capt. Tony's Saloon.** Arson struck this landmark bar in 1990, but this has only added to its legend. In the aftermath of the deliberately set Fantasy Fest blaze, owners turned up a $12.66 check made out to Tennessee Williams, endorsed to Captain Tony Tarracino from the playwright's publisher in the early 1960s. Captain Tony is the former bootlegger, smuggler, mercenary, gunrunner, gambler, raconteur/owner of the bar that was the original Sloppy Joe's (from 1933 to 1937), even though another more touristy bar a block away now uses the name. The building dates from 1851 when it was first used as a morgue and ice house; later it was Key West's first telegraph station. As for Captain Tony, in 1989—a year after he sold the bar—he was elected Mayor of Key West (unseated two years later after a colorful term), but his trace—his image on memorabilia that adorns the walls—can still be found in the saloon that reopened two months after the fire. Hemingway was a regular here, and Jimmy Buffet got his start at Capt. Tony's. Live country and rhythm-and-blues makes the scene nowadays, and the house drink, the Pirates' Punch, contains a secret rum-based formula. *428 Greene St., tel. 305/294–1838. No credit cards. Open 10 AM–4 AM.*

Havana Docks Lounge. A high-energy disco club popular with young locals and visitors, this lounge is in the old William R. Porter Docks Shipping Office, now part of the Pier House hotel. The Havana Docks deck is a good place to watch the sun set when Mallory Square gets too crowded. *1 Duval St., tel. 305/296–4600. AE, MC, V. Open Sun.–Thurs. 4 PM–2 AM, Fri.–Sat. 4 PM–4 AM, though sometimes closing at 2 AM.*

Margaritaville Cafe. This place is owned by Key West resident and MCA recording star Jimmy Buffett, who performs here several times a year. The menu, which changes often, serves an entree they call "cheeseburger in paradise." The house special drink is, of course, a margarita. *500 Duval St., tel. 305/292–1435. Live music nightly. Cover charge for special events. AE, MC, V. Open 11 AM–2 AM.*

Sloppy Joe's. Named for its founder, Captain Joe Russell, Sloppy Joe's started as a speakeasy. Ernest Hemingway liked to gamble in a partitioned club room in back. After Hemingway's death, the original manuscript of *To Have and Have Not*, sections of *Death in the Afternoon, The Fifth Column*, and notes for *A Farewell to Arms* were found among personal papers he had stored at the bar. Decorated with Hemingway memorabilia and marine flags, the bar is popular with tourists and is full and noisy all the time. There is live entertainment from noon to 2 AM by local and touring groups. *201 Duval St., Key West, tel. 305/294–5717. No reservations. Dress: shoes and shirt required. All customers must show proof of age at night. Usually a $1 cover charge after 8 PM. No credit cards at the bar; major cards accepted to purchase T-shirts. Open 9 AM–4 AM.*

The Top Lounge. Located on the seventh floor of the La Concha Holiday Inn, Key West's tallest building, this is one of the best places from which to view the sunset. The Top features Coconuts Comedy Club Wednesday through Sunday. Also at La Concha, on the ground floor, is Craizy Daizy's. *430 Duval St., tel. 305/296–2991, 800/227–6151 (FL) or 800/745–2191 (US). AE, D, DC, MC, V. Open 11 AM–2 AM. Craizy Daizy's open 11–1 AM serving deli food and presenting weekend entertainment.*

9 Disney World and the Orlando Area

Introduction

By David Wilkening

Orlando, a high-profile city of fast growth boosted by a robust business climate and thriving tourist trade, seems to be an area touched by pixie dust. A magical city. But it was not always that way.

A military outpost was established here in 1838, and the area became known as Fort Gatlin. In 1850, that name gave way to Jernigan, in deference to one of the region's most prosperous residents. It wasn't until 1875 that the one-square-mile-wide city was incorporated as Orlando. There are various theories why the name was chosen, but the most popular is that the new city was named after Orlando Reeves, a soldier killed fighting the Seminole Indians.

Upon its incorporation, Orlando had less than 100 residents. The town had no seaport or major waterway. There was no railroad to spur its growth. There was little to stimulate or sustain any prosperity. But Orlando had a sunny year-round climate. And it had something else—a location in the very center of what would become one of the fastest-growing states in the country.

Citrus and cattle were the dominant industries in Orlando's early years. The English arrived in the mid-1860s, bringing with them tennis, polo, and afternoon tea. The great freezes of 1884 and 1885 virtually ruined the citrus industry, and traditional farming returned. Orlando remained a clean, sleepy, handsome city, known for its lakes and for its sprawling oak trees planted by northerners who wanted to remember the world they had left behind.

In the 1950s, large corporations gave the area a solid business base on which to build. Today, in large part because of Walt Disney World, Orlando is known for its tourism. But it's also a growing center of national and international business activity.

In its graceful and quiet past Orlando enjoyed a small-town pace that earned it the title of "The City Beautiful." The city today is far more metropolitan, even cosmopolitan, but much of the original charm remains. Many residents have homes near the hundreds of clear spring-fed lakes, far from the south Orlando-based tourist corridor. The aroma here is often that of orange blossoms and citrus trees.

The population of the greater metropolitan area that includes Orange, Seminole, and Osceola counties is now over one million. Various surveys cite the greater Orlando area as among the fastest growing in the country.

With all its business activity, however, Orlando is better known as the world's number one tourist destination. Disneyland had long been a successful staple in California when Disney decided, in the early 1960s, to build another theme park in the eastern United States. By 1963, Florida was chosen as the best state. Orlando was chosen for a variety of reasons, including its transportation system and its large amounts of open, available land.

By 1964, property was quietly purchased. Eventually, a huge tract of 28,000 acres was bought. But it wasn't until late 1965 that news reports leaked out that Disney was buying those parcels of land in anticipation of a large-scale theme park.

Orlando Area

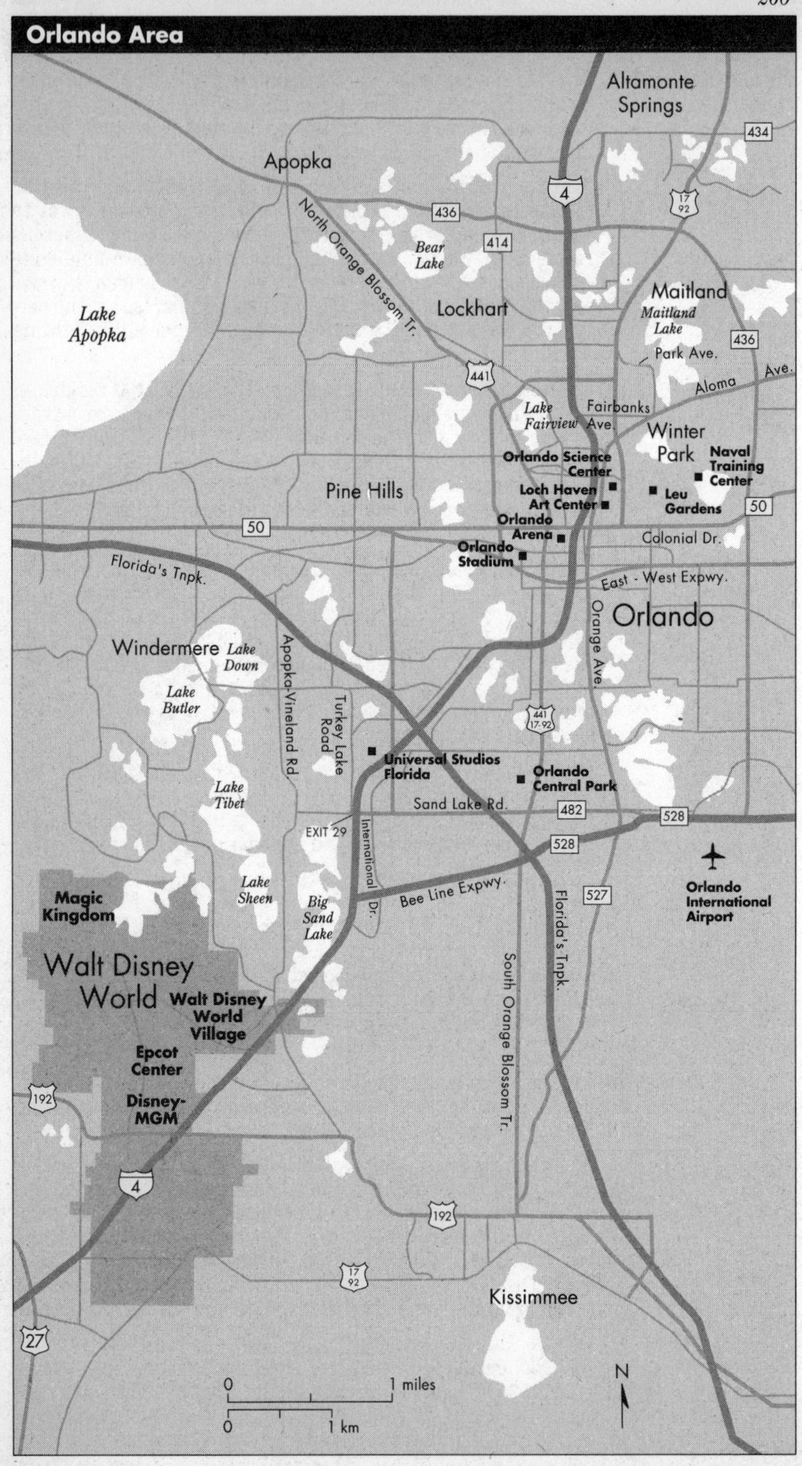

The accumulation of the land, often in small parcels purchased by agents working silently for Disney, was a dramatic story in itself. But seeing how the surrounding tourist areas around his California park had suffered rampant commercial sprawl, Disney was determined to buy enough land in Orlando to prevent that from happening again. This time, he would have *control of* the surrounding area.

On November 16, 1965, Walt Disney outlined his dream of an innovative working and living center that would provide a new way of life. He called it Experimental Prototype Community of Tomorrow (EPCOT). The first phase: the Magic Kingdom and a vacation complex. Walt Disney died the next year and never saw his dream come true. But construction began in 1969 on the park, which opened in 1971. New attractions were added continually, and, by the end of the fifth year, almost 11 million visitors annually were parading through the Magic Kingdom.

Plans were announced for another phase of the Disney master plan in 1975. That was EPCOT. On October 1, 1982, Epcot Center, as it is now called, opened its gates. It was not a quiet opening but included a month-long celebration that featured the West Point Glee Club, the 450-piece All American Marching Band, and World Showcase Festival performers representing 23 countries. The Epcot Center that emerged after Disney's death was not the one he envisioned—a living, working community set next to theme parks—apparently because it was later determined that the concept was not practical. But Epcot Center, standing on its own, was an immediate success. Almost 23 million visitors passed through its gates the very first year.

Walt Disney World added Disney–MGM Studios Theme Park in 1989. This park spans 135 acres and offers visitors an opportunity to get behind the scenes and sometimes in front of the cameras at a working movie and television studio reminiscent of Hollywood in the 1930s and '40s.

And for those visitors who want to dip their toes or their fishing lines into the ocean, the Cocoa Beach area is less than an hour from Orlando.

Essential Information

Arriving and Departing

By Plane More than 21 scheduled airlines and more than 30 charters operate in and out of Orlando's airport, with direct service to more than 100 U.S. cities. At last count, Delta, the official airline of Disney World, had more than 90 flights to and from the airport every day! Travel packages to Disney World are offered by Delta (tel. 800/872–7786).

In the fall of 1991 Orlando International became a major hub for United Airlines. United expanded from 18 to 47 daily flights to and from Orlando. Major airlines that serve Orlando include American, Bahamasair, British Airways, Continental, Delta, Icelandair, KLM, Mexicana, Northwest, TWA, United, and USAir.

Between the Airport and the Hotels You can catch a public bus between the airport and downtown Orlando, which goes to and from the main terminal of **Tri-County Transit Authority** (1200 W. South St., Orlando, tel. 407/841–8240). The cost is 75¢. The downtown area, however, is far from most hotels, so you might want to consider other options. **Mears Transportation Group** (tel. 407/423–5566) sends 11-passenger vans to Disney World and along Rte. 192 every 30 minutes. Prices begin at $12.50 one way for adults, $8.50 for children 4–11; to $22 round-trip adults, $16 children 4–11. **Town & Country Limo** (tel. 407/828–3035) and **First Class Transportation** (tel. 407/578–0022) also offer limousine service. **Suncoast Shuttle** (tel. 407/676–4557; in FL, 800/226–4557 or outside FL, 800/762–5466) services the Cocoa Beach area. One-way fares are $15, round-trip is $28. Suncoast Shuttle also provides round-trip service from the Space Coast to the major attractions. Round-trip to Walt Disney World is $28.

By Taxi Taxis are the fastest way to travel (25–30 minutes to hotels), but the ride won't be cheap. To Walt Disney World hotels or to hotels along West 192, a cab trip will cost about $35 plus tip. To the International Drive area, it will cost about $25 plus tip.

By Car When leaving the airport, a left turn onto the Beeline Expressway (Rte. 528) leads you past Sea World to I–4. A left turn on I–4 takes you to Walt Disney World Village and Epcot Center or to U.S. 192 and the Magic Kingdom entrance. A right turn on I–4 from the Beeline takes you past Highway 482 and into downtown Orlando. A right turn on the Bee Line from the airport takes you to the Atlantic Ocean coast and connects with the three major north-south ocean coast highways: I–95, U.S. 1, and S.R. A1A.

By Train **Amtrak** (tel. 800/USA–RAIL) Autotrain stops at Sanford (600 Persimmon Blvd.), and the passenger service makes stops at Sanford (800 Persimmon Blvd.), Winter Park (150 Morse Blvd.), Orlando (1400 Sligh Blvd.), and then, 20 minutes later, in Kissimmee (416 Pleasant St.).

By Bus Contact **Greyhound/Trailways** (tel. 407/843–7720) or consult your phone book or directory assistance for a local number that will automatically connect you with the national Greyhound/Trailways Information Center.

Getting Around

By Car The most important artery in the Orlando area is **Interstate 4 (I–4).** This interstate ties everything together, and you'll invariably receive directions in reference to it. The problem is that I–4 is considered an east-west expressway in our national road system (the even numbers refer to an east-west orientation, the odd numbers to a north-south orientation). I–4 does run from east to west *if* you follow it from the Atlantic Coast to Florida's Gulf of Mexico. But in the Orlando area, I–4 actually runs north-south. Always remember, therefore, that when the signs say east, you are often going north, and when the signs say west, you are often going south. Think north-east and south-west. Another main drag is **International Drive,** which has several major hotels, restaurants, and shopping centers. You can get onto International Drive from I–4 Exits 28, 29, and 30B.

The other main road, Irlo Bronson Memorial Highway (U.S. 192), cuts across I–4 at Exits 25A and 25B. This highway goes through the Kissimmee area and crosses Walt Disney World property.

By Bus If you are staying along International Drive, in Kissimmee, or in Orlando proper, you can take advantage of the limited public bus system, but only to get places locally. To find out which bus to take, ask your hotel clerk or call the Tri-County Transit Authority Information Office (tel. 407/841–8240) during business hours. A transfer will add 10¢ to the regular 75¢ fare.

By Taxi Taxi fares start at $2.45 and cost $1.40 for each mile thereafter. Call **Yellow Cab Co.** (tel. 407/699–9999) or **Town and Country Cab** (tel. 407/828–3035).

Guided Tours

General-Interest Tours **Globus Gateway/Cosmos** (150 S. Los Robles Ave., Suite 860, Pasadena, CA 91101, tel. 818/449–0919 or 800/556–5454) offers a comprehensive eight-day tour that includes entry to Disney World. If you live on the East Coast of the country, **Domenico Tours** (751 Broadway, Bayonne, NJ 07002, tel. 201/823–8687 or 800/554–TOUR) will take you to Orlando via coach tour or direct flight; from the west, it's air only.

Balloon Tours **Aerial Adventures.** This Church Street Station event is not cheap, but it's an experience you'll never forget. The flight is followed by brunch at Lili Marlene's. Aerial Adventures also offers bungee jumping and blimp rides. *124 W. Pine St., Orlando, tel. 407/841–UPUP. $150 per person.*

Rise and Float Balloon Tours. Depart at dawn and indulge yourself with an in-flight champagne breakfast. *5767 Major Blvd., Orlando, tel. 407/352–8191. $280–$350 per couple.*

Helicopter Tours **J.C. Helicopters.** Sign up for aerial tours of Walt Disney World, Sea World, and other attractions. The flights at dark are spectacular. *Orlando Hyatt Heliport at I–4 and U.S. 192 (next to Walt Disney World), tel. 407/857–7222. Prices start at $35 adults, $20 children.*

Important Addresses and Numbers

Visitors to **Mickey's Kingdom** can direct all inquiries to Walt Disney World (Box 10040, Lake Buena Vista, 32830, Attention: Guest letters, tel. 407/824–4321.) Request a free copy of the *Walt Disney World Vacation Guide.*

For information on the greater Orlando area, contact the **Visitor Information Center** (8445 International Dr., Orlando 32819, tel. 407/363–5800). Open 8–8. Ask for the free *Discover Orlando* guidebook.

Visitors to the Kissimmee area on U.S. 192 can get brochures from the **Kissimmee/St. Cloud Convention and Visitors' Bureau,** 1925 E. Irlo Bronson Memorial Hwy., Kissimmee 32742, tel. 407/847–5000, in FL 800/432–9199, outside FL 800/327–9159.

Emergency Dial 911 for **police** and **ambulance** in an emergency.

Doctors Hospital emergency rooms are open 24 hours a day. The most accessible hospital, located in the International Drive area, is the **Orlando Regional Medical Center/Sand Lake Hospital** (9400 Turkey Lake Rd., tel. 407/351–8500).

For hotel-room visits by physicians for minor medical care, contact a mobile minor emergency service called **Housemed** (tel. 407/648–9234 or 407/846–2093 in Kissimmee).

On the coast, **Cape Canaveral Hospital** is on the Highway 520 Causeway between Cocoa Beach and Merritt Island (tel. 407/799–7150).

24-Hour Pharmacies **Eckerd Drugs** (908 Lee Rd., Orlando, tel. 407/644–6908).
Walgreen Drug Store (2410 E. Colonial Dr., Orlando, tel. 407/894–6781).

Road Service **AAA Emergency Road Service** (tel. 407/877–2266 or 800/824–4432).

Disney World Walt Disney World Information, tel. 407/824–4321.
Accommodations Reservations, tel. 407/W–DISNEY.
Dinner Show Reservations, tel. 407/W–DISNEY.
Walt Disney World Resort Dining/Recreation Information, tel. 407/824–3737.
Tours: Magic Kingdom, Epcot Center, and Disney-MGM, tel. 407/824–4321.
Magic Kingdom Lost and Found, tel. 407/824–4521.
Epcot Center Lost and Found, tel. 407/560–6105.
Disney-MGM Lost and Found, tel. 407/420–4668.
Central Lost and Found, tel. 407/824–4245.
Car Care Center, tel. 407/824–4813.
Western Union at Walt Disney World, tel. 407/824–3456.
Banking Information (Sun Bank), tel. 407/824–5767.
Time and Weather, tel. 407/422–1611.
Walt Disney World Shopping Village Information, tel. 407/828–3058.
KinderCare Child Care, tel. 407/827–5444, private baby-sitting; 407/827–5437, group sitting.

Exploring Walt Disney World and the Orlando Area

Walt Disney World has its own complete transportation system to get you wherever you want to go. Yet because the property is so extensive—28,000 acres, 98 of them for the Magic Kingdom, 260 for Epcot Center, and another 135 for Disney-MGM—the system can be a bit confusing, even for an experienced visitor. Best-known is the elevated monorail, which connects Walt Disney World's biggest resorts and attractions. There are also extensive bus, motor-launch, and ferry systems. If you are staying at an on-site resort or a Walt Disney World Village hotel or if you hold a combination Magic Kingdom-Epcot Center ticket, transportation is free. If not, you can buy unlimited transportation within Walt Disney World for $2.50 a day.

By Monorail This elevated train of the future operates daily 7:30 AM–11 PM (or until 1 hour after the Magic Kingdom closes). It does not go everywhere. The central connecting station for the monorail is called the **Transportation and Ticket Center** (TTC). One monorail line goes from the TTC to the Magic Kingdom and back in a loop around Seven Seas Lagoon. This line is primarily for visitors who are not guests at the on-site resorts. Another line connects the TTC with the Contemporary Resort, the Magic Kingdom, the Grand Floridian, and the Polynesian. A third line goes directly from the TTC to Epcot Center. The TTC is where you can transfer between the Disney bus system and the monorail. When you get to a monorail station, ask an attendant if you can sit in the conductor's cabin, called "the nose" by the crew.

By Bus Each bus carries a small color-coded or letter-coded pennant on the front and sides. They come by at 15- to 25-minute intervals. Here's where the buses take you:

Green—Connects Disney Inn and Polynesian Village Resort with the TTC. This line operates from 7 AM to 2 AM. If there is an MK pennant on the bus, it connects Disney Inn with the Magic Kingdom and runs from 7 PM until two hours after the park closes.

Blue—Connects Fort Wilderness Resort Area with the TTC. These buses operate every eight minutes 7 AM to 2 AM.

Green-and-Gold—If the pennant has the letters EC on it, the bus connects Epcot, the Resort Villas, the Disney Village Marketplace, and Disney Village Clubhouse. If the bus has the letters MK on it, it travels between the Magic Kingdom and the villas during park hours. Before and after park hours it stops at the TTC. If the bus has ST/V on it, the bus connects Disney-MGM, Disney Village Marketplace, Pleasure Island, the Resort Villas, and Disney Village Clubhouse. These lines operate: EC 8 AM–2 AM; MK 7 AM–2 AM; and ST/V 8 AM–two hours after Disney-MGM closes, and 6 PM–2 AM to Pleasure Island.

Red-and-White—Connects Walt Disney World Village Hotel Plaza with the theme parks and Pleasure Island beginning at 8 AM and running until two hours after the respective parks close. EC goes to Epcot, MK to the Magic Kingdom, and ST goes to Disney-MGM. The V bus connects with Pleasure Island and Disney Village Marketplace and operates between 6 PM and 2 AM.

Red—Connects TTC, Disney Village Marketplace, and Epcot between 8 AM and 2 AM, and Typhoon Lagoon during park hours. It includes Pleasure Island from 6 PM to 2 AM.

Gold—Connects the Grand Floridian, Polynesian Resort, and Contemporary Resort with the TTC from 7 AM until the monorail begins at 7:30 AM. It picks up service again after the monorail closes (11 PM) until 2 AM.

Orange-and-White Stripe—If the pennant has the letters MK on it, the bus connects Caribbean Beach Resort with the Magic Kingdom while the park is open and stops at TTC only before and after park hours. The bus line is in operation from 7 AM to 2 AM. If the bus has the letters EC on it, it connects Epcot and Caribbean Beach Resort from 8 AM to two hours after Epcot closes. If the pennant is ST, the bus connects Caribbean Beach Resort with Disney-MGM from 8 AM to two hours after the park closes. If the letter is V, the bus connects Caribbean Beach Resort with Disney Marketplace between 8 AM and 2 AM, Typhoon Lagoon during park hours, and Pleasure Island between 6 AM and 2 AM.

Purple-and-Gold—These buses service the Epcot resorts: MK to the Magic Kingdom from 7 AM to 2 AM and to TTC before and after park hours, and V to Disney Village Marketplace (7:30 AM–2 AM), Typhoon Lagoon (park hours), and Pleasure Island (6 PM–2 AM).

Gold-and-Black—The STE bus takes a Disney-MGM, Fort Wilderness, Contemporary Resort route, while the STW bus stops at Disney-MGM, the Polynesian Village, the Grand Floridian, and Disney Inn. Both routes run from 8 AM until 2 AM and include Pleasure Island from 6 PM to 2 AM.

Blue-and-White—The EC connects Disney-MGM with Epcot, and the MK connects Disney-MGM with TTC. Both routes run from 8 AM to two hours after the parks close.

Brown—A Fort Wilderness Transportation Circle line connects Pioneer Hall, the Meadows Trading Post, Lodge/River Country parking lot, Creekside Meadows, and the Meadow complex with Loops 300, 500, 600, and 800–2800 from 7 AM to 2 AM.

Silver—This is another Fort Wilderness Transportation Circle line that connects Pioneer Hall, the Meadows Trading Post, Lodge/River Country parking lot, Creekside Meadows, and the Meadow complex with Loops 300, 500, 600, and 800–2800 from 7 AM to 2 AM.

Orange—The Caribbean Beach Resort internal transportation line operates from 7 AM to 2 AM.

Orange (tram)—The tram connects River Country to its parking lot, operating during River Country hours. If you are staying at one of the Epcot Center resorts, check with your hotel concierge for new bus routes and schedules.

Pink-and-Green—This line services the new Port Orleans resort. If the pennant is MK, the bus goes to the Magic Kingdom during park hours and the TTC before and after from 7 AM to 2 AM; if the pennant is EC, the bus goes to Epcot from 8 AM to two hours after the park closes; if the pennant is ST, the bus goes to Disney-MGM from 8 AM to two hours after the park closes; and if the pennant is V, the bus goes to the Disney Village Marketplace from 8 AM to 11 PM, Typhoon Lagoon during park hours, and Pleasure Island from 6:30 PM to 2 AM.

By Motor Launch These boats depart about every 20 minutes and use color-coded flags (except for the FriendShip) to identify their routes. They are for the use of Disney resort guests only, with the exception of day guests with special activity tickets to such places as Discovery Island and River Country.

Blue—Connects the Contemporary Resort with the Fort Wilderness Resort Area every 15 minutes 9 AM–10 PM. Another launch connects Fort Wilderness, Discovery Island, and the Magic Kingdom from 10 AM to 3:45 PM; pick-up from Discovery Island is extended after the park closes.

Gold—Connects the Grand Floridian, Magic Kingdom, and Polynesian Resort at 15- to 25-minute intervals from half an hour before the Magic Kingdom opens until it closes, with pick-up only from the Magic Kingdom until the park clears.

Green—Connects the Magic Kingdom, Fort Wilderness Resort Area, and Discovery Island (when it is open) every 20–25 minutes from half an hour before opening until closing time.

Friendship—Connects Disney-MGM with the Epcot resorts from 8 AM to 90 minutes after the park closes.

By Ferry A ferry service runs across Seven Seas Lagoon connecting the TTC with the Magic Kingdom. They depart from each side of the lagoon about every 12 minutes when the Magic Kingdom is open. They often get you to the Magic Kingdom faster than does the monorail. It is a comfortable ride, gliding over the lagoon's silky waters. Most people heading for the Magic Kingdom opt for the monorail and then take the ferry back at day's end, so if you want to avoid the worst of the lines for both the monorail and ferry, take the opposite tack.

By Car If you arrive at either the Magic Kingdom, Epcot, or Disney-MGM by car, there is a $4 parking charge. If you're staying at a Disney World hotel, show your guest ID for free parking. Remember or write down *exactly* where you park; you'll have a long wait before the sea of automobiles has departed and yours is the only one left. Trams make frequent trips between a park's turnstiles and its parking area.

Car Care If your car won't start or it breaks down in Disney World, the **Disney Car Care Center** (tel. 407/824-4813), an AAA facility near the Toll Plaza to the Magic Kingdom, offers emergency road service. Open weekdays 7 AM–5:30 PM. The gas islands stay open 90 minutes after the Magic Kingdom closes. If you need to drop your car off to be serviced, there is free shuttle service around the park.

Admission Visiting Walt Disney World is not cheap, especially if you have a child or two along. There are no discounted family tickets. Sixteen different types of admission tickets are sold in one of two categories—adult, meaning everyone aged 10 and older, and children aged 3–9. Children under age 3 get in free.

The word "ticket" is used by Disney World only to mean a single day's admission to the Magic Kingdom, Epcot, or the Disney-MGM Studios Theme Park. The price is $31 for adults and $25 for children. If you want to spend two or three days visiting the attractions, you have to buy a separate ticket each day. For more than three days, Disney World offers what it calls the All Three Parks Passport, which admits you to all three parks, along with unlimited use of the internal transportation system. Here is a list of prices. They are subject to change.

Italics indicate prices for visitors staying in a Disney World resort or in a resort in the WDW Village Hotel Plaza.

One-day ticket	$34 adults, $27 children
Four-day passport	$118 adults, $92 children
Five-day passport (includes 2 additional attractions)	$162 adults, $128 children
Annual Pass (new)	$190 adults, $165 children*
Annual Pass (renewal)	$170 adults, $145 children*
Annual Pass (charter renewal)	$150 adults, $125 children*
River Country, one day	$12 adults, $9.50 children; *$10.75/ $8.25*
River Country annual pass	$50 adults and children

Combined River Country/Discovery Island, one day	$15 adults, $11 children; *$14/$10*
Discovery Island, one day	$8 adults, $4.50 children
Typhoon Lagoon, one day	$18.50 adults, $14.75 children; *$16.25/ $13*
Typhoon Lagoon annual pass	$75 adults and children
Pleasure Island, one day	$12.95 adults and children
Pleasure Island, annual pass	$34.95 adults and children

**An additional $30 (or $27 if you're a Magic Kingdom Club member) entitles passholders to unlimited use of River Country and Discovery Island for the duration of their annual passes. An additional $26 ($20 for Magic Kingdom Club members) entitles passholders to unlimited use of Pleasure Island. An additional $60 ($54 for Magic Kingdom Club members) provides admission to Typhoon Lagoon.*

Passports are available for four or five days. They can save you a great deal of money and may be advisable even if you're staying in the area for only two days. Each time you use a Passport, the entry date is stamped on it; the remaining days may be used any time in the future. If you buy a one-day ticket and later decide to extend your visit, you can get full credit for it toward the purchase of any Passport. Exchanges can be made at City Hall in the Magic Kingdom, at Earth Station in Epcot, or at Guest Relations at Disney-MGM. Do this before leaving the park; once you've left, the ticket is worthless.

Tickets and Passports to Walt Disney World and Epcot Center may be purchased at admission booths at the TTC, in on-site or Hotel Plaza resorts (if you're a registered guest), or at the Walt Disney World kiosk on the second floor of the main terminal at Orlando International Airport. If you want to buy tickets before you arrive in Orlando, send a check or money order to Admissions, Walt Disney World, Box 10000, Lake Buena Vista, 32830. Remember, it usually takes four to six weeks for the order to be processed, so write well in advance.

If you want to leave the Magic Kingdom or Epcot Center and return on the same day, be sure to have your hand stamped on the way out. You'll need your ticket *and* the hand stamp to be readmitted.

Operating Hours Hours vary widely throughout the year and change for school and legal holidays. In general, the longest hours are during the summer months, when the Magic Kingdom is open until midnight, Epcot Center is open to 11 PM, and Disney-MGM is open to 9 PM. At other times of year, Epcot Center and Disney-MGM are open until 8 PM, and the Magic Kingdom to 6 PM, with Main Street remaining open until 7. Though each park usually opens at 9 AM, visitors can enter the grounds up to an hour earlier and get a significant head start on the crowds. A good bet for breakfast before 9 AM is the **Crystal Palace** in the Magic Kingdom (turn left at the end of Main St.). For current hours, tel. 407/824–4321.

When to Go The busiest days of the week are Monday, Tuesday, and Wednesday. You would think the weekend would be busiest, but it's not. Perhaps everyone tries to beat the crowds by going in the early part of the week, or perhaps vacationers leave on Friday, travel over the weekend, and begin their visits on Monday. Whatever the reason, Friday and Sunday are the slowest days, and Thursdays and Saturdays are only moderately busy.

The best time of the day to be at the parks is in the late afternoon and evening—especially during the summer months and holidays, when the attractions stay open late. It also helps to arrive as soon as the gates open, up to an hour before the "official" opening time. The most crowded time of the year is from Christmas through New Year's Day. The parks are also packed around Easter.

Memorial Day weekend is not only crowded, but hot. Other busy times of the year are mid-June—mid-August, Thanksgiving weekend, the week of Washington's Birthday in mid-February, and the weeks of college spring break in late March. The rest of the year is generally hassle-free, particularly from early September until just before Thanksgiving. The best time of all is from just after Thanksgiving weekend until the beginning of the Christmas holidays. Another excellent time is from early January through the first week of February. If you must go during summer, late August is best.

Magic Kingdom

You'll first see Town Square. City Hall is on your left. The railroad station is directly behind you.

Sprawling before you is Main Street—a shop-filled boulevard with Victorian-style stores, and dining spots. Walk two blocks along Main Street and you'll enter Central Plaza, with **Cinderella Castle** rising directly in front of you. This is the hub of the Kingdom; all the "lands" radiate out from it.

This is as good a place as any to see the daily parade at 3 PM. All Disney's characters are featured in the 20-minute show. In summer and during holidays, there's also an Electrical Parade of giant floats at 9 and 11 PM.

City Hall is a good place to pick up the *Magic Kingdom Guide Book* and a schedule of daily events. It is also the lost-and-found point for property and people. Nearby, beneath the railroad, are lockers where bags and gifts may be stored.

A great way to get an overview of the Kingdom is to hop aboard the WDW Railroad and take a 14-minute, 1½-mile ride around the perimeter of the park. You can board at the Victorian-style station you pass beneath to enter Town Square. Until recently, the only other station was in Frontierland, but there is now a Duckburg Station at Mickey's Starland on the border between Tomorrowland and Fantasyland.

The Magic Kingdom is the home of Mickey and Minnie Mouse, Goofy, Pluto, and dozens of other Disney characters. Seen on the streets, they're a child's delight, and even adults beam with pleasure as they shake hands with the fantasies they've grown up with. Characters are always willing to pose for photos. They're most often found next to City Hall.

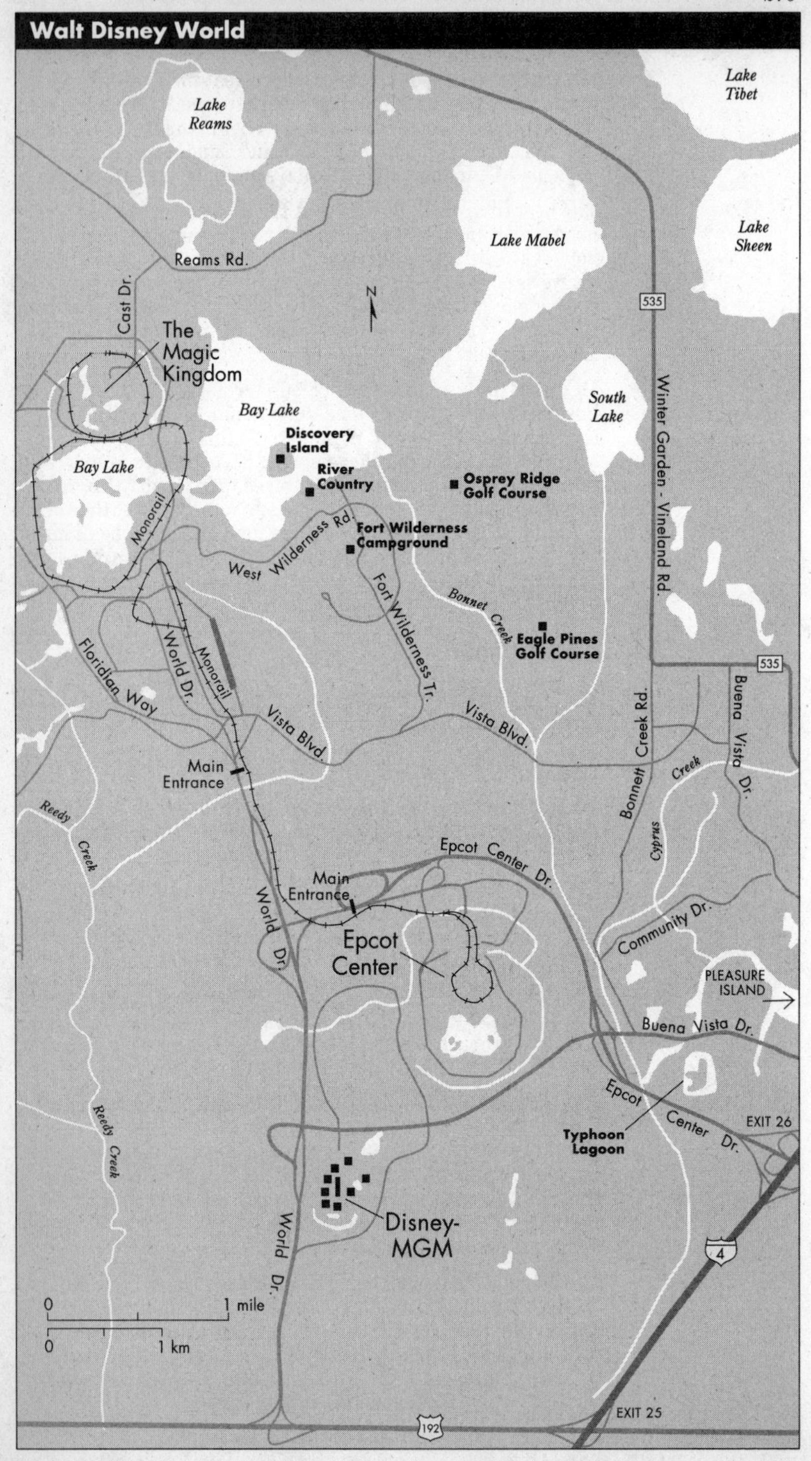
Walt Disney World
Lake Reams
Lake Tibet
Lake Mabel
Lake Sheen
Reams Rd.
Cast Dr.
N
535
The Magic Kingdom
Bay Lake
Discovery Island
River Country
Osprey Ridge Golf Course
South Lake
Winter Garden - Vineland Rd.
Bay Lake
Monorail
West Wilderness Rd.
Fort Wilderness Campground
Fort Wilderness Tr.
Bonnet Creek
Eagle Pines Golf Course
535
Floridian Way
World Dr.
Monorail
Vista Blvd.
Vista Blvd.
Bonnett Creek Rd.
Buena Vista Dr.
Main Entrance
Reedy Creek
Cypress Creek
Epcot Center Dr.
Main Entrance
World Dr.
Epcot Center
Community Dr.
PLEASURE ISLAND
Buena Vista Dr.
Epcot Center Dr.
EXIT 26
Typhoon Lagoon
Reedy Creek
Disney-MGM
World Dr.
4
0
1 mile
0
1 km
EXIT 25
192

The Magic Kingdom is divided into seven lands. Stories are told of tourists who spend an entire day in one land, thinking they have seen all the park; don't let that happen to you. The following is a selected list of Magic Kingdom attractions.

Adventureland These soft adventures to far-off lands are among the most crowded in the Kingdom. Visit as late in the afternoon as possible or, better yet, in the evening. Adventureland is the worst place to be in the morning, because other travel guides recommend it as a first stop.

Swiss Family Robinson Treehouse (popular; all ages) is a good way to get some exercise and a panoramic view of the park. Visitors walk up the many-staired tree in single file, a trip that can take up to a half hour.

Jungle Cruise (very popular; all ages) takes visitors along the Nile, across an Amazon jungle, and so on. The tour guide's narration is corny but nevertheless brings laughs. The ride itself takes only 10 minutes, but the line can take as long as an hour. Go during the parade time at 3 PM or after 5 PM. Avoid 10 AM–noon.

Pirates of the Caribbean (very popular; all ages) is a journey through a world of pirate strongholds and treasure-filled dungeons. The Audio-Animatronics pirates are first rate.

Tropical Serenade-Enchanted Tiki Birds (not very popular; for children) was one of the first Audio-Animatronic creations. The show's talking birds are somewhat charming, but the show itself can be confusing because it's difficult to tell what bird is speaking at any time. If you're in a hurry, you can safely skip this one.

Fantasyland This is a land in which storybook dreams come true and children are very much in their element.

There are a few traditional amusement-park rides with Disney themes, such as the Mad Tea Party, where teacups spin around a large teapot. Other favorites are Dumbo the Flying Elephant and a spectacular merry-go-round. There are also several indoor rides that spook and enchant children as they pass through a cartoon world filled with many familiar fairy-tale characters.

20,000 Leagues Under the Sea (very popular; all ages) is an underwater cruise inspired by the Jules Verne novel. Lines move slowly, but how often do you get to ride in a submarine and explore the world beneath the sea?

Frontierland "Frontier Fun" is the theme of this gold-rush town of the Southwest.

Big Thunder Mountain Railroad (very popular; all ages) is a scream-inducing roller coaster. Children must be at least 4′2″. For real rollercoaster fans, the ride is somewhat tame, but it's one of two fast rides in Walt Disney World (Space Mountain is the other one). Try to go in the evening when the mountain is lit up and lines are relatively short.

Country Bear Jamboree (moderately popular; for children) is a somewhat dated show with furry bears who sing and dance. A better show is put on at **Diamond Horseshow Jamboree** (popular; all ages)—a live stage show with singing, dancing, and innocently rowdy entertainment. You must make reservations early in the morning outside Disneyana Collectibles on Main Street, because there are only five shows daily. The strongest demand is usually for the noon and 1:30 shows. Other performances are at 3, 4:30, and 6 PM.

Splash Mountain (very popular; all ages). This elaborate water flume ride—the newest attraction at the Magic Kingdom—opened in the fall of 1992 and features a five-story drop. Spanning more than nine acres, the 87-foot-high ride is so elaborate that it forced Disney to move its Frontierland train station down the track to provide enough room for this addition. Based on Disney's 1946 film *Song of the South*, the ride includes characters from the movie as well as some of the songs. The eight-person hollowed-out log takes you on a half-mile journey that passes through Br'er Rabbit's habitat. Splash Mountain is also fun for visitors to watch: as the log hits Br'er Rabbit's briar-filled pond the last thing onlookers see are bubbles where the log went underwater. The final plunge is down Chickapin Hill at speeds reaching up to 40 mph.

Tom Sawyer Island (not very popular; all ages) has little to see but offers a happy respite from the crowds on the mainland. Adults can relax at **Aunt Polly's Landing** with lemonade and lunch while the kids scramble up Harper's Mill (a working windmill) or explore the caves and bridges.

Liberty Square This is a small land adjoining and blending into Frontierland. It's theme is Colonial history and it has a few decent but tame attractions.

Haunted Mansion (very popular; all ages) is the most popular attraction here. The spine-tingling effects, with ghosts, goblins, and graveyards, are realistic and may be too intense for the very young. The best time to go is in the morning when the lines are short. Avoid the noon–4 PM rush.

Liberty Square Riverboats (moderately popular; all ages) take visitors on a quiet, half-mile cruise through the rivers of America, passing Wild West scenes. It's not great entertainment, but it can be a comfortable escape from the crowds and the sun.

Hall of Presidents (moderately popular; adults or mature children) was a sensation when it first opened, but now it seems a bit slow and unexciting. Still, visitors of all ages find it interesting to see the Audio-Animatronics presidents in action. Adults find it educational; young children find it boring.

Mickey's Starland The newest of Disney's lands, it was called Mickey's Birthdayland when it was built in 1988 to celebrate Mickey Mouse's 60th birthday. Here, in Duckburg, visitors can view some of Mickey's cartoons and films, visit Mickey's house, and meet Mickey for some photos. For parents who don't have the same energy level as their youngsters, here is a good place to rest their feet while children explore a maze, pet young farm animals, or run around the playground.

Mickey's Hollywood Theatre (very popular; younger children). Here is the best opportunity to have your picture taken with Mickey Mouse when you meet him backstage in his dressing room.

Tomorrowland "Fun in the Future" is the motto of this land. Save it for the future if your time is limited because, except for Space Mountain, its rides are lackluster compared to others in the park. One major problem is that most attractions are sponsored by major corporations, and audiences are bombarded by commercial advertising. Plans are to make over Tomorrowland by 1996, changing it into an "intergalactic spaceport for arriving aliens."

Space Mountain (very popular, children must be at least 3 years old, and children under 7 must be accompanied by an adult) is about the only reason to stop here until the makeover. The space-age roller coaster may never reach speeds above 20 miles an hour, but the experience in the dark, with everyone screaming, is thrilling, even for hard-core roller-coaster fans. To see the interior without taking the ride, hop aboard the WEDway PeopleMover.

American Journeys, including **Carousel of Progress** and **Mission to Mars** (unpopular; all ages), is a series of 20-minute attractions that may be 20 minutes too long. Circle Vision's patriotic look at the landscape of America on nine movie screens is perhaps the best bet.

Grand Prix Raceway (popular) takes children in mini race cars to speeds up to 7 miles per hour. The ride is confining with little room to maneuver your vehicle. Children must be at least age 7 to ride alone, and there are usually long lines.

Epcot Center

Epcot Center is divided almost equally into two distinct areas separated by the 40-acre World Showcase Lagoon. The northern half, which is where the main admission gates are, is filled with the Future World pavilions, sponsored by major American corporations. The southern half is World Showcase, with an entrance through International Gateway next to the France pavilion. If you want to minimize the time spent waiting in line, do the opposite of what most people do. In the morning, visitors head for what's closest, which is Future World, so you should begin at World Showcase. In the afternoon, come back and explore Future World when the crowds have shifted to World Showcase. Evening hours, of course, are the best times for visiting either area.

Visitors who are familiar with the Magic Kingdom find something entirely different at Epcot Center. For one thing, Epcot is twice as large. For another, Epcot's attractions all have an educational dimension. **Future World** explores technological concepts, such as energy and communications, in entertaining ways. **World Showcase** is a series of pavilions in which various nations portray their cultures through a combination of films, exhibits, and seemingly endless shops. Bring a hearty appetite, because ethnic cuisines are featured in each foreign pavilion.

As you enter Epcot Center, you'll pass beneath **Spaceship Earth,** a 17-story sphere that marks the start of Future World. World Showcase is behind Future World. Stop first at Earth Station to pick up a guidebook and entertainment schedule. Also, make reservations for the busy, full-service restaurants here. Remember that it's not unusual for most restaurants to be fully reserved by 10 AM in the peak season. Remember also that guests who are staying in on-site properties can make their reservations ahead of time.

Future World The subjects explored at Future World include the ocean, agriculture, communications, energy, imagination, and transportation.

Communicore East and West (popular; all ages). These two buildings house exhibits by the various sponsoring companies of Epcot Center. The educational computer games are very popular with children.

Horizons (popular; all ages). A journey into the lifestyles of the next century, with robotic-staffed farms, ocean colonies, and space cities.

Journey Into Imagination (popular; for children). Two of the most popular characters, Dreamfinder and Figment, are your guides on a tour of the creative process that depicts how literature and art come from the sparks of ideas. Particularly popular with teenagers is **Captain EO,** a $17-million, 3-D film starring singer Michael Jackson. The experience here is well worth the wait in line, but try to go in the late afternoon when there are fewer people. Also be sure to see the "dancing waters" display in front of the entrance to Captain EO.

Listen to the Land (popular; for adults and mature children). The main event here is a boat ride through the experimental greenhouse that demonstrates how plants may be grown in the future, not only on Earth but in outer space. It's provocative for adults but somewhat dull for children. Those who are interested can arrange to join one of several walking tours. Reservations can be made in the morning on the lower floor, in the corner opposite the boat ride, behind the *Broccoli and Company* kiosk.

The Living Seas (popular; all ages). This is a new attraction and one of the most popular. It's the largest facility ever dedicated to the relationship of humans with the ocean and is sometimes known as the "eighth sea." Visitors take a gondola ride beneath the sea for a dynamic close-up look at marine life in a six-million-gallon aquarium more than four fathoms deep. There are more than 200 varieties of sea life among the 5,000 inhabitants. You can easily spend a half day here.

Spaceship Earth (very popular; all ages). This million-pound silver geosphere is so large that on clear days airline passengers on both coasts of Florida can see it. Inside the dome, visitors take a highly praised journey through the dramatic history of communications, from cave drawings to space-age technology. Visitors see the dome when they first get to Epcot Center and routinely make their way here. You would be well advised to wait until the late afternoon when the crowds have left **Universe of Energy** (very popular; all ages). This is a fast-paced exploration of the forces that fuel our lives and the universe. You'll ride on theater seats through a display on the Earth's beginnings, past battling dinosaurs, through earthquakes, and beneath volcanoes.

Wonders of Life (popular; all ages). The newest pavilion in Future World, which has something to do for all ages housed under a 60-foot gold dome, combines a thrill ride, a theater, exhibits, and hands-on activities while you learn about good health painlessly. Even the food offered in this pavilion is healthful.

World Showcase

World Showcase offers an adventure that is very different from what you will experience in either the world of the future in Epcot Center or the world of fairy tales in the Magic Kingdom. The Showcase presents an ideal image—a Disney version—of life in 11 countries. Native food, entertainment, and wares are on display in each of the pavilions. Most of the nations have done an imaginative and painstaking job of re-creating scale models of their best-known monuments, such as the Eiffel Tower in France, a Mayan temple in Mexico, and a majestic pagoda in Japan. During the day, these structures are impressive enough, but at night, when the darkness inhibits one's ability to judge their size, you get the sense that you are seeing the real thing. It's a wonderful illusion, indeed.

Unlike Future World and the Magic Kingdom, the Showcase doesn't offer amusement-park-type rides (except in Mexico and Norway). Instead, it features breathtaking films, ethnic art, cultural entertainment, Audio-Animatronics presentations, and dozens of fine shops and restaurants featuring national specialties. The most enjoyable diversions in World Showcase are not inside the national pavilions but in front of them. At various times of the day, each pavilion offers some sort of live street show, featuring comedy, song, or dance routines and demonstrations of folk arts and crafts. Don't be shy about trying to improve your foreign-language skills!

The only unfortunate note in this cultural smorgasbord is that with so many shops and restaurants, there seems to be more of an emphasis on commercialism than on education or entertainment. Know in advance that a taste of a nation may mean a bit out of your bank account.

The focal point of World Showcase, on the opposite side of the lagoon from Future World, is the host pavilion, the **American Adventure.** The pavilions of the other countries fan out from the right and left of American Adventure, encircling the lagoon. Going clockwise from the left as you enter World Showcase from Future World are the pavilions of Mexico, Norway, People's Republic of China, Germany, Italy, the United States, Japan, Morocco, France, United Kingdom, and Canada.

Mexico: This tame "boat ride" inside the pavilion is much like rides you have seen in the Magic Kingdom. The major tourist attractions of Mexico are its theme. Windows and doorways are filled with colorful video images, and rooms are full of dancing, costumed puppets, and Audio-Animatronics landscapes that roar, storm, and light up as you journey from the jungles of the Yucatán to the skyline of Mexico City. In front of the pavilion is **Cantina de San Angel**—a fast-food joint and bar that's good for burritos, margaritas, and, at night, a great view of the laser show, IllumiNations.

Norway: Visitors take a ride in small Viking vessels through the landscape and history of this Scandinavian country. You can tour a 10th-century Viking Village, sail through a fjord, and experience a storm and the midnight sun. The main spectacle of this pavilion is a re-creation of a 14th-century coastal fortress in Oslo called Akershus.

China: The much-talked about film should not be missed. It is a CircleVision presentation on the landscape of China, taking viewers on a fantastic journey from inner Mongolia to the Tibetan mountains, along the Great Wall, into Beijing, and through some of the most glorious landscape on Earth. The Chinese pavilion also has an art gallery with treasures never before displayed in the West and a wonderful shopping gallery with ivory goods, jade jewelry, hand-painted fans, opulent carpets, and inlaid furniture.

Germany: The main event in this replica of a small Bavarian village is the restaurant's oompah band show, with singers, dancers, and musicians. The indoor village is worth a quick look. There are four shows daily. You'll also find plenty of German wines, sweets, glassware, and porcelain for sale.

Italy: The main attraction is the architecture—a reproduction of St. Mark's Square in Venice, with the Campanile (bell tower) di San Marco as its centerpiece, and, behind it, the elegant and elaborately decorated Doges Palace. Complementing these buildings are Venetian bridges, gondolas, colorful barber poles, and the sculpture of the Lion of St. Mark atop a column. In the plaza of this pavilion, you can watch and participate in a comedy show put on by an Italian theater troupe. The show can be amusing, but only if there is a full, lively audience.

American Adventure: This is a 30-minute Audio-Animatronics show about the development of the United States. The huge, colonial-style theater features the most sophisticated and realistic animatronics characters in Disney World. The show takes visitors from the arrival of the Pilgrims through the revolutionary war, the Civil War, the taming of the West, the two world wars; and so on. The voyage is hosted by Benjamin Franklin and Mark Twain. Some will find the presentation a bit long, even though 30 minutes is not much time to cover 200 years of history. Many people find it inspiringly patriotic, but children may take this opportunity to catch a few winks—the dramatic music often puts them right to sleep.

Directly opposite the American Adventure pavilion, on the lagoon, is the open-air **American Gardens Theatre,** where live, high-energy, all-American shows are performed about four times a day. Show times vary but are posted each day on boards in front of the theater's entrances.

Japan: Elegant landscaping of rocks, streams, trees, and shrubs combines with traditional architecture to create this peaceful and charming pavilion. Inside the *torii* gates are monumental bronze sculptures and a pagoda. Of special interest are the Mitsukoshi Department Store, where lacquered dinnerware, teapots, vases, bonsai trees, and Japanese dolls and toys are for sale, and the Bijutsu-kan Gallery, featuring temporary exhibits of traditional Japanese crafts. The Yakitori House serves inexpensive Japanese fast food in a pleasant garden—a good bet for lunch.

Morocco: This is one of the more spectacular-looking of the pavilions. It has a replica of the Koutoubia Minaret from a famous prayer house in Marrakesh; a gallery of Moroccan art, tapestries, and traditional costumes; and a street with shops selling basketry, leather goods, samovars, and exquisite jewelry. Dancers move to the exotic rhythms of North Africa.

France: This 18-minute film is projected on a five-panel semicircular screen and takes viewers on a romantic tour of France—through the countryside, into the Alps, along the coast, and, of course, into Paris. It is a sophisticated visual adventure with little narration but much lyrical poetry and classical music.

The pavilion itself resembles a French boulevard, lined with shops and cafes. Of special interest are **Tout Pour le Gourmet** and **La Maison du Vin,** two shops featuring French culinary specialties, such as wines, cheeses, mustards, herbs, and pâtés. A little patisserie/boulangerie prepares all kinds of baked goods. Two restaurants, **Bistro de Paris** and **Au Petit Cafe,** are ideal for lunch. Also in this pavilion is an impressive model of the Eiffel Tower that was constructed using Alexandre-Gustave Eiffel's original blueprints.

United Kingdom: On this street from Old London are a variety of architectural styles, from thatch-roof cottages to Tudor and ornate Victorian homes. The city square and rural streets are filled with numerous food, toy, and souvenir shops. The very British **Rose and Crown Pub** serves Stilton cheese, ales, and simple English fare. Street artists and a minstrel troupe perform throughout the day.

Canada: A CircleVision film takes its audience into Canada's great outdoors, from the magnificent snow-peaked Rockies, down sprawling Arctic glaciers, and across the plains to Montreal. Peaceful gardens, a rocky gorge, an emporium selling everything from sheepskins to lumberjack shirts and maple syrup, and a cafeteria-style restaurant called **Le Cellier** are other highlights of this quaint pavilion.

Other Attractions in Disney World

Disney-MGM Studios Theme Park

Newly opened this year at Disney-MGM is the Muppet Studios, which includes a 3-D movie. The park, which started to expand almost as soon as it opened in 1989, has also added a Muppets parade; Here Come the Muppets, a musical show combining the characters with film; Dick Tracy Musical Revue; a Teenage Mutant Ninja Turtle performance; and a play area known as the Honey, I Shrunk the Kids Adventure Zone. Among the highlights at the park:

The **Backstage Studio Tour** and the **Animation Tour** are for those who want a close-up, behind-the-scenes look at a real studio. The Backstage Studio Tour takes up to two hours, but half of it is on a tram that will take you through costuming, into a shop where they make scenery, down a backlot "residential" street, and into Catastrophe Canyon for a look at special effects, and for a quick glance at more back-lot props before the walking part of the guided tour begins. As part of the walking tour you'll follow Roger Rabbit's pink paw prints through the Looney Bin. The walking portion takes in a water effects tank, special-effects workshops, soundstages, post-production work, and a theater showing previews of new movies. The Animation Tour takes visitors step-by-step through the process by looking over the artists' shoulders from a raised, glass-enclosed walkway.

Epic Stunt Spectacular is a live show with real stunt performers. Audience members are selected to join the actors on the set.

The Great Movie Ride begins tamely, like the Magic Kingdom's Pirates of the Caribbean, but soon the guide begins interacting with the Audio-Animatronics characters, and the action picks up to the delight of the younger children.

Jim Henson's Muppet Vision 3D is more than a 3D movie. A combination of Audio-Animatronics, live performances, and a 3D movie gets the audience into the middle of the action. Objects don't just fly off the screen, you actually get wet from a squirting boutonniere. Disney's "holding pen" (the portion of the line waiting to get in that you don't see from the outside) is cleverly designed as a production office and soundstage with plenty of movie props. There is nowhere to sit, but it is air-conditioned.

Star Tours is one of Disney's more recent simulator thrill rides. Created under the direction of George Lucas, the five 40-seat theaters become spaceships, and you are off to the moon of Endor. Be forwarned: lines are long and the ride is rough.

Typhoon Lagoon This 50-acre aquatic entertainment complex features the largest water-slide mountain in the world. The mountain is just under 100 feet high, with nine water slides shooting down it into white-water rivers and swirling pools. There are huge wave-making lagoons for swimming and surfing. The water park also includes a Swiss Family Robinson-type tropical island covered with lush greenery, where guests can play at being shipwrecked. A saltwater pool contains a coral reef where snorkelers come mask-to-face with all sorts of Caribbean sea creatures, such as groupers, parrotfish, and even baby sharks. *Typhoon Lagoon, tel. 407/824–4321.* See *Admission in Exploring Walt Disney World, above. Open 10–5, longer in summer.*

River Country In the backwoods setting of the Fort Wilderness Campground Resort, kids can slide, splash, and swim about in an aquatic playground, complete with white water inner-tubing channels and corkscrew water slides that splash down into a 300,000 gallon pond. The pool is heated during the winter, so kids can take a dip here year-round. During the summer, River Country can get very congested, so it's best to come late in the afternoon. *Fort Wilderness Resort, tel. 407/824–2760.* See *Admission in Exploring Walt Disney World, above. Open 10–5, longer in summer.*

Discovery Island Covered with exotic flora, small, furry animals, and colorful birdlife, this little island makes a great escape from the man-made tourist attractions of Walt Disney World. Visitors listen to nature as they stroll along winding pathways and across footbridges. Disney did not create these creatures—he just brought them here. Keep an eye out for the Galapagos tortoises, trumpeter swans, scarlet ibis, and bald eagles. Tickets are sold at Fort Wilderness's River Country, at the TTC, at guest service desks in the Disney resorts, and on the island itself. You can get there by watercraft from the Magic Kingdom, Contemporary Resort, Polynesian Village, Grand Floridian, and River Country in Fort Wilderness. *Discovery Island, tel. 407/824–2875.* See *Admission in Exploring Walt Disney World, above. Open 10–5, longer in summer.*

The Orlando Area

Numbers in the margin correspond to points of interest on the Orlando Area Attractions map.

❶ **Central Florida Zoological Park.** A 110-acre zoo. *U.S. 17–92, 1 mi east of I–4 and 4 mi west of Sanford, tel. 407/323–4450. Admission: $5 adults, $2 children 3–12. Open daily, 9–5.*

❷ **Mystery Fun House.** Magic mirrors, moving floors, laughing doors, barrels that roll, a shooting arcade—all are favorites with children, though the price is high for not much more than a few minutes' entertainment. *5767 Major Blvd., off Kirkman Rd. near International Dr., tel. 407/351–3355. Admission: $7.95 adults, children under 4 free; $4.95 for Starbase Omega, a laser tag game. Open daily 10–midnight.*

❸ **Universal Studios Florida.** The largest working film studio outside Hollywood, Universal opened its doors to tours in the summer of 1990. Patterned after the highly successful attraction in Los Angeles, the Florida facility has been developed to even more fully integrate the tour with studio production facilities, allowing visitors a closer and more interactive behind-the-scenes look at movie and TV production than does the West-Coast sibling. Visitors view live shows, participate in movie-themed attractions, and see back-lot sets. The attraction showcases the special-effects magic of creative consultant Steven Spielberg and the animation wizardry of Hanna-Barbera. In addition to the 40 movie street sets, popular stops include: Back to the Future; Earthquake—the Big One; E.T.'s Adventure; Jaws; King Kongfrontation; Nickelodeon Productions; and some of the many productions that demonstrate mixing, dubbing, sound and special effects, and set design. A **Hard Rock Cafe** is on the premises. To get to the studios, get off I–4 at Exit 29 and follow signs, or take exit 30B and go north on Kirkman Road and follow signs. *1000 Universal Studios Plaza, Orlando 32819, tel. 407/363–8000, 407/363–8210, or 407/363–8200. Admission: $33 adults, $26 children 3–9.*

❹ **Wet 'n Wild.** Water slides, flumes, rivers, and other water-related activities. *6200 International Dr., Orlando, tel. 407/351–WILD or 800/992–WILD. Admission: $20.95 adults, $18.95 children 3–12. Half-price discounts begin at 3 PM, 5 PM in summer. Hours vary but generally open 9–9 in summer, 10–5 in spring and fall; closed Jan.–mid-Feb.*

❺ **Fun 'n Wheels.** An expensive but active family theme park with go-cart tracks, rides, minigolf course, bumper boats, and cars. *6739 Sand Lake Rd. at International Dr., Orlando, tel. 407/351–5651. No general admission charge. Open Sun. 10 AM–11 PM, Mon.–Thurs. 4–11, Fri. 4–midnight, Sat 10–midnight.*

❻ **Gatorland Zoo.** Thousands of alligators and crocodiles sleeping in the sun are viewed from a walkway. Also snakes, flamingos, monkeys, and other Florida critters. *14501 S. Orange Blossom Trail, south of Orlando on U.S. 17–92 near Kissimmee, tel. 407/855–5496 or 800/393–JAWS. Admission: $8.95 adults, $5.95 children 3–11. Open daily 8 AM–6 PM.*

❼ **Sea World.** A major theme park celebrating sea life, including popular Baby Shamu and an awesome exhibit that guides you through a shark tank on a moving sidewalk. Marine animals perform in seven major shows. The park also has penguins, tropical fish, otter habitats, walrus training exhibits, botanical gardens, and other educational diversions in a setting more tranquil than that of most theme parks. *Located 10 mi south of*

Alligatorland Safari Zoo, **9**
Bok Tower Gardens, **11**
Central Florida Zoological Park, **1**
Cypress Gardens, **10**
Fun 'n Wheels, **5**
Gatorland Zoo, **6**
Mystery Fun House, **2**
Sea World, **7**
Universal Studios Florida, **3**
Wet 'n Wild, **4**
Xanadu, **8**

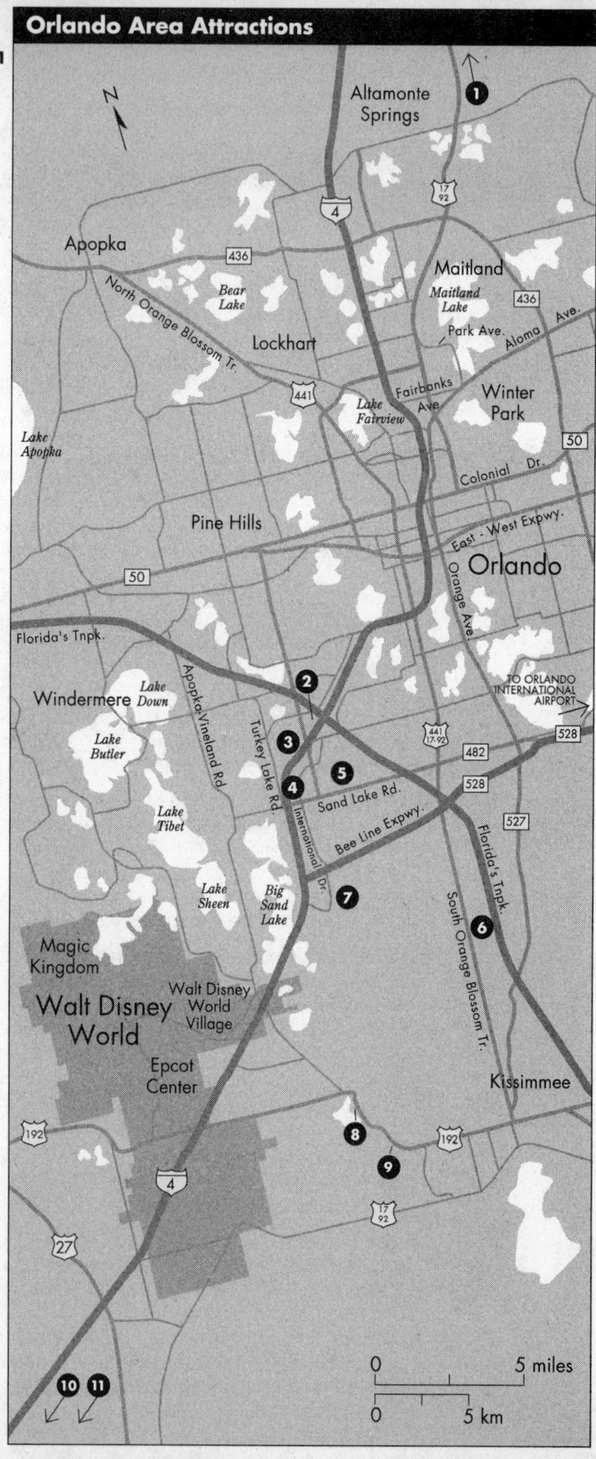

Orlando at the intersection of I-4 and the Bee Line Expressway, 7007 Sea World Dr., Orlando, tel. 407/351-3600 or 800/327-2420. Admission: $31.95 adults, $27.95 children 3-9. Open daily 9-8, with extended summer and holiday hours.

8 **Xanadu.** A dome-shaped home showcasing technological and electronic devices. Guided tours daily. *Located at the intersection of U.S. 192 and Rte. 535, Kissimmee, tel. 407/396-1992. Admission: $4.95 adults, children under 9 free.*

9 **Alligatorland Safari Zoo.** More than 1,600 exotic animals and birds in a natural setting. *U.S. 192 between Kissimmee and Walt Disney World, tel. 407/396-1012. Admission: $5.95 adults, $4.50 children 4-11. Open daily 8:30-dusk.*

10 **Cypress Gardens.** Central Florida's original theme park features exotic flowers, waterskiing shows, and bird and alligator shows. *East of Winter Haven off Rte. 540, tel. 813/324-2111. Admission: $19.95 adults, $13.95 children 3-9. Open daily 9-6.*

11 **Bok Tower Gardens.** A 128-acre garden with pine forests, shady paths, and a bell tower that rings daily at 3 PM. *Between Haines City and Lake Wales off U.S. 27, tel. 813/676-1408. Admission: $3 per person, children under 12 free. Open daily 8-5.*

The Cocoa Beach Area

Spaceport USA at the Kennedy Space Center. Free museum exhibits and films are featured, as well as guided bus tours and an IMAX theater film presentation, *The Dream Is Alive*, narrated by Walter Cronkite. The film alone is worth the trip. *Visitors' Center, tel. 407/452-2121. Bus tours: $6 adults, $3 children 3-12. IMAX theater admission: $2.75 adults, $1.75 children 3-12. Open daily 9-7. Closed Christmas.*

Cruises

Carnival Cruise Lines (tel. 800/327-9501). Three- and four-day cruises go to the Bahamas aboard *Carnivale*.

The Grand Romance, a replica of an old-time sidewheeler that used to cruise the inland waterways, has either three- or four-hour cruises daily beginning at 11 AM. Also offered is a romantic dinner-dance cruise Friday and Saturday evenings, and a RiverDaze Revue dinner and show Tuesday-Thursday. Prices range from $29.78 to $45.92, depending on the cruise; children 12 and under travel for $10 less than an adult-ticket price. Reservations are required. *433 N. Palmetto Ave., Sanford 32771, tel. 800/225-7999 in U.S.; 407/321-5091 or 800/423-7401 in FL.*

Orlando for Free

Kissimmee Livestock Market, Inc. Going, going, gone in a real cattle auction, one of the oldest in Florida. *850 E. Donegan Ave., Kissimmee 32742, tel. 407/847-3521. Open Wed. at 1 PM.*

Lake Wales Museum. Railroad memorabilia and area history. *325 S. Scenic Hwy., Lake Wales, tel. 813/676-5443. Open weekdays 9-5, Sat. 10-4.*

Monument of the States. A 50-foot-tall step pyramid built in the 1940s from concrete and stones donated by every state in the union. *Monument St., Lake Front Park, Kissimmee, tel. 407/847-3174.*

Slocum Water Gardens. An extensive display of water plants. *1101 Cypress Gardens, Winter Haven 33880, tel. 813/293-7151. Open weekdays 8-noon and 1-4, Sat. 8-noon.*

Tupperware World Headquarters. Narrated tours and displays depicting the evolution of food storage since the days of the ancient Egyptians. *U.S. 441 south of Orlando near Kissimmee, tel. 407/847–3111. Open weekdays 9–4.*

Water Ski Museum and Hall of Fame. Waterskiing fans will love what is probably the world's largest collection of equipment and memorabilia. *799 Overlook Dr., Winter Haven, tel. 813/324–2472. Open weekdays 10–5.*

Off the Beaten Track

Big Tree Park. One of the oldest and largest bald cypress trees in the country is featured in this moss-draped park with picnic tables. *U.S. 17–92 on General Hutchinson Pkwy., Longwood, tel. 407/323–9615. Open weekdays 8–sunset, weekends 9–sunset. Admission free.*

Cassadaga. The mystic's mecca, an eerily tree-shaded village started by Spiritualists. Many of the residents read palms, peer into the future, and relay messages from the world beyond. When the psychics meet from January to March, many of the lectures and seminars are open to the public. Visit anytime. *Located off I–4, 7 miles south of De Land. Southern Cassadaga Spiritualist Camp, Box 319, Cassadaga 32706, tel. 904/228–2880.*

Hontoon Island State Park. Take a ferry-boat ride to a 1,650-acre park and campground with six rustic cabins, 22 campsites, a floating marina with slips for 54 boats, and an 80-foot observation tower. The park is off Rte. 44 on Hontoon Road. *Hontoon Island, 2309 Riverridge Rd., De Land 32720, tel. 904/736–5309. Open daily 9 AM–sunset. The ferry operates from 9 AM until an hour before the park closes.*

Navy Graduation. Recruit graduation parade every Friday at 9:45 AM. *Orlando Naval Training Center, General Rees Rd., entrance off Corrine Dr., Orlando, tel. 407/646–5054. Admission free.*

Pioneer Settlement for the Creative Arts. Folk museum with demonstrations of day-to-day pioneer lifestyles, a turn-of-the-century country store, and a train depot. *Intersection of U.S. 40 and 17 in De Land, about 40 mi from Orlando, tel. 904/749–2959. Admission: $2.50 adults, $1.50 children under 17. Open weekdays 9–4, Sat. 9–2.*

Shopping

Altamonte Mall. The largest mall in central Florida was renovated in 1989 and a food court was added in 1990. Sears, Maison Blanche, Dillard's, and Burdine's department stores anchor the two-level mall with its 165 specialty shops. *A half mile east of I–4 on Rte. 436 in Altamonte Springs, tel. 407/830–4400. Open Mon.–Sat. 10 AM–9 PM, Sun. noon–5:50 (except holidays).*

Florida Mall. This is a newer, large-scale center in Orlando, closer to the Walt Disney World tourism corridor. More than 170 stores in an enclosed mall that has three distinctive shopping areas—Victorian, Mediterranean, and Art Deco. *On the corner of Sand Lake Rd. (Rte. 482) and S. Orange Blossom Trail and near International Dr., tel. 407/851–6255. Open Mon.–Sat. 10–9, Sun. noon–5:30.*

Flea World. Flea markets are scattered across the Orlando area, but this is the largest and most popular. Well over 1,500 booths, some air-conditioned, offer arts and crafts, auto parts, citrus produce, and so on. *Highway 17–92 between Orlando* *and Sanford, tel. 407/647–3976. Admission free. Open Fri., Sat., and Sun. 8–5.*

Park Avenue. This is the place to go for fashionable, upscale shopping in Winter Park. Most stores are open weekdays 9–5, but you can window-browse anytime and enjoy the many restaurants and ice-cream shops along the avenue. The shops range from Laura Ashley to small antiques shops.

Mercado Mediterranean Village. The latest trend in Orlando is "festive retail," where shopping is combined with entertainment. At Mercado, visitors wander along brick streets and browse through more than 50 specialty shops in the atmosphere of a Mediterranean village. Free entertainment nightly. Exotic foods are all under one roof at the International Food Pavilion. *8445 International Dr., tel. 407/345–9337. Open 10–10 daily.*

Old Town. Also in the tourist corridor is this collection of more than 60 specialty shops, an Elvis Presley museum, a train, and restaurants along pedestrian walks. Tethered balloon rides are available. *5770 Spacecoast Pkwy., Kissimmee, tel. 407/396–4888; 800/843–4202; or in FL, 800/331–5093. Open daily 10–10.*

Ron Jon Surf Shop. They have everything you will need for a day at the beach ranging from their distinctive T-shirts to surfboards. A scuba center at the back of the shop offers equipment, rentals, and lessons. *4151 N. Atlantic Ave., Cocoa Beach, tel. 407/799–8888. Open daily 9 AM–11 PM.*

Walt Disney World. For unusual and sophisticated shopping, try World Showcase, where each country offers unique native merchandise. Walt Disney World Village in Lake Buena Vista, only 2 miles from Epcot Center and 6 miles from the Magic Kingdom, is a collection of some 20 shops that offer everything from Christmas tree ornaments to Disney memorabilia.

Participant Sports

Bicycling The most scenic bike riding in Orlando is on the property of Walt Disney World, along roads that take you past forests, lakes, golf courses, and Disney's wooded resort villas and campgrounds. Bikes are available for rent at **Caribbean Beach Resort** (tel. 407/934–3400), **Fort Wilderness Bike Barn** (tel. 407/824–2742), and **Walt Disney World Village Villa Center** (tel. 407/824–6947). Bike rental is $3 an hour, $7 per day. In Cocoa Beach, **Ron Jon Surf Shop** (4151 N. Atlantic Ave., tel. 407/799–8888) has bikes to rent.

Fishing Central Florida is covered with freshwater lakes and rivers teeming with all kinds of fish, from largemouth black bass to perch, catfish, sunfish, and pike.

If you are staying at WDW, **Fort Wilderness Campground** (tel. 407/824–2900) is the starting point for two-hour fishing trips, departing at 8 AM and 3. Boats, equipment, and guide for up to five anglers cost $110.

Lake Tohopekaliga is a popular camping and fishing destination and convenient for most visitors to central Florida. Among the best fishing camps are: **Red's Fish Camp** (4715 Kissimmee Park Rd., St. Cloud, tel. 407/892–8795); **Richardson's Fish Camp** (1550 Scotty's Rd., Kissimmee, tel. 407/846–6540); **Scotty's Fish Camp & Mobil Home Park** (1554 Scotty's Rd., Kissimmee, tel. 407/847–3840); and **East Lake Fish Camp** (3705 Big Bass Rd., Kissimmee, tel. 407/348–2040).

Bass Challenger Guide (Box 679155, Orlando 32867, tel. 407/273–8045) takes you out in boats equipped with drinks and tackle. Transportation can be arranged to and from their location. Half day (1 or 2 persons) from $125, full day from $175. Their guarantee is "No bass, no pay!"

Bass Bustin' Guide (5935 Swoffield Dr., Orlando, tel. 407/281–0845) provides boat, tackle, transportation, and amenities for bass fishing on local lakes, and it guarantees fish! Half day from $125, full day from $175.

You can deep-sea troll in the Atlantic for blue and white marlin, sailfish, dolphin, king mackerel, tuna, and wahoo. Grouper, red snapper, and amberjack are deep-sea bottom-fishing prizes. Surf casting is popular for pompano, bluefish, flounder, and sea bass. From fishing piers, anglers pull in sheepshead, mackerel, trout, and tarpon. Most Atlantic beach communities have a lighted pier with a bait-and-tackle shop and rest rooms. Deep-sea charters are found at Port Canaveral. Call ahead for prices and reservations. **Cape Marina** (800 Scallop Dr., tel. 407/783–8410); **Miss Cape Canaveral** (630 Glen Cheek Dr., tel. 407/783–5274); **Pelican Princess** (665 Glen Cheek Dr., tel. 407/784–3474).

Golf Many resort hotels let nonguests use their golf facilities. Some hotels are affiliated with a particular country club and offer preferred rates. If you are staying near a resort with facilities you want to use, call and inquire about its policies. Be sure to call in advance to reserve tee times. What follows is a list of the best places that are open to the public.

Golfpac (Box 940490, Maitland, 32794, tel. 407/660–8559) packages golf vacations and prearranges tee times at over 30 courses around Orlando.

Poinciana Golf & Racquet Club (500 Cypress Pkwy., tel. 407/933–5300) has a par-72 course about 18 miles southeast of Walt Disney World.

Walt Disney World's three championship courses—all played by the PGA Tour—are among the busiest and most expensive in the region. Greens fees are $70 and $32 after 3 PM. In January 1992 WDW opened two more 18-hole courses, Osprey Ridge and Eagle Pines. Greens fees are $85.

Golf lessons are given in small groups at the Disney Inn courses, the Magnolia and the Palm. Private lessons are available both at these courses and at the Lake Buena Vista Club. There is also a nine-hole executive course on artificial turf with natural turf greens for $25 18 holes, $20 for nine holes. For private lessons at the Lake Buena Vista Club, phone tel. 407/828–3741. For all other information, phone tel. 407/824–2270.

Grenelefe Golf and Tennis Resort (3200 Rte. 546, Haines City, tel. 813/422–7511; 800/237–9546; in FL, 800/282–7875), about 45 minutes from Orlando, has three 18-hole courses over gentle hills. Make the West Course (18 holes, par 72, 7,325 yards) your first choice. East Course is 6,802 yards, par 72, and the South Course is 6,869 yards, par 71.

Orange Lake Country Club (8505 W. U.S. 192, Kissimmee, tel. 407/239–0000) offers three nine-hole courses and is about five minutes from Walt Disney World's main entrance. The Orange (with a 118-yard island hole) and the Cypress is the most challenging 18-hole combination. All three courses are par 36 and about 3,300 yards.

Other challenging courses open to the public are: **Marriott's Orlando World Center** (1 World Center Dr., Orlando, tel. 407/239–4200; 800/228–9290), 6,265 yards; **Cocoa Beach Municipal Golf Course** (5000 Tom Warriner Blvd., Cocoa Beach, tel. 407/783–5351, 6,968 yards); **Cypress Creek Country Club** (5353 Vineland Rd., Orlando, tel. 407/425–2319, 6,952 yards); **Hunter's Creek Golf Course** (14401 Sports Club Way, Orlando, tel. 407/240–4653, 7,432 yards); **Timacuan Golf and Country Club** (550 Timacuan Blvd., Lake Mary, tel. 407/321–0010, 7,027 yards); **Turtle Creek Golf Club** (1278 Admiralty Blvd., Rockledge, tel. 407/632–2520, 6,709 yards); **Wedgefield Golf and Country Club** (20550 Maxim Parkway, Orlando, tel. 407/568–2116, 6,378 yards); **MetroWest Country Club** (2100 S. Hiawassee Rd., Orlando, tel. 407/297–0052, 7,051 yards).

Horseback Riding

Grand Cypress Equestrian Center (tel. 407/239–4608) offers hunter, jumper, and dressage private lessons ($30 for 30 minutes, $50 for an hour). Novice ($25 an hour) and advanced ($30 an hour) trails are available.

Fort Wilderness Campground (tel. 407/824–2803) in Walt Disney World offers tame trail rides through the backwoods and along lakesides. Open to the general public. Call in advance to arrange an outing. Rides at 9, 10:30, noon, 1, and 2. Cost: $13 per person for 45 minutes. Children must be over 9.

Poinciana Riding Stables (tel. 407/847–4343) takes visitors for hour-long rides along old logging trails near Kissimmee. Cost: $15.99.

Ice Skating

Orlando Ice Skating Palace (3123 W. Colonial Dr., Parkwood Shopping Plaza Orlando, tel. 407/299–5440) isn't the most attractive rink, but if you are homesick for a winter chill, this should do the trick. Open Wed.–Fri. 7:30–10:30 PM, Sat. 12:30–3:30, 4–7, 7:30–10:30, and 11 PM–1 AM, and Sun. 2–5 and 7:30–10:30. Call for additional weekday hours.

Jogging

Walt Disney World has several scenic jogging trails. Pick up jogging maps at any Disney resort. **Fort Wilderness** (tel. 407/824–2900) has a 2.3-mile jogging course, with plenty of fresh air and woods, as well as numerous exercise stations along the way.

Tennis

For the following courts that aren't first-come, first-served, call to reserve courts.

Disney Inn (tel. 407/824–1469) has two courts, **Village Clubhouse** (tel. 407/828–3741) has three; the **Dolphin** and **Swan** (tel. 407/934–6000) share eight; the **Grand Floridian** (tel. 407/824–2438) has two composition courts; the **Yacht and Beach Club** (tel. 407/934–8000) has two; **Fort Wilderness Campground** (tel. 407/824–2900) has two (first come, first served); and the **Contemporary Resort** (tel. 407/824–3578) has six, where private and group lessons are available. All courts are lighted and open until 10 PM. Racquets may be rented by the hour.

Orange Lake Country Club (8505 W. U.S. 192, Kissimmee, tel. 407/239–2255) has 16 all-weather courts, 10 of them lighted.

Orlando Tennis Center (649 W. Livingston St., tel. 407/246–2162) has 16 lighted courts (nine clay, seven hard), two racquetball courts, and four tennis pros.

The Orlando Vacation Resort (west of I–4 on U.S. 27, tel. 407/394–6171) has 17 asphalt courts open only to guests.

Water Sports Marinas at **Caribbean Beach Resort, Contemporary Resort, Fort Wilderness, Polynesian Village,** and **Yacht and Beach Club, Walt Disney World Village** rent Sunfish, catamarans, motor-powered pontoon boats, pedal boats, and Water Sprites for the 450-acre Bay Lake, the adjoining 200-acres of the Seven Seas Lagoon, Club Lake, Lake Buena Vista, and Buena Vista Lagoon. The Polynesian Village marina rents outrigger canoes. Fort Wilderness rents canoes. For waterskiing ($65 per hour) reservations, phone 407/824–1000.

Airboat Rentals (4266 Vine St., Kissimmee, tel. 407/847–3672) rents airboats ($20 per hour) and canoes ($5 per hour) for use on Shingle Creek, with views of giant cypress trees and Spanish moss.

Ski Holidays (13323 Lake Bryan Dr., tel. 407/239–4444) has waterskiing, jetskiing, and parasailing on a private lake next to Walt Disney World. Boat rental: $60 per hour. Also available: wave runners, jet boats, and jetskis. To get there take I–4 to the Lake Buena Vista exit, turn south on Rte. 535 toward Kissimmee. Turn left onto a private dirt road about 300 yards down on the left.

Rent a powerful seven-seater ski boat at **Sanford Boat Rentals** (tel. 407/321–5906, in Florida 800/237–5105, outside Florida 800/692–3414) up the St. Johns River. Houseboats and pontoons are available for day, overnight, weekend, or week-long trips. Pontoon and ski boats $60 for 4 hours or $100 per day; 44-foot houseboat $350 per day, $560 for 2 days, $1,000 weekly. Rates vary seasonally.

Go Vacations (2280 Hontoon Dr., DeLand, tel. 800/262–3454 or 904/736–9422) rents luxury houseboats on the St. Johns River. Among the packages is a $759 weekend deal and a weekly price of $1,295. Rates vary seasonally.

Jetskiing, boardsailing, waterskiing, sailing, and powerboating are popular pastimes on the Atlantic Intracoastal Waterway. Rental equipment is available at **The Water Works** (1891 E. Merritt Island Causeway, Rte. 520, Merritt Island, tel. 407/452–2007).

Spectator Sports

Jai Alai **Orlando-Seminole Jai-Alai.** The sport is fun to watch even if you don't bet. *Tel. 407/331–9191. Admission: $1 general, $2 reserved seating. Open May–Jan. at 7:20 nightly except Sun. with noon matinees Mon., Thurs., Sat., and Sun.*

Dog Racing **Sanford Orlando Kennel Club** (301 Dog Track Rd., Longwood, tel. 407/831–1600) has dog racing and betting nightly except Sun. at 7:30. Matinees Mon., Wed., and Sat. at 1 PM. *Admission: $1. Open Dec.–May.*

Seminole Greyhound Park (2000 Seminola Blvd., Casselberry, tel. 407/699–4510) is a newer track with racing nightly at 7:45 except Sunday. Matinees Mon., Wed., and Sat. at 1 PM. *Admission: $1 general, clubhouse $2, children half price. Open May–Oct.*

Basketball **Orlando Magic** (Box 76, Orlando 32802, tel. 407/839–3900) joined the National Basketball Association in the 1989–90 season. The team plays in the new, 15,077-seat Orlando Arena.

Admission: $8–$28. Off I-4 at Amelia; the arena is 2 blocks west of the interstate.

Baseball The **Orlando SunRays** are Minnesota's Class AA Southern League affiliate. They play baseball at Tinker Field. *Tel. 407/872-7593. Get off I-4 at Colonial Ave. (Hwy. 50), go west to Tampa Ave. and south on Tampa to the stadium.*

The **Osceola Astros** (tel. 407/933-2520) are Houston's Class A team in the Florida State League. They play at Osceola County Stadium in Kissimmee.

The **Baseball City Royals** (tel. 813/424-2424) are Kansas City's Class-A team in the Florida State League. They play at the former Boardwalk and Baseball complex at I-4 and U.S. 27.

Football **The Orlando Thunder** play in the World League of American Football. Games are held from March to June at Orlando stadium. *Tel. 407/841-2078.*

Dining

If you want to try some local specialties, consider stone crabs, pompano (a mild white fish), Apalachicola oysters, small but tasty Florida lobsters, and conch chowder. Fresn hearts of palm are a treat, too.

Highly recommended restaurants are indicated by a star ★.

Category	Cost*
Very Expensive	over $40
Expensive	$30–$40
Moderate	$20–$30
Inexpensive	under $20

**per person, excluding drinks, service, and 6% sales tax*

In Epcot Center World Showcase offers some of the finest dining not only in Walt Disney World but in the entire Orlando area. The problem is that the restaurants are often crowded and difficult to book. Many of them are operated by the same people who own internationally famous restaurants in their home countries. The top-of-the-line places, such as those in the French, Italian, and Japanese pavilions, can be expensive, but they are not as pricey as comparable restaurants in large, cosmopolitan cities such as Paris or New York. One good thing about Epcot's restaurants, besides the food, is that most of them have limited-selection children's menus with drastically lower prices, so bringing the kids along to dinner won't break the bank.

Visitors are not expected to go all the way back to their hotels to change and clean up and then return for dinner, so casual dress is expected in all the restaurants, even the finest.

If you want to eat in one of the more popular restaurants, it will be much easier to get a reservation for lunch than for dinner. It won't be quite the same experience, but it will be cheaper. Another way to get a table is to have lunch before noon and dinner before 6 or after 8.

Both lunch and dinner reservations are strongly recommended at all the finer restaurants in Epcot. Unless you are staying at one of the Walt Disney World hotels, you cannot reserve in advance of the day on which you wish to eat, and you can't book by phone. Instead, you must reserve in person at each restaurant or head for Earth Station at the base of Spaceship Earth as soon as you get to Epcot Center. There you will find a bank of computer screens called WorldKey Information. You need to stand in line to get to one of these screens and place the reservation, and the lines form very early. On busy days, most top restaurants are filled within an hour of Epcot's opening time, so you may have to line up at the Epcot admissions booth before opening time and then, once you're through the gate, make a mad dash for the WorldKey computer terminals. If there is a long line when you get to Earth Station, remember that on the far side of Future World, just before the bridge to World Showcase, is an outdoor kiosk with five WorldKey terminals that few people notice. There is also another WorldKey kiosk on the far side of the Port of Entry gift shop, near the boat dock for the water taxi to the Moroccan pavilion. Having made the reservations, you can begin to enjoy your day at Epcot.

If you are a guest at an on-site Walt Disney World resort or at one of the Walt Disney World Village hotels, avoid the battle of the WorldKey by booking a table by phone (tel. 407/824–4000). Remember that if you are staying at one of these resorts, you cannot make a same-day reservation by phone but must book either one or two days in advance between noon and 9 PM. The restaurant will ask to see your resort identification card, so don't leave it in your hotel room. No matter how you book, try to show up at the restaurant a bit early to be sure of getting your table. You can pay with American Express, Visa, MasterCard, or, of course, cash. If you're a guest of a Disney hotel, you can charge the tab to your room.

British **Rose and Crown.** This is a very popular, friendly British pub, where visitors and Disney employees come at the end of the day to knock off a pint of crisp Bass ale or blood-thickening Guinness stout with a few morsels of Stilton cheese. "Wenches" serve up simple pub fare, such as steak-and-kidney pie, beef tenderloin, and fish and chips. The Rose and Crown sits on the shore of the lagoon, so on warm days it's nice to lunch on the patio at the water's edge and enjoy the soft breezes and the homiest atmosphere in Epcot Center. *Moderate.*

French **Bistro de Paris.** Located on the second floor of the French pavilion, above Chefs de France (*see* below), this is a relatively quiet and charming spot for lunch or dinner. The bistro specializes in regional cooking from southern France. A favorite is steamed filet of fresh grouper with tomato, mushrooms, fresh herbs, and white wine sauce, served with rice pilaf. Wines are moderately priced and available by the glass. *Expensive.*

★ **Chefs de France.** Three of France's most famous culinary artists came together to create this French restaurant. The most renowned of the three, Paul Bocuse, operates one restaurant north of Lyon and two in Tokyo and has published several famous books on French cuisine. Another, Gaston Lenôtre, has gained eminence for his pastries and ice creams. The third of this culinary triumvirate, Roger Vergé, operates one of France's most highly rated restaurants, near Cannes. The three don't actually prepare each meal, but they were the ones who created the menu and carefully trained the chefs. Some of their most popular classic dishes are roast duck with prunes and wine sauce; beef filet with fresh ground pepper, raisins, and Armagnac sauce; and filet of grouper topped with salmon-vegetable mousse and baked in puff pastry. *Expensive.*

German **Biergarten.** This popular spot boasts Oktoberfest 365 days a year. Visitors sit at long communal tables and are served by waitresses in typical Bavarian garb. The cheerful—some would say raucous—atmosphere is what one would expect from a place where performers yodel, sing, and dance to the rhythms of an oompah band. The crowd, pounding pitchers of beer or wine while consuming hot pretzels and hearty German fare, is usually pretty active when audience participation is called for and just as active when it is not. *Moderate.*

Italian **L'Originale Alfredo di Roma Ristorante.** This is a World Showcase hot spot, with some of the finest food in Walt Disney World. During dinner, waiters skip around singing Italian songs and bellowing arias. The restaurant is named for the man who invented the now-classic fettuccine Alfredo, a pasta served with a sauce of cream, butter, and loads of freshly grated Parmesan cheese. Another popular dish is *lo Chef Consiglia* (the chef's selections), which consists of an appetizer of spaghetti or fettuccine, a mixed green salad, and a chicken or veal entrée. The most popular veal dish is *piccata di vitello*—veal thinly sliced and panfried with lemon and white wine. *Expensive.*

Japanese **Mitsukoshi.** This isn't just a restaurant, it's a complex of dining areas on the second floor above the Mitsukoshi Department Store. Each of the five dining rooms (on your left as you enter) has four tables that seat eight and are equipped with a grill on which chefs prepare meats and fish with acrobatic precision. It's an American's idea of the real Japan, but fun nonetheless. *Moderate.*

Mexican **San Angel Inn.** The lush, tropical surroundings—cool, dark, almost surreal—make this one of the most exotic restaurants in Disney World. The ambience is at once romantic and lively. Tables are candlelit, but close together, and the restaurant is open to the pavilion, where folk singers perform and musicians play guitars or marimbas. One of the specialties is *langosta Baja California*—Baja lobster meat, sautéed with tomatoes, onions, olives, Mexican peppers, and white wine, and baked in its shell. Try the margaritas, and, for dessert, don't miss the chocolate Kahlúa mousse pie. *Moderate.*

Moroccan **Restaurant Marrakesh.** Belly dancers and a three-piece Moroccan band set the mood in this exotic restaurant, where you may feel as though you have stumbled onto the set of *Casablanca.* The food is mildly spicy and relatively inexpensive. At lunch, you may want to try the national dish of Morocco, *couscous,* served with garden vegetables. For dinner, try the *bastila,* an appetizer of sweet and spicy pork between many layers of thin pastry, with almonds, saffron, and cinnamon. *Moderate.*

Norwegian **Restaurant Akershus.** Norway's tradition of seafood and cold meat dishes is highlighted at the restaurant's *koldtbord,* or Norwegian buffet. Hosts and hostesses explain the dishes to guests and suggest which ones go together. It is traditional to make several trips to the koldtbord, so there is no need to shovel everything you see onto your plate at one time. The first trip is for appetizers, usually herring prepared in a number of ways. On your next trip choose cold seafood items—try gravlaks, salmon cured with salt, sugar, and dill. Pick up cold salads and meats on your next trip, and then you fill up with hot dishes on your fourth trip, usually a choice of lamb, veal, and venison. Desserts are offered à la carte, including cloudberries, delicate, seasonal fruits that grow on the tundra. There are four dining rooms, seating 220 in an impressive copy of Oslo's famous Akershus Castle. *Moderate.*

The Walt Disney World Area

These are restaurants close to Disney World, situated along International Drive or near Kissimmee, Disney Maingate, or Lake Buena Vista.

American

Empress Lilly. Disney's 220-foot, 19th-century Mississippi-style riverboat is a popular tourist dining spot at the far end of Disney Village Marketplace, right on Buena Vista Lagoon. The boat is permanently moored; it looks like an elegant old-fashioned Victorian showboat, complete with brass lamps, burgundy velvet love seats, mahogany wood, and several restaurants and lounges. Beef is served in the *Steerman's Quarters* and seafood in *Fisherman's Deck.* Only 5% of the tables are open for reservations, two days in advance. Visitors without reservations should arrive early, add their names to the list, then go and listen to banjo music in the *Baton Rouge Lounge.* The food is as predictable as it is expensive, but dining here can be an enjoyable experience for large families or groups who want a decent meal but do not want to feel inhibited by a stuffy atmosphere. The third restaurant on the showboat is the *Empress Room,* a plush, Victorian dining room filled with gilded reminders of another age. It is a luxurious (if gaudy) setting that might bring out the Rhett Butler or Scarlett O'Hara in you, but you will wish that the food were more palatable, especially at these prices. The menu reads elegantly, featuring such specialties as duck, pheasant, venison, and various seafood dishes, but the food is unlikely to live up to your elegant expectations. *Steerman's Quarters and Fisherman's Deck: Disney Village Marketplace, tel. 407/828–3900. Only a few reservations accepted. Dress: casual. AE, DC, MC, V. Moderate. Empress Room: Reservations required, up to a month in advance. Jacket required. AE, DC, MC, V. Expensive.*

★ **Chatham's Place.** In this elegant, simple, unpretentious restaurant the Chatham brothers show their skills with such entrées as black grouper with pecan butter, spaghetti à la Grecque, and duck breast, grilled to crispy perfection. It's a small space, and the office building exterior belies what's inside, but this is arguably one of Orlando's best. *7575 Dr. Phillips Blvd., Orlando, tel. 407/345–2992. Reservations advised. Dress: informal. MC, V. Moderate–Expensive.*

Hard Rock Cafe Orlando. The guitar-shaped structure is at Universal Studios Florida with an entrance from the studio or off the street. Hamburgers, barbecue, and sandwiches are served to the sound of rock music amidst rock memorabilia. *Universal Studios Florida, 5401 S. Kirkman Rd., tel. 407/363–ROLL. No reservations. Dress: casual. AE, MC, V. Inexpensive.*

Chinese

Ming Court. This is no take-out Chinese, but truly fine Oriental-style dining. Although some dishes will seem familiar, creative flairs make each dish unique. Try the jumbo shrimp in lobster sauce flavored with crushed black beans, or the Hunan *kung pao* chicken with peanuts, cashews, and walnuts. Prices may seem high, but the elegant surroundings—glass walls allow you to look out on the pond and floating gardens—make the

It's easy to recognize a good place when you see one.

American Express Cardmembers have been doing it for years.

The secret? Instead of just relying on what they see in the window, they look at the door. If there's an American Express Blue Box on it, they know they've found an establishment that cares about high standards.

Whether it's a place to eat, to sleep, to shop, or simply meet, they know they will be warmly welcomed.

So much so, they're rarely taken in by anything else.

Always a good sign.

check worthwhile. *Not far from the Orange County Convention Center. 9188 International Dr., Orlando, tel. 407/351–9988. Reservations advised. Dress: casual. AE, DC, MC, V. Moderate.*

Continental

Victoria and Albert's. The prix fixe menu changes daily but always offers a choice among beef, seafood, and poultry. The prices tend to be high, but help pay for the Royal Doulton china, Sambonet silver, Schott-Zweisel crystal, and turn-of-the-century costumes for your servers—a maid and butler named Victoria and Albert. The surroundings and treatment impress more than the food. *Grand Floridian Beach Resort, Walt Disney World, tel. 407/824–2323. Reservations required. Jacket required. AE, MC, V. Very Expensive.*

Dux. In the Peabody Hotel's gourmet restaurant, some creations are innovative, such as the grilled quail with poached quail eggs, served with wild rice in a carrot terrine nest. Others are a trifle self-conscious, like the avocado with sautéed salmon, artichoke chips, and champagne caviar sauce. For an entrée, consider the baked Florida lobster with chanterelle mushrooms, spinach, and champagne sauce. The selection of California wines is outstanding. *Peabody Hotel, 9801 International Dr., Orlando, tel. 407/352–4000. Reservations strongly recommended. Jacket required. AE, DC, MC, V. Expensive.*

La Coquina. This is a hotel restaurant with an emphasis on seafood and serious sauces. One popular meat specialty is loin of lamb with eggplant and goat cheese in grape leaves, served with grilled *polenta* (a type of cornmeal). The best bet here is Sunday brunch—a cornucopia of fruits, vegetables, pastries, pâtés, smoked fish, and a number of dishes cooked before your eyes. The $29 brunch is served with Domaine Chandon champagne; the $85 brunch with all the Dom Perignon champagne you can consume. If you're hungry and thirsty enough, you just might be able to put them out of business. *Hyatt Regency Grand Cypress Resort, 1 Grand Cypress Blvd., Orlando, tel. 407/239–1234. Reservations suggested. Jacket required. AE, DC, MC, V. Expensive.*

Indian

Darbar Exclusive House of Indian Cuisine. This lavishly decorated dining room features northern Indian cuisine. In addition to curries and pilafs, Darbar specializes in tandoori cooking—barbecuing with mesquite charcoal in a clay oven. Meats and vegetables are marinated in special sauces overnight and cooked to perfection. If you're not familiar with Indian cuisine, this is a good place to begin. The best bet is the tandoori dinner for two, with different types of lamb and chicken. *7600 Dr. Phillips Blvd., Orlando, tel. 407/345–8128. To get there, take Sand Lake Blvd. (exit 29 off I–4) and head west to the Marketplace Shopping Center (right after the 2nd stoplight). The restaurant is in the shopping center. Reservations advised on weekends. Dress: casual. AE, DC, MC, V. Moderate.*

Italian
★

Christini's. For traditional Italian cuisine, this is Orlando's finest. The restaurant is not about to win any awards for decor, but the food couldn't be fresher and the service couldn't be more efficient. The restaurant makes its own pastas daily and serves them with herbs, vegetables, and freshly grated Parmesan. Specialties include fresh fish; a fish soup with lobster, shrimp, and clams; and veal chops with fresh sage. *Intersection of Sand Lake Rd., and Dr. Phillips Blvd., in the Marketplace*

Shopping Center, tel. 407/345–8770. Reservations recommended. Jacket required. AE, DC, MC, V. Expensive.

Japanese ★ **Ran-Getsu.** The best Japanese food in town is served in this palatial setting. The atmosphere may seem a bit self-conscious—an American's idea of the Orient—but the food is fresh and carefully prepared. Sit at the curved, dragon's tail-shaped sushi bar for the Matsu platter—an assortment of *nigiri-* and *maki*-style sushis—or, if you are with a group, sit Japanese style at tables overlooking a carp-filled pond and decorative gardens. Specialties are sukiyaki and *shabu-shabu* (thinly sliced beef in a boiling seasoned broth, served with vegetables and prepared at your table). If you feel more adventurous, try the deep-fried alligator tail. *8400 International Dr., Orlando, tel. 407/345–0044. Reservations accepted. Dress: casual. AE, DC, MC, V. Moderate.*

Kosher **Palm Terrace.** This is a kosher restaurant supervised by a rabbi of the Orthodox Union. Diners who are guests at the Hyatt Orlando get a 20% discount. Specials begin at $25. There are fixed-price Shabbos meals, which must be prepaid on Friday, and reservations are required one-half hour before candle-lighting. Kosher breakfast and lunch items are available next door at the Marketplace Deli from 6 to 1 AM. (The Hyatt also has a shul, with services held twice daily.) *Hyatt Orlando, 6375 Irlo Bronson Memorial Hwy., Kissimmee, tel. 407/396–1234. Reservations required. Dress: casual. AE, DC, MC, V. Moderate.*

Middle Eastern **Phoenician.** *Hummus, baba ghanouj*, and *lebneh* are just some of the exotic dishes at this small cafe serving authentic Mediterranean and Middle Eastern cuisine. The best bet is to order a tableful of appetizers, *meza*, and sample as many as possible. *7600 Dr. Phillips Blvd., Suite 142, Orlando, tel. 407/345–1001. No reservations. Dress: casual. AE, MC, V. Inexpensive.*

Seafood **Hemingway's.** Located by the pool at the Hyatt Regency Grand Cypress, this restaurant serves all sorts of sea creatures, from conch, scallops, and squid to grouper, pompano, and monkfish. In addition to the regular menu, Hemingway's also has what is called a "Cuisine Naturelle" menu, featuring dishes that are low in fat, calories, sodium, and cholesterol—recipes that are approved by the American Heart Association and Weight Watchers. What more could you want other than a big hot-fudge sundae for dessert? *Hyatt Regency Grand Cypress Resort, 1 Grand Cypress Blvd., Orlando, tel. 407/239–1234. Reservations suggested. Dress: casual. AE, DC, MC, V. Moderate–Expensive.*

Thai **Siam Orchid.** Another in the trend of elegant Oriental restaurants offering fine dining, Siam Orchid is in a gorgeous structure and is a bit off the more beaten path of International Drive. Waitresses, in the attire of their homeland, serve authentic Thai cuisine. Some standouts are the Siam wings appetizer—stuffed chicken wings—and *pla lad prig* (a whole fish, deep-fried and covered with a sauce of red chili, bell peppers, and garlic). If you like your food spicy, ask for it "Thai hot," and grab a fire extinguisher. *7575 Republic Dr., Orlando, tel. 407/351–0821. Dress: casual. AE, DC, MC, V. Moderate.*

24 Hours **Beeline Diner.** This is a slick 1950s-style diner that's always open. It is in the Peabody Hotel, so it's not exactly cheap, but the salads, sandwiches, and griddle foods are tops. A good bet for breakfast or a late-night snack. And for just a little silver, you get to play a lot of old tunes on the jukebox. *Peabody Hotel, 9801 International Dr., Orlando, tel. 407/352–4000. Dress casual. AE, DC, MC, V. Moderate.*

The Orlando Area The following restaurants are in or near the city of Orlando and cater mostly to a local clientele.

American **Jordan's Grove.** This old house was built in 1912 and now holds one of Orlando's most popular restaurants. The menu changes daily and the prix fixe includes choice of soup or salad, appetizer, entrée with vegetables, and dessert. An à la carte menu was recently added. The changing menu allows for some creative flexing in the kitchen, and few people leave unsatisfied. Wine is the only alcoholic beverage served. The list is small but well-planned, featuring mostly American wines from smaller estates. *1300 S. Orlando Ave. (U.S. 17–92), Maitland, tel. 407/628–0020. Reservations advised. Dress: casual. AE, DC, MC, V. Moderate–Expensive.*

Pebbles. A favorite of Orlando residents, Pebbles serves a casual California cuisine using local ingredients. This restaurant in the suburbs was such a big hit, three more have opened—two in areas more easily accessible to tourists. Each of the four is noted for its fine service and an atmosphere of casual elegance. You'll feel at home in shorts as well as in a jacket, although the Longwood location tends to get a better-dressed crowd, probably because tourists aren't walking in off the street. You can make a delightful lunch out of soups and salads and blow your diet on the desserts. The more touristy locations are: Crossroads (at the Lake Buena Vista entrance to Walt Disney World), tel. 407/827–1111; and 17 W. Church St., tel. 407/839–0892. The fourth location is at 2516 Aloma Ave., Winter Park, tel. 407/678–7001. *2100 S.R. 434, Longwood, tel. 407/774–7111. No reservations. Dress: casual. AE, DC, MC, V. Moderate.*

Chinese ★ **4, 5, 6.** Pedestrian surroundings don't hide well-prepared and well-served traditional dishes, such as steamed sea bass and chicken with snow peas that are served in Chinatown fashion by cart-pushing waiters. *657 N. Primrose Dr., Orlando, tel. 407/898–1899. Reservations advised on weekends. Dress: casual. Open weekends to 2 AM. AE, MC, V. Inexpensive.*

Continental ★ **Chalet Suzanne.** If you like to drive or are returning from a day at Cypress Gardens, consider dining at this award-winning family-owned country inn and restaurant. It has been expanded bit by bit since it opened in the 1930s. Today, it looks like a small Swiss village—right in the middle of Florida's orange groves. The place settings, china, glasses, chairs, and even the tables are of different sizes, shapes, and origins. Strangely, however, it all works together as the expression of a single sensibility. For an appetizer, try broiled grapefruit. Recommended among the seven entrees are chicken Suzanne, shrimp curry, lobster Newburg, shad roe, and filet mignon. Crêpes Suzanne are a good bet for dessert. The seven-course meals begin at $40. This unlikely back-road country inn should provide one of the most memorable dining experiences one can have in Orlando. *U.S. 27 north of Lake Wales, about 10 mi past Cypress Gardens turnoff, tel. 813/676–6011. Reservations advised. Jacket required. AE, DC, MC, V. Closed Mon. during summer. Expensive.*

★ **Park Plaza Gardens.** To feel part of the Park Avenue crowd, you must dine at Park Plaza Gardens. The dining room is actually a courtyard with a glass roof (contrary to what most people think, Florida is not a great place to dine al fresco), but it feels like you are dining outdoors. Tuxedoed waiters serve such delights as grouper *escovitche* and roast rack of lamb. Atmosphere is high-class but not pretentious. *319 Park Ave. S., Winter Park; tel. 407/645–2475. Reservations advised. Dress: neat but casual. AE, DC, MC, V. Moderate–Expensive.*

★ **Basil's.** Standing apart from other fast-food restaurants, Basil's has a creative cuisine designed to take a little time. Red snapper Provençale and chicken diavolo are standouts. Specialty of the house is the painted desserts. Cheesecakes and pies are served on a vanilla sauce painted with chocolate sauce and raspberry coulis. *1009 W. Vine St., Kissimmee, tel. 407/846–1116. Reservations accepted. Dress: casual. AE, DC, MC, V. Moderate.*

Cuban

★ **Rolando's Cuban Restaurant.** Cuban cuisine is a Florida staple, and Rolando's is one of the best places to try it. Black bean soup, dirty rice, chicken with yellow rice, and minced meat are just a few of the specialties of this cuisine. *870 Sermoran Blvd., Casselberry, tel. 407/767–9677. No reservations. Dress: casual. MC, V. Inexpensive.*

French

★ **Le Coq au Vin.** The atmosphere here is "Mobile Home Modern", but the traditional French fare is first class. After dining here, you can pride yourself on discovering a place few tourists know about but that is nearly always filled with a friendly Orlando clientele. Owners Louis Perrotte and his wife, Magdalena (the hostess), are a charming couple who give the place its warmth and personality. The specialties include homemade chicken liver pâté, fresh rainbow trout with champagne, and roast Long Island duckling with green peppercorn sauce. For dessert, try the *crème brûlée. 4800 S. Orange Ave., Orlando, tel. 407/851–6980. Reservations suggested. Dress: casual. AE, DC, MC, V. Moderate.*

Mexican

Border Cantina. A new addition to Park Avenue, Border Cantina is trendy Tex-Mex. If you can forgive the pink walls and neon lights in this third-floor restaurant, you won't have any complaints about the food. The Border does fajitas better than you'll find in most places, and the salsa is a fresh, chunky mix that will suit all tastes. *329 Park Ave. S., Winter Park, tel. 407/740–7227. Reservations accepted for parties of 8 or more. Dress: casual. AE, MC, V. Inexpensive–Moderate.*

★ **Bee Line Mexican Restaurant.** It looks like another hole-in-the-wall eatery, but the burritos, taco salads, meat *chalupas*, and chili rellenos are among the best in the area. *4542 Hoffner Rd., Orlando (near the airport), tel. 407/857–0566. No reservations. Dress: casual. No credit cards, but checks are accepted. Inexpensive.*

★ **Paco's.** Good Mexican food in a cheerful but cramped little house. Guacomole is hand mashed from avocados on the premises; so are the refried beans. *1801 W. Fairbanks Ave., Winter Park, tel. 407/629–0149. No reservations. Dress: casual. No credit cards. Inexpensive.*

Pizza

Pizzeria Uno. It's a chain, but when the pizza tastes this good, you can't hold that against it. The decor is early Chicago, a tribute to the franchise's birthplace. The menu includes spinaccoli pizza, which gets its name from the two main ingredients: spinach and broccoli. *55 W. Church St., Orlando, tel. 407/839–1800. No reservations. Dress: casual. AE, MC, V. Inexpensive.*

Rossi's. This is a local pizza joint—a garlic bread pepperoni pizza and a pitcher of Bud or root beer type of spot. The food is not about to win any awards, but Rossi's is a good escape from the tourist/hotel scene, and the price is right. *5919 S. Orange Blossom Trail, Orlando, tel. 407/855–5755. Dress: casual. AE, MC, V. Inexpensive.*

Seafood

Gary's Duck Inn. This long-time Orlando favorite is known for its knotty-pine nautical motif and its fresh shrimp, crab, and fish dishes. This was the model for a seafood chain known as Red Lobster. *3974 S. Orange Blossom Trail, Orlando, tel. 407/843–0270. Reservations accepted. Dress: casual. AE, DC, MC, V. Moderate.*

Wekiwa Marina Restaurant. Plenty of local color here as customers ranging from three-piece-suited bankers to overall-clad farmers eat catfish, frog legs, and cheese grits in a Cracker-style wooden building on the wharf. *1000 Miami Springs Rd., Longwood (off I–4, about 20 min north of Orlando), tel. 407/862–9640. Reservations only for large parties. Dress: casual. AE, MC, V. Inexpensive.*

Steak

Cattle Ranch. If you're hungry and looking for a big, thick, juicy, down-home American steak, then steer for the Cattle Ranch. It's cheap and, if you're insanely hungry, it's free. Just take "The 6-pound Challenge," in which you're given 75 minutes to eat an entire six-pound steak dinner, including salad, potato, and bread. If you can do it, you won't have to pay a dime. If you can't, it will cost you just over $30. There is nothing fancy about this cowboy cafeteria except the steaks that come off the burning orangewood fire. And you won't see another tourist for miles around. *6129 Old Winter Garden Rd., Orlando (5 blocks west of Kirkman Rd.); tel. 407/298–7334. No reservations. Dress: casual. AE, MC, V. Closed Sun. and Mon. Inexpensive.*

Cocoa Beach Area

Moderate prices and fresh seafood are characteristic of Cocoa Beach dining. Here are some favorites.

American

Mango Tree Restaurant. Candles, fresh flowers, white linen tablecloths, rattan basket chairs, and eggshell-color walls adorned with tropical watercolors by local artists set a romantic mood at the Mango Tree. The intimate dining room overlooks a garden aviary that is home to exotic doves and pheasants. Try the grouper broiled and topped with scallops, shrimp, and hollandaise sauce. *Cottage Row, 118 N. Atlantic Ave., Cocoa Beach, tel. 407/799–0513. Reservations advised. Dress: casual. AE, MC, V. Expensive.*

Gatsby's Food and Spirits. This casual waterfront is the best of five eateries at the complex known as **Gatsby's World.** Inside the publike establishment you can order prime rib, steaks, and seafood. Early-bird special dinner prices are in effect between 4:30 and 6:30. *480 W. Cocoa Beach Causeway, Cocoa Beach, tel. 407/783–2380. Reservations advised. Dress: casual. AE, DC, MC, V. Moderate.*

Italian

Alma's Italian Restaurant. Five crowded, noisy dining rooms keep the waitresses busy. The specialties of the house are veal marsala and more than 200 imported and domestic wines. *306 N. Orlando Ave., Cocoa Beach, tel. 407/783–1981. Reservations advised. Dress: casual. AE, DC, MC, V. Inexpensive.*

Seafood

Bernard's Surf. Don't come to Bernard's for the view; there are no windows in the two main dining rooms. Come for steaks and local fish and a few unusual dishes like alligator and buffalo. A specialty is Doc Stahl's Skillet, a combination of shrimp, crabmeat, mushrooms, and wild rice sautéed and served in the skillet. *2 S. Atlantic Ave., Cocoa Beach, tel. 407/783–2401. Reservations advised. Dress: casual. AE, D, DC, MC, V. Closed Christmas. Expensive.*

Lodging

When you visit the Orlando area, you have a choice of properties that are (1) owned and operated by Disney on WDW grounds, (2) not owned or operated by Disney but located on Disney property, and (3) not located on WDW property. There are advantages to each.

The law of inertia seems to keep most Walt Disney World guests within the park. And if you are coming to Orlando for only a few days and are interested solely in the Magic Kingdom, Epcot Center, and the other Disney attractions, the resorts on Disney property—whether or not they're owned by Disney—are the most convenient. But if you plan to spend time sightseeing in and around Orlando or if you're traveling on a tight budget, it makes sense to look into the alternatives.

Let's look at the pros and cons of staying on-site. On the positive side, you won't need to drive. Walt Disney World buses and monorails—free to guests—are efficient enough to make it possible to visit the parks in the morning, return to your hotel for R&R when the crowds are thickest, and go back to the parks for uncrowded evening visiting.

Older children can travel on their own on the transportation system without inviting trouble. Younger children get a special thrill from knowing that they're actually living in Walt Disney World.

On-site hotels were built with families in mind. Rooms are usually large enough to accommodate up to five; villas sleep six or seven. All accommodations offer cable TV with the Disney Channel and a station providing the latest on daily events. In addition, on-site hotels offer many of their own special events such as theme dinner shows and breakfasts with appearances or entertainment by Disney cartoon characters. You don't need to stay in these hotels to enjoy such special programs, but it's nice to have them only an elevator ride or a short walk away.

As an on-site guest, you can call in advance to make reservations at any of the restaurants in Epcot Center. Outsiders can make reservations only in person in the park on the day they wish to dine, and their choice of seating times may be limited.

Then there are the small conveniences. On-site guests of Disney-owned properties are able to charge most meals and purchases throughout WDW to their room. To golfers, it's important that Disney guests also get first choice of tee times at the busy golf courses.

On the negative side, hotels with comparable facilities tend to cost more on Disney property than off. This is not offset by guest discounts on multiple-day passports and on some WDW activities. And if complete peace and quiet are what you're after, you'll want to stay very far from WDW—since most nearby hotels, on-site and not, are well-populated by excited children and socializing conventioneers. It is true that to the cost of an off-site hotel must be added to the expense of transportation to Walt Disney World, but shuttle service is frequent, convenient, and—if your family is small—relatively inexpensive.

Reservations

Central Reservations Office

All on-site accommodations may be booked through the Walt Disney World Central Reservations Office (Box 10100, Suite 300, Lake Buena Vista, FL 32830, tel. 407/WDISNEY). Be sure to tell the reservationist exactly what you are looking for—Disney-owned property or not, price range, the number of people in your party, and the dates of your visit. If possible, stay flexible about this. Many hotels and attractions offer discounts up to 40% from September to mid-December.

You must give a deposit for your first night's stay within three weeks of making your reservation. At many hotels you can get a refund if you cancel at least five days before your scheduled stay. However, individual hotel policies vary, and some properties may require up to 15 days notice for a full refund. Check before booking.

Reservations should be made several months in advance—as much as a year in advance for the best rooms during high season (historically, Christmas vacation, summer, and from mid-February through the week after Easter).

Other Options

If you can't get what you want, keep in mind that Delta Airlines (tel. 800/221–1212) has many rooms allotted to it for its travel packages. And since there are always cancellations, it's worth trying even at the last minute; for same-day bookings, call the property you're interested in directly.

Land packages, including admissions tickets, car rentals, and hotels either on or off Disney property can be made through **Walt Disney Travel Co.** (1675 Buena Vista Dr., Lake Buena Vista, FL 32830, tel. 407/828–3255).

Land/air packages, with accommodations both on and off Disney property, can be booked through **Disney Reservation Service** (tel. 800/828–0228).

Ratings

Highly recommended properties are indicated by a star ★. Unless otherwise noted, rates are for two adults traveling with up to two children under 18.

Category	Cost*
Very Expensive	over $150
Expensive	$120–$150
Moderate	$65–$120
Inexpensive	under $65

**double room; add 9% for taxes*

Disney-Owned Properties

When choosing among the Disney-run hotels, consider price and location. Many are on the expensive side. (The exceptions are the Caribbean Beach Resort, Dixie Landings, and Port Orleans, which are grouped together a short bus ride from Epcot Center, near Typhoon Lagoon.)

The Contemporary, Disney Inn, Grand Floridian, and Polynesian Village are closest to the Magic Kingdom. All but the Disney Inn are on the Magic Kingdom monorail loop, just minutes away from that park.

Other Disney-owned properties are a bus ride away from the Magic Kingdom and Epcot Center. Disney's Village Resort, a group of several town house and villa complexes, is near Disney Village Marketplace, which is roughly halfway between the Magic Kingdom and Epcot Center. Fort Wilderness Campground Resort, where you can rent completely equipped trailers as well as RV and tent sites, is about halfway between Epcot Center and the Magic Kingdom. Two relatively new hotels, the Beach Club and Yacht Club, are within walking distance of Epcot Center, not far from a couple of newer non-Disney properties, the Dolphin and the Swan.

Beyond that, it's a question of the resort's individual style.

Resort Hotels

Contemporary Resort. Since the monorail runs right through the middle, this awkwardly modern 15-story A-frame feels like something straight out of Tomorrowland. But otherwise, what you've got is a place that always seems to be bustling in the best '90s fashion, from the crack of dawn until after midnight. Half the rooms are in the Tower, the main building, and these are the hotel's most expensive because of their spectacular views. Those in the front look out toward the Magic Kingdom's Cinderella Castle, a great backdrop for the flaming Florida sunsets and a nightly fireworks show, while those on the back side have ringside seats for the Electrical Water Pageant and sunrise through the mists of Bay Lake. If you spring for 14th-floor all-suites, you'll enjoy the additional amenities of a new concierge package: free valet parking, wine and cheese at night, fruit and juice in the morning, nightly turndown. Tower rooms can be somewhat noisy at night—sounds rise through the busy atrium—so if you're a light sleeper, you may prefer a room in the hotel's North and South Gardens, where the other half of the rooms are located. Overlooking the hotel's pool and gardens, these cost less than Tower rooms; the best are on the shore of Bay Lake. (Try to avoid units described as having a view of the Magic Kingdom—they have an even better view of the parking lot.) Regardless of location, all rooms have a small terrace and most have two queen-size beds and a small additional bed, though you can request a room with a king-size bed and double sofa bed. Bathrooms are jumbo, with double sinks as well as tub and shower. Many recreational facilities are right on the property, including six tennis courts, two swimming pools (one of them WDW's largest), and many water sports at its own lake marina. There is also a co-ed health club. The fast-paced Top of the World offers nightly Broadway revues and live jazz with dinner or drinks (jackets are required here). The Concourse Grill serves breakfast, lunch, and dinner. Kids will enjoy meeting the Disney characters who show up for breakfast and dinner in the Contemporary Cafe. They'll also be happy to disappear into the Fiesta Fun Center, one of the biggest game rooms ever. It's also hard to beat the Contemporary's location. The monorail can take you to the Polynesian and Grand Floridian hotels as well as to the Magic Kingdom and Epcot Center; you can catch a motor launch to Discovery Island, Fort Wilderness, and River Country; and it's relatively easy to get everywhere else by bus. *WDW Central Reservations, Box*

10100, Lake Buena Vista 32830, tel. 407/W–DISNEY or 407/824–1000 for same-day reservations. 1,052 rooms. AE, MC, V. Very Expensive.

Disney Beach and Yacht Club Resort. These two relatively new properties, a short walk from Epcot Center, are New England inns on a grand scale. The five-story, 634-room Yacht Club recalls the turn-of-the-century New England seacoast with its hardwood floors, gleaming brass, gray clapboard facade, and evergreen landscaping; there's even a lighthouse on its pier. Equally impressive is the blue-and-white, three- to five-story, 580-room Beach Club, where a croquet lawn, cabana-dotted white-sand beach, and staffers' 19th-century "jams" and T-shirts set the scene. Each property has its own restaurants and shops and shares certain facilities—child-care facilities at the Sand Castle Club for children 3–12 years from 4:30 PM, game arcade, health club, and water-recreation area that includes water slides and a swimming pool with a sandy bottom. So far, Disney's attempts to introduce live freshwater fish here haven't worked. Maybe by the time you check in, this great idea will have panned out. *WDW Central Reservations, Box 10100, Lake Buena Vista 32830, tel. 407/W–DISNEY or 407/934–8000 (Beach) and 407/934–7000 (Yacht). 1,214 rooms. AE, MC, V. Very Expensive.*

Disney Inn. The smallest and quietest of the Disney hotels used to be called the Golf Resort, and non-golfers stayed away. That was unfortunate. Because although the resort does sit between two world-class golf courses, and a number of golfers do like to stay here, the place is a great spot for anyone who wants to get away from the more frenzied activity found at the other resorts. Replacing the "golf" in the name with the biggest name in tourism this side of Mecca, and changing "resort" to "inn" to signal the away-from-it-all quality of a country hostelry, has helped this comfortable place find its niche at last. Rooms are slightly larger than in most other Disney resorts and accommodate up to five in two queen-size beds and a comfortable sleeper sofa. The least expensive units have views of the gardens or the fairways. The most expensive overlook the pool, though these can be noisy. Aside from the pool, the main recreation is driving and putting, and two of WDW's three first-rate 18-hole courses are just outside, as is its separate 6-hole executive course. Although all these are open to the public, Disney guests are accommodated first. *WDW Central Reservations, Box 10100, Lake Buena Vista 32830, tel. 407/W–DISNEY or 407/824–2200 for same-day reservations. 288 rooms. AE, MC, V. Very Expensive.*

★ **The Grand Floridian.** At first you might think that Disney transported this gilded-age masterpiece from some turn-of-the-century coastal hot spot to the shores of the Seven Seas Lagoon. Not so. The gabled red roof, brick chimneys, and rambling verandas were all built from scratch on the site. Loving attention was paid to every detail from the crystal chandeliers and stained-glass domes to the ornate balconies and elaborate aviary. Though equipped with every convenience, the softly colored rooms share this vintage charm, especially the attic nooks, up under the eaves. Even the resort's monorail station carries the elegant Victorian theme. The hotel has five bustling restaurants, two lounges, many shops, a health club, spa, beach, outdoor pool, and a marina that offers a variety of water sports. On the monorail, the Grand Floridian is also served by

Best Western-Grosvenor Resort, **17**
Buena Vista Palace, **19**
Casa Rosa Inn, **25**
Chalet Suzanne, **32**
Comfort Inn Maingate, **33**
Crown Hotel, **36**
Days Inn Orlando/Lakeside, **6**
Embassy Suites, **9**
Embassy Suites at Plaza International, **7**
Embassy Suites Resort Orlando, **13**
The Enclave Suites at Orlando, **5**
Grand Cypress Resort, **12**
Guest Quarters, **14**
Hilton at WDW Village, **20**
Holiday Inn Lake Buena Vista, **21**
Holiday Inn Main Gate East, **30**
Howard Johnson, Lake Buena Vista, **18**
Hyatt Orlando Hotel, **31**
Marriott's Orlando World Center, **22**
Orlando Heritage Inn, **3**
Park Inn International, **28**
Park Plaza Hotel, **1**
Peabody Orlando, **4**
Quality Suites East of Maingate, **29**
Radisson Inn Maingate, **34**
Ramada Resort Maingate at the Parkway, **23**
The Residence Inn by Marriott on Lake Cicile, **26**
Royal Plaza, **16**
Sheraton Lakeside Inn, **35**
Sonesta Villa Resort Orlando, **10**
Stouffer Orlando Resort, **11**
Summerfield Suites Hotel, **8**
Travelodge Golden Triangle, **27**
Travelodge Hotel, **15**
Twin Towers Hotel and Convention Center, **2**
Vistana Resort, **24**

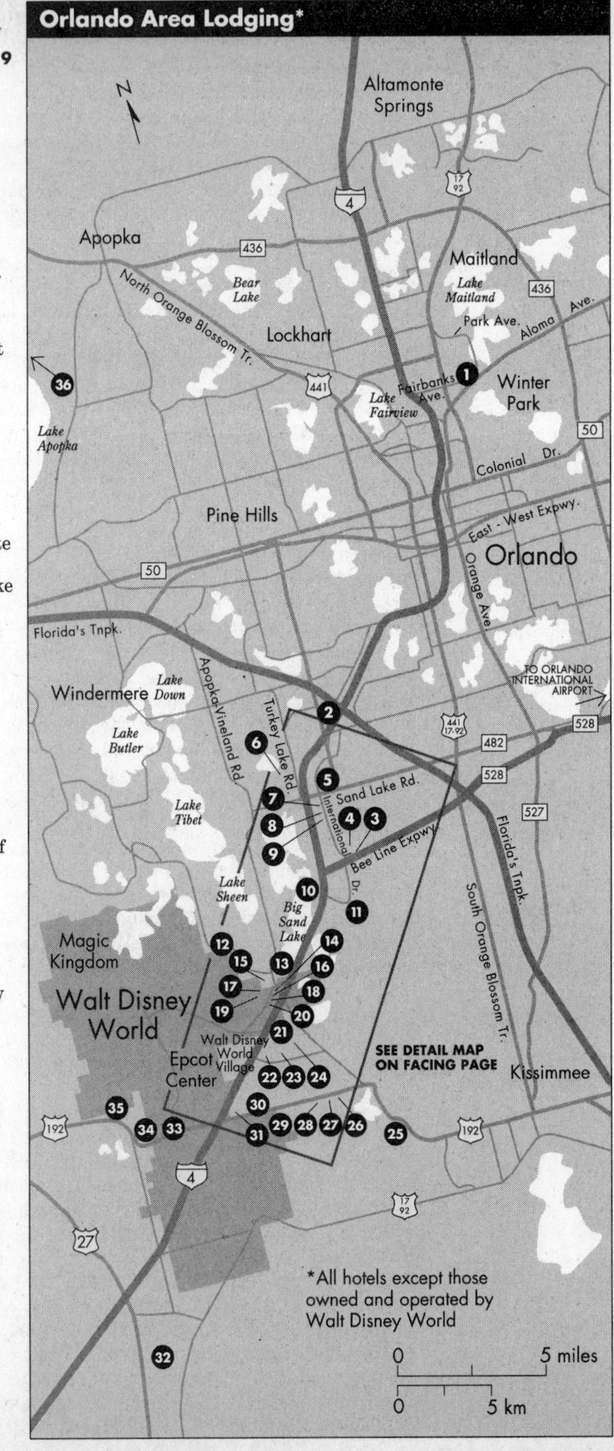

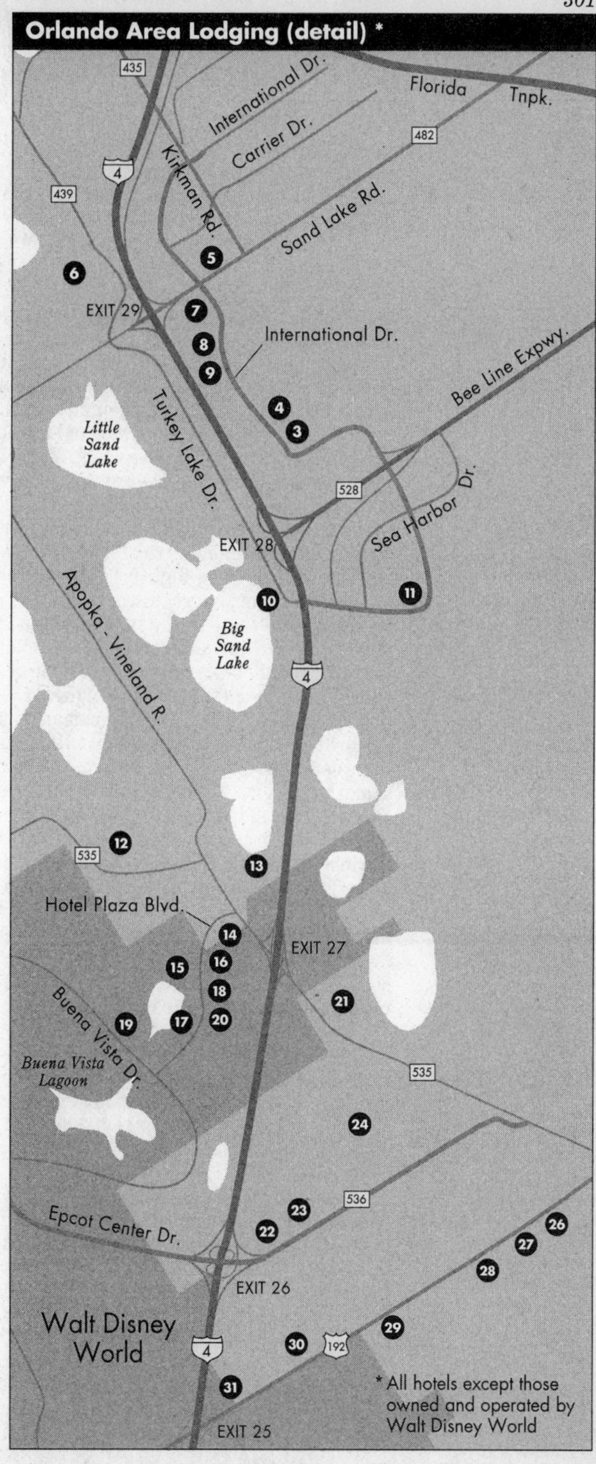
Orlando Area Lodging (detail) *
435
International Dr.
Florida
Tnpk.
Carrier Dr.
482
4
Kirkman Rd.
439
Sand Lake Rd.
5
6
EXIT 29
7
8
International Dr.
9
Bee Line Expwy.
4
3
Little Sand Lake
Turkey Lake Dr.
528
Sea Harbor Dr.
EXIT 28
10
11
Apopka - Vineland R.
Big Sand Lake
4
12
535
13
Hotel Plaza Blvd.
14
EXIT 27
15
16
18
21
Buena Vista Dr.
19
17
20
Buena Vista Lagoon
535
24
536
23
Epcot Center Dr.
22
26
27
28
EXIT 26
Walt Disney World
29
4
30
192
31
* All hotels except those owned and operated by Walt Disney World
EXIT 25

motor launches and buses. *WDW Central Reservations, 10100 Lake Buena Vista 32830, tel. 407/W–DISNEY or 407/824–3000. 652 standard rooms, 167 smaller "attic" chambers, 88 deluxe concierge suites, 35 suites. AE, MC, V. Very Expensive.*

Polynesian Village Resort. The Great Ceremonial House, where visitors check in, sets the mood at this resort, the most popular of all owned by Disney. Right in the middle of the atrium, orchids bloom alongside coconut palms and volcanic rock fountains create the constant sound of running water. If it weren't for the kids running around in Mickey Mouse caps, you might think you were in Fiji. Rooms are in 11 two- and three-story "longhouses" stretching from this main building. All offer two queen-size beds and a smaller sleeper sofa to accommodate up to five, and except for some second-floor rooms, all have a balcony or patio. If you want to be near the main building, request a room in the Bora Bora or Maui longhouses (named for exotic Pacific Islands, like all similar structures here). For the best view of the Magic Kingdom and the sandy, palm-trimmed Seven Seas Lagoon, stay in Samoa, Moorea, or Tonga. Lagoon-view rooms—the priciest—are the most peaceful and include a host of upgraded amenities and services that make them among the most sought after in Walt Disney World. They also have a perfect view of the Electrical Water Pageant. Rooms with garden and pool view are slightly less quiet and slightly less expensive; least expensive rooms overlook the other buildings, the monorail, and the parking lot across the street. There are two pools, one of them an extravagantly landscaped free-form affair with rocks and caverns; both can be overrun by children, so head for the beach to escape the squeals. Other recreational activities center on the hotel's marina, which rents sailboats, motorboats, and an eight-person outrigger canoe. Some 60% of the guests have been here before, so the resort must be doing something right. *WDW Central Reservations, Box 10100, Lake Buena Vista 32830, tel. 407/W–DISNEY or 824–2000 for same-day reservations. 855 rooms. AE, MC, V. Very Expensive.*

★ **Caribbean Beach Resort.** The first of Disney's moderately priced accommodations, this property is made up of "villages," two-story buildings on a 42-acre tropical lake. Each village is named for a different Caribbean island—Aruba, Barbados, Jamaica, Martinique, and Trinidad—and each has its own pool, self-service laundry, and stretch of white-sand beach. Bridges over the lake connect the mainland with one-acre, path-crossed Parrot Cay, where there's a play area for children. The attractive, pastel-hued rooms are smaller than rooms in the more expensive Disney resorts, but perfectly comfortable for smaller families. There is a 500-seat food court and 200-seat lounge. *WDW Central Reservations, 10100 Lake Buena Vista 32830, tel. 407/W–DISNEY or 407/934–3400. 2,112 one-bedroom units. AE, MC, V. Moderate.*

Dixie Landings. The Deep South's bayous and backwoods don't seem so far away when you're lodging in the columned plantation manor or the weathered, tin-roofed bayou cottages at this new, moderately priced resort complex. Rooms are designed to accommodate four and have every convenience. There is a pool. Book early—rooms go fast! *WDW Central Reservations, 10100 Lake Buena Vista 32830, tel. 407/W–DISNEY or 407/934–6000. 2,048 rooms. AE, MC, V. Moderate.*

Port Orleans. This Disney take on New Orleans's Jackson Square, WDW's newest moderately priced hotel, feels intimate despite its enormity. That's because rooms are clustered in small groups in faux row houses lined up around the perimeter of charming squares lavishly planted with magnolias and other typically Deep South trees. The two big dining areas do a commendable job with Crescent City specialties such as beignets and jambalaya, and the jazz lounge can really hop after dark. Kids love the pool, where Neptune sits astride a giant serpent that's actually a pool slide. Note that most rooms here have two double beds and accommodate four; for quarters with one king-size bed, book early. *WDW Central Reservations, 10100 Lake Buena Vista 32830, tel. 407/W–DISNEY or 407/934–5502. 1,008 rooms. AE, MC, V. Moderate.*

Villa Accommodations

If you're visiting WDW with your family or with other couples and want to stay together to avoid the expense of separate rooms, you may prefer to skip the WDW hotels in favor of the five clusters of villas at **Disney's Village Resort,** which share a single check-in point, the new Village Resort Reception Center. Since none are on the monorail, transportation to the parks can be slow, and a car or rented bike or golf cart is necessary to speed getting around within the village. Free shuttle buses operate every 20 minutes to take you anywhere on the property. In addition, the accommodations are not quite as plush as in the resort hotels. On the positive side, you get more space, not to mention proximity to great golf, WDW's most extensive shopping, and the lively after-dark action of Pleasure Island. *WDW Central Reservations, 10100 Lake Buena Vista 32830, tel. 407/W–DISNEY or 407/827–1100 for same-day reservations. AE, MC, V.*

Grand Vista Suites. These fully furnished, upscale accommodations were designed as prototypes for a housing development, but now they're available to rent. All the comforts of a luxury hotel are offered, including nightly turndown, stocked refrigerator, and quality furnishings. *5 units. Rates vary depending on dates and party size.*

One-Bedroom Suites. The smallest and least expensive of the villas, these were designed to meet the needs of business people attending meetings at the nearby WDW Conference Center. Built of cedar, they have one bedroom, a sofa bed in an adjacent sitting area, and a wet bar but no kitchen—they're the only villas without one. A few deluxe units with whirlpools sleep six, but most accommodate five. Facilities include two outdoor pools, a small game room, a playground, and boat rentals. *324 units. Expensive–Very Expensive.*

One- and Two-Bedroom Villas. Originally built as the Vacation Villas and refurbished in 1986, these have complete living facilities with equipped kitchens and either one or two bedrooms. The one-bedroom units have a king-size bed in one room and a queen-size sofa bed in the living room and sleep up to four. The two-bedroom units, which sleep six, have a sofa bed in the living room and either a king-size bed or two twins in each bedroom. The nearby Villa Recreation Center has two pools. *139 one-bedroom units, 87 two-bedroom units. Very Expensive.*

Two-Bedroom Deluxe Villas. Built of cedar like the Club Suite Villas, these villas are more tastefully decorated and very spacious. All have two bedrooms and a full loft and sleep up to six. They're right on the fairways of the Lake Buena Vista Golf Course, and swimming pools are not far away at the Villa Recreation Center or Disney World Clubhouse. *64 units. Very Expensive.*

Two-Bedroom Resort Villas with Study. To really get away from it all, these out-of-the-way forest retreats on stilts are the best bet. Isolated within a peaceful, heavily wooded area ribboned with canals, these "treehouse" villas won't exactly make you feel like Tarzan or Jane, but the woods do occasionally reverberate with a howl or two late at night. All units accommodate six and have a kitchen and breakfast bar, two bathrooms, and two bedrooms with queen-size beds on the main level, plus a double-bedded study and a utility room with washer/dryer on a lower level. Swimming pools are nearby at the Villa Recreation Center or Disney World Clubhouse. *60 units. Very Expensive.*

Camping

Fort Wilderness Campground Resort is 780 acres of scrubby pine, tiny streams, and peaceful canals on the shore of subtropical Bay Lake opposite the Contemporary. There's always a feeling of excitement in the air, but the mood is extremely relaxed (for Walt Disney World). There's also plenty to keep youngsters occupied: tennis courts and video arcades, tetherball and volleyball setups, a petting farm and horse barn, exercise trail, pool, fishing, and biking and canoeing (rentals are available), not to mention boating on Bay Lake. And though everyone has access to WDW's River Country water playground, it's right at the doorstep of those who lodge in Fort Wilderness by either bringing your own trailer or tent, or renting one of the fully equipped WDW RVs parked on the property. *WDW Central Reservations, Box 10100, Lake Buena Vista 32830, tel. 407/W–DISNEY or 407/824–2900 for same-day reservations.*

Rental trailers. For *House Beautiful* decor, stick to the resort hotels. Otherwise, these perfectly comfortable accommodations—more Motel 6 than Ritz-Carlton—are an excellent choice, since they put the relaxed friendliness of Fort Wilderness within reach of families who haven't brought their own RVs. Trailers are 60–80 feet long. Both types come with one bedroom, one bath, full kitchen, air-conditioning, heat, and daily housekeeping services. *Very Expensive.*

RV and tent sites. Bringing a tent or RV to Walt Disney World is one of the cheapest ways to actually stay on property, especially considering that sites accommodate up to 10. Tent sites with water and electricity are real bargains. RV sites cost more, but come equipped with electrical, water, and sewage hookups as well as outdoor charcoal grills and picnic tables; you can even get maid service for trailer homes. Of these, the most expensive sites (numbers 100 through 700) are nearest the lake; the least expensive (numbers 1,600 through 1,900) are far from the lake in denser vegetation. *827 tent sites, 363 sites (all with water and electrical power, 694 with sewage hookups).*

Other Hotels in Walt Disney World

While not owned or operated by the Disney organization, the Swan and the Dolphin just outside Epcot Center and the seven hotels at Hotel Plaza call themselves "official" Walt Disney World hotels. Having paid for the privilege, they are able to offer their guests many of the same courtesies available to guests at Disney-owned properties—for instance, guests can make telephone reservations for restaurants and dinner shows in Walt Disney World in advance of the general public. The convenience of the on-site location and the efficiency of the Walt Disney World Transportation System can't be underestimated either. If half the family wants to spend the afternoon in one of the parks and the other half wants to go back to the hotel pool, it's easy. This freedom does come with a price tag—the on-site hotels cost more than those with comparable facilities outside WDW. Only you can say whether the extra expense is warranted.

For reservations, call hotels directly, or book through the **Walt Disney World Central Reservations Office** (CRO, Box 10100, Lake Buena Vista 32830, tel. 407/W–DISNEY). Delta Airlines offers discount prices at these in their package deals.

Epcot Center Resorts

The attractively landscaped Epcot Center hotels are within walking distance of Disney-MGM Studios and Epcot Center. Dolphin, Swan, and Yacht and Beach all comprise Epcot Resort. All four properties are between the Disney-MGM Studios Theme Park and Epcot Center.

★ **Walt Disney World Dolphin.** Not everyone takes to this ITT Sheraton-operated bit of whimsy, where the wild and imaginative runs rampant. But no one questions that it's fast becoming a Disney landmark. Two mythical 56-foot sea creatures—labeled dolphins by the hotel's noted architect, Michael Graves—perch atop each end of the building; between them soars a 27-story pyramid, the highest structure in Walt Disney World Resort. A waterfall cascades down the facade from seashell to seashell and then into a 54-foot-wide clamshell supported by other giant dolphin sculptures; in true Florida spirit, the building's coral-and-turquoise facade displays a mural of giant banana leaves. Inside, chandeliers are shaped like monkeys and brightly painted wooden benches sprout wooden palm trees. Rooms are equally colorfully furnished and equipped with in-room safes, minibars, and large vanity areas. The best overlook Epcot Center and have a stunning view of its nightly fireworks-and-laser show, IllumiNations. Special registration and concierge services are available to those staying on the 12th–20th Tower floors. Hotel facilities include eight tennis courts, a health club, Camp Dolphin (a daily supervised youth activities program), game room, seven restaurants and four lounges, beauty salon, car rental, airlines desk, concierge service, three pools, and a white-sand beach. *1500 Epcot Resort Blvd., Lake Buena Vista 32830, tel. 407/934–4000 or 800/227–1500. 1,510 rooms (140 suites and 185 tower rooms). AE, DC, MC, V. Very Expensive.*

Walt Disney World Swan. Two 45-foot swans grace the rooftop of this coral-and-aquamarine hotel, which is connected by a covered causeway to the Dolphin. Inside, architect Michael Graves has canopied the ceiling with tall, gathered papyrus reeds and lined up a regiment of columns with palm-frond capitals. Located in the 12-story main building and two seven-story wings, rooms are decorated in coral, peach, teal, and yellow floral and geometric patterns. Facilities include an in-room safes, stocked refrigerators, car rental, youth hotel, baby-sitting service, three restaurants, two lounges, health club, heated pool, tropical grotto, white-sand beach, and eight lighted tennis courts. *1200 Epcot Resorts Blvd., Lake Buena Vista 32830, tel. 407/934–3000, 800/248–SWAN, or 800/228–3000. 758 rooms (45 concierge rooms on 11th and 12th floors). AE, DC, MC, V. Very Expensive.*

Hotel Plaza Resorts and Hotels

The attractively landscaped Walt Disney World Village Hotel Plaza at Lake Buena Vista, as this area is formally known, is just a short walk from Disney Village Marketplace, a pleasant outdoor mall full of shops and restaurants. Each of its hotels has its own restaurants, lounges, and sports facilities; those who stay here are considered Disney guests and are entitled to most of the privileges of guests at Disney-owned resorts. Most important, Hotel Plaza guests may reserve at Epcot Center restaurants in advance of the general public.

★ **Hilton at Walt Disney World Village.** One of the top establishments at Hotel Plaza, the Hilton is also among the most expensive. Its facade is unimpressive, but the interiors are richly decorated in peach, mauve, and green; tastefully carpeted; and full of gleaming brass and glass. The lobby was recently refurbished and enriched with tile and latticework, and the pool area received a new deck and gazebo. Guest rooms positively sparkle, and while not huge, they are cozy and contemporary. Rooms are furnished with a king-size bed and two double beds, and amenities include cable TV, in-room movies, and service bars. The most expensive have views of Disney Village Marketplace and Lake Buena Vista, but pool-view rooms are also good. Prices vary dramatically from one location, floor, and season to another. Keep in mind that if you book a room at the lowest rate—on a lower floor with a mediocre view—the check-in clerk can assign you to a better room if one is available, at an extra charge of $40. Rooms on the 9th and 10th floors have a private lounge and their own check-in and check-out; rates for the 84 luxurious rooms and suites include hors d'oeuvres in the late afternoon, complimentary Continental breakfast, and a newspaper each morning. Parents are particularly enthused about the Hilton's Youth Hotel, a supervised playroom with large-screen television and six-bed dormitory that operates daily from 4:30 PM to midnight; meals are served on schedule, and the cost is $6 an hour. Other facilities include two pools, two lighted tennis courts, a health club, outdoor spa, game room, business center, gift shop, and nine restaurants and lounges, including the American Vineyards, which serves seafood and steak. *1751 Hotel Plaza Blvd., Lake Buena Vista 32830, tel. 407/827–4000 or 800/782–4414 for reservations. 813 rooms. AE, DC, MC, V. Very Expensive.*

Best Western-Grosvenor Resort. Offering a wealth of facilities and comfortable rooms for a fair price, this attractive hotel is probably the best deal in the neighborhood. Rooms are average in size, but colorfully decorated, and have a refrigerator/in-room refreshment center and a VCR (movies are for rent in the lobby) and cable TV. Public areas are spacious, with columns, high ceilings, cheerful colors, and plenty of natural light. Baskerville's, decorated with Sherlock Holmes memorabilia, serves Continental fare, and the homey Moriarity's pub has live entertainment. Sports facilities will suit an active family: two heated pools, two lighted tennis courts, playground, and racquetball, shuffleboard, basketball, and volleyball courts. There's also a game room, and the lobby rents videocameras, so you can record your Disney visit on tape. *1850 Hotel Plaza Blvd., Lake Buena Vista 32830, tel. 407/828–4444 or 800/624–4109. 629 rooms. AE, DC, MC, V. Expensive–Very Expensive.*

Buena Vista Palace and Palace Suite Resort at Walt Disney World Village. This bold, modern hotel, the largest at Lake Buena Vista, seems small and quiet when you enter its lobby.

Don't be fooled. Better indications of its enormity are its sprawl of parking lots, the height of its taller tower—27 stories—and its huge roster of facilities: health club, beauty salon, game room, three heated pools, and three tennis courts, not to mention the airline assistance desk and the business center complete with translation and secretarial service and fax. Its nine restaurants and lounges include the Australian-theme Outback, which serves steaks and seafood; the Laughing Kookaburra Good Time Bar next door to the Outback; and, at the top of the hotel, the formal Arthurs 27 restaurant and the Top of the Palace Lounge, which offers a ringside seat on the local sunsets and Epcot Center's nightly laser-and-fireworks show. The original hotel underwent a $2 million redecoration in 1989; in 1991, $15 million more created an adjacent 200-suite hotel. Its suites, which accommodate up to eight people, offer a nice alternative for larger families or people who just want extra space; these have private balconies, living rooms with sleeper sofas, and dining areas with appliances (sink, coffee-maker, microwave, and refrigerator). The original and new rooms have small balconies. Upper-floor rooms in the main hotel are more expensive; the best ones look out toward Epcot Center. Ask for a room in the main tower, where original rooms are, to avoid the late-night noise that reverberates through the atrium from the Kookaburra nightclub. All bedrooms come with one king- or two queen-size beds. *1900 Lake Buena Vista Dr., Lake Buena Vista 32830, tel. 407/827–2727 or 800/327–2990. 1,028 rooms. AE, DC, MC, V. Expensive–Very Expensive.*

Guest Quarters. Consisting exclusively of suites, this hotel is convenient for small families who want to avoid the hassle of cots and the expense of two separate rooms; it attracts a quiet family crowd and few of the noisy conventioneers often found at larger, splashier properties. Each unit has a bedroom with two double beds or a king, plus a separate living area equipped with a sofa bed; each can accommodate up to six (if not particularly comfortably). There's a television in each room (including a small one in the bathroom), refrigerator, wet bar, and coffee-maker; microwave ovens are available on request. Among the public facilities are a kiddie pool, heated pool, pool bar, two exercise centers, a whirlpool, two tennis courts, a game room, and a children's play area. The terrace restaurant and bar are fine for the complimentary buffet breakfasts, but you will probably want to drink and dine elsewhere. *2305 Hotel Plaza Blvd., Lake Buena Vista 32830, tel. 407/934–1000 or 800/424–2900. 229 units. AE, DC, MC, V. Moderate–Very Expensive.*

Howard Johnson, Lake Buena Vista. Though somewhat charmless, with its lobbyful of white Formica and nondescript 14-story atrium, this is undeniably one of the most reasonably priced places to stay, and it's popular with young couples and senior citizens. There are two heated pools, a kiddie pool, a whirlpool, game room, and a better-than-average Howard Johnson's restaurant that's open until midnight. *1805 Hotel Plaza Blvd., Lake Buena Vista 32830, tel. 407/828–8888, 800/654–2000, 800/FLORIDA in FL, or 800/822–3950 in NY. 323 rooms. AE, DC, MC, V. Moderate–Very Expensive.*

Royal Plaza. Though dated in comparison to the slick hotels in the neighborhood, this casual, lively establishment is quite popular among families with young kids and teenagers. Each of the generously proportioned rooms has a terrace or balcony, and the best ones overlook the pool. Be sure your quarters aren't too close to the ground floor if you have any interest in sleeping late or napping in the afternoon. The hotel has four lighted tennis courts, a sauna, a pool, and a beauty salon. There are two restaurants. The Giraffe, the hotel's Top-40 nightclub, hops until the wee, wee hours. *1905 Hotel Plaza Blvd., Lake Buena Vista 32830, tel. 407/828–2828 or 800/248–7890. 396 rooms. AE, DC, MC, V. Moderate–Very Expensive.*

Travelodge Hotel. Although unexceptionally furnished, this is a good choice for families who can take advantage of its amenities—pool, playground, and game room. There's nightly entertainment in the 18th-floor Topper's Nightclub, which overlooks Epcot Center. *2000 Hotel Plaza Blvd., Lake Buena Vista 32830, tel. 407/828–2424, 800/423–1022 in FL, or 800/348–3765 outside FL. 325 rooms. AE, DC, MC, V. Expensive.*

The Orlando Area

Since its birth as a tourist mecca, Orlando's hotel business has boomed, and the number of hotels, motels, and resorts in the Orlando area is now simply astounding. There are more than 77,000 hotel rooms, and new ones of all sizes and varieties seem to open every day. Just about every American hotel chain has at least one hotel in the vicinity. In the early days of Walt Disney World, the largest hotels tended to be on Disney property, but this has changed as convention business has taken off, and plenty of big properties now keep company on International Drive with the smaller ones that have been around for a long time. Whether you're staying there, in the inexpensive Kissimmee area (with its smaller hotels), or in the Disney Maingate area (around WDW's northernmost entrance, just off 1–4), nearly all hotels provide frequent transportation to and from Walt Disney World. What matters most is that you choose a hotel within your price range, where you can be comfortable.

International Drive

If you plan on visiting other attractions besides Walt Disney World, the sprawl of newish hotels, restaurants, and shopping malls known as International—"I Drive" to locals and "Florida Center" in formal parlance—is a convenient point of departure. Paralleling I–4 (and accessible from Exits 28, 29, and 30), it's just a few minutes south of downtown Orlando. It's also near Sea World, Universal Studios, the vast Wet 'n Wild waterslide park, and several popular dinner theaters.

Many veteran Orlando visitors consider the area the territory's most comfortable home base and its hotels some of the best around. But each part of the drive has its own personality. The southern end is classier; the concentration of cheaper restaurants, fast-food joints, and inexpensive malls increases as you go north. Where you end up will depend as much on your budget as anything else.

Peabody Orlando. Built by the owners of the landmark Memphis, Tennessee, Peabody Hotel, this 27-story structure looks like a high-rise office building from afar. Don't be put off by its austere exterior. Inside, the place is very impressive and handsomely designed, from the lobby's rich marble floors and fountains to the sweeping views and the modern art throughout the hotel. As a grace note, there is also the famous Peabody tradition: Each day at 11, a flock of ducks waddles down a swathe of red carpet through the lobby to a marble fountain, where they frolic until 5, when they do the whole thing in reverse. The most panoramic rooms have views of Walt Disney World and a sea of orange trees that extends as far as the eye can see; those in the Peabody Clubs on the top three floors enjoy special concierge service. All guests have access to the pool, health club, and four lighted tennis courts. There are also three restaurants: Capriccio's, which serves Italian fare; Dux, where the cuisine is Continental; and the Beeline, a 24-hour 1950s-style diner. Located across the street from the Orlando Convention and Civic Center, the hotel attracts rock stars and other performers as well as conventioneers. *9801 International Dr., Orlando 32819, tel. 407/352–4000 or 800/PEABODY. 891 rooms. AE, DC, MC, V. Very Expensive.*

Stouffer Orlando Resort. From the folks who brought French bread pizza and Lean Cuisine to your grocery store comes an even more palatable product—the 10-story Stouffer Orlando Resort. Located directly across the street from Sea World, this bulky building looks more like a Federal Reserve Bank than a comfortable hotel. Longer than a football field, its atrium lobby is billed as the world's largest. Occupying the entire core of the building, it is full of waterfalls, goldfish ponds, and palm trees; as guests shoot skyward in sleek glass elevators, exotic birds twitter in a large, hand-carved, gilded Venetian aviary. It is nice to be greeted with a glass of champagne when you register, but the spaciousness of the guest rooms is even more pleasant. The most expensive rooms face the atrium, but if you're a light sleeper, ask for an outside room and avoid the music and party sounds that come from gatherings there. Facilities include five lighted tennis courts, pool, whirlpool, Nautilus-equipped fitness center, child-care center, game room, and two commendable restaurants, Haifeng (Chinese) and Atlantis (French and seafood); guests also have access to an 18-hole golf course. *6677 Sea Harbor Dr., Orlando 32821, tel. 407/351–5555 or 800/HOTELS–1. 780 rooms. AE, DC, MC, V. Very Expensive.*

Sonesta Villa Resort Orlando. In this complex of multiunit lakefront town houses not far from International Drive, each unit is a homey, comfortable apartment, small but fully equipped with a kitchenette, dining area, living room, small patio, bedroom, and private ground-floor entrance; some units are bilevel. Equally attractive are the conveniently located outdoor facilities—two lighted tennis courts, mini health club (sauna, exercise room, stationary bicycles, workout stations), pool, 11 whirlpools, and a kiddie pool. Guests can sail and water-ski on the lake or sun themselves on the sandy beach. There is a restaurant and a bar, but the only after-dark action is the outdoor barbecue buffet when available. If you want to cook at "home" but are too busy to shop, the hotel will pick up groceries for you and deliver them while you're out. Laundry is strictly self-service, and dry cleaning is available. *10000 Turkey Lake Rd., Orlando 32819, tel. 407/352–8051 or 800/SONESTA. 369 units. AE, DC, MC, V. Moderate–Very Expensive.*

Embassy Suites. The former Park Suite hotel seems part Deep South, part tropical. With its marble floors, pillars, hanging lamps, and ceiling fans, the lobby has an expansive, old-fashioned feel. Tropical gardens with mossy rock fountains give a distinctive southern humidity to the atrium. Elsewhere, ceramic tile walkways and brick arches carry out the tropical mood. The units, all suites, are comfortable, and the hotel has a restaurant, bar, and a fancy indoor pool with whirlpool, steam room, and sauna. Included in the rate is a complimentary breakfast and free cocktails daily from 5 to 7 PM. *8978 Interna-*

tional Dr., Orlando 32819, tel. 407/352–1400 or 800/432–7272. 245 suites. AE, DC, MC, V. Moderate–Expensive.

Embassy Suites Hotel at Plaza International. The concept of the all-suites hotel serving a free buffet breakfast with cooked-to-order items, pioneered by the Embassy Suites chain, has proved very popular in Orlando for a couple of reasons: The arrangement is comfortable. (Each unit has both a bedroom and a full living room equipped with wet bar, refrigerator, pull-out sofa, two TVs.) The even greater appeal is the modest cost—less than a single room in the topnotch hotels. The atrium at the center of the hotel—wide, but somewhat smaller than at the Stouffer—contains a lounge where a player piano sets the mood. Other facilities include one indoor/outdoor pool, an exercise room with whirlpool and sauna, a steam room, and a game room. *8250 Jamaican Ct., Orlando 32819, tel. 407/345–8250 or 800/327–9797. 246 rooms. AE, DC, MC, V. Moderate–Expensive.*

The Enclave Suites at Orlando. With three 10-story buildings surrounding an office, restaurant, and recreation area, this all-suite hotel is less a hotel than a condominium complex. Here, what you spend for a room in a fancy hotel gets you a complete apartment, with significantly more space than in other all-suite hotels. Accommodating up to six, the units have full kitchens, living rooms, two bedrooms, and small terraces. This is a great deal for families or small groups of friends who don't mind skipping the hotel hustle, and the single suites are wonderful for couples. Facilities include one indoor and two outdoor pools, whirlpool and sauna, exercise room, lighted tennis court, playground, and the Enclave Beach Cafe, which is popular with local yuppies. *6165 Carrier Dr., Orlando 32819, tel. 407/351–1155 or 800/457–0077. 321 suites. AE, DC, MC, V. Moderate–Expensive.*

Summerfield Suites Hotel. A great option for big families, the all-suites Summerfield is small enough that guests get plenty of personal attention, but accommodations are quite roomy. Two-bedroom units, the most popular, have fully equipped kitchens (complete with full-size stove, coffee-maker, microwave, jumbo refrigerator, dishes, and pots and pans), plus a living room with TV and VCR. All the bedrooms have full baths and TVs. The courtyard shelters a small but pretty pool, with a poolside bar where you can get hotdogs and burgers; cocktails are served at the lobby bar every evening. If you don't want to hassle with whipping up eggs in the morning, you can sample the hotel's free Continental buffet—or stop in at one of the nearby International Drive restaurants (since there's none on-site). The hotel also offers video rentals, a do-it-yourself laundry, game room, and exercise room. *8480 International Dr., Orlando 32819, tel. 407/352–2400 or 800/833–4353. 146 suites (42 with 1 bedroom, 104 with 2). AE, DC, MC, V. Moderate–Expensive.*

Twin Towers Hotel and Convention Center. While this hotel has a big convention center and caters to meetings, it's a good choice for tourists, too. Who wouldn't appreciate the we-try-harder attitude, or the great location just across from Universal Studios Florida? New owners have undertaken a $29.5 million renovation, refurbishing guest rooms, restaurants, lounges, and convention center. And don't worry about noisy conventioneers—the meeting and convention facilities are completely isolated from the guest towers. The comfortable if nondescript rooms have one king- or two queen-size beds, cable

TV, and in-room movies. There's also an exercise room, whirlpool, sauna, and a good range of dining-and-drinking options: 24-hour room service, a deli open around-the-clock, the Palm Court Restaurant (which serves three meals daily), and the Everglades Lounge (with live entertainment and a large-screen TV). The green neon that outlines the towers makes it easy to find your way home at night, and the swimming pool is surrounded by nicely landscaped grounds that include a playground. *5780 Major Blvd., Orlando 32819, tel. 407/351–1000 or 800/327–2110. 760 rooms, 30 suites. AE, DC, MC, V. Moderate–Expensive.*

Orlando Heritage Inn. If you want a small, simple hotel with reasonable rates but plenty of charm, look into this establishment next door to the towering Peabody. Recalling Victorian-era Florida, it's full of reproduction turn-of-the-century furnishings, French windows, and brass lamps, interspersed with 19th-century antiques. In the guest rooms, folk art hangs on the walls, lace curtains the double French doors, and quilted spreads cover the beds. The kitschy quaintness contrasts pleasantly with the anonymity of area's other hotels, and the staff is strong on southern hospitality. You'll also find a small saloon-type lounge and dinner shows in the rotunda several nights weekly. There is a swimming pool. *9861 International Dr., Orlando 32819, tel. 407/352–0008 or 800/447–1890. 150 rooms. AE, DC, MC, V. Moderate.*

Days Inn Orlando/Lakeside. Among the budget motels in the International Drive area, this Days Inn is tops. That's not only because of its location on the shores of Spring Lake, across 1–4 from International Drive, but also because of its good facilities: three pools, picnic areas, playgrounds, and a beach that's perfect for sunning, swimming, water sports, or volleyball. Rooms are basic but just fine, and suites with coffee-maker, microwave, and refrigerator are also available. Parents appreciate the chain-wide policy that lets accompanying children (age 12 and under) eat free with paying adult in its restaurants and cafeteria. Additional amenities include a gift shop, gas station, guest laundry, outdoor video arcade and Tiki bar (with patio). The one drawback: There is no swimming or fishing in the hotel's lake. *7335 Sand Lake Rd., Orlando 32819, tel. 407/351–1900 or 800/777–DAYS. 695 rooms. AE, DC, MC, V. Inexpensive–Moderate.*

Maingate Resorts

Outside the northernmost entrance to WDW, just off I–4, the Maingate area is full of large hotels unaffiliated with Walt Disney World, mostly sprawling, high-quality resorts catering to Walt Disney World vacationers. While they share a certain sameness with resorts the world over, they vary in size and price. As a rule, the bigger the resort and the more extensive the facilities, the more you can expect to pay. If you're looking for a clean, modern room, you cannot go wrong with any of them. All are equally convenient to Walt Disney World. One may emphasize one recreational activity more than another. So your ultimate decision may depend on how much time you plan to spend at your hotel and on which of your strokes—your drive or your backhand—requires most attention.

Grand Cypress Resort. If you polled those familiar with Orlando to name its most spectacular resort, few would hesitate to name the Grand Cypress. With more than 1,500 acres, it is so huge that there's a trolley system to help guests get around. It offers virtually every resort facility and then some: 12 tennis courts; 45 holes of Jack Nicklaus—designed golf (3 golf courses); a high-tech golf school; paddleboats, canoes, and sailboats for rent; scenic bicycling and jogging trails; racquetball courts; a complete health club; and a horse stable. The huge, 800,000-gallon swimming pool has three levels and is fed by 12 cascading waterfalls, and there's a 45-acre Audubon nature reserve. Even the service is attentive. And as you'd expect of a first-class Hyatt resort, the hotel has a striking 18-story glass atrium filled with tropical plants and Oriental paintings and sculptures. Accommodations are divided between the 750-room Hyatt Regency Grand Cypress and the 150-unit Villas of Grand Cypress. Rooms are unmemorable but spacious; those with the best views overlook the pool and Lake Windsong. Hemingway's Restaurant specializes in seafood and La Coquina serves upscale French fare; both are excellent. There are three other restaurants, a gift shop, beauty salon, and a supervised program for children age 5–15. This huge resort has just one drawback: the king-size conventions that it commonly attracts. *1 Grand Cypress Blvd., Orlando 32836, tel. 407/239–1234 or 800/233–1234. 750 rooms. AE, DC, MC, V. Very Expensive.*

Marriott's Orlando World Center. To call this Marriott massive would be an understatement. The 18-hole golf course, dozen tennis courts, health club, four pools (one of them the largest in the state), and 13 restaurants and bars are just the beginning of the facilities. The lobby is a huge, opulent atrium, and the rooms are clean and comfortable. Luxurious villas, the Royal Palms and Sabal Palms, are available for daily and weekly rentals. If you like your hostelries cozy, you'll consider the size of this place a definite negative; otherwise, its single unappealing aspect is the crowd of conventioneers it attracts. *8701 World Center Dr., Orlando 32821, tel. 407/239–4200 or 800/228–9290. 1,504 rooms. AE, DC, MC, V. Very Expensive.*

Vistana Resort. Consider this peaceful resort if you're interested in tennis: In addition to the five heated outdoor pools and full health club, there are clay and all-weather tennis courts that can be used without charge; private or semiprivate lessons are available for a fee. It's also a good bet if your family is large, or if you're traveling with a group of friends. The spacious, tastefully decorated villas and town houses spread over 95 landscaped acres and have two bedrooms each plus a living room and all the comforts of home, including a full kitchen, washer/dryer, and so on. The price may seem high, but considering that each unit can sleep six or eight, the place is a positive bargain. *8800 Vistana Centre Dr., Orlando 32821, tel. 407/239–3100 or 800/877–8787. 722 units. AE, DC, MC, V. Very Expensive.*

Embassy Suites Resort Orlando. Some local folks have been shocked by this hotel's wild turquoise, pink, and yellow facade. Clearly visible from I–4, it has become something of a local landmark. But it's an attractive option for other reasons. It's just one mile from Walt Disney World, five miles from Sea World, and seven miles from Universal Studios Florida. All rooms are suites; you can choose one with a king-size bed that sleeps four, or one with two double beds that sleeps six. Every morning, a free breakfast buffet is served in the pretty atrium lobby, which is loaded with tropical vegetation and soothed by a rushing fountain. Free beverages and cocktails are offered there in the evenings from 5:30 to 7:30 PM. Other features include a pool that's partially indoors, an adjacent kiddie pool and playground, a poolside snack bar, sauna, whirlpool, lighted tennis court, and basketball, volleyball, and shuffleboard courts. There is one restaurant. *8100 Lake Ave., Lake Buena Vista 32830, tel. 407/239-1144 or 800/EMBASSY. 280 suites. AE, DC, MC, V. Expensive–Very Expensive.*

Ramada Resort Maingate at the Parkway. With its attractive setting and competitive prices, this bright, spacious Ramada may offer the best deal in the neighborhood. It has two lighted tennis courts, a volleyball court, a pool with a waterfall, a kiddie pool, two whirlpools, a sauna, and a delicatessen that comes in handy for assembling picnics. Generously proportioned rooms are decked out in tropical patterns and pastel colors; those with the best view and light face the pool. *2900 Parkway Blvd., Kissimmee 34746, tel. 407/396-7000, 800/634-4774, or 800/225-3939 in FL. 716 rooms. AE, DC, MC, V. Moderate–Very Expensive.*

Holiday Inn Lake Buena Vista. From its sweeping, covered entrance to its striking, terra-cotta-colored facade, this big Holiday Inn is most impressive. It's also an excellent value. Furnished with two queen-size beds or one king and a sleeper, all rooms have a TV and VCR plus a kitchenette equipped with refrigerator, microwave, and coffee-maker. In the hotel courtyard is a wonderfully huge, free-form pool, plus a whirlpool and a vast wading pool. But what really earns the kudos here is Camp Holiday, a free children's program of magic shows, arts and crafts, movies, cartoons, and other supervised activities, day and night, for children ages 2–12. The hotel's only requirement is that children must be potty-trained to participate. A nifty touch is that the hotel rents beepers to parents who want to spend some time alone but stay in close touch with their children. *13351 Rte. 535, Lake Buena Vista, Lake Buena Vista 32821, tel. 407/239-4500, 800/366-6299, or 800/HOLIDAY. 507 rooms. AE, DC, MC, V. Moderate–Expensive.*

Hyatt Orlando Hotel. Instead of a single towering building, this very large hotel consists of nine two-story buildings in four clusters. Each cluster is a community with its own heated pool, whirlpool, park, and playground at its center. The rooms are spacious, but otherwise unmemorable. The lobby is vast and mall-like, with numerous shops and restaurants. One of the restaurants, the Palm Terrace, is kosher. There is also a very good take-out deli with great picnic snacks for those wise enough to avoid the lines and prices at amusement park fast-food stands. Aside from two lighted tennis courts, there's not much in the way of recreation except for a game room. However, if you'll be spending most of your time attacking Orlando attractions, that may matter less than the convenience and reasonable rates. *6375 W. Irlo Bronson Memorial Hwy., Kissimmee 34746, tel. 407/396-1234, 800/331-2003 in FL, or 800/544-7178 outside FL. 924 rooms. AE, DC, MC, V. Moderate.*

U.S. 192 Area

If you're looking for anything remotely quaint, charming, or sophisticated, move on. The U.S. 192 strip—aka the Irlo Bronson Memorial Highway, the Spacecoast Parkway, and Kissimmee—is crammed with mom-and-pop motels and bargain basement hotels, cheap restaurants, fast-food chains, nickel-and-dime attractions, gas stations, and minimarts in mind-numbing profusion. But if all you want is a decent room with perhaps a few extras for a manageable price, this is Wonderland. Room rates start at $20 a night—lower at the right time of year, if you can cut the right deal; otherwise, most cost $30–$70 a night, depending on facilities and proximity to Walt Disney World. Among the chain hotels—Best Western, Comfort Inn, Econolodge, Holiday Inn, Radisson, Sheraton, Travelodge, and so on—are a pride of family-owned properties, many of which are run by recent immigrants such as the Norwegian couple that operates the Viking Motel and the Chinese family in charge at the Casa Rosa.

Whatever your choice, you will find basic rooms, grounds, and public spaces that vary little from one establishment to the next. As a rule, the newer the property, the more comfortable your surroundings, and the greater the distance from Walt Disney World, the lower the room rates. Since a few minutes' drive may save you a significant amount of money, shop around. And if you wait until arrival to find a place, don't be bashful about asking to see rooms. Kissimmee is a buyer's market.

Quality Suites East of Maingate. This hotel, built in 1989, is an excellent option for a large family or groups of friends. The spacious rooms, designed to sleep six or 10, are decorated in green and gold and equipped with a microwave, refrigerator and dishwasher. A minimarket, game room, self-service laundry, heated pool, and poolside bar are located in the patio courtyard. Kids will enjoy the motel's restaurant: A toy train chugs along overhead. No-smoking suites are available. *5876 W. Irlo Bronson Memorial Hwy., Kissimmee 34746, tel. 407/396–8040, 800/221–2222, or 800/848–4148 in FL. 225 units. AE, D, DC, MC, V. Moderate–Very Expensive.*

The Residence Inn By Marriott on Lake Cicile. Of the all-suite hotels on U.S. 192, this complex of four-unit town houses is probably the best. One side of the complex faces the highway, the other overlooks an attractive lake, where you can sail, water-ski, Jet-ski, and fish. Forty units are penthouses accommodating four, with complete kitchens, small living rooms, loft bedrooms, and fireplaces. All others accommodate two and are like studio apartments, but still have full kitchens and fireplaces. Each suite has a private entrance. While the price may seem high considering the location, there is no charge for additional guests, so you can squeeze in the whole family at no extra charge, and both Continental breakfast and a grocery shopping service are complimentary. *4786 W. Irlo Bronson Memorial Hwy., Kissimmee 34746, tel. 407/396–2056, 800/648–7408 in FL, or 800/468–3027 outside FL. 160 units. AE, DC, MC, V. Moderate–Expensive.*

Radisson Inn Maingate. This sleek, modern hotel, just a few minutes from WDW's front door, has cheerful guest rooms, large bathrooms, and plenty of extras for the price: pool, whirlpool, two lighted tennis courts, and jogging trail. It's not fancy, but it is perfectly sufficient. The best rooms are those with a view of the pool. Two floors in each tower are reserved for nonsmokers. *7501 W. Irlo Bronson Memorial Hwy., Kissimmee 34746, tel. 407/396–1400 or 800/333–3333. 580 rooms. AE, DC, MC, V. Moderate.*

Sheraton Lakeside Inn. This comfortable if undistinguished resort, a complex of 15 two-story buildings spread over 27 acres, offers quite a few recreational facilities for the money. Facilities include heated pools, wading pools for tots, paddleboats, 18 holes of miniature golf, four tennis courts, two restaurants, a deli, and a bar. *7769 W. Irlo Bronson Memorial Hwy., Kissimmee 34746, tel. 407/239-7919, 800/325-3535, or 800/422-8250 in FL. 651 rooms. AE, DC, MC, V. Moderate.*

Holiday Inn Main Gate East. The service at this place is good, despite the fact that it's the world's biggest two-story Holiday Inn. But that's not the only reason to stay here. The rooms have TV, VCR, and kitchenettes with refrigerator, microwave, and coffee-maker; you can rent tapes and buy snacks and groceries in the lobby. There's also a free Camp Holiday, a supervised child-care program for kids ages 3–12. Facilities include two big pools (one heated), two whirlpool spas, a good-size children's pool, two playgrounds, two lighted tennis courts, and six eateries, some with buffet service. Also available is free shuttle service to Walt Disney World. *5678 W. Irlo Bronson Memorial Hwy., Kissimmee 34746, tel. 407/396-4488, 800/FON-KIDS, or 800/HOLIDAY. 670 rooms. AE, DC, MC, V. Moderate.*

Comfort Inn Maingate. This hotel is close to Walt Disney World—just a mile away. So you can save a bundle without unduly inconveniencing yourself. A swimming pool, game room, restaurant, lounge, and playground are available, and there's shuttle service to major attractions for a nominal charge. Children age 17 and under stay free. *7571 W. Irlo Bronson Memorial Hwy., Kissimmee 34746, tel. 407/396-7500 or 800/228-5150. 281 rooms. AE, DC, MC, V. Inexpensive–Moderate.*

Casa Rosa Inn. For simple motel living—no screaming kids or loud music, please—this pink, Spanish-motif spot run by a Chinese immigrant family is the place you want. It's simple and doesn't have much in the way of facilities aside from its little swimming pool, free in-room movies, and guest laundry. But it's a good, serviceable option, and the price is right. *4600 W. Irlo Bronson Memorial Hwy., Kissimmee 34746, tel. 407/396-2020 or 800/432-0665. 54 rooms. AE, DC, MC, V. Inexpensive.*

Park Inn International. The Mediterranean-style motel architecture is not likely to charm you off your feet, but the staff is friendly and the property has all the facilities you're likely to want—pool, whirlpool, and a lakefront beach with picnic areas, waterskiing, and sailing. Ask for a room as close to the lake as possible. There is a restaurant, but for an extra $10 you can get a room with a kitchenette. *4960 W. Irlo Bronson Memorial Hwy., Kissimmee 34741, tel. 407/396-1376 or 800/327-0072. 197 rooms. AE, D, DC, MC, V. Inexpensive.*

Travelodge Golden Triangle. Rooms at this plain Jane are adequate if not fancy. Try to get one as close to the lake as possible—it's prettier as well as quieter. *4944 W. Irlo Bronson Memorial Hwy., Kissimmee 34746, tel. 407/396-4455, 800/228-4427, or 800/432-1022 in FL. 222 rooms. AE, DC, MC, V. Inexpensive.*

Off the Beaten Track

Mention should be made of a trio of unusual hotels off the beaten track—close enough to be part of the immediate Orlando area, but well away from the areas that draw most area visitors.

Winter Park

Winter Park, Orlando's poshest and best-established neighborhood, is full of chi-chi shops and restaurants. Its heart is Central Park, a charming greensward dotted with huge trees hung with Spanish moss. It feels a million miles away from Orlando's tourist track, but it's still just a short drive away from the major attractions.

Park Plaza Hotel. Small and intimate, this 1922-vintage establishment feels almost like a private home, but there are nice touches: A newspaper is slid under your door each morning, for example. Rooms—mostly on the small side—have either a double-, queen-, or king-size bed; all open onto one long balcony abloom with ferns and flowers and punctuated by wicker chairs and tables, with views of Park Avenue or Central Park. This old-fashioned spot is definitely not for you if you want recreational facilities or other special amenities. But if you are hoping for real southern charm and hospitality, it's the only choice. On the first floor is one of Orlando's most popular restaurants, the Park Plaza Gardens, where you can see and be seen by the fashionable folk of Winter Park over good Continental cuisine. This property is not suitable for young children. *307 Park Ave. S, Winter Park 32789, tel. 407/647–1072 or 800/228–7220. 27 rooms. AE, DC, MC, V. Moderate–Expensive.*

Lake Wales

Chalet Suzanne. You'll find this conversation piece of a hotel in the orange grove territory of what seems the middle of nowhere. A homemade billboard directs you down a country road that turns into a palm-lined drive, then cobblestone paths lead to a balconied chalet-style house and cabins with thatched roofs. Fields and gardens extend to one side, a lake on the other. A friendly, homespun mom-and-pop operation, this assemblage has been in the Hinshaw family for generations; it became a country inn during the lean years of the Depression and has been added to bit-by-unlikely-bit over the years. The happily quirky grounds are decorated with colorful tilework from Portugal, ironwork from Spain, pottery from Italy, and porcelain from England and Germany. In the rooms and public spaces, furnishings vary wildly from the rare and valuable to the garage-sale one-of-a-kind. As in the home of someone's rich, crotchety old uncle, each room has its own personality; all have eccentrically tiled bathrooms with old-fashioned tubs and washbasins. The most charming rooms face the lake. There is a gourmet dining room. *Box AC, Lake Wales 33859, tel. 813/676–6011. 30 rooms. AE, DC, MC, V. Moderate–Expensive.*

Inverness

This small town is north of Tampa, an easy one-hour drive from Orlando.

Crown Hotel. Charming is a word all too often applied to hotels that don't really deserve it. This one does. Owners Jill and Nigel Sumner have given Florida's West Coast a bit of Merrie Old England, their native land, via special touches like the portraits of English royalty that hang below the curving lobby staircase; there's even a display case filled with replicas of the Crown Jewels. Guest rooms, on the second and third floors, have pretty flowered wallpaper and huge, old-fashioned washbasins with bright brass fixtures. Each room has a TV, and either two twin beds or one double or queen-size bed. There's a small but beautiful pool out back, with a vine-covered wall for privacy. Churchill's is well worth trying, for its Continental food as well as its wine list; the cozy, dark-paneled Fox and Hounds is a good bet for snacks, sandwiches, and British beers—and oh, those chicken wings! *109 N. Seminole Ave., In-*

verness 32650, tel. 904/344–5555. 34 rooms. AE, MC, V. Moderate.

Nightlife

Walt Disney World

Top of the World. This is Disney's sophisticated nighttime entertainment spot, located on the top floor of the Contemporary Resort. A spirited show called "Broadway at the Top" runs for about an hour after the two nightly seatings for dinner. A cast of high-energy dancers and singers bring to life some of Broadway's greatest hits. A single price includes the show and dinner. Tax, gratuity, and alcoholic drinks are extra. *Contemporary Resort, tel. 407/W–DISNEY. Reservations necessary months in advance. Jacket required. Admission: $42.50 adults, $19.50 children 3–11. Seatings at 6 and 9:15.*

Polynesian Revue and Mickey's Tropical Revue. Put on some comfortable, casual clothes and head over to the Polynesian Village Resort for an outdoor barbecue and a tropical luau, complete with fire jugglers and hula drum dancers. It's a colorful, South Pacific setting and an easygoing evening that families find relaxing and trouble free. There are two shows nightly of the Polynesian Revue and an earlier show for children called Mickey's Tropical Revue, where Disney characters perform decked out in costumes befitting these South Seas surroundings. *Polynesian Village Resort, tel. 407/W–DISNEY. Reservations necessary, usually months in advance. Dress: casual. Polynesian Review: $31 adults, $24 juniors 12–20, and $16 children 3–11. Seatings at 6:45 and 9:30. Mickey's Tropical Revue: adults $27, juniors $21, children $12. Seating at 4:30.*

Hoop-Dee-Doo Revue. This family entertainment dinner show may be corny, but it is also the liveliest and most rollicking. A troupe of jokers called the Pioneer Hall Players stomp their feet, wisecrack, and make merry in this Western mess-hall setting. The chow consists of barbecued ribs, fried chicken, corn on the cob, strawberry shortcake, and all the fixins. There are three shows nightly at Pioneer Hall in the Fort Wilderness area—not the easiest place to get to. *Fort Wilderness Resort, tel. 407/W–DISNEY. Reservations necessary, sometimes months in advance. Dress: informal. For same-day reservations, 407/824–2748. Admission: $33 adults, $25 juniors 12–20, $17 children 3–11. Seatings at 5, 7:30, and 10 PM.*

Pleasure Island. There is a single admission charge to this nightlife entertainment complex, which features a comedy club, teenage dance center, rock-and-roller skating-rink disco, numerous restaurants, lounges, shops, and even a 10-screen theater complex. Seven themed nightclubs offer everything from swinging jazz to foot-stompin' country and western to the latest pop video hits. The $16.95 admission charge gives you access to all clubs and shows except the theater. The newly added fireworks are at midnight on Friday and Saturday and 11 PM the rest of the week. The clubs and their opening hours are: **Adventurers Club,** live performers and special effects, 6:30 PM; **Baton Rouge Lounge,** live jazz and comedy, noon; **Cage,** progressive rock, over-21 crowd, 7 PM; **Comedy Warehouse,** improvisational comedy, 7:20, 8:40, 10, 11, and 12:40 AM on Fridays and Saturdays; **Mannequins Dance Palace,** dancing to top 40 music in a high-tech disco, 8 PM; **Neon Armadillo Music Saloon,** live country-and-western music and dancing, 7 PM; **XZFR Rock and Roll Beach Club,** dancing, dining, and drinking, with a live band and djs in a multilevel hall, 7 PM. *Pleasure Island, tel. 407/934–7781. Reservations not necessary. Dress: informal.*

IllumiNations. You won't want to miss Epcot Center's grand finale, a laser show that takes place along the shores of the World Showcase lagoon, every night just before Epcot closes. It is a show unlike any other. In the middle of the lagoon, laser projections of dancing images move across screens of spraying water. Orchestral music fills the air as multicolored neon lasers streak across the sky, pulsating to the rhythms of the music. Suddenly the night lights up with brilliant fireworks and the lagoon vibrates with the sounds of Tchaikovsky's 1812 Overture. Projections of the Earth's continents transform Spaceship Earth into a luminescent, spinning globe. The lasers used to create these images are powerful enough to project an identical image on a golf ball up to five miles away. The projections are called IllumiNations, and one of them creates a towering Mt. Fuji over the Japan pavilion. When the show is over, the crowds exit as Spaceship Earth continues to revolve. It is a stellar performance.

The Orlando Area

Until a few years ago Orlando's nightlife was more like that of Oskaloosa, Iowa, than of a booming tourist haven. But slowly an after-dark scene has developed, spreading farther and farther beyond the realm of Disney. Orlando entrepreneurs have now caught on that there is a fortune to be had by satisfying the fun-hungry night owls that flock to this city. New night spots open constantly, offering everything from flashy discos to ballroom dancing, country-and-western saloons, Broadway dinner theaters, and even medieval jousting tournaments.

The Arts

If all the fantasyland hype starts to wear thin, and you feel the need for more sophisticated entertainment, check out the local fine arts scene in *Orlando Magazine*, *Center Stage*, or the "Calendar" and "Arts and Entertainment" sections of Friday's and Sunday's *Orlando Sentinel*, available at any newsstand. The price of a ticket to performing arts events in the Orlando area rarely exceeds $12 and is often half that price.

Orlando has an active performing arts agenda of ballet, modern dance, classical music, opera, and theater, much of which takes place at the **Carr Performing Arts Centre** (401 Livingston St., tel. 407/849–2070). This community auditorium presents a different play each month (Wed.–Sat., with Sun. matinees). The Broadway series features performances on the way to Broadway or current road shows.

During the school year, **Rollins College** (tel. 407/646–2233) in Winter Park has a choral concert series that is open to the public and usually free. The first week of March, there is a **Bach Music Festival** (tel. 407/646–2182) that has been a Winter Park tradition for over 55 years. Also at the college is the **Annie Russell Theater** (tel. 407/646–2145), which has a regular series of productions.

Across the street from the Peabody Hotel on International Drive is the **Orange County Convention and Civic Center** (tel. 407/345–9800), which hosts many big-name performing artists.

Brevard Community College (1519 Clearlake Rd., Cocoa, tel. 407/632–1111, ext. 3660) each year sponsors the **Lyceum Series,** featuring a lineup of state, national, and international performing groups in the fields of music, theater, and dance.

Surfside Playhouse (Brevard Ave. and S. Fifth St., Cocoa Beach, tel. 407/783-3127), a community theater in operation since 1959, annually produces a season of high-standard performances.

Dinner Shows

Dinner shows have become an immensely popular form of nighttime entertainment around Orlando. A set price usually buys a multiple-course dinner and a theatrical production—a totally escapist experience. The food tends to be predictable—but not the major attractions. Always make reservations in advance, especially on weekends. A lively crowd can be an asset; a show playing to a small audience can be a pathetic and embarrassing sight. What the shows lack in substance and depth, the audience makes up for in color and enthusiasm. The result is an evening of light entertainment, which kids in particular will enjoy.

Arabian Nights. This attraction inside an Arabian Palace (home to eight breeds of horses from around the world) features 60 performing horses, music, special effects, a chariot race, and a four-course dinner. Low-cholesterol meals may be ordered when making reservations. *6225 W. Irlo Bronson Memorial Hwy. (U.S. 192), Kissimmee, tel. in Orlando, 407/239-9223, in Kissimmee, 407/396-7400 or 800/533-6116, in Canada, 800/533-3615. Reservations required. Dress: casual. Admission: $29.95 adults, $17.95 children 3–11. AE, DC, MC, V.*

Brazil Carnival Dinner Show. A two-hour extravaganza features the sights and sounds of Brazil. Native artists perform the dances of different cultures from throughout their country. Brazilian dancers bring the music to life in such numbers as "Carmen Miranda," the Bossa Nova, the Lambada, and the "Girls from Ipanema." Included in the price are a four-course meal served before the show, unlimited beer, wine, and soft drinks during the meal, and the 75-minute show. *7432 Republic Dr., Orlando, 32819, tel. 407/352-8666 or 800/821-4088 for reservations. Dinner begins at 8 PM, show begins at 9. Reservations necessary. Dress: casual. Admission: $28 adults, $17 children 3–12. D, MC, V.*

Fort Liberty. Run by the same company that operates Mardi Gras and King Henry's Feast, this dinner show whisks you out to the Wild West. The entertainment is a mixed bag of real Indian dances, foot-stompin' sing-alongs, and acrobatics. A British cowboy shows what he can do with bullwhips and lassos, and a musician plays the *1812 Overture* on the tuba and *America the Beautiful* on an old saw (yes, the kind that cuts wood). The show is full of slapstick theatrics and country-western shindigging that children really enjoy. The chow is what you might expect to eat with John Wayne out on the prairie: beef soup, fried chicken, corn on the cob, and pork and beans. You are served by a rowdy chorus of cavalry recruits who keep the food coming and beverages freely pouring. All tables seat 12, so unless you are in a big party, expect to develop pass-the-ketchup relationships. Fort Liberty is a stockade filled with Western-themed gifts and souvenirs, and a Brave Warrior Wax Museum ($4 adults, $2 children 2–11). The ambience is set by the photographers snapping photos of visitors dressed in cowboy garb. Forever trying to attract tourists, the Fort Liberty entertainers perform in the courtyard during the day. If the kids are more intent on seeing Marlboro country than you are, go at lunch time (11–2), pick up some fast-food fried chicken for $2, and see many of the acts that are in the dinner show. *5260*

Irlo Bronson Memorial Hwy. (U.S. 192), Kissimmee, tel. 407/351–5151 or 800/847–8181. Reservations required. Dress: casual. Admission: $28.95 adults, $19.95 children 3–11. AE, DC, MC, V.

King Henry's Feast. Driving along the strip of hotels and shopping malls on I–4 or International Drive, you may notice two Tudor-style buildings. One of them is the GoldStar International Motel, the other is the home of Orlando's King Henry VIII and his court of 16th-century jesters. The entertainment includes dancers, jesters, jugglers, magicians, and singers who encourage audience participation as King Henry celebrates his birthday and begins a quest for his seventh bride. Saucy wenches, who refer to customers as "me lords" and "me ladies," serve potato-leek soup, salad, chicken and ribs, and all the beer, wine, and soft drinks you can guzzle. Bar drinks are extra. *8984 International Dr., Orlando, tel. 407/351–5151 or 800/347–8181. Reservations required. Dress: casual. Admission: $28.95 adults, $19.95 children 3–11. AE, D, DC, MC, V.*

Mardi Gras. This recently expanded, jazzy, New Orleans–style show is the best of Orlando's dinner attractions. The set menu consists of vegetable soup, Caesar salad, chicken breast stuffed with herb dressing or a vegetarian plate; steamed broccoli, potatoes, and all the beer, wine, or soda you can drink. It is not an elaborate meal, but it is as good as one can expect from a dinner theater. A New Orleans jazz band plays during dinner, followed by a one-hour cabaret with colorful song-and-dance routines to rhythms of the Caribbean, Latin America, and Dixieland jazz. Although the kids are more likely to vote for the Wild West or medieval shows, adults tend to prefer Mardi Gras because it is more of a restaurant nightclub than a fantasyland. *At the Mercado Mediterranean Village, 8445 International Dr., Orlando, tel. 407/351–5151 or 800/347–5151. Reservations suggested. Dress: casual. Admission: $28.95 adults, $19.95 children 3–11. AE, D, DC, MC, V.*

Mark Two. This is the only true dinner theater in Orlando, with full Broadway musicals, such as *Oklahoma!*, *My Fair Lady*, *West Side Story* and *South Pacific*, staged through most of the year. During the Christmas holiday season, shorter Broadway musical revues are presented. A buffet and full-service cocktail bar open for business about two hours before the show. The food is nothing to write home about and should not be the reason to pay a visit. The buffet of seafood Newburg, baked whitefish, a variety of meats, and salad bar is only a few notches above cafeteria food. Best bets are the rich desserts that arrive during intermission. The shows are directed by the theater's owner, and the sets, costumes, music, and choreography are all done in-house. The actors are mostly from the Orlando area. It will not be the best performance you will ever see, but it can be a pleasure to hear the scores and see the routines of a favorite old musical while you sit comfortably at your table with a drink in hand. The cost of the show, including your meal, ranges from $28–$32 for adults and $23–$27 for children (12 and under). Performances start at 8 PM Wednesday–Saturday, with 1:15 PM matinees on Wednesday, Thursday, and Saturday, and a 6:30 PM show on Sunday. *Edgewater Center, 3376 Edgewater Dr., Orlando (from I–4, take Exit 44 and go west), tel. 407/843–6275. Reservations advised. Dress: casual. AE, MC, V. Closed Mon. and Tues.*

Medieval Times. In a huge, modern-medieval manor, visitors enjoy a four-course dinner while watching the struggle of good and evil in a tournament of games, sword fights, and jousting matches, including no less than 30 charging horses and a cast of 75 knights, nobles, and maidens. Sound silly? It is. Yet if you view it through the eyes of your children, this two-hour extravaganza of pageantry and meat-and-potatoes banquet fare can be amusing. Everyone faces forward along narrow banquet tables that are stepped auditorium-style above the tournament. If you and your family traveled the amusement-park route all day and are tired of looking and nagging at each other, you may get some respite, a bit of comic relief, and some vicarious pleasure from a night of crossing lances. *4510 W. Irlo Bronson Memorial Hwy. (U.S. 192), Kissimmee, tel. 407/239-0214 or 407/396-1518, in FL 800/432-0768, outside FL 800/327-4024. Reservations required. Dress: informal. Admission: $26 adults, $18 children. AE, MC, V.*

Church Street Station This downtown Orlando attraction is a complete entertainment experience. Widely popular among both tourists and locals, it single-handedly began Orlando's metamorphosis from a sleepy town, to the nighttime hot spot it now boasts to be and is on its way to becoming. Unlike much of what you see in Walt Disney World, this place doesn't just look authentic—it *is* authentic. The train on the tracks is an actual 19th-century steam engine, and the whistling calliope was especially rebuilt to blow its original tunes. The buildings have been completely redecorated with collectibles and memorabilia from around the world. You can spend an evening in part of the complex, or you can wander from area to area, soaking up the peculiar characteristics of each. For a single admission price of $14.95 adults or $9.95 children 4–12, you're permitted to wander freely, stay as long as you wish, and do what you want, whether it's drinking, dancing, dining, or people-watching. Food and drink cost extra and are not cheap, but they add to the fun. Parts of the complex are open during the day, but the place is usually quiet then; the pace picks up at night, especially on weekends, with crowds thickest 10–11. *129 W. Church St., Orlando, tel. 407/422-2434. Reservations not necessary. Dress: casual. AE, MC, V.*

Rosie O'Grady's Good Time Emporium. This is a turn-of-the-century saloon with dark wood, brass trim, a full Dixieland band blaring out of a gazebo, and countertop can-can dancers, tap dancers, and vaudeville singers. Is this a set for *The Music Man* or an evening at the Moulin Rouge? It's difficult to tell at first. The 90-minute shows begin at 7:30 PM. The last show starts at midnight. Multidecker sandwiches and hot dogs are sold in the Gay 90s Sandwich Parlour 4:30–11 PM.

Victorian Garden Bar. Formerly Apple Annies Courtyard, this relatively quiet nook features continuous live folk and bluegrass music from about 8 PM to 2 AM. It's a good place to rest your feet, have a drink, and people-watch. Salads, fruit platters, and exotic drinks are served 11–2 AM.

Lili Marlene's Aviator's Pub and Restaurant. Here you have a relaxed, wood-paneled English-pub atmosphere and the finest dining on Church Street. Food is hearty, upscale, and very American—mostly steaks, ribs, and seafood. Prices are not cheap. The walls have biplane-era memorabilia, and a large-scale model aircraft hangs from the ceiling. Open for lunch 11–4, and dinner 5:30–midnight.

Phineas Phogg's Balloon Works. This is a very popular disco filled with young singles over age 21 and a sprinkling of old-timers showing off their moves on the dance floor. It is a good-looking yuppie tourist crowd, leavened with locals. Contemporary dance tunes are played on a sound system that will blow your socks off. The place is jammed by midnight and open until 2 AM. Much of the young crowd feels it is worth the price of admission into the Church Street Station just to be able to come here.

Orchid Garden. Decorative lamps, iron latticework, arched ceilings, and stained-glass windows create a striking Victorian arcade where visitors sit, drink, and listen to first-rate bands pounding out popular tunes from the 1950s to the '80s. Open until 2 AM.

Cracker's Oyster Bar. Located behind the Orchid Garden, Cracker's is a good place to get a quick gumbo or chowder and slam down a few oysters with a beer chaser. It has one of the largest wine cellars in Florida. Dinner begins at 5; open 11 AM–midnight.

Cheyenne Saloon and Opera House. This is the biggest, fanciest, rootin'-tootin' saloon you may ever see. The former triple-level opera house is covered with moose racks, steer horns, buffalo heads, and Remington rifles; a seven-piece country-and-western band darn near brings the house down. This is a fun crowd to watch, with all the pickin', strummin', fiddlin', hollerin', and do-see-doin'. Make sure you come equipped with your best stompin' shoes, cowboy hat, and catcalls. An upstairs restaurant serves chicken-and-ribs saloon fare. The shows start at 8:30, 10, 11:30, and 1 AM.

Church Street Exchange. The newest addition to the complex, near Church Street Station, is a razzle-dazzle marketplace filled with more than 50 specialty shops and restaurants on the first two floors. The third floor has been taken over by **Commander Ragtime's Midway of Fun, Food, and Games.** The Exchange is free and open 11–2 AM, although most of the shops close by 11 PM.

Bars and Clubs

The bars and nightclubs have been divided into three sections. The first covers the tourist hotel districts in the Disney area, including Kissimmee, Lake Buena Vista, and International Drive. These places are usually filled with visitors to Disney World. The second section covers the city of Orlando and Winter Park, both of which cater to a more local crowd. The third hits some of the hot spots around Cocoa Beach. Remember that clubs on Disney property are allowed to stay open later than are bars elsewhere, and many of them don't have last call until 2:45 AM.

Disney Area

Wolfman Jack's Rock 'n Roll Palace. Shake, rattle, and roll the night away in this 1950s and '60s nostalgia nightclub. The interior looks like an opera house, with an orchestra-pit dance floor and a huge bandstand stage featuring famous old rock bands that still tour, such as The Drifters, Platters, and Bo Diddley. The crowd is a mix of young and old, singles and couples. The club features a very talented house band that serves up live music seven nights a week. Much of the menu is vintage '50s: Philly hot dogs, cheese-steak sandwiches, banana splits, but there also is prime rib. *Old Town, 5770 Spacecoast Pkwy., Kissimmee 34746, tel. 407/396–6499 or 407/827–6169. Dress: casual. Admission: $8.50, children under 3 free. AE, MC, V. Open 5–2 AM.*

Giraffe Lounge. Located inside the Hotel Royal Plaza, Lake Buena Vista (World Village), this flashy disco with spinning, colored lights is usually densely packed on weekends. It is a small place, and classy it ain't, but there's a lot going on, includ-

ing live bands five nights a week. Happy hour runs daily 4–9:30 PM. Music plays and the bartender pours until 2 AM. *Hotel Royal Plaza, Walt Disney World Village, Lake Buena Vista, tel. 407/828–2828. Dress: casual. No cover. AE, DC, MC, V. Open 4 PM–2 AM.*

Laughing Kookaburra Good Time Bar. A big hotel nightclub with live band music nightly and a serious singles crowd of all ages. The music is loud and the dance floor can get very crowded—a plus for some, a minus for others. The bar serves up 99 brands of beer, plus cocktails. Happy hour with free bar food runs daily 4–8 PM. Live bands play Tuesday through Saturday nights, and a Talent Showcase takes over on Sunday. *Buena Vista Palace Hotel, Walt Disney World Village, Lake Buena Vista, tel. 407/827–3520. Dress: casual. No cover. AE, DC, MC, V. Open 8 PM–2 AM.*

Bennigan's. A young singles' spot that draws crowds in the early evening and during happy hours, from 4–7 PM and 11 PM–2 AM. It caters mostly to nontourists who work in the area. Food is served almost until closing. *6324 International Dr., Orlando, tel. 407/351–4436. Open 11 AM–2 AM.*

Orlando Area

The nightclubs in Orlando have significantly more character than those in the Disney hotel area. If you have the energy to get in your car, you will probably find these spots more satisfying and less touristy—if you can find them.

Beacham's Jazz & Blues Club. This classy restaurant club in downtown Orlando offers local jazz and blues and occasional national acts. *54 N. Orange Ave., tel. 407/843–3078. Lunch served weekdays starting at 10 AM. Cover charge: $3 and up. Open nightly.*

Big Bang. A small, imaginatively Bohemian downtown night spot with a trendy but friendly atmosphere. The club, which features a mix of music from alternative to rap, keeps it pretty funky on weekends and has themes on weekday evenings. It is open after hours for dancing, coffee, and mineral water. Be sure to check out the Winnebago Room. *102 N. Orange Ave., tel. 407/425–9277. Cover charge: $3 on weekends. Open Fri. and Sat. 11 PM–4 AM; Tues. 10 PM–3 AM; Wed. 9 PM–2:30 AM; Thurs., Disco Hell, 11 PM–4 AM.*

Crocodile Club. This bar, inside a restaurant called Bailey's in Winter Park, collects a young, well-dressed college crowd from neighboring Rollins College. The atmosphere is more sophisticated and yuppified than most Orlando bars. Expect to hear jazz and Motown and dance to pop. *Bailey's Restaurant, 118 W. Fairbanks Ave., Winter Park, tel. 407/647–8501.*

J.J. Whispers. A classy, brassy singles crowd flocks to this trendy disco, which tries hard to maintain an image of cosmopolitan class. Expect to mingle with fashion-conscious locals in their tastefully outrageous attire. The club is equally popular with the over-30 set, who listen to music from the 1940s, '50s, and '60s in the Showroom. The young people do what young people do in a massive, multilevel, state-of-the-art disco. J.J.'s has one restaurant serving bar-food fare, and another that is open for lunch. It is also home to Bonkerz!, a comedy club. Live entertainment (Tues.–Sun., 8 PM–2 AM) includes all-male and all-female revues and live bands. *5100 Adanson St., Orlando 32804, tel. 407/629–4779. To get there, take I–4 to the Lee Rd. exit and go west for about half a mile on Lee Rd. Watch for a sharp left-hand turn at Adanson St. J.J.'s is located at the end of the Lee Rd. Shopping Center. Dress: tasteful but outra-*

geous—or just a jacket. Cover charge: $5 and up; $10 and up for Bonkerz, tel. 407/629–2665. AE, MC, V.

Sullivan's Trailways Lounge. A very popular place with much right-friendly charm, where people of all ages and many families come to strut their stuff on the largest dance floor in Florida. Even Yankees are welcome in this southern country-and-western dance hall. Big name performers entertain on occasion; local bands play Tuesday–Saturday. *1108 S. Orange Blossom Trail (U.S. 441), tel. 407/843–2934. Cover charge: $2 and up. Bands play 8 PM–2 AM.*

Cocoa Beach

Coconuts. The Saturday bikini contests and the April jet-ski rodeo, along with Mr. Muscle contests and dirt-in-the-face volleyball attract the under-40 set to this oceanside night spot. Patrons dance to live music most evenings, and there is a dining area. *2 Minuteman Causeway, tel. 407/784–1422. Dress: no cut-offs. Open Mon.–Sat. 11 AM–2 AM, Sun. 10 AM–midnight.*

Plum's Lounge/Holiday Inn Cocoa Beach. This lounge features dancing and live entertainment nightly. There is a beach deck on the ocean and a bar by the pool. *1300 N. Atlantic Ave., Cocoa Beach, tel. 407/783–2271. Dress: neat, but casual. Open noon–1 AM.*

Spinnaker's. In this entertainment center on an 800-foot pier extending into the ocean, visitors can find a boutique, fishing bait, and dining ranging from mesquite-grilled alligator snacks at a boardwalk bar to coconut-beer shrimp at the Pier House. *401 Meade Ave., tel. 407/783–7549. Dress: neat but casual. Reservations required. Dinner 5–10 PM. AE, DC, MC, V. Expensive–Moderate.*

10 Southwest Florida

Introduction

By Karen Feldman Smith and G. Stuart Smith

Updated by Peter Coan

Southwest Florida is no longer considered the state's left coast. Over the last 25 years the region has become fully developed, but has a much slower pace and a less commercial atmosphere than its right coast big brother. As a result, this is not so much a resort area as an integrated community that also happens to have some excellent beaches, and fine weather and several superior hotels that cater to families. Here, many hotels offer reasonably priced two-bedroom, two-bath suites with full kitchens and laundry facilities, in addition to supervised children's programs. Taking advantage of the facilities, mom and dad can pursue their own activities, which may include 18 holes of golf, or a couple of tennis matches organized by the property.

The area called Southwest Florida spans some 200 miles and includes a lot of beachfront, though the bays are polluted and the cloudy Gulf waters have poor visibility, making watersports such as scuba diving and snorkeling undesirable, if not unadvisable. However, boating and deep-sea fishing rank among the favorite pastimes here and such opportunities are aplenty.

As for cities, the closest resemblance to a metropolis you'll find in this region is Tampa, the crown jewel and entertainment hub, with the greatest concentration of restaurants, stores, and nightlife of any Southwest Florida city. Inland, and to the east of Tampa, the area is residential in standard Americana style: suburban sprawl, freeways, shopping malls, and—the main draw—Busch Gardens. The northern coast has been coined "Manatee Country," for its extensive nature preserves and parks designed to protect the water creatures and other wildlife indigenous to the area. To the south you'll discover a beach-resort atmosphere, especially in Naples, and on Sanibel, Captiva, and Marco islands. Relaxed and family-oriented—these are the keynotes of a Southwest Florida vacation.

Essential Information

Getting Around

By Plane Most major carriers fly into at least one of the area's three major airports, in Tampa, Sarasota, and Fort Myers.

Tampa International (tel. 813/870–8700) is 6 miles from downtown. It is served by Air Canada (tel. 800/776–3000), Air Jamaica (tel. 800/523–5585), American (tel. 800/433–7300), Bahamasair (tel. 800/222–4262), British Airways (tel. 800/247–9297), Canadian Holidays (tel. 800/282–4751), Cayman (tel. 800/422–9626), Continental (tel. 800/525–0280), Delta (tel. 800/221–1212), Mexicana (tel. 800/531–7921), Northwest (tel. 800/225–2525), Transworld (tel. 800/221–2000), United (tel. 800/241–6522), and USAir (tel. 800/428–4322).

Sarasota's Airport is **Sarasota-Bradenton** (tel. 813/359–5200), just north of the city. It is served by American, Continental, Delta, Northwest, Transworld, United, and USAir.

The Fort Myers/Naples area's airport is **Southwest Florida Regional Airport** (tel. 813/768–1000), about 12 miles south of Fort Myers, 25 miles north of Naples. It is served by Air Canada, American, Continental, Delta, Northwest, Transworld, United, USAir, and Canadian Holidays.

The Naples Airport (tel. 813/643–6875) is a small facility just east of the city, and is served by American Eagle (tel. 800/433–7300), ComAir (tel. 813/263–1101), and USAir Express (tel. 800/428–4322).

Between the Airport and the Hotels

Major car-rental companies and taxi and limousine companies service all three airports. Many hotels also operate shuttles.

In Tampa, major transportation services include **Central Florida Limousine** (tel. 813/276–3730), serving Hillsborough and Polk counties; **The Limo** (tel. 813/572–1111 or 800/282–6817 in St. Petersburg and Clearwater), serving Pinellas County; and **Florida Suncoast Limousines** (tel. 813/620–3597). Expect taxi fares to be about $12–$18 for most of Hillsborough County and about twice that for Pinellas County.

In Sarasota, transportation includes **Airport Limousine** (tel. 813/355–9645) and **Diplomat Taxi** (tel. 813/366–9822). Both deliver to most parts of the county. An average cab fare is $12–$20.

In Lee County, a taxi ride to downtown Fort Myers or the beaches (Sanibel, Captiva), costs about $30, and about twice that to Naples. Other transportation companies include **Aristocat Super Mini-Van Service** (tel. 813/275–7228), **Boca Limousine Service** (tel. 813/936–5466), **Personal Touch Limousines** (tel. 813/549–3643), and **Sanibel Island Limousine** (tel. 813/472–8888). Commercial shuttle service between the airport and Naples is generally $10 to $25 per person. Call **Naples Taxi** (tel. 813/643–2148) or, to get to nearby Marco Island, try **Marco Transportation, Inc.** (tel. 813/394–2257).

By Car

I–75 spans the region from north to south. Once you cross the border into Florida from Georgia, it should take about three hours to reach Tampa. Add an hour for Sarasota, two to Fort Myers, and three to Naples. Alligator Alley (Rte. 84) links up with I-75 at Naples and runs east to Fort Lauderdale. I-75 is being extended along the Alligator Alley right-of-way; expect construction delays.

U.S. 41 also runs the length of the region and serves as the business district in many communities. It's best to avoid all bridges and U.S. 41 during rush hours, 7–9 AM and 4–6 PM.

Rental car prices can vary dramatically, so it pays to shop around. Major companies serving Southwest Florida include **Alamo** (tel. 800/327–9633), **Avis** (tel. 800/331–1212), **Budget** (tel. 800/527–0700), **Dollar** (tel. 800/421–6868), **Enterprise** (tel. 800/325–8007), **Hertz** (tel. 800/654–3131), **Payless** (tel. 800/237–2804), **Superior** (tel. 800/237–8106), **Thrifty** (tel. 800/367–2277), and **Value** (tel. 800/327–2501).

By Train

Amtrak (tel. 800/872–7245) connects the Northeast, Midwest, and much of the South to Tampa. From Tampa, Amtrak heads east, across the coast, then up to Jacksonville and points north. Amtrak's Autotrain runs from Lorton, Virginia (near Washington, DC), to Sanford, Florida (near Orlando). In Tampa, the Amtrak station is at 601 N. Nebraska Avenue (tel. 813/221–7600).

By Bus

Greyhound/Trailways provides service to and throughout the state. Call the nearest office for schedules and fares (Fort

Myers, tel. 813/334–1011; St. Petersburg, tel. 813/898–1496; Sarasota, tel. 813/955–5735; and Tampa, tel. 813/229–2112).

Around Tampa, the **Hillsborough Area Regional Transit** (HART), (tel. 813/254–4278, 7 AM–6 PM) system serves most of the county.

In Sarasota, **Sarasota County Area Transit** (SCAT), (tel. 813/951–5850) is the public transit company. The **Lee County Transit System** (tel. 813/939–1303) serves Fort Myers and most of the county.

Scenic Drives

I–275 between St. Petersburg and **Terra Ceia.** Motorists get a bird's-eye view of bustling Tampa Bay along the Sunshine Skyway and its bright-yellow suspension bridge.

Head north or south on the **Bayshore Drive Causeway** for a spectacular view of Tampa Bay.

Rte. 679 takes you along two of St. Petersburg's most pristine islands, Cabbage and Mullet keys.

Rte. 789 carries you over several of the coast's slender barrier islands, past miles of green-blue Gulf waters, beaches, and waterfront homes. The road does not connect all the islands, however. It runs from Holmes Beach off the Bradenton coast south to Lido Beach in Sarasota, then begins again on Casey Key south of Osprey and runs south to Nokomis Beach.

Rte. 867 (McGregor Boulevard), Fort Myers's premier road, passes what were the winter homes of Thomas Edison and Henry Ford and goes southwest toward the beaches. The road is lined with thousands of royal palm trees and many large old homes.

J.N. "Ding" Darling National Wildlife Refuge. Drive along the 5-mile dirt road in Sanibel and, especially at low tide, you may see raccoons; alligators; and birds, such as roseate spoonbills, egrets, ospreys, herons, and anhingas.

Head west on **Mooringline Drive** in Naples for a drive past some of the cushiest coastline property in the state. Mooringline turns south and becomes Gulf Shore Boulevard. Condominiums, shops, hotels, and lots of beaches line this drive.

Just near the end of Gulf Shore Boulevard on Broad Avenue, you can pick up **2nd Street South,** which becomes Gordon Drive. It leads into Port Royale, where million-dollar homes are a dime a dozen. The architecture, landscaping, and statuary that are visible from the road make it a worthwhile expedition.

Guided Tours

Orientation Tours

Around the Town (tel. 813/932–7803) conducts tours for groups of 25 or more in the Tampa Bay area, plus Tarpon Springs and Sarasota, the dog tracks, and area theaters. Try to make reservations several weeks in advance.

Gulf Coast Gray Line (tel. 813/822–3577) makes daily trips from Tampa to Disney World, Epcot Center, Sea World, Busch Gardens, and other attractions.

Travel is Fun Tours of St. Petersburg (tel. 813/821–9479) offers day-long tours to area sights from St. Petersburg.

Boat Tours

Sea Escape Cruises (tel. 800/432-0900) are day-long excursions into the Gulf of Mexico on full-size cruise ships departing from St. Petersburg.

The ***Captain Anderson*** (tel. 813/367-7804) combines sightseeing and dinner cruises from the St. Petersburg Causeway, 3400 Pasadena Ave. It operates from October through May, St. Petersburg Beach.

The Admiral (tel. 813/462-2628 or 800/444-4814) is docked at Clearwater Beach Marina. It runs dinner and sightseeing cruises all year.

The ***Starlite Princess*** (tel. 813/595-1212) is a paddlewheel excursion boat offering three-hour, five-course meals from Hamlin's Landing, Indian Rocks Beach. Old-fashioned boat adds to the fun.

The ***Miss Cortez*** (tel. 813/794-1223) departs from Cortez, just north of Bradenton, every Tuesday, Thursday, and Sunday for Egmont Key, a small abandoned island just north of Anna Maria Island.

Le Barge Tropical Cruises (tel. 813/366-6116) offers a variety of half- and full-day cruises from Marina Plaza in downtown Sarasota.

Myakka Wildlife Tours (tel. 813/365-0100) is at Myakka River State Park, east of Sarasota on Rte. 72. *The Gator Gal*, a large airboat, conducts one-hour tours of the 29,000-acre wildlife and bird sanctuary. Four trips daily.

Epicurean Sailing Charters (tel. 813/964-0708) conducts half- and full-day cruises from Boca Grande to Useppa Island, Cabbage Key, and other area islands.

King Fisher Cruise Lines (tel. 813/639-0969) offers half-, full-day, and sunset cruises in Charlotte Harbor, Peace River, and Intracoastal Waterway from Fishermen's Village, Punta Gorda.

Babcock Wilderness Adventures (tel. 813/656-6104) conducts guided swamp-buggy tours through the Telegraph Cypress Swamp on the 90,000-acre Crescent B Ranch, south of Punta Gorda. Reservations required.

Everglades Jungle Cruises (tel. 813/334-7474) explores the Caloosahatchee and Orange rivers of Lee County. The ***Capt. J.P.***, a stern paddle wheeler, offers a variety of cruises on the Caloosahatchee River and environs from mid-November through mid-April. Brunch, lunch, and dinner cruises available, and depart from the Fort Myers Yacht Basin.

The ***Island Rover*** (tel. 813/765-SHIP) offers morning, afternoon, and sunset sails on a tall ship in the Gulf of Mexico that leave from Gulf Star Marina, Fort Myers Beach.

Jammin' Sailboat Cruises (tel. 813/463-3520) offers day and sunset cruises from Fort Myers Beach. Call for reservations.

Dalis Charter (tel. 813/262-4545) offers half-day fishing and sightseeing trips and sunset cruises. Also available for private cocktail cruises. It's docked at Old Marine Market Place at Tin City (1200 Fifth Ave. S., Naples).

Tiki Boat Tours (tel. 813/262-7577) conducts a variety of tours through the northern section of the Everglades' Ten Thousand Islands, including half-day fishing and shelling expeditions to Keewaydin Island and sightseeing along Naples Bay. Tours start at the dock behind Old Marine Market Place, Naples.

Wooten's Everglades (tel. 813/695-2781) runs a variety of airboat and swamp-buggy tours through the Everglades daily from Wooten's alligator farm, 35 miles east of Naples on U.S. 41.

Eden of the Everglades (tel. 813/695–2800) travels the wilderness wetlands of the Everglades' Ten Thousand Islands, departing from Everglades City in southern Collier County five times daily.

Florida Boat Tours (tel. 813/695–4400) depart from the heart of Everglades City. The 40-minute tours of the Ten Thousand Islands set off hourly.

Day in the Everglades (tel. 813/695–4000 or 800/638–5081, ext. 118) conducts swamp buggy tours of the Ten Thousand Islands and sunset dinner tours.

Swampland Airboat Tours and Guide (tel. 813/695–2740 or 800/638–5051, ext. 274) conducts hourly, half- and full-day tours of the Everglades from just outside Everglades City.

By Plane Helicopter tours of the Tampa Bay area and the west coast of Florida are offered by **Suncoast Helicopters** (tel. 813/872–6625), based at Tampa International Airport; and **West Florida Helicopters** (Albert Whitted Airport, tel. 813/823–5200). In the Charlotte Harbor area, sightseeing tours are offered by the **Boca Grande Seaplane Service** (tel. 813/964–0234), 4th and Bayou, Boca Grande.

Important Addresses and Numbers

Tourist Information All the following offices are open weekdays 9–5 and closed on holidays:

Charlotte County Chamber of Commerce (2702 Tamiami Trail, Port Charlotte, tel. 813/627–2222).

Lee County Visitor and Convention Bureau (2180 W. First St., Fort Myers, tel. 813/335–2631 or 800/237–6444).

Naples Area Chamber of Commerce (3620 N. Tamiami Trail, Naples, tel. 813/262–6141).

Sanibel-Captiva Chamber of Commerce (Causeway Rd., Sanibel, tel. 813/472–1080).

Sarasota Convention and Visitors Bureau (655 N. Tamiami Trail, tel. 813/957–1877 or 800/522–9799).

Tampa Bay Area **The Greater Tampa Chamber of Commerce** (Box 420, tel. 813/228–7777). For information on current area events, call the **Visitors Information Department** (tel. 813/223–1111).

Tampa/Hillsborough Convention and Visitors Association (111 Madison St., Suite 1010, tel. 800/826–8358).

Tarpon Springs Chamber of Commerce (210 S. Pinellas Ave., Suite 120, tel. 813/937–6109).

Treasure Island Chamber of Commerce (152 108th Ave., tel. 813/367–4529).

Greater Clearwater Chamber of Commerce (128 N. Osceola Ave., tel. 813/461–0011).

Greater Dunedin Chamber of Commerce (301 Main St., tel. 813/736–5066).

Gulf Beaches Chamber of Commerce (105 5th Ave., Indian Rocks Beach, tel. 813/595–4575).

Madeira Beach Chamber of Commerce (501 150th Ave., tel. 813/391–7373).

Pinellas Suncoast Tourist Development Council (4625 E. Bay Dr., Suite 109, Clearwater, tel. 813/530–6452).

St. Petersburg Chamber of Commerce (100 2nd Ave. N, tel. 813/821–4069).

Emergencies Dial 911 for **police** or **ambulance** in an emergency.

Hospitals Hospital emergency rooms are open 24 hours. In Tampa: **University Community Hospital** (3100 E. Fletcher Ave.). In St. Petersburg: **Bayfront Medical Center** (701 6th St. S). In Bradenton: **Manatee Memorial Hospital** (206 2nd St. E). In Sarasota: **Sarasota Memorial Hospital** (1700 S. Tamiami Trail, U.S. 41). In Fort Myers: **Lee Memorial Hospital** (2776 Cleveland Ave.). In Naples: **Naples Community** (350 7th St. N).

24-Hour Pharmacy **Eckerd Drugs** (11613 N. Nebraska, Tampa, tel. 813/978–0775).

Exploring Southwest Florida

The Tampa Bay Area

Numbers in the margin correspond to points of interest on the Tampa–St. Petersburg Area map.

Tampa boasts more business suits than any other part of the region. Its port is the country's seventh largest, with phosphate, shrimp, and bananas the primary cargo. The city's shrimp fleet, docked at Hooker's Point, is the state's largest. Industry flourishes as well, with millions of cigars rolled daily, phosphate mined from massive pits, and one major brewery—Busch—producing its wares here.

It's fitting that an area with a thriving international port should also be populated by a wealth of nationalities—Greeks, Scots, Hispanics, and Italians, to name only a few. American Indians were the sole inhabitants of the region for many years (Tampa is an Indian phrase meaning "sticks of fire"). The Spanish explorers Juan Ponce de Léon, Pánfilo de Narváez, and Hernando de Soto passed through in the mid-1500s. The U.S. Army and civilian settlers arrived in 1824; a military presence remains in the form of MacDill Air Force Base, where the U.S. Operations Command is located.

The Cubans brought their cigar-making industry to the area in 1866 and developed Ybor City. This east Tampa suburb is still primarily Cuban but contains a dwindling number of cigar makers.

Tampa does not have a Gulf beach, and Tampa Bay, though lovely to look at, is too polluted for swimming. For that, visitors should head to neighboring St. Petersburg, which sits on a peninsula bordered on three sides by bays and the Gulf of Mexico, filled with pleasure and commercial craft.

North of Tampa, in Tarpon Springs, there has been a large Greek population for decades, since sponge divers from the Dodecanese Islands of Greece moved to the area at the turn of the century. This was the world's largest sponge center during the 1930s. Although a bacterial blight wiped out the sponge beds in the 1940s, the Greeks held on, and the sponge industry has returned, though in lesser force than during its heyday. Today, the Greek influence remains evident in the churches, the restaurants, and, often, in the language spoken on the streets.

The accent is Scottish in Dunedin, just south of Tarpon Springs. Two Scots were responsible for giving the town its Gaelic name in the 1880s. If the sound of bagpipes played by men in kilts appeals to you, head to Dunedin in March or April, when the Highland games and the Dunedin Heather and Thistle holidays pay tribute to the Celtic heritage.

Tampa Tampa is the business and commercial hub of this part of the state, as you'll quickly notice when driving by the busy port. The major north-south route is I–75; if you're heading from Orlando, you'll likely drive in on east-west I–4.

Let's begin a tour of Tampa along that I–4 corridor at Exit 5 (Orient Rd., east of the city). The water tower with an arrow ❶ sticking through it gives it away: this is the **Seminole Indian Village,** which contains a village and museum displaying artifacts of the Seminole Indians, who inhabited Florida long before white settlers arrived. You'll also be treated to alligator wrestling and snake shows. *5221 N. Orient Rd., tel. 813/620–3077. Admission: $4.50 adults, $3.75 children under 12, $3.50 senior citizens. Open Mon.–Sat. 9–5, Sun. 10–5.*

❷ **Ybor City** is Tampa's Cuban melting pot, which thrived on the cigar-making industry at the turn of the century. To get there, take I–4 west to Exit 1 (22nd St.) and go south five blocks to 7th Avenue. You're in the heart of Ybor City, where the smell of cigars—hand-rolled by Cuban refugees—mingles with old-world architecture. Take a stroll past the ornately tiled Columbia Restaurant and the stores lining the street, or step back to the past at **Ybor Square.** The restored cigar factory (1901 13th St.) now is a mall with boutiques, offices, and several restaurants. You can watch as artisans continue the local practice of hand rolling cigars.

For something a little more modern, head for the new skyscrapers downtown. From 7th Avenue, go west to Nebraska Avenue and turn left. That will take you to Kennedy Boulevard; turn right and drive a few blocks to the vicinity of Franklin Street. You are now in one of Tampa's booming growth areas, with a pedestrian mall down the center of Franklin Street.

❸ A few more blocks to the east you'll find the **Tampa Museum of Art,** near Curtis Hixon Convention Center. Egyptian, Greek, and Roman artifacts are on display, as well as traveling exhibits. *601 Doyle Carlton Dr., tel. 813/223–8128. Donations accepted. Open Tues.–Sat. 10–5, Wed. 10–9, Sun. 1–5.*

❹ On another day, enjoy a romp through **Busch Gardens.** A safari simulating a journey to the Dark Continent will let you watch free-roaming zebras, giraffes, rhinos, lions, and more—all from the comfort of a monorail. There are many other rides and attractions in this 300-acre park, so allow at least six hours here. *3000 Busch Blvd. (Rte. 580), 2 mi east of I–275, tel. 813/987–5082. All-inclusive admission: $26.95, plus $3 parking charge. Open daily 9:30–6.*

❺ **Adventure Island,** one mile northeast of Busch Gardens, is a water wonderland in the heart of Tampa. Water slides, pools, and man-made waves are the highlights; the park also has convenient changing rooms, snack bars, a gift shop, and a video arcade. *4545 Bougainvillea Ave., tel. 813/987–5660. Admission: $13.95 per person, children under 2 free. Open daily. Closed Dec.–Feb.*

St. Petersburg St. Petersburg and the Pinellas Suncoast form the thumb of the hand jutting out of the west coast, holding in Tampa Bay. I–275 crosses the bay from Tampa through the heart of the city and

Adventure Island, **5**
Busch Gardens, **4**
Cedar Key, **15**
Crystal River, **14**
Fort Desoto Park, **8**
Great Explorations!, **6**
Homosassa Springs State Wildlife Park, **12**
Seminole Indian Village, **1**
State Wildlife Park, **12**
Suncoast Seabird Sanctuary, **9**
Sunken Gardens, **10**
Sunshine Skyway, **7**
Tampa Museum of Art, **3**
Weeki Wachee Spring, **11**
Ybor City, **2**
Yulee Sugar Mill State Historic Site, **13**

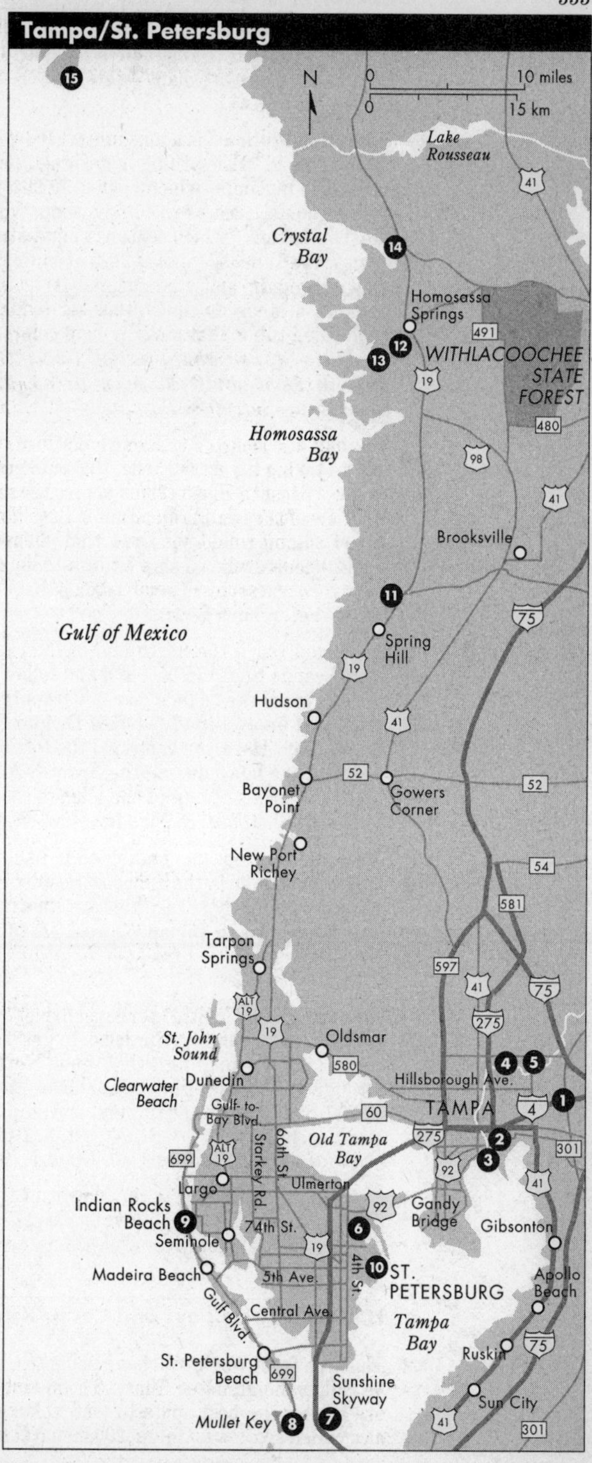

then crosses the bay again at the Sunshine Skyway into Bradenton. U.S. 19 is the major north–south artery. Traffic can be heavy, and there are many lights, so U.S. 19 should be avoided on lengthy trips.

6 **Great Explorations!** is a museum where you will never be told, "Don't touch!" Everything is designed for a hands-on experience. The museum, which opened in late 1987, is divided into theme rooms, such as the Body Shop, which explores health; the Think Tank, which features mind-stretching puzzles and games; the Touch Tunnel, a 90-foot-long, pitch-black maze you crawl through; and Phenomenal Arts, which displays such items as a Moog music synthesizer (which you can play) and neon-filled tubes that glow in vivid colors when touched. *1120 4th St. S, St. Petersburg just off I-275, tel. 813/821–8885. Admission: $4.50 adults, $3.50 children 4–17, $4 senior citizens. Open Mon.–Sat. 10–5, Sun. noon–5.*

The bay and beaches offer two distinct communities to visit. 7 Let's start with a trip over the **Sunshine Skyway.** Heading south, a $1 toll will carry you across the causeway for a bird's-eye view of the islands and Tampa Bay. You can also see what's left of the original twin span that collapsed and killed more than 30 people when a ship hit it in 1980. Heading north, you'll get a view of a series of small islands that dot the bay, and you'll see St. Petersburg Beach.

When you reach the north end of the causeway, turn left on 54th Avenue South (Rte. 682), and follow it to Rte. 679. Turn left and cross the islands you saw from the Sunshine Skyway. 8 You'll end up eventually at **Fort DeSoto Park** at the mouth of Tampa Bay. Here you can roam the fort that was built to protect Gulf sea lanes during the Spanish-American War or wander the beaches of any of the islands that make up the park. *Mullet Key, 34th St. S. No admission charge.*

When pelicans become entangled in fishing lines, locals some-9 times carry them to the **Suncoast Seabird Sanctuary,** a nonprofit organization whose facilities are open to the public. Drive up Gulf Boulevard to Indian Shores. *18328 Gulf Blvd., tel. 813/391–6211. Admission free, but donations welcome. Open daily 9–5:30.*

For a second day in St. Peterburg, drive to one of Florida's most 10 colorful spots, **Sunken Gardens.** To get there, take 4th Street North (a right turn) to 18th Avenue North. Visitors can walk through an aviary with tropical birds, stroll among more than 50,000 exotic plants and flowers, and stop to smell the rare, fragrant orchids. *1825 4th St. N., tel. 813/896–3186. Admission: $6.95 adults, $4 children 3–11. Open daily 9–5:30.*

For visitors spending several days in the Tampa Bay area, there are a couple of worthwhile excursions just to the north: the pristine Crystal River area (Manatee Coast) and rustic Cedar Key.

The Manatee Coast and Cedar Key

Manatee Coast The area from Weeki Wachee Spring to Crystal River can aptly be called the Manatee Coast. The springs, rivers, and creeks are among the best spots to view these endangered animals, also called sea cows. Only 1,200 manatees remain. It's believed ancient mariners spun tales of mermaids based on these curious mammals related to elephants.

U.S. 19 is the prime route through manatee country, but this highway is free-flowing, unlike the stop-and-go traffic on U.S. 19 in St. Petersburg.

11 Heading north on U.S. 19 out of St. Petersburg about 60 miles, you'll see **Weeki Wachee Spring** at the junction of Route 50. Here, an underwater theater presents mermaid shows and a nature trail through the subtropical wilderness, plus a jungle boat cruise to view local wildlife. Allow at least three hours to see everything. *At U.S. 19 and Rte. 50, Weeki Wachee, tel. 904/596–2062. Admission: $13.95 adults, $9.95 children 3–11. Open daily 9:30–5:30.*

12 About 15 miles further north on U.S. 19 is another of Florida's natural wonders: **Homosassa Springs State Wildlife Park.** Turn left on County Road 490-A and follow the signs to the attraction at Fish Bowl Drive. Here you may see manatees, but the "Spring of 10,000 Fish" is a main attraction, where you seem to mingle with the inhabitants in a floating observatory. A walk along the park's paths will lead you to reptile, alligator, and exotic bird shows. Jungle boat cruises on the Homosassa River are available across Fish Bowl Drive from the park's main entrance. *One mi west of U.S. 19, Homosassa Springs, tel. 904/628–2311. Admission: $6.95 adults, $3.95 children 3–11; 20% AARP discount with current card if presented before purchasing ticket. Open daily 9–5:30.*

13 The **Yulee Sugar Mill State Historic Site** is just a short drive from Homosassa Springs. The site of a ruined sugar plantation built by the state's first U.S. senator, this is a good spot for a picnic. *From Homosassa Springs Nature World, turn left on C.R. 490-A. Admission free. Open daily.*

14 The last stop could be a half-day or an all-day event. **Crystal River** is a U.S. Fish and Wildlife Service sanctuary for manatees. The Kings Bay area of the river is set aside to prevent human intrusion, but wide stretches are open for people to watch and swim with the sea cows. The main spring feeds crystal-clear water into the river at 72 degrees year-round and during winter months manatees congregate around the spring. During warmer months when manatees scatter, the main spring still makes an interesting swim. *Go north on U.S. 19 into the town of Crystal River, turn left on C.R. 44. Two marinas with boat and snorkel rentals are Port Paradise, tel. 904/563–2816 and Plantation Inn and Golf Resort, tel. 904/795–5797. Admission to refuge free.*

Cedar Key

Up in the area known as the Big Bend, Florida's long curving coastline north of Tampa, you won't find many beaches. But you will find an idyllic island village tucked in among the marshes and scenic streams feeding the Gulf of Mexico. From U.S. 19,
15 take Route 24 until the highway ends. This is **Cedar Key.**

Once a strategic port for the Confederate States of America, Cedar Key today is a commercial fishing center. Historical photographs dating to 1800 and exhibits that focus on the development of the area, visit **Cedar Key Historical Society Museum** *at Rte. 24 and Second St., tel. 904/543–5549. Admission: $1 adults, 50¢ children 6–12. Open daily 10–4.*

Bradenton/Sarasota Area

Numbers in the margin correspond to points of interest on the Bradenton/Sarasota Area map.

Sarasota is a city of two tales. Situated on the water, it is unquestionably a beach resort. But it also has a thriving cultural community, making it a suitable destination for those with a taste for the arts. Much of the credit for the city's diversity is due to the late John Ringling, founder of the Ringling Brothers Barnum & Bailey Circus, who chose to make Sarasota the winter home of his circus and his family.

For those who like statistics, here are a few: Sarasota County has 35 miles of Gulf beaches, 2 state parks, 22 municipal parks, and 46 golf courses, many of them open to the public.

Nearby Bradenton maintains a lower profile, but also has its share of sugar-sand beaches, golf courses, and historic sites dating back to the mid-1800s.

To the south is Venice, with its multitudinous canals crisscrossing the city. Besides being the winter home of the circus, the city contains the world's only clown college. And, though shell collecting is quite good, the beaches of Venice are best known for the wealth of shark teeth to be found.

Bradenton Bradenton is on a finger of land enclosing the southern end of Tampa Bay; the Manatee River also borders the city's north side. The barrier island, Anna Maria, lies off the mainland and fronts the Gulf of Mexico. The combined U.S. 41 and 301 cuts north-south through the center of the city. I–75 is to the east, and Rte. 64 connects the interstate to Bradenton and Anna Maria Island.

Hernando de Soto, one of the first Spanish explorers, set foot in Florida in 1539 near what is now Bradenton. Take Rte. 64 to ❶ 75th Street NW, turn north, and drive to **DeSoto National Memorial,** where park employees dressed in costumes of the period demonstrate various 16th-century weapons and show how the explorers who roamed the southeastern United States prepared and preserved food for their journeys through the untamed land. Films, demonstrations, and a short nature trail are on the grounds. *75th St. NW, tel. 813/792–0458. Admission: free. Open daily 8–5:30.*

Head back to the center of the city, to 10th Street West. A few ❷ blocks from the river is the **South Florida Museum,** where you can find artifacts on Florida's history, including displays of Indian culture and an excellent collection of Civil War memorabilia. The museum is also home to "Snooty," the oldest living manatee (or sea cow) in captivity. In the wild, manatees are endangered, but here Snooty likes to shake hands and perform other tricks at feeding time. *201 10th St.; tel. 813/746–4132. Admission: $5 adults, $2.50 children and students. Open Tues.–Sat. 10–5, Sun. noon–5.*

❸ Also part of the museum is the **Bishop Planetarium,** where, inside a domed theater, you can see star shows and special-effects laser light displays. *Tel. 813/746–4131. Admission: $5 adults, $2.50 children 5–12. Star show Tues.–Sun. at 1:30 and 3 PM plus Fri. and Sat. at 7:30 PM.*

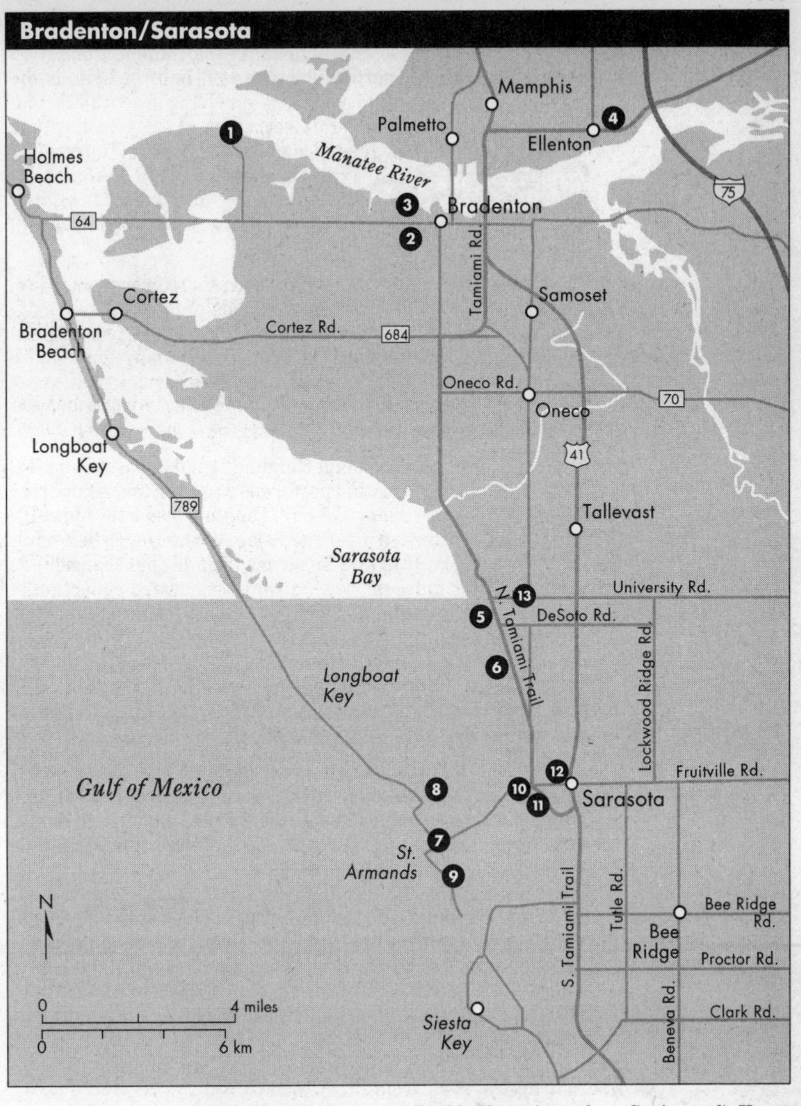

Bellm's Cars & Music of Yesterday, **13**
Bishop Planetarium, **3**
DeSoto National Memorial, **1**
Downtown Art District, **12**
Gamble Plantation and Confederate Memorial, **4**
Marie Selby Botanical Gardens, **11**
Marina Jack II, **10**
Mote Marine Aquarium, **8**
Ringling Museums, **5**
St. Armand's Key, **7**
Sarasota Jungle Gardens, **6**
South Florida Museum, **2**
South Lido Park, **9**

❹ Cross the river on U.S. 41 and turn right when U.S. 301 splits off. On the left, three miles ahead, is the **Gamble Plantation and Confederate Memorial.** The mansion, built in 1850, is the only pre-Civil War plantation house surviving in south Florida. This is where the Confederate secretary of state took refuge when the Confederacy fell to Union forces. Some of the original furnishings are on display in the mansion. *3708 Patten Ave., Ellenton, tel. 813/723–4536. Admission: $2 adults, $1 children 6–12. Open Thurs.–Mon. 8–5; closed Tues. and Wed. Tours of the house at 9:30, 10:30, 1, 2, 3, and 4.*

Sarasota The City of Sarasota sits on the eastern shore of Sarasota Bay. Across the water lie the barrier islands of Siesta Key, Longboat Key, and Lido Key, with myriad beaches, shops, hotels, condominiums, and houses. U.S. 41 is the main north-south thoroughfare in the city; further east, I-75 carries traffic past the city to Tampa or Fort Myers. Four state roads run west from the interstate highway into Sarasota.

❺ Long ago, circus tycoon John Ringling found Sarasota an ideal spot to bring his clowns and performers to train and recuperate during the winter. Along the bay, Ringling also built himself a fancy home, patterned after the Palace of the Doges in Venice, Italy. Today, the **Ringling Museums** include that mansion, as well as his art museum (with a world-renowned collection of Rubens paintings) and a museum of circus memorabilia. Also situated on the property is the Asolo State Theater. *Located ½ mi south of the Sarasota-Bradenton Airport on U.S. 41, tel. 813/355–5101. Combined admission (good for the mansion and both museums): $8.50 adult, $7.50 senior citizens, children 12 and under free. Open daily 10–5:30, Thurs. 10–10.*

❻ From the Ringling museums, head south on U.S. 41 about 1½ miles to **Sarasota Jungle Gardens.** Here you can stroll through 10 acres of tropical plants and watch the bird and reptile shows. *3701 Bayshore Rd., tel. 813/355–5305. Admission: $8 adults, $4 children 3–12. Open daily 9–5.*

Time Out **St. Armand's Circle.** It's time to swing out across the bay. Continue south on U.S. 41 to Rte. 789. Turn right, and cross the Ringling Causeway to the small island of St. Armand's Key, where you'll find this chic little circle of shops and restaurants. Some sure bets include: **Cafe L'Europe, The Columbia,** and **Charley's Crab.**

---

❼ ❽ Just up the road from **St. Armand's Key** is the **Mote Marine Aquarium.** On display in the aquarium are sharks, rays, fish, and other marine creatures native to the area. A huge outdoor shark tank lets you see its inhabitants from above and below the water's surface. To get there from Harding Circle, turn north on Ringling Boulevard. Before you reach the bridge leading to Longboat Key, turn right at the sign for City Island and Mote Marine Lab. *1600 City Island Park, tel. 813/388–2451. Admission: $5 adults, $3 children 6–17. Open daily 10–5.*

❾ You now have an option. One choice is to either head back south, past the public beach at Lido Key, to **South Lido Park,** where you can try your luck at fishing, take a dip in the waters of the bay or Gulf of Mexico, roam the paths of the 130-acre park, or picnic as the sun sets through the Australian pines into the Gulf. *Admission free. Open 8–sunset.*

The alternative is to turn back east across Sarasota Bay and turn right into the Marina Plaza along U.S. 41. Here you can enjoy an evening on the water in style, with a sunset dinner

10 cruise on board a stern-wheel paddleboat, the ***Marina Jack II.*** *Marina Plaza, Island Park, tel. 813/366–9255. Cost: $6 plus dinner. Reservations required. MC, V.*

11 Start out your second day of exploring Sarasota at **Marie Selby Botanical Gardens,** which are near the Island Park yacht basin. Here you can stroll through a world-class display of orchids and wander through 14 garden areas along Sarasota Bay. *800 S. Palm Ave., off U.S. 41, tel. 813/366–5730. Admission: $5 adults, free for children under 12 when accompanied by an adult. Open daily 10–5 except Christmas.*

12 In the heart of Sarasota, you'll discover a **downtown art district,** with galleries such as Art Uptown (1367 Main St.), Adley Gallery (1620 Main St.), Corbino Galleries (69 S. Palm Ave.), Apple & Carpenter Gallery of Fine Arts (1280 N. Palm Ave.), and J. E. Voorhees Gallery (1359 Main St.).

13 On the road to the airport (U.S. 41) is **Bellm's Cars & Music of Yesterday.** The display includes 130 classic cars, such as Pierce Arrows and Auburns, and 2,000 old-time music makers, such as hurdy-gurdies and calliopes. *5500 N. Tamiami Trail, tel. 813/355–6228. Admission: $6.50 adults, $3.25 children 6–12. Open Mon.–Sat. 8:30–6, Sun. 9:30–6.*

Fort Myers/Naples Area

Numbers in the margin correspond to points of interest on the Fort Myers/Naples Region map.

Lee County has a split personality. Its inland communities—Fort Myers and Cape Coral—are primarily commercial and residential. Its Gulf-front communities are composed mainly of beach resorts.

Fort Myers gets its nickname, the City of Palms, from the hundreds of towering royal palms that inventor Thomas Edison planted along a main residential street, McGregor Boulevard, on which his winter estate stood. Edison's idea caught on, and there are now more than 2,000 royal palms on McGregor Boulevard alone, with countless more throughout the city.

Along the county's western border are the resort islands of Estero, Sanibel, and Captiva. Estero contains Fort Myers Beach, a laid-back beach community favored by young singles and those who want to stay on the Gulf without paying the higher prices on Sanibel or Captiva. A few miles farther off the coast are Sanibel and Captiva, connected to the mainland by a mile-long causeway. In recent years development has threatened the charm of the islands. However, island dwellers have staunchly held the line on further development, keeping buildings low and somewhat farther apart than on the majority of Florida's barrier islands. Sanibel has long been a world-class shelling locale, with fine fishing, luxury hotels, and dozens of restaurants. You will not be able to see most of the houses, which are shielded by tall Australian pines, but the beaches and tranquil Gulf waters are readily accessible.

Once a small fishing village, Naples has grown into a thriving and sophisticated city, often likened to Palm Beach for its ambience. Its Third Street South and Fifth Avenue South offer shoppers a chance to make serious inroads in their disposable cash. The number of golf courses per capita in Naples is the highest in the world, a new, 1,200-seat performing arts hall attracts world-class performers, and the town is the west coast home of the Miami City Ballet.

Unlike Palm Beach, where public beaches are scarce, the Naples area prides itself on a multitude of access points along its 41 miles of beach. The yen to shell, sun, and fish can be indulged to excess on the sun-drenched white shores.

And, for a little local tradition, experience the twice-yearly swamp buggy races, where drivers plow through the Mile 'O' Mud track in their massive machines. Originally held to mark the start of the Everglades hunting season, the races have been running ever since.

South of Naples is yet another resort island, Marco. Here, high-rise condominiums and hotels line much of the waterfront, but many natural areas have been preserved, including the tiny fishing village of Goodland, where Old Florida lives on.

Fort Myers–Lee County ❶

Fort Myers is the heart of the county, but only a few major roads lead through it. I–75 runs north-south, as does the more commercial thoroughfare, U.S. 41 (called Cleveland Ave. in Fort Myers). McGregor Boulevard runs from downtown Fort Myers southwest to Sanibel-Captiva. Summerlin Road runs southwest from Colonial Boulevard in South Fort Myers to Sanibel-Captiva and Fort Myers Beach. Rte. 78 (Pine Island-Bayshore Rd.) leads from North Fort Myers through north Cape Coral onto Pine Island.

If you are headed downtown from the beaches, drive at least part of the way on palm-lined McGregor Boulevard (from College Parkway north into town is the most scenic).

Thomas Edison's Winter Home, containing a laboratory, botanical gardens, and a museum, is open for guided tours. The property straddles McGregor Boulevard (Rte. 867) about a mile west of U.S. 41 near downtown Fort Myers. The inventor spent his winters on the 14-acre estate, developing the phonograph and teletype, experimenting with rubber, and planting some 6,000 species of plants from those collected throughout the world. A recent addition to the Edison complex is **Mangoes,** the winter home of the inventor's long-time friend, automaker Henry Ford. The 3-acre grounds and renovated home opened to the public in early 1990. *2350 McGregor Blvd., Fort Myers, tel. 813/334–3614. Admission to the Edison home: $7 adults, $3 children 6–12; to the Ford home $5 adults, $3 children 6–12; combined tickets $9 adults, $4 children. Open daily except Thanksgiving and Christmas. Tours 9–4 daily except Sun. 12:30–4.*

Just a few blocks east is the **Fort Myers Historical Museum,** which is housed in a restored railroad depot. Its displays depict the area's history dating back to 1200 BC. *2300 Peck St., Fort Myers, tel. 813/332–5955. Open Mon.–Fri. 9–4:30, Sun. 1–5. Admission: $2 adults, 50¢ children 2–12.*

Head northwest to Edwards Drive, which borders the Caloosahatchee River. The **City Yacht Basin** has tour boats that offer sightseeing and luncheon cruises on the river. Also on Edwards Drive, you can find a plethora of shuffleboard courts that

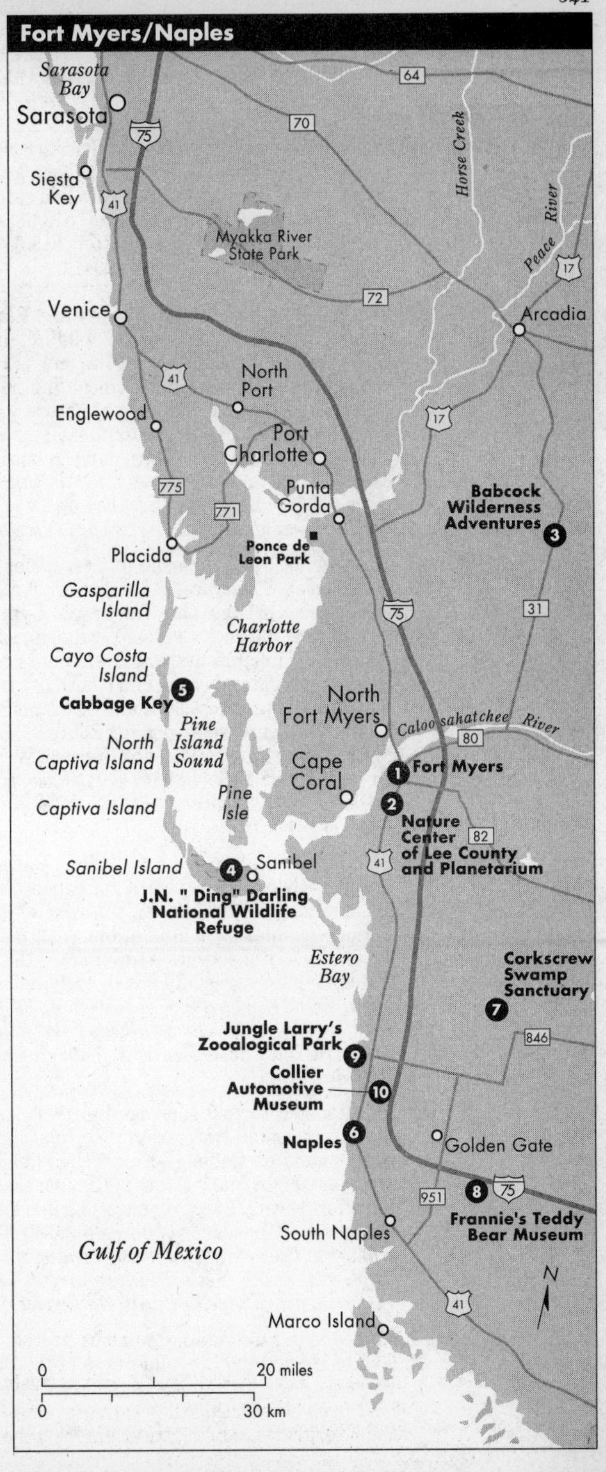
Fort Myers/Naples
Sarasota Bay
Sarasota
Siesta Key
Myakka River State Park
Horse Creek
Peace River
Venice
Arcadia
North Port
Englewood
Port Charlotte
Punta Gorda
Babcock Wilderness Adventures
Placida
Ponce de Leon Park
Gasparilla Island
Charlotte Harbor
Cayo Costa Island
Cabbage Key
Pine Island Sound
North Captiva Island
Captiva Island
Pine Isle
North Fort Myers
Caloosahatchee River
Cape Coral
Fort Myers
Nature Center of Lee County and Planetarium
Sanibel Island
Sanibel
J.N. " Ding" Darling National Wildlife Refuge
Estero Bay
Corkscrew Swamp Sanctuary
Jungle Larry's Zooalogical Park
Collier Automotive Museum
Naples
Golden Gate
Frannie's Teddy Bear Museum
South Naples
Gulf of Mexico
Marco Island
N
0
20 miles
0
30 km
64
70
75
41
72
17
775
771
31
80
82
846
951

weather heavy use on all but the hottest days. Adjacent to the courts is the **Hall of 50 States,** where the Fort Myers Chamber of Commerce dispenses information. *1365 Hendry St. Open weekdays 9–4.*

Time Out Walk another block in from the river to First Street, which runs through the heart of downtown Fort Myers. Stroll past the shops and have lunch at one of several eateries, including **Casa De Guerrero** (2225 First St., tel. 813/332–4674), **French Connection Café** (2282 First St., tel. 813/332–4443), and **April's** (2269 First St., tel. 813/337–4004).

---

❷ The **Nature Center of Lee County and Planetarium** offers frequently changing exhibits on wildlife, fossils, Florida's natives, and native habitats. An aviary is home to a variety of permanently disabled birds, including hawks, owls, and bald eagles, and there are 2 miles of nature walks through the cypress swamps. The planetarium offers star and laser light shows and Cinema-360 films. *3450 Ortiz Ave., Fort Myers, tel. 813/275–3435. Nature Center admission: $2 adults, 50¢ children 3–11; Planetarium admission: $3 adults, $2 children under 12. Open Mon–Sat. 9–4, Sun. 11–4:30.*

❸ To see what Florida looked like centuries ago, reserve a place on **Babcock Wilderness Adventures,** 90-minute swamp buggy excursions through the Telegraph Cypress Swamp on the 90,000-acre Babcock Crescent B Ranch, south of Punta Gorda. Among the inhabitants you are likely to see are turkey, deer, bobcats, alligators, cows, and a herd of bison. From downtown Fort Myers, head east on Route 80 (Palm Beach Blvd.) past the I-75 interchange, then look for Route 31. Make a left and drive until you see the entrance for Babcock Wilderness Adventures on your right. *Tel. 813/656–6104. Reservations required. Admission: $16.91 adults, $8.43 children. Four tours daily, weather permitting.*

❹ On Sanibel, explore the **J. N. "Ding" Darling National Wildlife Refuge**—by car, foot, bicycle, or canoe. The 5,014-acre refuge is home to some 290 species of birds, 50 types of reptiles, and various mammals. A 5-mile dirt road meanders through the sanctuary. An observation tower along the road is a prime birdwatching site, especially in the early morning and just before dusk. *Tel. 813/472–1100. Admission: $3 per car or $15 for a duck stamp (which covers all national wildlife refuges). Wildlife Drive open Sat.–Thurs. 7–5:45, closed Fri. Visitor Center open daily 9–5.*

❺ Board a boat to visit **Cabbage Key,** which sits at Marker 60 on the Intracoastal Waterway. Atop an ancient Calusa Indian shell mound on Cabbage Key is the friendly inn that novelist and playwright Mary Roberts Rinehart built in 1938. Now the inn offers several guest rooms, a marina, and a dining room that is papered in thousands of dollar bills, signed and posted by patrons over the years. *Lunch and dinner tours available through Captiva's South Seas Plantation (tel. 813/472–5111), and Fishermen's Village in Punta Gorda (tel. 813/639–0969).*

Naples ❻ **Naples** and surrounding suburbs are squeezed between the Gulf of Mexico and the wilderness of the Big Cypress National Preserve, which stretches to the Everglades. I–75 and U.S. 41 lead from the north. Alligator Alley and U.S. 41 cut through the Everglades to bring travelers from the east coast.

To get a feel for what this part of Florida was like before humans began draining the swamps, take a drive out Rte. 846 to

7 the **Corkscrew Swamp Sanctuary.** The National Audubon Society manages the 11,000-acre tract to help protect 500-year-old trees and endangered birds, such as the wood storks that nest high in the bald cypress. Visitors taking the 1¾-mile self-guided tour along the boardwalk can glimpse alligators, graceful wading birds, and unusual "air" plants that cling to the sides of trees. *16 mi east of I–75 on Rte. 846, tel. 813/657–3771. Admission: $5 adults, $2.50 children 5–12. Open daily 9–5.*

From Corkscrew Swamp Sanctuary, take Route 846 back to I–75 and head south to the next exit, Pine Ridge Road. Take that

8 west to **Frannie's Teddy Bear Museum.** Built by oil heiress and area resident Frances Pew Hayes, the $2 million museum houses more than 1,500 teddy bears. *2511 Pine Ridge Rd., tel. 813/598–2711. Admission: $4.50 adults, $2.50 senior citizens and youths, $1.50 children 4–12. Open Wed.–Sat. 10–5, Sun. 1–5.*

9 For some real wildlife, head for **Jungle Larry's Zooalogical Park.** Continue west on Pine Ridge Road to U.S. 41. Turn left and drive south, past Mooringime Drive until you see the big sign for Jungle Larry's, then turn left. Here you can see a tiglon—a cross between a tiger and a lion—and other exotic wildlife in a junglelike park. The kids will also enjoy the petting zoo. *1590 Goodlette Rd., tel. 813/262–4053. Admission: $9.95 adults, $5.95 children 3–15. Open 9:30–5:30; Closed Mon., May–Nov.*

Antique car enthusiasts should head to Naples' newest tourist

10 attraction, the **Collier Automotive Museum,** where 75 antique and classic sports cars now enjoy a splendid retirement. *2500 S. Horseshoe Dr., Collier Park of Commerce, off Airport-Pulling Rd., tel. 813/643–5252. Admission: $6 adults, $3 children 5–12. Open daily 10–5.*

Head back to U.S. 41 and go south to **Third Street South** or **Fifth Avenue South,** Naple's fashionable shopping areas.

Head south on U.S. 41 to the **Old Marine Market Place at Tin City** (1200 5th Ave. S.). In a collection of former fishing shacks along Naples Bay, entrepreneurs and artisans have set up 40 boutiques, studios, and souvenir shops offering everything from scrimshaw to Haitian art.

Time Out **Merriman's Wharf** (1200 5th Ave. S., tel. 813/261–1811), in the Old Marine Market Place, is a good bet for a drink or a seafood lunch—either along the dock or indoors in air-conditioned comfort. AE, DC, MC, V.

What to See and Do with Children

Adventure Island (*see* Exploring Tampa Bay Area, above).

Babcock Wilderness Adventures (*see* Fort Myers/Naples Region, above).

Busch Gardens (*see* Exploring the Tampa Bay Area, above).

Circus Galleries, Ringling Museum (*see* Bradenton and Sarasota, above).

Everglades Wonder Gardens captures the flavor of untamed Florida with its exhibit of native wildlife and natural surroundings. *U.S. 41, Bonita Springs, tel. 813/992-2591. Open daily 9-5. Admission: $5 adults, $3 children 5-15.*

Frannie's Teddy Bear Museum (*see* Fort Myers/Naples Region, above).

Great Explorations! (see Exploring the Tampa Bay Area, above).

Nature Center of Lee County and Planetarium (*see* Fort Myers/Naples Area, above).

Sarasota Jungle Gardens (*see* Bradenton and Sarasota, above).

Southwest Florida for Free

Bradenton

Manatee Village Historical Park. An 1860 courthouse, 1887 church, 1903 general store and museum, and 1912 settler's home are situated here, as is the Old Manatee Cemetery, which dates back to 1850 and contains the graves of early Manatee County settlers. (Appointments necessary to tour the cemetery.) *Rte. 64, 1 mi east of U.S. 41, tel. 813/749-7165. Open weekdays 9-4:30 and Sept.-June, Sun. 2-5. Closed Sun. the rest of the year.*

Fort Myers/ Naples Area

Youth Museum of Charlotte County. Mostly animal specimens from Africa and North America, plus dolls, shells, and a variety of programs, are displayed here. *260 W. Retta Esplanade, Punta Gorda. Open weekdays 10-5.*

St. Petersburg

Fort de Soto Park. This 900-acre park is composed of six keys: Mullet, Bonne Fortune, Cunningham, Madeleine, St. Christopher, and St. Jean. Fort de Soto, begun during the Spanish-American War, is on the southern end of Mullet Key. *Reach it via 34th St. S, U.S. 19, and the Bayway. Open daily sunrise-sunset.*

Tampa

Shrimp Docks. By late afternoon, the shrimp boats pull in at the 22nd Street Causeway to unload their catches.

The Suncoast Seabird Sanctuary. This refuge and rehabilitation center for injured birds houses brown pelicans, cormorants, white herons, ospreys, and many other species. Many are on exhibit for public viewing. *18328 Gulf Blvd., tel. 813/391-6211. Admission free; donations accepted. Open daily 9-5:30.*

Tampa Bay Downs. Women are admitted free here on Fri., senior citizens Thurs. *Rte. 580 (Hillsborough Ave.) in Oldsmar, tel. 813/855-4401. Races Dec.-early May; post time 1 PM. Parking $1.*

Tampa Jai Alai Fronton. This fast-paced and strenuous game is popular among Floridians, even those who don't like to bet (South Dale Mabry Highway and Gandy Boulevard, tel. 813/831-1411). Senior citizens admitted free to Wednesday and Saturday matinees. No one under age 18 admitted. Pari-mutuel betting.

University of Tampa. Tour the administration building, built as a luxury hotel in 1890, which served as Theodore Roosevelt's headquarters during the Spanish-American War. *Tel. 813/253-6220. Reservations required for groups. Tours Tues. and Thurs. at 1:30, Sept.-May. Closed holidays.*

Tampa Bay Area

Heritage Park and Museum. A collection of restored pioneer homes and buildings is spread on a 21-acre wooded site. The museum is the park's centerpiece, with exhibits depicting Pinellas County's pioneer lifestyle. Spinning, weaving, and other demonstrations are held regularly. *11909 125th St. N, Largo, tel. 813/462–3474. Donations accepted. Open Tues.–Sat. 10–4, Sun. 1–4.*

Off the Beaten Track

Boca Grande Before roads to southwest Florida were even talked about, the wealthy boarded trains to get to the Gasparilla Inn, built in 1912, on **Boca Grande.** From U.S. 41 in Murdock (in northern Port Charlotte) head southwest on Rte. 776, then south on Rte. 771 into Placida, where a causeway runs out to the island.

While condominiums and other forms of modern sprawl are creeping up on Gasparilla, parts of Boca Grande looks as it has for a century or more. The mood is set by the old Florida homes, many made of wood, with wide, inviting verandas and wicker rocking chairs. There is generally sleepy ambience to the island, except in the spring, when the tarpon fishermen descend with a vengeance on Boca Grande Pass, considered among the best tarpon-fishing spots in the world.

At the island's southern end is Old Lighthouse Beach, where a historic wooden lighthouse still stands and where there is ample parking and lots of Gulf-front beach space.

Fort Myers **Eden Vineyards Winery and Park** opened to the public in late 1989 claiming to be the southernmost bonded winery in the United States. The family-owned winery offers tours, tastings, picnics, and tram rides. *On the right side of Rte. 80, 10.2 mi east of the I–75 interchange, tel. 813/728–9463. Admission: $2.50 adults, children 12 and under free; tastings included in price. Open daily 1–5.*

North Fort Myers **ECHO** (Educational Concerns for Hunger Organization) is a small active group striving to solve the world's hunger problems. The group offers tours of its gardens that feature collections of tropical food plants, simulated rain forests, and fish farming. *17430 Durrance Rd., tel. 813/543–3246. Tour Tues., Fri., Sat. 10 AM or by appointment.*

North Port An early-morning journey in a **hot-air balloon** gives the adventurous a bird's-eye view of a portion of Southwest Florida (the portion depending on the prevailing winds). Rides commence (from North Port, south of Venice) early enough to watch the sunrise and are followed by leisurely breakfasts of quiche and champagne. *Contact Trans-America Balloons, North Port, tel. 813/426–7326. Cost: $129 per person, maximum 4 people.*

Palmdale You aren't likely to happen upon Palmdale, a speck of a town about 40 minutes east of Punta Gorda, unless you make a point of visiting either of two singular attractions. You know you're approaching the **Cypress Knee Museum** when you see spindly hand-carved signs along Rte. 27 with sayings such as Lady, If He Won't Stop, Hit Him on Head with a Shoe. In the museum are thousands of cypress knees, the knotty, gnarled protuberances that sprout mysteriously from the bases of some cypress trees and grow to resemble all manner of persons and things. There are specimens resembling dogs, bears, ballet dancers' feet, an anteater, Joseph Stalin, and Franklin D. Roosevelt. *1 mi south of the U.S. 27 and U.S. 29 junction, tel. 813/675–2951.*

Admission: $2 adults, $1 children 6–12. Open daily 8 AM–dusk.

Just 2 miles southeast on U.S. 27, **Gatorama's** 1,000 alligators and assorted crocodiles await visitors, smiling toothily. Visitors who want to take a good long gander at gators can get their fill here, where a variety of species and sizes cohabit. It's also a commercial gator farm, so you'll see how the "mink" of the leather trade is grown for profit. *Tel. 813/675-0623. Admission: $4.50 adults, $2.50 children 2–11. Open daily 8–6.*

Shopping

Most visitors eventually get their quota of sun, sand, and surf and find themselves in need of something else to do. For many, that something is shopping.

Gift Ideas It is a rare vacationer who does not leave the state with at least one sack of oranges or grapefruit. Most produce stands are open during the citrus season (Dec.–Mar.). You cannot take citrus out of state without a USDA inspection sticker, so make sure you take only those sacks that are properly sealed.

In Tarpon Springs, natural sponges are plentiful and reasonably priced. Many shops along Dodecanese Boulevard, the town's main street, sell a variety of locally harvested sponges.

Tampa's Ybor City is a thriving Cuban community where the art of cigar making lives on. There are many small cigar shops in the area on Tampa's east side.

Shell items—jewelry, lamps, plant hangers, and such—are among the more kitschy commodities found in abundance in the region. Sanibel Island, one of the world's premier shelling grounds, has numerous shops that sell shell products. **The Shell Factory** in North Fort Myers claims to have the world's largest display of seashells and coral. *2787 N. Tamiami Trail (U.S. 41). Open daily 9–6.*

In Clearwater Beach, **Boatyard Village** (16100 Fairchild Dr.) contains boutiques, galleries, and restaurants in an 1890s-style village.

Hamlin's Landing (401 2nd St. E.) at Indian Rocks Beach. You can shop and dine along the Intracoastal Waterway in a Victorian ambience.

Fine Shopping Those who gravitate toward exclusive boutiques should visit Harding Circle in St. Armand's Key (just west of downtown Sarasota). Here is a circular string of shops and restaurants that cater to consumers seeking out-of-the-ordinary, pricey items.

Head through St. Petersburg Beach and Treasure Island to Madeira Beach. Stop here at **John's Pass Village and Boardwalk** (12901 Gulf Blvd.), a collection of shops in an old-style fishing village, where you can shop and eat at a variety of restaurants or pass the time watching the pelicans cavorting and dive-bombing for food.

In Fort Myers, there are two such centers—**Bell Tower** (U.S. 41 and Daniels Rd., South Fort Myers) and **Royal Palm Square** (Colonial Blvd., between McGregor Blvd. and U.S. 41). Both have about 36 shops and restaurants. Both are worth visiting if just to look at the elegant tropical landscaping, which includes parrots that stand sentry from perches among the palms. Neither center is enclosed, but both have covered sidewalks. In Naples, 3rd Street South and 5th Avenue South are lined with boutiques selling resort wear and designer fashions, jewelry, and upscale gifts.

The finest shopping (and restaurants) in the region can be found in Tampa, especially at **Old Hyde Park Village** (tel. 813/251–3500), an elegant outdoor shopping center that stretches more than seven blocks along Swan Avenue, near Bayshore Boulevard.

On your way to the bayfront you can check out **The Pier** (800 2nd Ave. NE. Open daily 10–9), a five-story building that looks like an inverted pyramid and contains numerous shops and eateries.

Flea Markets

Wagonwheel is 100-plus acres containing some 2,000 vendors and a variety of food concessions. Parking costs $1. There is a tram from the parking lot to the vendor area. *7801 Park Blvd., Pinellas Park, tel. 813/544–5319. Open weekends 8–4.*

Red Barn has the requisite big red barn, in which vendors operate daily except Mondays. The number of vendors increases to about 1,000 on weekends. *1707 1st St. E, Bradenton, tel. 813/747–3794. Open Wed., Sat., Sun. 8–4.*

Dome has sheltered walkways under which can be found dozens of stalls selling new and recycled wares. *Rte. 775, west of U.S. 41, Venice, tel. 813/493–6773. Open Fri.–Sun. 9–4. Closed Aug.*

Ortiz also features covered walkways and hundreds of vendors selling new and used items. *Ortiz and Anderson avenues, east of Fort Myers, tel. 813/694–5019. Open Fri.–Sun. 6–4.*

Oldsmar Flea Market is a charming place to hunt for bargains. *Off Rte. 580 near Old Tampa Bay, tel. 813/855–5306. Open Fri.–Sun. 8–4.*

Beaches

The Gulf of Mexico tends to be murky or cloudy, so you probably won't find the crystal clear water and perfect white beaches that one may normally associate with the Caribbean. The best beaches in the region are on Sanibel and Captiva islands, and in the Naples and Tampa's Clearwater Beach areas—the latter being Southwest Florida's version of Daytona Beach. Avoid swimming in any of the bays, however, as the waters are polluted from boaters, marinas, and industry.

Charlotte County (Punta Gorda Area)

Englewood Beach, near the Charlotte-Sarasota county line, is popular with teenagers, although beachgoers of all ages frequent it. In addition to a wide and shell-littered beach, there are barbecue grills, picnic facilities, and a playground.

Collier County (Naples Area)

Barefoot Beach State Recreation Area, north of Wiggins Pass, is accessible only by boat and has no facilities or lifeguards.

Bonita Springs Public Beach is 10 minutes from the I–75 exit at Bonita Beach Road, on the southern end of Bonita Beach. There are picnic tables, free parking, and nearby refreshment stands and shopping.

Delnor-Wiggins Pass State Recreation Area is at the Gulf end of Bluebill Avenue, off Vanderbilt Drive in North Naples. The well-maintained park offers miles of sandy beaches, lifeguards, barbecue grills, picnic tables, a boat ramp, observation tower, rest rooms with wheelchair access, lots of parking space, bathhouses, and showers. Fishing is best in Wiggins Pass at the north end of the park. *Admission: Florida residents pay $1 for the operator of a vehicle, plus 50¢ per passenger; out-of-state drivers pay $2, $1 per passenger. Boat launching costs $1. No alcoholic beverages allowed.*

Lowdermilk Park stretches along Gulf Shore Boulevard in Naples. There are 1,000 feet of beach plus parking, rest rooms, showers, a pavilion, vending machines, and picnic tables. No alcoholic beverages or fires permitted.

Tigertail Beach is on Hernando Drive at the south end of Marco Island. Singles and families congregate here. Facilities: parking, concession stand, picnic area, sailboat rentals, volleyball, rest rooms, and showers.

Lee County (Fort Myers Area)

Carl E. Johnson Recreation Area is just south of Fort Myers Beach. The admission of $2 per adult, $1 per child includes a round-trip tram ride from the park entrance to Lovers Key, on which the park is situated. Shelling, bird-watching, fishing, canoeing, and nature walks in an unspoiled setting are the main attractions here. There are also rest rooms, picnic tables, a snack bar, and basic showers.

Estero Island, otherwise known as **Fort Myers Beach,** is 18 miles from downtown Fort Myers. It has numerous public accesses to the beach, which is frequented by families and young singles. In most areas, you are never far from civilization, with houses, condominiums, and hotels nestled along the shore. The island's shores slope gradually into the usually tranquil and warm Gulf waters, affording a safe swimming area for children. From Fort Myers, it is reached via San Carlos Boulevard; from Naples and Bonita Springs, via Hickory Boulevard.

Lynn Hall Memorial Park is on Estero Boulevard, in the more commercial northern part of Fort Myers Beach. Singles can be found playing in the gentle surf or sunning and socializing on shore. A number of night spots and restaurants are within easy walking distance. A free fishing pier adjoins the public beach. Facilities: picnic tables, barbecue grills, playground equipment, and a bathhouse with rest rooms.

Manatee County (Bradenton Area)

Anna Maria Island, just west of the Sunshine Skyway Bridge, boasts three public beaches. **Anna Maria Bayfront Park,** at the north end of the municipal pier, is a secluded beach fronting both the Intracoastal Waterway and the Gulf of Mexico. Facilities include picnic grounds, a playground, rest rooms, showers, and lifeguards. At mid-island, in the town of Holmes Beach, is **Manatee County Beach,** popular with all ages. It has picnic facilities, a snack bar, showers, rest rooms, and lifeguards. At the island's southern end is **Coquina Beach,** popular with singles and families. Facilities include: picnic area, boat ramp, playground, refreshment stand, rest rooms, showers, and lifeguards.

Cortez Beach, on the mainland, just north of Coquina, is on Gulf Boulevard in the town of Bradenton Beach. This one's popular with those who like their beaches without facilities—nothing but sand, water, and trees. The Palma Sola Causeway takes Manatee Avenue on the mainland to Anna Maria Island and also offers beachgoers a long, sandy beach fronting Palma Sola Bay. There are boat ramps, a dock, and picnic tables.

Egmont Key lies just off the northern tip of Anna Maria Island. On it is Fort Dade, a military fort built in 1900 during the Spanish-American War, and Florida's sixth-brightest lighthouse. The primary inhabitant of the 2-mile-long island is the threatened gopher tortoise. The only way to get to the island is by boat, and fare and admission to the Key is $12 adult, $6 children. Shellers will find the trip rewarding. An excursion boat makes trips on Tuesday, Thursday, and Sunday. The *Miss Cortez* departs from Cortez, just west of Bradenton (tel. 813/794–1223).

Greer Island Beach is at the northern tip of the next barrier island south on Longboat Key. It's accessible by boat or via North Shore Boulevard. The secluded peninsula has a wide beach and excellent shelling, but no facilities.

Pinellas County (Gulf Coast west of Tampa)

Caladesi Island State Park lies 3 miles off Dunedin's coast, across Hurricane Pass. The 600-acre park is one of the state's few remaining undeveloped barrier islands. It's accessible only by boat. There is a beach on the Gulf side and mangroves on the bay side. This is a good spot for swimming, fishing, shelling, boating, and nature study. A self-guided nature trail winds through the island's interior. Park rangers are available to answer questions. Facilities: boardwalks, picnic shelters, bathhouses, a ranger station, and concession stand. A ferry runs hourly 10–5 between Caladesi Island and Honeymoon Island to the north but it runs in good weather only. *Ferry admission: $4 adults, $2.50 children 2–10. Park admission extra. Call for ferry information (tel. 813/734–5263).*

Clearwater Beach is another popular, more accessible island beach that also serves as a hangout for teenagers and college students. It is south of Caladesi on a narrow island between Clearwater Harbor and the Gulf and is connected to downtown Clearwater by Memorial Causeway. Facilities: marina, concessions, showers, rest rooms, and lifeguards.

Tarpon Springs has two public beaches: **Howard Park Beach,** where a lifeguard is on duty daily 8:30–6 Easter through Labor Day, and **Sunset Beach,** where there is similar lifeguard duty as well as rest rooms, picnic tables, grills, and a boat ramp.

St. Petersburg Area

The St. Petersburg beaches are numerous and wide-ranging in character.

Bay Beach (North Shore Dr. and 13th Ave. NE, on Tampa Bay) charges 10¢ admission. It has showers and shelters.

Fort DeSoto Park consists of the southernmost beaches of St. Petersburg, on five islands totaling some 900 acres. Facilities: two fishing piers, picnic sites overlooking lagoons, a waterskiing and boating area, and miles of beaches for swimming. Open daily until dark. To get there, take the Pinellas Bayway through three toll gates (cost: 85¢).

Indian Rocks Beach (off Rte. 8 south of Clearwater Beach) attracts mostly couples.

Maximo Park Beach (34 St. and Pinellas Point Dr. S) is on Boca Ciega Bay. There is no lifeguard. There is a picnic area with grills, tables, shelters, and a boat ramp.

North Shore Beach (901 North Shore Dr. NE) charges $1 admission and has a pool, beach umbrellas, cabanas, windbreaks, and lounges.

Pass-a-Grille Beach, on the Gulf, has parking meters, a snack bar, rest rooms, and showers.

St. Petersburg Municipal Beach (11260 Gulf Blvd.) is a free beach on Treasure Island. There are dressing rooms, metered parking, and a snack bar.

Sanibel

Sanibel and **Captiva** islands are about 23 miles from Fort Myers and are reached via a toll bridge on the Sanibel Causeway. Though there is a $3 round-trip toll, avid shell collectors and nature enthusiasts are apt to get their money's worth. Sanibel beaches are rated among the best shelling grounds in the world. For the choicest pickings, get there as the tide is going out or just after a storm. Windsurfers need go only as far as the Sanibel Causeway to find a suitable place to set sail.

Bowman's Beach is mainly a family beach on Sanibel's northwest end, but nudists have been known to bathe unabashedly in more secluded areas of the beach.

Gulfside Park, off Casa Ybel Road, is a lesser-known and less-populated beach, ideal for those who seek solitude and do not require facilities.

Lighthouse Park, at Sanibel's southern end, attracts a mix of families, shellers, and singles. Rest rooms are available. One of the draws is a historic old lighthouse.

Sarasota County

The county contains 10 beaches, ranging from 5 to 113 acres.

Caspersen Beach, on Beach Drive in south Venice, is the county's largest park. It has a nature trail, fishing, picnicking, rest rooms, plus lots of beach for those who prefer space to a wealth of amenities. Along with a plentiful mix of shells, observant beachcombers are likely to find sharks' teeth on Venice beaches, washed up from the ancient shark burial grounds just offshore.

Manasota Key spans much of the county's southern coast, from south of Venice to Englewood. It has two choice beaches: *Manasota,* on Manasota Beach Road, with a boat ramp, picnic area and rest rooms; and *Blind Pass,* where you can fish and swim but will find no amenities.

Nokomis Beach is just north of North Jetty on Albee Road. Its facilities are similar to those at North Jetty, except that it has two boat ramps and no horseshoe court.

North Jetty Park is at the south end of Casey Key, a slender barrier island. It's a favorite for family outings. Amenities include rest rooms, a concession stand, play and picnic equipment, fishing, horseshoes, and a volleyball court.

Siesta Beach is on Beach Road on Siesta Key. The 40-acre park contains nature trails, a concession stand, soccer and softball fields, picnicking facilities, play equipment, rest rooms, and tennis and volleyball courts.

South Lido, at the southern tip of Lido Key, is among the largest and best beaches in the region. The sugar-sand beach offers little for shell collectors, but the interests of virtually all other beach lovers are served on its 100 acres, which probably accounts for the diverse mix of people it attracts. Facilities include fishing, nature trails, volleyball, playground, horseshoes, rest rooms, and picnic grounds.

Turtle Beach is farther south on Siesta Key's Midnight Pass Road. Though only 14 acres, it includes boat ramps, horseshoe courts, picnic and play facilities, a recreation building, rest rooms, and a volleyball court.

Participant Sports

Biking Call the nearest chamber of commerce or bike store for information about bike paths. Two of the best are at Boca Grande and Sanibel Island.

Tampa Bay. There are many places to rent bikes, but not much in the way of bike paths. Rental stores include **St. Petersburg:** *The Beach Cyclist* (7517 Blindpass Rd., tel. 813/367–5001); **Largo:** *D & S Bicycle Shop* (12073 Seminole Blvd., tel. 813/393–0300).

Sarasota/Bradenton. There are no bike paths but rental shops include **Bradenton:** *Bicycle Center* (2610 Cortez Rd., tel. 813/756–5480); **Sarasota:** *Mr. CB's* (1249 Stickney Point Rd., tel. 813/349–4400), and *Pedal N Wheels* (Merchants Pointe Shopping Center, 2881 Clark Rd., tel. 813/922–0481); and **Venice:** *The Bike Doctor* (291 Trott Circle, tel. 813/426–4807); and *Bicycles International* (1744 Tamiami Trail S, [U.S. 41], tel. 813/497–1590).

Fort Myers/Naples. There are several bike paths in the area. **Boca Grande,** an hour's drive from Fort Myers or Sarasota, has good bike paths. **Fort Myers:** The best choice here is the path along Summerlin Road. For rental, try *Trikes & Bikes & Mowers* (3224 Fowler St., tel. 813/936–4301). **Sanibel:** The island's extensive bike path is well used. It is in good condition and runs throughout the island, keeping bikers safely apart from the traffic and allowing them some time for reflection on the waterways and wildlife they will encounter. Rent bikes at *Finnimore's Cycle Shop* (2353 Periwinkle Way, Sanibel, tel. 813/472–5577), *Tarpon Bay Marina* (900 Tarpon Bay Rd., Sanibel, tel. 813/472–8900), and *Jim's Bike & Scooter Rental* (11534 Andy Rosse La., Captiva, tel. 813/472–1296). **Bonita Springs:** *Pop's Bicycles* (3685 Bonita Beach Rd., Bonita Springs, tel. 813/947–4442). **Naples:** *The Bicycle Shop* (813 Vanderbilt Beach Rd., Naples, tel. 813/566–3646); **Marco Island:** *Scootertown* (855 Bald Eagle Dr., tel. 813/394–8400).

Canoeing Canoe rentals abound in Southwest Florida. Among them are **Art's Swap Shop** (9608 Nebraska, Tampa, tel. 813/935–4011), canoe and car racks for rent; and **Myakka River State Park** (tel. 813/361–6511), 15 miles south of Sarasota near Venice, canoes, paddles, and life vests for rent. **Canoe Outpost** offers half-day, full-day, and overnight canoe-camping trips from a number of southwest Florida locations, including Little Manatee River (18001 U.S. 301 S, Wimauma, just south of Tampa, tel. 813/634–2228) and Peace River (Rte. 7, Box 301, Arcadia, 25 miles northeast of Port Charlotte, tel. 813/494–1215). **Lakes Park**

(tel. 813/481–7946) in Fort Myers rents canoes on waterways where you can see the carp swimming, and, if you are quiet enough, some herons and osprey fly overhead; **Canoe Safari** (Arcadia, tel. 813/494–7865) has half- and full-day trips, plus overnighters including camping equipment; and **Tarpon Bay Marina** (Sanibel, tel. 813/472–8900) has canoes and equipment for exploring the waters of the J. N. "Ding" Darling National Wildlife Refuge. **Estero River Tackle and Canoe Outfitters** (20991 Tamiami Trail S, Estero, tel. 813/992–4050) has canoes and equipment for use on the meandering Estero River.

Fishing Anglers flock to southwest Florida. Tarpon, kingfish, speckled trout, snapper, grouper, sea trout, snook, sheepshead, and shark are among the species to be found in coastal waters. Avoid fishing in Tampa Bay because the water is polluted. You can also charter your own boat or join a group on a party boat for full- or half-day outings.

Party boats in the area include **Florida Deep Sea Fishing** (4737 Gulf Blvd., St. Petersburg, tel. 813/360–2082), **Rainbow Party Fishing** (Clearwater Marina, Clearwater Beach, tel. 813/446–7389), **Flying Fish** (Marina Jack's, U.S. 41 and bay front, Sarasota, tel. 813/366–3373), **L-C Marine** (215 Tamiami Trail S., [U.S. 41], Venice, tel. 813/484–9044), **Kingfisher Charter** (Fishermen's Village, Punta Gorda, tel. 813/639–0969), **Deebold's Marina** (1071 San Carlos Blvd., Fort Myers, tel. 813/466–3525), **Gulf Star Marina** (708 Fisherman's Wharf, Fort Myers Beach, tel. 813/765–1500), **Deep Sea Charter Fishing** (Boat Haven, Naples, tel. 813/263–8171).

Golf Courses open to the public include **Apollo Beach Club** (Tampa, tel. 813/645–6212), **Babe Zaharias Golf Course** (Tampa, tel. 813/932–4401), **The Eagles** (Oldsmar, tel. 813/920–6681), **Rocky Point Golf Course** (Tampa, tel. 813/884–5141), **Clearwater Golf Park** (Clearwater, tel. 813/447–5272), **Largo Golf Course** (Largo, tel. 813/587–6724), **Dunedin Country Club** (Dunedin, tel. 813/733–7836), **Mangrove Bay Golf Course** (St. Petersburg, tel. 813/893–7797), **Twin Brooks Golf Course** (St. Petersburg, tel. 813/893–7445), **Manatee County Golf Course** (Bradenton, tel. 813/792–6773), **Bobby Jones Golf Course** (Sarasota, tel. 813/955–8097), **Forest Lake Golf Course** (Sarasota, tel. 813/922–1312), **Bird Bay Executive Golf Course** (Venice, tel. 813/485–9333), **North Port Golf Course** (North Port, tel. 813/426–2804), **Deep Creek Golf Club** (Charlotte Harbor, tel. 813/625–6911), **Burnt Store** (Punta Gorda, tel. 813/332–7334), **Eastwood Country Club** (Fort Myers, tel. 813/275–4848), **Lochmoor Country Club** (North Fort Myers, tel. 813/995–0501), **Bay Beach Club Executive Golf Course** (Fort Myers Beach, tel. 813/463–2064), **Cypress Pines Country Club** (Lehigh Acres, tel. 813/369–8216), **Fort Myers Country Club** (Fort Myers, tel. 813/936–2457), **The Dunes** (Sanibel, tel. 813/472–2535), **Wildcat Run** (Estero, tel. 813/936–7222), **Pelican's Nest Golf Course** (Bonita Springs, tel. 813/947–4600), **Hibiscus Country Club** (Naples, tel. 813/774–3559), **Lely Flamingo Island Club** (Naples, tel. 813/793–2223), **Naples Beach Golf Course** (Naples, tel. 813/261–2222), and **Oxbow** (LaBelle, tel. 813/334–3903).

Motorboating Much of southwest Florida's charm lies beyond its shoreline. Fortunately, there are many concerns that rent powerboats.

Florida Charter (tel. 813/347–SAIL) in South Pasadena has power and sailboats for rent, bareboat or captained.

Don and Mike's Boat and Jet Ski Rental (520 Blackburn Point Rd., Sarasota, tel. 813/966–4000) has water skis, jet skis, pontoon boats, and instruction for all activities.

Boat House of Sanibel (Sanibel Marina, tel. 813/472–2531) rents powerboats.

Getaway Bait and Boat Rental (1091 San Carlos Blvd., Fort Myers Beach, tel. 813/466–3200) rents powerboats and fishing equipment and sells bait.

Brookside Marina (2023 Davis Blvd., Naples, tel. 813/263–7250) rents 16- to 25-foot powerboats.

Sailing Sailing schools are plentiful. Spend a week learning the ropes or a few hours luxuriating on a sunset cruise.

La Gringa Sailing Services (400 2nd Ave. N.E., St. Petersburg, tel. 813/822–4323); **M&M Beach Service & Boat Rental** (5300 Gulf Blvd., St. Petersburg Beach, tel. 813/360–8295); **O'Leary's Sarasota Sailing School** (near Marina Jack's, U.S. 41 and the bay front, Sarasota, tel. 813/953–7505); **Southwest Florida Yachts** (3444 Marinatown La. N.W., Fort Myers, tel. 813/656–1339 or 800/262–7939); **Fort Myers Yacht Charters** (Port Sanibel Yacht Club, south Fort Myers, tel. 813/466–1800); and **Marco Island Sea Excursions** (1281 Jamaica Rd., Marco Island, tel. 813/642–6400).

Scuba Diving Dive shops are found all over the region. However, most make excursions to the Florida Keys or the east coast of Florida rather than dive in this area.

Tennis Most hotels and motels in Florida have outdoor tennis courts, some lighted for night use. For those who are motivated to find other courts, a list of public ones follows:

City of Tampa Courts (59 Columbia Dr., Davis Islands, Tampa, tel. 813/253–3997), **McMullen Park** (1000 Edenville Ave., Clearwater, tel. 813/462–6144), **Dunedin Community Center** (Pinehurst and Michigan Sts., Dunedin, tel. 813/734–3950), **Port Charlotte Tennis Club** (22400 Gleneagles Terr., Port Charlotte, tel. 813/625–7222), **Bay Beach Racquet Club** (120 Lenell St., Fort Myers Beach, tel. 813/463–4473), **Lochmoor Country Club** (3911 Orange Grove Blvd., North Fort Myers, tel. 813/995–0501), **The Dunes** (949 Sand Castle Rd., Sanibel, tel. 813/472–3522), and **Forest Hills Racquet Club** (100 Forest Hills Blvd., Naples, tel. 813/774–2442).

Windsurfing For sailboard rentals and lessons try **Gulf Water Sports Center** at the Colony Beach and Tennis Resort (1620 Gulf of Mexico Dr., Longboat Key, tel. 813/383–7692); or **Ocean Boulevard Sailboarding** (1233 Gulf Stream Ave. N., Sarasota, tel. 813/364–9463).

Spectator Sports

Baseball The season comes early to Florida with the annual convergence of the Grapefruit League—17 major league teams offer exhibitions in March and April. These teams hold their spring training in southwest Florida. For information on all the teams, tel. 904/488–0990. Home bases for area teams are Bradenton: **Pittsburgh Pirates** (McKechnie Field, 17th Ave. W and 9th St., tel. 813/747–3031); Clearwater: **Philadelphia Phillies** (Jack Russell Stadium, Seminole and Greenwood Ave., tel. 813/442–8496);

Dunedin: **Toronto Blue Jays** (Grant Field, 373 Douglas Ave., North of Rte. 88, tel. 813/733–9302); Fort Myers: **Minnesota Twins** (Lee County Sports Complex, 1410 Six Mile Cypress Pkwy., Fort Myers, tel. 813/768–4278); Port Charlotte: **Texas Rangers** (Charlotte County Stadium, Rte. 776, tel. 813/625–9500); St. Petersburg: **St. Louis Cardinals** (Al Lang Stadium, 1st St. and 2nd Ave., tel. 813/822–3384); Sarasota: **Chicago White Sox** (Ed Smith Stadium, 2700 12th St., tel. 813/954–7699).

Football NFL football comes in the form of the **Tampa Bay Buccaneers,** who play at Tampa Stadium (4201 N. Dale Mabry Hwy.). For information, tel. 813/461–2700 or 800/282–0683.

Soccer The lone competitor in the area is the **Tampa Bay Rowdies** (tel. 813/877–7800). The team plays May–September outdoors at Tampa Stadium in Tampa, the University of South Florida.

Gambling Casino gambling has yet to find its way into the state, but the odds are that there are more than enough alternatives to suit bettors. There is **horse racing** at Tampa Bay Downs (Race Track Rd. off Rte. 580, Oldsmar, tel. 813/855–4401, with Thoroughbred races mid-Dec.–early May). **Dog racing** occurs somewhere in the region all year: January–June at Derby Lane (10490 Gandy Blvd., St. Petersburg, tel. 813/576–1361); July–Dec. at Tampa Greyhound Track (8300 N. Nebraska Ave., Tampa, tel. 813/932–4313); late Dec.–June at the Sarasota Kennel Club (5400 Bradenton Rd., Sarasota, tel. 813/355–7744); and year-round at the Naples–Fort Myers Greyhound Track (10601 Bonita Beach Rd., Bonita Springs, tel. 813/992–2411). **Jai-alai** is offered at the Tampa Jai-Alai Fronton (S. Dale Mabry Hwy. and Gandy Blvd., Tampa, tel. 813/831–1411) year-round.

Dining and Lodging

Dining As in most coastal regions, fresh seafood is plentiful. Raw bars, serving just-plucked-from-the-bay oysters, clams, and mussels, are everywhere. The region's ethnic diversity is also well represented. Tarpon Springs adds a hearty helping of classic Greek specialties such as moussaka, a ground meat and eggplant pie, and baklava, delicate layers of pastry and nuts soaked in honey. In Tampa, the cuisine is Cuban. Standard menu items include black beans and rice and paella, a seafood, chicken, and saffroned-rice casserole. In Sarasota, the accent is on Continental fare, both in food and service. In Fort Myers and Naples, seafood reigns supreme, especially the succulent claw of the native stone crab, in season October 15–May 15. It's usually served with drawn butter or a tangy mustard sauce.

Highly recommended restaurants are indicated by a star ★.

Category	Cost*
Very Expensive	over $60
Expensive	$40–$60
Moderate	$20–$40
Inexpensive	under $20

**per person, excluding drinks, service, and 6% sales tax*

Lodging There are old historic hotels and ultramodern chrome-and-glass high rises, sprawling resorts and cozy inns, luxurious waterfront lodges and just-off-the-highway budget motels. In general, inland rooms are considerably cheaper than those on the islands. The most expensive accommodations are those with waterfront views. Rates are highest mid-December–mid-April. The lowest prices are available May–November. Many apartment-motels are springing up in the area and can prove economical for families that wish to prepare some of their own meals or for groups who can share an apartment. Price categories listed below apply to winter rates. Many drop to a less expensive category at other times of the year.

Category	Cost*
Very Expensive	over $120
Expensive	$90–$120
Moderate	$50–$90
Inexpensive	under $50

**per person, double occupancy, excluding 6% state sales tax and nominal (1%–3%) tourist tax*

Bradenton
Dining

Crab Trap. Rustic decor, ultrafresh seafood, gator tail, and wild pig are among the trademarks of this restaurant. *U.S. 19 at Terra Ceia Bridge, Palmetto, tel. 813/722–6255; and 4814 Memphis Rd., Ellenton, tel. 813/729–7777. No reservations. Dress: casual. D, MC, V. Moderate.*

Lodging

Holiday Inn Riverfront. A Spanish Mediterranean–style motor inn near the Manatee River. *100 Riverfront Dr. W 34205, tel. 813/747–3727. 153 rooms. Facilities: pool, whirlpool, restaurant, lounge. AE, DC, MC, V. Moderate.*

Cape Coral
Dining

Cape Crab House. Crabs are served Maryland-style—with mallet and pliers and heaped on a tablecloth of newspaper—or in the more refined atmosphere of a second dining room with linen tablecloths and a piano player. *Coralwood Mall, Del Prado Blvd., tel. 813/574–2722. Reservations accepted. Dress: casual. AE, MC, V. Moderate.*

Venezia. A small, neighborhood restaurant serving straightforward Italian food including pastas, pizza, chicken, veal, and fresh seafood. *1515 SE 47th Terr., tel. 813/542–0027. No reservations. Dress: casual. No lunch. MC, V. Moderate.*

★ **Siam Hut.** Thai music pings and twangs in the background while the dishes do the same to your tastebuds. Get it fiery hot or extra mild. Specialties: *pad thai* (a mixture of noodles, crushed peanuts, chicken, shrimp, egg, bean sprouts, and scallions) and crispy Siam rolls (spring rolls stuffed with ground chicken, bean thread, and vegetables). *1873 Del Prado Blvd. (Coral Pointe Shopping Center), tel. 813/772–3131. No reservations. Dress: casual. AE, MC, V. Inexpensive.*

Lodging

Cape Coral Golf & Tennis Resort. A resort for golf and tennis enthusiasts who also seek economy. Understated decor reflects the sporty atmosphere. *4003 Palm Tree Blvd. 33904, tel. 813/542–3191. 100 rooms. Facilities: pool, golf, driving range, tennis, baby-sitting, restaurant, lounge. AE, DC, MC, V. Moderate.*

Quality Inn. Conveniently located in downtown Cape Coral.

1538 Cape Coral Pkwy. 33904, tel. 813/542–2121. 146 rooms. Facilities: pool; pets accepted. AE, DC, MC, V. Moderate.

Cedar Key
Dining

The Captain's Table. This is a dockside seafood restaurant with a fine view of anglers on the pier and artists along the seawall. Broiled seafood is the house specialty, but there are chicken and steak dishes as well. *On Dock St., tel. 904/543–5441. Reservations advised at Sat. dinner. Dress: casual. MC, V. Moderate.*

The Heron Restaurant. The specialty at this island restaurant is seafood, served in Victorian comfort. *S.R. 24 and 2nd St., tel. 904/543–5666. Reservations advised. Dress: neat but casual. AE, MC, V. Moderate.*

Lodging

Island Place. One- and two-bedroom suites that sleep four are available at this small two-story condominium complex. The roof is tin, and the decks offer a view of the busy dock. *Box 687 32625, tel. 904/543–5307. 25 suites. Facilities: pool, sauna, Jacuzzi, laundry. MC, V. Expensive.*

Historic Island Hotel. Located in the historic district, this bed-and-breakfast hotel features 1850 Jamaican architecture and gourmet natural foods. *Main and B Sts. 32625, tel. 904/543–5111. 10 rooms. Facilities: cafe, bicycle built for 2. MC, V. Moderate.*

Clearwater
Dining

Bob Heilman's Beachcomber. Southern-fried chicken and mashed potatoes with gravy have long been the Sunday staple at this 40-year-old restaurant. Also known for its seafood, homemade desserts, and hearty portions. *447 Mandalay Ave., Clearwater Beach, tel. 813/442–4144. Reservations advised. Dress: casual. AE, DC, MC, V. Moderate.*

Lodging

Belleview Lido Resort and Hotel. This large, historic resort on Clearwater Bay has extensive facilities and transportation to the beach. *25 Belleview Blvd. 34616, tel. 813/442–6171. 350 rooms. Facilities: pools, whirlpools, saunas, golf, tennis, bicycles, playground, fishing, sailboats, restaurant, lounge. AE, DC, MC, V. Very Expensive.*

Sheraton Sand Key Resort. A resort for those who want lots of sun, sand, and surf. Balconies and patios overlook the Gulf and well-manicured grounds. *1160 Gulf Blvd., Clearwater Beach 33515, tel. 813/595–1611. 390 rooms. Facilities: pool, wading pool, beach, whirlpool, playground, tennis courts, windsurfing, sailboats, restaurant, lounge. AE, DC, MC, V. Expensive.*

New Comfort Inn. This is a comfortable, unpretentious motor inn near the airport and Tampa Bay. *3580 Ulmerton Rd. (Rte. 688) 34622, tel. 813/573–1171. 119 rooms. Facilities: pool, whirlpool, fitness center, restaurant. AE, DC, MC, V. Moderate.*

Crystal River
Dining

Charlie's Fish House Restaurant. This popular, no-frills seafood spot features locally caught fish, oysters, crab claws, and lobster. Only beer and wine served. *224 U.S. 19 N, tel. 904/795–3949. No reservations. Dress: casual. MC, V. Moderate.*

Lodging

Plantation Golf Resort. Set on the banks of Kings Bay, this is a colonial-style resort with many outdoor amenities. *C.R. 44, tel. 904/795–4211. 136 rooms. Facilities: lounge, pools, golf, saunas, canoes, rental boats, fishing, tennis, scuba rental, dining room. Pets permitted. AE, DC, MC, V. Expensive.*

Econo Lodge Crystal Resort. This cinder block roadside motel offers proximity to Kings Bay and its manatee population.

There's a marina within steps of the motel, with dive boats departing for scuba and snorkeling excursions. The only rooms that view the water are 114 and 128. *U.S. 19, 32629, tel. 904/795–3171. 94 rooms. Facilities: pool, waterfront restaurant. AE, DC, MC, V. Inexpensive.*

Fort Myers
Dining

Flute's. Dine alfresco or in the small, colorful dining room of this innovative restaurant serving California grill–style fare. *Royal Palm Sq., 1400 Colonial Blvd., tel. 813/278–1600. Reservations accepted. Dress: stylishly casual. AE, MC, V. Expensive.*

★ **Peter's La Cuisine.** The quiet elegance of this downtown restaurant blends perfectly with the fine Continental cuisine served within. The menu changes every few weeks but usually includes a fresh salmon dish, chateaubriand, and duck or some other exotic meat. *2224 Bay St., tel. 813/332–2228. Reservations advised. Dress: neat but casual. AE, DC, MC, V. Expensive.*

★ **The Prawnbroker.** Its ads urge you to scratch and sniff. There is no odor, says the ad, because fresh fish does not have one. What there is is an abundance of seafood seemingly just plucked from Gulf waters, plus some selections for landlubbers. Almost always crowded. *13451–16 McGregor Blvd., tel. 813/489–2226. Reservations accepted. Dress: casual. No lunch. AE, MC, V. Moderate.*

Sangeet of India. Indian melodies waft through the air mingling with fragrant spices used in traditional dishes of India. Buffet lunch served weekdays. *Villas Plaza, U.S. 41 and Crystal Dr., tel. 813/278–0101. Reservations accepted. Dress: casual. AE, MC, V. Moderate.*

The Veranda. Within a sprawling turn-of-the-century home is served an imaginative assortment of American regional cuisine. This is a popular place for business and governmental bigwigs to rub elbows. *2122 2nd St., tel. 813/332–2065. Reservations accepted. Dress: casual. AE, DC, MC, V. Moderate.*

Miami Connection. If you hunger for choice chopped liver, lean-but-tender corned beef, and a chewy bagel, this kosher-style deli can fill the bill. The sandwiches are huge. It is, as the local restaurant critic aptly said, "the real McCohen." *11506 Cleveland Ave., tel. 813/936–3811. No reservations. Dress: casual. No credit cards. No dinner. Inexpensive.*

Woody's Bar-B-Q. A no-frills barbecue pit featuring chicken, ribs, and beef in copious amounts at bargain-basement prices. *13101 N. Cleveland Ave. (U.S. 41), North Fort Myers, tel. 813/997–1424. No reservations. Dress: casual. AE, MC, V. Inexpensive.*

Lodging

Sonesta Sanibel Harbour Resort. This high-rise apartment hotel sits on the east side of the Sanibel Causeway, not quite in Fort Myers, not quite on Sanibel. It overlooks San Carlos Bay, has a full complement of amenities, and was once home to tennis great Jimmy Connors. *17260 Harbour Pointe 33908, tel. 813/466–4000. 240 rooms, 100 condominiums. Facilities: pools, health club, tennis, whirlpool, restaurant, lounge. AE, DC, MC, V. Very Expensive.*

Sheraton Harbor Place. This modern high-rise hotel commands a dominant spot on the downtown Fort Myers skyline, rising above the Caloosahatchee River and Fort Myers Yacht Basin. *2500 Edwards Dr. 33901, tel. 813/337–0300. 437 rooms. Facili-*

ties: pool, tennis, a game room, whirlpool, dock, exercise room. AE, DC, MC, V. Expensive.

Robert E. Lee Motor Best Western. Rooms are spacious, with patios or balconies overlooking the Caloosahatchee River. *6611 U.S. 41N, North Fort Myers 33903, tel. 813/997-5511. 108 rooms. Facilities: pool, dock, lounge. AE, DC, MC, V. Moderate.*

Fort Myers Beach

Dining

★ **The Mucky Duck.** Slightly more formal than its waterfront sister restaurant on Captiva, this restaurant concentrates on fresh, well-prepared seafood. A popular dish is the bacon-wrapped barbecued shrimp. *2500 Estero Blvd., tel. 813/463-5519 and Andy Rosse Lane, Captiva, tel. 813/472-3434. Reservations for large parties only. Dress: casual. MC, V. Moderate.*

Snug Harbor. Casual, rustic atmosphere is evident at this seafood restaurant on the harbor at Fort Myers Beach. *645 San Carlos Blvd., tel. 813/463-8077. No reservations. Dress: casual. AE, MC, V. Moderate.*

Lodging

Seawatch-on-the-Beach. A modern seven-story hotel with one- and two-bedroom suites. Each has a whirlpool, kitchen, and a view of the Gulf. *6550 Estero Blvd. 33931, tel. 813/463-4469 or 800/237-8906. 42 rooms. Facilities: beach, pool, tennis, baby-sitting. AE, MC, V. Very Expensive.*

The Boathouse Beach Resort. A nautical theme pervades this all-suite time-share resort, with lots of teak and brass throughout. *7630 Estero Blvd. 33931, tel. 813/481-3636 or 800/237-8906. 22 units. Facilities: kitchen, beach, pool, whirlpool, shuffleboard. AE, MC, V. Expensive.*

Sandpiper Gulf Resort. Gulf-front apartment-motel. *5550 Estero Blvd. 33931, tel. 813/463-5721. 63 rooms. Facilities: pools, beach, whirlpool, playground, shuffleboard. MC, V. Moderate.*

Homosassa Springs

Dining

K.C. Crump on the River. An 1870 Old Florida residence on the Homosassa River, K.C. Crump was restored in 1986, then opened as a restaurant in 1987. There is a marina on the river, lounge, and outdoor dining, plus large, airy dining rooms serving meat and seafood. *3900 Hall River Rd., tel. 904/628-1500. Reservations advised. Dress: neat but casual. AE, DC, MC, V. Expensive.*

Lodging

Homosassa Lodge. This is a simple motor inn that accepts pets and has a playground for the kids. *On U.S. 19 at C.R. 490A West, tel. 904/628-4311. 104 rooms. Facilities: pool, tennis, restaurant, lounge. AE, D, DC, MC, V. Moderate.*

Riverside Inn. A rustic little place, this inn boasts an intimate location across from Monkey Island—residence of six such mammals—and beside the Homosassa River. Complete with its own restaurant (The Yard Arm) and lounge (Ship's Lounge), the Riverside is also conveniently situated within walking distance of three local restaurants and near two others accessible by boat. Rent bicycles, canoes, or paddle boats to get a feel for these lovely surroundings. *Box 258, 32687, tel. 904/628-2474. 76 rooms. Facilities: marina, restaurant, lounge, pool, tennis courts, ship's store, bike and boat rentals. AE, MC, V. Moderate.*

Homosassa River Resort. Located right on the banks of the Homosassa River, this resort featuring nine cottages is well situated for outdoor adventuring. *10605 Hall's River Rd.,*

32646, tel. 904/628–7072. 9 cottages. Facilities: 2 boat docks, pontoon rentals, kitchen, laundry. MC, V. Inexpensive.

Weeki-Wachi Holiday Inn. Good, basic accommodations are available at this hotel where the Sunday brunch—at $7.25 a person—is great. *6172 Commercial Way, Weeki-Wachi 34606, tel. 904/596–2007. 122 rooms. Facilities: restaurant, lounge, pool. AE, D, DC, MC, V. Inexpensive.*

Marco Island
Dining

Marco Lodge Waterfront Restaurant & Lounge. Built in 1869, this is Marco's oldest landmark. Fresh local seafood and Cajun entrees are features, as is live Dixieland jazz Sundays at 2. *1 Papaya St., Goodland, tel. 813/394–3302. Reservations advised. Dress: casual. AE, DC, MC, V. Moderate.*

★ **Island Cafe.** A small and intimate European-style cafe specializing in seafood and Continental cuisine. Pompano is prepared in a multitude of ways. *918 N. Collier Blvd., tel. 813/394–7578. Reservations accepted. Dress: casual. MC, V. Inexpensive.*

Lodging

Eagle's Nest Beach Resort. This time-share resort contains one- and two-bedroom villas (with French doors opening onto screened patios) clustered around a large tropical garden and a high rise with two-bedroom suites overlooking the Gulf. *410 S. Collier Blvd. 33937, tel. 813/394–5167 or 800/237–8906. 96 rooms. Facilities: kitchen, beach, pool, whirlpool, sauna, exercise room, tennis, racquetball, sailing, windsurfing. AE, MC, V. Very Expensive.*

Marco Bay Resort. An all-suite motor inn on Marco Bay. *1001 N. Barfield Dr. 33937, tel. 813/394–8881. 320 rooms. Facilities: kitchens, pools, whirlpools, dock, fishing, putting green, transportation to beach, tennis, restaurant, lounge. AE, DC, MC, V. Very Expensive.*

★ **The Marco Beach Hilton.** With fewer than 300 rooms and wisely apportioned public areas, the Hilton is smaller than most resorts in the area. For this reason guests typically have no trouble taking advantage of the myriad recreational facilities available to them, including a brand-new, well-equipped fitness center adjacent to the three tennis courts. All of the rooms in this 11-story beachfront hotel have private balconies with unobstructed gulf views, a sitting area, wet bar, refrigerator, and plenty of space. Furnishings are cheerful, and unobtrusive—the same can be said about the staff. You're always made to feel at home here. *560 S. Collier Blvd., Marco Island 33937, tel. 813/394–5000 or 800/443–4550, fax 813/394–5251. 295 rooms. Facilities: restaurant, lounges, beach, pool, whirlpool, tennis, golf nearby, fitness center, sailing, sailboarding. AE, D, DC, MC, V. Very Expensive.*

Marriott's Marco Island Resort. Large rooms with balconies surrounded by lush, tropical grounds right next to the Gulf. *400 S. Collier Blvd. 33937, tel. 813/394–2511. 736 rooms, 86 suites. Facilities: pools, beach, whirlpool, waterskiing, sailboats, windsurfing, tennis, bicycles, golf, exercise room, restaurants, lounge. AE, DC, MC, V. Very Expensive.*

Radisson Beach Suite Resort. All 214 one- and two-bedroom suites plus 55 rooms in this medium high-rise resort contain kitchens fully equipped with utensils to give a home-away-from-home touch. The casual decor of the suites contrasts sharply with the marble floors and chandelier in the lobby. Built in 1986, the resort faces a large beachfront. *600 S. Collier Blvd., Marco Island 33937, tel. 813/394–4100 or 800/333–3333. 214 rooms. Facilities: pool, beach, whirlpool, exercise room,* *game room, water sports equipment, restaurant, lounge. AE, DC, MC, V. Very Expensive.*

Naples
Dining

★ **The Chef's Garden.** A mixture of Continental, traditional, and California cuisines has consistently won this restaurant awards over the past decade. Some daily specials include Scottish smoked salmon with avocado and caviar, roast rack of lamb, and spinach and fresh mango salad with toasted cashews and honey vinaigrette. The less formal Truffles bistro, upstairs, features sandwiches, pastas, and pastries to take-out or to eat in. *1300 3rd St. S, tel. 813/262–5500. Reservations advised. Jacket required during winter season. AE, DC, MC, V. Very Expensive.*

★ **Alexandra's.** This intimate eatery on Fifth Avenue South features American nouvelle cuisine in the casually elegant dining room, where flowers and linen napery are as fresh as the well-prepared food. Veal and proscuitto birds, shrimp and scallop diablo, and linguine with emerald sauce rank among house specialties. *878 Fifth Ave. S, tel. 813/262–7076. Reservations advised. Dress: neat but casual. Closed Sun. MC, V. Expensive.*

Villa Pescatore. Northern Italian cuisine is the theme of the vast menu found here. While half the menu remains constant, the other half is ever changing, to keep up with the chef's creative and high-quality flare. Specials such as duck randi in sage sauce, and saffron and linguine with salmon and tomatoes in a pepper-vodka cream sauce, may be found in this romantic restaurant with white linen, candlelight, crystal, and wicker furnishings. In another wing is Plum's Café, a bistro-style restaurant serving light fare. *8920 N. Tamiami Trail, tel. 813/597–8119. Reservations advised. Dress: neat but casual. AE, DC, MC, V. Expensive.*

Cafe La Playa. The soul is French, and from it comes classic offerings such as pâté de fois gras, veal in a Dijon mustard sauce, and vichyssoise. The view is of the Gulf, either indoors or from the broad-screened patio. *9891 Gulfshore Dr., tel. 813/597–3123. Reservations advised. Dress: neat but casual. AE, MC, V. Moderate.*

★ **St. George and the Dragon.** A long-lived seafood-and-beef restaurant, with a decor reminiscent of an old-fashioned men's club—heavy on brass, dark woods, and deep-red tones. Among the specialties are conch chowder, various cuts of prime rib, and shrimp steamed in beer. *936 5th Ave. S, tel. 813/262–6546. No reservations. Jacket suggested. AE, DC, MC, V. Moderate. Closed Sun. and Christmas.*

Lodging

Edgewater Beach Hotel. An all-suite Gulf-front hotel on fashionable Gulf Shore Drive, long an elegant address in Naples. Close to downtown. *1901 Gulfshore Blvd. N 33940, tel. 813/262–6511, or 800/821–0196; in FL, 800/282–3766. 124 rooms. Facilities: beach, pool, exercise room, restaurant. AE, DC, MC, V. Very Expensive.*

The Registry Resort. This modern, luxurious high-rise resort is a half mile from the beach and is known for its excellent tennis facilities: there are 15 courts, five of which can be lit for night play. *475 Seagate Dr. 33940, tel. 813/597–3232. 50 tennis villas, 29 suites, 395 rooms. Facilities: pools, whirlpools, bicycles, tennis, health club, restaurants, lounge. AE, DC, MC, V. Very Expensive.*

The Ritz–Carlton. If the size and elegance of your hotel room are the most important factors in your choice of lodging, you may as well head elsewhere. Equally fabulous hotel rooms can be had for less throughout Florida. What is priority here is that guests are treated like Royalty. High tea is better attended than high tide. The extensive network of lavishly appointed public rooms is astounding. At the Ritz, you're paying for the dozen meeting rooms of varying shapes and sizes, the estimable collection of 19th-century European oils, the twice daily housekeeping service, and the almost overwhelming array of creature comforts. It is considered by some to be the finest resort in Florida. But remember, you're probably going to feel a little uncomfortable traipsing through the lobby in tennis shoes. If you're seeking a younger crowd and a laid-back atmosphere, you might feel more at home on nearby Marco Island. Wherever you decide to stay, do at least drive by and gawk at this marvelous fairy castle. *280 Vanderbilt Beach Rd. 33941, tel. 813/598-3300. 463 rooms. Facilities: 4 restaurants, lounge, beach, pool, saunas, whirlpool, 6 tennis courts, access to nearby 27-hole golf course, fitness center, children's programs, sailboarding, sailing. AE, D, DC, MC, V. Very Expensive.*

La Playa Beach & Racquet Inn. This is a large Gulf-front motor inn where guests can stay close to the ground or get a gull's-eye view from one of the apartments in the mid-rise tower. *9891 Gulfshore Dr., 33963, tel. 813/597-3123. 137 units. Facilities: pool, beach, dock, tennis, restaurant, deli, lounge. AE, MC, V. Expensive.*

Comfort Inn. One of the more attractive chain motels along busy U.S. 41, this four-floor, pink-and-white stucco lodging on the banks of the Gordon River is centrally located—a 20-minute walk from the beaches. Rooms are clean, but stuffy; coffee, juice, and doughnuts are served every morning in a bright and spacious lounge. *1221 5th Ave. S (corner of U.S. 41), 33940, tel. 813/649-5800 or 800/221-2222. Facilities: pool. AE, D, DC, MC, V. Moderate.*

Port Charlotte/ Punta Gorda

Dining

Salty's Harborside. Seafood is served from a dining room that looks out on Burnt Store Marina and Charlotte Harbor. *Burnt Store Marina, Burnt Store Rd. Punta Gorda, tel. 813/639-3650. Reservations advised. Dress: casual. AE, DC, MC, V. Moderate.*

Mexican Hacienda. Tex-Mex of a high order is presented in humble surroundings. The building matches its well-worn neighbors; inside are well-interpreted guacamole dip and tacos made with tender shredded beef. *Harbour Inn, U.S. 41, Charlotte Harbor, tel. 813/625-4211. Reservations accepted for parties of 6 or more. Dress: casual. MC, V. Inexpensive.*

Lodging

Burnt Store Marina Resort. For golfing, boating, and getting away from it all, Burnt Store can fill the bill. One- and two-bedroom modern apartments are situated along a relatively undeveloped stretch of vast Charlotte Harbor. Two-bedroom units available only on a weekly or monthly basis. *3150 Matecumbe Key Rd., Punta Gorda 33955, tel. 813/639-4151. 46 1-bedroom condominiums. Facilities: kitchens, pool, golf, marina, boats, tennis, restaurant, lounge. AE, DC, MC, V. Expensive.*

Days Inn of Port Charlotte. A modern mid-rise motel on Charlotte County's major business route. *1941 Tamiami Trail (U.S. 41), Port Charlotte 33948, tel. 813/627-8900. 126 rooms. Facilities: pool. AE, DC, MC, V. Moderate.*

St. Petersburg

Dining

King Charles Room. Quiet elegance, attentive service, and soothing harp music are to be found in this restaurant on the fifth floor of the Don CeSar Beach Resort. Continental specialties include beluga caviar on ice and smoked salmon stuffed with crab mousse. *3400 Gulf Blvd., tel. 813/360–1881. Reservations advised. Dress: Jacket and tie suggested. AE, DC, MC, V. No lunch. Very Expensive.*

Pepin. The fish is fresh, the beef well aged, and the wine list broad ranging. *4125 4th St. N., tel. 813/821–3773. Dress: neat but casual. AE, MC, V. Expensive.*

Peter's Place at the Tower. This established St. Pete chef wants dinner to be an evening's entertainment in itself. Hence, his new restaurant serving Continental fare (breakfast, lunch, and dinner) in Egyptian decor circa 1350 BC promises extravagant fun. Although the menu changes regularly, you can always expect selections from around the world, including such dishes as Mexican chicken mole and French roast duckling in brandied peaches. *200 Central Ave., tel. 813/822–8436. Dress: neat but casual. MC, V. Moderate.*

★ **Hurricane Seafood Restaurant.** Located right on historic Pass-a-Grille Beach (also known as St. Pete Beach), this seafood joint is popular for its grilled, broiled, or blackened grouper; steamed shrimp; and homemade crab cakes. One of the few places in St. Petersburg with live jazz (Wed.–Sun.), it also has an adjacent disco called Stormy's at the Hurricane, so is a well-frequented place even after mealtime. Also, the sundeck on the third floor attracts crowds who come to see those gorgeous sunsets. *807 Gulf Way, tel. 813/360–9558. Reservations advised. Dress: casual. MC, V. Inexpensive.*

★ **Ted Peters Famous Smoked Fish.** The menu is limited to mackerel and mullet, but both are smoked and seasoned to perfection and served with heaping helpings of German potato salad. All meals are served outdoors. *1350 Pasadena Ave. S, Pasadena, tel. 813/381–7931. No reservations. Dress: casual. No dinner. Closed Tues. No credit cards. Inexpensive.*

Lodging

Don CeSar Beach Resort. This palatial, pink-rococo resort sprawls along the Gulf front. A favorite of author F. Scott Fitzgerald and baseball great Babe Ruth in the 1920s and '30s. *3400 Gulf Blvd., St. Petersburg Beach 33706, tel. 813/360–1881. 277 rooms. Facilities: pool, whirlpool, beach, saunas, tennis, children's program, exercise room, sailboats, parasails, jet skis, restaurants, lounge. AE, DC, MC, V. Very Expensive.*

Tradewinds on St. Petersburg Beach. Old Florida ambience is offered here, with white gazebos, gondolas gliding along canals, and hammocks swaying on 13 acres of beachfront property. *5500 Gulf Blvd., St. Petersburg Beach 33706, tel. 813/367–6461. 381 rooms. Facilities: kitchens, pools, wading pool, beach, sauna, whirlpools, boating, dock, fishing, tennis, racquetball, bicycles, playground, exercise room, scuba instruction, waterskiing, windsurfing, restaurant, lounge. AE, DC, MC, V. Very Expensive.*

Colonial Gateway Resort Inn. This Gulf-front hotel is family-oriented, with half of its 200 rooms equipped with kitchenettes. The resort was recently remodeled to give it a contemporary look for young families. *6300 Gulf Blvd., St. Petersburg Beach 33706, tel. 800/237–8918 outside FL, 800/282–5245 in FL. 200 rooms. Facilities: beach bar, pool, water sports, restaurants, lounge. AE, DC, MC, V. Moderate.*

Sanibel/Captiva
Dining

The Bubble Room. It's hard to say which is more eclectic here, the atmosphere or the menu. Waiters and waitresses wearing Boy Scout uniforms race amid a dizzying array of Art Deco, while music from the 1940s sets the mood. The aged prime rib is ample enough to satisfy two hearty eaters—at least. Chances are you'll be too full for dessert, but it can be wrapped to go. *Captiva Rd., Captiva, tel. 813/472-5558. No reservations. Dress: casual. AE, DC, MC, V. Expensive.*

The Greenhouse. Though the kitchen is in full view of the diminutive dining area, all is calm and quiet as you wend your way through the day's specials. Chef-owner Danny Melman changes his Continental-style menu every four to six weeks. Each menu features fresh seafood and game among its selections. *Captiva Rd., Captiva, tel. 813/472-6066. Reservations advised. Dress: neat but casual. No lunch. No credit cards. Expensive.*

★ **Jean Paul's French Corner.** French food, finely seasoned with everything but the highfalutin attitude often dished up in French establishments. Salmon in a creamy dill sauce, sautéed soft-shell crabs, and roast duckling in fruit sauce are among the few but well-prepared choices on the menu. *708 Tarpon Bay Rd., tel. 813/472-1493. Reservations advised. Dress: casual. No lunch. MC, V. Expensive.*

Windows on the Water. Savor a Gulf view and some of Sanibel's finest food, as Chef Peter Harman concocts cuisine with Continental and Cajun overtones, making the most of fresh seafood. Try the outstanding bronzed fish special, a take-off on blackened fish, but with garlic. *Sundial Beach & Tennis Resort, 1451 Middle Gulf Dr., tel. 813/472-4151. Reservations advised. Dress: neat but casual. AE, DC, MC, V. Expensive.*

McT's Shrimphouse and Tavern. Somewhat of a departure from most Sanibel establishments, McT's is lively and informal, featuring a host of fresh seafood specialties, including all-you-can-eat shrimp and crab. *1523 Periwinkle Way, Sanibel, tel. 813/472-3161. No reservations. Dress: casual. AE, DC, MC, V. Moderate.*

Lodging

Casa Ybel Resort. This time-share property features contemporary one- and two-bedroom Gulf-front condominium villas on 23 acres of tropical grounds, complete with palms, ponds, and a footbridge. *2255 W. Gulf Dr., Sanibel 33957, tel. 813/472-3145 or 800/237-8906. 40 1-bedroom units, 74 2-bedroom units. Facilities: kitchens, pool, whirlpool, biking, tennis, sailing, playground, shuffleboard, game room, baby-sitting, restaurant, lounge. AE, DC, MC, V. Very Expensive.*

★ **South Seas Plantation Resort and Yacht Harbour.** This quiet, elegant 330-acre property is more like a neighborhood community than a beach resort, with nine different types of accommodations, among them tennis and harborside villas, Gulf cottages, and private homes. Walk, cycle, or Rollerblade (rentals in town) along the well-paved one-mile path that runs through the neatly landscaped grounds that are fashionably overgrown with exotic vegetation. Better yet, sign up for some of the many outdoor activities organized by South Seas, including wave running, sailboarding, waterskiing, tennis, golf, and shelling—to mention a few. From the service in the posh restaurant—The King's Crown Dining Room—to the waterskiing instructors, the staff is five-star. You'll find a mix on the guest roster, as the property provides endless activities and good nightlife suited for singles and couples, as well as supervised children's programs for *all* ages (including toddlers)—a feature that attracts a good number of families. But somehow, even with all the options, the pace is satisfyingly slowed and the atmosphere is one that inspires calm and relaxation. Rates can drop as much as 40% off-season. *South Seas Plantation Rd., Captiva 33924, tel. 813/472–5111 or 800/237–1260. 600 rooms. Facilities: 4 restaurants, 2 lounges, kitchens, boating docks, fishing, golf, tennis, game room, playground, pools, parasailing, sailboats, wave runners, waterskiing, sailboarding, sailing school, beauty parlor, children's programs. AE, DC, MC, V. Very Expensive.*

Sundial Beach & Tennis Resort. The largest all-suite resort on the island; many suites look out upon the Gulf of Mexico, and all have full kitchens and laundry facilities, making them great for families. *1451 Middle Gulf Dr., Sanibel 33957, tel. 813/472–4151 or 800/237–4184. 200-plus suites. Facilities: kitchens, pools, beach, bicycles, tennis, sailboats, recreational program, children's program, baby-sitting, game room, shuffleboard, restaurants, lounge. AE, DC, MC, V. Very Expensive.*

Sarasota

Dining

★ **The Bijou Cafe.** Wood, brass, and sumptuous green carpeting surround diners in this gas station turned restaurant. Chef Jean Pierre Knaggs's Continental specialties include crispy roast duckling with tangerine brandy sauce or cassis and blackberry sauce, rack of lamb for two, and *crème brûlée*, a custard with a carmelized brown-sugar topping. *1287 1st St., tel. 813/366–8111. Reservations advised. Dress: neat but casual. DC, MC, V. Expensive.*

★ **Cafe L'Europe.** Located on fashionable St. Armand's Key, this greenery- and art-filled café specializes in fresh veal and seafood. Menus change frequently, but might include fillet of sole Picasso, Dover sole served with a choice of fruits, wiener schnitzel sautéed in butter and topped with anchovies, olives, and capers. *431 St. Armand's Circle, tel. 813/388–4415. Reservations advised. Dress: neat but casual. AE, DC, MC, V. Expensive.*

Marina Jack. Have a dinner cruise on the *Marina Jack II* or eat fresh seafood overlooking Sarasota Bay. *2 Marina Plaza, tel. 813/365–4232. Reservations advised. Dress: neat but casual. MC, V. Expensive.*

Ophelia's on the Bay. Sample mussel soup, eggplant crêpes, chicken pot pie, seafood spiedini or cioppino, among other things, at this waterfront restaurant. *9105 Midnight Pass Rd., Siesta Key, tel. 813/349–2212. Reservations advised. Dress: casual. AE, D, DC, MC, V. Moderate.*

Lodging

The Colony Beach. If tennis is your game, this is the place to play it, while you enjoy the luxury and relaxed atmosphere of this resort. Tennis greats such as Bjorn Borg make The Colony their home court, and for good reason. Complimentary games on 10 clay hydro courts and 11 hard courts are offered, as well as a wide variety of clinics and camps for all levels of players, with scaled-down racquets for children. Guaranteed matchmaking means guests play a pro if another guest is not free to be a partner. Every member of the tennis staff is USPTA certified and a video analysis of your game is available. After the game, or whenever, visit the Health Spas (separate for men and women) that offer seaweed body packs, facials, licensed shiastu and western massage, whirlpool, steambaths, and too much more to list. The Fitness Center is run by pros and provides Stairmasters, free weights, yoga, and aerobics classes. There are 235 suites and 25 VIP suites, some of which sleep up to 8. Private beach houses and lanais that open onto sand and sea are also available to rent. The rooms are done in four different styles, from Southwestern to more classic looks. As for dining, the Colony Restaurant has held *Wine Spectator's* Grand Award since 1982 and is one of the "outstanding restaurants of the world," according to *Travel-Holiday* magazine. It is much more formal than the relaxed, poolside Bamboos, where you can get everything from tropical cocktails to raw oysters. Special menus are available for kids, as is a complimentary children's program with indoor and outdoor activities. Conference facilities are impressive: a banquet seating up to 600 can be produced at the Beach Club, with a more modest one of up to 250 indoors; a reception can host 275, and more modest rooms are available, including one overlooking the tennis courts. Kitchen facilities for all settings are built in, so meals can be prepared for each meeting. Vacation packages are available, as are virtually all activities, including ecology trips and deep-sea fishing. The Colony calls itself "intentionally different," and it's worth a visit to find out why. *1620 Gulf of Mexico Dr., Longboat 34228, tel. 813/383–6464, 800/237–9443 outside FL, or 800/282–1138 in FL; fax 813/383–7549. 235 suites, 25 VIP rooms. Facilities: 3 restaurants, bar, spas, health club, tennis clinics, 21 tennis courts, pool, children's activities. Very Expensive. AE, D, MC, V.*

Hyatt Sarasota. Recently renovated, the Hyatt is contemporary in design and conveniently located in the heart of the city. Some rooms overlook Sarasota Bay. *1000 Blvd. of the Arts 34236, tel. 813/366–9000. 297 rooms. Facilities: pool, sauna, sailing, health club, dock, restaurant, lounge. AE, DC, MC, V. Very Expensive.*

The Resort at Longboat Key Club. This is not simply a refined luxury hotel, it's one of *the* places to golf in the state. All 45 holes of golf on the silver medal courses (most likely ranking gold in the near future) are known on Longboat Key as a watery challenge. The Islandside Course was designed by Billy Mitchell and opened in 1960 at par 72, and boasts 5,000 palm trees. The Harbourside Course, opened in 1982, is a championship layout designed by Willard Byrd. Both have excellent pro shops, lessons, and clinics. Additionally, there are 38 Har-tru tennis courts, ranked among the top 50 in the United States, and 1,000 acres of landscaped public areas with 56 new flower beds surrounding the club. The 228 suites are done up in tropical patterns with light wood furnishings, and are renovated completely every five years. Views of the golf course or beaches are to be had from huge private balconies; one even overlooks a private lagoon, where manatees can be seen from time to time. The deluxe suite sleeps up to six, with three TVs, five phones, washer/dryer, dressing room, and kitchen. Housekeeping is twice daily, and a safe, hairdryer, minibar, and coffeemaker are found in every room. The 228 suites accommodate up to four and have two rollaway beds, but the most economical are the 100 guest rooms, which do not include a kitchen. Voice-mail boxes are a great convenience, as are the security key cards, which also function as club charge cards. Choose from the five restaurants, among them, the award-winning Orchids' for gourmet dining, and the casual poolside Barefoots, and, after a game of golf, Spike and Tees. There is a library with materials in several languages. Hobie Cats, kayaks, Sunfish, deep-sea charters, and ecology trips are all available on the beach. The Club has been rated four stars, AAA, and four diamonds. *301 Gulf of Mexico Dr. (Box 15000), Longboat Key 34228, tel. 813/383–8821, 800/282–0113 in FL, or 800/237–8821 outside FL; fax 813/383–0359. 228 rooms. Facilities: 4 restaurants, golf* *courses, meeting rooms, library, 38 tennis courts, watersports and rentals, charters. Very Expensive. AE, DC, MC, V.*

Half Moon Beach Club. Conveniently located just minutes from St. Armand's Circle, this horseshoe-shaped hotel offers Lido Key's finest accommodations. Elegance begins with the alabaster-lit lobby, and continues as you pass through the glass doors to the hotel's masterful centerpiece: a tropical garden surrounding the pool. A $3 million renovation (begun in 1989), together with inspirational 1950s and 1960s architecture, has returned the Half Moon to its original adored state. Walk past the pool, the tiki huts, and yogurt bar to the spacious beach deck where you can enjoy a cool drink. Continue on to the wide beach where, to the left, the sand meets the forest—a sight of unadulterated beauty. Decorated in pink pastels, every asymmetrical room and suite is unique; four have direct Gulf views. Rooms on the inside of the horseshoe overlook the pool and garden. The quality bistro-style restaurant is open for all meals and the worldly chef prepares daily specials. *2050 Ben Franklin Dr., Lido Beach 34236, tel. 813/388–3694 or 800/358–3245; fax 813/388–1938. 74 rooms, 12 suites. Facilities: restaurant, bar, yogurt bar, pool. AE, DC, MC, V. Expensive.*

Days Inn Sarasota-Siesta Key. Modern, built in 1986, with earth-tone rooms, this inn is 1 mile from the beaches. *6600 S. Tamiami Trail (U.S. 41) 34231, tel. 813/924–4900. 132 rooms. Facilities: pool, whirlpool. AE, DC, MC, V. Moderate.*

Gulf Beach Resort Motel. Appreciating the enigma of a resort motel is perhaps the key to understanding this kitsch cinder-block palace. The stylized pink sign, enclosed in teal arching waves, gives new arrivals their first—and accurate—impression of this place. Guests sign in, meet others, and return year after year to re-acquaint with old friends, a number of whom are young Europeans. Maybe the management draws the clientele: three delightful women show you a choice of rooms, each unit differently furnished from the others. The best—both with sea views—are a modern two-bedroom, done in white, and the one-bedroom below it. Most of the 48 rooms are minimal, some have balconies, screened-in patios, or small private gardens with lime trees. All have kitchens, private baths, and basic cable TV. Shuffleboard, a heated pool, a large tiki hut on the beach, low rates, and a 1-mile walk to St. Armand's Circle through one of Florida's typical '50s residential neighborhoods are features you can count on. Daily, weekly, or monthly Sept.–Jan. rates available. *930 Ben Franklin Dr., Sarasota 34236, tel. 813/388–2127 or 800/232–2489 in U.S.; 800/331–2489 in Canada. 48 rooms. Facilities: pool, kitchens, shuffleboard, cable TV. MC, V. Moderate.*

Hampton Inn Sarasota Airport. On the main drag, convenient to beaches and downtown. *5000 N. Tamiami Trail (U.S. 41) 34234, tel. 813/351–7734. 100 rooms. Facilities: pool. AE, DC, MC, V. Moderate.*

Tampa
Dining

★ **Armani's.** Located in the Hyatt Regency Westshore, this northern Italian–style restaurant offers a great view of Old Tampa Bay and the city. For an even closer look, take a seat on the terrace, where you can have dessert and really get a good look around. The interior is appealing, with an elegant almond-and-black color scheme, dim lighting, and many windows. Someone at your table should order the tasty veal Armani—veal sautéed with mushrooms, cream, and cognac in black and white truffle sauce. If it strikes your fancy, give the extensive antipasto bar a try. *6200 Courtney Campbell Causeway, tel. 813/281–9165. Reservations advised. Jacket and tie required. AE, DC, MC, V. Closed lunch and Sun. Very Expensive.*

★ **Bern's Steak House.** Perhaps the best steak house, not just in Tampa but in all of Florida, Bern's offers specialties created with finely aged prime beef. Choose from an extensive wine list—some 7,000 choices, with selections ranging in price from $10 to $10,000 a bottle. The vegetables are grown on owner-chef Bern Lexer's organic farm. Upstairs are the dessert rooms: small, glass-enclosed rooms where sumptuous desserts are served. Each room is equipped with a control panel for TV, radio, or listening in to the live entertainment in the lounge. *1208 S. Howard Ave., tel. 813/251–2421. Reservations advised. Dress: neat but casual. AE, DC, MC, V. No lunch. Very Expensive.*

★ **Bella Trattoria.** Brightly lit, slightly noisy, and filled with the smells of such Italian fare as *capelli di l'Angelo*—smoked salmon and caviar tossed with spinach and angel-hair pasta in a vodka and cream sauce—and *Bella! Bella!*, a truffle torte of bittersweet, semisweet, and white chocolates. Crayons and paper tablecloths afford a public outlet for frustrated artists. *1413 S. Howard Ave., tel. 813/254–3355. No reservations. Dress: casual. AE, MC, V. Moderate.*

Colonnade. The wharfside location of this popular family restaurant is reflected in its nautical decor. Seafood—particularly grouper, red snapper, and lobster—is a specialty, but steak and chicken are also served. *3401 Bayshore Blvd., tel. 813/839–7558. No reservations. Dress: casual. AE, DC, MC, V. Moderate.*

★ **Columbia.** A Spanish fixture in Tampa's Ybor City for more than 85 years, this restaurant has several airy and spacious dining rooms and a sunny atrium with tile decor. Specialties include the Columbia 1905 salad—lettuce, ham, olives, cheese, and garlic; and paella—saffron rice with chicken, fish, and mussels. Flamenco dancing. *2117 E. 7th Ave., tel. 813/248–4961. Reservations accepted. Dress: casual weekdays, jacket suggested weekends. AE, DC, MC, V. Moderate.*

RG's. Both locations offer imaginative food in sophisticated settings served by a competent staff. Char-grilled duck and chocolate pecan toffee mousse are among the dishes found here. *RG's at City Center: 110 N. Franklin St., tel. 813/229–5536; RG's North: 3807 Northdale Blvd., tel. 813/963–2356. Reservations advised. Dress: neat but casual. AE, MC, V. At City Center, closed Sun. and lunch Sat.; at North, closed lunch. Moderate.*

Selena's. New Orleans Creole food served here with some Sicilian dishes as well, in antique-filled dining rooms. Shrimp scampi and other fresh seafood featured. *1623 Snow Ave., tel. 813/251–2116. Dress: casual. Reservations advised. AE, DC, MC, V. Moderate.*

The Cactus Club. Southwestern cuisine such as fajitas is what you'll get at this casual but fashionable restaurant. Also available is a pretty good pizza. *1601 Snow Ave. (in the Old Hyde Park Mall), tel. 813/251–4089. Reservations not needed. Dress: casual. AE, DC, MC, V. Inexpensive.*

Lodging

Hyatt Regency Westshore. This large, relatively new luxury hotel is well placed, right on Tampa Bay. *6200 Courtney Campbell Causeway, 33607, tel. 813/874–1234. 445 rooms. Facilities: 3 restaurants, 2 pools, sauna, Jacuzzi, health club. AE, D, DC, MC, V. Very Expensive.*

Saddlebrook. Arguably one of Florida's premier tennis (42 courts) and golf (36 holes) resorts, Saddlebrook rests on sprawling, heavily wooded grounds situated just 15 miles north of Tampa. A variety of accommodations and amenities are available. Families should find the two-bedroom, two-bath suites (with full kitchens) convenient and comfortable. *100 Saddlebrook Way, Wesley Chapel 34249, tel. 813/973-1111. 501 rooms. Facilities: kitchenettes, pools, wading pools, whirlpools, saunas, fishing, golf, tennis, bicycles, health club, restaurants, lounge. AE, DC, MC, V. Very Expensive.*

Wyndham Harbour Island Hotel. Elegant ambience, with lots of dark wood paneling, substantial furniture, and attentive service is featured here. Tennis players can enjoy excellent facilities. *725 S. Harbour Island Blvd., 33602, tel. 813/229-5000. 300 rooms. Facilities: pool, dock, sailboats, tennis, health club, restaurant, lounge. AE, DC, MC, V. Very Expensive.*

Embassy Suites Hotel. Modern all-suite hotel midway between Tampa International Airport and downtown Tampa. *555 N. Westshore Blvd. 33609, tel. 813/875-1555. 221 rooms. Facilities: pool, whirlpool, sauna, exercise room, transportation to airport, restaurant, lounge. Pets allowed. AE, DC, MC, V. Expensive.*

Hyatt Regency Tampa. A large, elegant high-rise hotel with a modern, mirrored ambience. *2 Tampa City Center, 211 N. Tampa St., 33602, tel. 813/225-1234. 517 rooms. Facilities: pool, whirlpool, sauna, exercise room, restaurant, lounge. AE, DC, MC, V. Expensive.*

Holiday Inn Busch Gardens. A family-oriented motor inn just 1 mile west of Busch Gardens. *2701 E. Fowler Ave., 33612, tel. 813/971-4710. 399 rooms. Facilities: pool, sauna, exercise room, restaurant, lounge, transportation to Busch Gardens. AE, DC, MC, V. Moderate.*

Tahitian Inn. This family-run motel offers comfortable rooms at budget prices. *601 S. Dale Mabry Hwy., 33609, tel. 813/877-6721. 79 rooms. Facilities: pool. AE, DC, MC, V. Inexpensive.*

Tarpon Springs
Dining

★ **Louis Pappas' Riverside Restaurant.** The decor consists mainly of wall-to-wall people who pour into this waterfront landmark for all manner of Greek fare, especially the Greek salad, made with lettuce, feta cheese chunks, onions, and olive oil. *10 W. Dodecanese Blvd., tel. 813/937-5101. Reservations advised. Dress: casual. AE, DC, MC, V. Moderate.*

Lodging

Innisbrook Resort. There are deluxe rooms and suites here, some with balconies or patios at this get-away-from-it-all resort on 1,000 wooded acres. *Box 1088, U.S. 19 34689, tel. 813/942-2000. 1,200 rooms. Facilities: golf, tennis, racquetball, pools, health club, children's program (May-Sept.), miniature golf, saunas, dining rooms, nightclub. AE, DC, MC, V. Very Expensive.*

Venice
Dining

Sharky's on the Pier. Gaze out on the beach and sparkling waters while dining on grilled fresh seafood. *1600 S. Harbor Dr., tel. 813/488-1456. Reservations advised. Dress: casual. MC, V. Moderate.*

Lodging

Holiday House. Comfortable rooms in motor inn on the main business route through town. *1710 S. Tamiami Trail (U.S. 41) 34293, tel. 813/493-4558. 72 rooms. Facilities: pool, restaurant, lounge. Pets allowed. AE, MC, V. Moderate.*

Veranda Inn–Venice. A landscaped pool is the focal point of this small but spacious inn. All rooms look out on the pool and courtyard. *625 S. Tamiami Trail (U.S. 41), tel. 813/484–9559. 37 rooms. Facilities: pool, restaurant. AE, DC, MC, V. Moderate.*

The Arts

Not too many years ago, southwest Florida was content to bask in the warmth of the sun and leave cultural matters to others. But as the population has boomed, a growing number of transplanted northerners have been unwilling to sacrifice the arts for nature. Hence, there are curtains going up at performing-arts centers throughout the region.

If you are interested in cultural events while staying in Florida, it's a good idea to purchase tickets before you arrive, especially during the busy winter tourist season. Most halls and theaters accept credit-card charges by phone. The area chambers of commerce (*see* Important Addresses and Numbers, above) can supply schedules of upcoming cultural events.

Ringling Museum of Art. (*See* Exploring Bradenton/Sarasota Area.)

The **Museum of Fine Arts** has outstanding examples of European, American, pre-Columbian, and Far Eastern art, as well as photographic exhibits. *255 Beach Dr., NE, St. Petersburg, tel. 813/896–2667. Suggested donation: $4. Open Tues.–Sat. 10–5, Sun. 1–5.*

Begin at the **Salvador Dali Museum.** Inside you'll find a large collection of paintings of melting watches, colorful landscapes, and thought-provoking works of the late Spanish surrealist. *Take I–275 and then follow I–175 toward the bay. At 3rd Street South, turn right. The museum is on the left, about two blocks ahead. 1000 3rd St. S, tel. 813/823–3767. Open Tues.–Sat. 10–5, Sun. noon–5. Admission: $5 adults, $3.50 students and senior citizens.*

The **Tampa Performing Arts Center** (1010 W. C. MacInnes Pl., Box 2877, tel. 813/221–1045 or 800/955–1045) occupies nine acres along the Hillsborough River and is one of the largest such complexes south of the Kennedy Center in Washington, DC. The festival hall, playhouse, and small theater accommodate opera, ballet, drama, and concerts.

Ruth Eckerd Hall (1111 McMullen Booth Rd., Clearwater, tel. 813/791–7400) also plays host to many national performers of pop, classical, and jazz music; ballet; and drama.

Sarasota's **Van Wezel Performing Arts Hall** (777 N. Tamiami Trail, tel. 813/953–3366) is easy to find. Just look for the purple shell rising along the bay front. It offers some 200 performances each year, including Broadway plays, ballet, jazz, rock concerts, symphonies, children's shows, and ice skating. For tickets and information, contact the box office.

The **Naples Philharmonic Center for the Arts** (5833 Pelican Bay Blvd., tel. 813/597–1111) comprises two theaters and two art galleries offering a variety of plays, concerts, and exhibits year-round.

Concerts
Bradenton/Sarasota

The **Sarasota Concert Band** (Van Wezel Hall, 777 N. Tamiami Trail [U.S. 41], Sarasota, tel. 813/955–6660) includes 50 players, many of whom are full-time musicians. The group performs monthly concerts.

Florida West Coast Symphony Center (709 N. Tamiami Trail, Sarasota, tel. 813/953-4252) consists of a number of area groups that perform in Manatee and Sarasota counties regularly. Included are the *Florida West Coast Symphony, The Florida String Quartet, Florida Brass Quintet, Florida Wind Quintet,* and *New Artists String Quartet.*

Sarasota The **Sarasota Opera** (61 N. Pineapple Ave., tel. 813/953-7030) operates from its home in a historic theater downtown at the corner of 1st and Pineapple streets. The company's season runs from February to March. Internationally known singing artists perform the principal roles, supported by a professional apprentice chorus—24 young singers studying with the company.

Tampa Bay Area **The Tampa Convention Center** (333 South Franklin St., tel. 813/223-8511) offers year-round events such as concerts, boxing matches, gift shows, and boat and car exhibits.

Dance

Tampa Bay Area The **St. Petersburg Concert Ballet** performs periodically throughout the year, mostly at the Bayfront Center in St. Petersburg.

The Tampa Ballet performs at the Tampa Bay Performing Arts Center.

Film All areas have conveniently located commercial movie houses. Check the local newspapers for shows, times, and locations.

Sarasota The **Sarasota Film Society** operates year-round, showing foreign and nonmainstream films daily at 2, 5:45, and 8 at the Cobb Cinema (100 N. Fruitville Rd., tel. 813/388-2441).

Theater

Bradenton/Sarasota The **Asolo Center for the Performing Arts** (Drawer E, tel. 813/351-8000) is a new $10 million facility that offers productions nearly year-round.

Florida Studio Theatre (1241 N. Palm Ave., Sarasota, tel. 813/366-9796) is a small professional theater that presents contemporary dramas, comedies, and musicals.

Golden Apple Dinner Theatre (25 N. Pineapple Ave., Sarasota, tel. 813/366-5454) combines a buffet dinner with musicals and comedies.

The **Players of Sarasota** (U.S. 41 and 9th St., tel. 813/365-2494), a long-lived troupe, provided opportunities for then-unknowns Pee-Wee Herman, Montgomery Clift, and Polly Holiday. The community theater features volunteer actors and technicians and performs comedies, thrillers, and musicals.

Theatre Works (1247 1st St., Venice, tel. 813/952-9170) presents professional, non-Equity productions at the Palm Tree Playhouse.

Venice Little Theatre (corner of Tampa and Nokomis Aves., Venice, tel. 813/488-1115) is a community theater offering comedies, musicals, and a few dramas during its October-May season.

Fort Myers/Naples **The Naples Dinner Theatre** (Immokalee Rd., halfway between U.S. 41 and the I-75 interchange, tel. 813/597-6031) is open October-August and features professional companies performing a variety of mostly musicals and comedies. Admission includes buffet.

The **Naples Players** (Harbour Town Shopping Center, 399 Goodlette Rd., tel. 813/263–7990) has winter and summer seasons. The winter shows often sell out well in advance.

Tampa Bay The **Tampa Theater** (711 N. Franklin St., tel. 813/223–8981) presents shows, musical performances, and films. Area dinner theaters include the **Showboat Dinner Theatre** (3405 Ulmerton Rd., Clearwater, tel. 813/223–2545). All offer dinner and a variety of Broadway and off-Broadway shows throughout the year.

Nightlife

Bars and Nightclubs **Harbour Island Hotel** (Harbour Island, Tampa, tel. 813/229–5000). Great view of the bay, large-screen television, and thickly padded, comfortable chairs.

Blueberry Hill (Harbour Island, Tampa, tel. 813/221–1157). Nightclub-restaurant with performing disc jockeys and large-screen TV. Couples, yuppie crowd.

Coliseum Ballroom (535 4th Ave. N, St. Petersburg, tel. 813/892–5202). Ballroom dancing Wednesday and Saturday night.

The Patio (Columbia Restaurant, St. Armand's Key, tel. 813/388–3987). A casual lounge with live music nightly.

'Tween Waters Inn (Captiva Rd., Captiva, tel. 813/472–5161). Live entertainment and large-screen TV catering to casual, over-30 crowd.

Harp & Thistle (650 Corey Ave., St. Petersburg Beach, tel. 813/360–4104). Live Irish music Wednesday–Saturday.

Yucatan Liquor Stand (4811 West Cypress, Tampa, tel. 813/289–8454). Trendy new spot with live music, dancing, performing disc jockey, and a nosh menu that includes seafood, burgers, and Mexican delights.

Comedy Clubs **Comedy Works** (3447 W. Kennedy Blvd., Tampa, tel. 813/875–9129).

Coconuts Comedy Club at Barnacle Bill's (Howard Johnson's, 6110 Gulf Blvd., St. Petersburg, tel. 813/367–NUTS).

Ron Bennington's Comedy Scene (Rodeway Inn, 401 U.S. 19 S, Clearwater, tel. 813/799–1181).

Bijou Comedy Club & Restaurant (McGregor Point Shopping Center, Fort Myers, tel. 813/481–6666).

Country-Western **Joyland Country Night Club** (11225 U.S. 19, St. Petersburg, tel. 813/573–1919).

Dallas Bull (8222 N. Hwy. 301, Tampa, tel. 813/985–6877).

Carlie's (5641 49th St., St. Petersburg, tel. 813/527–5214).

Maestro's Country Lounge (14727 N. Florida Ave., Tampa, tel. 813/961–5090).

Discos **Animal House** (1927 Ringling Blvd., Sarasota, tel. 813/366–3830). A rock-and-roll palace, complete with extensive light show, music videos, a DJ, and several bars. Especially popular with the younger set.

Club Mirage (4797 U.S. 41, Fort Myers, tel. 813/275–9997) packs in the singles (21 and up) with such events as hot legs and lip-sync contests, hot-tub night, live bands and disc jockeys.

Jazz Clubs Most offer jazz several nights a week. Call for details.

Baxters Lounge (714 S. Dale Mabry Hwy., Tampa, tel. 813/879–1161).

Cha Cha Coconuts (City Pier, St. Petersburg, tel. 813/822-6655). Overlooks the water from atop the pier.

Hurricane Lounge (807 Gulf Way, Pass-a-Grille Beach, tel. 813/360-9558).

Upstairs at Peter's (2224 Bay St., Fort Myers, tel. 813/332-2223).

Gatsby's (2840 Tamiami Trail N, Naples, tel. 813/262-2040).

Rock Clubs

The Barn (13815 Hillsborough Ave., Tampa, tel. 813/855-9818). Plays '50s and '60s hits.

306th Bomb Group (8301 N. Tamiami Trail, Sarasota, tel. 813/355-8591). Amid World War II gear, a DJ spins Top-40 tunes for a generally over-25 clientele.

Club Yesterdays (2224 S. Tamiami Trail, Venice, tel. 813/493-2900). Top-40 is king every night at this club popular with the under-30 set.

Edison's Electric Lounge (Holiday Inn, 13051 Bell Tower Dr., Fort Myers, tel. 813/482-2900). Top-40 tunes, usually live bands, rock nightly.

MacDintons (405 South Howard Ave., Tampa, tel. 813/254-1661). Live rock music daily starting at 10 PM at this trendy new playground that also has a full Continental menu for when the munchies strike.

11 The Panhandle

Introduction

By Ann Hughes

Northwest Florida resident Ann Hughes is former editor of Indiana Business *magazine and a contributing editor to other travel and trade publications.*

Because there are no everglades or palm trees here, some call northwest Florida "the other Florida." Instead, magnolias, live oaks, and loblolly pines flourish, just as they do in other parts of the Deep South. When the season winds down in south Florida, it picks up here (beginning in May). Northwest Florida is even in a different time zone: Crossing the Apalachicola River means an hour's difference between eastern and central times.

Others call this section of the state "Florida's best-kept secret." It was, until World War II when activity at the air bases in the area began to rev up. Also known as the Panhandle—because of the region's long, narrow shape—northwest Florida is nestled between the Gulf of Mexico, just west of Tallahassee, and the Alabama and Georgia state lines.

By the mid-1950s, the 100-mile stretch along the Panhandle coast between Pensacola and Panama City was dubbed the "Miracle Strip" because of the dramatic rise in property values of this beachfront land that in the 1940s sold for less than $100 an acre. Today, property fetches millions. But the movers and shakers of the area felt this sobriquet fell short of conveying the richness of the region, with its white sands and forever-green sparkling waters, swamps, bayous, and flora. And so the term "Emerald Coast" was coined.

This little green corner of Florida that snuggles up to Alabama is a land of superlatives: It has the biggest military installation in the Western Hemisphere (Eglin Air Force Base); the oldest city in the state (Pensacola, claiming a founding date of 1559); and the most prolific fishing village in the world (Destin). Thanks to restrictions against commercial development imposed by Eglin AFB and the Gulf Islands National Seashore, the Emerald Coast has been able to maintain several hundred linear miles of unspoiled beaches.

The Panhandle is also an ideal tourist destination. It has resorts that out-glitz the Gold Coast's and campgrounds where possums invite themselves to lunch. Lovers of antiquity can wander the many historic districts or visit archaeological digs. For sports enthusiasts, there's a different golf course or tennis court for each day of the week; and for those who decide to spend time with nature, there's a world of hunting, canoeing, biking, and hiking. And anything that happens on water happens here, from surfboarding and scuba diving to fishing off the end of a pier or casting a line from a deep-sea charter boat.

Essential Information

Getting Around

By Plane **Fort Walton Beach/Eglin AFB Airport/Okaloosa County Air Terminal** is served by ASA–The Delta Connection (tel. 800/282–3424), American Eagle (tel. 800/433–7300), and Northwest (tel. 800/225–2525). **Panama City–Bay County Airport** is served by ASA–The Delta Connection and Northwest (tel. 800/225–2525). A new, state-of-the-art terminal opened in 1991 at the **Pensacola Regional Airport,** which is served by American (tel. 800/433–7300) and Continental Airlines (tel. 800/525–

0280), Delta, Northwest Airlink (tel. 800/225–2525), and USAir (tel. 800/428–4322).

Tallahassee Regional Airport opened its new terminal in 1990. It is served by American Eagle (tel. 800/433–7300), Delta (tel. 800/221–1212), USAir (tel. 800/428–4322).

Accommodations for corporate jets, private planes, and charter services are offered by **Miracle Strip Aviation** (tel. 904/837–6135) in Destin and at **Bob Sikes Airport** (tel. 904/682–6395) in Crestview.

By Car The main east-west arteries across the top of the state are Interstate 10 and U.S. 90. I–10 tends to be monotonous, but a drive along U.S. 90 piques your interest by taking you down the main streets of several county-seat towns. Along the coast, U.S. 98 snakes eastward, forking (into 98 and 98A) at Inlet Beach before becoming U.S. 98 again at Panama City and continuing down to Port St. Joe and Apalachicola. Major north-south highways that weave through Florida's Panhandle are (from east to west) U.S. 231, U.S. 331, Rte. 85, and U.S. 29. The Emerald Coast is also accessible to yachtsmen and sailors from the Intracoastal Waterway, which turns inland at Apalachicola and runs through the bays around Panama City to Choctawhatchee Bay and into Santa Rosa Sound.

By Taxi or Car Service At the Panama City airport, **DeLuxe Coach Limo Service** (tel. 904/763–0211) provides van service to downtown Panama City for $5.25–$8.25 and to Panama City Beach for $11.25–$16.75. **Yellow Cab** (tel. 904/763–4691) taxi service charges about $15 to the beach area, depending on where your hotel is. A ride from the Fort Walton airport via **Yellow Cab** (tel. 904/244–3600) costs $11 to Fort Walton Beach and $18 to Destin or Niceville/Valparaiso. **A-I Taxi** (tel. 904/678–2424) charges $12 to Fort Walton Beach and $16–$18 to Destin. A trip from the Pensacola airport to downtown via **Yellow Cab** (tel. 904/433–1143) costs about $7 and $15 to Pensacola Beach. **Quick Service** (904/224–1121), **City Taxi** (904/893–4111), **Tallahassee Cab** (904/576–2227), and **Yellow Cab** (904/222–3070) all travel from Tallahassee Regional Airport to downtown for about $11. Some hotels provide free shuttle service.

By Train **Amtrack** (tel. 800/USA–RAIL) plans to begin a Los Angeles-to-Panhandle route sometime in late 1992. Among the towns served will be Pensacola, Crestview, Chipley, Lake City, and Pensacola.

By Bus The principal common carrier throughout the region is the **Greyhound/Trailways Bus Line** with stations in Crestview (tel. 904/682–6922), DeFuniak Springs (tel. 904/892–5913), Fort Walton Beach (tel. 904/243–1940), Panama City (tel. 904/785–7861), and Pensacola (tel. 904/476–4800). **Taltran** (tel. 904/574–5200) system provides service throughout the city limits of Tallahassee.

Scenic Drives

Route 399 between Pensacola Beach and Navarre Beach takes you down Santa Rosa Island, a spit of duneland that juts out into the turquoise and jade waters of the Gulf of Mexico. It's a scenic drive if the day is clear; otherwise, it's a study in gray.

The panorama of barge traffic and cabin cruisers on the twinkling waters of the Intracoastal Waterway will get your attention from **U.S. 331**, which runs over a causeway at the east end of Choctawhatchee Bay between Route 20 and U.S. 98.

Guided Tours

Right This Way, Pensacola (2875 W. Michigan Ave., tel. 904/944–1700) offers tours by reservation and tailors them according to individual preferences and interests.

Important Addresses and Numbers

Tourist Information

Apalachicola Chamber of Commerce. *128 Market St., tel. 904/653–9419. Open weekdays 9–4; closed noon–1.*
Crestview Chamber of Commerce. *502 S. Main St., tel. 904/682–3212. Open weekdays 9–5.*
Destin Chamber of Commerce. *Miracle Strip Pkwy., tel. 904/837–0087. Open weekdays 9–5.*
Fort Walton Beach Chamber of Commerce. *34 S.E. Miracle Strip Pkwy., U.S. 98, tel. 904/244–8191. Open weekdays 8–5.*
Niceville/Valparaiso Chamber of Commerce. *170 John Sims Pkwy., tel. 904/678–2323. Open weekdays 9–4:30.*
Panama City Beach Visitors & Convention Bureau. *12015 W. Front Beach Rd. tel. 800/PCBeach. Open Oct.–Apr., weekdays 8–5, May–Sept., weekends 9–5.*
Pensacola Convention & Visitor Information Center. *1401 E. Gregory St., tel. 904/434–1234, 800/343–4321, 800/874–1234 outside FL. Open daily 8:30–5.*
Tallahassee Area Convention and Visitor Bureau. *200 W. College Ave., tel. 904/681–9200 or 800/628–2866. Open weekdays 8–5.*
Walton County Chamber of Commerce. *200 W. Circle Dr., tel. 904/892–3191. Open weekdays 8–5.*
Walton County Chamber of Commerce Welcome Center. *U.S. 331 at U.S. 98, tel. 904/267–3511. Open weekdays 8–4, Sat. 9–4.*

Emergencies Dial 911 for **police** and **ambulance** in an emergency.

Hospitals Emergency rooms are open 24 hours at the following northwest Florida hospitals: **Physician Care** (tel. 904/385–2222) has three locations in Tallahassee, all open daily. **North Okaloosa Medical Center** (151 S.E. Redstone Ave., Crestview, tel. 904/682–9731), **Walton Regional Hospital** (21 College Ave., DeFuniak Springs, tel. 904/892–5171), **Humana Hospital-Destin** (996 Airport Rd., Destin, tel. 904/654–7600), **Humana Hospital-Fort Walton Beach** (1000 Mar-Walt Dr., Fort Walton Beach, tel. 904/862–1111), **HCA Twin Cities Hospital** (2190 N. Rte. 85, Niceville, tel. 904/678–4131), **HCA Gulf Coast Hospital** (449 W. 23rd St., Panama City, tel. 904/769–8341), **Bay Medical Center** (615 N. Bonita Ave., Panama City, tel. 904/769–1511), **Baptist Hospital** (1000 W. Marina St., Pensacola, tel. 904/434–4011), **HCA West Florida Regional Medical Center** (8383 N. Davis Hwy., Pensacola, tel. 904/478–4460).

Exploring the Panhandle

Numbers in the margin correspond to points of interest on the Panhandle map.

Pensacola, with its antebellum homes and historic landmarks, is a good place to start your trek through northwest Florida. After a browse through its museums and a stroll through the preservation districts, begin heading east on U.S. 98. Don't overlook the deserted beaches along the Gulf of Mexico, where the sugar-white quartz-crystal sand crunches underfoot like snow on a sub-zero night. The next point of interest is Fort Walton Beach, the Emerald Coast's largest city and the hub of its vacation activity, with shops and restaurants galore. From Fort Walton, swing north on Rte. 85 to Niceville/Valparaiso, on Choctawhatchee Bay, considered one of the world's most beautiful "sandboxes." The explorer's itinerary calls next for a run up Rte. 85 to Crestview, then to I–10 to DeFuniak Springs and down U.S. 331 to its junction with Rte. 20 at Freeport. A drive along Rte. 20— a two-laner that twists along Choctawhatchee Bay and through the piney woods past bait shacks and catfish restaurants— is a great way to see the other Florida. Proceed on Rte. 20 to Rte. 79 just beyond Ebro, then head south to Panama City Beach, a resort community with a wealth of varied leisure activities. Consider making this a base for some interesting side trips. Afterward, circle back toward Destin, but take time for a meander through the backwaters and byroads that spur off the main drag.

Pensacola

Spanish conquistadors, under the command of Don Tristan de Luna, made landfall on the shores of Pensacola Bay in 1559, but, discouraged by a succession of destructive tropical storms and dissension in the ranks, De Luna abandoned the settlement two years after its founding. In 1698, the Spanish once again established a fort at the site. During the early 18th century, control jockeyed back and forth between the Spanish, the French, and the British and ultimately, in 1819, landed in the hands of the United States. During the Civil War, **Pensacola** came under the governance of the Confederate States of America, so by the time the 20th century rolled around, the flags of five different nations had flown over this fine, old southern city; hence its nickname, the City of Five Flags.

1

Today, historic Pensacola consists of three distinct districts—Seville, Palafox, and North Hill—though they are easy to explore as a unit. Stroll down streets mapped out by the British and renamed by the Spanish, such as Cervantes, Palafox, Intendencia, and Tarragona. Be warned, though, that it is best to stick to the beaten path; Pensacola is a port town and can get rough around the edges, especially at night.

The best way to orient yourself is to stop at the **Pensacola Convention & Visitors Information Center** (1401 E. Gregory St., tel. 904/434–1234 or 800/874–1234). Located at the foot of the Three-Mile Bridge over Pensacola Bay, it's easy to find. You

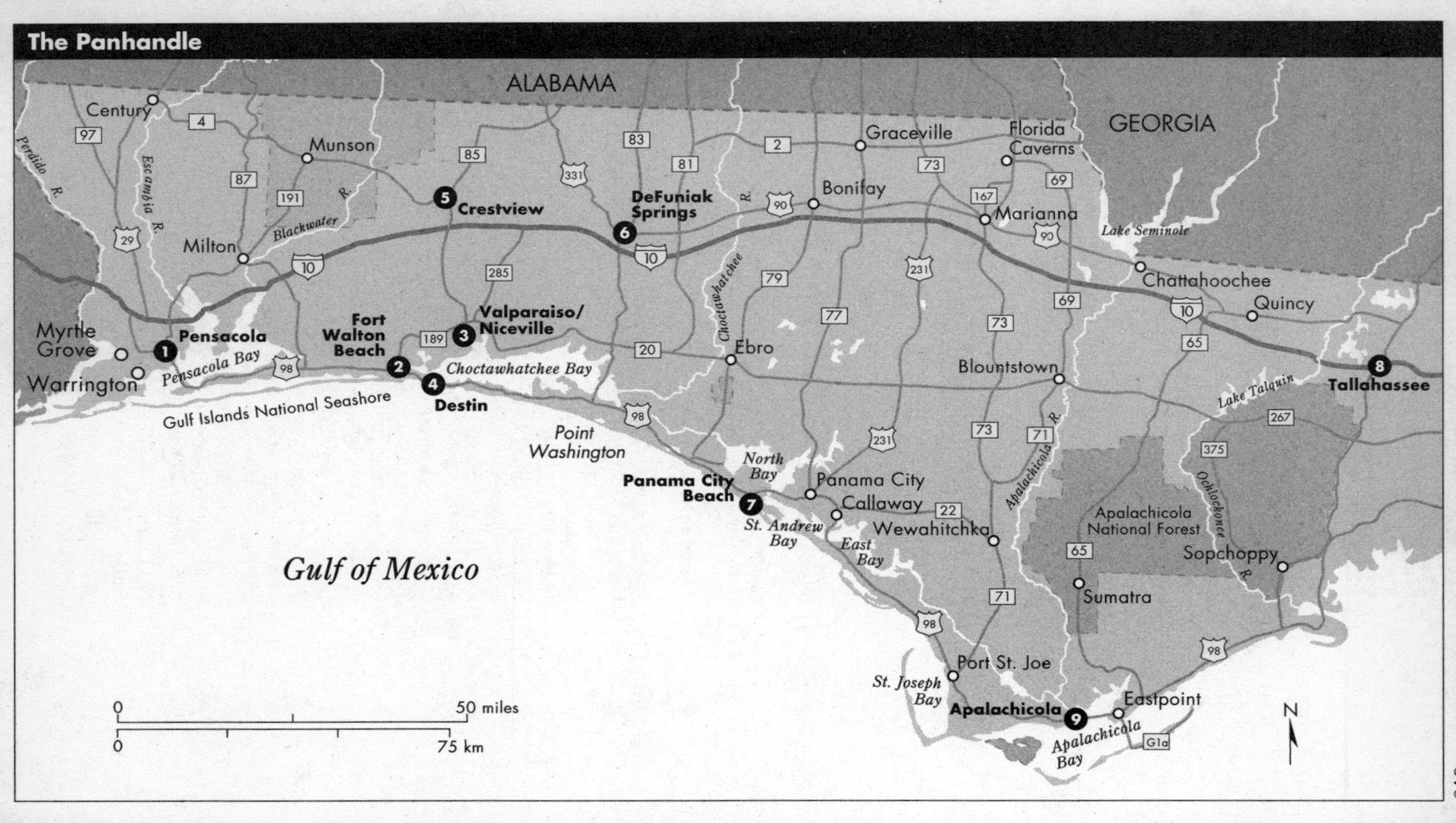
The Panhandle
ALABAMA
GEORGIA
Gulf of Mexico
Pensacola
Fort Walton Beach
Valparaiso/ Niceville
Destin
Crestview
DeFuniak Springs
Panama City Beach
Tallahassee
Apalachicola
Myrtle Grove
Warrington
Century
Milton
Munson
Graceville
Bonifay
Florida Caverns
Marianna
Chattahoochee
Quincy
Ebro
Blountstown
Panama City
Callaway
Wewahitchka
Port St. Joe
Sumatra
Sopchoppy
Eastpoint
Point Washington
Apalachicola National Forest
Gulf Islands National Seashore
Pensacola Bay
Choctawhatchee Bay
North Bay
St. Andrew Bay
East Bay
St. Joseph Bay
Apalachicola Bay
Lake Seminole
Lake Talquin
Perdido R.
Escambia R.
Blackwater R.
Choctawhatchee R.
Apalachicola R.
Ochlockonee R.
N
0
50 miles
0
75 km

can pick up maps of the self-guided historic district tours and other information.

Approaching from the east, the first historic district you reach is **Seville**—the site of Pensacola's first permanent Spanish colonial settlement. Its center is Seville Square, a live oak-shaded park bounded by Alcaniz, Adams, Zaragoza, and Government streets. Park your car and roam these brick streets past honeymoon cottages and bay-front homes. Many of the buildings have been restored and converted into restaurants, commercial offices, and shops where you can buy anything from wind socks to designer clothes.

Continue west to Palafox Street, the main stem of the **Palafox Historic District.** This was the commercial and government hub of old Pensacola. On Palafox Place, note the Spanish Renaissance-style Saenger Theater, Pensacola's old movie palace; and the Bear Block, a former wholesale grocery with wrought-iron balconies that are a legacy from Pensacola's Creole past. Though the San Carlos Hotel has been closed for many years, in its heyday the Mediterranean-style building at Palafox and Garden streets was the proper place for business tycoons and military officers to savor their cigars and brandies and where Pensacola's elite dined after the theater and introduced their daughters to society. Nearby, on Palafox between Government and Zaragoza streets, is a statue of Andrew Jackson that commemorates the formal transfer of Florida from Spain to the United States in 1821.

Palafox Street also funnels into the **North Hill Preservation District,** where Pensacola's affluent families, many made rich during the turn-of-the-century timber boom, built their homes on ground where British and Spanish fortresses once stood. To this day residents occasionally unearth cannonballs while digging in their gardens. North Hill occupies 50 blocks that consist of more than 500 homes in Queen Anne, neoclassical, Tudor Revival, and Mediterranean architectural styles. Take a drive through this community, but remember these are private residences not open to the public. Places of general interest in the district include the 1902 Spanish mission-style Christ Episcopal Church; Lee Square, where a 50-foot-high obelisk stands as Pensacola's tribute to the Old Confederacy; and Fort George, an undeveloped parcel of land at the site of the largest of three forts built by the British in 1778.

From the North Hill district, go south on Palafox Street to Zaragoza Street to reach the **Historic Pensacola Village,** a cluster of museums between Adams and Tarragona. The **Museum of Industry,** housed in a late 19th-century warehouse, hosts permanent exhibits dedicated to the lumber, maritime, and shipping industries—once mainstays of Pensacola's economy. A reproduction of a 19th-century streetscape is displayed in the **Museum of Commerce,** while the city's historical archives are kept in the **Pensacola Historical Museum**—what was once Old Christ Church, one of Florida's oldest churches. Also in the village are the **Julee Cottage Museum of Black History, Dorr House, Lavalle House,** and **Quina House.** *Pensacola Village Information Center, tel. 904/444–8905. Admission: free. Open Mon.–Sat. 10–4:30; Pensacola Historical Museum, tel. 904/433–1559. Open Mon.–Sat. 9–4:30.*

In the days of the horse-drawn paddy wagon the two-story mission revival building housing the **Pensacola Museum of Art** served as the city jail. *Admission free. 407 S. Jefferson St., tel. 904/432-5682. Open Tues.-Fri. 10-5, Sat. 10-4.*

Pensacola's 1908 old City Hall has been refurbished and reopened as the **T. T. Wentworth Jr., Florida State Museum.** The Wentworth displays some 150,000 artifacts ranging from Civil War weaponry to bottle caps. Representing more than 80 years of collecting, the assemblage is worth over $5 million. *333 S. Jefferson St., tel. 904/444-8905. Admission: $5 adults, $4.50 senior citizens, $2 children over 4. Open Mon.-Sat. 10-4:30.*

From the port, take Palafox Street to U.S. 98 (Garden St.) to reach the **Pensacola Naval Air Station** (tel. 904/452-2311). Established in 1914, it is the nation's oldest such facility. On display in the **National Museum of Naval Aviation** are more than 100 aircraft that have played an important role in naval aviation history. Among them are the NC-4, which in 1919 became the first plane to cross the Atlantic by air; the famous World War II fighter, the F6F *Hellcat;* and the *Skylab Command Module*. Thirty-minute films on aeronautical topics are shown, June-August. Call for details. The National Park Service-protected **Fort Barrancas,** established during the Civil War, is also located at the NAS. Nearby are picnic tables and a half-mile woodland nature trail. *Navy Blvd. (off U.S. 98), tel. 904/455-5167. Admission free. Open daily 9-5.*

Fort Walton Beach

❷ **Fort Walton Beach** dates from the Civil War years when patriots loyal to the Confederate cause organized Walton's Guard (named in honor of Colonel George Walton, one-time acting territorial governor of West Florida) and made camp on Santa Rosa Sound, the site that would come later to be known as Camp Walton. In 1940, fewer than 90 people lived in Fort Walton Beach, but thanks to the development of Eglin Field during World War II, and New Deal money spent for new roads and bridges, within a decade the city became a boom town. Today, Greater Fort Walton Beach has more than 78,000 residents, making it the largest urban area on the Emerald Coast. The military is Fort Walton Beach's main source of income, but tourism runs a close second to it.

Eglin Air Force Base encompasses 728 square miles of land, has 10 auxiliary fields (including Hurlburt and Duke fields), and a total of 21 runways. Jimmie Doolittle's Tokyo Raiders trained here, as did the Son Tay Raiders, a group that made a daring attempt to rescue American POWs from a North Vietnamese prison camp in 1970. Tours leave from the officers club at the base. The main gate is on U.S. 98 northeast of Fort Walton Beach. Tour tickets, which are free, may be picked up at the **Niceville/Valparaiso Chamber of Commerce,** or from the museum (*see* below). *Tel. 904/678-2323. Tours Jan.-Mar. and June-Aug., Mon., Wed., Fri. 9:30-noon.*

Just outside Eglin's main gate on U.S. 98, is the **Air Force Armament Museum,** with an uncluttered display of more than 5,000 articles of Air Force armaments from World Wars I and II, and the Korean and Vietnam wars. Included are uniforms, engines, weapons, aircraft, and flight simulators; larger craft such as transport planes and swept-wing jets are exhibited on the grounds outside the museum. A 32-minute movie about Eglin's history and its role in the development of armaments is presented continuously throughout the day. *Rte. 85, Eglin Air Force Base, tel. 904/882–4062. Admission free. Open daily 9:30–4:30.*

Artifacts reflecting the cultural, artistic, technological, and spiritual achievements of the many prehistoric peoples who have inhabited northwest Florida during the past 10,000 years are on exhibit at the **Indian Temple Mound Museum.** Of special interest are the funerary masks and weaponry of these pre-Columbian tribes. The museum is adjacent to the 600-year-old National Historic Landmark Temple Mound, which is a large earthwork built over saltwater. *139 Miracle Strip Pkwy. (U.S. 98), tel. 904/243–6521. Admission: 75¢ adults, children 12 and under free. Open Sept.–May, Mon.–Fri. 11–4, Sat. 9–4; June–Aug., Mon. to Sat. 9–4.*

A 2-mile jaunt east on U.S. 98 will bring you to the **Gulfarium**—a great way to spend a few hours when bad weather drives you off the beach. The Gulfarium's main attraction is its "Living Sea" presentation, in a 60,000-gallon tank, that simulates conditions on the ocean bottom. There are performances by trained porpoises, sea lion shows, and marine life exhibits featuring seals, otters, and penguins. There's also an extensive gift shop where you can buy anything from conch shells and sand-dollar earrings to children's beach toys. *U.S. 98E, tel. 904/244–5169. Admission: $12 adults, $8 children 4–11, children under 3 free. Open May–Sept., daily 9–6; Oct.–Apr., daily 9–4.*

Valparaiso/Niceville

There aren't many places in the country where you can find people who were involved in the city's chartering activities and who are alive and well and currently serving on the local boards of directors. You can in **Valparaiso** and **Niceville,** however. The Twin Cities, as they are often called, are still in their youth, having been granted their charters in 1921 and 1938, respectively.

Niceville evolved from a tiny fishing hamlet called Boggy, whose sandy-bottomed bays were rich in mullet. Valparaiso, on the other hand, didn't evolve. An entrepreneurial Chicagoan named John B. Perrine envisioned Valparaiso as an ideal city by the sea, or "vale of paradise." Together, the cities have maintained an uncomplicated and serene existence, one relatively untouched by the tourist trade farther south. But that may change as word gets out about the abundance of opportunities to waterski, fish, and sail.

The history of the Twin Cities and surrounding counties is on display in Valparaiso's **Historical Society Museum.** Take a step back in time among 8,000-year-old stone tools and early-20th-century iron pots and kettles. A rarity on display here is a steam-powered, belt-driven cotton gin. The museum also maintains a reference library of genealogical and historical research materials and official Civil War records. *115 Westview Ave., tel. 904/678–2615. Admission free. Open Tues.–Sat. 11–4.*

East of Niceville, off Rte. 20 on Rocky Bayou, are 50 excellent picnic areas, nature trails, boat ramps, and uncrowded campsites with electrical and water hookups in the **Fred Gannon Rocky Bayou State Recreational Area** (tel. 904/833-9144). It's quiet and secluded, yet easy-to-find, and a great venue for serious bikers.

Destin

4 A fishing village since the mid-1830s, **Destin** was founded by Leonard A. Destin, a New London, Connecticut, sea captain who sailed in and settled his family near the strait that connects Choctawhatchee Bay with the Gulf of Mexico. Life remained calm here until the strait, or East Pass, was bridged in 1935. Then, recreational anglers discovered its white sands, blue-green waters, and the abundance of some of the most sought-after sport fish in the world. More billfish are hauled in around Destin each year than from all other Gulf fishing ports combined. But you don't have to be the rod-and-reel type to love Destin. You could stay in Destin for a month and still not try every gourmet restaurant in the area. There's also plenty to entertain the sand-pail set as well as seniors who ask for nothing more than a chance to sprawl in the sun and soak up its rays.

The Destin Fishing Museum has a dry aquarium where lighting and sound effects create the sensation of being underwater. You can get the feeling of walking on a sandy bottom that's dotted with sponges while viewing the species of fish indigenous to the Gulf of Mexico. *35 U.S. 98E, tel. 904/654-1011. Admission: $1 adults, children under 12 free. Open Tues.-Sat. noon-4, Sun. 1-4.*

Drive east on U.S. 98 for about 8 miles to the **Museum of the Sea and Indian,** where there are exhibits on marine life in the Gulf of Mexico as well as the seven seas of the world. Artifacts from both North and South American Indian tribes also are displayed here. *4801 Beach Hwy. (off U.S. 98), tel. 904/837-6625. Admission: $3.75 adults, $2 children. Open summer, daily 8-7; winter, daily 9-4.*

In the **Eden State Gardens,** 25 miles east of Destin on U.S. 98, an antebellum mansion, with colonnaded porticoes and upstairs galleries that wrap the entire house, is set amid an arcade of moss-draped live oaks and is open to the public for touring. Furnishings in the spacious rooms date from several periods as far back as the 17th century. The surrounding gardens are beautiful year-round, but they're nothing short of spectacular in mid-March when the azaleas and dogwoods are in full bloom. *County Rte. 395, Point Washington, tel. 904/231-4214. Admission to gardens free; mansion tour $1.50. Open daily 8 AM-sunset. Mansion tours Thurs.-Mon. 9-4 hourly.*

Seaside has all the features of Cape Cod, right here in Florida. "A new town with the old ways," Seaside, with its Victorian fretwork, white picket fences, and captain's walks, is contrived. But the pastel paint jobs, latticework, and Adirondack chairs also make this community stunning. Open-air markets for shoppers and old-fashioned ice-cream parlors for the kids add up to a memorable way to spend a tranquil afternoon. *County Rte. 30A (off U.S. 98), 25 mi east of Destin, tel. 904/231-4224.*

Crestview/DeFuniak Springs

By linking Crestview and DeFuniak Springs to neighboring cities, the railroads did for these landlocked Panhandle towns what the military did for the settlements along the Gulf shore. When the Louisville & Nashville Railroad Company completed a line through northwest Florida in 1882, its surveyors dubbed the area **Crestview** because, at 235 feet above sea level, it had the highest altitude in the state. **DeFuniak Springs,** on the other hand, was so named to flatter the then-prominent L & N official Ernest A. DeFuniak.

The Okaloosa county seat of Crestview is also known as the Hub City of northwest Florida because of its location at the junction of three major highways. Crestview makes no bones about being a small town where folks enjoy roller-skating, playing softball, or packing a picnic lunch and taking off to the woods. But it is not without its cultural accomplishments, such as the **Robert L. F. Sikes Public Library** and research center that houses more than 44,000 volumes within a stately Greek Revival building.

DeFuniak Springs brags about its culture, too. In 1885 it was chosen as the location for the New York Chautauqua's winter assembly. It was also the site of the Knox Hill Academy, the only institution of higher learning in northwest Florida for more than half a century after its founding in 1848. The Chautauqua programs were discontinued in 1922, but DeFuniak Springs attempts to revive them, in spirit at least, with a county-wide Chautauqua Festival it sponsors every May.

Another legacy from the Chautauqua era is the **Walton-DeFuniak Public Library,** by all accounts Florida's oldest library continuously operating in its original building. This tiny facility, measuring 16 by 24 feet, opened in 1887 to make reference and recreational reading material available to the Chautauqua crowd. At present, it contains nearly 28,000 volumes, including rare books, many of which are older than the building itself. The collection has grown over the years to include an impressive display of European armor that can easily compete with similar exhibits twice its size. *100 Circle Dr., tel. 904/892-3624. Open Mon. 9–7, Tues.–Fri. 9–6, Sat. 9–3.*

Panama City Beach

A vacation spot with mass appeal, **Panama City Beach** is about 5 miles south and to the west of Panama City proper. In spite of shoulder-to-shoulder condominiums, motels, and amusement parks that make it seem like one big carnival ground, Panama City Beach has a natural beauty that excuses its overcommercialization. The incredible white sands, navigable waterways, and plentiful marine life that attracted Spanish conquistadors and gave sustenance to the settlers early on, are a lure to today's family-vacation industry. Peak season for Panama City is June–September, and during spring break.

Time Out **Pineapple Willie's** brings together the best elements of a discotheque and a Wild West saloon, and caters to the 25- to 40-year-old crowd. If you feel overwhelmed by the live entertainment, you can escape to the serenity of a seaside deck. *On Beach Blvd. at Thomas Dr., tel. 904/235-0928. AE, MC, V.*

At the eastern tip of Panama City Beach is the **St. Andrews State Recreation Area,** which comprises 1,038 acres of beaches, pinewoods, and marshes. There are complete camping facilities here, as well as ample opportunities to swim, pier fish, or hike the dunes over clearly marked nature trails. You can board a ferry to **Shell Island**—a barrier island in the Gulf of Mexico that offers some of the best shelling north of Sanibel Island.

About 40 miles southeast of Panama City Beach on U.S. 98 at **Port St. Joe** is the spot where Florida's first constitution was drafted in 1838. Most of the old town, including the original hall, is gone—wiped out by hurricanes—but the exhibits in the **Constitution Convention State Museum** recall the event. There are also provisions for camping and picnicking in a small park surrounding the museum. *200 Island Memorial Way, tel. 904/229–8029. Open Thurs.–Mon. 9–5. Closed noon–1. Admission: 50¢ per person, children under 6 free.*

From Panama City, head north for a two-hour drive on U.S. 231 to Rte. 167 to visit the 1,783-acre **Florida Caverns State Park.** Take a ranger-led spelunking tour to see an array of stalactites, stalagmites, and "waterfalls" of solid rock. If the underground bit isn't your thing, the park also has hiking trails, campsites, and areas for swimming and canoeing on the Chipola River. *Rte. 167, tel. 904/482–9598. Admission to park: $3.25 per vehicle and driver, 50¢ each additional person, children under 6 free; admission to caverns: $4 adults, $2 children 6–12. Open daily 8 AM–sunset; cavern tours 9–4.*

Falling Waters State Recreation Area is about an hour's drive north on Rte. 77 from Panama City. One of Florida's most recognized geological features is the Falling Waters Sink, a 100-foot-deep cylindrical pit that provides the background for a waterfall. There's an observation deck for viewing this natural phenomenon. *Rte. 77A, tel. 904/638–6130. Admission: $3.25 per vehicle with up to 8 people. Open daily 8 AM–sunset.*

Tallahassee

Interstate 10 rolls over the timid beginnings of the Appalachian foothills and through thick pines into the state capital, (8) **Tallahassee,** with its canopies of ancient oaks and spring bowers of azaleas. Among the best canopied roads are St. Augustine, Miccosukee, Meridian, Old Bainbridge, and Centerville. Country stores and antebellum plantation homes still dot these roads, much as they did in earlier days.

In the heart of the city, stop at the **Tallahassee Area Convention and Visitors Bureau** to pick up information about the capital and the surrounding area. The bureau, housed in **The Columns,** is the city's oldest structure, built in 1833 and moved in 1970 to its present location. *200 W. College Ave., tel. 904/681–9200 or 800/628–2866. Open weekdays 8–5.*

The downtown **Capitol Complex area** is compact enough for walking, but is also served by a free, continuous shuttle trolley. It's a pleasant walk to the **Old Capitol,** originally a pre-Civil War structure. It has been added to and subtracted from but now has been restored to the way it looked in 1902, with its jaunty awnings and combination gas-electric lights. *Monroe St. at Apalachee Pkwy., tel. 904/487–1902. Admission free.*

Self-guided or guided tours weekdays 9–4:30, Sat. 10–4:30, Sun. noon–4:30.

The **Union Bank Building,** built in 1833, is Florida's oldest bank building. Since the time it closed in 1843, it has played many roles, from ballet school to bakery. It's been restored to what is thought to be its original appearance as a bank. *Monroe St. at Apalachee Pkwy., tel. 904/487–3803. Admission free. Open Tues.–Fri. 10–1, weekends 1–4.*

At the **Museum of Florida History,** the long, intriguing story of the state's role in history—from prehistoric times of mastodons to the present, with the launching of space shuttles—is told in lucid and entertaining ways. *500 S. Bronough St., tel. 904/488–1673. Admission free. Open weekdays 9–4:30, Sat. 10–4:30, Sun. and holidays noon–4:30.*

On a clear day, from the 22nd floor of the **New Capitol,** you can catch a panoramic view of Tallahassee and its surrounding countryside. *Duvall St., tel. 904/488–6167. Admission free. Hourly tours of the New Capitol, weekdays 9–4, weekends 11–3.*

San Luis Archaeological and Historic Site focuses on the archaeology of 17th-century Spanish mission and Apalachee Indian townsites. In its heyday, in 1675, the Apalachee village here had a population of at least 1,400. Threatened by Creek Indians and British forces in 1704, the locals burned the village and fled. *2020 W. Mission Rd., tel. 904/487–3711. 1-hr guided tours weekdays noon, Sat. 11 and 3, Sun. 2.*

A short drive north of Tallahassee, off U.S. 27 is **Lake Jackson,** a resource bass fishermen hold in reverence. Sightseers view, along the shores of the lake, Indian mounds and the ruins of an early-19th-century plantation built by Colonel Robert Butler, adjutant to General Andrew Jackson during the siege of New Orleans. *Indian Mound Rd., off U.S. 27, tel. 904/562–0042. Admission free. Open 8 AM–sunset.*

Five miles north of town on U.S. 319 is the magnificent **Maclay State Gardens.** In springtime the grounds are afire with azaleas, dogwood, and other showy or rare annuals, trees, and shrubs. Allow at least half a day for wandering the paths past the reflecting pool, into the tiny walled garden, and around the lakes and woodlands. The Maclay residence, furnished as it was in the 1920s, as well as picnic grounds, and swimming and boating facilities, are open to the public. *3540 Thomasville Rd. (1 mi north of I–10), tel. 904/487–4556. Admission: $3.50 per vehicle, with up to 8 people. Open daily 8 AM–sunset.*

Lafayette Vineyards, a mile west of exit 31-A off I–10, is a gleaming, modern winery set among timeless vineyards. In 1812, these lands were granted by President Monroe to the Marquis de Lafayette in gratitude for his role in the American Revolution. French settlers planted the vines, and today award-winning wines catch the attention of oenophiles nationwide. Engage in the entertaining slide show, winery tour, and wine tastings (juice is also available). Wines are sold by the case or bottle at discount prices. *Tel. 904/878–9041 or 800/768–WINE. Admission free. Open Mon.–Sat. 10–6, Sun. noon–6.*

In 1865, Confederate soldiers stood firm against a Yankee advance on St. Marks. The Rebs held, saving Tallahassee—the only southern capital east of the Mississippi that never fell to the Union. The **Natural Bridge Battlefield State Historic Site,** about 10 miles southeast of the capital, marks the victory, and is a good place for a hike and a picnic. *Natural Bridge Rd. (Rte. 354), off U.S. 363 in Woodville, tel. 904/922–6007. Admission free. Open daily 8 AM–sunset.*

Wakulla Springs, about 15 miles south of Tallahassee on Rte. 61, is one of the deepest springs in the world. The wilderness remains relatively untouched, retaining the wild and exotic look it had in the 1930s, when Tarzan movies were made here. Aboard glass-bottom boats, visitors probe deep into the lush, jungle-lined waterways to catch glimpses of alligators, snakes, waterfowl, and nesting limpkin. More than 154 bird species can be spotted in a teeming wilderness that also hosts raccoon, gray squirrel, and an encyclopedia of southern flora. *1 Springs Dr., Wakulla Springs, tel. 904/222–7279. Admission: $3.25 per vehicle with up to 8 people. Boat tours $4.50 adults, $2.25 children. Tours daily 9–5:30. Springs open daily 8 AM–sunset.*

Time Out The **Wakulla Springs Lodge and Conference Center** (tel. 904/224–5950), located on the grounds, serves three meals a day in a sunny, spartan room that also seems little changed from the 1930s. Schedule lunch here to sample the famous bean soup, home-baked muffins, and a slab of pie.

About 25 miles south of Tallahassee along the coast is the **St. Marks Wildlife Refuge and Lighthouse.** The once-powerful Fort San Marcos de Apalache was built here in 1639. Stones salvaged from the fort went into building the lighthouse, which is still in operation today. Exhibits are on display at the visitor center. *C.R. 59 (3 mi south of the Newport and U.S. 98 intersection) in St. Marks, tel. 904/925–6121. Admission: $3 per car. Refuge open sunrise–sunset; visitor center open weekdays 8–4:15, weekends 10–5.*

Apalachicola

A scenic 90-minute drive west along U.S. 98, will bring you to **(9) Apalachicola,** the state's most important oyster fishery. Visit the **Raney House,** circa 1850; **Trinity Episcopal Church,** built from prefabricated parts in 1838; and the **John Gorrie State Museum.** In this museum, the physician who is credited with inventing ice-making and air-conditioning is honored. Exhibits of Apalachicola history are displayed here as well. *John Gorrie State Museum, Ave. C and Sixth St., tel. 904/653–9347. Admission: 50¢ adults, children under 6 free. Open Thurs.–Mon. 9–5.*

If the outdoors are an important part of your travels, explore **Fort Gadsden State Historic Site,** on the river north of Apalachicola at Sumatra, and **St. George Island State Park.** St. George is reached by a causeway from Eastpoint, where you can drive toward the sea along the narrow spit of land with its dunes, sea oats, and abundant bird life. *Fort Gadsden, tel. 904/670–8988. St. George Island State Park, tel. 904/927–2111. Admission: $3.25 per vehicle with up to 8 people. Open 8 AM–sunset.*

Spreading north of Apalachicola and west of Tallahassee is the **Apalachicola National Forest** where you can camp, hike, picnic, fish, or swim. Just above the forest, on the east bank of the Apalachicola River south of I–10, is **Torreya State Park,** with campsites, hiking trails, and an antebellum mansion. *Torreya State Park, tel. 904/643–2674. Admission: $2 per vehicle. Open daily 8 AM–sunset.*

What to See and Do with Children

Fast Eddie's Fun Center (W St. at Michigan, Pensacola, tel. 904/433–7735) features kiddie rides, a video room, air hockey, and basketball.

The Zoo (5701 Gulf Breeze Pkwy., Gulf Breeze, tel. 904/932–2229) is home to plants, animals, and 30 acres of ponds, lakes, and open plains.

Island Golf Center (1306 Miracle Strip Pkwy., Fort Walton Beach, tel. 904/244–1612) has 36 holes of miniature golf, a nine-hole par-three course, pool tables, and video games.

Museum of the Sea and Indian (4801 Beach Hwy., Destin. tel. 904/837–6625) (*see* Destin, above).

The Track Recreation Center (1125 U.S. 98, Destin, tel. 904/654–4668) is a special theme park with go-cart tracks and rides.

Big Kahuna's Lost Paradise (U.S. 98, Destin, tel. 904/837–4061) is a water park with miniature golf and an amphitheater.

Shipwreck Island (12000 U.S. 98W, Panama City Beach, tel. 904/234–2282) features 6 acres of water rides for kids and adults of all ages.

Miracle Strip Amusement Park (12000 U.S. 98W, Panama City Beach, tel. 904/234–5810) has 30 rides, including a roller coaster with a 65-foot drop.

Gulf World (15412 Front Beach Rd., Panama City Beach, tel. 904/234–5271) performers include a bottle-nosed dolphin, porpoises, seals, otters, and sea lions.

Tallahassee Junior Museum features a collection of old cars and carriages, a red caboose, nature trails, a snake exhibit, and a restored plantation home. *3945 Museum Dr., Tallahassee, tel. 904/576–1636. Admission: $5 adults, $4 senior citizens, $3 children 4–15, under 4 free. Open Mon.–Sat. 9–5, Sun. 12:30–5.*

Off the Beaten Track

Take I–110 from downtown Pensacola to I–10. About 40 miles northeast is **Blackwater River State Park** (tel. 904/623–2363), in Holt. Park the car, stretch your legs, and take advantage of what is regarded as one of the cleanest rivers in the country. Don't be fooled by the dark color of the Blackwater River, though. It's the result of the tannic acid that leaches into it from the cypress trees along its banks. The river's shallow waters offer the best canoeing in the area; the largest, whitest sandbars; plus the scenic beauty of the magnolias and cedars in the surrounding Blackwater River State Forest. Canoeing fans will enjoy the special challenges of a paddle up Sweetwater/Juniper Creek, whose sandbars and cliffs call for more maneuvering and technical skill. Okay—so you didn't bring your own canoe. Not to worry. **Blackwater Canoe Rental** (U.S. 90E, Milton, tel. 904/623–0235) provides complete round-trip service (*see* Participant Sports, below). These friendly folks will meet you at the end point of the trip, transport you upstream, and launch you on your way. The river winds around so that you'll end up back at your car, where you simply beach your canoe, without having to wait or load the gear yourself.

Back on U.S. 98, head east over the 3-mile-long Pensacola Bay Bridge and cross the bridge to Santa Rosa Island. This barrier reef offers more than seascapes and water sports. It's also a must-see for bird-watchers. Since 1971 more than 280 species of birds from the common loon to the majestic osprey have been spotted here. Two caveats for visitors: "Leave nothing behind but your footprints," and "don't pick the sea oats" (natural grasses that help keep the dunes intact). At Santa Rosa Island's western tip is **Fort Pickens National Park,** where there are a museum, nature exhibits, aquariums, and a campground with more than 180 campsites, many with electrical hookups. Fort Pickens's most famous resident was Apache Indian chief Geronimo. Legend has it that he became a fairly likable fellow before he was transferred to Oklahoma's Fort Sill for his final incarceration. *Ranger station at Fort Pickens Rd., tel. 904/934–2635. Admission: $3 per car. Open daily 8:30–4.*

Proceed along Rte. 399 from Fort Pickens to **Navarre Beach,** a small, relaxed niche without the traffic and congestion common to most resort areas, but with amenities ranging from luxury condominiums to unspoiled campgrounds. It's the halfway point between Pensacola and Fort Walton Beach. To reach Fort Walton Beach, cross over the Navarre Bridge to U.S. 98.

Shopping

Cordova Mall (511 N. Ninth Ave., Pensacola, tel. 904/477–7562) is anchored by four department stores in addition to its specialty shops and a food court with 13 fast-food outlets. **Harbourtown Shopping Village** (913 Gulf Breeze Pkwy., Gulf Breeze, no phone) has trendy shops and the ambience of a wharfside New England village. There are four department stores in the **Santa Rosa Mall** (300 Mary Esther Cut-off, Mary Esther, tel. 904/244–2172), as well as 118 other shops and 15 bistro-style eateries. Stores in the **Manufacturer's Outlet Centers** (127 U.S. 98W, Fort Walton Beach, and 105 W. 23rd St., Panama City, no phone) offer well-known brands of clothing and accessories at a substantial discount. **The Market at Sandestin** (5494 U.S. 98E, tel. 904/654–5588) has 27 upscale shops that peddle such wares as gourmet chocolates and designer clothes in an elegant minimall with boardwalks. **The Panama City Mall** (U.S. 231 and Rte. 77, Panama City, tel. 904/785–9587) has a mix of more than 100 franchise shops and national chain stores.

Participant Sports

Biking Some of the nation's best bike paths run through northwest Florida's woods and dunelands, particularly on Santa Rosa Island where you can pedal for 50 miles and never lose sight of the ocean. Routes through Eglin AFB Reservation present cyclists with a few challenges. Biking here requires a $3 permit, which may be obtained at **Jackson Guard Forestry** (tel. 904/882–4164). Rentals are available from **Bob's Bicycle Center** (Fort Walton Beach, tel. 904/243–5856) and at **The Wheel Works** (Fort Walton Beach, tel. 904/244–5252).

Boating There are niches for boaters of all classes in northwest Florida's sheltered inlets and lazy rivers, as well as in the open waters of its bays and the Gulf of Mexico. You can rent powerboats for fishing, skiing, and snorkeling at **Club Nautico** (320 U.S. 98E, Destin, tel. 904/837–6811, and U.S. 98E, Sandestin, tel. 904/267–8123). Pontoon-boat rentals for the more laid-back water enthusiast are available at **Consigned RV's** (101 W. Miracle Strip Pkwy., Fort Walton Beach, tel. 904/243–4488).

Canoeing Both beginners and veterans will get a kick out of canoeing the Florida Panhandle's abundance of rivers and streams. The shoals and rapids in the Blackwater River in the Blackwater River State Forest will challenge even the most seasoned canoeist, while the gentler currents in the sheltered marshes and inlets are less intimidating. Canoe rentals are readily available from **Blackwater Canoe Rental** (U.S. 90E., Milton, tel. 904/623–0235) and at **Adventures Unlimited** (12 mi north of Milton on Rte. 87, tel. 904/623–6197). For a trip down Econfina Creek, "Florida's most beautiful canoe trail," rentals are supplied by **Econfina Creek Canoe Livery, Inc.** (north of Rte. 20 on Strickland Rd., tel. 904/722–9032). Contact **TNT Hideway** (St. Marks, tel. 904/925–6412) to canoe the Wakulla River, near Tallahassee.

Diving A breathtaking world of adventure and beauty awaits below the water's surface where you can observe colorful fish and marine life or, if you're in the Panama City Beach area, investigate the wreckage of sunken tanker ships, tugboats, and cargo vessels. For snorkelers and beginning divers, the jetties of St. Andrews State Recreation Area, where there is no boat traffic, are safe. Wreck dives are offered by **Diver's Den** (3804 Thomas Dr., tel. 904/234–8717) or **Panama City Dive Center** (4823 Thomas Dr., tel. 904/235–3390). In the Destin-Fort Walton Beach area, you can arrange for diving instruction and excursions through **Aquanaut Scuba Center, Inc.** (24 U.S. 98W, Destin, tel. 904/837–0359) or **The Scuba Shop** (348 Miracle Strip Pkwy., Fort Walton Beach, tel. 904/243–1600).

Fishing Northwest Florida's fishing options range from fishing for pompano, snapper, marlin, and grouper—in the saltwater of the Gulf of Mexico—to angling for bass, catfish, and bluegill in the freshwaters of the region. All fisherfolk, except Florida residents 65 years or older, children under 16, and anyone fishing from a licensed charter boat, must have fishing licenses, which are available at tackle shops, and hardware and sporting-goods stores where fishing tackle is sold. You can buy bait and tackle at **Stewart's Outdoor Sports** (4 Eglin Pkwy., Fort Walton Beach, tel. 904/243–9443; 1025 Palm Plaza, Niceville, tel. 904/678–4804), at **Panama City Beach Pier Tackle Shop** (16101 Front Beach Rd., Panama City, tel. 904/235–2576), or at **Penny's Sporting Goods** (1800 Pace Blvd., Pensacola, tel. 904/438–9633). If your idea of fishing is to drop a line off the end of a pier, you can fish from **Old Pensacola Bay Bridge** or from the 3,000-foot-long **Destin Catwalk,** along the East Pass Bridge. For \$2 adults, \$1.50 children, \$1 observer, you can also fish from Panama City Beach's **city pier.**

Deep-Sea Fishing Charters When planning an excursion, be advised that rates for renting deep-sea fishing boat are usually quoted by the day (about \$550) or half day (about \$350). This is an immensely popular pastime on the Emerald Coast, so there are boat charters aplenty. Among them are **Miller's Charter Services**/*Barbi-Anne* (off U.S. 98 on the docks next to A.J.'s Restaurant, Destin, tel. 904/837–6059), **East Pass Charters** (at East Pass Marina, U.S. 98E, Destin, tel. 904/837–6412), **Lafitte Cove Marina** (1010 Ft. Pickens Rd., Pensacola Beach, tel. 904/932–9241), **The Moorings Marina** (655 Pensacola Beach Blvd., Pensacola Beach, tel. 904/932–0305), and **Rude Roy's Marina** (6400 U.S. 98W, Panama City Beach, tel. 904/235–2809).

Party boats that carry as many as 100 passengers at $35–$40 per head are the cheapest way to go, offering everything from half-day fishing excursions to dinner cruises. The old standbys are ***Capt. Anderson's*** (Captain Anderson Pier, 5550 N. Lagoon Dr., Panama City Beach, tel. 904/234–3435) and ***Emmanuel*** (U.S. 98E, Destin, tel. 904/837–6313).

Golf The Gulf is northwest Florida's number-one asset; golf is number two. **Perdido Bay Resort** (1 Doug Ford Dr., Pensacola, tel. 904/492–1223) has an 18-hole layout with four sets of tees, making it virtually four different courses. **Tiger Point Golf & Country Club** (1255 Country Club Rd., Gulf Breeze, tel. 904/932–1333) offers 36 holes of golf overlooking the natural wonderland of Santa Rosa Sound. **The Club at Hidden Creek** (3070 PGA Blvd., Gulf Breeze, tel. 904/939–4604) has 18 holes that wind through woods of hickory, magnolia, oak, and pine. The 18-hole course at the **Shalimar Pointe Golf & Country Club** (2 Country Club Dr., Shalimar, tel. 904/651–1416) presents a professional challenge, but is forgiving enough for players of all levels. Long, well-groomed fairways rank the 18-hole **Fort Walton Beach golf course** (Rte. 189, Fort Walton Beach, tel. 904/862–3314) one of the state's finest municipal routes. Heavily wooded and enhanced by water and rolling terrain, **Bluewater Bay**'s (Rte. 20, 6 mi east of Niceville, tel. 904/897–3241) 27 championship holes combine to make three different 18-hole courses. **Indian Bayou Golf & Country Club**'s (Airport Rd. off U.S. 98, Destin, tel. 904/837–6192) bunkered, undulating greens make this 7,000-yard course one of the most interesting on the Emerald Coast. **Baytowne Golf Club** (Emerald Coast Pkwy., Destin, tel. 904/267–8155) at the Sandestin Beach Resort is gentler than its sister course, the sticky **Sandestin Links** (Emerald Coast Pkwy., Destin, tel. 904/267–8144), but is no pushover. Tight fairways, cavernous sand traps, and water hazards make the 18-hole course at **Santa Rosa Golf & Beach Club** (County Rte. 30A, Santa Rosa Beach, tel. 904/267–2229) provoking yet memorable. Water, water everywhere and island fairways make the **Lagoon Legend** (100 Delwood Beach Rd., Panama City Beach, tel. 904/234–3307), at Marriott's Bay Point, northwest Florida's answer to the Blue Monster at Doral. Bruce Devlin and Bob von Hagge designed this one to punish the big boys; its complement, the **Club Meadows** (100 Delwood Beach Rd., Panama City Beach, tel. 904/234–3307) course, is kinder and gentler. **Killearn** (100 Tyron Circle, Tallahassee 32308, tel. 904/893–2144), holds the annual Centel Classic.

Sailing **Hobie Shop** (12705 Front Beach Rd., Panama City Beach, tel. 904/234–0023) rents Hobie Cats and Windsurfers. Sailing instruction as well as rentals are offered by **Friendship Charter Sailing** (404 U.S. 98, Destin, tel. 904/837–2694). Sailboat rentals come in a range of classes at **Cove Marina at Bluewater Bay** (300 Bay Dr., Niceville, tel. 904/897–2821). Renting sailboats, jet skis, or catamarans from **Bonifay Water Sports** (460 Pensacola Beach Blvd., Pensacola Beach, tel. 904/932–0633) includes safety and sailing instructions. Hobie Cats, Sunfish, jet skis, Windsurfers, and surfboards are available at **Key Sailing** (400 Quietwater Beach Blvd., Pensacola Beach, tel. 904/932–5520).

Tennis At **Marriott's Bay Point Resort**'s (100 Delwood Beach Rd., Panama City Beach, tel. 904/234–3307) tennis center there are 12 Har-Tru clay tennis courts. **Sandestin Resort** (U.S. 98E, Destin, tel. 904/267–8000), one of the nation's five-star tennis resorts, has 16 courts with grass, hard, or Rubico surfaces. **Destin Racquet & Fitness Center** (995 Airport Rd., Destin, tel. 904/837–7300) boasts six Rubico courts. The **Municipal Tennis Center** (45 W. Audrey, Fort Walton Beach, tel. 904/243–8789) has 12 lighted Laykold courts and four practice walls. You can play tennis day or night on seven Rubico and two hard courts at the **Ft. Walton Racquet Club** (23 Hurlburt Field Rd., Fort Walton Beach, tel. 904/862–2023). There are 21 courts (12 lighted) featuring three different playing surfaces at **Bluewater Bay Resort** (Tennis Center, Bay Dr., Niceville, tel. 904/897–3679). Tennis courts are available in more than 30 locations in the Pensacola area, among them the **Pensacola Racquet Club** (3450 Wimbledon Dr., Pensacola, tel. 904/434–2434).

Spectator Sports

Auto Racing Billed as the fastest half-mile track in the country, **Five Flags Speedway** (7450 Pine Forest Rd., Pensacola, tel. 904/944–0466) features action-packed racing every Friday with top-name stock-car drivers and special draw events such as the Snow Ball Derby and Super National Enduro.

Dog Racing Rain or shine, year-round, there's racing with pari-mutuel betting six nights a week and afternoons on Friday, Saturday, and Monday at the **Pensacola Greyhound Track.** Lounge and grandstand areas are fully enclosed, air-conditioned, and have instant-replay televisions throughout. *U.S. 98 at Dog Track Rd., W. Pensacola, tel. 904/455–8598. Open Mon.–Sat.; post time: 1:15 and 7:45* PM.

There's pari-mutuel betting and greyhound racing six nights a week at the **Ebro Dog Track.** *Rte. 20 at Rte. 79, Ebro, tel. 904/535–4048. Open Mar.–Labor Day, Mon.–Sat.; post time: 7:30* PM.

Football The top-notch **Florida State Seminoles** meeet other Atlantic Coast conference powerhouses in Tallahassee.

Beaches

Crystal Beach Wayside Park (tel. 904/837–6447). With something to appeal to just about everyone, this Gulf-side sanctuary is located just 5 miles east of Destin and is protected on each side by undeveloped state-owned land.

Eglin Reservation Beach (no phone). Situated on 5 miles of undeveloped military land and located about 3 miles west of the Brooks Bridge in Fort Walton Beach, this beach is a favorite haunt of local teenagers and young singles.

Grayton Beach State Recreation Area (tel. 904/231–4210). Sandwiched between Santa Rosa Beach and Grayton Beach, this is one of the most scenic spots along the Gulf Coast. Located about 30 miles east of Destin on Rte. 30A, this recreation area offers blue-green waters, white-sand beaches, salt marshes, and swimming, snorkeling, and campground facilities.

Gulf Island National Seashore (tel. 904/934–2631). This 150-mile stretch of pristine coastline runs all the way from Gulfport, Mississippi, to Destin. Managed by the National Park Service, these beach and recreational spots include the **Fort Pickens Area,** at the west end of Santa Rosa Island; the **Santa Rosa Day Use Area,** 10 miles east of Pensacola Beach; and **Johnson's Beach** on Perdido Key, about 20 miles northwest of Pensacola's historic districts. Check with the National Park Service for any restrictions that might apply.

John C. Beasley State Park (no phone). Located on Okaloosa Island, this is Fort Walton Beach's seaside playground. A boardwalk leads to the beach where you'll find covered picnic tables, changing rooms, and freshwater showers. Lifeguards are on duty during the summer. In the winter, the desolate, nostalgic quality is peaceful.

Panama City Beaches (tel. 800/PC–BEACH). These public beaches along the Miracle Strip combine with the plethora of video-game arcades, miniature golf courses, sidewalk cafes, souvenir shops, and shopping centers to lure people of all ages.

Pensacola Beach (tel. 904/932–2258). To get to Pensacola Beach, which is 5 miles south of Pensacola, take U.S. 98 to Gulf Breeze, then cross the Bob Sikes Bridge over to Santa Rosa Island. Beachcombers and sunbathers, sailboarders and sailors keep things going at a fever pitch in and out of the water. In season, no particular demographic group has a lock on Pensacola Beach. Off season, conventioneers keep things hopping.

St. Andrews State Park (tel. 904/233–5140). On the eastern tip of Panama City Beach, this is Florida's most visited park. An artificial reef creates a calm, shallow play area that is perfect for young children.

Dining and Lodging

Dining Since the Gulf of Mexico is only an hour's drive from any spot in the Panhandle, menus in restaurants from modest diners to elegant cafes feature seafood, most of which will be hauled out of the water and served that same day. Native fishes such as grouper, red snapper, amberjack, catfish, and mullet are the regional staples.

Restaurants are organized geographically. Unless otherwise noted, they are open for lunch and dinner.

Category	Cost*
Very Expensive	over $60
Expensive	$40–$60
Moderate	$20–$40
Inexpensive	under $20

**per person, excluding drinks, service, and 6% sales tax*

Lodging Northwest Florida offers everything from posh seaside resorts to modest roadside motels. The rule of thumb is: The closer you are to the water, the more you can expect to pay. If you're planning a lengthy stay, a condominium rental is a good idea. Most accept walk-ins, but to be on the safe side, reserve a spot through a property management service.

Category	Cost*
Very Expensive	over $120
Expensive	$90–$120
Moderate	$50–$90
Inexpensive	under $50

**All prices are for a standard double room, excluding service charge.*

Highly recommended restaurants and lodgings are indicated by a ★.

Crestview *Lodging*

Crestview Holiday Inn. Within this simple sandstone stucco motel is typical Florida decor: shell-shape ceramic lamps, seashell-print bedspreads, and oceanic art on the walls. It's right on the main drag and is the "in" place for local wedding receptions and high school proms. *Rte. 85 and I–10, Box 1355, 32536, tel. 904/682–6111. 120 rooms. Facilities: pool, restaurant, lounge. AE, DC, MC, V. Inexpensive.*

Destin *Dining*

★ **Flamingo Cafe.** Two types of atmosphere are presented at the Flamingo Cafe: the black, white, and pink color scheme, with waiters and waitresses dressed in tuxedos with pink bow ties, shouting nouveau; and the airy, seaside setting embraced by the panoramic view of Destin harbor seen from every seat in the house, or from a table on the full-length porch outside. Chef specialties include veal *Magenta* (baby white veal sautéed with lobster and shrimp, finished with raspberry beurre blanc and garlic butter) and grouper Flamingo (broiled with butter, Madeira wine, and bread crumbs, topped off with sautéed mushrooms and artichoke hearts in lemon-butter sauce). *414 U.S. 98E, tel. 904/837–0961. Reservations accepted. Dress: casual. AE, DC, MC, V. Moderate–Inexpensive.*

Vaccaro's. Black ashtrays and gray napkins on pink tablecloths cap off the art deco appointments in this restaurant's striking interior. The mostly Italian menu features a variety of selections, from pizza made with sun-dried tomatoes, roasted shallots, and mushrooms to *pollo saltimbocca* (sautéed breast of chicken with prosciutto, mozzarella, and tomato sauce). Join the happy hour festivities on the rooftop deck and watch the sun set over Destin harbor. *Morena Plaza, U.S. 98, tel. 904/654–5722. Reservations accepted. Dress: casual. AE, DC, MC, V. No lunch. Moderate–Inexpensive.*

Captain Dave's on the Gulf. This beachfront restaurant comprises three dining rooms: a central room with a glass dome overlooking the Gulf; a sports room filled with bats, helmets, jerseys, autographed baseballs, and photographs of professional atheletes; and finally, a more intimate dining area with small dim lights and potted plants. The hearty menu offers seafood entrées such as fillet of snapper sprinkled with crabmeat and covered with shrimp sauce and Parmesan cheese; and a medley of broiled seafood served with celery, onions, bell peppers, tomatoes, and topped with black olives and mozzarella cheese. Children's plates are available. Dancing and live entertainment are featured in the downstairs lounge. *3796 Old Hwy. 98, tel. 904/837-2627. No reservations. Dress: casual. No lunch. AE, MC, V. Inexpensive.*

Lodging

★ **Sandestin Beach Resort.** This 2,600-acre resort of villas, cottages, condominiums, and an inn seems to be a town unto itself. All rooms have a view, either of the Gulf, Choctawhatchee Bay, a golf course, lagoon, or bird sanctuary. This resort provides something for an assortment of tastes, from simple to extravagant, and offers special rates October–March. *Emerald Coast Pkwy., 32541, tel. 904/837-0044 or 800/342-7040. 175 rooms, 316 villas. Facilities: miles of private beach, several pools, 2 golf courses, 16 tennis courts, tennis and golf pro shops, marina, 5 restaurants, shopping mall. AE, MC, V. Very Expensive–Expensive.*

Summer Breeze. White picket fences and porches or patios outside each unit make this condominium complex look like a summer place out of the Gay Nineties. One-bedroom suites have fully equipped kitchens and can sleep up to six people in queen-size beds, sleeper sofas, or bunks. It's halfway between Destin and Sandestin and is across from a roadside park that gives it the feel of privacy and seclusion. *3885 U.S. 98E, 32541, tel. 904/837-4853; 800/874-8914 or 800/336-4853. 35 units. Facilities: pool, outdoor Jacuzzi, barbecue. MC, V. Moderate.*

Village Inn of Destin. This property, only minutes away from the Gulf, was built in 1983 with families in mind. A variety of amenities, including entertainment, are provided to occupy each member of the family in some way. Rooms have serviceable dressers and queen- or king-size beds. Senior citizen discounts are available. *215 U.S. 98E, 32541, tel. 904/837-7413. 100 rooms. Facilities: pool. AE, DC, MC, V. Moderate.*

Fort Walton Beach

Dining

★ **Seagull.** In addition to an unobstructed view of Brooks Bridge and the sound, this waterside restaurant has a 400-foot dock for its cruise-minded customers. Decorated with pictures from Fort Walton in the 1940s, and dimly lit, the Seagull is a comfortable place to dine. Choose between no-frills steak and prime rib or fancier fare such as fillet of snapper topped with almonds and Dijon mustard sauce. After the family business clears out, things liven up a bit when one of two bands provide live soft rock music. *U.S. 98E, by the Brooks Bridge, tel. 904/243-3413. Dress: casual. Reservations accepted. No lunch. AE, DC, MC, V. Moderate–Inexpensive.*

The Sound. Lean back and watch the action on Santa Rosa Sound from any seat in the house in this easygoing establishment where wood paneling and rattan fixtures make a happy marriage. The grouper del Rio sauced with Dijon mayonnaise and topped with bread crumbs and Parmesan cheese is touted, as is the prime rib. Let your appetite determine whether you order a junior or senior cut. A children's menu is available lunch and dinner. Cap off an evening meal with a wedge of Key lime pie, then move over to the adjacent lounge for live jazz and blues. *108 W. U.S. 98, tel. 904/243-7772. Reservations accepted. Dress: casual. AE, DC, MC, V. Inexpensive.*

Lodging

Holiday Inn. This U-shape hotel consists of a seven-story tower flanked on either side by three-story wings. Rooms feature pastel green-and-peach decor and have flowered bedspreads and complementing striped draperies and face either the Gulf or the pool, but even the poolside rooms have at least some view of the sea. There are four floors of suites in the middle tower, each with a spacious sitting area and access to an extensive veranda overlooking the Gulf. The lobby, with an upscale, contemporary design, boasts glass elevators, colored banners hanging from the ceiling, wicker furniture, and tiled floors. *1110 Santa Rosa Blvd., 32548, tel. 904/243–9181 or 800/465–4329 outside FL. 385 rooms. Facilities: 3 pools, 800-foot beach, tennis courts, exercise room, restaurants, lounge. AE, DC, MC, V. Expensive–Moderate.*

Ramada Beach Resort. The lobby and entrance presents a slick look: black marble and disco lights—what some locals feel is too much like the Las Vegas strip. Activity here centers around a pool with a five-story grotto and a swim-through waterfall, and along the 800-foot private beach. *U.S. 98E, 32548, tel. 904/243–9161, 800/874–8962 or 800/2–RAMADA. 454 rooms. Facilities: pools, whirlpool, tennis courts, game room, exercise room, restaurants, lounges. AE, DC, MC, V. Expensive–Moderate.*

Panama City Beach
Dining

Boar's Head. An exterior that looks like an oversize thatch cottage sets the mood for dining in this ever-popular ersatz-rustic restaurant and tavern. Prime rib has been the number-one people-pleaser since the house opened in 1978, but broiled shrimp with crabmeat and vegetable stuffing, and native seafood sprinkled with spices and blackened in a white-hot skillet are popular, too. For starters, try escargot in mushroom caps or a shrimp bisque. There's a special menu for the junior appetite. *17290 Front Beach Rd., tel. 904/234–6628. No reservations. Dress: casual. AE, DC, MC, V. No lunch. Moderate–Inexpensive.*

Capt. Anderson's. Come early to watch the boats unload the catch of the day, and be among the first to line up for one of the 600 seats in this noted eatery. The atmosphere is nautical, with tables made of hatch covers. The Greek specialties aren't limited to feta cheese and shriveled olives; charcoal-broiled fish and steaks have a prominent place on the menu, too. *5551 N. Lagoon Dr., tel. 904/234–2225. No reservations. Dress: casual. AE, DC, MC, V. No lunch. Closed Sun. and Nov.–Jan. Moderate–Inexpensive.*

Montego Bay. Queue up with vacationers and natives for a table at any one of the four restaurants in this local chain. Service is swift and the food's good. Some dishes, such as red beans and rice or oysters on the half shell, are no surprise. Others such as shrimp rolled in coconut and served with a honey mustard and orange marmalade sauce, or steak doused with Kentucky bourbon and presented with a bourbon marinade are real treats. *4920 Thomas Dr., tel. 904/234–8686; 9949 Thomas Dr., tel. 904/235–3585; The Shoppes at Edgewater, tel. 904/233–6033. 17118 Front Beach Rd., tel. 904/233–2900. No reservations. Dress: casual. MC, V. Inexpensive.*

Lodging

★ **Edgewater Beach Resort.** Luxurious one-, two-, or three-bedroom units in beachside towers or golf-course villas are elegantly furnished with wicker and rattan and done in the seaside colors of peach, aqua, and sand. The centerpiece of this resort is a Polynesian-style lagoon pool with waterfalls, reflecting ponds, footbridges, and more than 20,000 species of tropical plants. *11212 U.S. 98A, 32407, tel. 904/235–4044 or outside FL 800/874–8686. Facilities: golf, 12 tennis courts, game rooms, health club, shuffleboard, restaurants, lounge. MC, V. Very Expensive–Expensive.*

★ **Marriott's Bay Point Resort.** Sheer elegance is the hallmark of this pink stucco jewel on the shores of Grand Lagoon. Wing chairs, camel-back sofas, and Oriental-patterned carpets in the common areas re-create the ambience of an English manor house, which is sustained by the Queen Anne furnishings in the guest rooms. Gulf view or golf view—take your pick. Kitchen-equipped villas are a mere tee-shot away from the hotel. *100 Delwood Beach Rd., 32411, tel. 904/234–3307 or outside FL 800/874–7105. 400 rooms, suites, or villas. Facilities: 5 pools, including indoor pool with Jacuzzi, 2 golf courses, 12 lighted Har-Tru tennis courts, 145-slip marina, sailboat rentals, fishing charters, riverboat cruises, 5 restaurants, lounges. AE, DC, MC, V. Expensive–Moderate.*

Miracle Mile Resort. A mile of beachfront is awash with hotels: Miracle Mile Inn, Gulfside, Sands, Barefoot Beach Inn. These older properties target the family and convention trade. *9450 S. Thomas Dr., 32407, tel. 904/234–3484; in FL 800/342–8720; outside FL 800/874–6613. 632 units. Facilities: pools, tennis courts, restaurants, lounges. AE, DC, MC, V. Moderate–Inexpensive.*

Pensacola
Dining

Cap'n Jim's. Get a table by a picture window and gaze at Pensacola Bay while you savor a house special such as snapper Chardonnay (served with lobster-based wine and cream sauce, scallions, and mushrooms) or snapper Dean'o (broiled and served with fresh tomatoes, spring onions, and lemon butter sauce). *905 E. Gregory St., tel. 904/433–3562. Reservations accepted. Dress: casual. AE, DC, MC, V. Closed Sun. Inexpensive.*

★ **Jamie's.** This is one of a handful of Florida restaurants that are members of the prestigious Master Chef's Institute. Dining here is like spending the evening in the antiques-filled parlor of a fine, old southern home. If a visit to Florida has you fished-out, try the pâté du jour, followed with almond-coated breast of chicken accompanied by a champagne cream sauce and seedless grapes. The wine list boasts more than 200 labels. *424 E. Zaragoza St., tel. 904/434–2911. Reservations advised. Dress: casual. AE, DC, MC, V. Inexpensive.*

McGuire's Irish Pub. Drink cherry beer brewed right on the premises in copper and oaken casks, and eat your corned beef and cabbage while an Irish tenor croons in the background. Located in an old firehouse, the pub is replete with antiques, moose heads, Irish Tiffany lamps, and Erin-go-bragh memorabilia. More than 36,000 dollar bills signed and dated by the pub's patrons flutter from the ceiling. McGuire's also has a House Mug Club with more than 2,000 personalized mugs. The waitresses are chatty and aim to please. Menu items run from kosher-style sandwiches to chili con carne to Boston cream pie. *600 E. Gregory St., tel. 904/433–6789. No reservations. Dress: casual. AE, DC, MC, V. Inexpensive.*

Perry's Seafood House & Gazebo Oyster Bar. This vintage 1858 house, known locally as "the big red house," was a residence, a tollhouse, and a fraternity house before Perry purchased it in 1968 and turned it into a restaurant. Native fish are broiled with Perry's secret sauce and garlic butter, or baked and topped with garlic sauce and lemon juice. The menu varies depending on weather conditions, fishing boat schedule, and what was caught that day. *2140 S. Barrancas Ave. tel., 904/434–2995. No reservations. Dress: casual. AE, DC, MC, V. Closed Tues. Inexpensive.*

Lodging

Perdido Sun. This high rise is the perfect expression of Gulf-side resort living. After a stay here, you'll know why the Spanish explorers of 300 years ago called the area the "Lost Paradise." One-, two-, or three-bedroom decorator-furnished units all have seaside balconies with spectacular views of the water. You can choose to make this your home away from home—accommodations include fully equipped kitchens—or you can pamper yourself with daily maid service. *13753 Perdido Key Dr., 32507, tel. 904/492–2390 or outside FL 800/227–2390. 93 units. Facilities: glass-enclosed heated pool, outdoor pool, spa, health club. MC, V. Very Expensive–Expensive.*

Pensacola Hilton. The Hilton's lobby is in the renovated L & N train depot. Ticket and baggage counters are still intact and old railroad signs remind guests of the days when steam locomotives chugged up to these doors. The old train station connects via a canopied two-story galleria to a 15-story tower. Here's where the spittoons and hand trucks give way to upholstered furniture and deep-pile carpet; standard doubles are up-to-date and roomy. Bilevel penthouse suites have snazzy wet bars and whirlpool baths. The hotel is adjacent to the Pensacola Civic Center and only few blocks away from the historic districts. *200 E. Gregory St., 32501, tel. 904/433–3336 or 800/HILTONS. 212 rooms. Facilities: heated pool, restaurants, lounges, complimentary airport limo. AE, DC, MC, V. Expensive–Moderate.*

Holiday Inn/Pensacola Beach. This property enjoyed its finest hour during the filming of *Jaws II*, when the cast made this its headquarters. Inside, the lobby is simple, with potted plants, floral arrangements, and a coral-colored decor. Outside, the Holiday Inn has its own 1,500 feet of private beach. From the ninth-floor Penthouse Lounge, you can watch the goings-on in the Gulf, especially when the setting sun turns the western sky to lavender and orange. *165 Ft. Pickens Rd., Pensacola Beach, 32561, tel. 904/932–5361 or 800/HOLIDAY. 150 rooms. Facilities: outdoor pool, tennis courts, restaurant, lounge. AE, DC, MC, V. Moderate.*

★ **New World Inn.** This is Pensacola's little hotel, where celebrities who visit the city are likely to stay. Photos of dozens of the inn's famous guests (Lucille Ball, Shirley Jones, Charles Kuralt) hang behind the front desk in the lobby. The exquisite furnishings in the guest rooms take their inspiration from the five periods of Pensacola's past: French or Spanish provincial, early American, antebellum, or Queen Anne. The baths are handsomely appointed with brass fixtures and outfitted with oversize towels. *600 S. Palafox St., 32501, tel. 904/432–4111 or outside FL 800/258–1103. 14 rooms, 2 suites. Facilities: restaurant, lounge. AE, DC, MC, V. Moderate.*

Ramada Inn North. All the guest rooms at this hotel have been renovated. Suites have game tables and entertainment centers; some have whirlpools. This Ramada is conveniently located close to the airport. *6550 Pensacola Blvd., 32505, tel. 904/477–0711 or outside FL 800/2–RAMADA. 106 rooms. Facilities: pool, restaurant, lounge, courtesy airport transportation. AE, DC, MC, V. Inexpensive.*

Seaside

Dining

★ **Bud & Alley's.** This roadside restaurant grows its own herbs—rosemary, thyme, basil, fennel, and mint. The inside room has a unique, down-to-earth feel, with hardwood floors, ceiling fans, and six-foot windows looking out onto the garden. There is also a screened-in porch area with a view of the Gulf. The Gorgonzola salad with sweet peppers is a delightful introduction to one of the entrées, perhaps the seared duck breast with caramelized garlic, wild mushrooms, and Cabernet sauce. *County Rte. 30A, tel. 904/231–5900. Reservations accepted. Dress: casual. MC, V. Closed Tues. Inexpensive.*

Lodging ★ **Seaside.** Two- to five-bedroom porticoed Victorian cottages are furnished right down to the vacuum cleaners. Although there's no air-conditioning, the Gulf breezes blowing off the water will cool rooms and remind you of the miles of unspoiled beaches so nearby. *County Rte. 30A, 32459, tel. 904/231–1320. 133 units. Facilities: pool, tennis court, croquet, badminton, bicycles, Hobie Cats, and beach equipment rentals. AE, MC, V. Expensive.*

Tallahassee

Dining

★ **Andrew's 2nd Act.** Part of a smart complex in the heart of the political district, this is classic cuisine: elegant and understated. If you like pub hopping, there's Andrew's Upstairs, and the Adams Street Cafe (also by Andrew) is next door. For dinner, the veal Oscar is flawless or choose a chef's special from the chalkboard. You can't go wrong. *102 W. Jefferson St., tel. 904/222–2759. Reservations advised. Jacket and tie suggested. AE, DC, MC, V. Expensive.*

Anthony's. Often confused with Andrew's, but a different and equally deserving restaurant, this is the locals' choice for uncompromising Italian classics. Try one of the Italian-style grouper or salmon dishes. *1950 Thomasville Rd., tel. 904/224–1447. Reservations advised. Dress: casual. AE, MC, V. Moderate.*

Nicholson's Farmhouse. The name says a lot about this friendly, informal country place with its outside kitchen and grill. If you've never tried amberjack, discover this unusual, meaty fish—a specialty of the house. *Turn off Hwy. 27 to Hwy. 12 toward Quincy; follow signs, tel. 904/539–5931. Reservations advised on weekends. BYOB. Dress: casual. MC, V. Closed Sun.–Mon. Moderate.*

★ **Barnacle Bill's.** Don't be put off by the slummy decor. The seafood selection is whale-size and it's steamed to succulent perfection before your eyes, with fresh vegetables on the side. This popular hangout is famous for pasta dishes and home-smoked fish, too. Choose from complete weight-loss menus and daily chalkboard specials. Children eat free on Sunday. The full menu is available for carryout. *1830 N. Monroe St., tel. 904/385–8734. Reservations required for large groups. Dress: casual. AE, MC, V. Inexpensive.*

Lodging

★ **Governors Inn.** Only a block from the Capitol, this plushly restored historic warehouse is abuzz during the week with politicians, press, and lobbyists. It's a perfect location for business travelers involved with the state, and on weekends, for tourists who want to tour the Old Capitol and other downtown sites. Rooms are a rich blend of mahogany, brass, and classic prints. The VIP treatment includes airport pickup, breakfast, cocktails, robes, shoe shine, and a daily paper. *209 S. Adams St., 32301, tel. 904/681–6855 or in FL 800/342–7717. 41 units. AE, D, DC, MC, V. Expensive.*

Las Casas. The quiet courtyard with its own pool and the darkly welcoming cantina where a complimentary Continental breakfast and evening cocktail are served convey the look of old Spain. Rooms are furnished in heavy Mediterranean style. *2801 N. Monroe St. 32303, tel. 904/386–8286 or 800/521–0948 in*

FL. 112 rooms. Facilities: heated pool. AE, DC, MC, V. Moderate.

Tallahassee Sheraton. Bustling and upscale, the hotel hosts heavy hitters from the worlds of politics and media who can walk from here to the Capitol. *101 S. Adams St., 32301, tel. 904/224–5000 or 800/325–3535. 246 rooms. Facilities: pool, restaurant, lobby bar, lounge with entertainment, gift shop, valet service. AE, DC, MC, V. Moderate.*

Valparaiso/Niceville
Dining

Heidelberg Haus. Enjoy the best of the wurst with gemütlichkeit on the side, and don't be surprised if the couple at the next table is tête-à-têting in a foreign tongue. The biergarten atmosphere, as well as the food in this German-European restaurant, attracts visitors from overseas who are seeking such back-home specialties as schweinebraten, sauerbraten, or *rouladen* (sliced top sirloin rolled and stuffed with bacon, pickles, and herbs and served with *spätzle*). Consider starting with a glass of German beer or wine and ending with *Schwarzenwalder kirschtorte* (Black Forest cherry cake). *4400 Rte. 20E, Niceville, tel. 904/897–3338. Reservations accepted. Dress: casual. AE, MC, V. Inexpensive.*

Lodging
★

Bluewater Bay Resort. This upscale residential resort is carved out of 1,800 acres of pines and oaks on the shores of Choctawhatchee Bay. It's still woodsy around the edges, but showcase homes are surrounded by tenderly manicured gardens. Rentals run the gamut from motel rooms to villas, some with fireplaces and fully equipped kitchens, to patio homes. Check-out information in the rental units is translated into German for the benefit of the international visitors who flock to this golf course–rich region. *Rte. 20E., Box 247, Niceville, 32578, tel. 904/897–3613 or outside FL 800/874–2128. 134 units. Facilities: 2,000-ft private beach, several pools, 27 holes of golf, 21 tennis courts, marina, playground, exercise room, 2 restaurants, lounge. AE, MC, V. Expensive.*

The Arts and Nightlife

The Arts

Broadway touring shows, top-name entertainers, and concert artists are booked into the **Marina Civic Center** (8 Harrison Ave., Panama City, tel. 904/769–1217), the **Tallahassee-Leon County Civic Center** (Box 10604, Tallahassee, tel. 904/487–1691), and the **Saenger Theatre** (118 S. Palafox St., Pensacola, tel. 904/444–7686).

Concerts

Okaloosa Symphony Orchestra (tel. 904/244–3308) performs a series of concerts featuring guest artists at Rita Schaeffer Hall (38 S.W. Robinwood Dr.). **Pensacola Symphony Orchestra** (tel. 904/435–2533) presents a series of five concerts each season at the Saenger Theatre (118 S. Palafox St.).

Florida State University School of Music (tel. 904/644–4774), in Tallahassee, stages 350 concerts and recitals a year.

The **Tallahassee Symphony Orchestra** (tel. 904/224–0461) performs at Florida State University, September–April.

The **Capitol City Band** (tel. 904/893–8303) has been brandishing its brass in Tallahassee since 1924.

Dance

The Northwest Florida Ballet (101 S.E. Chicago Ave., Fort Walton Beach, tel. 904/664–7787) has a repertoire of the classics and performs in communities throughout the Panhandle.

Opera The **Monticello Opera House** (tel. 904/997–4242) presents operas in the restored gaslight-era playhouse, near Tallahassee.

Theater **The Pensacola Little Theatre** (186 N. Palafox St., tel. 904/432–8621) presents plays and musicals during a season that runs from fall through spring.

The **Florida State University** (tel. 904/644–6500) in Tallahassee presents 15–20 productions a year.

Nightlife Northwest Florida's nightlife falls on the scale somewhere between uptown Manhattan supper clubs and Las Vegas–style dinner shows. There are places that cater especially to the night owls, but some of the family restaurants also take on a different character when the sun goes down. A good way to find out what's hot and what's not is to ask locals.

Bars and Nightclubs **Pineapple Willie's** (9900 Beach Blvd., Panama City Beach, tel. 904/235–0928) alternately features big-band and rock music and caters to the post-college crowd. After dark, **McGuire's Irish Pub** (600 E. Gregory St., Pensacola, tel. 904/433–6789) welcomes anyone of legal drinking age, particularly those of Irish descent. If you don't like crowds, stay away from McGuire's on Friday nights and nights when Notre Dame games are televised. **Mesquite Charlie's** (5901 N. W St., Pensacola, tel. 904/434–0498) offers good, ol' down-home pickin' and grinnin' with live entertainment and singin' up a storm. Pensacola's **Seville Quarter** (130 E. Government St., tel. 904/434–6211) with five fabulous bars featuring music from disco to Dixieland is this city's equivalent to the New Orleans French Quarter. **Tickets** at the Pensacola Hilton (200 E. Gregory St., tel. 904/433–3336) is the spot for those who dip when they dance but still like to boogie. Catch the action at **Cash's Faux Pas Lounge** (106 Santa Rosa Blvd., Fort Walton Beach, tel. 904/244–2274) where anything goes. **Jamaica Joe's** (790 Santa Rosa Blvd., Fort Walton Beach, tel. 904/244–4137) features a deejay and drink specials that appeal to younger pub crawlers. **Nightown** (140 Palmetto St., Destin, tel. 904/837–6448) has a dance floor with laser lights and a New Orleans–style bar with live band music. In Tallahassee, stop by **Andrew's Upstairs** (228 S. Adams St., tel. 904/222–3446) to hear contemporary jazz and reggae music.

12 Northeast Florida

Introduction

By Janet and Gordon Groene

Updated by Ann Hughes

When Orlando's new cinema industry scouts for filming locations, it can find almost any setting it needs in Northeast Florida. Towering, tortured live oaks, plantations, and antebellum-style architecture symbolize the Old South, and the mossy marshes of Silver Springs and the St. Johns River look today as they did generations ago when Tarzan movies were filmed in the jungles here. Jacksonville is a modern metropolis abounding with skyscrapers; Payne's Prairie, near Gainesville, looks like it's a lost prehistoric stomping ground; while county seats such as De Land and Green Cove Springs are reminiscent of Thorton Wilder's *Our Town.*

Fishing villages of Big Bend country along the Gulf have a ramshackle, New England look. And the beaches, spreading in shimmering, sandy glory south from Fernandina, vary in likeness from the stony shores of the North Sea in Great Britain to the deep, hot sands of the Caribbean. In this chapter, we'll take you east from Jacksonville to Amelia Island, and south to New Smyrna Beach on the east coast.

Essential Information

Getting Around

By Plane

Daytona Beach Regional Airport is served by Delta (tel. 800/221–1212), American (tel. 800/433–7300), USAir (tel. 800/428–4322), Continental (tel. 800/525–0280), and TWA Express (tel. 800/221–2000).

Taxis meet every flight; fare to beach hotels is about $10. Taxis include **Yellow Cab** (tel. 904/252–5536), **City Shuttle** (tel. 904/255–8422), **Checker Cabs** (tel. 904/255–8421), **AAA Cab** (tel. 904/253–2522), and **City Cab** (tel. 904/253–0675).

Gainesville Regional Airport is served by Delta (tel. 800/221–1212), USAir (tel. 800/428–4322), Comair (tel. 800/354–9822), and ASA (tel. 800/282–3424).

Taxi fare to the center of town is about $10. Some hotels provide free airport pickup.

The main airport for the region is **Jacksonville International.** It is served by American (tel. 800/433–7300), Continental (tel. 800/525–0280), TWA (tel. 800/221–2000), United (tel. 800/241–6522), and USAir (tel. 800/428– 4322).

Vans from the airport to area hotels cost $15 per person. Taxi fare is about $20 to the downtown area, $40 to the beaches and Amelia Island. Among the limousine services, which must be booked in advance, is *AAA* **Limousine Service** (tel. 904/751–4800 or 800/780–1705). The charge is $20 for one or two persons to downtown, $5 for each additional person; $40 to the beaches and to Amelia Island.

By Car

East–west traffic travels the northern part of the state on I–10, which is a cross-country highway stretching from Los Angeles to Jacksonville. Farther south, I–4 rambles east from Tampa to Orlando, then northeast to the sea. Signs indicate this east–west orientation, which can be confusing when you're driving north (signs say east) from Orlando to Daytona Beach.

Chief north–south routes are I–95 along the east coast, and I–75, which enters Florida south of Valdosta, Georgia, and joins the Sunshine Parkway toll road at Wildwood. If you want to drive as close to the Atlantic as possible, and are not in a hurry, stick with A1A (although the name changes several times along the way). Where there are no bridges across inlets, cars must return to the mainland. Where there are bridges, openings and closings cause unexpected delays. While I–75 is the fast route from Georgia to Tampa and points south, U.S. 19–98 takes you closer to the Gulf, for quick forays into coastal communities, beaches, and fishing villages.

Car Rentals Rental cars include **Alamo** (tel. 800/327–9633), **Avis** (tel. 800/331–1212), **Budget** (tel. 800/572–0700), **Hertz** (tel. 800/654–3131), and **National** (tel. 800/227–7365).

Private Services **My Brother's Limousine** (tel. 904/437–5466), based in Bunnell, serves Flagler, Volusia, and St. Johns counties. Chauffeured limousines cost $40 per hour, with a two-hour minimum. The firm is also a National Car Rental center.

By Train **Amtrak** (tel. 800/USA–RAIL) schedules stops in Jacksonville, De Land, Waldo (near Gainesville), Ocala, and Palatka. The Auto Train serves Sanford from the Washington, D.C., area. Schedules vary depending on the season.

By Bus **Greyhound/Trailways** serves the region, with stations in Jacksonville (tel. 904/356–9976), St. Augustine (tel. 904/829–6401), Gainesville (tel. 904/376–5252), Daytona Beach (tel. 904/255–7076), and De Land (tel. 904/734–2747).

Daytona Beach has an excellent bus network, **Votran** (tel. 904/761–7600), that serves the beach area, airport, shopping malls, and major arteries. Exact fare is required.

DOTS Transit Service (tel. 904/257–5411) has scheduled service among the Daytona Beach Airport, Orlando International Airport, the Palm Coast Sheraton area, De Land, De Land's Amtrak station, and Deltona. Fares to the airport in Orlando are $24 one way and $42 round trip from Daytona; $18 one way and $32 round-trip from De Land or Deltona.

By Water Taxi Connecting the banks of the St. Johns River to different points of interest in the downtown Jacksonville area, this system makes many attractions within reach of one another. Fare is $3 round-trip adult, $2 senior citizens; $1.50 one way. Water taxis run every 15 minutes.

Scenic Drives

The **Buccaneer Trail** (Rte. A1A) on the Atlantic Coast goes from Mayport (where a ferry is part of the state highway system), through marshlands and beaches into Fort Clinch State Park, with its massive brick fortress, then into the 300-year-old seaport town of Fernandina Beach.

Rte. 13 takes you up one side of the St. Johns River, through has-been hamlets. **U.S. 17,** which was once the main highway between Miami and New York, travels the west side of the river, passing through Green Cove Springs and Palatka, where Ravine State Gardens' mountains of spring azaleas bloom.

S.R. 19 runs north and south through the Ocala National Forest, giving a nonstop view of stately pines and bold wildlife.

Short side roads lead to parks, springs, picnic areas, and campgrounds.

Riverside Drive, where New Smyrna Beach's grand old homes line the Intracoastal Waterway is a good bicycle path, in addition to being a picturesque throughway.

Guided Tours

Northeast Florida **Suwannee Country Tours** (White Springs, tel. 904/397–2347), run by the Florida Council of American Youth Hostels, organizes bicycle and canoe trips on some of the state's most unspoiled and unique roads and waters. Stay overnight in country inns, picnic in ghost towns, eat at country churches, and explore forgotten sites.

Daytona Beach Helicopter flights are booked at **Space Coast Helicopter Services** (tel. 904/724–4191) in Palm Bay. For a sightseeing flight, try **Flagler Aviation** (tel. 904/437–4547) at Bunnell. **Dixie Queen Riverboat Cruises** (tel. 904/255–1997 or 800/329–6225) runs lunch, brunch, dinner, and specialty cruises throughout the Daytona Beach area.

Jacksonville City tours of Jacksonville are offered by **Gray Line Tours** (tel. 904/632–2232) and **Jacksonville Historical Society Tours** (tel. 904/384–0849). **Europa Cruise Line Ltd.** (tel. 800/688–7529) sails daily from Mayport to "nowhere," wowing the entire family with boffo buffets, floor shows, games, dancing, and other cruise ship hoopla. For grown-ups only, there is casino gambling.

Important Addresses and Phone Numbers

Tourist Information

Amelia Island–Fernandina Beach Chamber of Commerce. *102 Centre St., tel. 904/261–3248. Open weekdays 9–5.*

Destination Daytona! *126 E. Orange Ave., tel. 904/255–0415 or 800/854–1234. Open weekdays 9–5.*

Gainesville Chamber of Commerce. *300 E. University Ave., tel. 904/336–7100. Open weekdays 8:30–5.*

Jacksonville and Its Beaches Convention & Visitors Bureau. *6 E. Bay St., Suite 200, tel. 904/353–9736. Open weekdays 8–5.*

Ocala–Marion County Chamber of Commerce. *110 E. Silver Springs Blvd., tel. 904/629–8051. Open weekdays 8:30–5.*

St. Augustine Visitor Information Center. *10 Castillo Dr., tel. 904/824–3334. Open daily 8:30–5:30.*

Emergencies Dial 911 for **police** or **ambulance** assistance in life-threatening situations.

Hospitals Emergency rooms are open 24 hours at the following: In Gainesville, **Alachua General** (801 S.W. 2nd Ave., tel. 904/372–4321); **North Florida Regional Medical Center** (Rte. 26 at I–75, across from the Oaks Mall, tel. 904/333–4000); **Shands Hospital** (at the University of Florida, tel. 904/395–0111). In Ocala, **Munroe Regional Medical Center** (131 S.W. 15th St., tel. 904/351–7200). In Daytona, **Halifax Medical Center** (303 N. Clyde Morris Blvd., tel. 904/254–4100); **Atlantic Shores Hospital** (841 Jimmy Ann Dr., tel. 904/274–5333) is a private psychiatric hospital with two hotlines for psychiatric emergencies, including drug and alcohol abuse. **Hotline** numbers are 800/237–0835 or 800/345–2647.

24-Hour Pharmacies The only 24-hour pharmacy in the area is **Eckerd Drug** (4397 Roosevelt Blvd., Jacksonville, tel. 904/389–0314).

Exploring Northeast Florida

Numbers in the margin correspond to points of interest on the Northeast Florida map.

Jacksonville/Jacksonville Beach

One of the oldest cities in Florida, in area the largest city in the United States, and an underrated tourist destination, (1) **Jacksonville** continues its battle against the stench of the sulfur pulp mill that keeps many travelers speeding straight on through. Improvements have been made, and winds shift, so if you stay you may be pleasantly surprised. The city has neighborhoods with a solid look and heritage and a strong business base. Its residents have a great love for the outdoors as well as the arts, and some of the best beaches in the state are located here.

Stop off in Jacksonville and savor remnants of the Old South that continue to flavor the city, and the sense of subtropical paradise for which Florida is famous. Because the city was settled around the river, many attractions are on or near one riverbank or the other. To avoid crossing back and forth, you may want to sit down with a map and plan your trip carefully. Some attractions can be reached by water taxi, but for others, a car is necessary.

On the south side of the river, the **Jacksonville Art Museum** brings together contemporary and classic arts. Especially noteworthy are the Koger collection of Oriental porcelains and the pre-Columbian collection of rare artifacts. Special exhibits, film and lecture series, and workshops make this destination worthy of more than one visit. Travel by car. *4160 Boulevard Center Dr., tel. 904/398–8336. Admission free. Open Tues., Wed., Fri. 10–4, Thurs. 10–10, weekends 1–5; closed Mon.*

The **Cummer Gallery of Art,** situated on the northwest side of the river, amidst leafy formal gardens, occupies a former baron's estate home. The permanent collection of more than 2,000 items includes one of the nation's largest troves of early Meissen porcelain as well as the works of some impressive Old Masters. Travel by car. *829 Riverside Ave., tel. 904/356–6857. Admission: $3 adults, $2 senior citizens, $1 students and children. Open Tues.–Fri. 10–4, Sat. noon–5, Sun. 2–5. Closed Mon.*

Jacksonville's Museum of Science and History presents hands-on exhibits, live animals, temporary displays, and a planetarium with free astronomy programs. Devote an entire day to this museum, and lunch in the cafe. Located downtown on the south bank, the museum can be reached by water taxi. *1025 Museum Cir., tel. 904/396–7062. Admission: $5 adults, $3 senior citizens, $3 children, children under 4 free. Open Mon.–Fri. 10–5, Sat. 10–6, Sun. 1–6.*

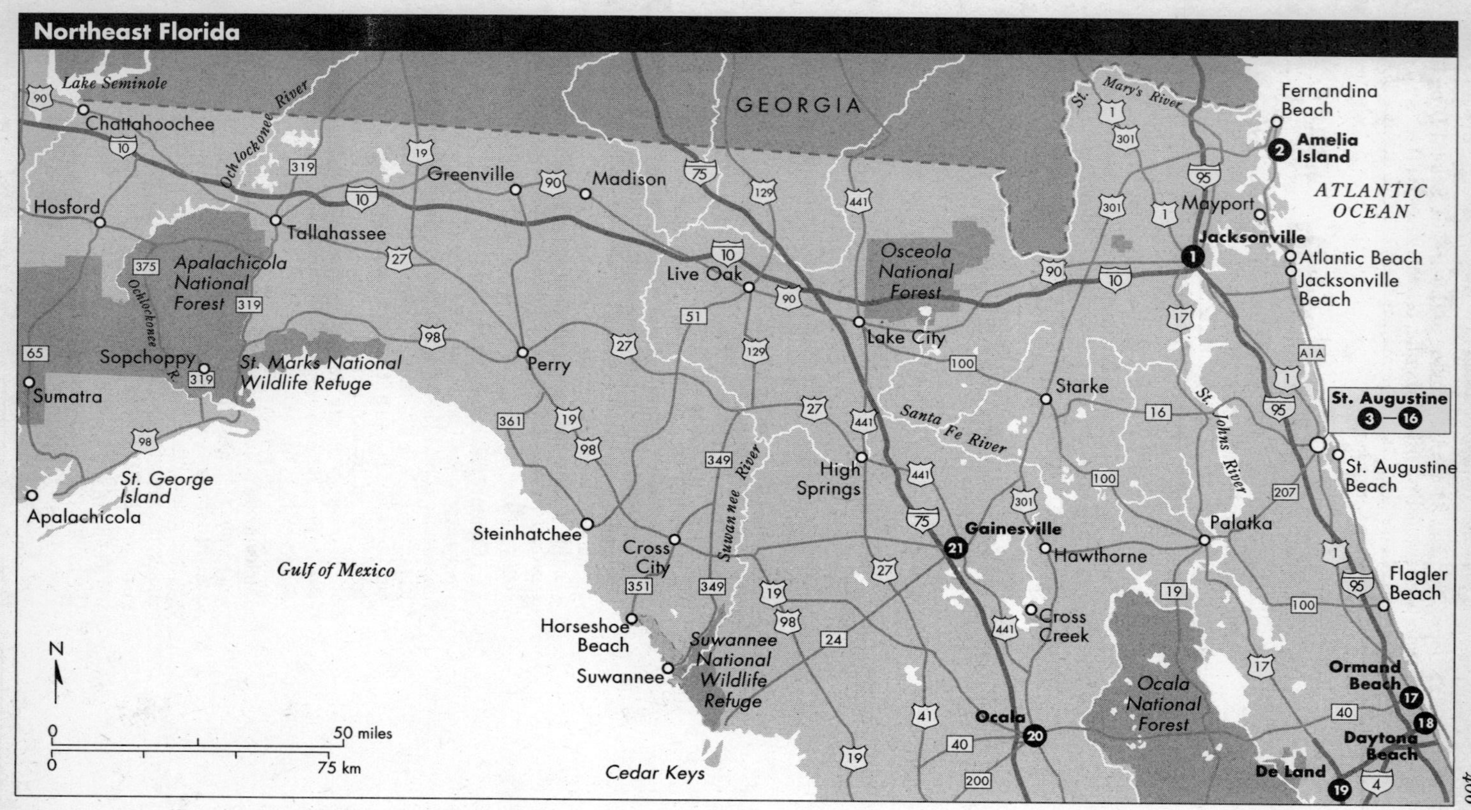
Northeast Florida
GEORGIA
ATLANTIC OCEAN
Gulf of Mexico
Lake Seminole
Chattahoochee
Hosford
Tallahassee
Greenville
Madison
Live Oak
Lake City
Osceola National Forest
Apalachicola National Forest
Ochlockonee River
St. Marks National Wildlife Refuge
Sopchoppy R.
Sumatra
Apalachicola
St. George Island
Perry
Steinhatchee
Cross City
Horseshoe Beach
Suwannee
Suwannee National Wildlife Refuge
Suwannee River
Cedar Keys
High Springs
Santa Fe River
Starke
Gainesville
Hawthorne
Cross Creek
Ocala
Ocala National Forest
Palatka
St. Johns River
St. Mary's River
Fernandina Beach
Amelia Island
Mayport
Jacksonville
Atlantic Beach
Jacksonville Beach
St. Augustine
3—16
St. Augustine Beach
Flagler Beach
Ormand Beach
Daytona Beach
De Land
N
0 50 miles
0 75 km

The **Alexander Brest Museum,** located on the campus of Jacksonville University, has a small but important collection of Stueben glass, Boehm porcelain, ivories, and pre-Columbian artifacts. The home of composer Frederick Delius is also on the campus and is open for tours, upon request. Travel by car. *2800 University Blvd. N., east bank of the St. Johns River, tel. 904/744–3950, ext. 3374. Admission free. Open weekdays 9–4:30, Sat. 12–5. Closed holidays.*

To experience some of Jacksonville's natural resources, start with the ferry to **Mayport** (located 3 miles east of A1A). Dating back more than 300 years, Mayport is one of the oldest fishing villages in the United States. Today it's home to a large commercial shrimp boat fleet and is the Navy's fourth-largest home port. *Ferry tel. 904/246–2922. Ferry admission: $1.50 per car, 50¢ pedestrians. Ferry runs daily 6:20 AM–10 PM, every ½ hour. Admission to naval station free. Naval station tel. 904/270–NAVY. Open Sat. 10–4:30, Sun. 1–4:30.*

Travel south on A1A to State Route 10; drive for about 2 miles to Girven Road; follow signs to the replica of **Fort Caroline National Monument.** The original fort was built in the 1560s by French Huguenots who were later slaughtered by the Spanish. The site, which is the scene of the first major clash between European powers for control of what would become the United States, maintains the memory of a brief French presence in this area. Today, it's a sunny place to picnic (bring your own food and drink), stretch your legs, and explore a small museum. *12713 Fort Caroline Rd., tel. 904/641–7111. Admission free. Museum open daily 9–5. Closed Christmas.*

Take Fort Caroline Road west to Rte. 9A, on which you'll travel for 3 miles, crossing the N.B. Brovard Bridge (locally known as Danes Point Bridge). Take the first exit (S.R. 105) and drive northeast for about 12 miles to Fort George Island, where signs will lead you to the **Kingsley Plantation.** Built by an eccentric slave trader, the Kingsley dates to 1792 and is the oldest remaining plantation in the state. Slave quarters, as well as the modest Kingsley home, are open to the public. *Tel. 904/251–3537. Admission: $1 adults, children under 6 free. Open daily 8–5. Guided tours Thurs.–Mon. 9, 11, 1:30, and 3.*

From the plantation, drive northeast on A1A for about 5 miles to **Little Talbot Island State Park**—a gorgeous stretch of sand dunes, endless beaches, and golden marshes that hum with birds and bugs. Come to picnic, fish, swim, snorkel, or camp. *Tel. 904/251–2320. Admission: $3.25 per vehicle with up to 8 people. Open daily 8 AM–sunset.*

Jacksonville's sensational beaches spread south from Mayport, but casual tourists can miss the boundaries between, as well as the distinctions among, the beaches. **Atlantic Beach** was another Henry Flagler project, developed in 1901 with the building of a hotel. A condo now stands on the site of the once-grand Atlantic Beach Hotel, built in 1929. Neighboring **Neptune Beach** is a quiet bedroom community, while **Jacksonville Beach,** once Ruby Beach and later Pablo Beach, was already a tent city in 1884 and was soon served by a narrow-gauge railway. Today it's a solid resort community, with new beach hotels replacing the original 350-guest resort hotel that burned in 1890. **Ponte Vedra Beach,** now the home of the Tournament Players Club and American Tennis Professionals, has been popular with golfers since 1922 when the National Lead Company built a 9-hole course for its workers to play.

Before heading on to St. Augustine, plan a visit to **Fernandina** ❷ **Beach,** which lies north of Jacksonville on **Amelia Island,** across the border from St. Marys, Georgia. Take A1A east off I–95 or, for a more fun and leisurely approach, drive north on A1A from the Jacksonville beaches; take the Mayport ferry across the St. Johns River, then drive the Buccaneer Trail (A1A).

Once an important political and commercial stronghold and now merely a quaint haven for in-the-know tourists, Fernandina Beach offers a wide range of accommodations from bed-and-breakfasts to Amelia Island Plantation (*see* Dining and Lodging, below), a sprawling landmark resort. The town's 30-block historic district includes the old cemetery where names on gravestones reveal the waves of immigrants who settled here: Spanish, French, Minorcan, Portuguese, and English. In **Old Town** you'll see some of the nation's finest examples of Queen Anne, Victorian, and Italianate mansions dating back to the haven's glory days of the mid-19th century. Begin your self-guided walking or driving tour of the historic district with a visit to the old railroad depot, originally a stopping point on the first cross-state railroad. Now the **Amelia Island–Fernandina Beach Chamber of Commerce,** this is a good place to pick up leaflets and information on the area. *102 Centre St., tel. 904/261–3248. Open weekdays 9–5.*

Follow Centre Street (which turns into Atlantic Avenue) for about 8 blocks to **St. Peter's Episcopal Church.** Founded in 1859, the church once served as a school for freed slaves. Continuing on Atlantic, you will reach the bridge. From here you can see the **Amelia Lighthouse,** built in 1839. It's a great background for photos, but the inside is not open to the public.

A couple of blocks farther is the **Fort Clinch State Park,** home to one of the best-preserved and most complete brick forts. Built around the rim of Florida and the Gulf states, the fort served to protect against further British intrusion after the War of 1812 and was occupied in 1847 by the Confederacy; a year later it was retaken by the north. During the Spanish-American War it was reactivated for a brief time but for the most part was not used. Today the park offers camping, nature trails, carriage rides, swimming, surf fishing, picnicking, and living history reenactments showing life in the garrison at the time of the Civil War. *Tel. 904/261–4212. Admission: $3.25 per vehicle with up to 8 people. Open daily 8 AM–sunset.*

Time Out **The Palace Saloon** (117 Centre St., tel. 904/261–6320) is the state's oldest continuously operating watering hole, still sporting swinging doors straight out of Dodge City. Stop in for a cold drink and a bowl of boiled shrimp. The menu is limited, but the place is unpretentious, comfortable, and as genuine as a silver dollar.

St. Augustine

❸ To reach **St. Augustine,** take U.S. 1 south and head straight for the **Visitor Information Center** (10 Castillo Dr., tel. 904/824–

Basilica Cathedral, **7**
Castillo de San Marcos, **4**
City Gate, **5**
Flagler College, **13**
Flagler Memorial Church, **14**
Fountain of Youth, **15**
Lightner Museum, **12**
Mission of Nombre de Dios, **16**
Museum Theatre, **6**
Oldest House, **11**
Oldest Store Museum, **10**
Plaza de la Constitution, **8**
Ximenez-Fatio House, **9**

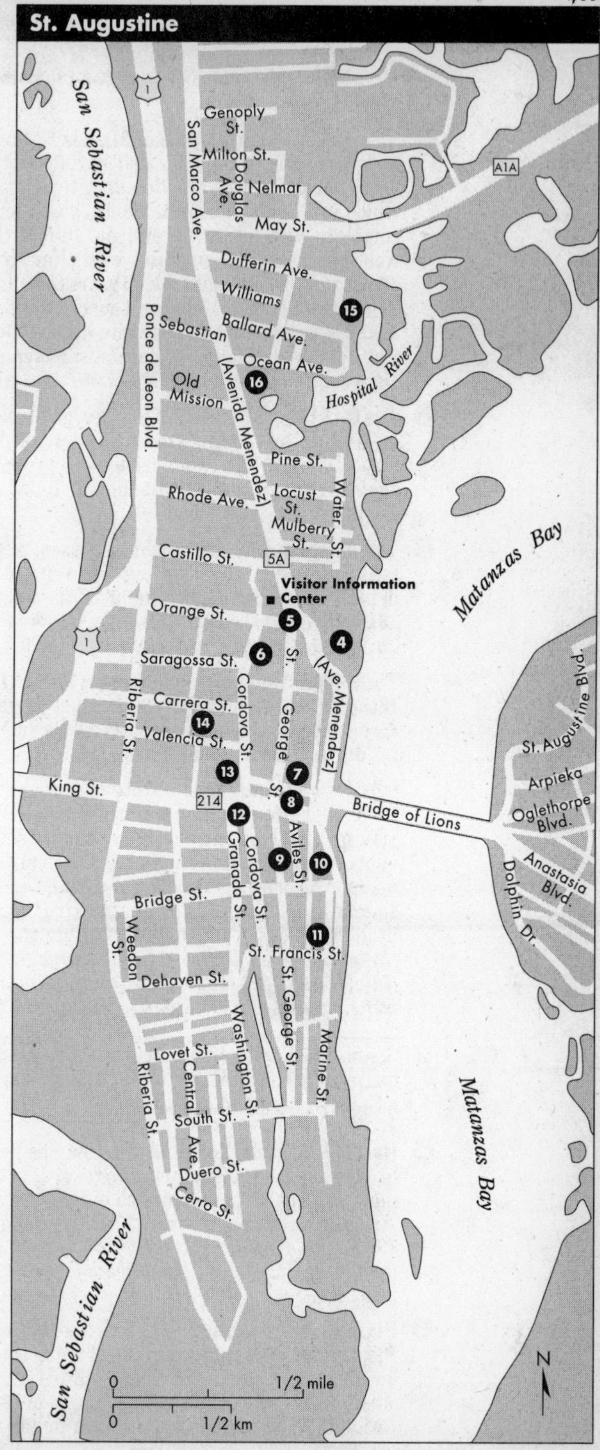

3334), where you'll find has loads of brochures, maps, and information about the nation's oldest city.

Numbers in the margin correspond to points of interest on the St. Augustine map.

4 The massive **Castillo de San Marcos National Monument** hunkers over Matanzas Bay, and looks every century of its 300 years. Park rangers provide an introductory narration, after which you're on your own. This is a wonderful fort to explore, complete with moat, turrets, and 16-foot-thick walls. The fort was constructed of coquina, a soft limestone made of broken shells and coral, and it took 25 years to build it. Garrison rooms depict the life of the era, and special artillery demonstrations are held periodically on the gun deck. *1 Castillo Dr., tel. 904/829–6506. Admission: $1 adults, children under 16 and senior citizens free. Open daily 8:30–5:30.*

5 The **City Gate,** at the top of St. George Street, is a relic from the days when the Castillo's moat ran westward to the river and the Cubo Defense Line (defensive wall) protected the settlement against approaches from the north. Today it is the entrance to the popular restored area.

6 The **Museum Theatre** screens a film several times daily. One tells the story of the founding of the city in 1565, and the other depicts life in St. Augustine in 1576. *5 Cordova St., tel. 904/824–0339. Admission: $3 adults, $1 children under 15. Open daily 9–5.*

The **Oldest Wooden Schoolhouse** (14 St. George St.) is a tiny 18th-century structure that, because it was the closest structure to the city gates, served as a guardhouse and sentry shelter during the Seminole Wars.

San Agustin Antiguo is a state-operated living-history village with eight sites; you can wander through the narrow streets at your own pace. Along your way you may see a Colonial soldier's wife cooking over an open fire; a blacksmith building his shop (a historic reconstruction); and craftsmen busy at candle dipping, spinning, weaving, and cabinetmaking. They are all making reproductions that will be used within the restored area. *Entrance at Triay House, 29 St. George St., near the Old City Gate, tel. 904/825–6830. Admission: $5 adults, $4.50 senior citizens, $2 students 6–18; $10 family ticket. Open daily 9–5.*

Time Out **Spanish Bakery,** behind Casa de Calcedo on St. George Street, has meat turnovers, cookies, and fresh-baked bread made from a Colonial recipe. *No credit cards.*

---

7 **Basilica Cathedral of St. Augustine** has parish records dating back to 1594, the oldest written records in the country. Following a fire in 1887, extensive changes were made to the current structure, which dates from 1797. It was remodeled in the mid-1960s. *40 Cathedral Pl., tel. 904/824–2806. Admission free, but donations requested. Open weekdays 5:30–5, weekends 5:30 AM–7 PM.*

8 **Plaza de la Constitution,** at St. George Street and Cathedral Place, is the central area of the original settlement. It was laid out in 1598 by decree of King Philip II, and little has changed since. At its center there is a monument to the Spanish constitution of 1812; at the east end is a public market dating from

early American days. Just beyond is a statue of Juan Ponce de León, who discovered Florida in 1513.

9 The **Ximenez-Fatio House** was built in 1797, and it became a boarding house for tourists in 1885. *20 Aviles St., tel. 904/829–3575. Admission free. Open Mar. 1–Aug. 31, Sun.–Thurs. 1–4.*

10 The **Oldest Store Museum** re-creates a turn-of-the-century general store. There are high-button shoes, lace-up corsets, patent drugs, and confectionery specialties. *4 Artillery La., tel. 904/829–9729. Admission: $3 adults, $2.50 senior citizens, $1.50 children 6–12. Open Mon.–Sat. 9–5, Sun. noon–5.*

11 Operated by the Historical Society, the **Oldest House** reflects much of the city's history through its changes and additions, from the coquina walls built soon after the town was burned in 1702 to the house's enlargement during the British occupation. *14 St. Francis St., tel. 904/824–2872. Admission: $5 adults, $4.50 senior citizens, $2.50 students. Open daily 9–5.*

12 The **Lightner Museum** is housed in one of two posh hotels built in 1888 by railroad magnate Henry Flagler, who wanted to create an American Riviera. The museum contains a collection of ornate antique music boxes (ask about demonstrations!), and the Lightner Antique Mall perches on three levels of what was the hotel's grandiose indoor pool. *75 King St., tel. 904/824–2874. Admission to museum: $4 adults, $1 students, children under 12 free. Museum open daily 9–5; mall open Tues.–Sun. 10–4.*

13 Across from the Lightner Museum, **Flagler College** occupies the second of Flagler's hotels. The riveting structure is replete with towers, turrets, and arcades decorated by Louis Comfort Tiffany. The front courtyard is open to the public.

14 At Valencia and Sevilla streets, behind Flagler College, the **Flagler Memorial Presbyterian Church,** which Flagler built in 1889, is a splendid Venetian Renaissance structure. The dome towers more than 100 feet, and it is topped by a 20-foot Greek cross. *Open Mon.–Sat. 9–5.*

15 The **Fountain of Youth** salutes Ponce de León. In the complex there is a springhouse, an explorer's globe, a planetarium, and an Indian village. *155 Magnolia Ave., tel. 904/829–3168. Admission: $4 adults, $3 senior citizens, $1.50 children 6–12, under 6 free. Open daily 9–5.*

16 The **Mission of Nombre de Dios** commemorates the site where America's first Christian mass was celebrated. A 208-foot stainless-steel cross marks the spot where the mission's first cross was planted. *San Marco Ave. and Old Mission Rd., tel. 904/824–2809. Admission free, but donations requested. Open weekdays 8–8, weekends 9–8 summer; weekdays 8–5:30, weekends 9–5 winter.*

Daytona Beach Area

Like most of coastal Florida, Daytona sprang up around the water, so its waterfront offers views of historic homes between expanses of natural marsh. As you venture along the Intracoastal Waterway, take note of the different names assigned to the passage. In the Daytona area, it's called the Halifax River, though it is not actually a river, but a tidal waterway that flows between the mainland and the barrier islands.

Numbers in the margin correspond to points of interest on the Northeast Florida map.

A good place to begin touring Daytona environs is along a segment of Old Dixie Highway. From I–95 north of Ormond Beach, take Exit 90 and travel east.

The first left off Old Dixie Highway (Kings Highway) will take you to the entrance of **Bulow Plantation Ruins State Historic Site,** built in 1821. From the entrance, a winding dirt road cuts through tangled vegetation and leads to a picnic area and day-use facilities facing Bulow Creek. All that remains of the plantation are the massive ruins of the sugar mill, which may be reached either by auto or bicycle along a one-way loop road, or on foot via a scenic walking trail from the picnic area. *Tel. 904/439–2219. Admission: $2 per car. Open daily 9–5.*

Continue southeast on Old Dixie Highway through a tunnel of vine-laced oaks and cabbage palms. Next stop is **Tomoka State Park,** site of a Timucuan Indian settlement discovered in 1605 by Spanish explorer Alvaro Mexia. Wooded campsites, bicycle and walking paths, and guided canoe tours on the Tomoka and Halifax rivers are the main attractions. *North Beach St., Ormond Beach, tel. 904/677–3931. Admission: June 1–Dec. 31, $8 per day; Jan. 1–May 31, $17 per day; electricity, $2 per day. Open daily 8 AM–sunset.*

17 Time moves forward and the canopy begins to thin as you travel east on Old Dixie Highway to **Ormond Beach.** Auto racing was born on this hard-packed beach back in 1902, when R. E. Olds and Alexander Winton staged the first race. **Birthplace of Speed Antique Car Show and Swap Meet** is an annual event, attracting enthusiasts from across the nation. Sportsmen and socialites flocked to Ormond Beach each winter and made the massive Ormond Hotel their headquarters. The grand old wooden hotel (built in 1888 to pamper Flagler's East Coast Railway passengers) still stands watch on the east bank of the Halifax, but it is now vacant and no longer entertains guests.

Across the street from the hotel is **The Casements,** the restored winter retreat of John D. Rockefeller, now serving as a cultural center and museum. The estate and its formal gardens, on the National Register of Historic Places, are the setting for an annual lineup of special events and exhibits. Tours of the estate also are offered. *25 Riverside Dr., Ormond Beach, tel. 904/673–4701. Admission free; donations accepted. Open Mon.–Thurs. 9–9, Fri. 9–5, Sat. 9–noon.*

From the Casements go 2 blocks east to the **Birthplace of Speed Museum.** Devoted to the most exciting moments in America's long love affair with the automobile, the museum exhibits a replica of the Stanley Steamer, old Model T and Model A Fords, and a wealth of auto racing memorabilia, including a commemoration to auto-aero pioneer Glenn Curtis. *160 E. Granada Blvd., Ormond Beach, tel. 904/672–5657. Admission: $1 adults; 50¢ children under 12. Open Tues.–Sat. 1–5.*

Take A1A about 8 miles south to Beach Street, on the mainland. In the old downtown section is the **Halifax Historical Society Museum.** Photographs, Indian artifacts, and war memorabilia relevant to this area's fascinating, varied past are on display here. You can also shop for gifts and antiques. *252 S. Beach St., tel. 904/255–6976. Admission free. Open Tues.–Sat. 10–4.*

Pick up Volusia Avenue and drive west to Nova Road. Go 2 blocks south and follow signs to Museum Boulevard and the **Museum of Arts and Sciences.** This competent little museum has two blockbuster features: One is a large collection of pre-Castro Cuban art; the other is a complete and eye-popping skeleton of a giant sloth. The sloth remains—found near here—are the most complete skeleton of its kind ever found in North America. *1040 Museum Blvd., tel. 904/255–0285. Admission: $3 adults, $1 children, students, and senior citizens. Members free Fri. Open Tues.–Fri. 9–4, weekends noon–5.*

18 To reach the famous beaches of **Daytona Beach** go east to A1A and follow signs to beach ramps, which lie for miles both north and south. During spring break, race weeks, and summer holidays, expect heavy traffic along this strip of garishly painted beach motels and tacky souvenir shops.

Several miles south of the Marriott, on A1A, is **Ponce Inlet,** which is frequented by locals and visitors who are familiar with the area. A manicured drive winds through low-growing shrubs and windblown scrub oaks to parking and picnic areas. Boardwalks traverse the delicate dunes and provide easy access to the wide beach. Marking this prime spot is a bright red century-old lighthouse, now a historic monument and museum. *Token admission. Open daily 10–5.*

Time Out **Lighthouse Landing** (4931 S. Peninsula Dr., tel. 904/761–1821), only yards from the historic light, is a good place for sipping cocktails and watching the sunset.

A 20-mile drive west on U.S. 92 (International Speedway) will 19 take you to little **De Land,** home of **Stetson University.** The **Gillespie Museum of Minerals,** on the stately campus, houses one of the largest private collections of gems and minerals in the world. *Michigan and Amelia aves., tel. 904/822–7330. Admission free. Open weekdays 9–noon and 1–4.*

Drive 4 miles south on 17–92, toward Orange City. Follow signs to the **Blue Spring State Park,** one of the best places to spot manatees. February is the top month for sightings, but you're likely to see one almost any time. The park, once a river port where paddle wheelers stopped to take on cargos of oranges, also includes a historic homestead that is open to the public. Park facilities include camping, picnicking, and hiking. *Off U.S. 17–92 in Orange City, tel. 904/775–3663. Admission: $3.25 per vehicle with up to 8 people. Open 8 AM–sunset.*

Ocala

20 To reach **Ocala,** take any of three Ocala exits off I–75. The city is on State Route 40, an east-west artery that runs from Yankeetown on the Gulf of Mexico to Ormond Beach. Once known only as the home of Silver Springs and the Ocala National Forest, the city has become a center for thoroughbred breeding and training. Along with the horses have come a new generation of glitterati, with their private jets and massive estates surrounded by green grazing grasses and white fencing.

As Ocala matures from country to gentry, its tourist appeal becomes more upscale. Trendy hotels and inns now dot the city; restaurants serve more innovative, international fare; and the Appleton Museum of Art is turning into a complex for all the arts, including theater, dance, and music.

Silver Springs, the state's oldest attraction (established 1890), and listed on the National Register of Historic Landmarks, features the world's largest collection of artesian springs. Today, the park presents wild animal displays, glass-bottom boat tours in the Silver River, a jungle cruise on the Fort King Waterway, Jungle Safari, an antique and classic car museum, and walks through natural habitats. A multimillion-dollar project is recapturing the look and atmosphere of the 1890s. The attraction promises visitors a journey to the wild kingdom above and below the water. *Rte. 40, 1 mi east of Ocala, tel. 904/236–2121. Open daily 9–5. Admission to all attractions: $19.95 adults, $14.95 children 3–10.*

Next door is Silver Springs's **Wild Waters,** a water theme park with a giant wave pool and seven water-flume rides. *Admission: $9.95 adults, $8.95 children 3–10. Open late Mar.–June 7, daily 10–5; Aug., daily 10–7; Sept. 4–30, weekends only 10–5.*

Farther east on Rte. 40 is the entrance to **Ocala National Forest,** a 366,000-acre wilderness with lakes, springs, rivers, hiking trails, campgrounds, and historic sites. Area residents recall the filming of *The Yearling* at several sites within the forest. The **Visitor Information Center** (tel. 904/625–7470) on the left just over the bridge, is the site of old-fashioned sugar-cane grinding and cane-syrup making during the first two weeks of November each year. The syrup is bottled and sold on the premises. **Lake Waldena Resort & Campground** (tel. 904/625–2851), several miles farther east into the national forest on Rte. 40, features a white-sand bathing beach and crystal-clear freshwater lake. Noncampers pay day-use fees for picnicking and access to the beach.

South of Rte. 40 (via Rte. 314-A) is **Moss Bluff,** on the Oklawaha River, which forms the southern boundary of Ocala National Forest. Three major recreational areas are found in the national forest: **Juniper Springs,** off Rte. 40, featuring a picturesque stone waterwheel house, campground, natural-spring swimming pool, and hiking and canoe trails; **Salt Springs,** off Rte. 40 (via Rte. 19 North), featuring a natural saltwater spring, where Atlantic blue crabs come to spawn each summer; and **Alexander Springs,** off Rte. 40 (via Rte. 445 South), featuring a swimming lake and campground.

Just outside the eastern boundary of the forest, at the crossroads of Rte. 40 and U.S. 17, are **Barberville** and the **Pioneer Settlement for the Creative Arts, Inc.** A bridge house, moved from the St. Johns River at Astor, forms the entrance to the museum. On the grounds are an old-time caboose, a railroad depot, the commissary store of a turpentine camp, and a newly constructed "post-and-beam" barn, built of wood milled on the premises. During the first weekend in May and November each year, the museum hosts a Country Jamboree, which features arts, crafts, folk music, and country cooking. *U.S. 17 and Rte. 40, Barberville, tel. 904/749–2959. Admission: $2.50 adults, $1 children 3–12. Open weekdays 9–3.*

North of Barberville on U.S. 17 is another 1800s steamboat stop, **Crescent City,** where the historic **Sprague House Inn** (125 Central Ave., Crescent City, tel. 904/698–2430) traces steamboat-era history through the inn's collection of stained-glass windows. The three-room bed-and-breakfast inn also features a full-service restaurant.

South on U.S. 17 is **DeLeon Springs State Recreation Area,** promoted as a fountain of youth to 1889 winter tourists. Today, visitors come to picnic, swim, fish, and hike the nature trails. *Tel. 904/985–4212. Admission: $3.25 per vehicle with up to 8 people. Open daily 8 AM–sunset.*

Gainesville

The University of Florida and its beloved Gators football games bring most visitors to this city, so styles and prices are geared primarily to modest budgets. In addition to sporting activities and the excellent theater, concerts, film series, and other activ- 21 ities typical of campus life, tourists come to the **Gainesville** area for its strange geological features.

During the 1600s, the largest cattle ranch in Spanish Florida flourished on these great savannas. The area, written about in Marjorie Kinnan Rawlings's *The Yearling* and made more famous by the film *Cross Creek*, is a place of great vitality and energy—to be discovered by the diligent hiker. Be warned, though, that the shimmering heat can be stupefying to even the most knowledgeable outdoorsperson.

The **Florida State Museum,** on the campus of the University of Florida, will be of interest to the entire family. Explore a replica Mayan palace, see a typical Timucuan household, and walk through a full-size replica of a Florida cave. There are outstanding collections from throughout Florida's history, so spend at least half a day here. *Museum Rd. at Newell Dr., tel. 904/392–1721. Admission free. Open Tues.–Sat. 10–4, Sun. and holidays 1–4; closed Christmas.*

About 11 miles south of Gainesville on U.S. 441 is the village of **Micanopy** (micka-*no*-pee), where Timucuan Indians settled. There was a Spanish mission here, but little remains from before white settlement, which began in 1821. Today, the streets are lined with antiques shops and live oaks. Browse the shops on the main street, or come in the fall for a major antiques event involving 200 dealers.

Paynes Prairie, situated between I–75 and U.S. 441 in Micanopy, is a strangely out-of-context site that attests to Florida's fragile, highly volatile ecology. Evidence of Indian habitation dated as early as 7,000 BC has been found on this 18,000-acre wilderness that was once a vast lake. Only a century ago, the lake drained so abruptly that thousands of beached fish died in the mud. The remains of a ferry, stranded here in the 1880s can still be seen. In recent years buffalo lived here; today persimmon trees, planted by settlers long ago, flourish, and wild cattle and horses roam. Swimming, boating, picnicking, and camping are permitted in the park. *Tel. 904/836–4281. Admission: $3.25 per vehicle with up to 8 people. Open daily 8 AM–sunset.*

At the **Marjorie Kinnan Rawlings State Historic Site,** Rawlings's readers will feel her presence. A typewriter rusts on the ramshackle porch; the closet where she hid her booze during Prohibition yawns open; and clippings from her scrapbook reveal her legal battles and marital problems. Bring lunch and picnic in the shade of one of Rawlings's trees. Then visit her grave a few miles away at peaceful Island Grove. *S.R. 325 at Hawthorn, southeast of Gainesville, tel. 904/466–3672. Small admission fee. Open Thurs.–Mon. 10–11:30 and 1–4:30; closed Thanksgiving, Christmas, and New Year's day. Tours every half hour.*

The **Devil's Millhopper State Geological Site** is a botanical wonderland of exotic, subtropical ferns and trees, with a waterfall. The state geological site is situated in and around an enormous 1,100-foot-deep sinkhole. *Off U.S. 441 north of Gainesville, tel. 904/336–2008. Admission: $2 per vehicle, $1 pedestrians. Open daily 9 AM–sunset.*

Off the Beaten Track

About 55 miles south of Jacksonville in Palatka is **Ravine State Gardens,** which began during the depression as a WPA project, and blossomed into one of the area's great azalea gardens. The ravines are atypical in flat Florida. They're steep and deep, threaded with brooks and rocky outcroppings, and floored with little flatlands that make for a perfect intimate picnic. Although any month is a good time to hike the shaded glens here, the azaleas are in full bloom February and March. The gardens can be easily reached from Gainesville and St. Augustine. *Off Twig St., from U.S. 17S, tel. 904/329–3721. Admission: $3.25 per vehicle with up to 8 people. Open daily 8–sunset.*

Perry, 26 miles south of I–10 between Tallahassee and Jacksonville, was once the largest single source of naval stores in the world and the home of a 1929 sawmill that was the largest one east of the Mississippi. The **Forest Capitol Museum,** on U.S. 19–98 a mile south of the city, includes lively, likeable forestry exhibits, a picnic area, and a pioneer homestead typical of this area. *Tel. 904/584–3227. Admission: $1. Open Thurs.–Mon. 9–5; closed noon–1 and major holidays.*

Far off the beaten byway, on Dog Island, is the **Pelican Inn** (tel. 800/451–5294), with pristine beaches, an eyeful of bird life, and peacefulness that can't be matched. Reached only by plane or boat, the inn provides a guaranteed island get-away. The kitchen is furnished, you supply the food and cook it yourself.

What to See and Do with Children

Castle Adventure is a slick update of an old-style family fun park, where you can play miniature golf, wander through a giant maze, explore waterfalls, caves, and lush tropical landscaping. *200 Hagen Terr., Daytona Beach, on U.S. 92, tel. 904/238–3887. Admission: $7 adults, $6 children and senior citizens. Golf alone or maze alone, $4.50 adults, $3.50 children. Open daily 10–10.*

Jacksonville Zoo is best known for its rare white rhinos and an outstanding collection of rare waterfowl. On a 7-acre veldt, see 10 species of African birds and animals. *I–95 north to Hecksher Dr. E., Jacksonville, tel. 904/757–4463. Admission: $4 adults, $2.50 children 3–12, $3 senior citizens. Open daily 9–5.*

Marineland, one of the first of such attractions in the United States is still a magic place. Dolphins grin, sea lions bark, and seals slither seductively to everyone's delight. *South of St. Augustine on A1A, tel. 904/471-1111 or in FL 800/824-4218. Admission: $12 adults, $7 children 3-11. Open daily 9-5:45, shows continuously.*

The Fred Bear Museum displays archery artifacts dating to the Stone Age, and a wealth of natural history exhibits all seeable in a one-hour guided tour. *Fred Bear Dr. at Archer Rd., Gainesville, tel. 904/376-2411. Admission: $2.50 adults, $1.50 children 6-12. Open Wed.-Sun. 10-6.*

At the **Florida Sports Hall of Fame** children can see mementos of more than 100 of their favorite sports heroes. *601 Hall of Fame Dr., off U.S. 90 W., Lake City, tel. 904/758-1310. Admission: $2 adults, children 12 and under free. Open Mon.-Sat. 9-9, Sun. 10-7.*

Shopping

Souvenirs unique to northeast Florida include stuffed manatees, citrus fruits, gems and minerals from De Land, beach and surf-theme merchandise from along the coast, award-winning Lafayette wines from Tallahassee, and auto racing items from Daytona Beach.

For specialty shops, roam around **Jacksonville Landing**, downtown at the Main Street Bridge.

Brand-name items are sold at discount prices at the **Daytona Beach Outlet Mall** (2400 S. Ridgewood Ave., South Daytona, tel. 904/756-8700). Daytona's **Flea Market** is one of the South's largest (I-4 at U.S. 92).

Beaches

Beaches in northeastern Florida are the most varied in the state, ranging from the rocky moonscape of Washington Oaks State Park, just below St. Augustine, to the slick sands of Daytona.

Amelia Island's lower half is mostly covered by the Amelia Island Plantation resort. However, on the island's extreme southern tip you can go horseback riding along the wide, almost deserted beaches.

Atlantic Beach, north of Neptune Beach, is the other favored surfing area. Around the popular Sea Turtle Inn, you'll find catamaran rentals and instruction. Five areas have lifeguards on duty in the summer 10-6.

Daytona, which bills itself as the "World's Most Famous Beach," permits cars to drive right up to your beachsite, spread out a blanket, and have all your belongings at hand; this is especially convenient for elderly or handicapped beachgoers.

Flagler Beach is a vast, windswept swath of sand with easy access.

Fort Clinch State Park, on Amelia Island's northern tip, includes a municipal beach and pier. That's where Fernandina Beach's city beaches are, meaning you pay a state-park entrance fee to reach them. But the beaches are broad and lovely, and there is parking right on the beach, bathhouses, picnic areas, and all the facilities of the park itself, including the fort.

Jacksonville Beach is the liveliest of the long line of Jacksonville Beaches. Young people flock to the beach, where there are all sorts of games to play and also beach concessions, rental shops, and a fishing pier.

Kathryn Abbey Hanna Park, near Mayport, is the Jacksonville area's showplace park, drawing families and singles alike. It offers beaches, showers, and snack bars that operate April–Labor Day.

Neptune Beach, adjoining Jacksonville Beach to the north, is more residential and offers easy access to quieter beaches. Surfers take to the waves, and consider it one of the area's two best surfing sites.

St. Augustine has 43 miles of wide, white, level beaches. The young gravitate toward the public beaches at St. Augustine Beach and Vilano Beach, while families prefer the Anastasia State Recreation Area. All three are accessible via Rte. A1A: Vilano Beach is to the north, across North River, and Anastasia State Park and St. Augustine Beach are both on Anastasia Island, across the Bridge of Lions.

Participant Sports

Boating
Rentals

Pontoon boats, houseboats, and bass boats for the St. Johns River are available from **Hontoon Landing Marina** (De Land, tel. 904/734–2474, or in FL 800/248–2474). Boats for the Tomoka River are offered by **Daytona Recreational Sales & Rentals** (Ormond Beach, tel. 904/672–5631). **Club Nauticos** rents boats to members and nonmembers (Amelia Island, tel. 904/277–2484; St. Augustine, tel. 904/825–4848; Jacksonville Beach, tel. 904/241–2628). Other rentals are available from **The Boat Club** (Daytona Beach, tel. 904/258–2991). Explore the silver waters of the St. Johns River system, with its many springs, lakes, and tributaries, aboard **Houseboat Vacations** (Astor, tel. 904/736–9422 or 800/262–3454).

Rental boats and motors for fishing the St. Johns are available from **Highland Park Fish Camp** (De Land, tel. 904/734–2334), **Blair's Jungle Den Fish Camp** (near Astor, tel. 904/749–2264), **Tropical Apartments & Marina** (De Land, tel. 904/734–3080), and **South Moon Fishing Camp** (near Astor, tel. 904/749–2383).

Canoeing

Float down sparkling clear spring "runs" that may be mere tunnels through tangled jungle growth. Try the 7-mile Juniper Springs run in the Ocala National Forest (tel. 904/625–2808) and the Sante Fe River at High Springs (tel. 904/454–1853).

Fishing

Your options range from cane-pole fishing in a roadside canal or off a fishing pier, to luxury charters. On the cheaper end of the scale, **Jacksonville Beach Fishing Pier** extends 1,200 feet into the Atlantic, and the cost for fishing is $3 for adults, $1.50 for children and senior citizens, or 50¢ for watching.

Charters

Deep-sea fishing charters are provided by **Critter Fleet Marina,** (Daytona Beach, tel. 904/767–7676 or in FL, 800/338–0850) and **Cindy Jay Charters** (Ponce Inlet, tel. 904/788–3469).

For sportfishing, charter the *Sea Love II* (St. Augustine, 904/824–3328) or contact **Critter Fleet Marina** (Daytona Beach, tel. 904/767–7676). One of the savviest guides to St. Johns River bass fishing is **Bob Stonewater** (De Land, tel. 904/736–7120). He'll tow his boat to whatever launch ramp is best for the day's fishing, and meet clients there.

Golf Florida is famed for its golf facilities, and no section of the state has better courses than the Northeast.

In Daytona Beach, the **Indigo Lakes Course** (tel. 904/258–6333) is now developing a headquarters course and golfing community for the LPGA (tel. 904/254–8800). The **Tournament Players Club at Sawgrass** (tel. 904/273–3235) in Ponte Vedra is home to the championship of that name; **Spruce Creek Golf & Country Club** (tel. 904/756–6114), near Daytona, has 18 holes of championship golf and its own fly-in runway for private planes.

At **Amelia Island Plantation** (tel. 904/261–6161), three stunning oceanfront holes are true "links" in the old Scottish golf tradition.

Ocala's **Golden Ocala Course** (tel. 904/622–0172) is rated among the state's top 25. Each of its holes is modeled after one of the world's most famous, from St. Andrews to Troon.

Horseback Riding Ocala's bluegrass horse country can be explored during trail rides organized by **Oakview Stable** (S.W. 27th Ave., behind the Paddock Mall, tel. 904/237–8844).

Skydiving Anybody who wants to jump out of an airplane when it's thousands of feet up in the air can do so with the help of **Skydive De Land** (tel. 904/738–3539), open daily 8 AM–sunset.

Tennis Resorts especially well known for their tennis programs include **Amelia Island Plantation** (tel. 904/261–6161), site of the nationally televised WTA Championships; the **St. Augustine Beach and Tennis Resort** (tel. 904/471–0909); **Ponce de Leon Lodge and Country Club** (tel. 904/824–2821); the **Ponte Vedra Club** (tel. 904/285–6911); and the **Marriott at Sawgrass** (tel. 904/285–7777).

Water Sports
Rentals Most larger beachfront hotels offer water sports equipment for rent. Other sources for renting sailboards, surfboards, or boogie boards include **The Surf Station** (1002 Anastasia Blvd., St. Augustine Beach, tel. 904/471–9463); **Salty Dog** (700 Broadway, Daytona Beach, tel. 904/258–0457); **Sandy Point Sailboards** (1114 Riverside Dr., Holly Hill, tel. 904/255–4977).

For jet-ski rentals try **J&J** (841 Ballough Rd., Daytona Beach, tel. 904/255–1917) or **Jet Ski Headquarters** (3537 Halifax Dr., Port Orange, tel. 904/788–4143).

Diving/Snorkeling Northeast Florida offers, in addition to ocean diving, a wide range of cave diving and snorkeling over spring "boils." For information about scuba diving in springs and caves, instruction, and rental equipment, call **Drive & Tour Inc.** (1403 E. New York Ave., De Land, tel. 904/736–0571).

Scuba equipment, trips, refills, and lessons are available from **Adventure Diving** (3127 S. Ridgewood Ave., S. Daytona, tel. 904/788–8050).

Spectator Sports

Auto Racing The massive **Daytona International Speedway** on U.S. 92 (Daytona Beach's major east–west artery) is home of year-round auto and motorcycle racing including the annual Daytona 500 in February and Pepsi 400 in July. Twenty-minute narrated tours of the historic track are offered daily 9–5 except on race days. For racing schedules, call 904/254–2700.

The Gatornationals of the **National Hot Rod Association** (tel. 818/914–4761) are held each year in late-winter in Gainesville.

Baseball The **Jacksonville Suns,** a Class AA Southern League professional team, play home games in Wolfson Park, Gator Bowl complex (1201 E. Duval St., Jacksonville, tel. 904/358–2846).

Football The blockbuster event in Northeast Florida is Jacksonville's **Gator Bowl** (tel. 904/396–1800). Other major events include **Florida Gators** games in Gainesville.

Golf The Tournament Players Championship is a March event at the **Tournament Players Club** (near Sawgrass in Ponte Vedra Beach, tel. 904/285–7888), which is national headquarters of the PGA Tour.

Greyhound Races Year-round, you can bet on the dogs every night but Sunday at the **Daytona Beach Kennel Club** (on U.S. 92 near the International Speedway, tel. 904/252–6484).

Greyhounds race year-round in the Jacksonville area, with seasons split among three tracks: **Jacksonville Kennel Club,** May–September (1440 N. McDuff Ave., tel. 904/646–0001); **Orange Park Kennel Club,** November–April (U.S. 17, about ½ mi south of I–295, tel. 904/646–0001); and **St. John's Greyhound Park,** March and April (7 miles south of I–95 on U.S. 1, tel. 904/646–0001).

Jai Alai The speediest of sports, jai-alai is played year-round at **Ocala Jai-Alai** (Rte. 318, Orange Lake, tel. 904/591–2345) and at **Daytona Beach Jai Alai** (U.S. 92, across from the Daytona International Speedway, tel. 904/255–0222).

Tennis The top-rated Women's Tennis Association Championships is held in April, and the Men's All-American Tennis Championship in September, both at **Amelia Island Plantation** (Amelia Island, tel. 904/277–5145).

Dining and Lodging

Dining The state is embraced by the Atlantic Ocean and the Gulf of Mexico and is laced with waterways, which means that seafood is prominently featured. In coastal towns, the catches often come straight from the restaurant's own fleet. Shrimp, oysters, snapper, and grouper are especially popular.

Restaurants are organized geographically. Unless otherwise noted, they serve lunch and dinner.

Category	Cost*
Very Expensive	over $60
Expensive	$40–$60

Moderate	$20–$40
Inexpensive	under $20

**per person, excluding drinks, service, and 6% sales tax*

Lodging Accommodations range from splashy beachfront resorts and glitzy condominiums to cozy inns and bed-and-breakfasts nestled in historic districts. As a general rule, the closer you are to the center of activity in the coastal resorts, the more you'll pay. You'll save a few dollars if you stay across from the beach rather than on it, and you'll save even more if you select a place that's a bit removed from the action.

Category	Cost*
Very Expensive	over $120
Expensive	$90–$120
Moderate	$50–$90
Inexpensive	under $50

**per double room, excluding 6% state sales tax and nominal tourist tax*

Highly recommended restaurants and lodgings are indicated by a star ★.

Amelia Island
Lodging
★ **Amelia Island Plantation.** One of the first "environmentally sensitive" resorts, Amelia Island's grounds ramble through ancient live-oak forests and behind some of the highest dunes in the state. A warm sense of community prevails; some homes are occupied year-round, and accommodations range from home and condo rentals to rooms in a full-service hotel. The resort is best known for its golf and tennis programs, but hiking and biking trails thread through the 1,300 acres. Restaurants range from casual to ultraelegant. *3000 First Coast Hwy., 32034, tel. 904/261–6161 or outside FL 800/874–6878. 125 rooms in the inn; 475 villa apartments; home rentals by arrangement. Facilities: private indoor pools in honeymoon villas, water sports, 25 tennis courts, 2 golf courses, fishing, racquetball, fitness center, instruction, pro shops, children's activities, restaurants, shopping, entertainment. AE, D, DC, MC, V. Expensive.*

Daytona Beach
Dining
Gene's Steak House. This family-operated restaurant, located west of town, in the middle of nowhere, has long upheld its reputation as the place for steaks. The wine list is one of the state's most comprehensive, and there are seafood specialties, but it's basically a meat-and-potatoes paradise for power beef-eaters. *U.S. 92, 4.5 mi west of the I–95/I–4 interchange, tel. 904/255–2059. Reservations advised. Dress: neat but casual. Closed Mon. AE, DC, MC, V. Expensive.*

★ **Top of Daytona.** Especially dazzling at sundown, this 29th-floor supper club has a 360° view of the beach, Intracoastal, and the city. It's a project of television personality and cookbook author Sophie Kay, who is famous for her shrimp dishes, chicken inventions, and delicate veal recipes. *2625 S. Atlantic Ave., tel. 904/767–5791. Reservations advised. Dress: casual. AE, DC, MC, V. Moderate.*

Lodging

Captain's Quarters Inn. It may look like just another mid-rise hotel, but inside, this is a home away from home with an antique desk, Victorian love seat, and tropical greenery set in the lobby of this beachfront inn. Fresh-baked goodies and coffee are served in The Galley, which overlooks the ocean and looks like grandma's kitchen with a few extra tables and chairs. Each guest suite features rich oak furnishings, a complete kitchen, and private balcony. *3711 S. Atlantic Ave., Daytona Beach Shores 32127, tel. 904/767–3119. 25 suites. Facilities: heated pool, sunbathing deck. AE, D, MC, V. Expensive.*

Daytona Beach Hilton. A towering landmark, this Hilton is situated on a 22-mile beach. Most rooms have balconies; some have a kitchenette, patio, or terrace. Convenient touches include an extra lavatory in every room, hair dryer, lighted makeup mirror, and a bar with refrigerator. *2637 S. Atlantic Ave., 32118, tel. 904/767–7350 or 800/525–7350. 214 rooms. Facilities: heated outdoor pool, children's pool, Jacuzzi, exercise room, sauna, game room, playground, gift shop, laundry. AE, D, DC, MC, V. Expensive.*

★ **Daytona Beach Marriott.** The location is a bombshell: The Ocean Center is in one direction and the best of the beach, boardwalk, and band shell is in the other. Fresh and flowery pastels set a buoyant tone for a beach vacation and every room views the ocean. *100 N. Atlantic Ave., 32118, tel. 904/254–8200. 402 rooms. Facilities: indoor-outdoor pool, 2 whirlpools, children's pool and playground, poolside bar, 2 restaurants, 30 specialty shops. AE, DC, MC, V. Expensive.*

Howard Johnson Hotel. Straight out of the glamour films of the 1930s, this 14-story hotel on the beach is an oldie that has been brought back to the splendor of its Deco years. Kitchenette suites are available. *600 N. Atlantic Ave., 32018, tel. 904/255–4471 or 800/767–4471. 324 rooms. Facilities: pool, restaurant, lounge with live entertainment and dancing. AE, DC, MC, V. Moderate.*

★ **Indigo Lakes Resort & Conference Center.** Home of the Ladies Professional Golf Association, this sprawling inland resort offers sports galore. The championship golf course measures 7,123 yards and has the largest greens in the state. Rooms are light and lavish in Florida tones. *U.S. 92 and I–95, Box 10859, 32120, tel. 904/258–6333; in FL, 800/223–4161; outside FL, 800/874–9918. 212 rooms, 64 condo suites. Facilities: Olympic-size pool, racquetball, tennis, golf, archery, pro shops, 2 restaurants, nightclub, courtesy transportation to airport and around resort, in-room coffee, nonsmoker and handicapped rooms available. AE, MC, V. Moderate.*

Perry's Ocean-Edge. Long regarded as a family resort, Perry's enjoys one of the highest percentages of repeat visitors in the state. Spacious grounds are set with picnic tables. Free homemade doughnuts and coffee—a breakfast ritual here—are served in the lush solarium, a good way to get acquainted. *2209 S. Atlantic Ave., 32118, tel. 904/255–0581; in FL, 800/342–0102; outside FL, 800/447–0002. 204 rooms. Facilities: heated indoor pool, whirlpools, golf privileges, planned activities, cafe open for breakfast and lunch, shops. AE, D, DC, MC, V. Moderate.*

Aku Tiki Inn. Located right on the beach, the family-owned inn has a Polynesian theme inside and out. You can bake by the large heated pool or snooze under a shady tree on the spacious grounds. *2225 S. Atlantic Ave., 32118, tel. 904/252–9631 or 800/528–1234. 132 rooms, some with efficiencies. Facilities: pool,* *shuffleboard, game room, restaurant, 2 lounges with live entertainment, pool bar, gift shop, laundry. AE, DC, MC, V. Moderate–Inexpensive.*

De Land
Dining

★ **Karlings Inn.** This facility is best described as a Bavarian Brigadoon set beside a forgotten highway near the has-been hamlet of DeLeon Springs and decorated like a Black Forest inn. Karl Caeners personally oversees preparation of the sauerbraten, red cabbage, succulent roast duckling, sumptuous soups, and tender schnitzels. Ask to see the dessert tray. *4640 N. U.S. 17, tel. 904/985–5535. Reservations advised. Dress: neat but casual. Closed Sun.–Mon. No lunch. AE, MC, V. Moderate.*

★ **Pondo's.** You lose a couple of decades as you step into what was once a romantic hideaway for young pilots who trained in De Land during the war. The owner/chef specializes in whimsical veal dishes, but he also does fish, beef, and chicken—always with fresh vegetables, a platter-size salad, and oven-baked breads. The old-fashioned bar is "Cheers"-y, and a pianist entertains. *1915 Old New York Ave., tel. 904/734–1995. Reservations advised. Dress: neat but casual. AE, MC, V. Moderate.*

Rose Room. A quiet, multilevel corner of the Hilton offers seating at tables or in romantic booths. In addition to the blackboard dinner specials are a Mediterranean concoction called Grouper De Land, boneless breast of chicken, pasta du jour, and a couple of steak items. Come here for breakfast, too. *De Land Hilton, 350 International Speedway Blvd. (U.S. 92), tel. 904/738–5200. Reservations accepted. Dress: neat but casual. AE, DC, MC, V. Moderate.*

The Original Holiday House. This, the original of what has become a small chain of buffet restaurants in Florida, is enormously popular with senior citizens, families, and college students. Patrons can choose from three categories: salads only, salads and vegetables only, or the full buffet. *704 N. Woodland Blvd., tel. 904/734–6319. No reservations. Dress: neat but casual. MC, V. Inexpensive.*

Lodging

De Land Country Inn. This home, replete with spacious verandas and glowing hardwoods, was built in 1903 and is furnished in an eclectic blend of restored antiques and reproductions. Hosts Raisa and Bill Lilley serve a complimentary Continental breakfast to start your day. *228 W. Howry Ave., 32720, tel. 904/736–4244. 5 rooms with baths. Facilities: pool. AE, MC, V. Moderate.*

De Land Hilton. Picture a snazzy, big-city hotel in a little college town, run by friendly, small-town folks with city savvy. An enormous painting by nationally known local artist Fred Messersmith dominates the plush lobby. Rooms are done in subdued colors and styles; prestige suites have housed the likes of Tom Cruise and the New Kids on the Block. *350 International Speedway Blvd. (U.S. 92) 32724, tel. 904/738–5200 or 800/826–3233. 150 rooms. Facilities: pool, tennis and golf privileges, restaurant, nightclub, bar. AE, MC, V. Moderate.*

University Inn. For years this has been the choice of business travelers and visitors to the university. Located on campus, and across from the popular Holiday House restaurant, this motel is in a convenient location, has clean, comfortable rooms, and offers a Continental breakfast each morning. *644 N. Woodland Blvd., 32720, tel. 904/734–5711, or 800/345–8991. 60 rooms, some with kitchenette. Facilities: pool. AE, DC, MC, V. Inexpensive.*

Flagler Beach
Dining
★

Topaz Café. An unexpected treasure on a quiet stretch of the beach highway, this intimate restaurant is operated by two sisters who do all their own cooking and baking: vegetables are bright and appealing and meats and fish are artistically presented. The menu changes weekly. Though the selection is limited, there are always enough choices, including a vegetarian entrée. The decor is a whimsical combination of enamel-top tables, unmatched settings and linens, and wildflowers. *1224 S. Ocean Shore Blvd. 32136, tel. 904/439–3275. Dress: neat but casual. Reservations advised. Closed Sun.–Mon. Lunch Fri. only. MC, V. Moderate.*

Lodging
★

Topaz Motel/Hotel. This lovingly restored 1920s beach house is lavishly furnished in museum-quality Victoriana. It's a popular beachfront honeymoon hideaway—romantic and undiscovered. *1224 S. A1A, 32136, tel. 904/439–3301. 48 units, including efficiencies. Facilities: pool, restaurant, laundry. D, MC, V. Moderate.*

Flagler Beach Motel. If you yearn for the mom-and-pop motels of old Florida, at 1950s prices, this is it in plain vanilla. It's on a quiet stretch of beach, away from the Daytona crowds, and dressed with old-fashioned informality and friendliness. *1820 S. Ocean Shore Blvd., 32136, tel. 904/439–2340. 23 units, including efficiencies, cottages, and apartments. Facilities: pool, shuffleboard, cable TV. MC, V. Inexpensive.*

Gainesville
Dining

Sovereign. Crystal, candlelight, and a jazz pianist set a theme of restrained elegance in this 1878 carriage house. The veal specialties are notable, particularly the *saltimbocca* (veal sautéed with spinach and cheese). Duckling and rack of baby lamb are dependable choices as well. *12 S.E. Second Ave., tel. 904/378–6307. Reservations advised. Jacket suggested. AE, DC, MC, V. Expensive.*

Capriccio. This rooftop restaurant is a celebration spot for locals and a dependable place for travelers who are looking for a good meal. The superb view and classic Italian cuisine make for a relaxing evening. The pastries and breads are home-baked. *University Centre Hotel, 1535 S.W. Archer Rd., tel. 904/371–3333. Reservations advised. Jacket and tie requested. AE, DC, MC, V. Moderate.*

Lodging

Herlong Mansion. Adorned with old relics at every turn, this late-19th-century home screams out its antiquity. Continental breakfasts and evening cordials with petit fours, provided by caring hosts, strengthens the appeal. Although the nearest restaurants are in Gainesville, this inn has much to offer. There's no street address; just look for the big, brick house on the short main street of Micanopy. *Tel. 904/466–3322. 6 rooms with private baths. Facilities: library, parlor with TV. D, MC, V. Expensive.*

Holiday Inn University Center. An upbeat, casual look sets the scene for business, medical, and vacation travelers. It's downtown and near the university and football stadium, jogging paths, and tennis courts. *1250 W. University Ave., 32601, tel. 904/376–1661 or 800/HOLIDAY. 167 rooms. Facilities: rooftop pool, remote control TV, rental cars on property, restaurant, lounge, airport transportation. AE, DC, MC, V. Moderate.*

Residence Inn by Marriott. Studios and two-bedroom suites with kitchen and fireplace make a cozy pied-à-terre. Cocktails, Continental breakfast, and a daily paper are part of the hospitality. The central location is convenient for the university or business traveler. *4001 S.W. 13th St., (at U.S. 441 and S. R. 331), 32608, tel. 904/371–2101 or 800/331–3131. 80 suites. Facilities: outdoor pool, whirlpool, exercise equipment, microwave, laundry, complimentary Continental breakfast daily and hospitality hour Mon.–Thurs. AE, DC, MC, V. Moderate.*

Cabot Lodge. Included in the room rate is a Continental breakfast and a chummy two-hour cocktail reception. Spacious rooms and a clublike ambience make this a favorite with business and university travelers. *3726 S.W. 40th Blvd., 32608, tel. 904/375–2400 or outside FL 800/843–8735. Facilities: satellite TV. AE, D, DC, MC, V. Inexpensive.*

Jacksonville/ Jacksonville Beach
Dining

Cafe on the Square. This 1920 building, the oldest on San Marco Square, is an unpretentious place for an after-theater meal, tête-à-tête dining, or Sunday brunch. Dine indoors or out and choose from a menu ranging from steak sandwiches to quiche, marinated chicken, or pasta—all choices with a Continental flair. *1974 San Marco Blvd., Jacksonville, tel. 904/399–4848. Reservations accepted Mon.–Thurs. Dress: casual. AE, MC, V. No lunch. Moderate.*

Crustaceans. With the Intracoastal in the background, hearty hard-shell crabs or juicy grilled fillet will taste all the better. The menu also offers steak and homemade bakery specialties. It's especially festive on summer weekends when there's live entertainment. *2321 Beach Blvd., Jacksonville Beach, tel. 904/247–4288. Reservations advised. Dress: casual. AE, MC, V. No lunch. Moderate.*

Ragtime. A New Orleans theme threads through everything from the Sunday jazz brunch to the beignets. It's loud, crowded, and alive with a sophisticated young bunch. If you aren't into Creole and Cajun classics, have a simple po-boy sandwich or fish sizzled on the grill. *207 Atlantic Blvd., Atlantic Beach, tel. 904/241–7877. No reservations. Dress: casual. AE, DC, MC, V. Moderate.*

Angelo's. A cozy, inelegant, hospitable family spot where you can dive into mountainous portions of southern Italian standards, including a socko eggplant parmigiana. House specials change daily. *2111 University Blvd. N., Jacksonville, tel. 904/743–3400. Reservations accepted. Dress: casual. AE, DC, MC, V. Inexpensive.*

Beach Road Chicken Dinner. If down-home chicken, potatoes, and biscuits are your comfort food, this is the place. It's the best of basic roadside diner stuff at Depression-era prices. Eat in or take out. *4132 Atlantic Blvd., Jacksonville, tel. 904/398–7980. Reservations accepted. Dress: casual. No credit cards. Inexpensive.*

Crawdaddy's. Take it Cajun or cool, this riverfront fish shack is the place for seafood, jambalaya, and country chicken. Dig into the house specialty, catfish—all you can eat—then dance to a fe-do-do beat. Sunday brunch served. *1643 Prudential Dr. (just off I–10 at I–95), Jacksonville, tel. 904/396–3546. Reservations accepted. Dress: casual. AE, D, DC, MC, V. Inexpensive.*

★ **Homestead.** A down-home place with several dining rooms, a huge fireplace, and country cooking, this restaurant specializes in skillet-fried chicken, which comes with rice and gravy. Chicken and dumplings, deep-fried chicken gizzards, buttermilk biscuits, and strawberry shortcake also draw in the locals. *1712 Beach Blvd., Jacksonville Beach, tel. 904/249–5240.*

Dress: informal. Reservations accepted for parties of 6 or more. AE, D, MC, V. Inexpensive.

The Tree Steakhouse. You select your steak and watch the staff cook it over a charcoal fire. Charbroiled chicken is also on the list, and there are several seafood dishes, too. The atmosphere is low-key and casual. *942 Arlington Rd., in Arlington Plaza, Jacksonville, tel. 904/725–0066. Reservations accepted. Dress: casual. AE, DC, MC, V. Inexpensive.*

Lodging

Jacksonville Omni Hotel. The city's newest hotel is a 16-story, ultramodern facility with a splashy lobby atrium and large, stylish guest rooms. All rooms have either a king-size or two double beds. You'll feel pampered anywhere in the hotel, but the extra frills are to be found in the two floors of the concierge level. *245 Water St., Jacksonville 32202, tel. 904/355–6664. 354 rooms. Facilities: heated pool, restaurant, lounge, exercise room, nonsmoker rooms, cable TV. AE, D, DC, MC, V. Expensive.*

Marina Hotel at St. Johns Place. This five-story luxury hotel, connected to the Riverwalk complex, has modern rooms with either a king-size or two double beds. It's located right in the center of things, and the hotel bustles with activity inside and out. Rooms overlooking the St. Johns River command the highest prices. *1515 Prudential Dr., Jacksonville 32207, tel. 904/396–5100. 321 rooms, 18 suites. Facilities: outdoor pool, 2 lighted tennis courts, restaurant, lounge, shopping arcade, privileges at Downtown Athletic Club, nonsmoker rooms, facilities for handicapped persons. AE, DC, MC, V. Expensive.*

Comfort Suites Hotel. Located in bustling Baymeadows, central to the currently "in" restaurants, nightclubs, and shops, this all-suites hotel is an unbeatable value. Suites, which are decorated in breezy, radiant Florida hues, include refrigerators, remote control TV, and sofa sleepers. Microwaves and VCRs come with master suites. Daily Continental breakfast and cocktail hour during the week are included in rates. *8333 Dix Ellis Trail, Jacksonville 32256, tel. 904/739–1155. 128 suites. Facilities: outdoor pool, heated spa, laundry. AE, DC, MC, V. Moderate.*

House on Cherry St. This early 20th-century treasure is furnished with pewter, oriental rugs, woven coverlets, and other remnants of a rich past. Carol Anderson welcomes her guests to her riverside home with wine and hors d'oeuvres and serves full breakfast every morning. Walk to the parks and gardens of the chic Avondale district. Call for restrictions. *1844 Cherry St., Jacksonville 32205, tel. 904/384–1999. 4 rooms with private bath. Facilities: free use of bicycles. MC, V. Moderate.*

Sea Turtle Inn. Every room in this inn has a view of the Atlantic. Let the staff arrange special outings for you: golf, deep-sea fishing, or a visit to a Nautilus fitness center. You'll be welcomed each evening with a complimentary cocktail reception, and in the morning you'll be awakened with hot coffee and a newspaper. *One Ocean Blvd., Atlantic Beach 32233, tel. 904/249–7402. 198 rooms. Facilities: oceanfront pool with cabana bar, restaurant, lounge with live entertainment, room service, free airport shuttle. AE, DC, MC, V. Moderate.*

New Smyrna Beach

Dining

The Skyline. Watch private airplanes land and take off at the New Smyrna Beach airport as you dine on secretly seasoned Tony Barbera steaks, veal, shrimp, chicken, and fish. A tray will be brought for your selection: order steaks by the ounce, cut to order if you wish. House specialties include the *zuppa di* *pesce*, served in a crock; fresh homemade pastas; and a New England clam chowder that took first place in the 1988 Chowder Debate. The building, once an officers club for American and RAF pilots, is filled with aeronautical nostalgia. *2004 N. Dixie Freeway, tel. 904/428–5325. Reservations advised. Dress: neat but casual; no jeans or T-shirts. AE, MC, V. No lunch. Moderate.*

Riverview Charlie's. Look out over the Intracoastal Waterway while you choose from a menu loaded with local and imported fish, all available broiled, blackened, or grilled. The shore platters are piled high; landlubbers can choose steaks and chicken dishes instead. *101 Flagler Ave., tel. 904/428–1865. Reservations advised. Dress: neat but casual. AE, D, DC, MC, V. Moderate–Inexpensive.*

Blackbeard's Inn. An array of seafood comes in fresh from the nearby docks. It's hard to beat the shrimp Louie, which is served at lunchtime, the stuffed grouper, or mountainous combo platters, but the inn is also known for its prime beef and barbecues. *701 N. Dixie Hwy., tel. 904/427–0414 in Daytona, 904/788–9476 elsewhere. No reservations except for parties of 15 or more. Dress: casual. AE, DC, MC, V. No lunch weekends. Inexpensive.*

Franco's. Begun as a pizza joint in 1983, Franco's has become a high-voltage Italian specialty house. Light concoctions include spinach or broccoli pies, pasta salads, and what could possibly be the best Greek salad you've ever had. There's a long list of fish, Italian classics, including a captivating zucchini parmigiana, seven styles of veal, and gourmet pizzas. *1518 S. Dixie Freeway (U.S. 1, ½ mi south of S.R. 44), tel. 904/423–3600. Reservations advised. Dress: casual. No lunch Sun. MC, V. Inexpensive.*

Goodrich Seafood & Restaurant. For those who like mullet, this is a piscatorial Shangri-la. Gorge on steamed oysters, fried fish, hush puppies, clams, shrimp, and chowders. Fresh and frozen seafood is also sold over the counter. *253 River Dr., tel. 904/345–3397. Reservations required for all-you-can-eat buffet (Sept.–May). Dress: casual. No credit cards. Closed Sun. Inexpensive.*

Lodging

Riverview Hotel. A landmark since 1886, this was once a bridge tender's home. Verandas look over the Intracoastal, dunes, and marshes, while inside, Haitian prints and wicker furniture add to the feeling that this is an island getaway. Complimentary Continental breakfast is served in your room, on the balcony, or poolside. *103 Flagler Ave., 32169, tel. 904/428–5858. 18 rooms with private bath. Facilities: restaurant, pool, bicycle rentals. AE, D, DC, MC, V. Moderate.*

Sea Woods Resort Community. Get the best of the beach plus 50 acres of rolling dunes and hammocks. A true community of homes, condos, and villas, this has a rhythm of doing, going, and playing. Most people rent by the week, month, or season, but nightly rates are available. *4400 S. Atlantic Ave., 32169, tel. 904/423–7796 or 800/826–8614. 180 units. Facilities: racquetball, tennis, Nautilus fitness center, outdoor heated pool planned activities in winter. No credit cards. Moderate.*

Ocean Air Motel. One of those modest little "finds," this motel is operated by a caring British couple who, in the English manner, groom the grounds as carefully as they do the neat and commodious rooms. It's only a five-minute walk from the beach. *1161 N. Dixie Freeway, 32069, tel. 904/428–5748. 14* *rooms. Facilities: pool, picnic tables. AE, DC, MC, V. Inexpensive.*

Ocala
Lodging

Ocala Hilton. A winding, tree-lined boulevard leads to this nine-story pink tower, nestled in a forested patch of countryside just off I–75. The marble-floor lobby, with piano bar, greets you before you enter your spacious guest room, decorated in deep, tropical hues. *3600 S.W. 36th Ave., 32674, tel. 904/854–1400. 198 rooms. Facilities: outdoor heated pool and Jacuzzi, tennis courts, restaurant, pub, live entertainment on weekends. AE, DC, MC, V. Expensive.*

Seven Sisters Inn. This showplace Queen Anne mansion is now a bed and breakfast. Each room has been glowingly furnished with period antiques and has its own bath; some have a fireplace. Rates include a gourmet breakfast. *820 S.E. Fort King St., 32671, tel. 904/867–1170. 7 rooms; wicker-furnished loft sleeps 4. No facilities. Moderate. AE, MC, V.*

Ormond Beach
Dining

Shogun II. The largest of this area's Japanese steak and seafood houses, this is the place for flashy tableside food preparation, a sushi bar, and a tropical bar. It's a fun, family place; call ahead if you want to celebrate a special occasion in traditional Japanese style. The steak and shrimp are stellar, but the lobster and chicken are also tempting. *630 S. Atlantic Ave. (A1A), in the Ellinor Village Shopping Center, tel. 904/673–1110. Reservations accepted. Dress: casual. AE, MC, V. Inexpensive.*

Ponte Vedra Beach
Dining

The Augustine Room. For a very special night out, come here not just to dine but for a look at the Marriott Sawgrass's emerald exterior and grounds filled with lagoons and waterfalls. Gaze at pleasing original paintings and enjoy the fresh flowers on your table while pondering a menu of fine steaks, native seafood, and veal specialties. The wine list is one of the area's most comprehensive. *1000 TPC Blvd., tel. 904/285–7777. Reservations advised. Jacket required. AE, MC, V. Closed Sun.–Mon. Very Expensive.*

Lodging

The Lodge at Ponte Vedra Beach. The look of this plush new resort is Mediterranean villa grand luxe, aimed at serving an elite clientele whose passions are golf and tennis. The PGA Tour, Tournament Players Club, and Association of Tennis Professionals are based here. Rooms, designed with a country-French flair, have private balconies and cozy window seats. *607 Ponte Vedra Blvd., 32080, tel. 904/273–9500. 66 rooms, 24 suites, some with private whirlpool and fireplace. Facilities: 54 holes of golf, water sports, deep-sea fishing, horseback riding, two beachside pools with bar and grill, exercise room, restaurant, lounge. AE, DC, MC, V. Very Expensive.*

Marriott at Sawgrass. A tropical design is conveyed throughout this luxury hotel. Pick a room with a fireplace or private balcony. Fine details, from the private lounge and special services on the concierge level to the mood set by the lagoon and waterfall in the complex, enhance this resort. *1000 TPC Blvd., 32082, tel. 904/285–7777. 546 units. Facilities: 2 pools, children's program and pool, lighted tennis courts, 99 holes of golf and complete golf program, bicycling, croquet, boating, exercise facilities, restaurants, valet, gift shop, private beach privileges. AE, D, MC, V. Very Expensive.*

St. Augustine
Dining
★

Columbia. An heir to the cherished reputation of the original Columbia founded in Tampa in 1905, this one serves time-honored dishes including *arroz con pollo* (chicken with rice), filet salteado, shrimp and scallops Marbella, and a fragrant, flagrant paella. The Fiesta Brunch on Sunday is a Spanish gala. *98 St. George St., tel. 904/824-3341 or 800/227-1905 in FL. Reservations advised. Dress: neat but casual. AE, D, MC, V. Moderate.*

La Parisienne. Tiny and attentive, pleasantly lusty in its approach to honest bistro cuisine, this little place is a true find—and weekend brunches are available, too. Save room for the pastries. *60 Hypolita St., tel. 904/829-0055. Reservations required at dinner. Dress: neat but casual. MC, V. Closed Mon. Moderate.*

Le Pavilion. The Continental approach spills over from France to Germany with a wow of a schnitzel with spätzle. Hearty soups and good breads make a budget meal, or you can splurge on the rack of lamb or escargot. *45 San Marco Ave., tel. 904/824-6202. Reservations advised; required for 6 or more. Dress: neat but casual. D, DC, MC, V. Moderate.*

★ **Raintree.** The oldest home in this part of the city, this building has been lovingly restored. The buttery breads and pastries are baked on the premises. Try the brandied pepper steak or the Maine lobster special. The Raintree's Madrigal or Champagne dinners are especially fun. The wine list is impressive, and there are two dozen beers to choose from. Courtesy pickup is available from any lodging in the city. *102 San Marco Ave., tel. 904/824-7211. Reservations accepted. Dress: neat but casual. DC, MC, V. No lunch. Moderate.*

Santa Maria. This ramshackle landmark, run by the same family since the 1950s, perches over the water beside the colorful city marina. Seafood is the focus, but there are also steaks, chicken, prime rib, and a children's menu. Have drinks first in the salty lounge or feed the fish from the open-air porch. *135 Avenida Menendez, tel. 904/829-6578. No reservations. Dress: casual. Moderate-Inexpensive. AE, DC, MC, V.*

Zaharias. The room is big, busy, and buzzing with openhanded hospitality. Serve yourself from an enormous buffet instead of, or in addition to, ordering from the menu. Greek and Italian specialties include homemade pizza, a big gyro dinner served with a side order of spaghetti, shish kebab, steaks, seafood, and sandwiches. *3945 A1AS, tel. 904/471-4799. Reservations accepted. Dress: casual. AE, MC, V. Inexpensive.*

Lodging

★ **Sheraton Palm Coast.** This is a bright, nautical-style resort hotel near the beach, and easily accessed by the nearby newly built bridge. Rooms have private patios that overlook the Intracoastal. *300 Club House Dr., 32137, tel. 904/445-3000 or 800/325-3535. 154 rooms, suites. Facilities: 2 heated pools, children's pool, marina, 16 tennis courts, access to 5 championship golf courses, whirlpool, exercise equipment, sauna, restaurant, bar, shops, refrigerators, free transportation around resort and to beach. AE, D, DC, MC, V. Very Expensive.*

Casa Solana. A hushed air of yesteryear hangs over this gracious, antiques-filled, 225-year-old home where you'll be welcomed like an old friend. Complimentary sherry and chocolates and a breakfast of fresh fruits and homemade specialties further convey the mellow but comfortable tone of this inn. *21 Aviles St. 32084, tel. 904/824-3555. 4 suites with bath. Facilities: bicycles. AE, D, MC, V. Expensive.*

★ **Colony's Ponce de Leon Golf and Conference Resort.** Pick your site to loll in the sun from the 350 lavishly landscaped subtropical acres or seek the shade of century-old live oaks in spacious contrast to the narrow streets and crowding of the old city. Insiders reserve well in advance to stay here for special events occurring in and around the area. *4000 U.S. 1N, 32085, tel. 904/824–2821; in FL 800/228–2821. 200 rooms, 99 condos. Facilities: pool, tennis, 18-hole championship golf course, 18-hole poolside putting course, volleyball, horseshoes, restaurant. AE, D, DC, MC, V. Expensive.*

★ **Kenwood Inn.** For more than a century this stately Victorian inn has been welcoming wayfarers, and the Constant family continues the tradition. Located in the heart of the historic district, the inn is within walking distance of restaurants and sightseeing. A Continental breakfast of home-baked cakes and breads is included. Call for restrictions. *38 Marine St., 32084, tel. 904/824–2116. 10 rooms, 4 suites. Facilities: walled-in courtyard with pool, fish pond, street parking and off-street parking 1 block away. D, MC, V. Moderate.*

The Old Powder House Inn. Part of an 1899 Flagler development of winter cottages for the rich, this inn stands on the site of an 18th-century Spanish gunpowder magazine. Imaginative decor makes every room, from "Granny's Attic" to "Queen Anne's Lace," unique. Try the two-night package, which includes a romantic room, full breakfast and afternoon tea daily, wine and hors d'oeuvres nightly, and a moonlight carriage ride with champagne. *38 Cordova St., 32084, tel. 904/824–4149. 9 rooms with bath. Facilities: bicycles. MC, V. Moderate.*

Beacher's Lodge. An all-suites hotel on the dazzling white beach of Anastasia Island provides complimentary coffee, juice, newspaper, and a glimpse of the sun rising over the Atlantic. *6970 A1AS 32086, tel. 904/471–8849 or 800/527–8849. 132 suites. Facilities: pool, fully equipped kitchen, laundry. D, MC, V. Moderate–Inexpensive.*

Carriage Way Bed and Breakfast. A Victorian mansion grandly restored in 1984, this B&B is within walking distance of restaurants and historic sites. Innkeepers Karen Burkley-Kovacik and husband Frank see to welcoming touches such as fresh flowers and home-baked breads. Special-occasion breakfasts, flowers, picnic lunches or romantic dinners, or a simple family supper can be arranged with advance notice. *70 Cuna St. 32084, tel. 904/829–2467. 7 rooms with bath. Facilities: bicycles. D, MC, V. Moderate–Inexpensive.*

St. Francis Inn. If only the walls could whisper, this late-18th-century house would tell tales of slave uprisings, buried doubloons, and Confederate spies. The inn, which was a boarding house a century ago, now offers rooms, suites, an apartment, and a cottage. Rates include Continental breakfast. *279 St. George St., 32084, tel. 904/824–6068. Facilities: pool, some fireplaces, bicycles. MC, V. Moderate–Inexpensive.*

The Arts and Nightlife

The Arts Broadway touring shows, top-name entertainers, and other major events are booked at the **Florida Theater Performing Arts Center** (128 E. Forsyth St., Jacksonville, tel. 904/355–5661), the **Jacksonville Civic Auditorium** (300 Water St., Jacksonville, tel. 904/630–0701), and **The Ocean Center** (101 N. Atlantic Ave., Daytona Beach, tel. 904/254–4545 or in FL 800/858–6444).

Concerts

Peabody Auditorium (600 Auditorium Blvd., Daytona Beach, tel. 904/255–1314) is used for many concerts and programs throughout the year.

The **Jacksonville Symphony Orchestra** (tel. 904/354–5479) presents a variety of concerts and hosts visiting artists.

Theater

Seaside Music Theater (901 6th St., Holly Hill, tel. 904/252–3394) presents professional musicals January–March and June–August.

Alhambra Dinner Theater (12000 Beach Blvd., Jacksonville, tel. 904/641–1212) offers professional theater and complete menus that change with each play.

Nightlife

Bars and Nightclubs

Finky's (640 N. Grandview, Daytona Beach, tel. 904/255–5059) brings in name entertainers you've seen on the Nashville Network and MTV. **Waves** in the Daytona Beach Marriott (100 N. Atlantic Ave., tel. 904/254–8200) is the area's hot, upscale place to drink, dance, and nosh while you listen to Top 40 and mellow standards. **Ocean Pier** (1200 Main St., Daytona Beach, tel. 904/253–1212), located on the ocean, has four bars and one of the biggest dance floors in town.

In St. Augustine, **Richard's Jazz Restaurant** (77 San Marco Ave., tel. 904/829–9910), **Scarlett O'Hara's** (70 Hypolita St., tel. 904/824–6535), the **White Lion** (20 Cuna St., tel. 904/829–2388), and **Trade Winds** (Charlotte St., tel. 904/829–9336) offer live music from bluegrass to classic rock. Call for information on specific performances.

Index

Personal Itinerary

Departure *Date*

Time

Transportation

Arrival *Date* *Time*

Departure *Date* *Time*

Transportation

Accommodations

Arrival *Date* *Time*

Departure *Date* *Time*

Transportation

Accommodations

Arrival *Date* *Time*

Departure *Date* *Time*

Transportation

Accommodations

Addresses

Name

Address

Telephone

Name

Address

Telephone

Name

Address

Telephone

Name

Address

Telephone

Name

Address

Telephone

Name

Address

Telephone

Name

Address

Telephone

Name

Address

Telephone

Name

Address

Telephone

Name

Address

Telephone

Name

Address

Telephone

Name

Address

Telephone

Name

Address

Telephone

Name

Address

Telephone

Name

Address

Telephone

Name

Address

Telephone